Barbarian Migrations and the Roman West, 376–568

This is a major new survey of the barbarian migrations and their role in the fall of the Roman Empire and the creation of early medieval Europe, one of the key events in European history. Unlike previous studies it integrates historical and archaeological evidence and discusses Britain, Ireland, mainland Europe and North Africa, demonstrating that the Roman Empire and its neighbours were inextricably linked. A narrative account of the turbulent fifth and early sixth centuries is followed by a description of society and politics during the migration period and an analysis of the mechanisms of settlement and the changes of identity. Guy Halsall reveals that the creation and maintenance of kingdoms and empires was impossible without the active involvement of people in the communities of Europe and North Africa. He concludes that, contrary to most opinions, the fall of the Roman Empire produced the barbarian migrations, not vice versa.

GUY HALSALL is Professor of History at the University of York. His recent publications include *Settlement and Social Organization* (Cambridge, 1995) and *Humour, History and Politics in Late Antiquity and the Early Middle Ages* (Cambridge, 2002).

D1610505

Cambridge Medieval Textbooks

This is a series of introductions to important topics in medieval history aimed primarily at advanced students and faculty, and is designed to complement the monograph series *Cambridge Studies in Medieval Life and Thought*. It includes both chronological and thematic approaches and addresses both British and European topics.

For a list of titles in the series, see end of book.

BARBARIAN MIGRATIONS AND THE ROMAN WEST, 376–568

GUY HALSALL
University of York

CAMBRIDGE
UNIVERSITY PRESS

University Printing House, Cambridge CB2 8BS, United Kingdom

Published in the United States of America by Cambridge University Press, New York

Cambridge University Press is part of the University of Cambridge.

It furthers the University's mission by disseminating knowledge in the pursuit of
education, learning and research at the highest international levels of excellence.

www.cambridge.org
Information on this title: www.cambridge.org/9780521435437

First published 2007
5th printing 2014

A catalogue record for this publication is available from the British Library

ISBN 978-0-521-43491-1 Hardback
ISBN 978-0-521-43543-7 Paperback

For My Friends,
without whom this book would have been finished sooner

CONTENTS

———————— • ————————

Contents

Contents

MAPS AND FIGURE

_____ • _____

FIGURE

ACKNOWLEDGEMENTS

———————— • ————————

This volume was commissioned a long time ago, and delivered very late. It is only right, therefore, that my editor for much of this time, Bill Davies, heads my list of acknowledgements. I thank him for his faith in this project, and the syndics of Cambridge University Press for their patience and understanding. Simon Whitmore cracked the whip fairly and in thoroughly amiable fashion in the latter period of the book's composition, and Michael Watson was most helpful at the very end. I hope the book has been improved by the fact that I am older and – perhaps – wiser than I would have been had it been delivered on time.

The people I have to thank above all else are my own 'barbarian horde', my students, especially the 'tradition-bearers' of this group, the 140 or so undergraduates who have studied the barbarian migrations (in various forms) with me over the past eight years at York and London. Their essays, seminar contributions and stubborn refusal just to take my word for it have kept me on my toes and stimulated my thinking about the issues discussed in this book. They have provided me, moreover, with many very fond memories, and will find much in the following pages that is extremely familiar. Two, Anthony Dee and Adrian Smith, read earlier drafts of this book, for which many thanks.

This is a book that touches on dozens of areas of specialist research, in all of which there are many people more expert than I. I owe an enormous debt to those scholars whose work I have drawn upon; if I have any perspective at all on the huge problems with which this book deals, it is very much one derived from a vantage point perched 'on the shoulders of giants'. Numerous scholars have kindly sent me off-prints of their works, which have proved invaluable. Of these learned ladies and gentlemen some deserve additional thanks. In the reinterpretation of 'Germanic' archaeology I have benefited from discussions with, and the encouragement of fellow-subversives: Sebastian Brather, Frans Theuws and Philipp von Rummel (vive la révolution!). Philipp also read the entire book in draft and made numerous helpful suggestions, saving me from many an error. Many others have helped too, as supporters, readers, discussants, always amiable (and patient!) sparring partners and in numerous other ways: Kate Cooper, Mayke de Jong, Bonnie Effros, Paul Fouracre, Mark Handley, Heinrich Härke, Peter Heather, Mark Humphries, Charlie Insley, Edward James, Ralph Mathisen, Walter Pohl, Susan Reynolds, Danuta Shanzer, Alan Thacker, Chris Wickham, and Ian Wood.

This book was mostly written in York but it owes much to Toronto. The influence of Walter Goffart's ideas will be readily apparent. His claim, following a lecture at Kalamazoo, to have 'liked half of [my] paper', is one which I will carry with pride to my grave as, by Goffartian standards, unstinting flattery. Michael Kulikowski read and offered a thorough critique of the narrative section. I have benefited greatly from discussions with him, as well as from his many publications, as a cursory inspection of this book's footnotes will attest. Finally, as well as learning much from his excellent volume on political communication in this era, I owe the term 'post-imperial', so much more appropriate than the usual, but in many ways misleading, 'post-Roman', to another product of the Toronto school, Andrew Gillett.

I must also give my deepest thanks to the fellow members of staff of the Department of History and the Centre for Medieval Studies of the University of York. It is a privilege to work with colleagues who are actually collegial, but they are much more than that. In particular I must thank Mark Ormrod for his unfailing support and friendship throughout.

Before moving to York, much of the period spent working on this book represented an unhappy phase of my personal and professional life, at least increasing my perception of the irony of the historical process! In addition to my family, who have remained the real bedrock of my existence, I have been blessed with wonderful friends who have served, way beyond the call of duty, in helping me through these difficulties. By calling me away from my word-processor they have doubtless significantly delayed the appearance of this tome, but the book and its author have been much improved as a result. It is a pleasure and an honour to record my debt to them. It would have taken too much space to name them all and I'd doubtless have forgotten someone. The enforced anonymity of this acknowledgement in no way reduces its sincerity. You know who you are! The one person who cannot remain anonymous is Emma Campbell, who, in addition to providing invaluable assistance with my discussions of gender and its theorisation, has reassured me that this book *would* get finished, and continued to make my life a much brighter place.

Guy Halsall
August 2006.

A NOTE ON SPELLINGS

———————— • ————————

Place-names within the Western Empire (where modern towns often preserve one element or another of their Roman name) have generally been given in their current form. Further east and south, in the Empire's Balkan, Asian and African provinces (where they frequently do not), I have used the ancient form, with the modern place-name given in brackets after the first occurrence. In the West, where there is no significantly different, generally accepted and thus more familiar, English form, I have employed the spelling used in the country within which the town now lies: thus Reims, Lyon, Mainz and Trier rather than Rheims, Lyons, Mayence and Trèves; but Cologne, Seville, Milan and Rome rather than Köln, Sevilla, Milano and Roma.

Roman provinces have always been given their ancient titles, even where a modern region derives its name from the same source: thus 'Aquitania Secunda' rather than 'Second Aquitaine'. Germanic personal names, rarely spelt consistently in contemporary sources, have usually been given in a Germanic rather than Graeco-Latinised form: Wulfila rather than Ulfilas; Theoderic rather than Theodericus. Some names, however, have forms which are too accepted to change. Therefore Radagaisus retains his Latinised name rather than his Germanic original (presumably something like Radegis or Ratchis) and Clovis keeps the later antiquarian, artificial but (in French and English) usual, back-formation from 'Louis' instead of his actual name of Chlodovech.

PART I

ROMANS AND BARBARIANS
IN THE IMPERIAL WORLD

I

HOW THE WEST WAS LOST AND WHERE
IT GOT US

·

SABA, ROMANUS AND GUNTRAMN BOSO: THE PROBLEMS OF GOVERNMENT

The rulers of the Gothic kingdoms had decided to persecute the Christians, and ordered religious ceremonies that they would find unacceptable.[1] In refusing to participate, the Christians would reveal themselves and, by spurning communal ritual, apparently state that they were neither part of the community nor interested in its well-being. This would bring down their neighbours' enmity upon them. However, as with the last Roman persecutions of Christians,[2] things did not quite work out that way. One Gothic community decided to cheat their leaders at the ritual feast by giving their Christians meat that had *not* been sacrificed to the gods and thus would not upset Christian sensibilities. One Christian, Saba, refused to go along with this deception and made a public statement of his belief, adding that anyone who did participate in the feast was not a proper Christian. The elders, unsurprisingly, threw him out of the village.

---

[1] This story is taken from *The Passion of St Saba the Goth*. The Gothic kingdoms in question lay north of the Danube in modern Romania. For discussion of the *Passion* and its significance, see Heather (1991), pp. 103–6; Thompson, E. A. (1966), pp. 64–77; Wolfram (1988), pp. 103–9.

[2] See, e.g. Jones, A. H. M. (1964), pp. 74–6, for the lengths to which Roman officials went to avoid persecuting their local Christians, and the lengths to which the latter had to go to achieve martyrdom.

Next, at another communal sacrifice overseen by a political leader of a higher level, the local Goths swore that there were no Christians in their midst, again deciding to leave them in peace. Saba (having returned to his village) thwarted them, striding into the meeting and declaring himself a Christian. The unnamed 'persecutor' asked the villagers whether Saba was a rich man, to which they replied that he had 'nothing except the clothes he wears'. Declaring that Saba was no threat to anyone, the 'persecutor' again had him expelled.

Now royal Goths appeared on the scene, in the form of 'Atharidus, son of Rotestheus of royal rank'. Atharid with his 'gang of lawless bandits' swooped on a village where Saba and the local priest had celebrated Easter and captured them both. Thoroughly beating up Saba, they left him tied to the wheel of a wagon (although miraculously unscathed) but during the night a local woman untied him. Saba refused to run away so next day Atharid's gang immediately recaptured him. After Saba refused to eat sacrificial meat and claimed to be immune to pain, Atharid ordered some warriors to take him away and drown him in the river Mousaios.[3] Even now, Atharid's men mooted the possibility of just letting Saba go and claiming to have drowned him: 'How will Atharid ever find out?' Yet again, Saba harangued them and told them to carry out their orders. Rather wearily, they held Saba under water with a log and drowned him. Leaving his body by the river, they went away. It was Thursday, 12 April 372.

There are serious grounds for not taking this story literally. The strategy adopted by its author, which succeeds so well in putting modern readers firmly on the side of Atharid and the pagan Goths, originally worked to show the uncompromising depth of Saba's Christianity. Thus all the chances that Saba was given to save himself might simply be a device to show his piety. Nevertheless aspects of the tale can be corroborated from other sources and it has a very human ring.[4] One might suppose that the difficulties in getting anything done which beset Rothesteus, at the apex of the political hierarchy described in the *Passion of St Saba*, or the great Gothic leader Athanaric (†381), who lies behind the whole episode, stemmed simply from the fact that this was a barbarian kingdom or confederacy with no literary instruments of government. However, things were

---

[3] Possibly the Buzau in Wallachia: Heather and Matthews (trans.) (1991), p. 110.
[4] Heather and Matthews (trans.) (1991), pp. 109–11.

not very different in the enormous bureaucratic edifice which was the Roman Empire.

North Africa was a prosperous area of the Roman world, something that often surprises modern students whose images of the region revolve around barren mountains and the great Saharan sand-sea. Here, and at more or less exactly the same time as Saba was so assiduously seeking martyrdom, was played out the story of Count Romanus.[5] The tale is unlikely to be as simple as Ammianus Marcellinus makes it appear, writing twenty years after it ended, and it is doubtful that we will ever get to the bottom of it, but the outlines of the case are as follows. In 363–4 a tribe called the *Austoriani* raided the people of Lepcis Magna (Lebda, Libya) in *Tripolitania* after one of the former was burnt at the stake, apparently for brigandage. The citizens called upon Romanus, the newly arrived count of Africa, who came with his troops but demanded large amounts of provisions and 4,000 camels. These the locals refused to produce so after forty days in the neighbourhood Romanus departed, leaving the citizens of Lepcis to the Austoriani. The Tripolitanians sent envoys to Emperor Valentinian I (364–75) to complain but Romanus had a relative at court and tried to get the affair heard by him. As it was, the emperor heard the envoys' complaint and a defence by Romanus' supporters, believed neither and promised a full inquiry. This, however, was delayed and meanwhile the North Africans again fell victim to serious attacks, which Romanus allegedly did nothing to avert. Valentinian was unhappy at the news of these raids and sent a tribune called Palladius with money to pay the African army and report on the situation.

Romanus persuaded the officers of his command to lodge the bulk of their pay with Palladius so, when two local townsmen showed Palladius the damage and the extent of Romanus' negligence, Romanus threatened to report Palladius as a corrupt official who had pocketed the pay entrusted to him. To save himself, Palladius agreed to inform the emperor that the Tripolitanians had no cause for complaint. The townsmen who had reported to Palladius were condemned to have their tongues cut out for lying, but fled. Valentinian, wholly deceived in the affair and never lenient at the

---

[5] The main story is recounted in Amm. Marc. 28.6 but see also 27.9.1, 29.5.1–2, 30.2.10. For discussion see MacMullen (1988), pp. 154–5, 179–80; Matthews (1989), pp. 281–2, 383–7. On Ammianus, see Drijvers and Hunt (eds.) (1999); Matthews (1989).

best of times, also ordered that the previous ambassadors from the province and the governor be executed although, again, at least one escaped into hiding. Eventually a number of the (in Ammianus' account) guilty parties, including Palladius, were driven to suicide and some were burnt alive by Count Theodosius, who led the military expedition in 373 which finally quelled the unrest of the North African tribes. Romanus, it seems, despite a short spell in prison, got away with it.

There is much more to this story than the simple apportioning of blame and Romanus' version might have been rather different.[6] The region's convoluted politics probably led to the execution of Count Theodosius, the father of the Emperor Theodosius who reigned when Ammianus was writing. This probably prevented Ammianus from giving a full account of what happened. Certainly, he never mentions Count Theodosius' execution.[7] The saga nevertheless illustrates the difficulty which emperors had in finding out what was happening 'on the ground' in their huge empire and the ways in which this difficulty could be exploited by local parties.

The final story in this trilogy comes from the *Histories* of Gregory of Tours (*c.*539–594). We now move on to the very end of the period covered by this volume, 200 years after the stories of Saba and Romanus. By 583 Gaul was divided into three kingdoms – Austrasia, Neustria and Burgundy – ruled by Franks of the Merovingian dynasty. Civil war broke out when a certain Gundovald sailed to Gaul from Constantinople (Istanbul, Turkey) and claimed to be a Merovingian.[8] Duke Guntramn Boso, a leading figure at the Austrasian court, was with Gundovald when he originally arrived but by 583 circumstances had changed and Boso had deserted the 'pretender', taking with him the gold sent by the eastern Roman (Byzantine) Empire to support the revolt. Gundovald fled to a Mediterranean island while Mummolus, a famous general who had defected to him from King Guntramn of Burgundy, held out in Avignon. Guntramn Boso was arrested and brought before King Guntramn, but bought his freedom by promising to capture Mummolus.

---

[6] Matthews (1989), pp. 282, 375; below, pp. 65–8 for commentary.

[7] Jerome, *Chronicle. a.* 376; Oros. 7.33.7; Matthews (1989), pp. 222, 382. Romanus' avarice is also attested by Zos. 4.15.

[8] For this story, see Gregory of Tours, *LH* 6.26. The classic discussion of the 'Gundovald affair' is Goffart (1957). See also Wood (1994a), pp. 93–8. For an introduction to Gregory, see Wood (1994b).

Leaving his son as a hostage with King Guntramn, Boso returned to the Auvergne. Using his title of *dux* (military commander) he raised the troops of the Austrasian city-districts of Clermont and Le Velay, and set out to besiege Mummolus in Avignon. Mummolus, however, thwarted Boso's attempts to capture him through force or persuasion. Now Boso was joined by Burgundian troops sent by King Guntramn and the two sides settled down to a siege. At this juncture the fourteen-year-old king of Austrasia, Childebert II, heard that Guntramn Boso was using Austrasian troops, without permission, to help the king of Burgundy in a campaign to which Austrasia was seemingly opposed, not least because Avignon was Austrasian territory. Childebert or his advisers sent to the spot another duke, Gundulf, a relative of Gregory of Tours. Gundulf raised the siege by ordering the Auvergnat levies home, whereupon the unsupported Burgundians also withdrew. He then took Mummolus to Clermont but shortly thereafter let him return to Avignon, further suggesting that his defection and flight to Austrasian soil had official sanction.

There are many problems with understanding this story, not least the fact that Gregory of Tours wrote about it during the supremacy of King Guntramn, who was implacable in his pursuit of anyone possibly involved in Gundovald's rebellion. Gregory's relative Gundulf played some role as an intermediary between Austrasia and the pretender's supporters and Gregory himself might have been involved.[9] Nevertheless, it illustrates more late antique problems of government. Acting a long way from the royal court, an unscrupulous royal officer like Guntramn Boso could call out the troops on the strength of his title and use them illegitimately to pursue his own ends. Order was restored, as it turned out, by another aristocrat, Gundulf, arriving from the court and invoking *his* royally bestowed authority to send the levies home. But what would have happened if Gundulf, like Boso, had only been invoking the king's name, without authority, for his own ends? Who, in the camp before Avignon, would have known?

This anecdotal triptych highlights the problems facing anyone trying to govern a late antique kingdom or empire. Europe and North Africa are difficult areas to rule. Three excellent books appeared in the early 1980s,[10] covering the early medieval history of most of mainland Europe: all began by stressing the geographical

---

[9] Halsall (2002); Wood (1993).
[10] Collins (1995), pp. 6–7; James (1982a), p. 1; Wickham (1981), pp. 1–6.

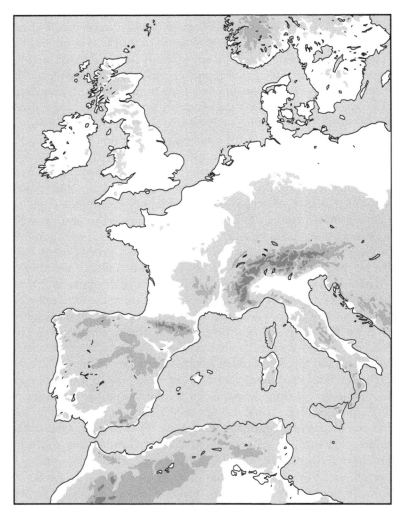

Map 1   Europe: physical relief

disunity and thus the problems of governing the area in question. Mountain ranges, barren high plateaux, broad rivers, marshlands and forests cut Europe up into innumerable micro-regions (map 1). Within each were people actively trying to do the best for themselves and their families. Sometimes this brought them into competition with their neighbours or with those trying to rule them in the name of outside powers. When one considers the difficulties of travel and communication in this period, the problems of effective rule become all too clear. We can see why Valentinian was so dependent upon taking on trust reports from possibly unreliable officers; just how scheming aristocrats could manipulate Auvergnat levies by claiming to bear the authority of a distant king. In Saba's tale Atharid's warriors began to consider how to avoid carrying out his orders when they were literally only just out of his sight; in Gothic territory, even the banks of the river Mousaios posed a barrier to the effective implementation of a ruler's writ.

As recent events in Iraq, the Balkans and the former Soviet Union have shown, and as Valentinian probably knew over 1600 years earlier, force and terror are implements of limited value in holding states together when local communities no longer wish to be incorporated in them. 'Nor is there any military power so great that it can last for long under the weight of fear.'[11] Making an example of a provincial governor and a couple of leading citizens might persuade other locally important figures to throw in their lot with the imperial forces or illustrate graphically what might happen if one got on the wrong side of the emperor but such measures were inefficient. At least two of those whom Valentinian ordered to be killed escaped into hiding with their fellow citizens' help. The local Goths' reluctance to rend their little community through persecution emerges very clearly from the account of Saba's martyrdom.

The problem of late antique government was how to bind all those communities, like Saba's, into one political entity. Large political units were the norm in this period, even after the western Empire's disintegration, something which heightens rather than reduces the importance of understanding this issue.[12] How could late antique rulers succeed where later leaders, even in the modern world with its mass armies, high technology, chemical weapons, cluster-bombs and helicopter gunships, have failed? Political change was brought about not by the imposition of authority but by the active subscription to new governments by inhabitants of all the communities in the different regions of the west. Yet discussions of the end of the western

[11] Cicero, On Duties 2.26. Compare the Burmese democratic leader Aung San Suu Kyi, quoted in The Observer 9 Feb. 1997: 'All [dictatorships] are shored up by arms and they all collapse in the end.'
[12] Gellner (1973), p. 1.

Roman Empire and the processes known to historians as 'the barbarian migrations' have rarely featured the role of individuals in small communities away from the core of 'high politics', like the Gothic villagers, the North African provincials or the troops before Avignon. This book seeks to restore to these people their important, indeed crucial, role in shaping western European history between 376 and 568.

THE BARBARIANS' ROLE IN HISTORY

Previous works have not generally featured people like these because – following the concerns of contemporary narratives – they have concentrated upon high political events. The barbarian migrations and the fall of Rome are inextricably linked. The end of the Roman Empire (by which, as has been endlessly pointed out, we mean only the *western* Roman Empire) has traditionally been thought to have been brought about by the influx of barbarians. The latter have a historical role but their movement is rarely explained, except as a primeval surge towards the Mediterranean or a late antique domino theory initiated by the pressure from tribes behind, ultimately fleeing from the Huns. On the other side, though, the inhabitants of the Roman Empire have hardly been given any part to play at all. They are usually passive, indeed apathetic, cowardly observers of the movements of armies and the transfers of political power.[13]

The historiography of this topic reflects Europe's strange, almost schizophrenic, attitude to its barbarian past.[14] This is manifest in the way that in popular speech barbarian means a savage, a destroyer of civilised values, yet a fascination with the heroic barbarian exists simultaneously: Conan the Barbarian is the prime example from western popular culture. Similarly, in some histories the end of the western Empire and the entry of the barbarians were believed to constitute a 'Bad Thing', bringing about the end of civilisation and the introduction of a Dark Age. In this way of seeing history, common amongst French and Italian historians, the movement of non-Romans into the Empire has generally been referred to as 'the barbarian invasions': 'les invasions barbares'; 'le invasioni barbariche'.

---

[13] Jones, A. H. M. (1964), pp. 1046, 1059–60, for the classic castigation of the apathetic Roman population, especially its aristocracy.

[14] Geary (2002), pp. 1–14.

On the other hand, especially amongst German historians, these events acquired a more heroic dimension. The movement of Germanic-speaking tribes was 'a Good Thing', bringing about the collapse of a decadent and effete Mediterranean society or, alternatively, a top-heavy, despotic and corrupt autocracy, and its replacement by a virile, martial society, sometimes seen as having political norms based on a proto-democracy of free peasants or the reciprocal bonds between warlord and retinue. These approaches led to different ways of emploting the period's history, as the tragedy of the Empire's demise or as the heroic epic of barbarian peoples culminating in their settlement and establishment of a kingdom in one of the former provinces. Both views, however, were in agreement about one essential fact: the barbarians brought down the Roman Empire.

It will come as no shock that these historical views were produced by the political circumstances in which they were written. Most national histories in the west begin with barbarians, which is hardly surprising given that many modern states and regions owe their names to the migrating peoples of late antiquity: England, Scotland, France, Burgundy and Lombardy. Other appellations equally derive from the ethnic shifts of the period. The French call their German neighbours 'allemands', the *Alamanni*, the barbarian confederation that neighboured that of the Franks. The Germans refer to France as Frankreich, the kingdom of the Franks. In the British Isles the English call the inhabitants of the western peninsula 'Welsh', a Germanic word meaning 'foreigner', whereas the Welsh call the English 'Saes' – Saxons.

National historiographical traditions frequently go back to a work of the early Middle Ages wherein a people's history is described, often from mythical origins to their settlement in the former Empire. Such 'national histories' are normally thought to include Jordanes' mid-sixth-century *Origin and Deeds of the Goths* (the *Getica*), Gregory of Tours' *History of the Franks* (late sixth century), Isidore of Seville's early seventh-century *History of the Goths*, Bede's *Ecclesiastical History of the English People* from about a century later and Paul the Deacon's *History of the Lombards*, belonging to the end of the eighth century. This is a problematic grouping of texts, which does little justice to their complexity.[15] Bede's work, as its name implies, belongs to the genre of ecclesiastical history and Gregory never wrote a *History of the Franks* at all. Some manuscripts of an anonymous early

---

[15] On which see Goffart (1988).

seventh-century six-book abridgement of his *Ten Books of Histories* bear the title *The History of the Franks*, and it was this name that stuck. The other texts are far more complex works than simple narrations of a people's history.

Even where a modern land is not named after a group of barbarians the latter can still play a hugely important role. The Visigoths have been influential in Iberian historiography. The Christian rulers who led the Reconquista – the later medieval 'reconquest' of territory from Islamic rulers – claimed to be the successors of the Visigothic kings of Toledo. The Visigothic monarchs' Catholicism gave them a particular importance in Spanish views of the past. In Italy, by contrast, the Lombards who invaded the peninsula at the very end of the period covered by this book have a much less favourable image. They are blamed for shattering the peninsula's unity and bringing about the fragmentation that endured until the nineteenth-century Risorgimento (the reunification of Italy).[16] It is noteworthy that in recent decades, as regionalism has become important in Italian politics, an interest in the Lombards has revived.[17]

Sometimes the barbarians were used within kingdoms to justify the social order, particularly in France, where early Frankish society was claimed to justify either absolute monarchy or aristocratic claims to share (or limit) royal power.[18] The Franks were seen as the founders of both monarchy and aristocracy, the Gallo-Romans sometimes being seen as the ancestors of the peasantry. These views were not necessarily disputed at the Revolution but their moral overtones were sometimes reversed. The Gallo-Romans, ancient possessors of the land, had been able to throw off the Frankish yoke. 'Do you not see what is happening in France?' asked Catherine the Great of Russia. 'The Gauls are driving out the Franks.'[19] This interpretation was to some extent responsible for the revival of Romanising political vocabulary: the Republic with its senate, its consuls and its Ecole de Mars. The common assumption that the classical world is somehow more recognisable, more 'modern' than the superstitious 'otherness' of the medieval is partly contingent upon the outcome of these late eighteenth- and nineteenth-century political struggles.

[16] Wickham (1981), p. 1, for the reification of unità in Italian politics and history.
[17] I. Barbiera, paper given to conference on 'Archäologie und Identität', Vienna, March 2006.
[18] I am grateful to Ian Wood for advice on this topic.   [19] James (1988), p. 240.

In England, by contrast, ideas of democracy were associated not with classical Rome but with the barbarians. Such key aspects of modern British[20] identity such as parliamentary democracy and constitutional monarchy were held to derive from the immigration of free Anglo-Saxon communities from the forests of northern Germany. The Whig view of historical progress took it as axiomatic that the innate superiority of British political institutions derived from the Anglo-Saxon migration. Nevertheless, this idea too grew out of opposition to the view that traced all British history to the Norman Conquest. Though there are certain similarities with the French situation, the political event under debate was different.

Perhaps the most historiographically important developments in the views of the barbarians stemmed from German politics. Germany, obviously, lay outside the Roman Empire, and was thus cut off from the Roman inheritance so proudly trumpeted in Renaissance Europe. An alternative past had to be found and the barbarians who had heroically resisted the might of Rome and then conquered her Empire became its focus. The late fifteenth-century rediscovery of Tacitus' tract *Germania* provided a particular boost. The term 'barbarian migrations' (Völkerwanderung) appeared in the sixteenth century and in the nineteenth the idea that all Germans owed a shared origin to these barbarians found new political currency in the moves towards German unification. Centuries of political rivalry and armed conflict between Bavarians and Saxons, Hessians and Prussians, were countered by the argument that all Germans were fundamentally alike. This similarity was not simply racial but expressed in a shared ethos and customs, support for which was found in the classical sources. Thus the reports of ancient writers who lumped all Germanic-speakers together out of Graeco-Roman chauvinism and a sense that all barbarians were basically the same became – ironically – the basis for German nationalism and unification. This did not stop with ideas about 'Germany' and the pre-migration 'Germans'. Espousing the heroic view of the end of the Roman Empire, German scholars could argue that the barbarians replaced the classical world with a new social order. The whole Middle Ages was viewed as a 'German' creation and its literary output, including the works of

[20] I use the word British deliberately to reflect the dominant political identity of the eighteenth and nineteenth centuries; it is *not* an early twenty-first-century elision of English and British.

writers as indisputably Roman as Cassiodorus, Venantius Fortunatus and Gregory of Tours, could be appropriated for the series of *Monumenta Germaniae Historica* (Historical Monuments of Germany).[21] This move and its use of history and archaeology have had an enormous impact upon the study of the barbarians and indeed of the early Middle Ages. Surprisingly, given that its origins in the contingencies of nineteenth-century politics are so obvious, it continues to exert an influence today, albeit usually implicitly.

This nineteenth-century use of history was not restricted to Germany. It was representative of the growth of the idea of the nation state.[22] A state's inhabitants were thought to be racially distinct and to have particular social and moral characteristics. It was, for example, felt that one could distinguish the skeletons of 'Germans' from those of 'Celts' or Slavs by the measurement of skulls, long-skulled (dolichocephalic) individuals being the former and round-skulled (brachycephalic) people representing the latter.

In the twentieth century, building upon this tradition, the barbarians played a significant role in Nazi ideology. The Nazis drew upon the work of a philologist called Gustav Kossinna, who adopted archaeological data to help prove his model of the German origins of Aryan Indo-European peoples.[23] Studies of the early Middle Ages justified the annexation of northern France, regarded as an ancestral German territory conquered in the fifth century.[24] The story of the Gothic migration and the fact that the fourth-century Goths lived in the area excused the conquest of the Ukraine and the Crimea. Indeed Sevastopol was to be renamed Theoderichshafen (Theoderic's Port) after the great Ostrogothic king.[25] The Nazis affected the ways in which the early 'Germans' were seen, rejecting the free proto-democracies of earlier historical theories in favour of a more martial society structured around reciprocal ties to a military leader. After the Third Reich fell some revision of these views was undertaken. In particular, Reinhard Wenskus developed a theory whereby the barbarian migrations were not the movements of whole peoples but instead the wanderings of noble bands who were guardians of a 'core of tradition' (Traditionskern), origin stories and other unifying legends.[26] Their military success attracted

---

[21] On which, see Knowles (1963), pp. 65–97.   [22] Geary (2002), pp. 15–40.
[23] Trigger (1989), pp. 163–7.   [24] Fehr (2002).   [25] Wolfram (1988), p. 3.
[26] Wenskus (1961).

warriors and other people to join the band. Membership of the group was defined by subscription to the ideas of the Traditionskern and thus new peoples were formed. This process of forming ethnic units – peoples – was later called ethnogenesis (the term is not Wenskus'; it seems to have been introduced by Soviet scholars such as Bromlej). It has recently been argued forcefully that, although moving away from the Nazis' extreme position, Wenskus' view was less of a break with traditional German historiography than has been claimed.[27] The focus on aristocratic leadership and the ties that bound the warband (Gefolgschaft) made a clear point of contact with theories of Germanic social structure that had been popular with Nazi historians.

Be that as it may, Wenskus' model was employed most notably by Herwig Wolfram, professor at the Institute for Austrian Historical Research and author of much important work on the Goths and the Danubian region.[28] The bulk of Wolfram's research centres on several key ideas. One is that early medieval origin legends reflect social and political changes of the distant past. According to a Germanic philological scheme, a chronology of types of tribal name and of religious developments associated with social transformation is proposed. Grounded in the traditions of German-language constitutional history (Verfassungsgeschichte) is the idea that different types of ruler had differing political capabilities relating to their constitutional position within the people. However, Wolfram also sees the Germanic peoples as dependent upon the Roman Empire. Again, a strongly constitutional/legal approach leads to the barbarian kings being viewed as positioning themselves within a Roman constitutional framework with particular formal relationships with the emperor. Wolfram, as has been argued recently, has sometimes had a tendency to reify concepts that were in fact very fluid and to use Latin phrases, quite misleadingly, as though they were well-recognised legal terms. Some Spanish scholars, notably Luis García Moreno and his school, have enthusiastically taken up the more traditional aspects of Wolfram's work.[29] It should, however, be stressed that Wolfram is

[27] Callander Murray (2002).
[28] Reference to Wolfram's voluminous oeuvre will be found scattered amongst the subsequent chapters. See above all his two key works translated into English: Wolfram (1988); (1997a).
[29] See, e.g. Pampliega (1998).

a much more intellectually agile scholar than many critiques make him appear, demonstrating a greater willingness and ability to change his mind than some of his key opponents.[30]

Wolfram's most influential student amongst the so-called 'Vienna School' has been Walter Pohl, whose work began with the Avars, extending the ethnogenesis model to a steppes people, and developed subsequently into studies of the Lombards and other Germanic peoples.[31] Pohl's work, whilst owing much to the traditions of Wenskus and Wolfram, is much more fluid and has been profoundly influenced by the so-called 'linguistic turn', in which the works of sociologists, philosophers of language and critical theorists were employed to understand how language and its use shaped past power structures.[32] Pohl has been careful not to reject the origin myths of the post-Roman kingdoms as complete fabrications. His analyses subtly study the ways in which extant components can be thrown together for particular purposes. Pohl has also worked on the meaning of early medieval ethnic identity, showing how it too was created by the contingent selection from a range of possible markers or 'signs of distinction'.[33] What Pohl has never, to my knowledge, argued – although his work has been traduced by some archaeological writers as claiming this – is that ethnicity was unimportant.

Pohl has found British and American allies. In Britain, much post-war German scholarship was mediated through the writings of J. M. Wallace-Hadrill, a great founder of early medieval European history in Britain. Many, indeed most, of the current leading scholars of early medieval Europe in Britain studied at Oxford University when Wallace-Hadrill taught there, though not all were supervised by him in their doctoral research.[34] Amongst this generation the most prominent student of barbarian history has been Ian Wood, professor at the University of Leeds. Wood's work has generally focused upon criticism of the literary sources, showing how their context and the agendas of individual writers shaped their presentation of the period

---

[30] See, e.g. Wolfram (2005a), and his views on barbarian settlement discussed below.
[31] E.g. Pohl (2002).
[32] For excellent discussion in relation to early medieval sources see Fouracre (1990). Also Pohl (2001). There is a brief account in Halsall (2005a).
[33] Pohl (1998a); (1998b).
[34] Notably Roger Collins, Edward James, Chris Wickham and Ian Wood.

and leading to a nuanced view of the barbarians' political take-over of the Roman west.[35]

In the USA Professor Patrick Geary has led analysis of the barbarians. Profoundly influenced by the 'Vienna School', Geary's work *Before France and Germany* demonstrated how Frankish settlers and Roman magnates gradually bought into Merovingian hegemony. From the introduction to this work comes Geary's famous dictum that 'the Germanic world was perhaps the greatest and most enduring creation of Roman political and military genius'.[36] In another very influential article he argued that ethnicity was a 'situational construct'.[37] Most recently, Geary has written a thought-provoking work on how modern European ideologies have coloured our view of the early Middle Ages and especially of the role of the 'nations' believed to have migrated into the Roman Empire to found the kingdoms from which modern states claim descent.[38]

Further north, at the University of Toronto, Walter Goffart launched an attack upon the prevailing Germanism[39] of barbarian studies. In the devastatingly effective opening chapter of his *Barbarians and Romans: Techniques of Accommodation*[40] he demonstrated how ideas of the 'Germanic barbarian' are contingent upon developments in early modern and modern political history (as sketched above). Goffart argued that no unifying ethos, no sense of shared identity, existed between Germanic-speaking barbarians. Roman ethnographers, to be sure, grouped the inhabitants of the lands north of the Rhine and upper Danube together as *Germani* but there is no evidence that these people felt themselves to be unified by language. The idea that a shared language created a common identity between Franks and Goths was first attested during eighth-century warfare against the Arabs in Spain. Goffart has followed up this line of argument in several, ever more polemical articles emphasising the associations between some Germanist historiography and Nazi

---

[35] Wood (1998a); Wood (1994a) for an extended application of his methodology to a post-imperial kingdom. Also Wood (2003).
[36] Geary (1988), p. vi.   [37] Geary (1983); see further below, chapter 2.
[38] Geary (2002).
[39] By which term we mean the belief in the cultural unity of the Germanic-speaking northern barbarians and in their particular importance in introducing crucial new features into fifth-century and later western European history.
[40] Goffart (1980); see also Goffart (1989a) and below, chapter 13, for further discussion.

ideology.[41] Elsewhere, he has further striven to deny any role to the Germanic-speaking barbarians in creating early medieval socio-political structures, showing the continuity of Roman institutions, an aspect of his work pursued by his student Alexander Callander Murray in a series of excellent works on the administrative and legal institutions of post-Roman Gaul.[42] Although Callander Murray has taken up Goffart's line of attack on Germanism[43] and on the 'Germanic' nature of post-Roman institutions, he has also argued against the idea that ethnic identity is a mutable, situational construct.[44] Thus he appears ready to believe that the people who called themselves Franks, *Alamanni* and Goths, for example, were indeed members of such migrating peoples, but that these people had little or no real effect. Goffart, Callander Murray and their colleagues at Toronto have established a 'school' of younger scholars re-engaging critically with the history of the barbarians and addressing in particular the work of the 'Vienna School' and its model of ethnogenesis.[45]

An American scholar who studied at Cambridge University, Patrick Amory, penned perhaps the most radical reassessment of the barbarian migrations.[46] Adopting Goffart's ideas, Amory argued that barbarian ethnicity was an identity adopted within the context of the break-up of the Roman Empire, one shaped by roles within society (such as churchman, soldier or administrator) and drawing heavily upon classical ethnographic views of the barbarian. Thus there was little or no role for 'Germanic' culture and social structures in the post-Roman world. Whether or not Amory's views stand the test of time, his book threw down the gauntlet and forced a number of key issues to be reconsidered.[47]

The general historical trend of the past fifty years has been to downplay the scale and effects of the barbarian migrations. The most important exception to this has been the work of the British historian Peter Heather, who, like many of the other leading students of this topic in recent decades, has worked primarily on the Goths.[48] Heather's work began with a scholarly and thoroughly convincing

[41] E.g. Goffart (1995); (2002a); (2000b).
[42] Callander Murray (1983); (1986); (1988); (1994).
[43] See Callander Murray (2002).   [44] Callander Murray (2002), pp. 58–9.
[45] Gillett (ed.) (2002).   [46] Amory (1997).
[47] See, for example, Heather (2003) for formidable critique.
[48] Heather (1991); (1996).

critique of the use to which historians following the Traditionskern approach had put Jordanes' *Getica*. From this basis, Heather attacked the idea that the barbarian peoples were simple aristocratic kernels carrying with them a core of tradition about their origins. Instead, Heather argued that a people like the Goths was constituted in large part by a numerically important social stratum of freemen. These were indeed Goths, descended from people who had crossed into the Empire from the barbarian territories in the late fourth century, and long played an important role in maintaining the exclusivity of their ethnic identity. It will be noted that the present book differs fundamentally from Heather's approach.[49] Heather and I would agree that the key factor in the break-up of the Empire was the exposure of a critical fault-line between the imperial government and the interests of the regional élites. However, while Heather sees the appearance of the Huns as decisive in exposing this fault-line,[50] the thesis proposed here is that the reasons for the Huns' profound effects on barbarian politics are themselves to be sought in the processes, originating *inside* the Empire, that uncovered the weaknesses of the ties binding the Empire together.

TRANSFORMATION OR FALL?

Recently the idea of the 'Fall of the Roman Empire' and to some extent that of 'the barbarian migrations' have lost in importance as historians have developed the paradigm of the 'transformation of the Roman world'. This was the title originally of a collection of essays edited by Lynn White Jr.[51] but has been popularised in a major European Science Foundation (ESF) funded project in the later 1990s, taking the whole period between the fourth century and the ninth as its remit. This development espouses a move away from traditional ideas of the end of the Roman Empire to look at slower processes of transformation and, especially, the ways in which elements of the Roman world survived beyond the traditional date of 476 to be taken up and modified in post-imperial Europe. The *transformation* of the Roman *world* moves away from the narrow

---

[49] For my critique of some of Heather's core arguments see Halsall (1999a), where, however, I also expressed the view that Heather (1996) represented the best overview of a single barbarian group. Certainly, I owe much to the lessons and inspiration provided by Heather's works.

[50] Heather (1995a) for lucid exposition of this thesis.   [51] White, L. (ed.) (1966).

political view of history often implicit in the phrase the *fall* of the Roman *Empire*. This title was also chosen for the ESF project because it enabled the participation of students of the eastern Roman Empire, inevitably excluded by a title based upon the idea of the 'fall' of the Roman west.[52] In the light of the historiographical sketch above this move towards 'transformation' is not surprising, and many of the scholars mentioned were participants in the ESF project, which produced a great deal of very good work upon which the present volume has drawn considerably.

In some ways this continues a long-standing historiographical tradition. While historians had tended to agree that the barbarians destroyed the Roman Empire but to disagree about whether this was a 'Good' or 'a Bad Thing', a great nineteenth-century French historian, N. D. Fustel de Coulanges, argued that the invasions or migrations had actually had very little effect on the society and institutions of Gaul.[53] Most such institutions were continuations from the Roman situation or were new creations born out of the events of the period. Fustel deserves more attention than he receives from modern British historians but even in his own day had to fend off attacks from both French and German scholars. Nevertheless his way of thinking was taken up in the study of the economy first by the Austrian Alfons Dopsch and later, most famously, by the Belgian scholar Henri Pirenne.[54] Pirenne's famous 'thesis' was that the Roman world was an economic unity around the Mediterranean that survived the barbarian invasions with little change and only collapsed when the seventh-century Arab conquests ruptured the coherence of the Mediterranean, dividing Christian north from Islamic south. Pirenne's work has stimulated debate to the present day. The foundations laid in different spheres by Fustel and Pirenne have been built upon in a number of areas, moving away from the 'catastrophic' view of the barbarian migrations and the fall of the Empire. Many of the views of the barbarians discussed above manifest this and there was an especially marked trend towards 'continuity' in British archaeology in the 1970s and 1980s. Similarly, one strand of French scholarship,

[52] Ian Wood *pers. comm.* July 2004.
[53] Fustel de Coulanges (1904–8). The notion had been propounded before by some earlier historians such as the Abbé Dubos but was not fashionable by the late nineteenth century; I am grateful to Ian Wood for pointing this out.
[54] Dopsch (1937); Pirenne (1939).

represented by Jean Durliat and Elisabeth Magnou-Nortier, has argued that imperial fiscal and other structures survived the fifth century to live on into the Carolingian era.[55] It is fair to say that the 'transformation' approach represents the currently dominant scholarly paradigm for work on this period.

Nevertheless, the approach has its problems. In one very interesting article written within this framework, for example, the transformations (by the ninth century) in the status of women perceived as being of major import are linked to differences in legal systems between those areas where Roman law had remained in force and those where non-Roman, 'Germanic' custom had come to prevail.[56] Therefore, leaving aside the vexed issue of whether these legal developments *can* be attributed to the introduction of 'Germanic' custom,[57] the changes are associated with the political take-over of the Roman Empire by 'Germanic' peoples. This does not move us very far from decline and fall. Another recent survey espouses long-term transformation and claims that the date of 476 is of no importance except to historians locked into traditional narratives of decline and fall. Yet its authors' explanation for the failure of the Roman Empire revolves around pressure on the frontiers, the causes of which were to be sought outside the Empire and the army's inability to cope with the influx of barbarians who conquered the provinces: a very traditional narrative.[58]

We might ask what is wrong with decline and fall. The Roman Empire *did* come to an end, admittedly at different times in different places, and when it did so people noticed.[59] Furthermore, between 376, when Emperor Valens allowed Gothic refugees to cross the Danube into the Empire, and 476, when Odoacer deposed Emperor Romulus, the western Empire lost control, one by one, of

---

[55] Durliat (1990); Magnou Nortier (1989); Wickham (1998) for devastating critique.
[56] Smith, J. M. H. (2001), esp. pp. 30–1. The choice of example is made out of respect for the work, which inspired Halsall (2004).
[57] Compare Barnwell (2000); Collins (1998); and Wormald (2003). Below, chapter 14.
[58] Garnsey and Humphress (2001), esp. pp. 2–3, 5. As far as these issues are concerned, I find myself in complete disagreement with this excellent survey.
[59] For the argument that the end of the Roman Empire was not really noticed at the time, being a construct of the 520s, emerging from ideological conflict between Ravenna and Constantinople, see Amory (1997); Croke (1983). For the alternative view, see below, chapters 9, 11 and 12. See also Harries (1994), p. 5, and recently Heather (2005).

its provinces. Whether this resulted from a weakening ability to project its power and make its writ run in distant regions, or to defend its territories by force, or to prevent local societies from breaking away from its political control, or all three at once,[60] matters little. In all cases it is reasonable to call this a decline in effective imperial rule: again, a decline which was felt in the ways in which people organised their identities and their relationships, in short their world. The power of the western Roman Empire declined and, as a political institution, it fell. This is as close as one can get to a matter of neutral reportage in fifth-century history, and implies no moral judgement on the process. This volume presents the end of the Roman Empire and the barbarian migrations as a dramatic, bewildering, massively important and comparatively short-term sequence of events, whose results were all the more dramatic and bewildering for being unintended.

GERMANISM AND CELTICISM

One of the problems that has most beset the study of early medieval Europe is, as noted, that of Germanism. This book aims to tackle this issue. A recent study claimed that the differences between the 'Germanic' peoples could be ignored.[61] In technological terms the diverse peoples who inhabited the region between the Rhine and the Baltic differed little from one another; most practised fairly similar burial rites. This does not mean that 'Germans is Germans'. To lump all Germanic-speaking tribes together is simply to repeat the assumptions of Roman ethnographers or the politically contingent Germanist interpretations of the nineteenth and early twentieth centuries.[62] There is, furthermore, the danger of assuming a linkage between Germanic-speaking barbarians of antiquity and the Germans of modern Europe. This was an approach adopted equally by nineteenth-century historians working in the context of German unification, by the Nazis and at the same time, polemically, by their enemies. Writing at the height of nineteenth-century attempts to prove an eternal unifying German-ness, Nietzsche was unconvinced that anything meaningfully connected the *Germani* of the past with the Germans of his own day.[63]

---

[60] See below, chapters 7–9.   [61] Elton (1996a), pp. 15–44.
[62] Above, pp. 13–14.
[63] Nietzsche (1994), pp. 25–6. I am immensely grateful to Conrad Leyser for drawing my attention to this passage.

That the peoples from the Frisians in the west to the Goths in the
east spoke Germanic languages does not create a fundamental unity
amongst them any more than the fact that people from Portugal to
Romania speak Romance languages permits us to treat them inter-
changeably. These strictures may sound self-evident, but there are
many occasions where modern historians and, especially, archaeologists, treat the different Germanic-speaking groups as sharing some
sort of unifying ethos. Two examples may suffice. Furnished burials
with weaponry are identified as the graves of migrating 'Germanic'
peoples, in spite of the fact that these people have never before
practised this rite; they are assumed to do so now for no better reason
than that this is supposedly a 'Germanic' custom, because other
groups (or another group) somewhere in the enormous 'Germanic'
region between the North Sea and the Ukraine at some point or other
disposed of their dead in this general fashion.[64] Similarly, buildings of
a particular type have been associated with migrating 'Germanic'
peoples, because, even if the people in question had never before used
such structures, examples are known from other areas occupied by
'Germanic' peoples; the building-type is therefore 'Germanic'. It is
implicit in such interpretations that all 'Germanic' peoples somehow
share a common mentality. In their minds is a common stock of
cultural traits which all 'Germanic' people can draw upon as and
when they see fit. This may be claimed to be a *reductio ad absurdam* of
traditional assumptions. It is, but only because these assumptions *are*
fundamentally absurd.

What is known as the Sapir–Whorf hypothesis (after the socio-
linguists who developed it) famously argues that people perceive and
structure their worlds according to the linguistic resources available to
them. This is surely true and there has been much very good work on
how the study of vocabulary can elucidate social and cultural ideas.[65]
Nevertheless, as the Romance analogue (to which many others could
be added) demonstrates, this does not create political, social or cultural uniformity amongst all speakers of a particular language-group.
Therefore, in order to provide no excuse for thinking that there was
anything interchangeable between Franks and Goths, Saxons and

[64] See Härke (1989), though the choice of a specific example is unfair; the
fundamental assumption is more or less universal in early Anglo-Saxon
archaeology.
[65] Green, D. H. (1998).

Lombards or that the *Germani* were the ancestors of modern
Germans, you will find few references to 'Germans' in this book. In
particular you will find no phrases like 'the German onslaught on the
west',[66] which seriously misrepresent this important period. This
comes at a certain cost: references to 'Germanic-speaking barbarians',
'barbarians north of the Rhine and Danube' or 'trans-Rhenan
barbarians' are certainly more long-winded (though I occasionally
use the term *Germani* to refer to all those so described by the
Romans).[67] Nevertheless it seems a price worth paying to avoid
giving a number of entrenched but misleading impressions. Germanic
will only be used to mean the Germanic languages or aspects relating
to those languages except, when placed in inverted commas, in discussing previous historical or archaeological views.[68]

The problems of Germanism have long been recognised. Alas,
entirely analogous developments are currently taking place, also in the
course of modern political movements, with the 'Celts'. It is presently
more fashionable and acceptable to talk of the 'Celtic' peoples as
sharing a unified culture so that evidence from one area (Ireland,
Scotland, Wales, Cornwall or Brittany) can be transferred unproblematically to the elucidation of another, sometimes regardless of
chronological context. This is no more acceptable than Germanism.
There is no evidence at all from antiquity that the speakers of either
Q-Celtic or P-Celtic (let alone speakers of both languages) regarded
themselves as a unified group. This changed in the later part of the
early Middle Ages when common resistance to English hegemony
occasionally led to appeals to a shared culture[69] but even in the
seventh century this sense does not appear to have existed. Scots,
Britons, Irish and Picts fought each other, frequently alongside the
English and sometimes even under kings of English birth.[70] The
modern political uses of Celticism could all too easily produce results

---

[66] Blockley (1998), p. 118.
[67] Modern German distinguishes between 'die Deutsche' (modern Germans) and
'die Germanen' (ancient *Germani*). Similarly, 'allemand' and 'germain' carry
different meanings in French. Alas, since the word 'German' replaced 'Dutch'
and 'Almain' no such resource exists in English.
[68] See Jarnut (2004) for the problems with the term 'Germanic'.
[69] See, e.g. the tenth-century poem 'Armes Prydein' ('The Prophecy of Britain').
[70] James (2001) correctly, and bravely, discusses politics not in terms of Anglo-
Saxons versus Celts but in terms of northern and southern British political
spheres.

as unfortunate as those earlier produced by Germanism.[71] Thus I have again avoided giving any impression that all Celtic-speakers formed a united group. This is easier to the extent that natural geographical divisions make it easier to talk of Irish, Britons and Picts. Celtic will, like Germanic, only refer to language and, when enclosed in inverted commas, to historiographical perspectives.

THE PRESENT STUDY

Discussion of the terminological peculiarities of the current volume leads to the setting and justification of an agenda. In its approach to written evidence, the book contextualises sources in time and space as rigidly as possible, for a number of reasons. First, because of the comparative scarcity of contemporary sources, there has too often been a tendency to aggregate written evidence from different times and places, which inclines towards the homogenisation of diverse situations and masks change.[72] Second, it is important to understand the sources and their stories as far as possible on their own terms. It is too easy to read the information of late antique works in the light of what we know happened later. Third, we must understand the production of written sources as deliberate and meaningful, a response to particular circumstances – circumstances that should, again, be understood as they appeared to the writers of sources rather than as things that would eventually lead to a specific future outcome.

The present volume integrates written material with archaeology, so it will be valuable to present some of the archaeological methodological approaches upon which it is based. There is no room for a detailed account of the development of the archaeology of the migrations.[73] A brief and necessarily over-simplified sketch might nevertheless be valuable, as many of the approaches are either still followed or have bequeathed legacies in the form of assumptions that still underlie modern work.

Most early approaches fell under the heading of 'culture history'. Artefacts and other material traces such as building, grave and cemetery types were classified according to their repeated association with

---

[71] James (2001), p. 137, for a salutary tale.   [72] See Halsall (1995a), pp. 1–3.

[73] A good account of the development of funerary archaeology may be found in Effros (2003), pp. 12–70. For the development of settlement archaeology, see Hamerow (2002), pp. 4–8. On the history of archaeology, see Trigger (1989).

each other.[74] These archaeological cultures were then equated with historically attested 'peoples', which, in line with historical assumptions of the time (see above), were believed to be genetic or otherwise biologically distinct 'races'. The spread of archaeological cultures was assumed to indicate the movement of the people represented by the culture. The replacement of earlier cultures revealed the conquest and displacement of those 'people' and so on. Thus culture history served mainly to extend national political histories into periods and places devoid of written sources. Culture history in one form or another remains a common approach to the archaeology of the migrations and the underlying Germanist assumptions still exercise a profound influence even if they are often not openly recognised. Post-Roman culture history has often been employed without the standards of logical proof that would – in other, especially prehistoric, periods – be demanded even within that paradigm.

After the Second World War culture history fell into disrepute, largely as a result of the uses to which the Nazi and Stalinist regimes had put it, in admittedly very different ways. By the 1960s a new paradigm appeared called 'processual archaeology' (at first called the 'New Archaeology'), essentially a reaction against North American culture history. Influenced strongly by anthropology and the natural sciences it sought normative rules, even laws, explaining human behaviour. Societies were seen as systems, within which different components (economies, political structures and so on) interacted with each other to work towards stasis or equilibrium within the system. Change would therefore primarily be introduced by external agents, especially the climate or environment. When a component of the system was placed under stress the other elements would either interact with it to negate any change, or would in turn be affected by it, having knock-on and increasingly dramatic effects on the system's other elements. A search to establish normative explanations for the collapse of complex societies led to some consideration of the end of the Roman Empire.[75] Processual archaeology was caught in something of a dilemma, being, on one hand, implacably opposed to

---

[74] Leeds (1913), which predates the more famous definition of V. G. Childe ('certain types of remains – pots, implements, ornaments, burial rites, house forms – constantly recurring together': Childe (1929), pp. v–vi) by sixteen years. See Dark, K. R. (1995), pp. 5–6.

[75] Bowersock (1988) – a historian's rather traditional commentary on this work; Tainter (1988).

migration as an explanation (seen as too 'historical') whilst, on the other, not seeing transformation as caused by stresses and strains within systems, which it thought worked functionally to maintain a status quo. Processualism had little impact upon post-Roman archaeology until the 1980s, when it was drawn into debates minimising the effects of the migrations, principally those of the Anglo-Saxons.[76]

However, at about this time processualism was severely criticised on a number of accounts: its insistence on universalising laws; its use of material culture as a simple passive reflection of social reality; its exclusion of internal causal factors; its removal of the individual from history. An opposition to these factors unified so-called 'post-processual' archaeology more than any cohesive body of ideas. Post-processualists agreed about the active use of material culture to create as well as to reflect social reality. Context and short-term change, as well as a more positive attitude to documentary evidence, were espoused (the last of these with little or no meaningful result). Post-processualism has affected late and post-Roman archaeology, especially the study of cemeteries. In the present work I shall approach the archaeological data in ways that are strongly influenced by post-processual thinking. Material culture will be understood as deliberately and meaningfully constituted.

This will be particularly significant in the examination of graves, the archaeological evidence longest analysed in studies of the migrations. The prominence of burials stems mainly from their archaeological visibility. Accompanied by grave-goods, deposited in distinctive cremation urns, placed in stone-lined tombs or sarcophagi or, less commonly, under earthen mounds and in churches, late antique graves are easily detectable.[77] Traditionally, burial has been seen as passively reflecting religion, ethnicity and social class. For example, inhumations containing grave-goods have been seen as marking the burials of 'Germanic' invaders (Anglo-Saxons, Franks or Visigoths), or of pagans (grave-goods being understood as indicating a non-Christian view of the afterlife). The numbers and, in some cases, types of grave-goods have also been analysed as reflecting social classes, sometimes legally attested ranks. Lavishly furnished graves, those with particular qualities of artefacts, or even those containing specified types of artefacts like swords, have been held to be those

---

[76] E.g. Arnold (1984); Hodges (1989).   [77] Halsall (1995b) for a brief survey.

of rich individuals, occasionally supposed to be nobles. Less well furnished burials or those with other types of grave-goods have been seen as less well-off members of society or the poor free, half-free or even slaves.[78]

All of these assumptions have been widely criticised, though these criticisms have not everywhere been accepted or replaced with more sophisticated analyses.[79] Paganism has no necessary connection with furnished inhumation.[80] This rite was, moreover, uncommon within the barbarian regions of *Germania* and there is little or no *prima facie* evidence to suggest its introduction by migrating barbarians.[81] The absence of clearly religious or 'ethnic' traditional explanations for the custom means that it is difficult to see how it could simply have reflected, in the differing degrees of lavishness, established ranks or classes of society. Broader study of such burials' context and of the nature of the displays made in the graves suggests (as will repeatedly be argued below) that furnished inhumation occurs in periods of stress and is symptomatic of social instability and competition for local power. Thus it is an active strategy employed to maintain and enhance standing. It does not simply mirror established wealth and authority. To make the point in an obvious way, a family with assured local dominance would not need to compete with its neighbours in demonstrating who had the most wealth, through a transient burial ritual. Where the social order was more established other forms of funerary display were employed, notably in the use of permanently visible above-ground monuments. Where we see a transition from one form of display to the other it seems to indicate change towards a more established social hierarchy.

The various means of disposing of the dead and the different uses of funerary display reveal much about social structure. Where people in one place cremate their dead and bury the ashes in fairly nondescript fashion in huge community graveyards, whereas in another area the rule is for small cemeteries wherein the ashes of people of one sex only are deposited, whilst in a third region, the local aristocracy has suddenly taken to distinguishing itself by inhuming its dead with large numbers of grave-goods, or in separate cemeteries, these variations speak eloquently about local politics and social organisation, and

---

[78] For useful English summaries of these ideas, see James (1989a); Samson (1987).
[79] For critiques, see Halsall (1995b), pp. 65–6; James (1989a); Samson (1987).
[80] See, above all, Young (1975).   [81] See below, pp. 153–9.

changes from one to another are similarly articulate testimony to real social developments.

Archaeological study of post-Roman settlements has been a much more recent development.[82] Roman villas have, of course, long been known. Their substantial masonry, mosaic floors and the debris of tile roofs made them, like post-Roman graves, easy to detect during agriculture. Other categories of rural settlement, however, were less easily discovered, as were the settlements of the post-Roman period. This was because, as timber buildings, their remains required a greater technical level of expertise for their recognition and excavation. The more ephemeral traces of any such structures that overlay Roman settlements were often destroyed in the process of uncovering the latter. Thus the study of the settlement pattern began between the world wars but only started to reach a high analytical level in recent decades.

Again, traditional views, still widely held, have seen the forms of architecture employed in these settlements in terms of migration and ethnicity. Though the empirical support for such views is, in some cases, rather stronger than for the ethnic explanation of furnished burial, it nevertheless simplifies a more complex situation and often begs important questions, not least because of underlying Germanist assumptions. Otherwise settlement studies have principally and understandably focused upon the important economic data to be derived from such sites. Handled with care, the excavation of rural settlements and the regional study of settlement patterns can reveal much about subsistence agricultural techniques, more specialised aspects of production and exchange between settlements. Nonetheless, this evidence can be put to more uses.

One potential of the increasing quantity and quality of settlement archaeology is that it allows us to think about cosmologies. Whether or not human beings lived under the same roof as their livestock, as was the case in the longhouses excavated across much of north-western Europe, says much about how people viewed their relationship with the natural world. Similarly if a change took place in this, as it did in the fifth century, towards the stabling of animals in separate structures, this development, quite apart from the economic or environmental factors that might have produced it, surely indicates a profound mental shift. The spatial organisation of settlements and

---

[82] Hamerow (2002) for an excellent survey of north-western Europe.

individual buildings is also a rich source of information, although requiring high quality excavation. We might be able to analyse which activities went on in which areas. If we can establish the gendering of these activities, though this is extremely difficult, it can reveal social attitudes. Where and how was rubbish disposed of? How did the main dwelling relate to ancillary structures, and what activities went on in these buildings? A settlement's layout suggests other aspects of social structure. Is centralised planning implied? Do there appear to be communal areas? Are individual areas fenced off, suggesting a clearer idea of individual property?

If, during a settlement's development, one farmstead or building unit becomes significantly larger than all the others and retains that difference in size over time it probably suggests the existence of a more powerful family or kin-group within the settlement. If higher-status settlements appear that are physically separated from other settlements, that too implies the emergence of a more powerful élite. We can investigate whether the layout of such settlements, or that of the dominant farms just mentioned, is designed to restrict social interaction, for instance by making certain areas inaccessible and limiting access from outside to particular zones within which status, and ideas of what defined it, might be publicly displayed (for instance through mosaics). Examination of high-status sites can reveal where specific items were manufactured for distribution to the élite's followers. Fortification suggests an ability to organise and mobilise manpower, as well as revealing how power was expressed through a military idiom. Such investigations are not limited to the rural settlement pattern. Studies of urban sites too have revealed profound shifts in attitudes to public building and to what was expected from a town.[83] Changes in spatial hierarchy within towns manifest develop-ments in ideas, just as the fortunes of towns are graphic indices of socio-economic complexity.

Note that in all of the possibilities mooted above, material culture does not simply reflect social structures; through the treatment of the body and the organisation of space, it creates them in the first place. Many surviving artefacts are items of costume and in late antiquity, as today, costume was a clear way of indicating various aspects of social identity: age, gender, ethnic identity, wealth, social class. Similarly,

---

[83] See, e.g. Brogiolo, Christie and Gauthier (eds.) (2002); Brogiolo and Ward-Perkins (eds.) (1999); Christie and Loseby (eds.) (1996).

stylistic forms also conveyed information to an audience: they could express authority and the origins and legitimacy of such power. The late Roman Empire produced large quantities of official metalwork for distribution to its civil and military services. The decorative style employed on such artefacts, principally brooches and belt-sets, expressed a link with the Empire and its power structures. So important was this in the contemporary thought-world that elements of these designs were occasionally transferred to objects of female attire and, more importantly, the same motifs also displayed status and power in barbarian territory. Thus the alteration of artistic motifs that occurred around the time of the western Empire's political demise is extremely significant, expressing changes in ideas and social structures and ways of coping with those transformations.

As well as allowing an appreciation of geographical diversity, the increasingly voluminous archaeological material reveals that change was dynamic. All the evidential forms discussed above manifest repeated transformations in our period. Burial rituals underwent frequent and significant change and the disposal of the dead is an extremely important focus for ideas of religion, cosmology, social relations and so on. Similarly, the layout and structure of settlements underwent regular and noteworthy developments. These too are central to ideas of social structure, the organisation of life and relations with the natural world. Alterations to any of these areas were not made lightly. The archaeologically revealed dynamism of the period is extremely important, permitting a vital insight into the changes surrounding the collapse of the western Roman Empire and a rounded appreciation of their causes and of how people in the myriad communities of western Europe participated in and responded to them.

This dynamism is enhanced by a multi-disciplinary approach, using all of the sources of evidence available, written, archaeological, epigraphic and numismatic. The multi-disciplinary model involves the close and contextualised study of each form of evidence separately and on its own merits, before bringing conclusions together at a higher level.[84] This approach permits an appreciation of the diversity of experiences during these centuries. In the different regions of Europe differing types of evidence survive, painting varying pictures of social and political transformation. This allows us to return to the

---

[84] See, e.g. Halsall (1995a); (1997).

issues raised in the first section of this chapter. With the attempt to integrate regional diversity of experience comes an effort to incorporate political history in the social and, at the same time, to give the social a place in the political. In so doing an attempt is made to restore to the individual a role in moulding the period's political history. The outcome of struggles and decisions within countless communities like those of Saba's village, Lepcis Magna or the Merovingian Auvergne determined the success or failure of kingdoms. At the same time the results of battles and high political events were responded to, and had effects in, all of these communities, shaping the precise nature of those identities that were most politically efficacious. Social identities cross-cut each other. In this period the ideas of the Roman Empire and the relationship between its civilisation and the barbarians also governed views of correct political behaviour, which incorporated the proper conduct of men and women. Thus our analysis has to be one of mentalities as well as social and political structures. The latter after all are constituted by worldviews; they are not extrinsic to them. Gender, therefore, had an important role in these political renegotiations.

This book opens in the mid-fourth century, with the Roman Empire at the height of the period sometimes called the Dominate and looking as strong as ever. This allows us to sketch late Roman social structures and those of the barbarians and the relationships between the Empire and the polities beyond its borders before the migrations began. Although the narrative section begins in 376 with the Gothic crisis, the traditional starting date for all discussions of the barbarians and the fall of Rome, this is in order to argue that this date and this crisis have been exaggerated in importance. The story really begins in 388. After narrating the period's political events up to the early sixth century the book surveys social and political structures in western Europe within and without the former frontiers before moving on to analyse some key areas: the mechanisms of migration and settlement and the creation of new identities. The volume closes with the Justinianic wars of 533–61. The book's terminal point shifts according to geographical area and thematic topic, but might conveniently be set in 568, on the eve of the Lombard invasion of Italy. Although it would have been ideal to have taken the story of the migrations into the middle of the seventh century in order to encompass early Lombard Italy and the emergence of the Anglo-Saxon kingdoms into documentary history, this would have made the book prohibitively lengthy. The rounded, contextualised analysis of the western Roman Empire's collapse and its replacement by non-Roman kingdoms is complex enough. Furthermore, the end of the sixth century saw another period of profound social, economic and political change, in many ways dependent upon Justinian's reconquests, which redefined the outlines of western European politics. These wars also put an end to two barbarian kingdoms, those of the Vandals and the Ostrogoths. The Visigothic kingdom went into a period of crisis as a result of Justinian's attack and the Franks destroyed the Burgundian and Thuringian realms at about the same time. For all these reasons the conclusion of Justinian's wars makes a suitable place to end this study.

The nature of the project thus explains this book's chronological parameters but it also accounts for its geographical coverage. The argument presented here traces the fifth-century changes to the specific social and political structures of the fourth-century western Roman Empire and to its particular relationships with the barbarians on its northern frontiers. The western Roman Empire and the polities beyond its borders were inextricably linked. Thus, to understand the migrations we must consider barbarian territory not just before the migrations, as is usually the case, but throughout the period. Comparison between the barbarians east of the Rhine and those of northern Britain, Ireland and North Africa and their relations with the Empire furthers this argument. The eastern Empire is excluded largely because it plays little part in this analysis. Things appear to have been different there, in terms of social and economic structures and the relationships between regional élites and central government.[85] When these resembled those of the fourth- and fifth-century west, in the later sixth and seventh centuries, the eastern Empire underwent similar changes and its own profound crisis.[86] Admittedly, to make this argument fully rounded, a detailed comparison with the east would have been ideal. This would however have necessitated close consideration of the barbarians of the Danube frontier up to the Slavic migrations. Quite apart from lengthening the book out of all proportion, such a study would for linguistic and other reasons have

---

[85] See, e.g. Cameron, A. M. (ed.) (1995); Cameron, A. M., and King, G. R. D. (eds.) (1994).
[86] Below, pp. 512–13.

exceeded my competence. What remains is, I hope, ambitious enough and has taxed my competence accordingly.

The east–west, Mediterranean axis has dominated the historiography of this period and this is understandable, especially if one wishes to study the transformation of classical culture. However, this book argues that a north–south axis, from Scandinavia to the Sahara, should be seen as of equal importance in understanding the specificities of fifth-century western European history.

Much simplified, the thesis of this book can be stated thus. The early Roman period was altogether exceptional in European history but the circumstances that brought about this situation had ceased to pertain by the third century. Late Roman western Europe was increasingly socially and economically fragmented and therefore difficult to govern. A solution was adopted which relied heavily upon a particular form of rule and the management of patronage in various forms to bind the peripheries into the centre. The Roman and non-Roman (barbarian) worlds were inextricably linked in the late imperial period and barbarian society, economics and politics were dependent upon particular relationships with the Empire. When the nature of imperial rule changed around 400 this produced social and political stress, particularly in the key north-western provinces and in the barbarian territories. This stress created political vacuums at local and regional levels in the western Empire, into which non-Roman political, social and military units were drawn. At the same time as, and inextricably linked with, this development it also impelled the movement of political factions from *barbaricum* into the Empire. In these circumstances new political identities were forged, which effectively replaced the political role of the Roman Empire, although other aspects of Roman identity were sometimes maintained. The ideological abandonment of Rome and concepts of empire, civilisation and barbarism was, however, never easy and the barbarians could not furnish an alternative before the Empire's political demise; renegotiating identities therefore had to involve existing Roman ideologies, particularly those associated with the army. In all of these areas the role of lower-level community, local and regional politics were indissolubly linked to high political developments. The 'barbarian migrations' were, therefore, the product of the 'end of the Roman Empire', and not vice versa.

2

DEFINING IDENTITIES

_____ . _____

ETHNICITY

There is no room here for an extended discussion of the complex historiography of ethnicity.[1] A brief, simplified outline must suffice, followed by my own understanding of ethnicity. The roots of the word lie in the Greek *ethnos* (pl. *ethne*) or people. Thus ethnicity should simply mean membership of a people. However that only relocates the problem of definition: what is a people? In the nineteenth century a people was held to be commensurate with the nation and thence with the state, and to be physically, morally and psychologically distinct.[2] The biological, or more usually pseudo-biological, idea of race was confused with the sociological concept of ethnicity.

Such views of ethnicity are called 'primordialist'. Even as students of the subject moved towards the idea that ethnicity was culturally rather than biologically defined, the notion persisted that it was a given, something you were born with. In the second quarter of the twentieth century the appalling uses to which these ideas could be put

---

[1] Ethnicity studies since *c.*1960 form an enormous bibliography. I have found Eriksen (1993) the most useful overview. There is a helpful introduction in Heather (1996), pp. 3–7; Brather (2004), pp. 29–96. Numerous ethnicity readers, e.g., Guibernau and Rex (1997); Hutchinson and Smith (1996). Anderson, B. (1983) and Smith, A. D. (1986) have been important in the development of the historical study of ethnicity but I have found both difficult to apply to late antiquity.

[2] Above, p. 14.

became all too clear. However, equally dreadful applications of notions of race and national characteristics had occurred much earlier in the processes of European colonisation. The horrific activities of Leopold II (1865–1909) of Belgium's 'force publique' in his private state of the Congo represent an extreme example. It is salutary to ponder the fact that only the use of racist concepts to justify genocide *within* Europe forced their reconsideration. Racial characteristics and physical anthropological ideas of race were questioned and largely abandoned, though such attitudes long survived even in ostensibly scholarly work[3] and were revived to devastating effect in the twentieth century's last decade, during the break-up of the communist bloc in the Balkans.

By the 1960s ethnicity was seen above all as a matter of belief in one's membership of a group. A milestone was the publication of *Ethnic Groups and Boundaries*, edited by Fredrik Barth.[4] Barth himself worked amongst the Swat Pathans of Afghanistan and Pakistan and noted that some Pathans, finding themselves in situations where they could no longer excel in the activities that they held to constitute Pathan identity, 'became' Baluchis or Kohistanis.[5] This 'instrumentalist' interpretation sees ethnicity as something one can adopt and discard according to social situations and has much relevance to our study. Many peoples simply disappeared from the historical record: the Gauls in what is now France, the Britons in England and the Ostrogoths in Italy, to take three examples. Hitherto these disappearances had been interpreted, following statements by early medieval authors pondering the issue, to imply physical displacement at best and extermination at worst.[6] Instrumentalist approaches to ethnicity have consequently become very influential amongst scholars questioning these interpretations of late antiquity and the early Middle Ages.

Attempts have been made to revive primordialist notions and develop instrumentalist ideas,[7] as well as to bridge the gap between the two camps through the use of other theory.[8] By the 1980s the

[3] Baker (1974).   [4] Barth (ed.) (1969).   [5] Barth (1969b).
[6] Heather (2003) revives this notion in relationship to the Ostrogoths.
[7] Controversially, van den Berghe applied evolutionary biological ideas: van den Berghe (1978); critique in Reynolds, V. (1980a); response: van den Berghe (1980) with comment: Reynolds, V. (1980b). On the other hand, and equally provocatively, Banton developed instrumentalism into 'rational choice theory', e.g. Banton (1998), pp. 196–219. See *ERS* for debates.
[8] Bentley (1987), drawing upon the work of Pierre Bourdieu (1977).

instrumentalist view had given rise to the theory of 'situational ethnicity', that ethnicity was employed as and when the situation demanded.[9] Patrick Geary applied this theory to the study of the barbarian migrations. More recently, by contrast, Peter Heather has presented strong objections to the idea that ethnic identities can simply be adopted and changed according to an individual's intentions or circumstances. Heather argues forcefully that the disappearance and reappearance of ethnic units demonstrates incomplete assimilation of subordinated groups and thus the relative impermeability of the boundaries between such units. Ethnicity continues to be hotly debated.

What people think defines ethnicity is endlessly fluid. Belief in shared descent is common. Language can also determine ethnicity. Elsewhere, religion or unifying social customs, even law, are invoked, as occasionally is one's place of residence. All these factors can be employed to give shape to an ethnic group yet, for every case where a particular factor is deployed, another exists where there is no correlation between it and ethnicity. Religious beliefs, for example, helped define late antique *ethne*, with the Arianism of the Goths, Burgundians and Vandals or the Anglo-Saxons' paganism and, in the modern world, with Catholicism or Protestantism in Northern Ireland or the Catholicism or Orthodoxy of Croats and Serbs. There are, however, equally numerous cases where shared religion did not prevent violently hostile relationships. The mutual Catholicism of the French and Spanish in the early modern period is one illustration. At the same time there might be religious divisions within ethnic units: again, early modern France provides an example. Equally, the shared language of Ulster Protestants and Catholics or of Serbs and Croats has not prevented violent division. Although ethnicity might be defined by habitation within a defined area, different ethnic groups have overlapped geographically and shared residential locations for centuries (the evils of 'ethnic cleansing' would not have been possible without this fact). Distinct (often antagonistic) ethnic groups (for example the Nuer and Dinka in eastern Africa) can share customs and other cultural practices, which in other cases define membership of an *ethnos*. They can also be *believed* to delineate an ethnic group whilst in reality being little used, or shared with other people![10] Even ideas of

[9] Okamura, J.Y. (1981) for a useful survey.
[10] Moerman (1968); below, pp. 61–2.

common origin are not universal and there are cases where different
ethnic groups believed in descent from a single ancestor.[11]
The only common factor in defining ethnicity is belief: in the
reality of your group and the difference of others. Ethnicity is *cognitive*: a state of mind. It is not, however, simply identity. There are
many types of social identity – religion, class, gender and age – but
ethnicity does not necessarily correlate with any of these. It occupies a
distinct arc within the spectrum of social identities. Sometimes certain classes were equated with particular ethnic identities, and ethnicity has sometimes apparently been gendered. Nevertheless in no
case did the occupation of a particular class situation or the possession
of specific sex attributes define the ethnic group.

A common mistake is to assume that ethnicity has only one layer. A
modern male inhabitant of London might, for example, see himself as
British, English, a 'southerner', a Londoner or as from Brixton. All
these levels might be important within social interaction, either to
proclaim a shared identity with individuals with whom it is advan-
tageous to stress similarity or alternatively to proclaim difference from
other individuals (or even from the same individuals in other situations). To take another example, Yorkshiremen might see themselves as a different group from Lancastrians when discussing the
annual 'roses' cricket matches between Yorkshire and Lancashire.
They might, however, come together as northerners when a
northern team plays one from southern England and all, northerners
and southerners, might join forces when England play Scotland. At
another level Englishmen and Scotsmen all carry British passports
when abroad and it is this level to which all refer in cases of difficulty.
Some Britons at the start of the twenty-first century also regard
themselves as Europeans and, at the other end of the scale, there are
lower levels of ethnicity: the 'Londoner', 'south Londoner' and
'Brixtonian' levels in the case above. If the individual were also of
Chinese, Indian or West African descent yet other dimensions of his
identity would exist. We could think of similar hierarchies of identity
in any country and it was the same in late antiquity. Theodehad, who
became king of the Goths in Italy in 534,[12] was a Goth but also

[11] According to Jordanes' *Getica* (17.94–5, 24.122–3), the Goths envisaged some
sort of ancient kinship with Gepids and Huns. Fredegar, *Chronicle* 2.6, claimed
common descent for Franks and Turks.
[12] See below, p. 501.

appears to have seen himself as a Tuscan landlord and as a Roman nobleman, involving himself in the traditional cultural pursuits of that class. Ethnicity is *multi-layered*. This point is vital to my argument in this book and has been given insufficient attention in many studies.

One might object that some of these levels are 'residential' rather than 'ethnic' but the difference is, on reflection, very blurred. 'From Brixton' might mean that one was born there rather than living there, implying importance attached to descent. Even a very local identity can go beyond mere shared residence. Think of the phrase 'we don't do things like that round here', suggesting common beliefs about correct behaviour. Some people from particular regions invoke a history giving them a distinct identity. Reference to 'Viking' ancestry is not uncommon in northern England, for example, as, in distinguishing Lancastrians from Yorkshiremen, is appeal to a history of strife based upon myths of the Wars of the Roses.[13] The denial of an ethnic character to the lower rungs of this ladder is equivalent to the refusal to acknowledge broader regional ethnic identities by the governments of modern nation states. Furthermore, it might only be true that these identities lack a fully ethnic character *at the moment*. In a changed political context, a hypothetical break-up of the United Kingdom for example, they might become vitally important dimensions of social identity. All such levels provide a potential resource within social interaction that can only meaningfully be termed ethnic. At the other end of the scale, dominant or default identities are, equally, frequently denied ethnic status. In many studies, ethnic identity implies minority status.[14] Yet there are many occasions in history when such 'high-level' ethnicities are actively sought and stressed by members of groups that in other social, spatial or chronological contexts might proclaim a more local and distinctive identity. The competition to become Roman during the early imperial centuries is a case in point. The contingencies of political history have also made some inhabitants of certain areas of Europe stress their Europeanness: Germans embarrassed by the Third Reich, Irish seeking to escape from an English-dominated 'British' archipelago, Spaniards relieved at the end of the Franco era's isolation,

---

[13] Smith, A. D. (1979, e.g.) is therefore, in my view, mistaken to distinguish English northerners from an ethnic group.

[14] This is especially true of studies of ethnicity in the USA.

and so on. In other circumstances, the emphasis upon this level of ethnicity might become more general.

As these examples make clear, ethnicity is, furthermore, *performative*.[15] It has nothing innate or immanent. Everything that proclaims the membership of an ethnic group, be it clothing, customs or whatever, and whether learnt almost subconsciously in the process of socialisation or adopted more deliberately later, must to some extent be performed. It is important, though, to note that ethnic relations are frequently unequal. 'Performed ethnicity' might be *forced* upon members of one group by those of another more powerful ethnic body. For example, many white inhabitants of the southern United States expected (and some still expect) their black neighbours to behave in a particular way in relationships with them, and many black people behaved accordingly in those circumstances as a result. There is nothing natural about such behaviour. As well as being enforced upon the weak, the latter might adopt it in order either to evade violence or to try to improve their situation with the help of the more powerful. It is not unlikely that Roman expectations of non-Romans produced similar situations.

Furthermore, ethnicity is performed in particular circumstances. In the multi-layered British identity just discussed, the different levels were invoked in different specific situations to proclaim either shared identity or difference. Ethnicity is therefore also *situational*. However, such a statement, nowadays a core tenet of instrumentalism, should be understood as incorporating four clarifying points. The first is that 'situation' must be understood at micro- and macro-levels. Following Okamura,[16] the micro-level might properly be called the *situation*, the specific social encounter within which an individual finds him- or herself interacting with another individual at a particular place and time. The second, macro-level can be called the *setting*: the wider social, economic and political context within which the situation is located. This might define the relative power available to members of different ethnic groups. Moving beyond Okamura's discussion, we should stress the reciprocal relationship between *setting* and *situation*. The *setting* establishes the terms for the playing out of the *situation* but it is, and can only be, constituted by knowledge of the outcomes

---

[15] In for example Barth's studies, Pashto (Pathan language and identity) was definitely something to be *done* rather than spoken. Barth (1969b).
[16] Okamura, J. Y. (1981).

of myriad *situations*, those thought right and proper and those considered inappropriate and wrong. Every interaction between members of particular ethnic groups has the potential to alter, in however minute a fashion, the broader setting. For example, if, bit by bit, every member of the white ruling class of a racially segregated state came (for whatever reason) to decide that it suited their purposes better to ignore the rules and behavioural codes of segregation then that state would disappear. Similar processes lie behind late antique western European ethnic changes. In recognising this fact we give the local communities discussed in chapter 1 their place in shaping continental history.

The second clarifying point, following from the first, is that one does not always have a free choice. The setting might determine the possibilities of employing or avoiding ethnicity. Further, an individual does not choose all of the identities that he or she can possess. An individual is born to one, or more usually several, identities within the ethnic arc of the spectrum. A group might deny membership to an outsider who wished to join. There may be physical traits that contemporary ideology has focused upon in the ordering of society, making the adoption of another identity far from straightforward. Skin colour is the clearest example. As noted, ethnicity can be ascribed by others and the performance of such an identity demanded by a more powerful group. A change (or the ignorance) of identity can be refused by others and, on the other hand, many people might not wish to alter their ethnicity. To say that ethnicity can be changed does not necessarily mean that this is done lightly. The logical extension of the view that concepts of ethnic difference are entirely socially contingent must be to accept that in some social formations it might be understood that a person *cannot* change identity. Whatever its material or instrumental advantages or disadvantages, ethnic affiliation can have an affective importance that often overrides material or 'rational' factors.

Thus, third, the instrumentalism involved in choosing to deploy ethnicity in particular situations should *not* be understood, as it frequently is by both instrumentalists and their critics, as representing only material advantage. One criticism aimed at instrumentalism is that it makes the members of persecuted or otherwise dominated groups instruments of their own repression. Members of subordinate groups might deploy their ethnicity to claim the support of networks within that group, to enhance their own group identity and to foster means of resistance (more often subtle and subversive than violent). The creation of an African-American identity in the USA is a clear example. An effective political identity has been forged, in a situation of domination and by using the dominant group's classificatory system (race and colour), from diverse groups that, even where they were aware of each other's existence, would frequently have seen themselves as having little in common, or even as being mutually antagonistic, before the European slave trade. The deployment of such an ethnicity can be used to avoid persecution and even as a means of resistance in itself. If a dominant ethnic group believes a subordinate one to be lazy and stupid, members of the latter can effectively resist their overlords by feigning miscomprehension of commands and working as slowly as possible.

The fourth clarification of the situational–instrumental position is that the relations between ethnic groups are by no means uniform. Within poly-ethnic societies they are rarely based upon an even distribution of power but there are other forms of relationship ranging from absolute domination, through joking relationships to hostility based on an equality of power, all of which alter the precise ways in which ethnic identity is deployed instrumentally.

Finally, ethnicity is *dynamic*. Just as situations and settings change through social and geographical context, their interrelationship means they vary through time. Ethnicities can be reordered in importance, new identities can become available and old ones dwindle in significance, only, perhaps, to be rediscovered later. This is very clear in Europe during the break-up of the Roman Empire and the barbarian migrations.

Seeing ethnicity as cognitive, multi-layered, performative, situational and dynamic allows us to counter some objections to instrumentalism in the study of late antique ethnic change. These have not always used appropriate examples, employing modern nation states with defined borders, legal notions of citizenship, formal passports and more or less orderly immigration procedures.[17] Obviously, one cannot simply turn up at the border or at an airport passport control and claim to be British, French, German or what have you, at whim. However, these examples ignore the point that, once within a modern state, identities are as mutable as ever. The example of the USA is a case in point. Once past the formal and,

---

[17] E.g. Heather (1996), p. 6.

theoretically, rigorous border and immigration controls, incomers from countless countries of origin have forged a common American identity, usually (and this is the real point) on top of or besides other ethnic identities (African-American, Latino, Italian-American and so on). Recognition of this fact gave the lie to what was called the 'melting pot' theory of ethnicity. Such examples also evade the question of knowledge. To deny someone membership of a particular group requires awareness of his or her background, family origins and so on. This is rarely to be had, even in close-knit communities, if reference is made to ancestors two generations back. Who, for example, would have the knowledge to deny a claim that someone who had lived all of her life in England and had a strong English accent had in fact had a Scottish grandfather? In a late antique situation who, within a mobile and fluid group of Goths could gainsay the claim of a Roman provincial to have had a Gothic grandfather?

The fact that individuals possess a series of identities, which we might think of as ethnic, and can order and reorder them in terms of importance, further facilitates such strategies. There were members of numerous ethnic groups within Theoderic's Ostrogoths.[18] Here people had been accepted as Gothic despite additional identities. Once acknowledged as having both identities, however, one might very well play up one at the expense of the other until, in this example, the individual was more Gothic than Roman. In extreme cases, through marriage, name change and so on – both strategies well attested in late antiquity – the individual might to all intents and purposes lose his Roman identity completely.

Even ethnic markers which might seem immutable – physical traits, skin colour and so on – are on reflection not as decisive as we might expect from a modern western perspective. A physical anthropological characteristic needs to be understood as signifying difference within a cultural system. Some cultures might regard hair or eye colour as signifying a particular identity and give them prominence in social differentiation, whereas others might note skin colour and others might attach importance to none of these aspects. The Romans, for example, do not appear to have attached overriding importance to skin colour. The sheer spectrum of skin pigmentation (or hair colours), especially around the Mediterranean, makes it very difficult to define a sharp dividing line between 'black' and 'white'

[18] See, e.g. Wolfram (1988), pp. 300–2.

skin. Thus there are dark-skinned 'white' people and pale-skinned 'black' people.[19] The difference between the two and the importance assigned to that difference depend upon culturally specific ideas about race, biology and identity, about how humanity can be divided up. Where these factors are not decisive it is cultural attributes, adopted by individuals, that allow the ascription to one or other 'racial' group. Even at the extremes, where there can be little debate about skin colour, it is difficult to gainsay a claim to descent from another group. Who could deny that someone with very dark skin had a white grandmother, or grandfather, unless they actually knew that individual's family-tree? Decisions to accept or reject the claim rest on other factors. The failure to appreciate these points produced heated debate over the extent of 'black' input into classical culture. Certain individuals might or might not have had skin that we would today think of as 'black' but 'black' and 'white' are modern racial constructs. Both parties in this debate divide past society according to contingent, modern notions of race, which is far from helpful.[20]

All of the discussion above about the theoretical fluidity of ethnic identity would, however, be pointless if late antique people had no concept of themselves except as belonging to immutable groups. To change ethnicity, a culture must have a notion of the individual, or the self, made up of particular identities that can be changed. It has been claimed that the classification of societies and styles of life into groups, which could be chosen, following models and becoming models for others, was a 'discovery' of the twelfth century. This does not seem to be the case.[21] The Romans divided the world up into groups but saw membership of their own as a matter of proper conduct, which one could choose to adopt or ignore. Ambrose (bishop of Milan, †397) exhorted each member of his flock to 'look upon himself and his own conscience' and follow

[19] See, e.g. the story recounted by Dave Chapelle, a black comedian, in *The Chicago Tribune*, 5 May 2004, about how his light-skinned grandfather boarded a bus in a black neighbourhood in Washington DC the day after Martin Luther King's assassination. Being blind, Chapelle's grandfather did not at first realise that the 'foolish' 'white fellow' abused by the passengers was himself.
[20] Thompson, L. A. (1989) is excellent on this issue.
[21] Walker Bynum (1982). This interesting discussion of the twelfth-century situation does not demonstrate, or indeed argue except by assertion, any difference from preceding centuries.

a godly path.[22] The idea of distinct groups with associated patterns of behaviour, where one could decide to change from one to another, was hardly alien to late antiquity (especially in a world of religious conversion). This did not, however, mean that a change of ethnicity was easily made.

None of the above denies ethnicity's importance. It is often overlooked that Barth himself, often mistakenly thought to have invented instrumentalism, said that the fluidity of ethnic boundaries did not reduce their importance.[23] Ethnic identities, whilst mutable, are amongst the most powerful means by which people organise their world. That they are essentially fictive in no way diminishes their significance. One does not have to look very far to see people killing, and dying, for the sake of ethnic identity. That is the great tragedy of ethnicity.

'MEN WHO HAVE NOTHING HUMAN BEYOND THEIR LIMBS AND VOICES'? THE ROMAN VIEW[24]

Scipio: Now tell me, was Romulus a king of the barbarians?
Laelius: If, as the Greeks say, all men are either Greeks or barbarians, I am afraid he was; but if that name ought to be applied on the basis of men's manners rather than their language, I do not consider the Greeks less barbarous than the Romans.
Scipio: For the purposes of our present subject we consider only character, not race (*gens*).[25]

Analysing Roman views of the barbarian requires us to view the problem as an archaeological site with many layers to be stripped away. At the surface level the Roman concept of the barbarian was derived ultimately from that of the Greeks. The *barbarus*, in the first instance, was someone who spoke an unintelligible language, literally someone who burbled. For the Greeks this included the Romans, as Laelius says in the extract from Cicero's (†43 BC) *Republic* above,

[22] Ambrose, *The Soul* 8.79. Augustine's writings, notably *Free Will* and the *Confessions*, make similar points. See Brown, P. R. L. (1998a) for an introduction to late antique ideas of the self, and the changes that took place in this period.
[23] Barth (1969a), p. 9.
[24] For useful introductions see Brather (2004), pp. 117–38; Geary (1999); (2002); Heather (1999); (2005); Jones, W. (1971); Ladner (1976). The quote refers to *Germani* and comes from Velleius Paterculus, *Roman History* 2.117.
[25] Cicero, *Republic* 1.37.58.

necessitating some modifications for Roman usage of the term. During the struggle for dominance in Italy and the Mediterranean, Rome had appropriated the Greek vocabulary of the barbarian,[26] so that by the early Empire, the barbarians were primarily those who lived beyond the political limits of, and were opposed to, Roman rule.

The second layer to be excavated in studying ideas of the barbarian involves political geography. The Roman Empire stood at the centre of the world, surrounded by barbarians.[27] As an anonymous late fourth-century writer said:

> Above all it must be noted that wild nations are pressing upon the Roman Empire and howling about it everywhere, and treacherous barbarians, covered by natural positions, are assailing every frontier.[28]

Since Herodotus in the fifth century BC it had been believed that the further one progressed from the shores of the Mediterranean, the more outlandish these 'wild nations' became.[29] The Romans retained this idea[30] and used natural 'scientific' reasons to justify it. The Greeks evolved a climatic theory of human nature. Placing themselves at the centre of the world, they perceived the characteristics of the surrounding peoples according to the fact that they lived too close to one or other equinox or too far to the north or south. Asiatics, for example, lived too far to the east, where things grew easily and where seasonal changes were not dramatic. As a result they became slothful and allowed themselves to become subjugated to monarchy. Scythians and Egyptians suffered from living too far north and south respectively. In the centre of the world, the Greeks, with pronounced seasonal changes and mixed geography, combined the best of all worlds. The coexistence of different features made them the best warriors and, naturally, prone to the best forms of government.[31]

---

[26] Dench (1995).

[27] Balsdon (1979), pp. 214–59, is an interesting if undigested catalogue of Roman descriptions of 'funny foreigners'.

[28] *On Matters Military* 6.1, written in the 360s or 370s.

[29] Pliny the Elder, *Natural History* 7.1–2, discusses the human race and odd customs and manners, especially 'those of people living more remote from the sea'.

[30] Pliny, *Natural History* 7.1–2, gives a series of examples from the inhabitants of the furthest reaches of the earth, including Scythians, Chinese and Ethiopians, of people with truly weird and wonderful characteristics: cannibals, people who are half male and half female, people who can kill with a stare, and so on.

[31] *Airs, Waters, Places* 12–24 is the earliest expression of this theory. See also Plato, *Republic* 4.11; Aristotle, *Politics* 1327b.

Perhaps not surprisingly, since they lived well to the west of the
Greeks, by Augustus' time the Romans had evolved a rather more
'banded' view of the world and of national characteristics.[32] People
like the Ethiopians, living in southern regions too close to the sun, or
those like the Germans who lived too far from it in the north, were
held to suffer certain damaging consequences. However, around the
Mediterranean things were just right:

In the middle of the earth, owing to a healthy blending of both elements [fire
and moisture], there are tracts that are fertile for all sorts of produce, and men
are of medium bodily stature, with a marked blending even in the matter of
complexion; customs are gentle, senses clear, intellects fertile and able to grasp
the whole of nature; and they also have governments, which the outer races
never have possessed, any more than they have ever been subject to the central
races, being quite detached and solitary on account of the savagery of the
nature which broods over those regions.[33]

The Romans had taken up a strand of Hellenistic thought that
derived 'moderation' not from having examples of both extremes but
from being midway between them. It is important to note how
rational behaviour and subjection to government were central to the
difference between civilised and barbarian. Character rather than race
is crucial. Pliny's (†79) explanation shows why the races beyond the
frontiers do not, and perhaps cannot, share this character.[34]

There also existed a belief that the barbarian represented a more
primitive form of life, which the process of civilisation in the
Mediterranean had, for good or ill, left behind. Lucretius' (†55 BC)
account of earliest man is reminiscent of accounts of the more remote
barbarian tribes. The civilising process largely involved the restriction
of sexual activity to married partners and the acquisition of law.[35]
Pliny supported the plausibility of his accounts of the weird and
wonderful human types to be found at the earth's edges by claiming
that vestiges of such things could still be found in Italy.[36] Propertius

---

[32] Vitruvius, *Architecture* 6.1 expresses this particularly clearly.

[33] Pliny the Elder, *Natural History*, 2.80.190.

[34] In the late Roman period the same view was expressed clearly by Vegetius,
Epitome 1.2. Balsdon (1979), pp. 59–60.

[35] Lucretius, *Nature of Things* 5.925–1090. The sexually licentious, berry-eating
man, living under branches and leaves, calls to mind Tacitus' account of the
Fenni, quoted below.

[36] *Natural History* 7.2.9.

described the ancestors of the Romans in terms usually reserved for the barbarians: wearing skins.[37] There was thus a physical geographical, a biological and a historical dimension to Graeco-Roman bipartite division of the world into civilisation and barbarism.

These ideas are also manifest in the ways in which Greek and Roman ethnographers habitually equated new barbarian political groupings with old tribes. Huns and Goths were called Scythians and *Getae*, and Sassanid Persians were referred to as Parthians or Medes. Partly this resulted from the demands of the genres in which these writers worked. Greek writers were expected to ape the great writers of 'Attic' Greek (that written during the heyday of the Athenian state) in precise vocabulary as well as in style and content. No Huns and Sassanids were to be found in the pages of Herodotus or Thucydides but there were Scythians and Medes aplenty. Latin writers inherited a less pronounced concern with ethnographic detail, and a lesser aversion to new words, but were still expected to use the language of their models. The stylistic replacement of 'modern' names for ethnic groups like Franks with more classical names like Sicambri persisted throughout our period and beyond. Quite aside from the exigencies of style, however, an idea underlay this practice that, fundamentally, barbarians from particular areas were all the same, no matter how they changed their names.[38]

Beneath the overarching division into civilised men and barbarians was a concern to describe and classify the different peoples of the world. A survey of the principal barbarian types, moving clockwise around the imperial frontiers reveals the stylised and compartmentalised way in which Mediterranean writers viewed the savage lands round about. Whether or not these barbarians were really like this does not concern us. Such matters will be examined in the next chapter. To the north and north-west of the Roman frontiers lived the barbarians grouped, sometimes by the Romans and much more commonly by later scholars, under the headings of Celts and Germans. In the Roman period these stereotypes covered the Gauls, the inhabitants of Britain – Britons, Irish and Picts – and the peoples who lived north of the Rhine and upper Danube frontiers. Strabo (†29) said that the whole race of Gauls was war-mad: very brave when victorious but cowardly when not. The *Belgae* in the north were, he claimed, the bravest, and the Britons taller, less yellow-haired and

---

[37] Propertius, *Elegies* 4.1, lines 11–12.   [38] Procopius, *Wars* 3.2.2–5.

looser built.[39] Dio Cassius (†235) said that the Gauls 'seize eagerly
upon what they desire and cling most tenaciously to their successes,
but if they meet with the slightest obstacle, have no hope at all left for
the future'; 'in brief time they rush abruptly to the very opposite
extremes, since they can furnish no sound reason for either course'.
Further on, the Gauls are 'unreasonably insatiate in all their passions,
know no moderation in either courage or fear' and plunge from one
to the other.[40] The Gauls' mercurial nature had a long life in ethnography.[41] These accounts illustrate the Roman idea that moderation and reason were things of which the barbarians were incapable.
Although Tacitus (†117) apparently considered the Irish to be much
like the British,[42] Strabo had earlier heard that they were more savage,
were man-eaters and enjoyed complete sexual licence, even with their
own mothers and sisters:[43] a good example of a hearsay description
of a people living, to Roman eyes, at the edge of the world.

Across the North Sea from these 'Celtic' peoples, and north of the
Rhine and upper Danube frontiers lived the *Germani*. The first classic
description of the *Germani* was Julius Caesar's (†44 BC).[44] Caesar's
account itself shows how the Romans thought that time could
modify the characteristics of people. The Gauls, he thought, had lost
their martial valour from too much contact with civilisation. The
Germani by contrast retained an insatiable appetite for war, their
society and its institutions were much simpler, and they retained
some virtues especially as regards chastity and hospitality. Caesar
thought that society and settlement patterns were much more fluid
east of the Rhine, though his account seems demonstrably misguided.
Strabo considered these peoples to be wilder, taller and to have
yellower hair than the Celts, but otherwise to be similar to them.[45]
Pliny believed that there were five races of *Germani*: Vandals,
Ingvaones, Istiaeones, Hermiones, and the race of the *Peucini* and
Bastarnae.[46] Tacitus, in his *Histories*, set out the key characteristics of

[39] Strabo, *Geography* 4.4.2 (war-mad), 4.4.3 (*Belgae*), 4.4.5 (brave when victorious but cowardly when not), 4.5.2 (Britons).
[40] *Roman History* 12.50.2–3, 14.57.6b, 39.45.7.
[41] See Gerald of Wales' description of the Welsh, esp. *Journey through Wales* 2.1, 2.3.
[42] *Agricola* 24.   [43] Strabo, *Geography* 4.5.4.   [44] *Gallic War* 6.21–4.
[45] Strabo, *Geography* 7.1.2; see also 4.4.2.
[46] The ethnic affiliation of the Bastarnae was a matter of some debate. Dio, *Roman History* 38.10.3, thought they were Scythians but then he believed that the *Suebi* – the archetypal *Germani* for Caesar – were *Keltoi*.

the 'Germanic' barbarian, which lived long in the minds of Roman authors.[47] Like the Gauls, the *Germani* are emboldened by success. Wild and incautious, they obey only blind fury. Following lost work by the elder Pliny, Tacitus' *Germania* presented a detailed geography of these peoples but, as is still too often forgotten, did this for moral purposes, to highlight Roman shortcomings, rather than to present a factual ethnographic report. This is especially apparent when one considers the ways in which the *Germani* become more stereotypical and extreme the further from the Empire they live, culminating in the Fenni, who:

are astonishingly wild and poor. They have no arms, no horses and no homes. They eat grass, dress in skins and sleep on the ground. Their only hope is in their arrows, which, for lack of iron, they tip with bone. The same hunt provides food for men and women alike; for the women go everywhere with the men and claim a share in securing the prey. The only way they can protect their babies against wild beasts is to hide them under a makeshift network of branches. This is the hovel to which the young men come back; this is where the old must lie. Yet they count their lot happier than that of others who groan over field labour, sweat over house building, or hazard their own or other men's fortunes to the wild lottery of hope and fear. They care for nobody, man or god, and have gained the ultimate release: they have nothing to pray for. What comes after them is the stuff of fables – Hellusii and Oxiones with the faces and features of men but the bodies and limbs of animals. On such unverifiable stories I will express no opinion.[48]

Here, at the ends of the earth, lay the complete opposite of the civilised life, with all its good and bad points, found at its centre. Dio Cassius repeated the main characteristics of the *Germani*: that they were like the Gauls, numerous, big, violent, reckless and impetuous, ferocious in their charges but soon exhausted by them.[49] By the fourth century, the political configurations of the *Germani* had changed[50] but Roman writers continued to repeat traditional views, and to hold that all the peoples between the rivers Rhine and Danube and the island (as they thought) of Scandinavia were *Germani* and could be treated together as such.

Further down the Danube, beyond *Germani* like the *Quadi* and extending into the lands north of the Black Sea, things became more complex. In classical ethnography, the middle Danube was the land of

[47] Tacitus, *Histories* 4.23, 2.22, 4.29.   [48] Tacitus, *Germania* 46.
[49] Dio, *Roman History* 38.47.5.   [50] See pp. 118–20 below.

peoples variously called Getic or Scythian. These peoples had included the *Bastarnae*, according to some definitions, and the Dacians, whom Dio Cassius divided into those who were Getic and those who were 'Scythians of a sort', illustrating the rather blurred ideas about this part of the world. The *Getae*, said he, were related to the Thracians of old.[51] Roman authors (and, later, Gothic ones), when searching for a more respectable, classical version of the name of the Goths, sometimes called them *Getae*.

The region north of the Danube was sometimes referred to as *Scythia*, the land of the 'Scythian', the horse-borne nomad. The classic descriptions of the Scythians come from Herodotus and Hippocrates. Ethnographic accounts of *Scythia*, like Ammianus', share characteristics with Tacitus' geography of the *Germani*.[52] Here again, the further one progressed from the Roman borders the wilder and more extreme became the peoples, culminating in the *Vidini* and *Geloni* who made clothes from the skins of dead enemies, the Agathyrsi who, for reasons best known to themselves, painted themselves blue and finally the nomadic and cannibalistic *Melanchlaenae* and *Anthropophagoi*, whose names were, conveniently if unconvincingly, Greek for 'black-cloaks' and 'man-eaters'. On the edge of this region lived, according to report, the Amazons and it was from here that came, to late Roman eyes, the most inhuman of all the barbarians: the Huns.[53]

Although the Scythians were long gone, their name was still applied to the inhabitants of these regions: Taifals and Sarmatians, Alans and Goths. Although the Goths (or at least some of them) spoke a Germanic language, it is significant that when Graeco-Roman writers wanted a classical term for them they tended to use 'Scythian' rather than 'German'. This implies that, as Cicero's Scipio thought, lifestyle was more important than language in ethnographic categorisation.[54] Whatever their language, it seems likely that a semi-nomadic

---

[51] *Roman History* 51.22–3, 26. Dio included the Moesians (Roman provincials by our period) amongst the *Getae*; *Roman History* 51.26.6.

[52] The outer regions of Tacitus' *Germania* appear to be in the same sort of geographical area as the further extremes of *Scythia*, beyond the Sarmatians to the north and east, by the 'ice-bound ocean'.

[53] Amm. Marc. 31.2. See below, pp. 171–3.

[54] This tells against traditional Germanist views, which assume blithely that the Goths were settled agriculturalists, like all other 'Germans'. Also significant is the fact that, as mentioned, when not using 'Scythian', these writers used *Getae* as a

pastoral lifestyle unified the various peoples beyond the middle and lower Danube.[55]

The peoples bordering the Roman Empire to the east will not concern us, but brief description of them and of Mediterranean attitudes to them is necessary in order to underline the general points about Graeco-Roman concepts. South of Scythia and east of the Roman frontiers lay peoples like the Armenians and then, further south, Iran, ruled by the Sassanid dynasty. The Persians continued to be equated with the ancient Medes and Parthians but, while writers in the Greek tradition still referred to the Persians as barbarians, unsurprisingly (the Medes were the archetypal *barbaroi* of classical Greek literature),[56] Latin authors such as Ammianus Marcellinus did not classify Sassanid Iranians as barbarians at all. Again, there was more to being barbarian than simply living outside the Roman Empire. Moving south again, beyond the Syrian and Palestinian frontiers, lived the nomadic Arabs, whom the Romans certainly viewed as barbaric.[57] Across the Red Sea, beyond the borders of Egypt, lived other peoples like the *Blemmyes* and *Nobades*. Pliny believed that the *Blemmyes* had no heads but had mouths and eyes in the middle of their chests.[58]

Finally, around rather than beyond the southern frontier of Roman North Africa lived a bewildering array of peoples, generally classified as *Mauri*, Moors, by Graeco-Roman authors. Beyond them lived the Ethiopians.[59] Living, according to the Romans, too close to the sun, Africans of all sorts had their blood drawn to their heads and had their blood thinned in this way. This, thought the Romans, made them dangerous enemies: clever and crafty but cowardly in a stand-up fight. Dio, drawing on classical accounts of Carthaginians, believed that harshness and cruelty were African characteristics.[60] Even amongst the relatively well-known African peoples, Roman geographers placed the usual array of the weird and wonderful. For Pliny, members of the Atlas tribe had no names and did not dream normal

synonym for Goths, rather than (as modern historians do) associating the Goths with the *Gutones*, who had a respectable pedigree going back to Pliny at least (*Natural History* 4.13.99).

[55] See below, p. 132.   [56] Themistius, *Orations* 5.69b.

[57] Amm. Marc. 14.4.1–7.

[58] *Natural History* 5.8.46. The idea still informed the thirteenth-century compiler of the Hereford *Mappa Mundi*, which shows headless Blemmyes.

[59] On whom see Thompson, L. A. (1989); Balsdon (1979), pp. 217–19.

[60] *Roman History* 78.6.1a.

dreams; there were cave-dwellers who lived on snake flesh alone and had no voice but only squeaked; the *Garamantes* (by late antiquity all too well-known as raiders of Libya) were promiscuous and had no marriages (stereotypical of extreme barbarism); *Gamphasantes* went naked, fought no battles and had no dealings with foreigners; the *Blemmyes* we have just met; after them came Satyrs, Goat-Pans (*Aegipani*) and *Himantopedes* (Strap-Feet).[61] Pliny drew examples of the strangest and most unbelievable types of people from the Ethiopians,[62] once again illustrating the Graeco-Roman notion that the further from the Mediterranean one went, the more outlandish things became.

It is thus easy enough to compile a list of typical features of the barbarian, 'Germanic', 'Celtic', steppes nomadic or African, but here we encounter the next layer of the problem. Even after the grant of universal citizenship in 212, which in some ways did make the difference between Romans and barbarians synonymous with that between those living within the imperial borders and those without, ethnography did not begin at the frontiers. It was still not a straightforward matter of contrasting undifferentiated Romans with stereotypical barbarians. Although clearly pinned at various points to the socio-biological and other concepts underlying the uppermost 'layer' (the bi-polar distinction between civilisation and barbarism), the next, 'taxonomic layer'[63] drew less sharp divisions along the Empire's political boundaries. Because the Roman state had, from early days, incorporated people who had hitherto been foreigners or barbarians, it was believed that the disparate peoples within the Empire also had their own particular characteristics. Dio thought that the emperor Antoninus 'Caracalla' (211–17), author of the grant of universal citizenship, derived the different aspects of his character from the various provinces whence his family hailed.[64] Ammianus wrote a lengthy ethnographic excursus about the Gauls, comparing them favourably with the Italians.[65]

Identities based upon one's home region, province or even city could be used to differentiate between inhabitants of the Empire. Some drew upon pre- and therefore non-Roman characteristics,

---

[61] *Natural History* 5.8.45–6.   [62] *Natural History* 5.43–6.

[63] I have adopted the term 'taxonomic' from discussions with Michael Kulikowski, who is working on a detailed study of this issue.

[64] *Roman History* 78.6.1a.   [65] Amm. Marc. 15.12.

unsurprisingly given that most western *civitates* outside Spain and Italy were based on pre-existing tribal groups. Ausonius (†394), tutor and later praetorian prefect to Emperor Gratian (367–83), famously declared that

> Bordeaux is my homeland: but Rome stands over all homelands
> I love Bordeaux, and cherish Rome; I am citizen in one
> Consul in both; here my cradle, there my chair of office.[66]

Other writers could claim membership of particular *civitates* through paternal and maternal descent and other factors complicated Roman ethnicity. 'I am a Frankish citizen but a Roman soldier in arms' stated one tombstone,[67] clearly illustrating the multi-layered nature of ethnicity.

In the later imperial period, Roman identity was vital but these other levels of ethnic identity could be equally important. As the period covered by this book developed we can see an opposition growing between the Gallic and the Italian senatorial nobility, for example, an opposition given more shape by the creation in 418 of a council where the former could meet.[68] Ausonius ridiculed a rival for his Britishness and claimed that the Britons were shifty and dishonest.[69]

Romanitas (the term is uncommon in contemporary writings[70]) was something therefore which overlay one's place of birth. It was part of a discourse which, while not separate from them, operated at a higher level than the regional and other 'taxonomic' levels of identity. Perhaps not surprisingly after the above catalogue, it was largely a matter of reasoned behaviour and living according to law. As we have seen, it was these related concepts – internal law or self-government and subjection to, and participation in, reasoned law-abiding political government – which the inhabitants of the Mediterranean had acquired on the road to civilisation, perhaps for climatic reasons, and which the barbarian had not. Other aspects, such as dress (as Tertullian [†c.230] noted) – the wearing of the toga – were visible signifiers of this, but of only secondary importance in defining the Roman. In the late Roman period, since nearly all inhabitants were born citizens, distinction from others was now achieved through the

---

[66] Ausonius, *Order of Famous Cities* 20, lines 40–1.   [67] *CIL* 3.3567.
[68] Heather (1998a), pp. 201–4.
[69] Ausonius, *Epigrams* 107–12. Jones, M. E. (1996), pp. 153–5, overplays this as evidence of Roman disdain for the British provinces.
[70] Tertullian, *Pallium* 4: a rare instance.

correct *performance* of Roman-ness rather than by the acquisition of citizenship.[71]

This is important; Roman identity was itself fluid. One definitive characteristic of the barbarian (at least in the wild) was his inability to live according to the law. Thus other people who refused to live by (Roman) law, like bandits and brigands, were, regardless of their origins, assimilated with barbarians. The elision of barbarians with all other enemies of the public order, or wielders of illegitimate or illegal force, was common in Roman thinking. Since legitimacy lay in the eye of the beholder, central governments labelled usurpers, especially failed usurpers, as exercisers of illegitimate force who had rejected legal rule.[72] Successful usurpers, of course, branded the previous regime as tyranny: equally a rejection of the law. And because barbarians were incapable of accepting law, barbarism could be equated with any unauthorised authority – with anyone who (in the central government's view) refused to be governed by law.

The common stock of ethnographic stereotypes was available to people within the Empire to highlight difference in other ways. The barbarians' reputation for ferocity and the association of Roman-ness with civil life added to the separation of civilian and military career-paths in the late Roman Empire and led the army to adopt con-sciously barbarian imagery and identities.[73] The barbarian:Roman dichotomy also intruded into the definition of class identities. Whilst gentlemen officers were forbidden from wearing military cloaks and trousers within the city of Rome a law of 382 permitted slaves to wear the shaggy coats and hoods associated with barbarians.[74] The employment of ethnographic ideas to shape identities *within* Roman society is vital.

Just as Romans who behaved the wrong way could be decried for casting off their Roman-ness, in the process becoming slaves, barbarians or animals or even acting like women (self-control and reason also distinguished man from woman[75]), non-Romans could enter the fold by subscription to correct behaviour. Though their non-Roman birth might not entirely be forgotten they might be praised for being as Roman as, or even more Roman than, the Romans. Significantly, the barbarian antecedents of some 'tyrants' were conveniently only remembered once they had fallen foul of

---

[71] See below, pp. 98–9.   [72] Shaw (1984), p. 6; Van Dam (1985), pp. 32–3.
[73] Below, pp. 102–9.   [74] *CTh* 14.10.3.   [75] Below, p. 98.

'legitimate' authority. Roman identity was, then, much more than a simple matter of birth and geographical origins.

Late Roman people were very familiar with ethnic stereotypes and could use, and subvert, them actively, as they saw fit. These stereotypes must be considered within the context of classical ethnography and its rules of genre. In contemplating the purposes served by Roman descriptions of barbarians and the uses to which such stereotypes were put we encounter the really interesting layer of problems. Roman depictions of barbarians are not part of a dialogue between 'us' and 'them' ('*we* are like this whereas *you* are like that') but between 'us' and 'us', between Romans ('*we* are [or, more often, ought to be] like this because *they* are like that').[76]

This rather obvious point has not always been fully taken into account in studies of late antiquity and the 'barbarian migrations'. Efforts persist to establish an ancient writer's view of the barbarians, as if a writer could have a single 'positive' or 'negative' opinion, and as if the barbarians were such a uniform reality that it could be possible to hold such a view. Much has been written trying to reconcile the fifth-century Christian apologist Orosius' apparently contradictory views of the barbarians in his *History Against the Pagans*, with some writers proposing that he modified his mind about them as he wrote, as political circumstances changed.[77] Yet the barbarian was a floating, rhetorical category which could be deployed in different ways to support the argument being made at a given point, usually about Romans or Christians. Thus the barbarian is wild, ferocious and cruel when an author wishes to play up the Roman army's, or its commanders', martial prowess or, conversely, to account for a defeat. In the latter circumstance the craftiness or cunning of the barbarian was also adduced. That the Romans saw no difficulty in having barbarians who were both stupid and sly neatly illustrates the rhetorical nature of the barbarian construct.

When a writer wished to denigrate the Romans' corruption or sinfulness, the barbarian became a noble savage: even the barbarians behave better than we do.[78] If barbarians appear virtuous and brave in

[76] For rhetorical use of the barbarian see Hall (1989); Dench (1995).
[77] Goetz (1980) and refs. for the literature on this problem.
[78] This point lies behind much of Tacitus' *Germania*. See also Claudius Mammertinus, *Speech of Thanks to Julian* 4.2. The idea was taken up and developed by the great Christian apologists of the earlier fifth century: Augustine, Orosius and Salvian.

one part of a work but wild and mad in the next this is not evidence of a contradictory or changeable view. We must examine the precise context and the argument being made, whenever the barbarian is mentioned. As Scipio says in the quote from Cicero's *Republic*, barbarism is a question of character, not race, and this alone should alert us to the indistinct nature of Roman categories of 'barbarian' and 'civilised'.

We cannot, however, end our discussion simply by stressing the fluidity of Roman ideas of barbarism, the permeability of the frontier between Roman and non-Roman and the fact that the Romans divided the Empire's inhabitants into ethnic groups just as they did the barbarians. The idea of the barbarian as non-human could find chilling expression. Captured barbarians could be thrown to the beasts. As ferocious sub-humans it was only fitting that wild animals should prey upon them. When the Empire wished to underline its political supremacy the army was unleashed upon the people beyond the frontiers with instructions to kill everyone they could catch, regardless of age or sex. The idea of the barbarian was mutable and rhetorical but, as with all ethnic identities, the rhetoric could be translated into a horrific reality for the people considered to have 'nothing human beyond their limbs and voices' and we must not forget that. To do so denies the barbarians their humanity just as securely as did Roman ideology.

THE BARBARIAN VIEW?

Thus far we have considered the Romans' worldview and their construction of the barbarian. Can we examine non-Roman views of identity and difference? This is very difficult without written sources from *barbaricum* but we can make some suggestions. By the late Roman period the barbarian peoples had been neighbours of a mighty world power for three or four centuries. The Empire habitually interfered in their politics, setting up and knocking down kings, paying gifts and so on.[79] Not surprisingly, any ideas of power and prestige that we can perceive in *barbaricum* had by this time come to be entirely based upon the Roman Empire. In the mid-third century in central Germany, for example, a burst of lavishly furnished inhumations, known as the Haßleben-Leuna group, appears amidst the usual cremations, probably as a response to crisis.[80] The display of

---

[79] See below, pp. 147–8. [80] Todd (1987), pp. 49–52.

material in these graves revolves around imported Roman silverware. In fourth-century northern Germany items of official Roman metal-work, especially belt-sets and brooches, are found in male cremation burials. Women were often buried with imported Roman jewellery too.[81] In the hillforts of southern Germany, Alamannic kings had brooches made, presumably to distribute to their followers as badges of rank. They were clear copies of the brooches used as insignia in imperial service. At the opposite end of *Germania*, on the island of Fyn, a local king based his authority upon controlling the import of goods from the Empire. Artistic styles and even the forms of metal dress-fasteners and other costume adornments made in Germany were heavily derivative of Roman originals.[82] Roman ideas of power, mediated through objects associated with the Empire, satu-rated barbarian life.[83] In a parallel with some Romans' use of ideas associated with barbarian ethnicity to signal particular identities within *their* society the barbarians employed Roman material to emphasise status, or differential access to power, within their own.

There can be no question of a general overriding 'Germanic' or 'Celtic' identity amongst the different barbarian groups. Shared lan-guage might have facilitated communication and alliance but there is no evidence for or reason to suppose a higher level of ethnic identity on this basis. It is not impossible that a knowledge that all were considered alike by the Romans might have created understandings but in fact it is difficult to find genuine instances of alliance between barbarians of different confederacies. In one, admittedly rather unlikely, instance – the barbarian conspiracy (*barbarica conspiratio*) of 367 – Irish, Picts and Saxons were involved.[84] This alliance tran-scended linguistic barriers but no one would suggest a pan-barbarian identity. The short-term partnerships between Goths of various sorts, Huns and Alans during the Gothic crisis of 376–82 are clearer examples but these were produced in exceptional circumstances and they too crossed linguistic bounds.[85]

[81] Following my reinterpretation of the origins of this jewellery. See further below, pp. 157–9.

[82] Thomas, S. (1966); (1967).   [83] See further below, pp. 126–8.

[84] The precise nature of this 'conspiracy' is obscure and the idea that Scots, Picts and Saxons were working in conjunction seems extremely unlikely. See Bartholomew (1984); Tomlin (1974); Blockley (1980).

[85] Below, pp. 177–80.

Discussion of barbarian identity must then start at the level of the confederacy. The barbarians, like the Romans, had a series of layers of ethnic identity. As far as the Romans were concerned the larger-scale confederacy was their prime means of identification. Nevertheless even Roman writers admitted that there were lesser tribes subsumed within the confederacies of the Picts, Franks and Alamans. Others still, especially in more distant confederacies like that of the Saxons, probably went unrecorded but their reappearance during the Empire's break-up argues that they had always existed. The Angles, Jutes and Frisians are recorded by early Roman writers but all disappear from the record between then and their reappearance in the 'migration period'. It is unlikely that these 'reappearing tribes'[86] represent incomplete acculturation. The contrary view is based upon the discredited 'melting-pot' theory of ethnicity. Rather, the persistence of these names is testimony, again, to ethnicity's multilayered nature. During late antiquity this level of ethnicity might have been less important, especially in dealings with the Romans, than the higher-level confederate identity. There were doubtless situations within the confederacies when such ethnicities and perhaps even lower-level ones (such as village community) were more usefully employed. In the changing political circumstances of the later fourth, fifth and sixth centuries, situations reappeared when these 'tribal' levels of affiliation became more important. Association with the Roman Empire might have created another level of identity amongst the barbarians. As well as signalling a difference in class and wealth it might well be the case that barbarians who had served the Empire thought of and presented themselves as *Romani* within their own society.

Enormous problems arise when confronting the archaeological data to explore the employment of material culture to give shape to barbarian ethnic groups. These require consideration, as they will crop up again when we try to identify barbarian newcomers inside the Empire in the late fourth to sixth centuries. A number of archaeological groupings can be listed between the Rhine and the Vistula, and north of the Carpathians,[87] usually defined by the style of their

[86] Borrowing the phrase of Heather (1998b).
[87] Todd (1987), pp. 39–76, is a very useful introduction. He discusses fifteen archaeological Kulturgruppen. See also *Autorenkollektiv* (1983), still important for more detailed information even if the interpretations are questionable.

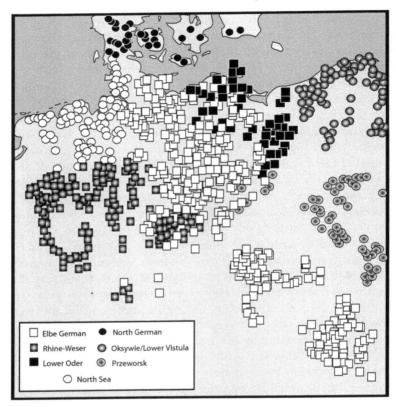

Map 2 Barbarian culture groups between the Rhine and the Baltic

ceramics but occasionally, too, by types of metalwork or burial rites (map 2).[88] That pottery has been the defining characteristic of culture groups in 'free Germany' was justified by Malcolm Todd on the not unreasonable grounds that, unlike metalwork, these sorts of coarse handmade wares were unlikely to travel very far through mechanisms such as trade or gift exchange (quite apart from the fact that their lack of durability makes them unsuitable for long-distance, overland transport), and are indeed fairly local in their distribution.[89]

In support of this view, we can say that material culture is often manipulated in the creation of ethnic difference. The production and,

[88] See above, pp. 25–6 for cultures and culture history.
[89] Todd (1987), p. 39.

especially, decoration of ceramics is also very frequently imbued with a great deal of tradition and even ideas of the social, natural and cosmological order.[90] Furthermore, pottery-types can reflect closely such culturally specific things as cuisine, culinary practices and diet. These ideas form the very substance of ethnic identity in primordialist interpretations. On the other hand, as noted, beliefs about the structure of the social, natural and supernatural universe do not necessarily correspond to ethnic identity. Indeed, different sections within a single 'ethnic' group might use material culture to create and maintain that difference. To complicate matters further, such intra-group identities might be structured around ideas about, and use material culture related to, neighbouring ethnic groupings.[91] We have seen instances of this within the Roman Empire and amongst the *Germani*. All these objections, it should be admitted, relate more easily to fine wares, metalwork and the components of dress than to the coarse wares, which usually form the basis of the identification of 'Germanic' Kulturgruppen, but they must nevertheless be borne in mind. It ought to be noted that the basic types of pottery, or ceramic decoration, under discussion do not differ enormously from one Kulturgruppe to another. It should also be mentioned that these groups are not hermetically sealed. There is significant overlap between them, especially if different types of ceramics are viewed separately. These culture groups are formed around cores of associated artefact-types, but there is considerable blurring around the edges. Finally, we must repeat that ethnic identity is multi-layered. Even when a culture group can be linked with a historically defined confederacy, as it can in the case of the Sîntana de Mureş-Çernjachov culture and the Goths, it would not tell us whether a user of this material culture was a Tervingian or Greuthungian Goth or whether s/he was not also a Sarmatian, a Dacian or a Taifal (or which of these s/he was).[92] Roman authors in the fifth and sixth centuries further stressed such (usually) archaeologically invisible features as hairstyles. Finally, it is worth repeating the lesson of Moerman's classic study of the Lue.[93] Group members can give long lists of characteristics,

[90] See Miller, D. (1985). Hines (1998) for similar points.
[91] A splendid cautionary tale is provided by Larrick's (1986) study of the Loikop Samburu, amongst whom different age-grades define themselves by adopting spearheads associated with neighbouring groups.
[92] Ellis (1996).   [93] Moerman (1968).

largely to do with dress and appearance, which they believe mark people out as a member of their group. Yet, when investigated, the bulk of such traits turn out to be shared with neighbouring groups or are rarely worn or practised any more.

Although we now only see Roman imports or imitations of imperial designs it is important to recognise that they might have been given significantly different interpretations and employed in distinctive ways in *barbaricum*,[94] even if the details now escape us. A clue might be found in the use of Roman metalwork and decorative motifs east of the Rhine, which might suggest a subtly different gendering of power. Although it too lies beyond our purview it must also be a strong possibility that with the closeness of the contacts between the Empire and the barbarians, Roman ethnographic ideas about the barbarians (to north or south) could have been adopted and played upon by the barbarians themselves. The Roman belief in the fierceness of barbarians might provide a significant basis for identity amongst the latter. After all, the name of the Frankish confederacy probably means 'the fierce people'.[95]

The barbarians' dependence upon Roman ideas, but their ability to manipulate these for their own purposes, the fluidity and multi-layered nature of barbarian ethnicity and the difficulty of associating material culture with defined ethnic groups are all features to which we will return in the following chapters.

---

[94] See, e.g. Wells (2001), pp. 121–2.   [95] James (1988), p. 6.

3

THE LATE ROMAN EMPIRE IN THE WEST

In 1964 A. H. M. Jones published his enormous social, economic and administrative survey, which I shall use as a paradigm of traditional ways of seeing the late Roman Empire. This is both fair, in that Jones was a very fine scholar who kept abreast of historical developments and in that his views have been enormously influential, and unfair, in that using a particular author as an example of a view of history subsequently modified – especially in a brief survey such as this – runs the risk of oversimplification and parody. Jones' book was based upon an unsurpassed knowledge of the evidence and, although now looking dated in places, especially where archaeological data (of which there was little in his day) has made a difference, for detailed depiction of the Empire's offices and institutions it is unlikely ever to be entirely replaced. And it was subtle and nuanced as only a work of nearly 1,100 pages of text and over 200 of endnotes can be. Nevertheless important features can be identified, which typify traditional thinking. Jones saw the late Roman state as authoritarian, at least in theory and often in practice. Marxist historians had deployed this idea before; Walbank, for example, saw the Empire's collapse as resulting from an oppressive bureaucracy and military, unsupportable by the period's stagnant productive forces.[1] Theories like Walbank's

---

[1] Walbank (1969). For another, more or less contemporary, discussion of the later Empire, see Vogt (1967). General works on the late Empire are too numerous to list. In English, Jones' mainly thematic work succeeded the essentially narrative history of J. B. Bury (1958).

profoundly influenced Jones' explanation, which also relied on the idea of a top-heavy state.

It is difficult to avoid being taken in by the Empire's totalitarian ideology.[2] Although the Empire was still referred to as the *Res Publica*, the Republic, the emperors abandoned any pretence of being simply the first citizen. Whereas the early Roman period is known as the Principate, the late Roman is called the Dominate. After Constantine, the emperors' claim to rule as Christ's vice-gerent on earth underpinned this, far more effectively one imagines than earlier claims to be divine. Statues depict the emperors as grim and authoritarian, in military garb and brandishing the insignia of their worldly power and divine legitimation, or enthroned in majesty, surrounded by their guards and humble barbarian petitioners.[3] The enactments gathered in the Theodosian and Justinianic codes present them as all-powerful figures whose word was law, threatening terrible punishments for those who thwart their will. Even late Roman imperial architecture can underline this view. The huge *Aula Palatina*, the imperial audience chamber still standing in Trier, broods over the archbishop-elector's pink-stuccoed baroque palace, its unrelieved brick and tile contrasting with the plaster and ornament of the latter, its massive plain rectangular form looming above the archiepiscopal palace's elaborate architecture.[4] Here is a building to capture the spirit of the autocratic late Empire.

This monster state with its absolute ruler at its head was seen as allying with the great landholders. The Empire relied upon the aristocracy who, thought Jones, used the Empire to increase their wealth through the opportunities for corruption and exploitation that it offered. Slaves, given their own small-holdings as a more cost-effective way of maintaining them, and freemen forced by corruption and oppression into selling their land and becoming tenants of the great landholders, fused into a downtrodden social group resembling later medieval serfs: the *coloni*. Managing this state were thousands of civil servants. To ensure that protest and opposition were stifled, the emperors used palatine officials to report on provincial government and on each other. The *agentes in rebus* ('agents in affairs': imperial

[2] As, e.g. is Grant (1990), pp. 100–10.
[3] See, e.g. L'Orange (1965), pp. 110–25; Reece (1999), pp. 19–44; Smith, R. R. R. (1997).
[4] L'Orange (1965) for this sort of view of the *Aula Palatina*. See, further, below, n. 16.

couriers and inspectors of the post) were seen by some (though not by Jones) as a sinister secret police.[5] Imperial notaries were even more dangerous, most notoriously Paulus *Catena*, who acquired his nickname from his ability to link people to each other in a chain (*catena*) of alleged conspiracy and whose activities are vividly depicted by Ammianus Marcellinus.[6]

The Empire was viewed as fairly monolithic. Some regions, like Egypt, were distinctive, to be sure, and the east was recognised as different from the west but by and large the social picture painted in Jones' work appears to apply across the Empire. The powerful and wealthy aristocracy cared little for the Empire except in so far as it provided opportunities for fleecing the poor, evading taxes and staying ahead of one's rivals in all-important matters of precedence. All told, in this view the Empire was oppressive, drab, uniform and regimented, governed by puritanical autocrats and self-seeking officials. Its resemblance to Stalin's USSR or Hitler's Third Reich was not surprising. Jones was writing when memories of the latter dictatorship were still fresh and when, after the Hungarian uprising, the Soviet Union had finally been seen in its true colours, even by most left-leaning British academics. State intervention – the welfare state in post-war Britain and the civil rights movement and social reform policies of presidents Kennedy and Johnson in the 1960s United States – was then very important in political vocabulary.

This interpretation has not been unchallenged. Again the historiography must be seen in its context. As right-wing governments avowedly 'rolled back the frontiers of the state' in the 1980s, so historians began to question whether the late Roman Empire was, or indeed could have been, as all-pervasive as it had seemed in Jones' day. The Soviet Union creaked, tottered and fell and understanding grew of the workings of Hitler's Germany, so that it was now appreciated that, rather than simply being imposed autocratically, the active involvement of elements of society in every locality within these regimes was essential. A new, more nuanced view of the Roman Empire emerged. Despite seeing the state as absolutist and

---

[5] Though some were certainly active in the culture of suspicion and denunciation that emerged in the reign of Constantius II (337–61) and they were certainly important in monitoring local government, they wielded little power.

[6] Amm. Marc. 14.5.8. This view of the Empire is nicely recreated in Alfred Duggan's novel *The Little Emperors* (1951), which may still be recommended as an imaginative evocation of the events of 406–10 in Britain.

bureaucratic, Jones had recognised that the emperors' will could not always have been very efficiently implemented. Quite apart from the problems of physical geography and the vagaries of maritime travel, he acknowledged that local élites could frustrate imperial commands, often with impunity.[7] Ramsay MacMullen's *Corruption and the Decline of Rome* further brought this aspect to the fore.[8] MacMullen argued that the late Roman state was highly inefficient, its power everywhere employed by its officials for their own benefit, selling privilege and exemptions, pocketing the army's pay or uniform allowances and so on. Whether this 'corruption' was as deleterious to the Empire as MacMullen believed is questionable,[9] as is the extent of change from the early Roman situation. MacMullen's view was still based upon a 'top-down' view of the state and its efficiency. Nevertheless his interesting study marshalled a great deal of data showing that the emperor's thundering pronouncements were not necessarily, or indeed very often, effective in the localities. The story of Romanus related in chapter 1 has thus become something of a cause célèbre of late Roman history.[10] Unofficial sources like letters, notably those of the Libyan bishop Synesius of Cyrene and the Antiochene rhetor Libanius, or Ammianus' extensive narrative could be scrutinised to present a more complex picture of the state's operation. Jones had not ignored this, although he does not seem to have thought it very significant in evaluating the Empire's overall efficiency or explaining its demise.

At about the same time as MacMullen's work appeared, other historians, influenced by the 'linguistic turn' in modern historiography, studying élite culture, language and behaviour, uncovered the checks and balances placed upon imperial autocracy. Averil Cameron's *Christianity and the Rhetoric of Empire* was particularly instructive and Peter Brown's *Power and Persuasion* revealed the negotiation involved at every level of government.[11] Roman politics were carried out using a learned rhetorical language, the acquisition of which marked out the élite from other levels of society and permitted entry into the powerful circles of the Empire. But this culture of *paidaea* (a Greek word which may be translated loosely as

---

[7] Jones, A. H. M. (1964), pp. 406–10.   [8] MacMullen (1988).
[9] Kelly (1998), pp. 175–80, for excellent discussion.
[10] E.g. Kelly (1998), pp. 158, 162.
[11] Cameron, A. M. (1991); Brown, P. R. L. (1992).

'being cultured') went beyond the simple ability to address importan gatherings in suitably learned rhetorical language. It was a whole mode of behaviour, into which one was inducted.[12] Emperors and their officers were expected to abide by it. Indeed it shaped attitudes to all aspects of Roman life and social structure, not always because it was accepted but because it became a focus for debate, a site of discourse, and as such a central part of the processes which we call the barbarian migrations and the fall of the Roman Empire. Simultaneously, more subtle study of the legislation was carried out, which, rather than assuming that the emperors' pronouncements were automatically implemented and thus reflected reality, instead saw a large dose of negotiation in law-making.[13] The study of discourse and negotiation should be stressed as it has moved the debate beyond simple ideas of efficiency and autocracy versus disobedience and inefficiency. By examining ideas and the ways in which language was used to create as well as describe power and to situate individuals within a worldview we come closer to an understanding of the crises and complexity of the end of the western Empire.

If Jones had to some extent recognised the weaknesses inherent in the operation of the state – and, though one might not now state them in quite the same way, many of his ideas are reasonable enough – and if subsequent work has furthered the debate in these areas, the idea of the socially monolithic Empire has proved more pervasive. Discussions of late Roman society still see the Jonesian image of an often massively wealthy aristocracy dominating an oppressed rural proletariat as of general application.[14] Here, however, the picture was circumscribed by the evidence from which Jones worked. This was overwhelmingly documentary (though he made use of numismatics and, very occasionally, of an excavated site) and usually from the Empire's Mediterranean heartlands. Many western European regions left no, or almost no, written data from the late imperial period and the extent to which the norms of the literate élite of eastern Spain, Italy and southern Gaul apply there is debatable. Archaeology can importantly modify this picture. The study of settlement patterns, urban and rural sites, high status and lower-ranking habitations, cemeteries and means of social distinction, reveals decisive variation in the nature of social structure from one

---

[12] Brown, P. R. L. (1992), esp. pp. 37–41.
[13] Harries (1999); Mathisen (ed.) (2001); Matthews (2000a).   [14] Marcone (1998).

area to another, and the examination of these aspects through our period demonstrates how the different regions of the western Empire related to the imperial state and in turn how they were able to negotiate its political demise.[15]

The brickwork of the *Aula Palatina*, the building used above as a metaphor for the autocratic state, was originally covered with white plaster with red false-jointing. The interior was lavishly ornamented with acanthus scroll mouldings, wall paintings and mosaics.[16] Far from being the grim monstrosity that stands today, it once had something common with its baroque neighbour. Much of the time, too, especially during periods of imperial absence, one imagines that it could all too easily look a little run-down. Perhaps as a symbol of the late Empire it is, in its own way, not so inappropriate.

RULING EUROPE: THE EARLY ROMAN SOLUTION

This book deals with Britain, Gaul (including the Rhineland provinces of *Germania*), Spain, Italy and North Africa. The Alps and the Pyrenees to some extent define the main geographical units, delineating modern Spain, Italy and southern France. As well as these impressive mountains there are lesser ranges, like the Vosges or the Apennines, high plateaux like the Massif Central or the Meseta, and areas of forest and marshland. The Rhine forms an effective frontier to the north of Gaul but huge rivers, such as the Loire, could be important barriers to, as well as arteries of, communication. The western Roman Empire was separated into numberless regions and lesser localities. These were not simply geographical divisions. They often had different ecologies, supporting divergent ways of life – pastoralism, settled agriculture and so on – producing different forms of surplus with varying levels of ease.[17] No modern state has ever been able effectively to hold these diverse areas together even with advanced communications and military technology. How could they be brought into a single state in antiquity?

---

[15] For some overviews of archaeological evidence from the later Empire, see Reece (1999); Swift (2000).

[16] Cüppers (ed.) (1984), pp. 139–57 (pp. 145–54 on decoration); Allison (2003), pp. 226–30.

[17] On the Roman economy see, e.g.: Duncan Jones (1974); (1990); Garnsey (1998); Garnsey and Saller (1987), pp. 43–82; Mattingly and Salmon (eds.) (2001); Shipley and Salmon (eds.) (1996); Whittaker (1993a).

During the early Empire this problem had been solved comparatively easily. In this most unusual period of European history *romanitas* was a commodity much sought after. The Roman absorption of western Europe was facilitated by the fact that much of Iron Age society in Gaul, Spain, Britain and elsewhere was closely tied into the Roman economic system.[18] Roman artefacts were greatly desired and their distribution a means by which kings in these areas maintained their power. The Roman conquest was traumatic and within a couple of generations had produced revolutionary changes.[19] Local élites, prevented from exercising their power in traditional ways, adapted to the Roman system. Service in, or the formation of, auxiliary cohorts, important vehicles for Romanisation, enabled a military career path.[20] Alternatively, local status and prestige could be acquired by service on municipal councils. Indeed, participation in the Roman form of urban life was possibly the most important means by which regions were bound into the Empire. Towns competed in acquiring the different statuses and privileges of the varying Roman categories of town.[21] Constructing public buildings along Roman architectural lines was an important element of this competition. Élite families also contended with each other within the tribal units now reorganised as *civitates* (city districts) in providing such monuments for their town and fellow citizens. Private resources went into public building. The rewards for such participation in Roman-style urban politics could be considerable. Citizenship, a great prize, might be obtained. A local leader might rise as far as the senate. The nature of such competition varied but the point remained that, within a couple of generations, local and regional politics were played out through investment in Roman urbanism. Involvement in municipal politics meant that the provincials largely did

---

[18] See, e.g. Collis (1984), esp. pp. 158–80; Wells (1980); (2001); Williams, D. F. (1989).

[19] Blagg and Millett (eds.) (1990); Keay and Terrenato (2001); Millett (1990); Woolf, G. (1998). See also below, n. 21.

[20] Haynes (1993); (1999).

[21] There is an enormous bibliography on towns, urbanisation, Romanisation and early Roman society. See, e.g.: Cunliffe and Keay (eds.) (1998); Fentress (ed.) (2000); Grew and Hobley (eds.) (1985); Jones, A. H. M. (1954); (1955); Jones, R. F. J. (1987); (1991); Keay (1988), pp. 47–94; Lomas (1998); Potter (1987), pp. 63–93; Rich and Wallace Hadrill (eds.) 1991; Wacher (1974); Wightman (1985), pp. 75–100. See also above, n. 19.

the work of government. The Empire was run with a minuscule central bureaucracy of at most a couple of hundred imperial freed-men. Roman aristocrats moved out from the centre to the periphery to serve as governors but on the whole the regions of the Empire bound themselves into the state.

Roman conquest may have enabled the reorganisation of land-holding, replacing clientship with landlord–tenant relationships, much, as A. L. F. Rivet long ago suggested, as took place in Scotland after the clearances, to the great advantage of the existing élite.[22] The material expression of these changed relationships and the altered ways by which local authority was expressed was the villa.[23] The villa's precise definition and socio-economic function has been debated but it seems beyond doubt that it represents a focus for the expenditure of surplus. Whether the villa served as the operational centre of a landed estate (as a working farm) or stood outside the mechanisms of agricultural production, simply as a high-status country house, is perhaps irrelevant. Both forms were doubtless represented by different villas within and between regions but in all cases it was the extraction of surplus that permitted the expression of power through such a permanent mark on the landscape. Villa architecture regulated social interaction with lesser groups and dis-played status to visitors through the manipulation of routes of approach.[24] These élite dwellings differed significantly in size, elabo-ration and plan but were quite different from pre-existing high-status settlements and show clearly the change in mentalité, the move towards expressing status and identity in recognisably Roman ways.

At the same time the Empire represented an economic unity. Roman goods and their distribution were as important after the conquest as they had been before. Prestigious items were produced in the core of the Empire and taken out to the provinces, whilst raw materials, taxes and other economic goods such as slaves moved inwards towards the centre.[25] Thus for a while some new urban foundations continued to prosper as ports of trade. London is a clear example, flourishing in the initial post-conquest period as a point

[22] Rivet (1969), pp. 182–3.
[23] For fine overviews, see Dyson (2003); Percival (1976); Smith, J. T. (1997).
[24] Scott (1990).
[25] On the early Roman economy, Hopkins (1978) was influential but controversial; Rathbone (1983) for important modification. See also above, n. 17.

through which Roman imports flowed, continuing to support the local élite. By the early second century, however, the *civitas*-capitals were established and thrived as new centres for aristocratic display and competition. They also had their own markets and, as the province became saturated with Roman goods, Roman London began to decline.[26] The establishment of interlocking markets nevertheless underlined the incorporation of the diverse regions of western Europe into a single, wholly exceptional political, social and economic unit.

The processes delineated above have generally been described under the heading of 'Romanisation', a term that has attracted much criticism of late.[27] Here, Romanisation is understood to be at least as much the conscious activity of the inhabitants of the conquered provinces as of the conquering Empire (itself no uniform entity). Yet *Roman*-isation it was nevertheless. However the situation is nuanced, the cultural forms adopted, in all their diverse manifestations, usually differed dramatically from those in use before the conquest and they were, again in all their variety, recognisably Roman in inspiration. Sometimes they have their precursors in late pre-Roman Iron Age society, as for instance in the evidence for orthogonal street planning in pre-Roman Silchester, but even here they were adopted in imitation of the Romans.[28] The provincials bought into Roman culture for their own purposes but this facilitated the political unification and coherence of early Roman western Europe.

THE 'THIRD-CENTURY CRISIS'[29]

This state of affairs could not last. The economy gradually fragmented.[30] The provinces began to manufacture the material expressions of Roman culture for themselves. High quality pottery was produced in southern and central Gaul (the famous Samian Ware) and then in northern Gaul as well as in other provinces. Regions specialised in different types of production; Spain manufactured olive oil and *garum* (a sort of fish relish) for example. None

[26] On Roman London, see Milne (1993); (1995); Perring (1991); Roskams (1991); Wacher (1974), pp. 87–103; Watson (ed.) (1998).
[27] See, e.g. Grahame (1998); Mattingly (2004); Webster and Cooper (eds.) (1996).
[28] Fulford (1993).
[29] Garnsey and Humfress (2001), pp. 10–24, and Witschel (2004) for fine overviews.
[30] Reece (1981) is now dated but still thought-provoking.

of this meant economic decline or stagnation; many provinces prospered. Nor did it imply any end to Romanness. It did, however, erode those factors that had transcended Europe's economic, ecological and physical geographical diversity to bind it into a single unit. This put social and economic realities out of step with the mechanisms used to govern and bind the Empire together.

Other forces led in a similar direction. In 212 Emperor Antoninus 'Caracalla' granted citizenship to all the Empire's inhabitants. Whilst ostensibly an imperial taxation policy, enabling the emperor to levy all sorts of taxes on the whole Empire, it ended citizenship as something to be competed for. Citizenship no longer brought the special privileges or social distinction it had hitherto afforded. Simultaneously, the other means by which local élites had invested in the Empire ceased to be as attractive. Public building provided decreasing rewards in local prestige. To simplify, if a town already had a forum furnished with all the monuments necessary for the full manifestation of its Roman identity there was little scope or motivation for further embellishment. Building a new bath complex for a town that already possessed three public bath houses was unlikely to yield the same prestige and influence that the construction of the first complex had given *its* builder. A law of diminishing returns operated and public building declined. In some areas the extraordinary investment in Roman urban forms was made even clearer. In the Rhône valley a number of towns went into terminal decline from the third century. The area had been over-urbanised during the first centuries of Roman government and when the exceptional circumstances behind the investment in towns ended, the region's economy simply could not support that level of urbanisation.[31] Except in North Africa and possibly Spain, service on municipal councils became ever less popular. The reasons, as with the decline of public building, were to be sought in the decreasing political benefits of such activity, not in a reduction in the ability to pay for it. The curial classes (the local aristocracy that manned the municipal councils, or *curiae*) naturally explained their reluctance in terms of the expense of duties. However, in the early Empire acts of public munificence could reach absurd levels. Roman politicians sometimes paid the entire tax bill of

---

[31] Loseby (2000a). See also Witschel (2004), p. 264 for a similar explanation of analogous changes in Italy.

a city or even province as an act of generosity.[32] Even the costliest
curial duties never ran to that level! What was at stake was political
will not economic wherewithal.

Further issues combined to make the third century a critical
period. The late second-century civil wars led the Severan dynasty
(193–235 AD) to ensure the army's loyalty by increasing its pay, a
process that spiralled, especially as political instability set in after
Caracalla's assassination. Without concomitant increases in revenue
the all-too-obvious consequence was the debasement of the coinage
and inflation. Grain prices rose by 200,000 per cent in half a century.[33] The large number of coin hoards buried at this time in the
west probably also attests to economic turbulence and inflation.[34]
The 'great inflation', and whether it produced a real economic
'third-century crisis', can be overstated.[35] Most western provinces
seem to have remained prosperous and North Africa underwent
something of a boom. Britain shows barely any trace of a third-
century crisis and the dramatic down-turn in northern Gaul only
seems to have occurred in the last quarter of the century, after
Emperor Aurelian's subjugation of the break-away Gallic Empire.[36]
The real problem caused by inflation was that, by reducing local
exchange to barter and other forms of socially embedded interaction, much of the economy came to take place within the tiny
geographical arena of the 'face-to-face community', emphasising
the Empire's geographical disunity.

Political instability at the centre did not help. Between Alexander
Severus' assassination in 235 and Diocletian's accession in 284 there
were no fewer than twenty legitimate emperors, discounting usurpers
and other rebels. Of these, only three were not assassinated: Decius
was killed in battle against the Goths, Valerian perished in Persian
captivity and Claudius II Gothicus died of the plague! Empires
appeared in Gaul and in Palmyra in the east. Banditry afflicted large
swathes of territory although, since *latrocinium* (banditry) and associated terms could simply refer to unsanctioned local rule, it is not
always easy to know what this meant in practice.[37] Beyond the
frontiers, as the Romans were distracted from any coherent 'foreign
policy', dangerous barbarian confederacies appeared, those units that

---

[32] Millar (1981), p. 94.   [33] Jones, A. H. M. (1953); (1964), pp. 26–32, 438–43.
[34] Witschel (2004).   [35] Garnsey and Humfress (2001), pp. 19–20.
[36] Drinkwater (1983), pp. 212–27.   [37] Shaw (1984a); (1993); Grünewald (2004).

concern this volume. The Franks, Alamans, and Goths are all first attested in the third century. In the east a resurgent Iran posed even greater problems. Instability and insecurity exacerbated the Empire's economic fragmentation and the decline in willingness to buy into the Roman state at the local level. It undermined the legitimacy, or belief in the durability, of imperial rule and presented the reality of plural empires. The rapid turnover of regimes and the repeated punishment of the losing sides' supporters can only have added to the unwillingness to invest in power at the centre. The Empire was springing apart and with only a few slightly different conjunctures might well have done so permanently.

THE NEW EMPIRE OF THE FOURTH CENTURY

Unity and security were re-established by the emperors Claudius II and Aurelian, but the real restoration was begun during the long reign of Diocletian (284–305) and his colleagues and successors.[38] Between 284 and 395 the Empire was governed by what have been termed 'problem-solving emperors'.[39] Their solutions were all the more remarkable for the seriousness of the problems facing them. By the third century Europe's natural diversity had triumphed over the exceptional cultural and political unity that characterised the early Roman period. This made the problem with which this book began especially acute. Indeed during the fourth century other factors may have emphasised it. Nevertheless, for all that, the century was a period of strong government. A case can be made that the reigns of the emperors from Diocletian to Theodosius I represent a high point of Roman imperial rule: a long sequence of consistently able rulers.

Administratively, the basic building block of the Empire remained the *civitas*, the city-district, although there were some modifications to these.[40] More important changes took place at higher levels. The provinces were drastically reduced in size to make their government easier and their number doubled, eventually to 114 (map 3). This

---

[38] For detailed description of the Tetrarchic reforms, see Barnes (1982). Williams, S. (1985) is accessible but not always up-to-date. Modéran (2003a), pp. 61–92.

[39] Collins (1999), p. 1.

[40] A succinct and useful summary of imperial administrative organisation may be found in Barnwell (1992), pp. 53–70. For more detail, see Jones, A. H. M. (1964), pp. 373–7; Barnes (1982); Corcoran (1996), pp. 75–94, 234–53.

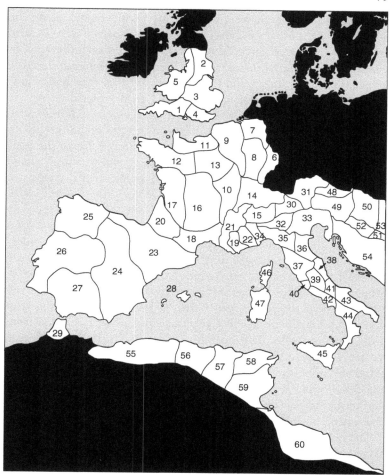

Map 3 The western Empire: administrative units (see page 592 for key)

obviously raised some cities to the status of provincial capitals; other towns declined in relative importance. The provinces were then grouped into dioceses, each ruled by a *vicarius*. In the area covered by this book there were seven dioceses: the Britains, the Gauls, the Seven Provinces (Gaul south of the Loire), the Spains, *Italia annonaria* (northern Italy and the provinces of Raetia, north of the Alps), *Italia suburbicaria* (the remainder of Italy, plus Sicily, Sardinia and Corsica), and Africa (North Africa east of *Mauretania Tingitania* – roughly northern Morocco – and west of Libya). By an uneven process during the reigns of Constantine I and his sons, the dioceses were in turn grouped into Praetorian Prefectures. There were two in the regions that concern us: Gaul (including 'the Britains' and 'the Spains' as well as 'the Gauls' and 'the Seven Provinces'), and Italy (the Italian dioceses and Africa). Rome remained as the Urban Prefecture.

All the rulers of these different regions had their own administrative staffs. Atop this administrative pyramid stood the emperor and his palatine officials. At the court were located the officials of the bedchamber, the financial ministries (the *sacrae largitiones* – the 'sacred largesses' – and the *res privatae* – the 'private affairs'), the corps of notaries, the imperial writing offices (*sacra scrinia*), the *agentes in rebus* (the couriers) and so on.[41] These totalled a veritable army (especially when added to the imperial bodyguards). Lactantius and other writers bemoaned the ever-increasing numbers of bureaucrats, and understandably:[42] the late Roman imperial civil service has been estimated at between 25,000 and 35,000 men. The growth in the number of provinces, the institution of two intermediate administrative levels between them and the emperor and, above all, the uncoupling of military and civil service effectively ended the danger of revolt from provincial governors. The separation of the two branches of imperial service was especially important. Henceforth governors would not command the troops within their territories, and military commanders would not control the supply of food and pay to their soldiers. Furthermore, military districts like the Saxon Shore or the *Tractus Armoricanus* no longer corresponded to civil administrative units.

The imperial bureaucracy's size did not result from a coherent plan. To some extent it was a development of early Roman military staffs seconded to provincial administration, which gradually turned into permanent bodies.[43] Partly, too, it is likely that the municipal councils' increasing inefficiency in raising taxes and carrying out effective government, through evasion and a lack of will, drew the emperors to install their own officers to oversee such activities. This bureaucracy may have been chronically inefficient but its importance lay in the fact that it came to replace municipal government as the means by which local élites bought into the Roman state. Service in it

[41] On these officials see Jones, A. H. M. (1964), pp. 366–73, 411–35, 566–86.
[42] Lactantius, *On the Deaths of the Persecutors* 7.1–5.
[43] Jones, A. H. M. (1964), pp. 563–6; Garnsey and Humfress (2001), pp. 36–41.

yielded many of the rewards hitherto provided by service on the
curiae. Most imperial offices brought entry into the different grades of
the aristocracy (see below) and attendant privilege and status. Certain
tax exemptions came with such service, as well as reduced (or escape
from) liability for unpopular curial duties. The imperial bureaucracy
permitted aristocrats to widen their political horizons through service
in other regions but at the same time it provided opportunities for the
operation of power at local level, through influencing legal and other
decisions, arbitration and the distribution of one's own patronage.[44]
Such public building as was done in the later Empire, which tended
to comprise restoration rather than the construction of new monuments, was carried out at public expense but the local official
responsible could still claim some credit.[45] Imperial service brought
honorific titles, determining local and regional hierarchies of prestige
and privilege. For all of these reasons, throughout the western Empire
involvement in the imperial civil service was much sought after and
the object of competition.

The importance of rank, status and precedence in the later Roman
world cannot be overestimated. Traditionally there had been only
two aristocratic orders, the equestrian and the senatorial. Constantine
added a third, the *comitiva*, the emperor's companions, in other words
those who had risen through imperial service.[46] The equestrian order
was divided into grades of precedence: the *egregii* (outstanding), the
perfectissimi (most perfect) and the *eminentissimi* (most eminent). The
senatorial order had originally been made up simply of *clarissimi* (most
shining). The *comitiva* was subdivided into three grades. Within all
groups were complex rules of precedence depending upon whether a
rank had been bestowed personally by the emperor, or in absentia, or
whether an *honoratus* (holder of an honour) had actually held the
requisite office or had been bestowed an honorary title such as
ex-*vicarius*. Imperial service brought entry into the equestrian order or
the *comitiva* and, as the fourth century progressed, an inflation of
honours set in so that offices that had carried equestrian status brought
senatorial rank. The equestrian order and the *comitiva* were devalued

---

[44] Heather (1998a) is excellent on the workings of imperial bureaucracy in local
  society. See also Cameron, A. M. (1993a), pp. 99–112; Kelly (1998) and now,
  especially, (2004); Matthews (1989), pp. 253–78.
[45] On late Roman public building, see Ward-Perkins (1984).
[46] On the grades of aristocracy, see Jones, A. H. M. (1964), pp. 523–54.

and the former more or less disappeared. The senatorial order expanded so that extra honorific grades had to be created: the *spectabiles*, the *illustres* and the *gloriosi*. Eventually the rank of *clarissimus* became a mere title. A leading senator's son was automatically a *clarissimus* but he needed to serve in the higher echelons of imperial service in order to gain his father's title of *illustris*. Thousands of offices existed at any time and, at the higher levels, most were not held for more than a year or two. By the end of the fourth century command of a regiment or the governorship of a province brought entry to the clarissimate. It has been estimated that about 3,000 jobs per generation in each half of the Empire brought senatorial status.[47] Some aristocrats possessed enormous wealth but this meant little in politics, even within their class, without the imperial service that guaranteed an honorific title and a higher place in precedence. Furthermore, traditional Roman aristocratic culture required periods (however brief) of service (*negotium*) between spells of *otium* (leisure) on one's estates.[48] The bureaucracy moreover provided aristocrats with opportunities to exercise their own patronage by placing people in posts within it, even when themselves not serving the state in an official capacity. As Averil Cameron has stated '[t]he fourth century witnessed the transformation of the old "orders", still closely linked to birth and wealth, into a service aristocracy, in which rank depended on office'.[49] The precise way in which this linked regional élites into the Empire varied. In some areas an aristocrat would, in local or regional socio-economic terms, have been an aristocrat with or without the existence of the Empire and its offices. In others it might have been the opportunities provided by imperial service that raised an individual or his family above the others in the locality. These variations made the Empire a socially and politically more variegated entity than is often appreciated, and are decisive in explaining the fate of different regions in the fifth century and later.

Continuing a trend begun during the third century, the emperors adopted a more autocratic governmental style.[50] They also moved the

---

[47] Heather (1998a), p. 196.
[48] Jones, A. H. M. (1964), pp. 557–62; Matthews (1975), pp. 1–31.
[49] Cameron, A. M. (1993a), p. 104.
[50] Kelly (1998), pp. 139–62; (1999); and Garnsey and Humfress (2001), pp. 25–36, are excellent introductions. Barnwell (1992), pp. 11–19; Corcoran (1996), pp. 254–65; Jones, A. H. M. (1964), pp. 321–65; Matthews (1989), pp. 231–52; McCormick (1986), pp. 36–46, 80–130.

political core of the Empire to the geographical periphery. Through the reigns of Maximian, Constantine and his sons, of the usurper Magnentius, of Julian as Caesar in Gaul and into those of Valentinian I and Gratian, the emperor was to be found, as often as not, in the far north of Gaul at Trier, or on the Rhine–Danube frontier itself. The other imperial capitals were places like Sirmium in *Pannonia* (Sremska Mitrovica, Serbia) and Antioch (Antakya, Turkey) in the east. Even the great new city of Constantinople was indicative of this trend. This made much strategic sense. There was a great deal of movement within the enormous pyramid of interlocking patronage networks that was the bureaucracy and thus a vast store of patronage for the emperors, their higher officials and powerful noblemen to acquire, distribute and redistribute. The problem, which should be stressed, was that although this system served effectively to bind the different regions of western Europe back into a single political unit and thus replaced early Roman municipal service and competition comparatively well, it was nevertheless somewhat passive. Early Roman regional élites worked to associate themselves with the Empire – they spent their money doing Rome's work. In the later Empire, the interest in imperial service lay in what the Empire could provide. Put another way, in the late Roman Empire aristocrats ceased to ask what they could do for their Empire and instead increasingly asked what the Empire could do for them.

THE REGIONS

A brief survey of the key areas of the Roman west reveals the dynamics of the relationships between political core and periphery and the diversity of social structures and the ways in which this affected the Empire's importance in local social structures. We can begin in Britain. *Britanniae* – the Britains – was a diocese of two halves (map 4).[51] To the south and east of a line roughly from the Bristol Channel to the Humber estuary, to which I shall refer as lowland Britain, lay the villas, the more elaborate manufacturing industries and craft specialisations and most towns. The highland zone, north and west of that line, generally – though not entirely – lacked these

---

[51] By far the best work on late Roman Britain remains Esmonde Cleary (1989). Dark, K. R. (1994); (2002); Faulkner (2000); Higham (1992); Jones, M. E. (1996) contain interesting ideas but all require some caution. Johnson (1980) provides much useful information but now looks dated.

Map 4 Britain

features. This rough division is worth stressing as it appears again and again in the late Roman period, through the fifth century and into the early Anglo-Saxon era. The division between 'Anglo-Saxon' and 'Celtic' cultural zones might originate in the late Roman period. Roman Britain survived the third century well. Villas continued to be occupied and new ones were built. These were usually small to middling affairs, but some were larger. As has long been known, these larger and often more sumptuously decorated villas generally lie on the fringe of the lowland zone, along that line between Somerset and the East Riding of Yorkshire.[52] This region appears to have been the economic powerhouse of late Roman Britain. The mosaic industries

[52] Rivet (1969), p. 213.

were located here, to serve the wealthier villas. Towns in this part of Britain also appear to have been more prosperous in the later Roman period than those further to the south and west.

The cemeteries suggest stability. That at Poundbury (Dorset) is particularly instructive.[53] Here the local élite constructed mausolea for its dead. The graves of the remainder of the community were simple, with no above-ground markers, and organised into rows. These have few grave-goods and thus show little evidence that the interment of the deceased was an occasion for competitive demonstrations of status. The mausolea display their distinction from the remainder of the community by ignoring the general alignment of these rows. The display made in their construction, unlike the transient display of grave-goods, was above-ground and permanent, or aimed at being so. At least one tomb was intended to be revisited. The competitive element here probably lay within the peer group that constructed these monuments. The evidence suggests a hierarchical and fairly stable society. When compared with those in mainland Europe, the villas point to an élite that was not, except perhaps on some fringes of the lowlands, hugely wealthy. It does not seem unreasonable to suppose that what kept this élite, which might be thought of as a 'squirearchy', in place was service in the bureaucracy and perhaps the army, with the rewards that that brought. The apparatus of the Roman state supported these local leaders against any potential rivals. It has been suggested that Britain's fourth-century prosperity was largely dependent upon involvement in the Empire. British grain was sent to feed the Rhine armies. Industries producing the standard items of Roman culture, such as fine tablewares, were well established in Britain. The mosaic industries were a late Roman phenomenon, further underlining the region's prosperity in this period. Britain was, furthermore, keyed into the Empire's long-distance trade networks, which ran as far as the eastern Mediterranean.

Across the channel in Gaul, things were also diverse.[54] Gaul is a huge region with many different ecological and climatic zones within it (map 5). Major rivers – the Seine, the Loire, the Garonne, the Meuse, the Moselle and the Saône/Rhône – define some areas.

---

[53] Sparey Green (1993); (1982) for summary.

[54] There is no recent overview of late Roman Gaul in English, but see Knight (1999), pp. 25–127. Esmonde Cleary (1989), pp. 16–40, *passim*, is useful. For the north, see Wightman (1985), pp. 202–311, now rather dated.

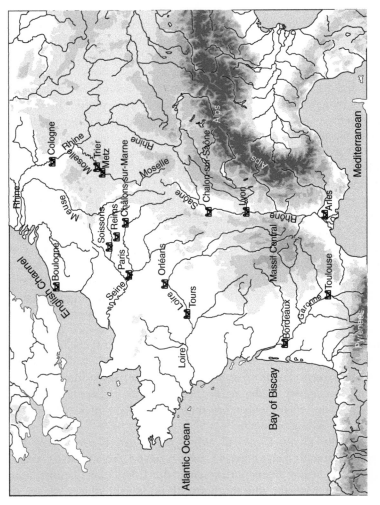

Map 5   Gaul

Modern Brittany in the west forms a distinctive zone, as does the Massif Central west and south of Lyon. There are also mountain ranges such as the Jura and the Vosges and large areas of forest. A very rough division can be made into northern and southern Gaul, along a line from the mouth of the Loire to modern Basel. This is much too crude but it will serve as useful shorthand. Many Gaulish regions traced their distinctiveness back to pre-Roman days.

The north had suffered badly at the end of the third century. Many villas occupied in the late second century were abandoned by the fourth. The extent of complete abandonment has been overestimated;[55] many continued on a reduced scale, but should probably not be considered villas. Nevertheless between a third and half (and sometimes more) were abandoned. Many sites in the countryside were now clearly fortified, or at least defensible. It is not unlikely that the military presence in the north was an important factor in the changes visible in the northern Gallic settlement pattern. Land might have been acquired by the state at the expense of landowners and geared towards production of foodstuffs and other materials to provision the armies and the central bureaucracy often located in the area, at Trier. In the south, by contrast, villas are frequently rather larger, such as at the famous site of Montmaurin.[56] Indeed archaeology suggests significantly greater prosperity in the rural settlement pattern in the south. Mosaic and sarcophagus manufacture was elaborate and flourishing.

Public building is rarely attested. Exceptions occur in towns with imperial connections. The Empire's rulers furnished Trier with numerous large public buildings.[57] About a quarter of the intra-mural area appears to have been given over to a huge palace complex. The *Aula Palatina* forms part of this but so did the Kaiserthermen (the imperial baths), and the double cathedral, circus and amphitheatre on its fringes were arenas of imperial ritual. Unlike British towns, which acquired their walls around the late second century, Gallic towns received defensive circuits after the final quarter of the third century. Throughout Gaul, these were generally short, enclosing only a fraction

[55] Wightman (1985) for traditional views; van Ossel (1992); van Ossel and Ouzoulias (2000) is a splendid overview. Regional surveys: Halsall (1995a), pp. 175–88; Louis (2004).

[56] Fouet (1983); Esmonde-Cleary (1989), fig.7.

[57] Allison (2003), pp. 226–30; Cüppers (ed.) (1984); Wightman (1971); (1985), pp. 234–41.

of the early Roman area of occupation. Tours' amphitheatre became a bastion (a phenomenon encountered across Gaul, at for example Périgueux) and enclosed only about a quarter of the early city.[58] Clermont's walls were shorter still. The extreme example of the phenomenon, however, appears to be Bavay in the far north, where the fortifications enclosed only the forum. At Paris the left bank forum also seems to have been fortified, but the main defended citadel was the Ile de la Cité.[59] When excavated, such walls are often found to contain fragments of earlier buildings, funerary monuments and inscriptions. In some cases they run across the line of earlier occupation. Taken together, this data was frequently assumed to represent a hasty, emergency response to the late third-century barbarian attacks.

Gallic city walls might, however, have been constructed over a much longer period than was once thought. Their dating to the late third century was often based upon that of the latest funerary inscriptions discovered in their foundations. Yet fourth-century inscriptions are much rarer than third-century ones, so this is a shaky basis for chronology. Better archaeology and clearer stratigraphy sometimes make clear that defences were built as late as the mid-fourth century.[60] Some might belong even later, in the early Middle Ages. Another support for the 'emergency' thesis, their supposedly hasty construction, is also unfounded. The funerary monuments, inscriptions and reused masonry are, unsurprisingly given the nature of archaeology, usually from the walls' foundations. Where the defences survive above ground, they are carefully constructed, often with fairly elaborate mural designs.[61] They do not look like walls hurriedly thrown up to fend off barbarian attackers.

The shortness of the walled circuits, adduced to suggest hasty construction and the decline in the cities' size, needs further consideration. It is perhaps not unlikely that the scale of their construction reflected the general late antique unwillingness to spend money on public building. In support of this hypothesis, we might cite the length of the walled circuit of Metz, the longest enceinte of

---

[58] Galinié (1988); (1999).
[59] Clermont: Pietri (1980); Bavay: Wightman (1985), pp. 224–7; Paris: Velay (1992), pp. 69–75.
[60] See, e.g. Halsall (1995a), pp. 203, 219.
[61] Esmonde-Cleary (1989), pp. 24–7; Knight (1999), pp. 26–34.

certain late Roman date in Gaul, enclosing 72 hectares.[62] Metz was the next *civitas* to Trier, on the imperial capital's lifeline to the Mediterranean. Troops and imperial finances were available for the construction of a lengthy circuit, leaving few areas outside the fortifications. Where, as was generally the case, such resources were not available, walls were kept almost to the minimum. Across Gaul, fortified late Roman towns were considerably smaller than their early Roman predecessors. This phenomenon can be seen further afield, too, in Spain and Italy, though the extent of contraction is rarely as drastic as that in some northern Gallic towns. It was, therefore, not only towns in areas prone to external attack that were fortified. Nevertheless, that these circuits are shortest in Gaul might indicate that at least in some cases the economic ability to fortify was also absent. Whether or not, as was once assumed, walled areas reflect the scale of occupation is more debatable. In extreme cases like Bavay this cannot have been the case. At Tours extramural sites were still used. However, it has been suggested that these bear witness to manufacture and other activities, but not to actual inhabitation, which was restricted to the fortified zone.[63] A degree of contraction is suggested across the Gauls. At Metz, even with its long walled circuit and (for northern Gaul) unusual prosperity, there is evidence of abandonment and dereliction on a number of sites inside the defensive circuit and outside.[64] Arles, too, in the far south, though another city with strong imperial connections, shows desertion and dereliction.[65] Urban decay and contraction, if perhaps not as dramatic as once thought, was still considerable. As in Britain, the information we have suggests that towns were less important as centres for markets, craft specialisation and manufacture than they had once been. Instead they appear to have been political and governmental centres.

Economically, southern Gaul was more keyed into the Mediterranean trade patterns reflected, for example, by the distribution of African Red Slip Ware (ARS). It produced its own finewares and other materials. However, the north forms a distinct economic zone. ARS, the 'barium meal' of late Roman long-distance trade-routes, does not reach this region except in a few instances on the upper Rhine.[66] Northern Gaul manufactured its own finewares, Argonne

---

[62] Halsall (1995a), p. 219.   [63] Above, n. 58.
[64] Halsall (1995a), pp. 223–8; (1996), pp. 239–41.
[65] Loseby (1996).   [66] Hayes (1972), maps at pp. 453–61.

Ware, and other prestigious products. Nonetheless, this area also had its own hinterland beyond the Rhine. Northern Gallic finewares, glass and bronze vessels, as well as imperial metalwork, are all found in *Germania* as far as Scandinavia.[67] This is important. The spread of these cultural influences northwards overwhelmingly outweighs the slender evidence for any spread of 'Germanic' culture into northern Gaul. It also suggests that the economic dislocation of northern and southern Gaul, assumed by Henri Pirenne to post-date the seventh-century Arab conquests,[68] can in fact be traced to the late Roman period. Overall, the Gaulish evidence suggests two distinct zones: the prosperous south, whose aristocrats were wealthy and, in the fourth century, politically important and the militarised north, where the élite was less prosperous but, like that of Britain, albeit in a rather different fashion, closely bound into the structures of the Empire.

Geographically, Spain forms a number of different regions (map 6). Much of the peninsula's interior is taken up with high plateaux, less barren in late antiquity than today. Major river valleys run on generally east–west lines: the Ebro (the only major river to run west–east), the Duero/Douro, the Tajo, the Guadiana, and the Guadalquivir. The north-west is mountainous and ranges like the Sierra Nevada ring the south-east. Other mountains divide up the interior and ecology can change dramatically from one side of a range to the other. Although Pyrenean Basques may have posed problems of law and order it no longer seems that the far north-west was separated off by an internal *limes hispanicus*.[69] From the late third century, *Mauretania Tingitania* was added to 'the Spains'. This was to help defend the peninsula from attacks from the Moorish tribe of the *Baquates*, who had caused much damage in the third century, but also to provide a designated area of logistical back-up for the Mauretanian defences.[70]

Late Roman Spain shows some similarities to southern Gaul.[71] Urban public building went into serious decline after the second

[67] Halsall (2000), p. 172.   [68] Pirenne (1939).

[69] See, e.g. Blazquez (1974); (1980), *contra* de Palol (1977); García Moreno (1990). Rodriguez-Aragon (1992) attempts to revive the notion.

[70] Kulikowski (2004), pp. 71–82, prefigured, to some extent by López-Pardo (1991).

[71] Kulikowski (2004) is essential. For a good English introduction concentrating upon archaeological evidence, see Keay (1988), chs. 8–9, updated with Keay (2003), pp. 198–210. Richardson (1996), ch. 8, is more document-based and adds more detail on political history and Christianity.

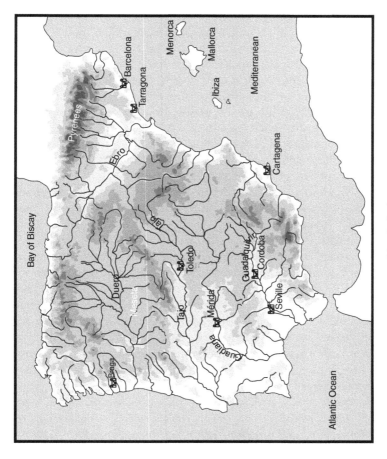

Map 6 Spain

century and some structures were completely abandoned.[72] The theatre at Málaga was derelict. That at Baelo (Bolonia) was turned into a rubbish dump whilst the city's main street silted over. The aqueduct at Termes fell into disuse, Empurias' (Emporiae) harbour was allowed to silt up, and so on. A couple of towns were deserted completely. As in Gaul, towns were now fortified, sometimes involving the levelling of buildings and the stripping of monuments, and the late imperial walls enclosed smaller areas than those covered by the early towns. The main factor behind these developments, as elsewhere, was the end of local aristocratic willingness to spend money on public building, as is proved by its common correlate, the continued ability to dispense large sums on private constructions, urban and rural. Within towns, private houses could be impressive and richly furnished with mosaics. From the fourth century, money was also spent upon church building.

Rural villas continued to be built. Spanish villas had long been luxurious but many late Roman examples were especially so, as at the famous villa of La Olmeda.[73] Many Spanish *villae* are very large and their construction went on right through the fourth century and beyond.[74] In an interesting late burst of 'Romanisation', the villa spread into the north of the Meseta in the fourth century. Study suggests that they are not an organic outgrowth of local landholding patterns but relate to the introduction of new landowners into the region.[75] The exact role of these villas is not always certain, and their fate in the fifth century further suggests a disjunction between their owners and local society. This possibly relates to a growth in the Spanish aristocracy's prosperity, associated with the rise to power of the Spaniard, Theodosius. Throughout Spain, many *villae* appear to have been the centres of large-scale production and the consumption of wealth derived from it.[76] On the coast, an extensive apparently private building was associated with fish sauce manufacture at Santa Pola.[77] The wealth of the Spanish aristocracy is also shown by sites like Centcelles[78] and underscored by the written sources.

---

[72] For detail on specific towns, see Cunliffe and Keay (eds.) (1995).
[73] Keay (1988), p. 193.
[74] Keay (2003), p. 206; E.g. Rodríguez Martín (1995); Tremoleda *et al.* (1995).
[75] Julio Escalona Monge, *pers. comm.* June 2003.   [76] Witschel (2004), p. 266.
[77] Reynolds, P. (1993), p. 10.   [78] Arce (1994).

Spain, like the other main regions of the western Empire, did not form a single economic unity. The coast remained involved in Mediterranean trade networks but imports from such trade did not penetrate far into the interior. Here, a Spanish fineware predominated: Terra Sigillata Hispanica Tardía (TSHT), produced north of the middle Duero valley.[79] The coastal and inland regions do not appear to have interacted with each other to a marked degree. Other economic changes took place. The Baetican fish sauce industry declined in the face of competition from *Lusitania*[80] and its olive oil industry lost out to that of North Africa. Spanish oil appears largely to have been exported to Gaul.

Italy is also divided into different regions by physical geography (map 7). In the north the wide Po valley provides an area of fertile land, but the Apennines, running down the spine of Italy from north-west to south-east, bisect the peninsula. Apart from separating east from west, these mountains divide society into myriad small valleys as

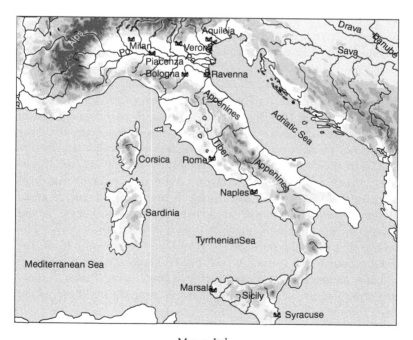

Map 7 Italy

[79] Keay (1988), pp. 190–1; (2003), pp. 208–9.   [80] Etienne and Mayet (1993–4).

water-courses drain to east or west. This feature, of mountainous valley after valley, made the Allied conquest of Italy in 1943–5 such a difficult, tortuous and bloody affair. Other regional variations existed, especially between north and south, which will become clear in discussion.

In its late Roman social and economic developments, Italy resembles Spain in many ways.[81] The changes in the nature of the Empire and the imperial responses meant that Italy effectively became a province, even if an ideologically important and fairly prosperous one. Under Diocletian it was divided into sixteen provinces ruled by senatorial *correctores* and the most important city of the region, in terms of realpolitik if not ideology, was Milan, a frequent capital since the mid-third century. Like Trier it lay close to the frontiers, covering key Alpine passes into the heart of *barbaricum*. The outlines of developments in Italy will be all too familiar. Urban decay had set in, even to some degree in Rome itself. The *fora* of a number of Italian towns reveal dereliction, decay and abandonment – and occasionally the transfer of the area to quite other activities, such as agriculture.[82] Within Italian towns, the importance of the old secular town centres, around the forum, was being transferred to new Christian religious foci around churches.

There was, again, a significant decline in public building, charted by Bryan Ward-Perkins: 'There are, to the best of my knowledge, no fourth-century or later inscriptions recording work carried out at the initiative of a town administration more important than the erection or re-erection of statues.'[83] Anzio's baths were described as 'sordid in their ruinous state and dangerous in their structural insecurity, and the threat of collapse frightened people and kept them away'.[84] Exceptions, as in Gaul, were connected with imperial presence. Milan benefited from large-scale monuments, as did Ravenna, the imperial capital after 402, in the fifth century. The central imperial government was responsible for much of the visible construction and repair of public buildings. Ostia received a set of baths on governmental initiative in 375–6. Ward-Perkins argues that attention focused on a fairly narrow range of buildings: walls,

---

[81] Potter (1987), pp. 192–209, is a convenient, if sketchy, place to begin. More detail can be found in Giardina (ed.) (1986). Humphries (2000a).

[82] On *fora*, churches and spatial realignments, see Potter (1995), pp. 90–8.

[83] Ward-Perkins (1984), p. 24.   [84] *CIL* 10.6656; Ward-Perkins (1984), p. 34.

palaces, aqueducts and baths. Other exceptions to the general rule of neglect, also instructive, were in Campania, a centre of the old Roman senatorial nobility, as ever marking itself out from the parvenus of the late imperial system through its adherence to traditional values.

The rural settlement pattern also showed diversity.[85] There were lavish villas, as one would expect in an area that was home to some of the wealthiest and most powerful families in the entire Empire. Piazza Armerina (Sicily) is a fine example.[86] Yet there are also traces of contraction and decline. Sometimes the field survey evidence upon which this conclusion is based is problematic. Field survey in South Etruria (just north of Rome) suggested that 75 per cent of the rural settlements that had existed in the second century had disappeared by the fourth.[87] Although this picture might have resulted from problematic data and methodology, its outlines have been confirmed by more recent work.[88] It remains clear that a profound reorganisation of the settlement pattern was under way.[89] This possibly involved a concentration of people in fewer but larger settlements rather than a fall in the overall population. This might stem from a reorganisation of the region's landholding patterns and reflect a growth of aristocratic power. Certainly there is evidence of a change in the focus of production. Some villas switched to intensive cereal cultivation and others, it seems, to large-scale rearing of pigs. Both are probably connected with the provisioning of Rome and in some areas this led to considerable prosperity for the local aristocracy.[90]

Agri deserti also existed in Italy. These 'deserted fields' were traditionally understood as evidence of falling population, leading to an increase in uncultivated land. However, closer examination, particularly of the legislation regarding such lands, suggests that *agri deserti* are rather to be understood as lands for which no tax-paying landowner could be identified. Some legislation makes clear that people fraudulently claimed rents from them and thus that people lived and worked on them.[91]

---

[85] Christie (1996) for overview.   [86] Wilson (1983).
[87] Potter (1979), pp. 140–2.   [88] Hemphill (2000).
[89] For other surveys, see Barker (1995); Saggioro (2004).   [90] Noyé (1996).
[91] *Agri deserti*: Jones, A. H. M. (1964), pp. 812–23; Whittaker (1976).

Rome deserves individual attention.[92] The fourth-century emperors rarely visited the city, Constantius II's visit of 357 being perhaps the best-known instance. Rome thus lost much political importance and probably declined in population as a result. It has even been argued that in the late Roman political context the city became something of an overgrown provincial town, with the senate as a grandiose *curia*.[93] This is probably going too far. Rome retained her ideological importance. Her population, which even in decline dwarfed that of any other western town, and the damage that it could do in times of crisis and revolt – hitting the houses of the rich and the standing of the emperor – meant that she had to be taken seriously. Consequently the absentee emperors spent lavishly on public building in Rome. The walls were refurbished; new baths were built by Diocletian and Constantine; Valentinian I and Theodosius built or rebuilt bridges; Constantius II provided an obelisk from Egypt; and so on. The city was lavishly provided with churches, including St Peter's on the Vatican. Emperors continued to inscribe their political identities and programmes on the much over-written architectural palimpsest that was Rome. They were not the only writers either. Until the early fifth century the senatorial nobility went on providing memorials to their wealth and status.

The Italian nobility was the wealthiest élite group within the Empire. It was also the most conscious of its position and its distinction from the remainder of society. Yet this wealth and class-consciousness did not always match its *de facto* power. Third-century changes and the new styles of imperial rule had removed the old dynasties from the real core of imperial politics. Italy, or at least Rome, was important ideologically, but strategically it was not as central to the western government as northern Gaul or even Africa. To some extent, especially once the administrative reforms had reduced the danger of regional aristocratic revolt, the emperors could afford to leave Italy to look after itself. It should not, however, be supposed that this was always, or often, a harmonious solution; the senatorial nobility resented its removal from the core of political power. Tension between emperor and nobility came to a head in Valentinian's persecution of the Roman senatorial aristocracy from

---

[92] On Rome, see Curran (1999); Giardina (ed.) (1986), vol. 3; Humphries (2000b);
     Krautheimer (1980), pp. 3–58; Lançon (2000); Ward-Perkins (1984), pp. 38–48.
[93] Robinson (1992), p. 23.

368. Supposedly motivated by Valentinian's puritan disapproval of adultery and corruption – there is scant evidence of any real conspiracy – it might equally have been fuelled by the emperor's wariness of these powerful magnates.[94] Yet at the same time as its members excoriated the emperors' and their provincial officers' lack of culture and breeding, they also competed for those high offices still available to them and necessary to maintain their traditional aristocratic culture of *otium* and *negotium*.

Especially after the foregoing discussion, which has catalogued regional variations on a general late Roman theme, North Africa can be seen as an unusual province.[95] North Africa is essentially made up of a series of geographical bands, running on a line roughly west-south-west to east-north-east (map 8). Ecologically the northernmost band is defined by the 400mm isohyet (the area within which 400mm of rain falls every year) and within this area grain and olives were produced in abundance. The next zone, which incorporates diverse regions such as the Tunisian steppe, the Algerian high plateaux and various mountain

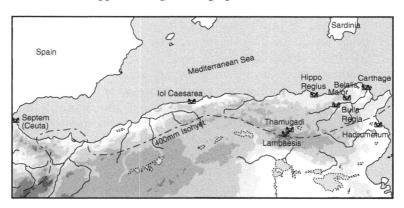

Map 8 North Africa

[94] Alföldi, A. (1952a); Arnheim (1972), pp. 93–8; Matthews (1975), pp. 32–63; (1989), pp. 209–17.

[95] The recent introduction of Roman Africa as an option for the French *agrégation* qualification has led to the appearance of a spate of solid text-books in 2005–6, which appeared too late to be used here. Of these, Prévot, Blaudeau, Voisin and Najar (2006) seems the most thorough. Bertrandi and Coltelloni-Trannoy (2005) is an excellent, thematic annotated bibliography. Raven (1993), chs. 10–12 is a readable English introduction but should be used with care. Shaw (1980). Mattingly (1995) is essential for Tripolitania; Mattingly and Hitchner (1995); Warmington (1954) is dated but still an excellent place to begin.

ranges is defined by the 100mm isohyet. This area can produce olives and sometimes cereals depending on the degree to which particular regions are watered (often by harnessing run-off from the mountains), as well as providing good grazing. Beyond this ecological zone, running along a series of mountain ranges, lay the desert, although in antiquity more cultivation was possible even here than is the case today. The Empire placed its southern frontier on this ecological boundary.[96]

Africa's distinctive place within the Roman Empire stems partly from the paradox that whilst in many ways (geographical and ecological) a peripheral, frontier zone, in other ways it was simultaneously a central, core region. Economically, it was essential to the governance of Rome itself and the higher aristocracy of the area had very close links with the Italian senatorial dynasties. Geographically it was also very close to Italy and all of these factors made Africa strategically and politically extremely important. In the third century it was prosperous, as manifested by elaborate, one might say baroque, mosaics adorning town houses and rural villas.[97] As elsewhere, the adornment of private building had been accompanied by a decline in public building. However, this changed in the fourth century. Public building revived, especially in *Africa Proconsularis*, and continued through to the end of the century.[98] There was an imperial dimension to this. The governors appear to have sponsored much of the building. What is more interesting, and unusual, is that urban councils, the *ordo* and the *curia*, are mentioned on inscriptions, even if the provincial governor is mentioned first. There are regional variations. In *Numidia* and *Mauretania*, frontier regions where there was less public building and where some decline seems to have begun to set in during the fourth century, the governor alone usually dedicated buildings to the emperor but in the more economically developed regions of *Proconsularis* and *Byzacena*, closer to the sea, the *ordo* took a prominent role.[99]

Also interesting is the continued use of inscriptions in local power struggles. At Lambaesis (Tazoult, Algeria) a veritable epigraphic debate took place between the local Christians and Pagans. At Thamugadi (Timgad, Algeria), famously, a lengthy inscription, the 'Album', sets out the names and achievements of the local *honorati*

---

[96] Daniels (1987), pp. 233–4. [97] Witschel (2004), pp. 267–9. [98] Lepelley (1992).
[99] Warmington (1954), p. 32.

and *curia*.[100] This sort of behaviour was not common in the rest of the western Empire and demonstrates the continuing importance of involvement with Rome in maintaining status in North African society. Of a kind with this is the evidence that the imperial cult, with its *duumviri* and *flamines* (priests), continued to be significant in North African cities, even under a Christian Empire and in a region as militantly Christian as North Africa.[101] Old-style participation in municipal politics had remained strategically valuable in African local politics. Furthermore, Africans continued to employ old-fashioned naming practices.[102] Not only was the conscious display of *romanitas* and involvement with Rome important in local politics, the North Africans were also conscious of their importance within late Roman politics – it was, crucially, North African grain that fed Rome – and could demonstrate this by being almost more Roman than the Romans.

Regional surveys have produced evidence of rural prosperity.[103] In some areas like *Africa Proconsularis* villas increased in the fourth century. In the south of that province settlement appears to nucleate around dominant farms, perhaps reflecting tenurial relationships.[104] Some villas seem not to have been the residences of the land-owner, even where, as at Nador (Algeria) the latter is named in an inscription.[105] This prosperity stems from the fourth-century blossoming of the North African export of products such as olive oil and *garum* and the African Red Slip (ARS) finewares.[106] Much of this trade might have piggy-backed on the compulsory export of grain to feed Rome and the employees of the state.

Fourth-century Africa saw intense religious dispute, centred on the Donatist schism.[107] Stemming from disagreement over whether those who had handed over scriptures during the Diocletianic persecution could serve as priests or bishops, this split North African society, there frequently being rival Christian communities in each city. This,

[100] Lambaesis: Warmington (1954), p. 36; Thamugadi: Chastagnol (1978); Lepelley (1992), pp. 63–4.
[101] Lepelley (1979), pp. 165–7, 362–9; (1992), pp. 62–3. [102] Lepelley (1992), p. 61.
[103] E.g. Leveau (1984); Dietz, Sebaï and Ben Hassen (eds.) (1995).
[104] Whittaker and Garnsey (1998), p. 285.
[105] Whittaker and Garnsey (1998), p. 300; Brett and Fentress (1996), p. 73.
[106] ARS production: Hayes (1974), pp. 13–299; Mackensen and Schneider (2002); Peacock, Bejaoui and Ben Lazreg (1990); Reynolds, P. (1995), pp. 6–34.
[107] There is a huge bibliography. Frend (1952) sparked this debate. For classic responses see, e.g. Brown, P. R. L. (1961); Markus (1972).

however, can be claimed to show North Africa's unusual place within the Empire. The intensity of persecution in the region, which brought about the schism in the first place, was unique in the west and might further illustrate the importance of demonstrating Romanness as a strategy in local politics.[108] The Donatist controversy turned upon an appeal to imperial arbitration by the Donatists themselves. Disappointed by Constantine's failure to uphold their cause, meaning that their opponents could claim the legitimacy of association with the government, the Donatists employed an alternative strategy to claim superior *romanitas*, based on Africa's distinctiveness and importance within the Empire and their unwillingness to be told what to do by Rome. Both sides, in their own ways, played upon Africa's unusual Romanness.

Africa was, then, prosperous but internally divided and always paradoxical. As well as a wealthy aristocracy closely associated with that of Italy there were also important military officials from the semi-barbarous tribes around the region's frontiers, whom we shall discuss in the next chapter.

GENDER

As we have just seen, the socio-economic structures of the western Empire were diverse. Elites were wealthier in some areas than others, with implications for the relative importance of the state aristocracy versus the traditional nobility and for the significance of less wealthy free classes and of slavery and the colonate. Other areas of social organisation also differed. That which concerns us here is gender. The study of women in the late Roman world has produced much important work.[109] What must be stressed is, again, regional variety. Most work on late Roman women has concentrated upon sources from the heart of the Empire and on legislation.[110] The pronouncements of the Theodosian code, although full of interesting

---

[108] On the continuing importance of paganism in African urban society, often overshadowed by concentration on Christian schisms, see Riggs (2001).

[109] By far the best introduction is Clark, G. N. (1993), with bibliography. Salzman (2002), pp. 138–77. A superb bibliography compiled by Antti Arjava may be found on-line at http://www.nipissingu.ca/department/history/MUHLBERGER/ORB/arjava3.htm. On the family, see Evans Grubbs (1995); Nathan (2000); Shaw (1984b); (1987).

[110] Arjava (1996) is comprehensive.

and useful material about women's legal status, should not be assumed to represent the totality of customary restraints on female behaviour. There was a broad spectrum of vulgar law and local custom, which can only be dimly perceived.

A few general points can be made. Legally, women lived under the control of men. Although legal guardianship (*tutela*) of an adult woman by her husband or male relatives had withered by the fourth century, this change seems to have made little difference.[111] Husbands still controlled a couple's property. Similarly, fathers retained some authority over their children through *patria potestas* (fatherly power). Inheritance was supposed to be equal between children of either sex, though the use of wills allowed considerable freedom. Fathers also granted their children a measure of autonomy by bestowing property upon them before they died (*peculium*).[112] Although traditional ideas about the primacy of agnatic kin (related only in the male line) persisted, families increasingly saw themselves as bilateral, claiming descent from both sides. Old ideas about different male and female sexual standards continued.[113]

One of the principal challenges of late antique history has been to bring the work on gender history together with the similarly voluminous literature on the end, or transformation, of the Roman world.[114] It is important not only to see gender as affected by high level political transformations but also to attempt to give gender a role in producing those changes. Gayle Rubin's concept of the 'sex–gender system' is helpful here.[115] Reduced to essentials, and at the risk of oversimplification, this sees the exchange of women in society as more important than any other aspect of gift exchange in that, in order to participate in the politics of marriage and all the social and economic links that it brings, it compels every member of society to be gendered male or female and renders heterosexuality obligatory.

This is very important. The Empire took considerable interest in legislating about marriage: whom it was possible between (going much further than simple incest legislation); the rights of inheritance of the groups joined by marriage; rights of guardianship over children; and so on.[116] At the same time, marriage and correct

[111] Arjava (1996), pp. 155–6.   [112] Arjava (1998).

[113] E.g. Clark, G. N. (1993), pp. 35–41.

[114] Halsall (2004); Noble (1999), p. 275; Smith, J. M. H. (2001).   [115] Rubin, G. (1975).

[116] Evans Grubbs (1995).

marital behaviour were essential for participation in Roman politics. 'The organisation of power within Roman society at large was thus grounded in the gender relationships that marriage enabled.'[117] The relationship between gender and politics was reciprocal and dialogical.

Traditionally, Roman gender relations had revolved around the idea of civic masculinity.[118] A man was supposed to control his emotions and to behave with reason, justifying his authority over the women of his family, who might allow their passions to govern their actions. Female behaviour was judged according to ideas of sexual and marital propriety but reflected principally upon a family's menfolk. A man had to maintain control over his relatives. In politics a man's fitness to rule was impugned by the accusation that he had been swayed by the opinions of his female relatives.[119] This is significant because what marked a good political leader out from someone unsuited to office was the same as what distinguished a man from a woman and, at the same time, crucially, what differentiated the civilised man from the barbarian.

There must have been regional variations in this situation. Archaeological cemetery evidence suggests different costume in some areas for younger and older women, presumably relating to married and unmarried status.[120] Written sources also attest that young and old, married and unmarried women were distinguished by their clothing[121] but quite how this key aspect of the sex-gender system was manifested will have changed from one area to another. There was also variation in ideals. It has been argued that late antiquity saw an increase in the depiction of female education on sarcophagi.[122] Whilst education had earlier been a male preserve and the depiction of a woman acquiring such virtue might have been intended to reflect well upon her male relatives, it also seems that women were appropriating such imagery. This in turn might have led to an increase in the portrayal of hunting scenes on male sarcophagi, as men sought an exclusively male ideal to depict.

This discussion is of especial significance because of the fact that, after the universal grant of citizenship in 212, Romanness was performed. In the later Roman Empire imperial service was crucially

[117] Smith, J. M. H. (2001), p. 29.
[118] Cooper and Leyser (2001).   [119] Cooper (1992).   [120] Swift (2000), p. 40.
[121] Clark, G. N. (1993), pp. 105–18.   [122] Huskinson (1999).

important in local politics (if in different ways in different areas). To secure a place in the hierarchy of offices one had to acquire a specific education, which emphasised subscription to the models of civic masculinity. Suitability for posts in the government was judged according to the success with which one lived out these ideals. This performance also determined one's eligibility for marriage, essential in maintaining or enhancing a family's standing and one's conduct within marriage was, simultaneously, an essential masculine virtue. Thus the Roman Empire was, to its core, a gendered edifice. This is vital to understanding the changes of the fifth century and the creation of the barbarian kingdoms. The performance of Roman identity was essential to involvement in the Empire. However, the equation of the difference between man and woman, between good and bad rule, and between civilised and barbarian meant that to turn one's back upon Roman identity, to adopt a barbarian ethnicity, could mean calling into question one's masculinity, one's ability to manage a family and one's suitability to rule (at whatever level). This should have had profound effects upon the political choices open to people in local and regional communities as the Roman Empire began to fall apart.

THE CHURCH[123]

Two further Roman institutions require attention as both played crucial roles in helping the people of the west to negotiate the change to the post-imperial world: the church and the army. The Christian church in western Europe was a comparatively recent introduction. At the start of our period it had been an official feature of imperial politics for less than three generations. Before Constantine I's conversion and the end of the last persecutions, Christianity was, outside Africa, a tiny minority religion in the western Empire with few significant communities. By 376 it had survived Emperor Julian's attempt to restore paganism and was securely entrenched within imperial administrative and political structures. Nevertheless, at this point it had still to make significant inroads into the rural poor of the north-west in particular and the senatorial nobility of Rome still clung tenaciously to their ancestral beliefs.[124] Constantine's

---

[123] For a good introduction, see Hunt (1998).
[124] On the conversion of the aristocracy see Salzman (2002).

conversion had been decisive.[125] Whatever personal piety lay behind
it, it cannot have been lost upon him that a well organised, exclusive
monotheism provided the best religious underpinning for the new
Empire's totalitarian ideology. In that sense Constantine's conversion
can, ironically, be seen as the logical extension of the pagan Diocletian's
reforms. Nevertheless, it is always worth repeating that contemporaries
in 312 had no more idea that the persecution just closed would be the
last than they knew that Constantine would turn out to be less
ephemeral than the supposedly Christian Emperor Philip the Arab had
been in the 240s. The key to Christianity's dramatic spread was the
importance of imperial patronage.[126] As we have seen, imperial service
was, in various ways, vital in local politics. As Constantine's success
grew it became apparent that to receive his patronage one would
need to be Christian. There were, furthermore, dramatic illustrations
of Constantine's favours to converts. Conversion was, thus, drawn
down through Roman society along the arteries of patronage. This
mechanism explains why those groups largely untouched by the new
religion by *c.*375 had remained so. The north-western rural poor
stood outside the system and the senatorial nobility liked to maintain
its distinction from those who had risen through such networks.

The church was organised around imperial administrative structures. With some exceptions, each *civitas* became a bishopric. The
bishop of a province's capital city became a metropolitan (renamed,
long after our period, an archbishop) and, though his rights and
privileges were yet to be securely established, had the right to ordain
the other bishops within his province. Above the metropolitans
were the patriarchs, although these too had ill-defined rights and
responsibilities (and even membership) at this time. Even the
patriarch of Rome's supremacy was a matter of some debate. It was an
unpopular decision when the 381 Council of Constantinople, called,
not coincidentally, by a western Catholic, the Spanish-born Theodosius I, recognised the Pope's superiority over the patriarchs of
Constantinople, Antioch and Alexandria. The church controlled
ever more wealth, which, unlike private fortunes, could not be

---

[125] Jones, A. H. M. (1948).
[126] MacMullen (1984); Salzman (2002), pp. 178–99. None of this should be taken as
dismissing genuinely pious motivation. On the religious context of the age, see,
e.g. Brown, P. R. L. (1978); (1992); (1995); (1998a); (1998b); (2002), pp. 54–
122; Cameron, A. M. (1991); Fowden (1993); (1999); Herrin (1987), pp. 54–89;
Markus (1990).

dissipated through inheritance, wedding gifts and so on. The bishop was becoming a very powerful figure in local politics and service in the church now provided an alternative route to the imperial presence. Since the time of Constantine, the bishops had gradually acquired important roles within the city, taking over to some degree from earlier authorities like the *curia*. This trend would be exaggerated in succeeding centuries. The bishops still had a monopoly on baptism and preaching and Christians within their sees were expected to come to the cathedral church for the major festivals of the year.

The Christian church's significance in the development of western Europe from a series of Roman provinces to a congeries of barbarian kingdoms does not, however, simply lie in material advantage or even in the fact that it had come to be an institution as thoroughly Roman as the bureaucracy. Christian discourse touched upon vital areas of social interaction and comportment. The Christians took on many traditional Roman ideas about correct behaviour. Bishop Ambrose of Milan, for example, repeatedly stressed that moderation should be sought in allowing the soul to overcome the temptations of the body.[127] The behaviour of women was held to reflect the moral probity of their husbands and other male relatives and a strand of Christian thinking continued to valorise the married matron.[128] Nevertheless other currents in Christian thinking parted company with their pagan predecessors. These stressed the extremes of ascetic self-denial, virginity and the renunciation of family ties.[129] This competitive approach to asceticism had little to do with the traditional Roman virtues of moderation and presented an alternative model of behaviour for men and women.

THE ARMY[130]

The late imperial army deserves separate treatment because the relationship between civilian and soldier in many ways foreshadows

---

[127] Ambrose, *The Soul* 2.5, 8.65, 8.79. On Ambrose himself, see McLynn (1994); Moorhead (1999).

[128] Cooper (1996). On Christianity and changes in the construction of men and women see, above all, Brown, P. R. L. (1988).

[129] Cooper and Leyser (2001).

[130] On the Roman army see the still classic description of Jones, A. H. M. (1964), pp. 607–86; more recently Elton (1996a); Lee (1998); Southern and Dixon (1996); Tomlin (1987).

that between 'Roman' and 'barbarian' in the post-imperial west. Furthermore, it is widely believed that the army was largely made up of barbarians and so represented an 'advance guard' or 'fifth column' in the history of the migrations. The late Roman army was not divided, as that of the Principate had been, simply into legions and *auxilia*. Instead, from the mid-third century, the emperors had begun to keep large field armies under their immediate command. These came to be called the *comitatenses*, or (loosely) companions. During the fourth century smaller field armies were created to help defend particular frontiers. This left a gradation of troops from the imperial guards (the *scholae* and the *domestici*), through the 'palatine' units, the 'praesental' field armies (in the presence of the emperor) and down to the regional field armies. Those forces left on the frontiers were called *ripenses* (riverside troops, referring to the Rhine and Danube) or *limitanei*, borderers. It has often been assumed that because the field armies were closer to the emperors they rose in status whilst the *limitanei* declined until they were little more than a frontier peasant militia. Although the *comitatenses* were certainly paid better and were probably less subject to demoralising abuses from their officers than the *limitanei*, the latter were not the hopeless farmer-soldiers that they have been supposed.[131] Many were transferred to the field armies, becoming *pseudocomitatenses*, which implies that they were considered capable of some battlefield role, even if only as reserves.

The army was, as it had always been, a community of its own, developing its own set of identities.[132] What is interesting, for our purposes, is that in the late Empire these identities were so clearly constructed around 'barbarian' imagery. Partly this was because the army recruited heavily in the regions beyond the frontier so that many officers and men were barbarians. However, the Romans had always used barbarian troops and the extent to which the army was being 'barbarised' before *c*.400 in the west has probably been overestimated.[133] What is clear is a late Roman confusion between

---

[131] Jones, A. H. M. (1964), pp. 644–5, for differing opportunities for officers to fleece their soldiers.

[132] Goldsworthy and Haynes (eds.) (1999).

[133] Elton (1996a), pp. 134–52 is an important and persuasive critique of the barbarisation thesis, whose literature is too voluminous to be cited here. In spite of referring to the 'all-destructive barbarization of the army' (p. 230), Speidel (1975) sees these 'savages' (p. 229) as prolonging the Empire's life. For a clear if crude

'soldiers' and 'barbarians', which in many ways resulted from the military's adoption of barbarian styles. Whereas the late Republican or early imperial army was a vehicle of 'Romanisation', in some respects the opposite was the case in the later Empire; the Roman army adopted 'barbarism', even if the latter may well have been a rather artificial Roman creation. When and why this happened is mysterious. One might postulate that it originated in Diocletian's and Constantine's reforms, which separated the military and civil branches of imperial service, removing governors from military command and largely ending senatorial involvement in the army. It seems plausible that this may have led the army to play upon its difference from 'Roman' civilian life.[134]

The late Roman army's barbarisation is often supposed to be manifest in the *barritus*, its war-cry. This is alleged to have originally been a 'German' battle-cry,[135] later adopted by the whole army.[136] Ammianus twice calls it a barbarian word, though the etymology is questionable.[137] Tacitus uses the word *barditus* (*quem barditum vocant*) but Ammianus set out to be Tacitus' continuator. The word *barritus* is also, simply enough, the sound made by a *barrus*, an elephant.[138] Ammianus' description of the *barritus* as a sound swelling to a discordant climax could easily be applied to an elephant's trumpeting. If so, the word is simply a descriptive, perhaps onomatopoeic, word for a particular kind of shout and has no ethnic connotation at all.[139] Whatever its precise origins, it is at least significant that

---

statement of the idea that the Roman Empire fell because of the army's barbarisation, see Ferrill (1986). Liebeschuetz (1991), pp. 11–25, presents reasons for the Empire's increasing reliance on recruitment in *barbaricum*. Jones, A. H. M. (1964), pp. 619–23 wisely offers no comment on *increasing* barbarian numbers and argues convincingly against the idea that such recruitment was necessarily a bad thing. Lee (1998), pp. 222–4, is judicious.

[134] Amory (1997), pp. 27–32, inspired these thoughts. He suggests that another reason for the creation of a 'barbarian' military identity may have been that governmental troops might have been seen as outsiders in the provinces and played upon this.

[135] As Tacitus, *Germania* 3.

[136] Amm. Marc. 16.12.43, 31.7.11; Vegetius, *Epitome* 3.18. See, e.g. N. P. Milner's note to Vegetius, *Epitome* 3.18: Milner (trans.) (1996), p. 101, n. 2.

[137] Amm. Marc. 26.7.17: *quem barbari dicunt barritum*; 31.7.11: *quam gentilitate barritum vocant*.

[138] Vegetius, *Epitome* 3.18, 3.24.

[139] The Germanic etymology for *barritus* given by Lewis and Short (1879), p. 223, unsusceptible of direct proof in any case, would thus be spurious.

gentlemen-officers like Ammianus thought the word was barbaric, although that could be because of its *bar-* stem. It is impossible to know whether this cry was genuinely taken over from the barbarians or whether it was adopted because it was perceived, thanks to classical ethnography, to be what barbarians did.

Another supposedly barbarian custom of the late Roman army is the raising of leaders on a shield. Perhaps the best-known instance of this is Julian's elevation by the Gallic army at Paris in 360.[140] This custom is recorded by Tacitus amongst the *Canninefates* in 69 AD but is otherwise unknown outside the Empire.[141] The link with real barbarians is tenuous. Ammianus does not call it a barbarian custom and even if he had done, classical ethnography, specifically that of Tacitus, his model, would get in the way. The raising of leaders on a shield became more common in the post-imperial period[142] and was occasionally held to be a barbaric, ancestral custom[143] but it is probable that in fact it derives from the practices of the late Roman army. Another, mentioned by Vegetius as of barbarian origin, was the use of whips by officers.[144] Whether this custom really reflects barbarian practice is debatable.

We might also consider the late imperial army's costume. Fourth- and fifth-century Roman troops looked very different from the soldier of the early Empire, who forms the basis for the popular image of the Roman legionary. The late Roman soldier wore trousers and a shorter, long-sleeved tunic, gathered in at the waist with a heavy, thick belt, the buckle of which proclaimed rank. Cloaks were worn, fastened with brooches that again displayed the wearer's status and rank. Armour was usually mail and helmets were simple, mass-produced items. The now circular or oval shield bore fairly simple regimental patterns quite different from early imperial types. Swords were longer (*spatha*) and were joined by axes and a different array of spears and throwing weapons, including heavy, lead-weighted darts. The overall effect, when compared with earlier military appearance, traditional Roman garb and classical descriptions of the Empire's enemies, was of barbarism, especially in the army's adoption of trousers and weapons with barbarian associations like long swords.

---

[140] Amm. Marc. 20.4.17.   [141] Tacitus, *Histories* 4.15.
[142] See, e.g. the reference, possibly purely rhetorical, to Wittigis' elevation by the Goths: Cassiodorus, *Variae* 10.31; the account of the elevation of various Merovingian kings and usurpers: *LH* 2.40, 4.51, 7.10; the elevation of the emperor Justin II: Corippus, *In Praise of Justin* 2, lines 137 ff.
[143] Cassiodorus, *Variae* 10.31.   [144] *Epitome* 3.6.

Imperial bodyguards, according to Synesius of Cyrene, were tall and blond,[145] and pictorial representations appear to show them wearing torques, classic barbarian items.[146] Indeed the standard bearer of the *petulantes* lent his torque to Julian on the occasion of his elevation.[147] Archaeology nevertheless does not suggest that torques were common apparel in the late antique *barbaricum*. Vegetius believed that much of the cavalry armour of his day was of Gothic, Hunnic or Alanic inspiration, although when fighting the Empire little mention is made of such armour,[148] though this might be because such accounts were imprisoned within the demands of Graeco-Roman ethnography. In the *Notitia Dignitatum* the workshops producing ornamented armour are called *barbaricaria*; elaborate military finery, especially gilding, is associated with barbarism.[149] The later imperial army also adopted the *draco* standard, a sort of wind-sock in the form of a dragon. This is depicted as used by Dacians on Trajan's Column, but called Scythian in literature.[150] Again, it may have been adopted for its vague, generally 'barbarian' overtones. The impression is given of an army adopting what it thought were barbarian styles and customs, but ones which are very likely to have been inspired by classical ethnic stereotypes rather than actually being imported by the barbarians employed in the army.

It is impossible to quantify the recruitment of non-Romans into the army. Recent analysis of known members of the imperial bodyguard regiments suggests that at least half, and perhaps as many as three quarters, were Roman.[151] It had long been customary for emperors to have bodyguards of *Germani*, so it is likely that 'German' fashion, as above, had become 'de rigueur' for the Palatine and *scholae* regiments, whatever the origin of their recruits.

---

[145] Synesius, *Kingship* 18. See Cameron, A. D, and Long (1993), p. 207.

[146] The Missorium of Theodosius shows this clearly: Williams and Friel (1994), pl. 1, for an illustration.

[147] Amm. Marc. 20.4.18. Speidel (1985).

[148] Vegetius, *Epitome* 1.20. Cp. Amm. Marc. 27.5, 31.2 (esp. 31.2.8); 31.5.9, 31.6.3, 31.7.6–16, 31.9.3–4, 31.11.4, 31.12.15–17, 31.13.

[149] Not. Dig. Occ.11. See also *CTh* 10.22.1, where *barbaricarius* is a goldsmith. This usage continued into the sixth century in the East: cp. *CJ* 12.24.7.

[150] Vegetius, *Epitome* 2.13; Amm. Marc. 16.10.7; Sid. Ap., *Poems*. 5, lines 402–4. For a full description, see Southern and Dixon (1996), p. 126.

[151] Elton (1996a), pp. 151–2. The methods are problematic but the results definitely suggestive.

Many units of the army bore barbarian names, including *Franci*, *Salii*, *Sarmati*, *Attecotti* and *Vesi* (Goths).[152] This may be, at least partly, because they were recruited amongst the peoples in question. A. H. M. Jones noted long ago that it is unlikely that these later regiments were exclusively made up of recruits from the people whose name they bore.[153] The reality seems rather more complex, and one might even question whether there was much of a connection between regiment and tribal group.

Classical ethnographic stereotyping dwelt heavily upon peoples' military characteristics. The early Roman army recruited specialist troops from particular ethnic groups and these units seem to have retained their function and name whatever their subsequent recruiting history. This might well have led to ethnic names being given to troops of specific types, regardless of their origin. Thus, in the *Notitia Dignitatum* we find numerous regiments of *Mauri*.[154] It seems that this ethnic name has simply been given to regiments of light cavalry – the warriors for which the Moors were famous – perhaps initially recruited from or trained by Moors. Regiments of *Mauri* often have another component to their unit name: *Mauri Feroces* (Ferocious Moors), *Mauri Tonantes* (Thundering Moors) and even *Mauri Illyriciani* (Illyrian Moors – referring to the province where the unit was formed). A number of regiments also have ethnic names which derive from areas *within* the Empire, and some of these might derive from 'functional' stereotyping; the *Dalmatae* regiments seem similarly to be particular types of cavalry.[155] One wonders whether the titles of other ethnically named units similarly derived from their function and from ethnographic stereotyping. It is noteworthy that regiments of mounted archers stationed in Gaul and Italy took the name *Parthi* (Parthians) – the great horse-archers of

---

[152] *Not. Dig.* occ. 5, or. 5, 9, 28, 31. The indispensable study is Hoffman (1969–70). Speidel (1975) provides a comprehensive and scholarly overview in English. My suggestions, however, differ significantly from both.

[153] Jones, A. H. M. (1964), p. 620.

[154] Speidel (1975), pp. 208–24 for discussion. Speidel shows epitaphs of troops of clearly non-Moorish origin in regiments of *mauri*.

[155] Hence *Equites Dalmatae Illyriciani* (*Not. Dig.* or. 33, 35, 37), *cuneus equitum dalmatarum Divitensium* ('Dalmatians from Deutz'; *Not. Dig.* or. 42). Speidel (1975), pp. 225–6, argues that Gallienus originally formed these regiments from units in Dalmatia to create a cavalry strike-force.

antiquity.[156] Whatever their origin, it is unlikely that they were still composed of Parthians in the fourth century.

Many units with older barbarian ethnic names (such as the *Batavi*, for example) might have descended from earlier imperial auxiliary units. However, what is noteworthy is that these units had so risen in status that they were grouped, as Palatine Auxiliaries (*auxilia palatina*), in the more prestigious field armies, unlike many of the old legions. Whilst they had retained the ethnic component of their names, though, they had altered their titles, so that they are listed simply as, for example, *Batavi Seniores* (Elder Batavians), rather than keeping older forms of title, like those retained by lower-status units on the frontiers: the *Cohors Prima Batavorum* on Hadrian's Wall, for example.[157] Given that it is unlikely that these troops were still recruited from Batavians, the retention of the old name is interesting. It has been possible to reconstruct plausibly the specific political circumstances in which some of the regiments recorded in the *Notitia* were enlisted. Nevertheless the evidence upon which historians have constructed genealogies of the Roman army's units, and theories about the development of military organisation, are never very secure. The discovery of one new inscription or papyrus fragment can demolish them. Hoffmann and Tomlin, for example, both produced very different theories about the origin of the division of some late fourth-century field army units into *iuniores* and *seniores*, which they dated to the 360s.[158] The subsequent discovery of an inscription of the 350s, referring to the *iuniores*, showed both to be mistaken[159] and a unit of *mauri iuniores* is even referred to in an inscription of 227.[160]

More significantly, some palatine auxiliary regiments took 'antique' ethnic titles from within and without the Empire: *Cimbri*, *Medii*, *Celtae*, *Latini* or *Sabini*. No one has suggested that Sabines were being recruited into the late Roman army! The argument that ethnic names might have been artificial, inspired by particular barbarian groups' connotations, is strengthened by further consideration of the context

---

[156] *Not. Dig.* occ. 6.   [157] *Not. Dig.* occ. 5, 6, 7, 40.

[158] Hoffmann (1969–70); Tomlin (1972).

[159] Kulikowski (2000a), pp. 370–1; Lee (1998).

[160] *CIL* 8.20996. Speidel (1975), p. 216, n. 56, claims that this must represent a quite different phenomenon and is probably right but, given the inscription from the 350s, we should not automatically assume this, and his alternative explanation does not carry conviction.

where such bodies of soldiers are found. Other Palatine regiments were named after wild animals or took names that stressed warlike or animal qualities: *Cornuti* (Horned Ones – probably bullocks), *Leones* (Lions – though see below), *Petulantes* (Vicious[161]), *Feroces* (Fierce), *Felices* (Lucky), *Invicti* (Undefeated) or *Victores*.[162] Some 80 per cent of units stationed in the west with 'barbarian' ethnic names, and over 70 per cent of western units with 'warlike' components to their names, are to be found amongst the Palatine auxiliary regiments.[163] Units seem to have competed in their ferocity or martial valour. With a huge corpus of ethnography and ethnic stereotypes to hand, much of which stressed the barbarians' warlike ferocity, it is not unlikely that regiments took these names to claim such characteristics for themselves. The similarity between 'animal' and 'barbarian' ferocity is strengthened by the fact that Emperor Caracalla recruited barbarian bodyguards among the *Germani* and called them the *leones*. These 'Lions' might be those of the *Notitia* but the genealogy is far from certain (note that it was the Roman emperor who bestowed this name upon them). The costumes and customs mentioned above may have been part of this appropriation of barbarian ferocity.

Growing numbers of non-Romans, especially from the Germanic-speaking peoples, gained high military rank in the fourth century. Nevertheless, we must remember that with the separation of the now much enlarged civil service from the military, Romans had to choose between the two, leaving more space for non-Romans to advance in the military arm. In the context of the army's valorising of barbarian characteristics, this is even less surprising and so is the fact that as the fourth century wore on many more kept their Germanic names. Early in the century non-Romans took Roman names: Silvanus and the Sarmatian Victor are examples. One early fourth-century Alamannic king even named his son Serapion.[164] By the second half

---

[161] Translated as an animal quality following Columella, *On Agriculture* 7.6.4: *Cornuti* [n.b. the name of another regiment] *fere perniciosi sunt propter petulantiam*: Most horned [goats] are destructive because of their viciousness.

[162] *Not. Dig.* occ. 5–6.

[163] *Not. Dig.* occ. 5–6. The exceptions are a few 'Moorish' units stationed in the Balkans, Armorica and Britain (*Not. Dig.* occ. 33–4, 37, 40) and a larger number of units in the British garrison with names like 'explorers', 'watchers', 'anticipators' and 'defenders' (*Not. Dig.* occ. 40).

[164] Amm. Marc. 16.12.25.

of the century, officers with clearly non-Roman names like Bauto, Arbogast, Merobaudes and Stilicho were common.

All this suggests that the army had created for itself a particularly 'barbarian' identity, but one which was a construct, owing much to classical ethnographic traditions. A parallel might be drawn from the types of gladiator used in classical circus games, which included the ethnic stereotypes Gauls, Thracians and Samnites.[165] As a modern comparison we might think of the Hollywood image of the 'Red Indian', a mythologised hotchpotch of authentic native American elements and idealised and fictional components, thrown together regardless of date or geographical origin. Alternatively, and in a more specifically military context, we could cite the Highland regiments of the British army, largely but far from exclusively recruited from the Scottish Highlands but wearing a uniform which was an English idea of what Highlanders looked like, based loosely around traditional costume. The nineteenth-century French army's Zouave regiments are perhaps an even better analogy. Deriving their name from the Algerian *zaouia*, but rapidly recruited entirely from Frenchmen, they wore a uniform which was a French version of North African dress. Both Zouaves and Highlanders derived a ferocious esprit de corps from the distinctiveness, which their 'ethnic' costume gave them. This is probably how we should view the 'barbarism' of the late imperial army.

The provincial aristocracy continued to serve in the army. Eastern papyrus sources, most famously the 'Abinnaeus Archive' from Egypt, document attempts by provincials to obtain army commands and promotion. The less detailed western sources suggest that the all too often assumed demilitarisation of the provincial aristocracy has been greatly overestimated. The Theodosian code contains legislation, parallel to that for the civil service, concerning absentee officers.[166] Officers who stay away for between one and three years are demoted ten to thirty places on the list of seniority (and thus promotion). Only an officer who absents himself from the colours for more than four years is dismissed from the service. This strikingly lenient system seems to be a governmental attempt to allow the provincial aristocracy to incorporate military service, like civil, within the traditional structures of *otium* and *negotium*. The career of the Antiochene gentleman-officer Ammianus Marcellinus, which involved apparently lengthy spells away from the army between periods of

---

[165] Grant (1967), p. 56.   [166] *CTh* 7.18.16.

active service, would seem to support this.[167] Emperor Theodosius himself came from a provincial aristocratic family that rose to the imperial throne through military service.

These western aristocrats appear to have enjoyed swaggering about in their military dress, which, as discussed above, included consciously barbarian elements. Unsurprisingly the emperors legislated to restrict such posturing. No senator (by this time any regimental commander earned senatorial rank) was to wear military garb within Rome. Instead they 'shall lay aside the awe-inspiring military cloak' and wear a sober civilian one.[168] Similar legislation against such 'barbarian chic' covered the wearing of trousers, archetypal barbarian costume and universal in the army.[169]

This discussion presents a number of important conclusions. The barbarisation of the army appears to have been largely (though not entirely) a Roman artefact. The western Roman provincial aristocracy continued to view service in the army as a career-choice, which meant participation in this barbarised culture. More importantly perhaps, the army, like the church, presented an alternative to the traditional civic model of masculinity. The field army units discussed above claimed, through their titles, the whole spectrum of features antithetical to civic masculinity. They are barbarian, fierce, animal even. There is no room for moderation and control of passions in this competitive discourse of ferocity. Nevertheless, whilst their new identities might have been adopted in rivalry with the civil service and its traditional ideas of Roman comportment, the army personnel did not see themselves as any less Roman. This martial model of late Roman masculinity provided an important resource for provincial society in navigating the dramas of the fifth century.

THE LATE ROMAN EMPIRE: THE PROBLEM REMAINS

The best way of representing the effective power of the Roman emperor and thus the state he headed would be to build a three-dimensional relief map of the Empire and represent the emperor on it by a small, and not especially powerful, light-bulb. This would graphically represent where, and with what efficiency, the imperial writ ran. The brighter the light, the greater the effectiveness of the imperial government; the dimmer the light, or the greater the shade,

---

[167] Matthews (1989).   [168] *CTh* 14.10.1.   [169] *CTh* 14.10.2.

the less the efficiency of the administration. Close to the emperor the light would be strong, and government effective, but the further one moved away from this source the dimmer the light would become. Difficult terrain, especially mountains like the Alps and Pyrenees, would cast substantial areas into shade, representing not only the near impossibility of effective governance within such regions but also the problems which they presented to communications between the emperor and the areas behind the obstacle. Clearly there were ways around this and all were tried during the fourth century. Moving the emperor around would enable the light, at least periodically, to reach most areas of the Empire; clever positioning of more than one emperor would similarly reduce the areas of shade. If our model could be built out of a weakly luminous substance, so that moving the emperor away from an area still left a residual glow, and if our imperial bulb were powered by a battery which, as well as weakening over time, could be, partially at least, recharged by military or political success and depleted by failure the representation would be even better.

The fourth-century emperors had managed this situation well. They were mobile and usually resident on the frontier, involving strategically important frontier areas in the government. They were also militarily capable and until 375 all succeeded as adults. This meant that they were skilfully able to manage the patronage network which the Empire had become. Nevertheless the system's weaknesses should be apparent. It required the effective management of its checks and balances. What would happen if these could no longer be managed?

One possible counter to this structural weakness was, however, the strength of the idea of Empire. The model of civic masculinity was crucial to a whole series of social identities. It would not be easy to turn one's back on Rome without calling into question other aspects of one's identity. The late Empire did, however, offer other models. How these were used to negotiate the difficulties of Roman life in a post-imperial world will be explored in chapter 14.

SOCIETY BEYOND THE FRONTIER

WEST OF THE IRISH SEA: THE *SCOTTI*

Beyond the seas west of Britain, lived the *Scotti*, the Irish, who might already have been moving into Argyll, if they had not lived there all along.[1] The examination of barbarian society west of the Irish Sea is plagued by the employment of later Irish sources, held to have a timeless 'Celtic' value and indeed to be applicable to other parts of the Celtic-speaking world.[2] Leaving aside the debate between 'nativists', who see the information in seventh-century and later sources as representing unalloyed Irish tradition, and anti-nativists, who argue that these accounts are heavily influenced by Christian ideas, to project our sources' information back 300 years or more must be unacceptable. Viewing later 'Celtic' sources as a 'window on the Iron Age' is simplistic and denies change. The archaeological record is unequivocal in revealing dramatic change in most areas of Irish life, beginning in the fourth century,[3] changes that created the situation

---

[1] It has been mooted recently that the linguistic frontier between Irish Q-Celtic and mainland British P-Celtic, rather than being formed by the Irish Sea and moving east with the Scottish migration, might always have lain between Argyll and the rest of modern Scotland. Nevertheless the name of the tribe in the region, the *Epidii* (horse-people), argues for a P-Celtic language. I am grateful to Katherine Forsyth and Simon Taylor for discussion of this topic. See also Harbison (1988), p. 185.

[2] See, classically, Jackson (1964).

[3] Cooney (2000); Cooney and Grogan (1994); Harbison (1988), pp. 155–94; Mytum (1992), pp. 21–8, 43–52; and Stout (2000), form the basis for my comments.

attested in the documents and buried the social structures of earlier Iron Age Ireland for good.

Archaeology suggests that society in Ireland was largely pastoral and, as far as can be told, had not changed significantly for some time. The archaeological data suggest a social structure based upon wide kinship groups with weak, but perhaps extensive, political authority based upon communal ritual practices. After a 'late iron age lull', settlement appears to pick up in the fourth century, with evidence of clearance of woodland and scrub and the beginnings of a change to dairy farming.[4] Cattle farming left its legacy in the primacy of loans of cattle in establishing later clientship but whether similar mechanisms for cementing social ties existed in the Iron Age is difficult to know. The large hillforts of various types, built at the end of the Bronze Age or the beginning of the Iron Age, continued to be, albeit sparsely, occupied. The major Bronze Age ritual sites (e.g. the Navan Fort) also went on being used. Some ritual or sacral aspects of Irish rulership might have bequeathed something to the strange royal inauguration ceremonies known in the historical period but we are unlikely to know which ones, or how. A political leader's important religious role in ensuring fertility might have bound diverse communities into particular units. Craft specialisation does not appear to have been widespread, though the technical level of craftsmanship was high. Artefacts were seemingly produced at the courts of the Irish kings for distribution to their followers. St Patrick caused offence by refusing gifts of jewellery from female members of an Irish royal family, which might support the notion that the gift of such objects was a means by which political allegiance was secured.[5] In later periods a hierarchy of kings is recorded from those ruling a very small local social group, the *túath* or people, through to powerful overkings.[6] This political structure might have existed earlier, although the principal material cultural traces of such hierarchies, the small forts ('raths', 'cashels' and 'crannogs' – earth-, stone-built and those on islands respectively), are absent before the fifth and sixth centuries.[7]

Ireland was increasingly drawn into the Roman world in the fourth century. Mercenaries served in the imperial armies and these warriors and other settlers will have come into contact with the more complex

---

[4] Stout (2000), pp. 87–8.   [5] Patrick, *Confession* 49, and cp. 37.
[6] Mac Niocaill (1972), pp. 29–32, for useful description.
[7] See further below, p. 374.

social and political structures of the Empire and transmitted information about these back across the Irish Sea. That apart, raiding was the principal form of contact. Irish raiders captured Patrick himself in his youth. The extent of trade with the Empire is debatable.[8] Roman material is never abundant in Ireland but is found from the early imperial period. After an evident break in the third century, the nature of Roman imports appears to change, with some significant hoards. This evidence might be of more political contacts than the sporadic exchange represented by the early Roman finds. Some elements of Irish society were being more closely bound into the imperial orbit. Fourth-century pottery from the eastern Mediterranean is found at Dalkey Island, near Dublin, though it is admittedly very rare; only in the seventh century does imported pottery become significant in Ireland. It has been suggested that 'Bordgal' place-names, which derive from the Latin name for Bordeaux (*Burdigala*), might indicate trade with Gaul, but it seems unlikely that they refer to a period this early, and the meaning of the name is disputed.[9] These contacts might have helped to stimulate fifth-century migration and change around the Irish Sea.

NORTH OF HADRIAN'S WALL: THE *PICTI*

Across the North Channel, in the north of Britain, lived the Picts, first attested in the third century as divided into *Verturiones* and *Dicalydones*.[10] Somewhere in the same general region dwelt the mysterious Attecotti, rarely attested by Roman writers but apparently renowned for ferocity.[11] Traditionally it is thought that Pictish territory began at the Forth and that between there and Hadrian's Wall lived 'British' groups like the *Votadini*. However, these 'British' peoples are, like many of the smaller groups east of the Rhine, not

---

[8] On Roman trade with Ireland: Edwards (1990), pp. 1–5; Freeman (2001); *Proceedings of the Royal Irish Academy* (1976).

[9] Mytum (1992), p. 263; James (1982b), pp. 383–4, is sceptical.

[10] Amm. Marc. 27.8.5.

[11] Amm. Marc. 27.8.5: *bellicosa hominum natio* (a warlike race of men). This is supported to some extent by the fact that two Roman regiments, the *Honoriani Atecotti Seniores* and *Juniores* adopted their name: *Not. Dig.* occ. 5.197, 200. Jerome (*Against Jovinianus* 2.7) said, allegedly on the basis of an eyewitness account, that the *Attecotti* were cannibals. Cannibalism was commonly attributed to barbarians at the world's edges.

mentioned between the early imperial geographers and early medieval sources. Whether there was any meaningful difference between 'Pictish' and 'British' peoples is arguable. It is now generally believed that the Picts spoke a P-Celtic language like their neighbours, though Bede (on what authority is unknown) considered it sufficiently distinctive to count as a separate tongue.[12] The Picts left no written sources to permit us to see what they called themselves and Irish sources refer to the Picts as 'Cruithne', a Q-Celtic rendition of a P-Celtic word like Pritani – Britons.

The usually envisaged political geography of the region, limiting Pictish power to the area north of the Forth, seems to be based entirely upon documentary and toponymic (place-name) data from the historic period (seventh century and later). There is no reason to suppose that this information is applicable to the fourth century. When Roman writers mention *picti* it seems clear, first, that the word is a general descriptive name ('painted men') rather than a genuine ethnonym,[13] and, second, that they refer to any and all peoples north of the Wall. Such sources universally use this term when discussing trouble in northern Britain, and of raids on the province. To assume that this refers to groups only from beyond the Forth, that the people between there and the Wall remained steadfastly peaceable and that Roman campaigns against the 'Picts' involved traversing a large tranquil zone between Tyne and Forth before military action began, seems extremely ill-judged. If Roman writers are correct that the later Roman period saw the formation of two more powerful confederations, *Verturiones* and *Dicalydones*, in a process paralleled east of the Rhine and elsewhere, there is nothing in our evidence, when shorn of assumptions derived from the seventh century and later, that precludes the supposition that the territory of the southernmost confederacy started at the Wall. Comparison with the trans-Rhenan situation suggests that the new confederations tended to be formed directly on the frontier. It is therefore proposed that on the northern British *limes*, the late Roman period saw the formation of new confederacies, which submerged some of the smaller tribes attested earlier. The Romans called these groups *picti* but it seems most unlikely that the name was used by these people themselves.

---

[12] *HE* 1.1.

[13] I am grateful to my former student Tom McCartney for discussions of Pictish ethnogenesis.

The Pictish example illustrates clearly how the Romans used the barbarian stereotype. Roman authors deploy the 'Picts', as inhabitants of the northern reaches of the earth, menacing the Empire's furthest-flung frontiers whenever they wish to emphasise the geographical extent of an emperor's or a general's power and whether or not the 'Picts' can really have been encountered.[14] Nevertheless, the *Picti* could make considerable trouble for the British provinces. Constantine I's father, Constantius I, and his son, Constans, were both required to lead expeditions to deal with their incursions. Later Count Theodosius and Magnus Maximus both had to conduct Pictish campaigns.

It is very difficult to know much about social and political structures. The archaeology of northern Britain is a difficult but vibrant field of research and offers ever more ways of investigating late Iron Age society and economy in the region.[15] The debate has now moved far beyond the 'problem of the Picts', attempts to identify and study the origins of the Picts in the archaeological record.[16] The *Verturiones* and *Dicalydones* represent political allegiances like the other barbarian confederate identities that appeared at the same time, and similar problems arise in linking them neatly to particular classes of material culture as were discussed for the *Germani*.[17] The area's economy was a mixture of pastoral and arable farming, making the colourful old idea that its inhabitants were 'Celtic cowboys' unsustainable. The impact of the Roman Empire is difficult to unravel. The well-known souterrains, whose extensive underground spaces are best interpreted as for grain storage, had died out by the fourth century. This increased storage capacity might have been linked somehow to the existence of the frontier but any such connection cannot have been straightforward and such sites appeared in the first century, before the Romans' presence in the north had much effect. Their disappearance might be further evidence of social change and reorganisation in the third-century *barbaricum*. Surplus was possibly being redirected to the leaders of the new confederacies.[18]

[14] E.g. Claudian, *Consulship of Stilicho* 3, line 54.
[15] I have found the following useful: Armit (1998); (2003); Armit (ed.) (1990); Armit and Ralston (2003); Ballin Smith and Bainks (eds.) (2002); Ralston and Armit (2003).
[16] The classic work was Wainwright (ed.) (1955).
[17] Above, pp. 60–2.
[18] Ralston and Armit (2003), p. 218.

Roman imports are found throughout the region but appear to be less common than in *Germania Magna* and perhaps to have played a less important role in society and politics.[19] Unsurprisingly, they are commonest between the Solway/Tyne and Clyde/Forth. The Romans had other links with elements of society north of the Wall. In the obscure *barbarica conspiratio* of 367 some blame for the catastrophe was placed upon the *areani* (often emended to *arcani* – spies) north of the frontier, allegedly derelict in their duty.[20]

Higher status sites were generally less clearly fortified in the Roman period than had been the case earlier but again this is a development that began too early to have a direct link with Roman military presence and intervention. The nature of their occupation has been debated.[21] Nevertheless some socio-economic hierarchy can be reconstructed from these sites. It has been suggested that the presence of the Roman frontier brought some stability and prosperity to the region immediately to the north. Further north, the famous brochs (towers) were no longer constructed but many sites continued to be occupied in somewhat different form, with often cellular structures built into the rubble.

Another change in the north of the region is an apparent shift towards an increasing focus upon dress and personal adornment at the expense of pottery, which becomes plainer in this period. This is difficult to interpret. It might relate to a situation in which status and gender was more clearly proclaimed through costume. This could imply that marriage and descent had become more important because of a greater emphasis upon inherited property. Alternatively it might relate to a more fluid situation wherein local standing was based around marriage alliances. Another explanation for changes in the later Roman period and after is a switch from kinship networks to clientship systems. This is very possible, but the difference between kinship and clientship is probably overstated. Early medieval Irish society, after all, was based heavily around both.

A picture can be constructed of a steadily more hierarchical and politically centralised society during the Roman period, much as can be proposed for the *Germani* and the Goths. Overall, however, as with the *Scotti*, it does not, except in the area between the Wall and

---

[19] Armit and Ralston (2003), pp. 182–3.
[20] Amm. Marc. 28.3.8. On the *barbarica conspiratio*, see above, p. 58.
[21] Cp. Armit and Ralston (2003), pp. 180–2; Close-Brooks (1987); Hill (1987).

the Clyde–Forth isthmus, appear that barbarian society and politics north of Hadrian's Wall were very closely entwined with the Empire. In this the *Scotti* and *Picti* present an interesting contrast with the barbarians across the Rhine and Danube.

EAST OF THE RHINE: THE *GERMANI*[22]

Pre-migration society east of the Rhine is essentially an archaeological topic, although some aspects of political structures can be illuminated from Roman written sources. A major problem has been the view of Tacitus' *Germania* as applicable across 'Germanic' society and across the historical gulf between his writing and Ammianus'.[23] The view is untenable and Tacitus' testimony is difficult to accept as an accurate report of Germanic society even in his own day. Where similarities exist between the two writers' statements, we must be careful that these do not result simply from the fact that Ammianus saw himself as Tacitus' continuator. We should acknowledge that the pre-migration societies of *Germania Magna*[24] were diverse and dynamic. To do so we must treat the archaeological data in more sophisticated ways.[25] If we do this we can demolish ideas about the interchangeability of 'Germanic' peoples.

In political–geographical terms we need only locate the major groupings of peoples facing the fourth-century Empire (map 9). At the mouth of the Rhine, and along that river as far as Worms, lived the Franks, the 'Fierce People', a confederacy first mentioned in the third century, apparently including earlier tribes like the *Chamavi*, *Chattoari*, *Sicambri*, *Bructuari* and (probably) the *Chatti*. In the angle formed by the upper Rhine and Danube frontiers lived the *Alamanni* (All men; Men United), again first reported in the third century. Within this confederacy were the *Bucinobantes*, the *Brisigavi*, the *Lentienses* and the *Juthungi*. Moving further down the Danube, we come to the *Quadi*, a people known hereabouts since the early

---

[22] The best recent introduction is Pohl (2000). Todd (1972) and (1987) retain their value as introductions. Hedeager (1992) is a thought-provoking regional case-study.

[23] See Wallace-Hadrill, J. M. (1971), pp. 1–20: a good example.

[24] This appears to have been the Roman designation. I have avoided the terms 'Free Germany' or *Germania libera*, which were only invented in the twentieth century: Alföldi, M. R.- (1997); Neumaier (1997).

[25] See above, pp. 28–31.

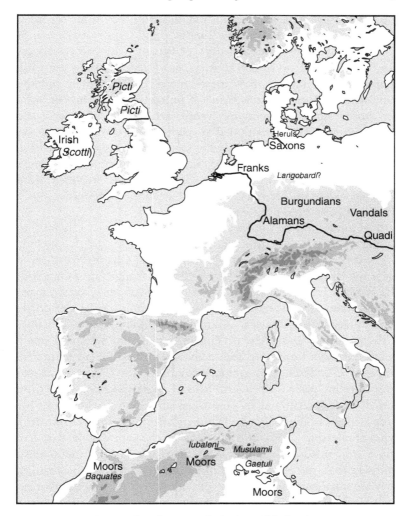

Map 9 Fourth-century barbarian political units

Empire, and we occasionally get the last faint glimpses of their old allies, the *Marcomanni* (Border Men), who had caused the Empire enormous difficulties in the first and second centuries.

Behind the Franks, along the North Sea coast of the modern northern Netherlands, Germany and Denmark lived the people the Romans referred to as 'Saxons', first recorded, once again, in the third-century troubles. These probably included, at least as far as the Romans were concerned or cared, the Jutes and 'Angli' recorded earlier as *Eudoses* and *Anglii* by Tacitus[26] and who re-emerged, of course, in the post-imperial history of Britain.[27] Probably amongst the Saxons' ranks were the Frisians, also attested during the early Empire but unnoticed in written sources between then and the early Middle Ages, and the *Heruli* of Jutland. Behind the *Alamanni* and bordering with them, by Ammianus' day at least, were the Burgundians. Pliny mentioned a people called the *Burgodiones* amongst the Vandal *gentes.*[28] In the same general region may have been the Longobards (Lombards), although they attracted no one's attention in the fourth century; some had been repelled from *Pannonia* in the late second century.[29] East of the Burgundians were the Vandals, attested since early imperial times.

It is interesting to note that the 'new' confederacies tended to border on the imperial frontiers (if, as the Romans did, we include the Saxons as bordering on the North Sea and Channel frontiers of Gaul and Britain). These may very well result from relationships with the Roman Empire. It is worth pausing to wonder what we make of the continuity over time of particular ethnic names, especially those further into *Germania*. We might note the similarity of names such as *Eudoses* and Jutes, or *Gutones* and Goths but how much continuity does this imply, especially when the different names are recorded in different geographical locations? This linkage of names over time and place is a principal basis of migration theory, and from it a distinguished strand of Germanist philological scholarship has proposed ideas about the development of ethnic names, and even types of rulership.[30] We must also consider the nature of the names of tribes or confederacies. Many are theogonistic (like the Goths), unifying (like the *Alamanni*) or 'boasting' (like that of the Franks): they are not dissimilar from the types of name chosen by late Roman regiments. Given this, we ought to be careful in assuming, when a name is attested in one area by one writer and a similar name is reported somewhere else by a later author, that the peoples in question are necessarily the same or that there need have been a migration from the first region to the second.

[26] *Germania* 40.2.   [27] Most famously in *HE* 1.15.
[28] Pliny, *Natural History* 4.13.99.   [29] Dio Cassius, *Roman History* 72.3.1.
[30] E.g. Wolfram (1997a), pp. 32–3.

The nature of kingship east of the Rhine is difficult to examine. Traditionally, the development of 'Germanic' kingship is discussed on the basis of Roman accounts, most notably those of Caesar and Tacitus, joining these accounts up with Ammianus where possible. The perils of this methodology have already been noted. Caesar doubtless had relevant information but, besides writing within the rules of traditional Roman ethnography, his vocabulary may not have been well suited to describing the barbarian political structures he encountered. Furthermore it is unlikely that the situation which pertained in the mid-first century BC was at all relevant to the late Roman period. Tacitus' *Germania* is a minefield probably best avoided. Above all, it is a critique of Roman society at the end of the first century AD, holding the barbaric *Germani* up as a mirror. With this in mind, many of Tacitus' remarks about political leadership amongst the *Germani* (notably their kings' nobility and the heed they always give to their council of leading men) can be seen as comments on the faults of imperial rule and the senate. Tacitus' historical writings probably give a better insight into political leadership in the region but the same problem arises as with Caesar. How valid is his information for the fourth century? Archaeology and even political history drawn from Roman documents show that society underwent considerable change in the third century, as we might expect given the 'crisis' in the Empire during that period and the close links between Rome and her neighbours.[31]

In examining fourth-century rulership in *Germania* we must be cautious in employing Roman sources. Roman writers were locked into old modes of writing and trying to make 'their' barbarians resemble those of canonical authors like Tacitus and Caesar. Moreover they too were probably trying to wrestle non-Roman structures into a Roman political vocabulary. Ammianus' celebrated description of the Alamannic army during its defeat by Emperor Julian at the battle of Strasbourg in 357 (at which Ammianus was not present), is a case in point. He appears to depict a pyramid of kings, from Chnodomar, the confederacy's leader, through 'those kings who come next in power' down to *regales* ('minor royals') and *optimates* (chieftains).[32] Ammianus' vague account will not support the weight of the constitutional theories often heaped upon it. It is unlikely that this was any more than a *de facto* hierarchy. Simply

[31] See further below, pp. 128–9.   [32] Amm. Marc. 16.12.26.

enough, some rulers were wealthier and commanded more warriors, and thus were able to dominate others. Scholars have tried to employ Germanic philology to unlock the different types of king east of the Rhine.[33] This too has proved unconvincing, not least because historians have not always been able to agree about what the relevant Germanic words were.

It has often been argued that the trans-Rhenan barbarians had a form of dual kingship, coupling a sacral king from a noble family, holding long-term but fairly circumscribed, largely religious powers, with a war-leader king, chosen according to prowess and whose kingship might endure only as long as military necessity. This, it is claimed, still existed in the fourth century but was being replaced by a new form of kingship, modelled on Roman imperial rule, combining sacral and military leadership.[34] The evidence for sacral kingship is, however, very weak. One key support is Tacitus' famous statement that the *Germani* 'choose their kings according to their nobility and their generals according to their prowess' (*reges ex nobilitate, duces ex virtute sumunt*).[35] Given the nature of Tacitus' work, however, this is clearly a comment on the shortcomings of the Romans during the reign of Tacitus' bête noir, Domitian; the unspoken 'unlike us' is almost audible. Even leaving this aside, it is unlikely that Tacitus was clearly distinguishing two constitutionally different types of rulership.[36] Ammianus states that the Burgundians had a dual kingship combining a sacral king with a military king.[37] However, it has been shown that here Ammianus is working from an archaic source and thus not necessarily describing fourth-century reality.[38]

Writers who have avoided the Scylla of classical ethnography have sometimes been sucked into the Charybdis of Old Norse myth. Some have attempted, on the basis of imagery on gold objects, to import the thought-world of the central medieval Icelandic and Norwegian Eddas (accounts of Norse religion) in order to understand late antique politics and religion.[39] This methodology

[33] E.g. Wolfram (1997a), pp. 15–20.
[34] See, e.g. Wallace-Hadrill (1962), pp. 154–5; Thompson, E. A. (1965), pp. 32–48; Todd (1972), pp. 26–7; Geary (1988), pp. 55–6; Wolfram (1988), p. 342; Yorke (1990), p. 15; Kirby (2000), p. 16; Wolfram (1997a), p. 15; Myrhe (2003), p. 72. The German historiography is outlined in Pohl (2000), pp. 65–8.
[35] *Germania* 7. The quote even has its own index entry in Wolfram (1988).
[36] Rives (1999), p. 146.   [37] Amm. Marc. 28.5.14.
[38] Wood (1977), pp. 27–8.   [39] Hedeager (2000).

cannot stand.[40] Although the images on some objects such as bracteates (Scandinavian gold discs) are identifiable with episodes in
Scandinavian mythology, the details given in the Eddas cannot
simply be transported backwards by 800 years.[41] Even ignoring
the fact that such sources were written by Christians, it is hugely
problematic to read the iconography of a scene depicted in *c*.400 in
the light of a written account of *c*.1200. One would make enormous
errors reading central medieval christological ideas into late antique
depictions of Christ. The Christ of the Saxon epic, the *Heliand*, is
hardly recognisable as the Christ discussed by St Augustine 400 years
earlier but the bishop of Hippo and the author of the poem would
both have recognised a pictorial depiction of the crucifixion. These
differences occurred even with written scripture, such as did not
exist for 'Germanic' paganism, to anchor ideas.

It is thus difficult to say much about pre-migration kingship east of
the Rhine from written sources. Some points can, however, be made.
The first is to repeat the point that Roman imperial ideology and
symbols permeated trans-Rhenan society. Roman material culture
was vital to the underpinning of barbarian kingship, frequently being
used in ritual contexts to display power and status.[42] It could come
from booty but also through trade and diplomatic gifts. The *Germani*
seem to have used Roman badges of office as rank insignia. If it is not
itself an import, it is very significant that the 'throne' found in a lavish
burial at Fallward in Saxony dated to *c*.400 is decorated in precisely
the geometric motifs used to adorn official 'chip-carved' Roman
metalwork.[43] After centuries of domination by the Empire it is not
surprising that ideas of power and legitimate rule in *barbaricum* should
have become centred on Roman models. It might even be that by this
time there were no truly distinctive ideas of kingship between the
Baltic and the Rhine. Certainly, during the late Empire it is difficult
to find anything that might be a characteristically 'Germanic' style
of kingship. Real power meant the emperor. It might therefore be
that there was less difficulty in assimilating trans-Rhenan political
structures into Roman vocabulary. Indeed many rulers were installed
by the Romans and might have been given titles and powers very

---

[40] The defence of the approach by Dickinson (2005), p. 112, uncharacteristically
carries no conviction.
[41] Hawkes (1997), esp. p. 315, for important critique.
[42] Above, pp. 57–8.   [43] Schön (1999).

much on Roman terms. That said, though, we should acknowledge that even if these largely aped the emperor the difference between the Roman situation and their perception of it probably allowed for significant variation and creativity.

The other approach to political leadership might be to consider solutions to the problems of binding local communities into a larger polity. This was a big enough problem for the Roman Empire with its 400,000 soldiers and 25,000 bureaucrats. It was surely much greater for barbarian rulers. Certain strategies can be isolated, however. The first is military leadership. Barbarian rulers appear to have derived kudos from success in war and to have been undermined by failure. Military success might give prestige and increase the local political benefits of association with the king but the royal role as a protector against external aggressors was also important. Associated with the issue of force and protection is that of law. If a king could gain a role as an arbiter and adjudicator in local disputes, if the contending parties both submitted themselves to his decision, then that too should have led to his rule extending over those communities. There is little specific evidence that kings east of the Rhine had legal functions like this but it seems likely. Moreover it was a key aspect of the government of their imperial models and, as a further analogy, the leader of the Tervingian confederacy on the Danube was styled a 'judge'.[44] Another solution was religious. If kings could claim a particular role in interceding with the gods in the important rituals that were held to guarantee such vital matters as the harvest then that too might lead local communities to subject themselves to their rule. Although the written and linguistic evidence for religious kingship is weak there is some archaeological data that suggests its existence.

Support from the leaders of local communities could also be bought by bestowing prestigious items, usually Roman imports, in return for loyalty. *Barbaricum* does not seem to have been monetised and an important part of the economy must have comprised reciprocal gift exchange. The control of trade with the Roman Empire and thus access to certain prestige items was therefore very important. In addition, gifts paid by the Empire itself were particularly valuable as they had the additional value of a direct and formal link with the mighty emperor.

[44] Amm. Marc. 27.5.6.

Another solution to the problem was to rule through subordinates. These were less likely to be subordinates introduced into the area than less powerful local rulers suborned, through the threat of force and the reward of gifts, into involvement in the wider polity. This situation produced the loose royal hierarchies seen not only in *Germania* in, for example, Ammianus' account of Strasbourg but also amongst the Goths. It is probably better to see this as a potentially fluid state of affairs, involving negotiation as well as force and turning on the contingencies of the current political situation, rather than envisaging (unlike, perhaps, in Ireland) a formal hierarchy of different types of king. Nevertheless the Romans viewed dominant kings with suspicion and worked hard to prevent their emergence. Treachery, murder and kidnap were all employed, lesser leaders were supported in attempts to topple mightier rulers and rival tribes paid to attack threateningly effective kings.[45] The Romans generally managed this policy efficiently when not distracted by internal troubles. When they were, however, powerful overkings rapidly emerged and one has the impression that lavish Roman use of bribes and diplomatic gifts only served to raise the stakes of barbarian politics.[46]

Several conclusions can be drawn. The first is the potential insecurity of most forms of barbarian leadership. Quite apart from the Romans' frequent interference, bases for kingship east of the Rhine were fluid and easily removed. Related to this is the dependence of such kings upon the Roman world for economic as well as political support. Nevertheless, shaky though they were, these bases provided a platform from which more lasting institutions of government might be consolidated. These points can be underlined by considering settlement, society and economy.

The evidence for social structures east of the Rhine mainly comprises settlements, burials and votive deposits. In surveying this evidence, beginning with the settlement evidence, we should pay due attention to geography. Immediately north of the lower and middle Rhine late antique settlements are badly understood. Perhaps the best-known settlement lies about 100 km north of the *limes* at Wijster.[47] The stimulus for this major site seems clearly to have been trade with the Roman frontier garrisons and it reached its zenith in the fourth century. At this stage it was clearly planned and home to at least 200 people. A site at Heeten (Overijssel, Netherlands) has

---

[45] Elton (1996a), pp. 181–92.   [46] Heather (1994).   [47] Van Es (1967).

yielded evidence of organised large-scale iron-working, where production (estimated at 20 tonnes of pig iron) was controlled by a fortified settlement.[48] It is likely that this was at least partly stimulated by the imperial frontier's proximity but it is simultaneously possible that the regional leaders used it to ensure their access to good iron products, which could be distributed to their followers or traded. In the Ruhr valley, a settlement at the Oespeler Bach near Dortmund shows how Roman products dominated life in the *barbaricum*.[49] The finds assemblage from this rural settlement, with evidence of its own craft-working, contained large quantities of Roman finewares as well as jewellery, glass and bronze wares and weaponry.

Further north, in the area believed by the Romans to be home to the Saxon confederacy, the classic form of settlement in the marshy coastal regions is known as a Terp or a Wurt – a mound formed by the build-up of occupation debris and periodic raising of the settlement. The most famous Terp is Feddersen Wierde, which also reached its apogee in the fourth century.[50] At this time a large long-house (Herrenhof), interpreted as the dwelling of the village headman, came to dominate the site and a craft-working zone has been identified, associated with this building. A nearby settlement at Bennekom also prospered in the fourth century.

Something of a phase of reorganisation of settlements in the north of *Germania* took place at the end of the third and the beginning of the fourth century.[51] Further north in Denmark the site at Vorbasse was rearranged at this time and that at Nørre Snede, 40 km to the east, shifted its location.[52] Vorbasse, like Wijster and Bennekom, reached its apogee in the fourth century. With twenty long-houses occupied, it may have had a population equivalent to Wijster's and likewise shows evidence of planning. In Denmark from the third century there was apparently an increased concern with the marking out of private property through boundary fences, as at Vorbasse, and this trend is revealed elsewhere in Scandinavia, as in Norway.[53]

[48] Verlinde and Erdrich (1998); Groenewoudt and van Nie (1995).
[49] Brink-Kloke and Meurers-Balke (2003).   [50] Haarnagel (1979).
[51] Hvass (1989).   [52] Hvass (1983).
[53] Myrhe (2003), p. 70. Also Solberg (1999) for greater social stratification in Norway.

It has been argued at length that Danish society and politics became more complex in the late Roman period.[54] Generally this has been envisaged, employing processual models of social progression from bands through chiefdoms to kingdoms and states, as a move from kin-based tribes to more hierarchically organised chiefdoms and even kingdoms. We should be wary of the view of linear social development based upon anthropological models from the 1960s. It is also simplistic to see the increased emphasis upon delineated private property as a move away from kin-based society. The opposition between kin-based and hierarchical social structures is misconceived. In a more stratified society birth and kinship acquire a new importance as they define one's membership of a particular social stratum. Furthermore private property raises issues of inheritance, and rights to inheritance are universally based around kinship relations. Nevertheless, the evidence clearly indicates a stable and more complex society than had existed before the third century.

In the fourth century prestigious new settlements appeared, based upon trade with the Roman Empire. These were not large settlements. Generally they were only small farmsteads but are characterised by unusual evidence of imported Roman material and of the production of other specialist items. One such site is at Dankirke on the west of Jutland whereas another, much better known and the subject of much analysis, has been found at Lundeborg on the island of Fyn in the Baltic.[55] The latter is associated with an extremely high-status settlement just inland, at Gudme, which appears to be the residence of a local leader whom, given the wealth of the site, it would seem unduly cautious not to think of as a king. These sites illustrate graphically the importance of controlling access to traded Roman material culture in maintaining political leadership. Indeed study of the region, which had long traded with the Empire, suggests that in the fourth century high-status imports were channelled to fewer sites. It might be, especially in considering sites like that at the Oespeler Bach, that access to Roman goods was more restricted further into *Germania* and thus that it was more politically important. It has certainly been thought

[54] Especially Hedeager (1992).
[55] Dankirke: Hansen (1989); Gudme-Lundeborg: Nielsen, Randsborg and Thrane (eds.) (1994).

possible to divide *Germania* into political-economic zones on the basis of the distribution-patterns of such Roman exports.[56]

The fourth century saw the growth of other forms of high-status settlement in Scandinavia.[57] Hillforts were intensively occupied, as, in flatter areas such as the islands of Öland and Gotland, were ring fortresses. The walls of Torsburgen, the largest ring fortress on Gotland, were strengthened to reach 7 m in height. This fort could be defended by 1,000 men, a significant number even in Roman terms. In Norway a series of large boathouses was constructed, associated with high-status centres. Given that the boats assembled at these houses would require more manpower than the high-status settlement itself could provide, their crews might have been conscripted from the surrounding region.[58]

In the Alamannic territories the late Roman period saw the occupation of important fortified sites, the Höhensiedlungen or hillforts. The best known of these is at the Runder Berg near Urach, which was a high-status settlement with evidence of craft specialisation. It may be unwise to generalise from this site, however.[59] Others might have fulfilled somewhat different functions. In sites such as the Geißkopf, large quantities of official Roman metalwork have been found, which the local rulers distributed to their own followers as rank insignia.[60] The manpower mustered to construct these fortified sites also implies considerable political authority. In the same region, some of the *Alamanni*, who it has been suggested were formed at least partly by the Romans themselves from inhabitants of the *agri decumates* and authorised barbarian settlers,[61] occupied former Roman villa sites, such as at Wurmlingen in Baden Württemberg.[62]

The third century also left evidence of stress in the barbarian polities in the form of clusters of lavishly furnished inhumations. The Haßleben–Leuna group, appearing in the Elbe–Saale region at the end of the century, has been mentioned.[63] Some rich burials appeared slightly earlier in the North Sea coast area, again employing Roman imports, and others are known from the north in Mecklenburg. A further group of lavish graves, the Sakrau group, is known from the

[56] Hedeager (1987).   [57] Myrhe (2003), p. 75 for a brief survey.
[58] Myrhe (1997).   [59] Hoeper (1998).
[60] Hoeper and Steuer (1999).   [61] Nuber (1993); (1998).
[62] Reuter, M. (1996). See also Carroll (2001), pp. 145–6.
[63] Above, pp. 57–8.

end of the third century in the Przeworsk culture associated, somewhat dubiously, with the Vandals.[64] These displays of wealth to an audience should be seen, as in other instances of such ritual during this period,[65] as attempts to smooth over the tension following the death of a family member by a lavish display of wealth, probably associated with gift-giving. On the whole, however, the fourth-century norm for burial in *Germania* was in large cremation cemeteries, which do not, as a rule, contain many grave goods. Indeed in the regions north of the lower Rhine, where the documentary sources place the Franks, burial is more or less archaeologically invisible. There is little evidence that funerary ritual was being used competitively to maintain and enhance status. This, perhaps, is what one might expect in view of the settlement data's stress on increasing social stratification and organisation. In some areas, however, inhumation begins to increase in numbers, as in the Middle Elbe.

A number of dramatic finds of votive deposits have been made in Denmark and the far north of Germany at sites like Nydam, Ejsbøl and Illerup. Here the matériel from defeated armies was thrown into a bog.[66] Such deposits are difficult to explain. Clearly they differ from the burial of grave-goods. It might be suggested that whereas the transient display of grave-goods was a mechanism for the creation or maintenance of individual families' status, the votive bog deposits were more of a communal rite. This should by no means be seen as egalitarian. The nature of the finds themselves suggests some sort of organisation. The objects disposed of in these rituals were precisely the things that would normally have become booty, for the distribution of which war leaders were responsible.[67] By disposing of large quantities of potential booty, presumably in a gift to the gods, the leader at once demonstrated his authority, removed from circulation valuable items that might have been used by others as gifts, and enhanced the value of those items that he *did* bestow upon his followers. We should not assume that everything was thrown into the marsh and this should make us sceptical of attempts to read too

[64] On these prestigious burials, see Todd (1987), pp. 46–7, 57, 71. Map: Todd (1987), p. 40.

[65] See below, pp. 350–1.

[66] For good recent studies of the phenomenon see Jørgensen, Storgaard and Gebauer Thomsen (eds.) (2003).

[67] See *LH* 2.27 for a late fifth-century Frankish analogy.

much detailed military organisation into the precise numbers of different types of weapons. Caution is also required by practical issues, such as the greater ability of mounted men to escape from a battle leading to an under-representation of horse furniture. Nonetheless the fourth-century bog finds stand as graphic indicators of the ability of the barbarians of the north to raise substantial armed forces, illustrating their leaders' political power.

The changes in social structure east of the Rhine during the later Roman period must also have affected gender. If, as seems likely from the archaeological data, private property became more important, this would, as mentioned, have affected inheritance systems. This would in turn have had an effect upon the social significance of marriage if, as is probable, kin-groups were considered to be bilateral (claiming descent from the father's and the mother's sides). The use of marriage as a strategy within local politics, binding families together, would have taken on added significance and a woman's family identity as well as her marriageable status emphasised. Thus women are now everywhere buried in communal cemeteries (there had been some areas in *Germania*, such as the Bardengau, where separate cemeteries for men and women had apparently existed[68]). In the cremations of northern Germany, women were buried with jewellery imported from the Empire, occasionally decorated with the motifs used on masculine items to proclaim status and power.[69] Given the social status brought by association with the Empire, this seems somewhat different from the situation in the northern provinces. In the Empire a woman's behaviour was very important in determining a man's standing but his status seems not to have been translated into her standing. In *Germania Magna* however, a family's power and claims to authority were also manifested in the costume of its women. This is very important. As private property, inheritance and, consequently, marriage grew in importance the significance of each member of society became (as in the Empire) related to their ability to marry. Thus they all had to be gendered male or female,[70] this and their suitability for marriage being judged according to ideas about

---

[68] Christie (1995), p. 7.

[69] See the distribution maps in Böhme (1974), but read as Roman imports, with Halsall (2000).

[70] Once again I adopt Gayle Rubin's idea of the sex-gender system.

particular modes of behaviour. As has been made clear, success and standing east of the Rhine were very often displayed through Roman artefacts.

During the Roman Iron Age the territories of particular 'culture groups' could change. One culture group, fairly plausibly to be loosely associated with the Saxon confederacy, spread to incorporate most of the lower Elbe region.[71] The Przeworsk culture expanded to the Carpathian basin from the third century and the neighbouring Wielbark culture spread out from the Baltic along the rivers draining into that sea.[72] Culture groups cannot be identified straightforwardly with peoples so their spread, equally, cannot be interpreted simplistically as showing population movement. That said, if material culture gave cohesion to loosely knit ethnic groups then its adoption might signal an area's ascription to new political leadership, and the acquisition of a new level of ethnic identity. As long as we are clear about what we mean in using such ethnic descriptions, the expansion of 'Saxon' material culture might indeed imply the spread of people called Saxons. It need not imply that anyone moved. The way in which such culture groups appear to spread along major rivers is particularly interesting. Many of these, such as the Elbe, were important trade routes, especially for the movement of amber from Scandinavia to the Roman Empire. Political authority seems to have grown along these trade arteries, probably in association with the control of such traffic.

East of the Rhine, the fourth century was a period of change. Society was becoming more complex, with much evidence of more powerful political leadership. This increase in authority might have been based upon Roman gifts and payments but there are indications that it was becoming more entrenched. Further away from the frontier, politics might have been more fluid and dependent upon Roman diplomatic gifts for stability.

NORTH OF THE DANUBE: THE GOTHS

The complex nature of society and politics north of the Danube does not directly concern this volume, which concentrates on western Europe, and excellent surveys of fourth-century Gothic society are

[71] Todd (1987), p. 56   [72] Heather (1996), pp. 36–7.

readily available in English.[73] Nevertheless a brief account is necessary
to underline the points made above about barbarian society and to act
as a background to the Gothic crisis of 376, with which accounts of
'the migrations' usually begin. Archaeologically, the Gothic confederacy is associated with the Sîntana de Mureş-Černjachov culture
which spreads from Romania through Moldavia to the Ukraine as far
as Kharkov.

The Černjachov culture comprises cemeteries and settlements.
The latter demonstrate that, although the Goths practised pastoralism
to a significant degree,[74] they had significant settlements based around
agriculture as fixed points within their economy – a point probably
underlined by the *Passion of St Saba*. Archaeology confirms that
herding was a significant element within the economy but these sites
also reveal evidence of significant craft specialisation and Černjachov
glass was exported as far as the Baltic. Iron-working too is attested.
Some settlements were elaborate stone-built affairs with tile roofs.[75]
Others, especially closer to the frontier were elaborate planned sites,
analogous to Wijster. The cemeteries contain a mixture of cremation
and inhumation, the latter frequently with grave-goods. Funerary
ritual was clearly, then, an occasion for the display of identity and the
maintenance of status. It is difficult to know what the different forms
of burial marked: ethnic affiliation, social class or religious identity.

The Černjachov culture is a mixture of all sorts of influences but
most come from the existing cultures in the region. It has been argued
that it evolves directly from the Wielbark culture of the lower Vistula
and that the spread from Wielbark to Černjachov is archaeological
proof of the Goths' migration from the shores of the Baltic. This
notion should not be entirely rejected but it needs considerable
modification. The source for the Gothic migration from Scandinavia

---

[73] In English, the best are by Peter Heather, especially, and John Matthews:
Heather (1998c), pp. 488–96; Heather and Matthews (1991), chs. 3–4; Matthews
(1989), pp. 318–32. See also Kazanski (1991), pp. 29–59. The following account is
based heavily upon these but with some differences of interpretation. See also:
Thompson, E. A. (1961); Wolfram (1988), pp. 89–116; (1997), pp. 69–89.

[74] See, e.g. Elton (1996a), pp. 22–9, drawing upon the unpublished Oxford D.Phil.
thesis of Roger Batty. Were the Goths, as often claimed, mainly settled
agriculturists then they were the only such people to occupy that part of the
world between the appearance of written descriptions in the fifth century BC and
the end of the nineteenth century.

[75] E.g. at Sobari in Moldova: Popa (1997).

is Jordanes' *Getica*, which is deeply problematic and certainly cannot be used as evidence for migration.[76] The Wielbark culture begins earlier than the Černjachov but its later phases cover the same period as the latter. There is thus no chronological development from one to the other. Furthermore, although the Wielbark culture does spread up the Vistula during its history, its geographical overlap with the Černjachov culture is minimal.[77] These facts make it improbable that the Černjachov culture was descended from the Wielbark. Although it is often claimed that Černjachov metalwork derives from Wielbark types, close examination reveals no more than a few types with general similarities to Wielbark analogues.[78] Migration from the Wielbark territories is also proposed from the supposedly distinctive mix of cremation and inhumation.[79] However, burial customs are rarely static and more than one area of *barbaricum* employed, at various times, a mixture of rites. The fourth century, in particular, saw widespread change in such practices. This evidence will not support the idea of a substantial migration.[80]

However, the Goths clearly spoke an east Germanic language, preserved in their apostle Wulfila's translation of the Gospels and other texts. Their personal names are Germanic and runes are known from the Černjachov area.[81] This probably implies some migration into the region (although there were people regarded as 'Germanic' in the region before), probably during the third century, when imperial sources first attest the Goths north of the Danube.[82] Where these newcomers came from cannot now be ascertained but the territory of the Wielbark culture is probable, though not on the basis of the archaeological evidence, as just discussed. A key trade artery between Scandinavia and the Black Sea was the amber route that passed up the rivers flowing into the Baltic and then down the Dniepr or Dniester. Indeed most of the Černjachov sites are clustered along

---

[76] See, e.g. Amory (1997), pp. 291–307; Goffart (1988), pp. 20–111; Heather (1991), pp. 34–67. Below, pp. 458–62.

[77] Heather (1996), pp. 36–7.

[78] There is a useful diagram of the artefact-types in Bierbrauer (1994a), p. 42.

[79] Heather (1996), p. 22.

[80] For further critical discussion of traditional views of archaeology and Tervingian ethnogenesis, see Curta (2005); Kulikowski (2006), pp. 87–99.

[81] For example on a pot in grave 36 from the cemetery at Letçani: Heather (1996), p. 87.

[82] See Heather (1996), pp. 38–43, for plausible reconstruction of the circumstances.

these two rivers and it was via this trade route that Černjachov glass spread to the Baltic. Similarly the expansion of the Wielbark culture took place along this artery. Political authority in *barbaricum* often spread up and down these important routes, probably on the basis of the power that their control bestowed. It seems most likely that in the confusion of the third century and, specifically, the Roman abandonment of the Carpathian basin a Germanic-speaking élite was able to spread its power down the amber routes into the lands of the Sarmatians, Dacians and *Carpi* and found a number of kingdoms, some grouped into a powerful confederacy. Much later on, Scandinavian settlers created various polities including an important realm in Kiev in the same general region and in much the same way.[83]

It seems that the Gothic confederacy, like those of the Saxons, Franks and Alamanni, comprised a number of other ethnic identities: former Roman provincials, Dacians, *Carpi*, Sarmatians, *Taifali* and so on. Even Gothic identity itself operated on more than one level, those of the kingdom and confederacy. Inhabitants of the region thus, like most other people, possessed a hierarchy of ethnic identities. Some might have been more restricted than others, or were acquired through entry into political and military circles. Political circumstances might determine the efficacy of a particular identity or the desire to signal it. Nevertheless we should not assume that because other ethnic identities persisted within *Gútthiuda*, as Gothic sources call the Tervingian homeland (presumably adapting the Roman term *Gothia*), this means that ethnic boundaries were rigid. In some way all inhabitants could probably think of themselves as Goths.

There were two principal Gothic groups before 376, although Peter Heather argues convincingly that this oversimplifies the situation.[84] We know most about the western confederacy, the *Tervingi*, inhabiting the lands north of the lower Danube. Beyond them, on the steppes, lay the *Greuthungi*, although whether the Greuthungi comprised all the non-Tervingian Goths is debatable. The *Tervingi* were ruled by an overlord with the title of judge. It was suggested above that a legal role might be one means by which a political leader could bind groups into his sphere of authority. The office of judge seems to have been more or less permanent although the sources leave room for debate. Analogy with the trans-Rhenan situation would suggest that such an overlord would be unlikely to meet with unequivocal Roman approval. Those whom we hear about occur at times of conflict with the Empire, although the Romans say little or nothing of Gothic politics in any other circumstances.[85] It might be that, as with barbarian politics east of the Rhine, overkingship appeared when the Romans were distracted from efficient frontier management. It has been argued that the judgeship passed through three generations of the same family[86] but, whilst this is possible, it is fundamentally based only upon the alliterative similarity of the names Ariaric, Aoric and Athanaric.

Below the judge or overking lay lesser rulers, equivalents to the less powerful kings mentioned among the *Germani*. These included people like the Rothesteus and Atharid encountered in the *Passion of St Saba*, the Winguric mentioned in another source relating to the persecution of Christians[87] or the *regalis* Alica mentioned by the 'Anonymous Valesianus' in his account of Constantine's reign.[88] If the *Passion of St Saba* is anything to go by, these rulers seem to have exacted tribute from dependent villages, touring them (presumably from a central high-status settlement) with a retinue of mounted warriors. Belonging to such a warband may very well have been the principal determinant of Gothic identity, though we should not assume that such membership was in any way closed. The Goths fought in much the same fashion as people in that region had done – and were to do – for centuries, forming their wagons into a defensive laager around which their cavalry strike force operated.[89] Although the Gothic ruling stratum, at least, were Germanic-speaking immigrants they soon picked up 'local' fighting techniques, arguing that their warriors included many from the region's existing population.

We are badly informed about Greuthungian political organisation. They were ruled by a king but we only know about one, Ermanaric,

---

[85] Heather (1998c), pp. 495–6, argues forcefully in favour of a permanent overlord. However, Heather (1994) also argued very convincingly that overkings among the western *Germani* only arose during periods of Roman neglect of frontier policy. Chnodomar of the Alamanni looked as much a monarch to Ammianus' informants as the Gothic rulers did to Themistius or the 'Anonymous Valesianus', yet his supremacy clearly arose as a result of a period of Roman internal disputes.

[86] E.g. Wolfram (1988), p. 62.   [87] Heather and Matthews (1991), pp. 126–7.

[88] Anonymous Valesianus 5.27.   [89] See, e.g. Amm. Marc. 31.7.7, 31.13.

a figure mentioned by Ammianus but obscured by later legend.[90] According to these stories he was a mighty ruler exercising hegemony over an enormous area. Unfortunately it is likely that our source for his great power, Jordanes (or his source, Cassiodorus), has built Ermanaric into this fearsome monarch for reasons entirely contingent upon sixth-century Gothic politics. After removing Jordanes' account from the equation we are left with very little. It might be that the Greuthungi were only one of a number of Gothic groups beyond the Tervingi and possibly not especially powerful.

Study of the Černjachov culture and the written sources relating to the fourth-century Goths paints a picture quite similar to that available for the barbarians east of the Rhine. Again we see a group in which ethnicity was multi-layered. The importance of the amber routes between the Baltic and the Roman Empire as arteries for political expansion is underlined, as is the fact that the fourth century was a period of change. Political structures were fluid and dependent upon the Empire but it is also clear that this was a period of increasing socio-economic complexity and growing potential for authority. There was, increasingly, a lot at stake in Gothic politics.

AROUND THE AFRICAN FRONTIER: THE *MAURI*[91]

The barbarians referred to by the Romans as *Mauri* (Moors) existed in close symbiosis with the formal structures of the African provinces. This can make it difficult to discuss those who technically lived beyond the frontiers separately from those who dwelt inside the Empire.[92] Some comments have, therefore, already been made.[93] Ecological reasons also render it difficult to distinguish society within the Empire from that outside. Contacts between sedentary and nomadic populations on both sides of the formal frontier remained strong so that here, unlike any frontier other than the lower Danube, Christianity spread beyond the Roman borders. In the far west in *Mauretania Tingitania*, the imperial withdrawal nevertheless left a very

---

[90] Amm. Marc. 31.3.1. Jordanes, *Getica* 23.116–20.
[91] Brett and Fentress (1996), pp. 50–77, is an excellent introduction. Modéran's (2003b) comprehensive study came to hand too late in this book's production for me to make much use of it.
[92] Modéran (2003b) makes an interesting attempt to distinguish the two.
[93] Above, pp. 93–6.

Romanised area behind, so that the degree of Roman abandonment has been debated.

Tribal leaders owned large estates, were very wealthy and had close relationships with the Empire. They had also acquired important military roles on the frontier, taking these over from earlier Roman prefects. They employed Roman vocabulary and symbols to express legitimate rule. Two brothers from the *Iubaleni* tribe, Firmus and Gildo rebelled against the Empire in the late fourth century, whilst a third brother, Mascezel, was employed in suppressing Firmus. Yet these rebellions were firmly within Roman political structures.[94] Firmus, whose revolt brought down Count Romanus, styled himself *augustus* and Gildo was count of Africa and rebelled as part of the struggle between Stilicho and the east.[95] Gildo was described as a typical African barbarian by Claudian, but Claudian was the court poet of Gildo's enemy, Stilicho.[96] Claudian also describes Gildo as a tyrant and a robber.[97] The case nicely illustrates Roman rhetorical use of the barbarian figure and the elision of barbarians with brigands and other wielders of illegitimate force.

---

[94] See, in particular, the analysis by Blackhurst (2004).
[95] See below, p. 200.
[96] Claudian, *Gildonic War*. On Claudian, see Cameron, A. D. (1970).
[97] E.g. *Gildonic War* I, lines 147, 162.

5

ROMANS AND BARBARIANS BEFORE 376

Having considered society, economy and politics inside the western Roman Empire and amongst the barbarians, we now examine the inter-relationships of the two worlds. A number of issues require attention. The first is military: we must explore the nature of the Roman–barbarian frontier and that of the 'barbarian threat'. Second, there are political issues: the barbarians' use by the Roman Empire and vice versa, and the interconnectedness of Roman and barbarian politics. Finally, we must consider the culture and identities of those barbarians who entered and lived within the Roman Empire.

During the mid-third-century political and military crises the Empire gave up several tracts of land. In the 260s it abandoned the *agri decumates* (Tithe Lands) between the upper Rhine and Danube and the *Alamanni* settled this area.[2] In the next decade it abandoned Dacia, which was taken over by Sarmatians and Goths. At some time apparently in the early 280s the Romans withdrew to some extent

---

[1] The best modern overview of the Roman frontiers is Whittaker (1994). Elton (1996b) contains some useful points and information, and Lee (1998) discusses the problems of information gathering. For regional overviews of the frontier lines, see Maxfield (1987) (mainland Europe); Breeze (1987) (Britain); and Daniels (1987) (Africa). For specific, mostly military detail, see the proceedings of the *Limeskongressen*. See also Vallet and Kazanski (eds.) (1993) and the less 'metaphorical' studies in Mathisen and Sivan (eds.) (1996).
[2] Okamura, L. (1996).

from the southern part of *MauretaniaTingitania*, around Volubilis (Ksar Faraoun, Morocco).[3]

In Britain the north of the province continued to be marked by Hadrian's Wall. Effective control may have shaded out as one approached the western highland regions, particularly in the mountains of Gwynedd, although there are traces of fourth-century occupation around the north Welsh coast and a new fort was constructed at Cardiff, perhaps against Irish raiding.[4] In the south and east, from the late third century, a series of forts was constructed from the Wash to the Solent. Their purpose is disputed, as is the extent to which they formed a 'system', but they may still for convenience be referred to by the title given them in the *Notitia Dignitatum*: the Saxon Shore.[5]

A series of coastal forts like Oudenburg in modern Belgium mark the mainland component of the Saxon Shore and maritime defence continued down the Channel coast in the *tractus Armoricanus*. In the Rhine delta it seems that, rather than the frontier being withdrawn to the Waal, some forts were maintained on the early imperial *limes*, like Utrecht. A chain of outposts ran along the lower Rhine, including Nijmegen and Krefeld-Gellep, ensuring free use of the river system by transport ships from Britain. The delta region was difficult to manage during this period of rising sea levels and flooding, however, and Franks may have settled much of it in more or less vague treaty relationships with the Empire. Here, the first real line of fortifications lay along the road running from the Channel at Boulogne to Cologne, where it joined the Rhine frontier. No longer regarded as a formal system, a *limes Belgicus*, the Boulogne–Cologne road nevertheless seems to have marked an important defensive and administrative line.[6] From Cologne the frontier lay along the Rhine. East of Lake Constance, it followed the Iller to join the upper Danube, whence it ran down that river to the Black Sea.

In North Africa, the Riff were never part of imperial territory, but east of those mountains, the Roman *limites* remained roughly where

[3] Warmington (1954), pp. 70–1. On the politics of the region, see Shaw (1986). See also below, p. 407, n.143.
[4] Jarrett (1967); Dornier (1971); Livens (1974); (1986).
[5] *Not. Dig.* 1, 5, 28, 37, 38. Cotterill (1993); Johnson (1979); Maxfield (ed.) (1989); Pearson (2002); White, D. A. (1961).
[6] Mertens (1977); (1980); (1986); Brulet (1993).

they always had been, along the border between the fertile Tell and the more arid steppe to the south. The African provinces, however, never had a clearly delineated border. Occasional ditch systems and watch towers have been noted, and were once compared with Hadrian's Wall, but the function of these is debatable. They may have aimed at the surveillance of transhumance patterns or perhaps at the defence of well-watered agricultural areas but are unlikely to have marked the Empire's political limits.[7]

Frontiers have been the subject of much work in recent years, and those of the Roman Empire have always attracted scholarly attention. Partly this is because they were, sometimes, very clearly marked. Hadrian's Wall was built, as one fourth-century writer said, 'to separate Romans and barbarians',[8] and the great river frontiers of the Rhine and Danube are studded with fine examples of border fortification. The Romans themselves could see their Empire as very clearly divided from the lands of the barbarians: *barbaria* or *barbaricum*. We have seen how Roman writers viewed the Empire as surrounded by barbarians. The strengthening of a clear frontier line with forts, walls and garrisons was therefore seen as a sign of good imperial management.[9] Ideological statements about the barbarians' ferocity and the threat they posed could then enhance the importance of such work.[10] Imperial propaganda underlined this view. A medallion struck under the Tetrarchy (*c.*296–324) shows *Germani* crossing the Rhine bridge at Mainz, waving goodbye to their barbaric homes and stepping into the warmth and glow of the Roman Empire, where the emperor himself receives them.[11] The river marks the edge of civilisation. These views could be expressed just as vividly by those manning the frontiers 'at the sharp end'. The blunt epitaph of a soldier killed next to Deutz (*iuxta Divitia*), the bridgehead fort for Cologne, and thus within sight of that city's fine Roman monuments, says

---

[7] Euzennat (1986); Daniels (1987); Whittaker (1994), pp. 145–52; Elton (1996b), pp. 101–4; Shaw (1982), pp. 39–42 for critique and the attractive proposal that at least some walls defended areas watered by run-off from the mountains.

[8] *SHA Hadrian* 2.21.

[9] *On Matters Military* 20. See also Zos. 2.34, which praises Diocletian for strengthening the 'preclusive' frontier line and condemns Constantine for removing troops to the interior.

[10] See Drinkwater (1996) for a thought-provoking discussion of this theme. See also below, p. 150.

[11] The medallion is illustrated in Burns (1994), p. 14.

that he was slain by a Frank (*a franco*) *in barbarico*.[12] The carver of this tombstone had no doubt that as soon as you set foot outside the fort's main gate you were out of the Empire and in wild country; *barbaricum* lapped around the fort's walls and up to the Rhine.

It was once common for modern historians to take a similar view and to see Roman frontiers, following Roman ideology about 'barbarians', as marking clear psychological as well as political lines of demarcation.[13] More recently the tendency has been reversed: through the recognition of the importance of frontiers as zones rather than lines; by stressing that political, cultural, linguistic, religious or economic frontiers are rarely coterminous; and by stressing the very permeability of Roman borders, with much movement across them in both directions. Furthermore we cannot overlook the very fluidity of political boundaries in areas like North Africa or the existence of internal frontier zones where, ideologically, banditry shaded into barbarism.[14] Imperial attention to the frontier may have served domestic political needs more than external military requirements.[15]

This work has been important in revising the traditional view of 'the moral barrier on the Rhine and Danube'. The argument has, however, often become facile: the frontier did not keep everyone out or stop all contact across it; therefore it was unimportant.[16] To show how mistaken this is, let us take a very obvious recent example, the so-called Iron Curtain. This line across Germany, and along the borders of the then Czechoslovakia, was heavily defended (on both sides), and marked with walls, barbed wire, minefields and watch-towers. No one could claim that it bore any relationship to linguistic frontiers; it marked no religious division; many people legitimately crossed the line back and forth every day, others did so one-way and illegitimately and others still died in the attempt; economically the 'wall' was breached very frequently on the open and 'black' markets; communist parties existed on the western side of the divide, and pro-democratic dissidents to the east, so the line did not even mark a political–ideological frontier particularly well; military–political activity and posturing and ideological use of 'the other side'

[12] *CIL* 13.2.2 8274.   [13] The classic statement is Alföldi, A. (1952b).
[14] The *migrans gens barbara* referred to by Paulinus of Nola (*Poems* 10.218–20) in 393 must be the Basques. On the context of this poem, see Trout (1999), pp. 78–86. For the elision of barbarism and banditry, see above, p. 55.
[15] Drinkwater (1996); Goffart (1989).   [16] E.g. Elton (1996b); (1996c).

as bogey-men served domestic political purposes far more than any real defensive needs; one could even, adopting a 'longue durée' approach, argue that after 'only' forty-five years the line collapsed and politics 'reverted' to pre-war patterns. The Iron Curtain was at least as permeable as the Roman *limites* in mainland Europe. Yet who would deny that for two generations the existence of this frontier line exerted a powerful force upon the mentalities and everyday lives of millions of people? This was a very real frontier: except perhaps in Africa, Roman borders were no less real.

The Empire could pay attention to fairly clearly marked frontiers and at the same time see itself as an Empire without limit (*sine finis*, meaning 'without end' both temporally and geographically) because the Roman *fines* were like a membrane.[17] They marked the edge of the territory administratively and politically organised by the Empire, into which none might enter unbidden, yet the Romans were not bound in any way by these lines and could pass through them at will. It was simply that the rest of the world, which could be and was described as part of the *imperium Romanum*, had not yet been integrated into the state. This ideology weighed heavily upon imperial shoulders; Valentinian I died of apoplexy when ambassadors from the *Quadi* dared to suggest that his construction of a fort across the Danube in 'their' territory was provocative, justifying their attack on its builders.[18] It has been suggested that this changed in the period after about 350, with the barbarians adopting the previously Roman view of the frontier as a membrane that only they could pass through.[19] Valentinian's death argues against this. However impractical campaigning beyond their frontiers became, nothing indicates that the Romans ever felt constrained by them.

The military aspects of the frontier have been much studied. Historians and archaeologists have been hamstrung by the chimera of 'frontier policy'. In our period, we are told, the emperors gave up on the Hadrianic idea of 'preclusive security', first in favour of a deepened frontier line under Diocletian, and then for a more extensive system of 'defence in depth'.[20] The *limitanei* would deal

---

[17] Whittaker (1994), pp. 10–30.   [18] Amm. Marc. 30.6.2–6.

[19] Whittaker (1994), pp. 241–2. Roberts, M. (1984) argues persuasively that Ausonius, in his *Moselle*, presents the view that the frontier should not be transgressed by the Romans. However, his opinions mattered little to his emperor, Valentinian I.

[20] Luttwak (1976); Ferrill (1986) for statements of this 'policy'.

with small-scale frontier disturbances and raids, and delay larger invasions for as long as possible by retreating into heavily fortified strong-points. This would deny the invaders supplies, whilst the field army moved up and destroyed them. So runs the traditional argument.

This view has been refuted in detail.[21] The deployment of troops in deeper defensive frontier zones or in the heart of the provinces probably has more to do with ease of supply, especially when many taxes were raised, and many troops paid, in kind. The central field armies, furthermore, almost certainly resulted more from a desire to place potentially dangerous bodies of soldiers under direct control, and counter internal threats to authority, banditry and brigandage, than from a 'grand strategy' of imperial defence.[22] That said, the creation of regional field armies surely has something to do with defence against external attacks. However, the heavy investment in frontier fortification along the Rhine and Danube[23] in the late fourth century hardly argues that the traditional ideas of heavily defended, preclusive *limites* had been abandoned.

It is too simple, however, to view the frontier as a marginal zone, in a straightforward core–periphery relationship with the Empire's Mediterranean heartlands. From the last decades of the third century onwards, northern Gaul and Roman Germany were, with the emperor's presence there, very often the political centre of the Empire. This may have been very important in maintaining the Empire's very existence. Until 388 in the west, the geographical periphery was the political core, and this is important to remember.

This part of the Empire was beginning to form an economic unit, separate from the Empire's Mediterranean core, with its own periphery in *barbaricum*.[24] It has become fashionable to see the economic, social and cultural frontier zones of the Empire 'deepening' progressively, particularly as north Gallic society became 'Germanicised' and militarised. A 'longue durée' approach can even see this 'process' as a reversion to more fundamental pre-Roman

---

[21] A clear refutation of Luttwak's thesis of Roman 'grand strategy' can be found in Mann (1979). Whittaker (1994), pp. 202–9 is robust on the subject: 'demonstrably rubbish' (p. 206).

[22] On the problems of banditry, see Grünewald (2004); Shaw (1984a); (1993).

[23] For useful descriptive summary, see Elton (1996a), pp. 155–74; Southern and Dixon (1996), pp. 127–47.

[24] Above, pp. 85–6.

economic patterns, with the early Roman period as an aberration.[25] Although the early imperial period in western Europe was truly exceptional in economic and cultural terms, it is a mistake to see the frontier zone as deepening into the Empire in the fourth century, and even into the fifth. If there was a deep economic zone, it was extending from the Gallic and Germanic provinces northwards into Germany. 'Germanic' influence in late Roman Gaul has been massively overestimated,[26] especially when compared to influences in the opposite direction, and to discuss the late and post-Roman period as a 'reversion' to pre-Roman patterns is to be misled by superficial descriptive similarities, and to mask the period's true dynamics.

THE BARBARIAN THREAT?

Roman emperors spent much of their time on the frontier, where they spent lavishly on defences aimed at keeping out the peoples beyond. The emperor was expected to win battles against the hostile peoples and be a *domitor gentium* – a pacifier of the nations. The greatest part of imperial expenditure went on the army – equally justified by the need for defence against the 'wild nations . . . assailing every frontier'.[27] What sort of a military threat was posed by the western barbarians? What was the real balance of power?

There can be little doubt that the Empire possessed considerably greater reserves of manpower than the barbarians. Estimating the barbarians' numerical strength is fraught with difficulties. The Romans were used to thinking of northern barbarians as innumerable and to describing their armies accordingly. This however stemmed from the ideas of bio-geography discussed in chapter 2 and need not worry us unduly. Writers in the classical tradition repeatedly employed large numbers like 80,000. Their audience expected such figures, deployed as a short-hand to describe a huge horde. A more solid basis would be provided by archaeology.[28] *Germania Magna* and Britain north of the Wall were not urbanised societies. The economy and the surplus extracted from agriculture did not permit large numbers of people to remove themselves from subsistence farming – it often did not maintain a massively wealthy élite. Settlements were, on the whole, small; the largest sheltered populations of only a couple

---

[25] Miller, D. H. (1996).   [26] See below, pp. 153–60.
[27] *On Matters Military* 6.1.   [28] Above, pp. 125–8.

of hundred. Within these parameters it does not seem likely that barbarian armies can have been very big. The Alamannic army at the battle of Strasbourg (357) cannot have approached the 35,000 mentioned by Ammianus. Indeed it is most unlikely it matched the (according to Ammianus) 13,000 Roman troops facing them.[29] A better indication of the numbers involved, taken from the same author, when not describing a pitched battle in a set piece of Latin literature, is that 600 Franks posed a serious military problem for Julian.[30] It is also telling that it was thought sufficient, in quelling political disturbances in Britain probably including significant barbarian incursions, to dispatch four regiments, totalling only about 2,000 men.[31] Similar points have been made about the military forces of the more nomadic or pastoral barbarian groups on the Danube frontier. These too cannot have mustered huge armies. The most generous sober estimates of the size of barbarian armies, proposed by historians who envisage the barbarian migrations as the movements of whole peoples, do not put them higher than between 20,000 and 30,000.[32] These, furthermore, refer to exceptional and short-lived circumstances. Even if these estimates, which seem optimistic, were accepted, they pale into insignificance alongside the 400,000 men or more that the Empire could muster.

Technologically, too, the barbarians were no match for the Romans. Roman troops, according to Vegetius, only abandoned heavy armour after the reign of Valens.[33] Archaeology and pictorial sources suggest that the Roman heavy infantry, who still formed the tactical core of the Empire's armies, wore helmets and mail or lamellar body armour.[34] The Empire had official state workshops producing helmets, armour, shields and iron weaponry. Though the technological and manufacturing capabilities of the northern barbarians have probably been underestimated and evidence suggests organised iron-working, it is probably going too far to envisage their armies as being uniformly heavily armoured. In addition, the Romans had developed artillery and, on the whole, well-constructed stone fortifications.[35] Their logistical organisation, though far from faultless, far surpassed that of the northern barbarians and they had organised and generally

---

[29] Amm. Marc. 16.12 on the battle of Strasbourg.   [30] Amm. Marc. 17.2.
[31] Amm. Marc. 27.8.7.   [32] E.g. Heather (1991), p. 147.
[33] Vegetius, *Epitome* 1.20.   [34] See, e.g. Southern and Dixon (1996), pp. 96–9.
[35] Above, n. 1.

effective communication networks. In none of these areas of military technology could the barbarians north of Hadrian's Wall or the Rhine–Danube line compete on remotely even terms.

Where the barbarians might have been more nearly able to match the Romans was in military skill. Man for man the barbarian warrior might have been the equal or even the superior of the Roman soldier but this is a difficult proposition to test. All accounts of warfare against the barbarians are of course written by the Romans and thus mired in all the usual stereotypes about barbarian ferocity. Ammianus' account of Strasbourg is a case in point.[36] He contrasts the Alamannic wild charge with the Roman infantry's solid discipline. The barbarians weary themselves in their fierce attacks whilst the disciplined and cool Roman line absorbs the rush and eventually drives back the enemy. After what was said in chapter 2 it is difficult to see this other than as the deployment of stereotypes. The account is not implausible but the ethnographic clichés hinder our acceptance of it as neutral reportage. That said, the regular drill and training of the better Roman regiments would give them an advantage over less well disciplined warbands. This seems undeniable, at least for the Palatine and comitatensian units, but it is difficult to generalise. Corruption was rife in some sections of the Roman army. The sale of horses by the officers of a mounted archer regiment in Libya and the pocketing of pay and uniform allowances are all attested.[37] The evidence for corrupt practices in the army can, individually, be explained away in terms of the nature of the sources, but cumulatively the volume of such evidence is very significant.

It is perhaps dangerous to assume that *limitanei* and other border troops away from the centre of imperial rule were constantly drilled and trained, or well equipped. Experienced barbarian warbands are likely to have been superior to such troops, at least in open battle. Recognition of this fact might have led to the greater reliance on small heavily fortified redoubts in the frontier zones, which would negate barbarian advantages in open warfare. Given the disparity in numbers, training and equipment, the fact that the Romans rarely lost is scarcely surprising. More remarkable is the fact that the barbarians sometimes won and, more frequently, caused the Romans serious

---

[36] Amm. Marc. 16.12.
[37] Jones, A. H. M. (1964), pp. 644–6, 1055; Lee (1998) for caution; MacMullen (1988), pp. 171–9.

problems. This might lead us to question common assumptions about the quality of the Roman regular army.

The recruitment of barbarians into the Roman army might suggest that, as the preceding paragraph implies, they were held to be of greater military value but there are reasons for caution. The army's increased size, even if not as drastic as Lactantius would have us believe, would still have presented recruitment difficulties, since the Empire's population was not rising; if anything, in some areas of the west, it may have been falling.[38] The Empire's large landowners, furthermore, resented the conscription of their tenants. Recruitment from outside the imperial borders would evade this. Troops raised from prisoners of war (*laeti*) or barbarians who had voluntarily surrendered themselves (*dediticii*) might not be significantly better than Roman conscripts.[39] The barbarisation of the army has probably been overstated and the Romans were, as we have seen, enmeshed in ideas about the barbarians and their ferocity.[40] This itself might have governed ideas about the desirability of recruiting beyond the frontiers. Even with these caveats in mind, some points still argue for the military value of barbarian recruits. A barbarian volunteer, especially one with experience in the warbands, might very well have made a better soldier than an impressed provincial peasant, especially if the latter found himself in one of the poorer-quality frontier units. The fact that the 'barbarian' units appear in the field armies must suggest, even with due attention paid to the reservations made in chapter 3, that barbarian recruits were held to be of most use in the army's élite units. The overall impression must be that barbarian warriors were at least the equals of Roman troops in terms of military skill, but that the numbers, equipment and (in the case of the better regiments) discipline and training of the latter usually offset this.

Another factor leaning heavily in the Empire's favour was the political disunity of the peoples beyond the frontiers. Roman policy worked towards the maintenance of barbarian fragmentation into small groups. The barbarians were certainly not above fighting each other, especially when Roman gold was at stake. There is no support in the evidence for any sense of 'Germanic' or 'Celtic' unity, a point

---

[38] Lactantius *On the Deaths of the Persecutors* 7; Liebeschuetz (1991), pp. 11–25, for reasons for recruiting barbarians.

[39] See below, pp. 152–3, for discussion of various types of barbarian recruit.

[40] Above, pp. 102–9.

backed up by the fact that there are almost no instances of barbarian
recruits betraying the Romans to their enemies. The handful of
exceptions concerns, in all cases, actions against the specific homeland
of the soldier in question.[41] On the other hand, even when it was
divided politically, the rulers of the Empire could mobilise the
resources of huge territories against incursions. The point was rather
that in times of Roman disunity imperial rulers were more concerned
with Roman politics than with the barbarian threat, a graphic indication of the real hierarchy of military dangers posed to an emperor.
Further, at such times, the management of the frontier broke down,
allowing larger groups of barbarians to coalesce, such as the confederacy defeated by Julian at Strasbourg in 357. The emergence of
such groupings posed a double problem. First, any political factions
that lost out in the formation of these larger units were almost
inevitably driven to seek refuge in the Empire. This process had
occurred over and over in Roman frontier politics since Julius
Caesar's days and was to happen again, repeatedly and with disastrous
results, in the generations after 376. Second, the ruler of such a
confederacy was inevitably either not legitimised by the Romans or
was sanctioned only in order to persuade him to attack the territory of
a Roman political rival. In the former case the ruler needed to acquire
the prestige and the Roman goods, in booty, that would maintain
him in power. In either instance the only result was an attack on
Roman territory by militarily more significant forces.

    The alleged increase in the scale of the barbarian threat has been
assumed to have led to a number of changes in the Gallic frontier
provinces: the fortification of towns and the abandonment of villas.
These assumptions, however, cannot be accepted at face value. The
new city walls cannot be seen as products of haste.[42] Furthermore,
the ubiquity of the phenomenon in the west must make the construction of walls something other than an emergency response to
particular attacks. Nonetheless, urban fortification surely reflects a
perceived lack of security. Whether that was entirely the result of
barbarian attacks is debatable. Internal security was doubtless
important, with the necessary fortification of taxation and administrative centres. The contraction of the settlement pattern cannot be

---

[41] Amm. Marc. 14.10.7–8 (Alamannic officers *suspected* of betraying Roman plans);
    31.10.3 (loose talk gives away planned troop movements).
[42] Above, pp. 83–5.

understood as consequent upon barbarian attacks. Greater structural reorganisation appears to have been at work. That said, it cannot be denied that the late Roman northern Gallic settlement pattern reflected changed circumstances, with a far greater degree of forti-fication.[43] This must represent a response to the danger of barbarian incursion at least in part. Even where it was not, it is surely likely that the expenditure on fortifications was justified in terms of defence against such raids. A small but highly mobile barbarian army, like the 600 Franks whose campaign against Julian is described by Ammianus, could cause a huge amount of damage and disruption, especially given the slow speed of communications and, consequently, Roman response.[44]

ROMAN USE OF THE BARBARIANS

The barbarians were extremely useful to the Romans. The Empire employed the barbarians to reduce the military threat on the frontier by engaging one group to attack another: a principal means by which the frontier was managed.[45] Valentinian I, campaigning against the Alamans in the 360s, allied with the Burgundians, encouraging them to attack the Alamans in the rear whilst Roman troops invaded Alamannic territory from across the Rhine.[46] Roman leaders also employed barbarians to attack their own political rivals. The Emperor Constantius made a pact with the *Alamanni*, engaging them to attack his cousin Julian when the latter was declared *augustus* in 361 in an act of rebellion.[47] With this in mind it might be that the Alamannic attack on Gaul during Constantius' war against the western usurper Magnentius (351–3) was undertaken with similar imperial encour-agement.[48] As noted, this policy could have serious and deleteri-ous consequences. Constantius' barbarian alliance produced Chnodomarius' confederacy and the serious upheavals in Gaul that had to be rectified by the *caesar* Julian. Within the Empire, settled barbarians, *laeti*, *gentiles* or *dediticii*,[49] fulfilled useful functions as farmers, taxpayers and soldiers and volunteers from beyond the borders helped solve recruiting problems.

[43] Van Ossel (1995); van Ossel and Ouzoulias (2000).   [44] Amm. Marc. 17.2.
[45] Heather (2001).   [46] Amm. Marc. 28.5.8–15.   [47] Amm. Marc. 21.4.
[48] On this attack, see Amm. Marc. 15.8.1, 6; Zos. 3.1. Elton (1996a), pp. 1–2, 38, 54.
[49] Below, pp. 152–3.

Valuable though the barbarians were in all these respects, however, it should be apparent by now that the barbarians' most important role in Roman politics was ideological. To simplify the situation, participation in the imperial bureaucracy was much sought after. The advantages it brought stemmed in no small measure from association with the emperor and thus the system worked as a huge patronage network. To manage this system most effectively the emperor needed to be positioned on the periphery and his position there was justified by his duty to protect the Empire against hostile peoples. The legitimacy of his rule was demonstrated by lavish expenditure on frontier works. He needed a large army in order to maintain his grip on authority in the face of rivals but this army's size was, again, justified by the need to defend the Empire against the barbarians. Paying for the army and frontier fortification justified taxation, which was the principal duty of the bureaucracy and it was participation in the bureaucracy that bound the diverse regions of the Empire into a single unit. Thus in a sense the whole late Roman imperial system was dependent upon the perception of a barbarian threat. Geary's famous dictum was that 'the Germanic world was perhaps the greatest and most enduring creation of Roman political and military genius'.[50] At the same time, though, as Alexander Callander Murray has correctly said in response,[51] the late Roman world was a creation of the barbarian threat. In constructing the barbarian world the Roman Empire defined itself.

BARBARIAN USE OF THE ROMAN EMPIRE

The barbarians were very important to the Romans but, as Geary implied, the Romans were also vital to the barbarians. The principal supports for rule over a barbarian polity originated with the Romans. Roman imports were crucial signs of status and wealth within barbarian society, something nowhere made clearer than by the Roman goods present in the furnished inhumations that appeared in *barbaricum* in times of stress (as in the Haßleben-Leuna group).[52] We have seen how social status and political authority was often manifest through the use of Roman stylistic motifs, often derived from official Roman metalwork and other objects.[53] Such goods could be

---

[50] Geary (1988), p. vi.   [51] Callander Murray (2002), p. 45, n. 24.
[52] Above, pp. 57–8.   [53] Above, pp. 57–8.

obtained through three principal mechanisms: gifts, trade and raiding. One imagines that the direct association with the emperor himself that gifts implied made this the preferred means of procuring them. The Romans appreciated the importance of trade to the barbarians,[54] to the extent that closing border markets was a tried and tested policy designed to hurt a barbarian ruler. Raiding might in certain circumstances be part of the relationship that brought diplomatic gifts. Roman material was so important to barbarian politics that, where trading and diplomatic payments were not possible, plundering them would have been almost compulsory.[55]

Raiding the Empire was doubtless important to the construction of barbarian rulership in other ways. Though we know practically nothing about barbarian kingship, it is more than likely that war-leadership was a significant component of it. This is all the more likely if, as seems reasonable, the emperors themselves provided the model of good rulership. Yet the very importance of the Empire within barbarian political structures, in so far as we can reconstruct them, might give us pause when considering the place of raiding the Empire in non-Roman political thinking. It might not have been a simple matter to attack the font of ideas of political legitimacy. Warfare against other barbarian groups, especially when sanctioned and paid for by the Romans, was probably simpler and more attractive in demonstrating the ability to rule through war-leadership.

The purpose of barbarian raids might therefore have been more complex than the simple acquisition of loot and prisoners. It ought perhaps to be viewed more as a bargaining strategy, aimed at pro-curing a more favourable relationship and the payment of gifts or the permitting of trade that would add to a barbarian ruler's prestige and security. The *Alamanni*, for example, attacked the Empire in 364 to protest at Valentinian I's bestowal on them of gifts inferior to those they were expecting.[56] Certainly, before the fifth century it is difficult to find a single instance of a barbarian group attempting the conquest of imperial territory.[57]

---

[54] Above, pp. 127–8.

[55] Elton (1996a), pp. 48–54, for typology of barbarian raiding. The analysis is blurred somewhat by taking the whole period between 350 and 425 together, when Roman–barbarian relations changed importantly during that time.

[56] Amm. Marc. 26.5.7.

[57] Elton (1996a), p. 47, and cp. p. 54. Elton believes there was an Alamannic attempt to conquer territory in 352–3.

However, as noted in chapter 4, there are clear signs that some barbarian political units, especially just beyond the frontier, were increasing in power and stability during the fourth century. They may have been dependent upon Roman support in rather different ways from those peoples further into 'free Germany'. Their power might have been more secure, but they still relied upon Rome to some degree. Treaties remained important. The vocabulary of power was resolutely Roman. What would happen to such groups if the Empire ceased to exist as a valid model for legitimate rule? These units could be destabilised and, when they were, the threat to the security of the frontiers was that much greater.

BARBARIANS WITHIN THE ROMAN EMPIRE

One of the most important means by which the barbarians used the political structures of the Roman Empire was, of course by settling within it and employing them to their own advantage. Much discussion of barbarian settlement is heavily technical, making considerable and precise use of Roman vocabulary and assigning a constitutional significance to such terms. However, close inspection of the sources reveals that the situation was much less clearly defined.[58] The terms by which barbarian groups were settled within the Empire were rarely if ever recorded in any detail. Sometimes historians have reconstructed these from the barbarians' subsequent behaviour but this seems a risky strategy. The main categories of barbarians in formal relationships with the Empire were as follows. There were *dediticii*, barbarians who had surrendered themselves to the Empire and been received into the state for settlement.[59] These were possibly the most numerous element of the non-Roman population. Another quite widespread category from the third century were the *laeti*: barbarians captured by the Romans and settled on the land rather than being, as was usual, butchered out of hand or thrown to the beasts.[60] Their name, which translates as 'the joyous' (we might think of it better as 'the lucky ones'), is a characteristic example of grim late antique humour.[61] There were also *foederati*,

---

[58] Elton (1996a), pp. 129–30.   [59] Burns (1994), pp. 12–13; Liebeschuetz (1991), p. 14.

[60] Elton (1996a), pp. 129–33; Liebeschuetz (1991), p. 12.

[61] On which see Shanzer (2002a). The numbers of *praefecti laetorum* in the *Not. Dig.* make me prefer this translation to that which relates it to the Alamannic tribe of

barbarians in a treaty (*foedus*) relationship with the Empire but in the fourth century such barbarians lived entirely outside the effective imperial frontiers.[62] There was no concept of the Empire entering into a treaty relationship with its own subjects. *Foederati* who turned out to be the losers in barbarian politics might be admitted into the Empire as refugees in reward for their support, but in so doing they became *dediticii*. Some barbarians fell into none of these categories; they were those in the regular army, of whom there were many. If settled inside the Empire, they became citizens after completing their service. The usurpers Magnentius (350–53) and Silvanus (355) were (allegedly in Magnentius' case) sons of barbarians.[63] Had they not rebelled or found themselves on the wrong side of the imperial authorities – whereupon their barbarian antecedents were emphasised – there would be no reason to see them as other than Roman.

The major debate over the archaeological manifestation of such barbarians within the Empire concerns a new form of burial appearing in late fourth-century northern Gaul. Such graves are widely distributed north of the Loire but are more frequent towards the north-west, in modern Belgium and Picardie (map 10). They are associated with all types of site – forts, *villae*, small towns and *civitas* capitals – and usually occur in small groups.[64] Even within larger cemeteries there are usually only small clusters of such interments. The principal exception is the cemetery of the fort at Oudenburg, where about ninety such graves were found.[65] Essentially these graves are typical late Roman inhumations but with more numerous grave-goods, often of a novel form. Above all, the deceased was interred in a more elaborate funerary costume than had previously been the norm, manifested in female graves above all by the presence of brooches and other dress accessories. The costume of the dead males is revealed mainly by late Roman official belt-sets but these burials, especially in the north of the region, frequently also contain weapons: usually axes or spears but some swords and occasional shields (map 11). The

---

the *Laeti* – cp. Elton (1996a), pp. 131–2. The usurper Magnentius was described as having been brought up among the *Laeti* in Gaul (Zos. 2.54) but has no known Alamannic antecedents. His mother may have been Frankish.

[62] Heather (1997); Wirth (1997). Below, pp. 183–4, for later *foederati* units.

[63] Magnentius: Zos. 2.54; Silvanus: Amm. Marc. 15.5.33.

[64] The best description of this material may be found in Böhme (1974).

[65] Mertens (1963); (1971).

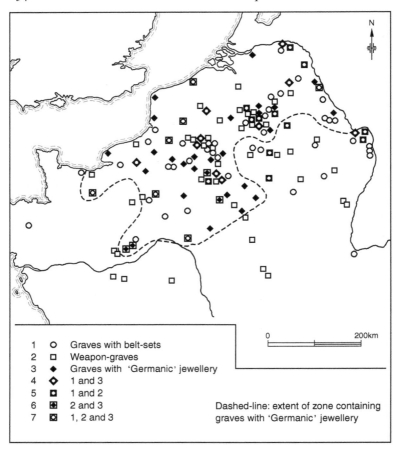

Map 10 Distribution of supposedly 'Germanic' furnished burials in late Roman
northern Gaul

Oudenburg graves generally lacked weapons, in spite of overwhelmingly being of male subjects.

 These burials have traditionally been associated with 'Germanic'
settlers, and this remains the most common interpretation of this
data. Originally identified as the burials of *laeti*, they are now most
frequently understood as those of *foederati* (a problem in itself).[66]
However, numerous problems arise, stemming from the weakness of

---

[66] *Laeti*: Werner (1950); *Foederati*: Böhme (1974).

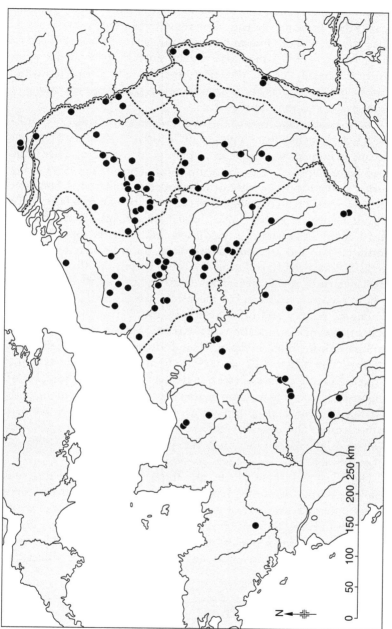

Map 11 Warrior burials in northern Gaul

the archaeological supports for such a conclusion.[67] The arguments against the traditional interpretation require restating for two reasons. First, the 'Germanic' interpretation continues to be widely cited in unquestioned fashion, in spite of the flimsiness of the evidence upon which it is based. Second, the rejection of the 'ethnic' or 'Germanic' reading of these graves opens up new readings of furnished burials in other parts of western Europe.

The principal objection to the traditional reading is that the burial ritual is nothing like that employed in the homelands of the Franks or Saxons, whom these burials are supposed to represent. There, the dead were disposed of by cremation, the ashes of the dead being buried, either in pots or without a container, or scattered.[68] The latter methods leave no archaeological trace. Thus the Frankish homelands remain blanks on archaeological distribution maps of cemetery or burial finds. Inhumation is unknown until *after* its appearance in northern Gaul and its eventual introduction can be linked to similar social factors as had produced this ritual within the Empire. Even small details of the furnished inhumation, such as the burial of a coin in the deceased's hand or mouth ('Charon's obol') or the positioning of pottery and other vessels by the feet of the corpse, are straightforward continuations of Roman funerary practice. The material culture found in the graves is, furthermore, overwhelmingly Roman. The belt-sets are, as has long been known, products of the Roman Empire, badges of office in the civil and military branches of imperial service. There is no reason at all to associate them with 'Germans'. The same is true of the weaponry. All is of Roman manufacture. The ceramics, bronze and glass vessels are equally of Roman origin. Only a few handmade pots in the north of the region might possibly have been made elsewhere.[69]

The idea that these graves are those of incoming barbarians employs a series of mostly very weak arguments. First, it has been assumed that the presence of weapons excludes the subjects of these graves from being Roman citizens, legally forbidden to carry arms. Furthermore, Roman soldiers did not own their weapons but were issued them by the state. It is also assumed that weapon burial is

[67] On these problems see Halsall (1992); (2000); Theuws and Alkemade (1999); Theuws and Hiddink (1997), pp. 69–71.

[68] Reichmann (1997), pp. 64–5.

[69] On this Roman material culture, see Halsall (1992); (2000).

somehow an inherently 'Germanic' rite. Roman law did ban civilians
from carrying weapons, but aristocrats and others must have possessed
weaponry for hunting and the civil defence actions that the state
sometimes permitted, such as bandit-chasing. Roman troops disposed
of weaponry in ritual contexts, in bog deposits for example, and
written sources make it clear that retiring troops took their weapons
with them. Weapon burial is extremely rare in the fourth-century
barbaricum east of the Rhine, whence these settlers are supposed to
have come (map 11). Indeed there is no *prima facie* archaeological
evidence from the ritual which makes any connection at all with the
Frankish or Saxon homelands. It has been argued that the axe is a
weapon with purely barbarian antecedents but this proposal is
problematic. The celebrated *francisca* (throwing axe) is never mentioned in association with the Franks until after their settlement in
Gaul. Archaeologically it has no precedent from the Frankish
homelands (although burial methods render artefactual evidence
scarce there). Indeed it is only known from Gaul during this period,
so that one recent survey has used it as an index of sixth-century
Frankish identity. The axe is probably a very late Roman weapon.[70]
The one area where a few inhumations with weapons (albeit of a
quite different type) are found is the south-western Alamannic
regions.[71] However, to propose an Alamannic origin for the
occupants of these graves drastically contradicts the best argument for
their non-Roman origin.

   A weightier argument has been proposed concerning the jewellery
found in female graves. Distribution maps of these items appear to
reveal links between northern Gaul and the north-west of 'free
Germany', the Saxon homeland.[72] It must first be repeated that the
apparent 'blank' between these areas and northern Gaul results largely
from the archaeologically invisible methods of disposing of the dead
employed there. However, closer study reveals that, rather than
originating in northern Germany and being taken by barbarian settlers into Gaul, it is far more likely that these items were made inside
the Empire and exported, or taken back, to Germany. Many of these
types of jewellery derive from Roman prototypes and are found first
inside the imperial frontiers and only later in Germany (map 12).
There is also a distinction between those types which are found in

---

[70] Halsall (2000), p. 174, and refs.   [71] Böhner (1963).
[72] Above all: Böhme (1974).

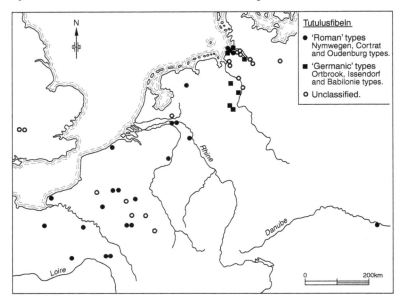

Map 12 Distribution of Tutulusfibeln

Gaul and in Germany and those which are found only in northern
Germany. The latter are later and appear to be copies of the former.
The distribution of these types of dress adjunct matches very closely
that of many of the types of official belt-set and other metalwork
manufactured in Gaul and taken back to northern Germany by
Saxons who had, presumably, served the Roman Empire. Other
distribution maps, of ceramics and bronze vessels, underline that the
trend was for material to be made in Gaul and exported into the
region's trans-Rhenan hinterland. The classic study of this jewellery
reveals a clear division between those items that are found in northern
Gaul and in northern Germany, but not in Britain, and those that are
found in northern Germany and Britain but not Gaul.[73] The latter,
largely of fifth-century date, clearly represent the Anglo-Saxon
migration to Britain; the artefacts' chronology makes this clear. The
former, however, represent the export of Roman fashions and
dress items into *Germania*. Furthermore, these forms of jewellery are
found within only a part of the region where furnished burials are
found (map 10). Finally, were one to accept the non-Roman origins

[73] Böhme (1974).

of the women interred with these items of jewellery, this would be impossible to square with the weapon burials, unknown in inhum-ations (there are occasional cremations with weapons) in north Germany until after the rite's appearance in Gaul. The only way in which a putatively Alamannic weapon rite can be reconciled with a Saxon origin for the jewellery (unless one assumes that Saxon women migrated into Gaul to meet and marry Alamannic male immigrants) is to appeal to the common 'Germanic' culture of the two groups, which will not withstand scrutiny.[74]

The archaeological data permit no association of these graves with trans-Rhenan settlers. Without assumptions based on the simplistic use of written sources no archaeologist would assume these were the graves of immigrants. A prehistorian, for example, would have no basis upon which to make such a claim and would search for more interesting explanations. In the climate of archaeological hostility towards documentary history it is ironic that this explanation remains so dominant. We must seek an alternative, social explanation.[75]

Barbarian settlers within the Empire have left little or no material cultural trace. Some supposed markers of barbarian presence, such as particular buildings are, like furnished burials, more dubious on closer inspection. In the north of Gaul and the German provinces long houses incorporating byres (*Wohnstallhäuser*) are found on the sites of villas abandoned in the third century. These houses are analogous to those found across the frontier but they are also of a type found in the region before the Roman conquest and up to at least the third century.[76] The socio-economic changes and constrictions that pro-duced the dereliction of the villas probably brought about a shift in architectural techniques. Buildings incorporating a sunken area with a tent-like structure erected over the pit, known as sunken-floored (or sunken-featured) buildings (SFBs) or *Grubenhäuser* are more characteristic of the *barbaricum*. However, they too begin to appear in Gaul in areas quite distant from the frontier during late antiquity and become a common feature of the period's architectural repertoire. Their ubiquity probably makes it too simplistic to equate their appearance with that of barbarian settlers.[77] Artefacts from *Germania*

---

[74] Above, pp. 22–4.   [75] See below, pp. 350–1.

[76] See, e.g. Carroll (2001), p. 65.

[77] For sensible comments on the ethnic associations of *Wohnstallhäuser* and *Grubenhäuser*, see van Ossel and Ouzoulias (2000), pp. 149–50.

Magna are rare, which is perhaps not surprising. The situation is different to some extent on the Danube, where the artefactual evidence from the late fourth century suggests material cultural blurring of the frontier line, and often a difficulty in deciding on which side of the frontier particular forms of artefact were produced.[78]

Where we have indubitable evidence of barbarians inside the Empire it all points in the same direction, towards their rapid subscription to Roman cultural norms. We only know that Chnothfrith's warband (the *numerus Hnaudifridi*) served on Hadrian's Wall from a thoroughly Roman record – a Latin inscription.[79] Hariulf, son of a Burgundian king, lived in Trier and served in the imperial guard. We know about him not because he was interred according to the traditional rites of his people or because he brought with him large quantities of non-Roman material culture, but because he erected an inscription in the best Roman fashion.[80] It has often been pointed out that the generalissimo Stilicho's Vandal antecedents would remain entirely hidden from historians – he would simply be a 'Roman general with a peculiar name'[81] – had he not fallen foul of the imperial court. In material cultural terms he has left us only a consular diptych of typical Roman style. The military fashion for 'barbarian chic' has been alluded to but that was something created very much on Roman terms and has left little material trace.[82]

Thus very little material culture suggests barbarian settlement. This, it must be stressed, is not to argue that there was no such settlement. Written and epigraphic sources are clear enough that there was and the appearance of some *Grubenhäuser* is suggestive. There are nevertheless vitally important conclusions to be drawn. First, material cultural influences spread overwhelmingly from the Empire into *Germania*. Given all that has been said about the importance of the Empire, its goods and symbols in barbarian life, this should not astonish us. Second, closely related to the first point and equally unsurprising on reflection, barbarians in the Empire rapidly

---

[78] It is not impossible that this material needs reassessment, freed from traditional assumptions about barbarian settlement.

[79] *RIB* 1576.   [80] *CIL* 13.3682; *RICG* 15*. Cüppers (ed.) (1984), pp. 349–50.

[81] M. Kulikowski, reviewing Pohl (2002) in *EME* 12 (2003): 196–7, at p. 196.

[82] The evidence for the presence of 'Elbe Germans' in the frontier garrisons usually turns out to be the items of jewellery referred to above in discussion of the burials and which are proposed to have been Roman products.

and completely adopted Roman material culture. As stated in chapter
1, material culture is active, not a passive reflection of reality. That
there were indisputably people of non-Roman birth inside the
Empire is no reason to suppose that the archaeological record should
reflect that fact. The Empire's ideological dominance beyond the
frontier, the well-attested barbarian desire to be associated with the
Empire and its structures, and Roman attitudes to non-Romans all
provide sound reasons why immigrants should have rapidly adopted
Roman culture. There might have been ways in which, or situations
wherein, barbarian identity could have been played to advantage
within the Empire (particularly in the army) but it is difficult to see
how or why non-Romanness should be proclaimed in the material
cultural contexts that form the archaeological evidence for the period.

CONCLUSION

It is not unlikely that there was increased pressure on the imperial
frontiers in the late Roman period but this should not be viewed as
the result of a pile-up of migrating peoples pushing each other against
the straining Roman defences. Furthermore, even if the pressure was
increasing, we cannot escape the conclusion that in the fourth century the struggle was still a hopelessly unequal one. The barbarians
north of the Rhine–Danube line and Hadrian's Wall and across the
Irish Sea could hardly, even in concerted action have contemplated
the conquest of the Empire. Perhaps for that reason, before 376 and
for a long time afterwards, none ever tried it. The 'barbarian threat'
was as much a Roman creation as a barbarian reality.

If pressure increased on the imperial *limes* then this probably
resulted largely from the symbiosis of Roman Empire and barbarian
peoples. The problem must principally lie at the door of the confederacies that emerged in the third century but the fact that one of
these, the Alamanni, was probably a Roman creation[83] only underlines the general point. So does the fact that these confederacies
appeared at the high-point of Roman internal weakness and
instability, which disrupted the political and social structures within
barbaricum. Payments to non-Roman rulers during imperial frontier
management in the end only raised the stakes in barbarian politics.
Their reliance upon Roman prestige and gifts made the barbarian

[83] Nüber (1993); (1998).

polities as dependent upon the efficient handling of the imperial
office and the management of its patronage as were the provincial
societies within the frontiers. In the decades either side of 400 AD
imperial patronage ceased to be managed effectively, and the results
were dramatic. In the following chapters, we shall examine the fate of
the western Empire in its last century and see how frequently the
lesson of the interdependence of Roman and barbarian politics is
underlined.

PART II

A WORLD RENEGOTIATED:
WESTERN EUROPE, 376–550

6

THE GOTHIC CRISIS, 376–382

·

INTRODUCTION: HISTORY AND IRONY

People know what they do; frequently they know why they do what they do;
but what they don't know is what what they do does.

Michel Foucault[1]

The central part of this book is a narrative history from the Gothic
crossing of the Danube in 376 to the deposition of the western
emperor, Romulus, in 476 and then on to the mid-sixth century. A
general political history is important for several reasons. We must
place the social, economic and ideological changes analysed in
chapters 11–14 in their specific historical context. They resulted from
choices influenced by, and often responses to, those political happenings. The narrative also highlights the conjunctures between high
political events in different parts of the Empire, perhaps allowing a
greater understanding of the circumstances that produced the changes
visible in local society. Recasting the narrative of the 'long fifth
century' also helps us to move away from seeing these developments
as inevitable. It is difficult to find a point at which the end of the
western Roman Empire was inescapable, certainly before 471; our
narrative must reflect this.

Writing a narrative means imposing a linear and coherent structure
upon the protean mass of past happenings: in selecting and shaping
the material of *history* into a *story*. This self-reflexivity about the

---

[1] A personal communication quoted in Dreyfus and Rabinow (1982), p. 187.

process of history writing, is often associated with the linguistic turn and the ideas usually lumped together as 'post-modernism'. In fact, though, the point was made by Thomas Carlyle more or less as soon as history-writing of a recognisably 'modern' form had begun in Britain,[2] and repeated in most generations since. In writing the history of this 'long fifth century' the problems are made even more acute by the frequent unavailability of the historian-storyteller's basic raw material, a precise chronology of happenings.

That contemporary or near-contemporary narratives of the fifth century were always written from particular ideological standpoints is no revelation. Their authors, like modern historians, selected events from all the goings-on of which they were aware, arranged them in series and interpreted them to suit their purposes. Even ostensibly straightforward chronographic records moved and re-dated events for rhetorical effect.[3] Perhaps more importantly many of these sources survive only in fragments, often further reshaped and glossed by later excerpters. As a result there is something of an industry of detailed chronographical study for this period and many articles shifting events backwards or forwards by a year or more, or showing how generally accepted dates are either based upon mis-understandings or errors, or historical constructs.[4] My story of the fifth century is therefore my creation, even more than a historian's account of the past normally is. I have chosen between equally plausible alternative chronologies according to what seems to make the most sense (itself, naturally, dependent upon my interpretation of what making sense means). The distinction between history and historical fiction becomes more blurred than usual.

This point is underlined when one considers the emplotment of histories of the fifth century.[5] As mentioned in chapter 1, the barbarian migrations and the end of the western Roman Empire have been viewed variously, as 'good' or 'bad' things, and consequently the story has been cast in diverse ways so that most of the classic forms of story are to be found. Many narratives are tragedies, with the demise of the western Empire (or perhaps the fall of the Gothic kingdom of

[2] Carlyle (1830).   [3] See, e.g. Wood (1987).

[4] As a fairly random selection, see Cesa (1992–3); Gillett (1999); Kulikowski (2000b); Halsall (2001), pp. 117–19; Schwarcz (2001), pp. 15–18; Wood (1992).

[5] On the emplotment of historical narrative, see, classically White, H. (1978), esp. pp. 81–100. See also Frye (1968). These thoughts are inspired by, but definitely not an 'application' of these writers' works.

Italy) as their final act.[6] Historians writing their work as tragedy have a tendency to consider particular decisions as mistakes with 'fatal' consequences (admitting the Goths, recognising non-Roman kingship, failing to destroy barbarian groups when the chance presented itself, and so on).[7] Others take a more positive line, rendering their works comedies (in the classical sense as the opposite of tragedy, representing the triumph of heroes over adversity), and see the period as a story of the rise to pre-eminence of particular peoples or of the new, medieval world. Others still, especially those following the migrations of particular tribes, write history along the lines of medieval romance or epic, narrating the strange and exciting adventures of particular heroes.

One reason why all these literary renderings are possible is that all historical writers and most of their readers – unlike the audience of a novel – know what is going to happen in the end.[8] This produces the 'grand narrative': the story of the fifth century as the fall of the Roman Empire, or as the rise of the barbarian kingdoms. This is true even of approaches that take as their outline the story of how the Roman world was *transformed* into ninth-century 'medieval' Europe. Events are given great significance because in the end they gave rise to other particular happenings – they can be seen from a later perspective as the 'origins' of events or institutions. The Gothic settlement in Aquitaine in 418/19, for example, is viewed as hugely important because ultimately the kingdom of Toulouse could trace its origins to this act. Even authors writing shortly after events could adopt the same attitude so that mid-fifth-century writers could ascribe to earlier actions an importance that escaped exact contemporaries in the late fourth or early fifth century. This produces the teleology, the explanation of events according to their outcomes, all too frequent in historical writing about late antiquity.[9]

I have argued against grand narratives before.[10] One might be able to alter the details here and there more easily than in better-documented historical eras but it is, clearly, as impossible to

---

[6] See, e.g. Mazzarino (1973), pp. 794–8: 'La tragedia di Stilicone'.

[7] An extreme example: 'Had Theodosius ... seen into the future, he would have rewarded Alaric [for his service against Arbogast] with a sword thrust to the heart': Burns (1994), p. 110.

[8] Lot (1933), p. 581: 'We who, in the eyes of our ancestors, are gods, because we know their future ... '

[9] Moroney (1989).   [10] Halsall (1995a), pp. 1–3; (1995c).

change the course of development in western Europe between 376 and 568 as it is in any other period. Whether you or I like it or not, the western Roman Empire is going to fall at the end of chapter 9 (I assume I am not giving anything away here). We can however write history so that events are not represented as inevitable stages on the road to a particular outcome. In what follows I have tried to avoid representing events as leading inexorably towards a specific final result, whether tragic, romantic or comedic. Whereas most writers about this period write history backwards, either in seeking to explain a particular predetermined end-result or in tracing the origins of a specific institution, I have attempted to depict history as unfolding. I have endeavoured to give primacy to those sources closest in date to the actions under discussion in the belief that, paradoxically perhaps, we come closer to an appreciation of the decisions that led to particular outcomes by looking at writers who did not comprehend their historical significance.

To understand a particular course of events we must be aware of the other alternatives open to contemporaries, of the other results that they might have desired. The restoration to the actors in our story of the choices available to them gives us a much better understanding of how history took the path that it did. Thus history unfolds not according to some master-plan but as the cumulative effect of myriad choices by countless people who did not know the 'plot', who were not being swept along helplessly by a tide of events leading to the end of the western Empire or the creation of the Frankish kingdom.

The decisions made by historical actors are shaped only by their understanding of current situations and by their knowledge of previous similar events and choices. This raises a further aspect of the problem. The actors in our story generally modelled themselves upon ideals from the past: civic Roman masculinity for example. The model for a good ruler was a Trajan (emperor, 98–117) or an Alexander the Great. In a period where much attention is given to changes in identities it is also worth remembering that identity means 'likeness'. To adopt a social identity is to stress likeness with a particular social category. Some idea of what *identifies* that social category must already exist. The creation of 'new identities' therefore must involve the employment of existing concepts, in other words things from the (however recent) past. Moreover, the ways in which social actors expressed themselves or the sources in which their actions were depicted were also, invariably, moulded by those of the past. Ammianus wished to be a new Tacitus; Sidonius a new Pliny. Late antique people made choices according to what they thought would bring about, for them, the best result. Their actions, however, frequently had cumulative effects quite different from those intended and unfolded in a fashion that no one can have foreseen. The force that informed their actions and weighed heaviest upon them, and which imposes itself most forcefully upon our perception of them and their deeds, was the past. The actors in this story were, simply enough, walking backwards into the future.

My rendition of western European history between 376 and 550 might still be read as a tragedy or as a heroic epic depending upon any predisposition that the reader might have, but it is presented as a dynamic sequence of events in which people acted according to their awareness of their situation and their own aims. They did not know that they were part of a particular story or how it would end. However, while the actors did not know this, the audience of history, that is both the author of this account and his readers, do, and this can only give this narrative a heavily and repeatedly ironic character. Tragedy and comedy can involve irony; irony can be tragic or comic. Comedy, tragedy, epic and romance all revolve around a unified, linear narrative structure and a particular ending, which informs the actions of the characters. Similarly, whilst history presented as tragedy, comedy, romance or epic has in all cases aimed to instruct, it can only do so – indeed it can only be written – by imposing a teleological structure on the narrative, preventing a full awareness of historical dynamics. A hero, for example, is often presented as such by ascribing to him (or occasionally her) an intention, rarely justified by the evidence, to produce a long-term result. Tragedy, by contrast, comes about by the characters' inability to produce a particular outcome and evade another fate. But historically such fates rarely seem inevitable. Consequently, this story unfolds as the disjunction between the intended results of people's actions and their actual outcomes. The end of the western Roman Empire was brought about by people frequently, if not always, trying to do the opposite. This disjuncture subverts any unified narrative.

The story begins in 376, the year when 'the narrative of the barbarian invasions and settlements can be said to have begun',[11]

[11] Wood (1998a), p. 517.

with the admission of the Goths into the Empire. At this point, the Empire was ruled by the Emperor Valens in the east and in the west by his nephews, the *augusti* Gratian and Valentinian II, sons of Valentinian I, who had died the previous year.

THE HUNNIC STORM[12]

'Troubles, I don't need to tell you, don't come at a gallop, like the Huns.'[13]

In 376 Roman officers on the Danube received word of serious disturbances beyond the river. Grim reality followed hard on the heels of these reports. Large groups of Goths began to appear on the north bank, and before long a mass of terrified humanity assembled there. The Goths had been defeated by a new and terrible people: the Huns. Now these refugees from what modern historians call the 'Hunnic storm' begged to be allowed into the Empire and safety.

The thirty-first and final book of Ammianus Marcellinus' *Res Gestae* is our main source for these events, which lent themselves to some of Ammianus' most powerful and memorable writing.[14] In his account the Huns subjected the Alans, who lived around the Don, and then attacked the *Greuthungi*. After valiant resistance, the semi-legendary Greuthungian king, Ermenaric, was forced to commit suicide. Vidimir, his successor, was slain, despite hiring some Huns to help him. Vidimir's son Videric was only a child so two experienced leaders, Alatheus and Saphrax, took over as regents. They retreated to the lands of the *Tervingi*. Athanaric, the Tervingian judge, marched against the Huns, pitching his camp close to the withdrawing Greuthungi but sending out an advance guard. The Huns, 'clever at guessing such things'[15] simply bypassed these scouts and launched a surprise attack, routing the main Gothic force. Athanaric, defeated

[12] Up to the aftermath of the battle of Adrianople, events are best followed in Amm. Marc. 31. See also Oros. 7.33.9–7.34–5; Soc. 4.34–8; Soz. 6.37, 6.39–40; Zos. 4.20–59. For the most detailed modern accounts, see Burns (1994), pp. 1–91; Heather (1991), pp. 122–92, and Lenski (2002), pp. 320–67. See also Burns (1973); Curran (1998); Heather (1996), pp. 131–8; (1998c); (2005), pp. 145–90; Wolfram (1988), pp. 117–39. Kulikowski (2002a) sets out a sensible narrative and judicious warnings against over-elaborate interpretations.

[13] P. Levi, *The Periodic Table* (London, 1986), p. 206.

[14] Barnes (1998) argues for an original composition in thirty-six books.

[15] Amm. Marc. 31.3.6: *in conjectura sagaces*.

again by the speed of the Hunnic attack whilst allegedly trying to build some sort of linear defence against them, fled into the Carpathians with his followers. The 'greater part of the people', however, according to Ammianus, deserted their ruler and, under Alaviv and Fritigern, fled to the Danube, where they petitioned Emperor Valens for entry into the Empire.

Ammianus' colourful description of these events has led to most interpretations of them invoking the similar imagery of the Blitzkrieg of 1939–41: hordes of homeless, hopeless refugees, with the pitiful remains of their homes packed onto carts, driving a few head of cattle with them, clogging the roads towards the Danube, anxious eyes scanning the horizon for the dreaded Hunnic cavalry, the Stukas of the scenario. A whole people took fright and fled for the border. How realistic is this picture? Two issues must be addressed: the nature of the Huns, supposedly so new and terrifying that they wrecked the whole fabric of Gothic society and drove the people abroad; and Gothic society and politics before the Hunnic arrival.

Ammianus' account of the Huns is famous.[16] The Huns, says he, are barely human, incredibly ugly and, having no use of fire, eat roots and half-raw animal flesh. They have no buildings and their clothes are of linen or the skins of mice; they live entirely on horseback or in their wagons; they have no religion, no kings, nor any government beyond the 'tumultuous' rule of a general council of their leading men; they know no laws and are faithless and unreliable.

Elements of Ammianus' description seem plausible, especially when compared with other steppe nomads of history. However, perhaps too much attention has been given to trying to establish the 'truth' behind the components of this portrait.[17] Ammianus' account is heavily infused with classical ethnographic stereotypes. He says the Huns were previously known only vaguely[18] and exceed every form of savagery. As a new people from 'beyond the Maeotic Sea [the Sea of Azov] near the icebound ocean', it is unsurprising that he links the Huns explicitly with no people attested earlier.[19] Although parts of

---

[16] Amm. Marc. 31.2.1–12.

[17] See, e.g. Maenchen Helfen (1973), pp. 1–15; Matthews (1989), pp. 332–42; Thompson, E. A. (1996), pp. 9–11.

[18] *Leviter.* Amm. Marc. 31.2.1. The word is all too often overlooked.

[19] Unlike Eunapius (fr. 41, at Zos. 4.20.3), who identified them with the 'Royal Scyths' of Herodotus, although via rather poor scholarship! Matthews (1989), pp. 335–6.

his description of their nomadic lifestyle are borrowed from his accounts of the Saracens and he uses similar terms to describe the Alans, the stereotypes used most are, as might readily be seen from the summary above, those of people from the ends of the earth. Like Tacitus' *Fenni*,[20] from, as he saw it, a similar part of the world, the Huns surpass the normal bounds of savagery, have no knowledge of the rudiments of architecture or fire and their clothing is most basic. Like the *Fenni*, they tip their arrows with bone for want of anything better, and are without settled abodes. Similarly like extreme barbarians, they lack religion, proper government or law[21] and their faithlessness and mercurial behaviour are characteristic of such people, incapable even of ruling their own passions. These aspects of Ammianus' portrait are thus to be understood firmly within the traditions of antique ethnography and can probably be taken with a pinch of salt.

That leaves elements which are either taken from stock descriptions of pastoral nomads or which hardly distinguish the Huns from their neighbours, who, after all, are similarly described as 'Scythians'. The Goths themselves were pastoralists to some degree as well.[22] It is extremely unlikely that the Huns were so new and terrible that, by their very nature, they induced a mass Gothic panic. The conflict between the Greuthungians and the Huns is generally agreed to have been going on for longer than Ammianus implies. It is also telling that Ammianus informs us that soon after the Huns' 'appearance' Vidimir allied with some of them. Furthermore, Jordanes' sixth-century account makes the Huns into descendants of Gothic witches,[23] suggesting that in Gothic legend the two peoples were kin to some degree. This possibly stems from the fifth-century linkage of the two groups but it could go further back. If the Huns were not completely

---

[20] Tacitus, *Germania* 91. See above, p. 50. Tacitus' account of the Fenni was influential. It clearly lies at the origins of Procopius' (*Wars* 6.15.16–23) description of the 'Skrithiphinoi', whom he places in Thule, and of Jordanes' (*Getica* 3.21) of the Scerefennae, located in 'Scandza'. It is assumed that these passages derive from Priscus (thus Blockley places them as Priscus fr. 66) but it seems to me that there is more Tacitean influence on Procopius than is often supposed: Halsall (2002b).

[21] In the monarchical late Roman Empire, their lack of royal constraint can no longer be taken as a 'good thing'. Heather (1995a) goes too far in reading this as an accurate description of Hunnic political structures.

[22] See above, p. 132.   [23] Jordanes, *Getica* 24.121–2.

unknown and terrifying to the Goths, we must consider the second element in the equation: internal Gothic politics.

We have already seen the difficulties of governing the *Tervingi*. The *Greuthungi* were ruled by someone whom Roman sources and later tradition called a king, rather than a judge, but similar problems probably arose. They might not have been a powerful confederacy at all, but just one of several non-Tervingian Gothic groups.[24] It is likely that the blame for the crisis of 376 should be laid ultimately at the doors of the Romans themselves. Valens had waged a major war against the Goths during the campaign seasons of 367–9 and, although he was unable to win a decisive victory in the field, his forces nevertheless caused huge damage.[25] In 369 Athanaric was put to flight and a defeat was also inflicted upon the *Greuthungi*. Roman plundering and the cutting off of commerce created severe hardships for the Goths, who sued for peace. Valens, now having to deal with trouble on the Persian front, acceded.

A treaty was signed on a boat in the middle of the Danube, ending any further payments and restricting to two the points at which the Goths could trade with the Empire.[26] This was clearly not the outcome the Romans wanted. Valens had failed to win the great victory that imperial ideology and internal Roman politics demanded if he was to be seen as a worthy emperor in his own right and not just Valentinian I's little brother. The Goths had not surrendered and Valens had been unable to impose a settlement with clearly defined obligations upon them.[27] Yet attempts to portray the treaty as a meaningful victory for the Goths are unconvincing.[28] Athanaric had avoided Roman domination but he had not been able to negotiate good terms either and the fall-out from the war was extremely detrimental to his rule. The restriction of commerce and the end of diplomatic payments both reduced access to the Roman-made prestige-goods and treasure which oiled Gothic (as other barbarian) politics.[29] These and the military defeats and devastation put severe

---

[24] Heather (1996), pp. 53–7.   [25] For this war, see Amm. Marc. 27.1–2.

[26] Amm. Marc. 27.5.7–10; Themistius, *Orations* 10; Zos. 4.11.4. Heather (1996), p. 62; Lenski (2002), pp. 133–7.

[27] Heather (1998c); Lenski (2002), p. 137.

[28] Heather (1991), pp. 118–21; (2005), pp. 72–6; Heather and Matthews (trans.) (1991), pp. 19–26.

[29] The restriction of such trade might have been a general policy of Valentinian I and Valens: Lenski (2002), pp. 135–7.

stress on the Gothic realms. During this period Athanaric launched
the persecution of potentially pro-Roman Christians, during which
Saba found martyrdom as related at the beginning of this book.[30] The
fifth-century historians Socrates Scholasticus and Sozomen mention
that subsequently some sort of warfare broke out amongst the
Goths.[31] They name Fritigern as the leader who opposed the defeated
and probably discredited Athanaric and state that Roman *limitanei*
supported Fritigern.[32] The Romans apparently used Christianity to
bind Fritigern's faction to them. Ammianus lets slip that Athanaric
was eventually driven out by a faction of his compatriots.[33] It is not
unlikely that the *Greuthungi* were similarly shaken up by the war.
Apparently the Alans too were divided, given that some were evidently to be found on the 'Hunnic' side, whilst others fled and,
judging from his name, Saphrax may have been an Alan. This volatile
situation tipped the scales in the Huns' favour.

Nevertheless, if it is unlikely that the Huns would have had such
dramatic effects without Valens' destabilising of the region, their role
was still crucial. We might compare the situation with that on the
upper Rhine. Valentinian's Alamannic war (368–74) had been almost
as indecisive as his brother's Gothic campaign and, although he did
win one significant (if lucky) victory, he too ended up making peace
with the Alamannic king, Macrianus, on a boat in the middle of the
boundary river.[34] The Rhine frontier was heavily fortified in the
aftermath (as Themistius implies the Danube was after 369[35]) and
archaeology suggests a hiatus in the hitherto close links between the
Empire and Alamannic settlements. Alamans ceased to reach the high
ranks of the army, henceforth being replaced by Franks.[36] Alas we are
ill-informed about late fourth-century Alamannic politics. They too
might have been riven by faction. In many ways this was no bad thing
for the Empire. Thus Athanaric's discomfiture and the destabilising of

---

[30] Lenski (2002), pp. 320–1.
[31] Here, as throughout this section, my analysis accords with that of Lenski (1995),
who (p. 85) points out that the letter describing the recovery of Saba's body in
373 implies a Roman ability to intervene militarily in Gútthiuda.
[32] Soc. 4.33; Soz. 6.37.
[33] Amm. Marc. 27.5.10. This took place later, in 381. Zos. 4.10 is very confused but
still links Athanaric's flight to intra-Gothic politics.
[34] Drinkwater (1997). Amm. Marc. 30.3.3–6.
[35] *Orations* 10.136–8. Lenski (2002), pp. 130–1, 375–9.
[36] Martin (1997), pp. 122–4; (1998).

the Goths were probably viewed with satisfaction. Goths ceased to bother anyone for seven years whilst Roman troops were able to carry out operations beyond the border and, without the intervention of the Huns, it is unlikely that the Danube frontier would have worried Valens again for some time. On the Alamannic front, the emperor remained close by, in Trier, until 388. As on the Danube the situation was kept under control with periodic raids. Although after 388 Roman payments to Alamannic leaders to secure the frontier during the civil wars might have elevated these figures to a more powerful position, there are few clear references to an Alamannic overking thereafter.[37] Valens might have taken his eye off the Danube, though military intervention in the early 370s argues that this cannot have been done completely even during his Persian war. The real decisive factor was the Huns. Nomadic groups on the steppe generally have close and often predatory relationships with their more settled neighbours. The unstable political situation of the early 370s provided a golden opportunity for their intervention. Rival factions could form around them, adopting a new political identity and deploying the military support that they provided. Overall, the episode is typical of steppes political history and was to be repeated many times. The intervention of the Huns was vital but it was not the *deus ex machina* that it is often supposed to have been.

THE GOTHIC ENTRY INTO THE EMPIRE

It seems most likely, therefore, that the crowds assembling on the north bank of the Danube in 376 represented one Gothic faction, their followers and dependants: those with most to lose from the turbulent situation within Gútthiuda. This, nevertheless, may have amounted to a substantial number of people. Guesses in the region of 15,000–20,000 warriors and their dependants are precisely that – guesses – but plausible ones nonetheless. Some have argued that the numbers involved far surpassed those ever managed by the Romans in a process of *receptio* but we do not know this. The Empire had incorporated groups of barbarians before, for whom the same inflated and rounded figures were employed as for the Goths of 376. The appeal to the size of the immigrant body stems from a need to explain the scale of its consequences.

---

[37] See further below, pp. 400–01.

Valens, campaigning against the Persians, allowed the *Tervingi* over the Danube, largely ferrying them across on Roman boats: 'diligent care was taken that no future destroyer of the Roman state be left behind, even if he were smitten with a fatal disease', comments Ammianus dryly.[38] Even people writing within two decades after the event could appreciate history's ironies. Eunapius states that the Tervingi were supposed to be disarmed on their entry, but this task was left, at best, incomplete.[39] The motives for Valens' decision are fairly clear. As contemporaries said, the Goths would provide a large number of recruits for the army, the numbers and quality of which were a constant source of imperial concern. Settled throughout the Empire, they could also bring land back into cultivation, and thus increase tax revenue.[40] These, in spite of Ammianus' damnation, were sound reasons, and they were repeatedly presented as such in Themistius' works.[41] Furthermore, the Empire had efficiently incorporated substantial numbers of barbarians before;[42] Constantine's reception of the Sarmatians in very similar circumstances in 334 is perhaps the best analogy.[43] The Empire was responding in tried and tested fashion to circumstances similar to those faced in the past, and in a way favourable to its own interests.

Valens also acted from a position of strength. It has been argued that he had no choice,[44] but this seems unconvincing. The emperor himself and the best units of the eastern army were indeed far away but the Danube defences were strong and well manned. The Goths' position and thus their likely crossing points were, moreover, well known to Roman intelligence. We must also consider the Danube fleet, whose vessels presumably ferried the *Tervingi* across. As events in 386 would show, an attempt by barbarians to cross in the teeth of resistance by the fleet would end only in their slaughter.[45] The Roman ability to refuse admittance to Saphrax, Alatheus and the *Greuthungi* until the mismanagement of the Tervingian *receptio* was well under way strengthens this point.[46]

---

[38] Amm. Marc. 31.4.5.   [39] Eunapius, fr. 42; Zos. 4.20.   [40] Amm. Marc. 31.4.4.
[41] E.g. Themistius, *Orations* 16.211.   [42] Pitts (1989).   [43] Cesa (1994a), p. 18.
[44] Heather (1991), pp. 122–35.
[45] Zos. 4.38–39. Eunapius, fr. 42, says that an attempt by Tervingian hotheads to force a crossing in 376 was easily destroyed.
[46] Amm. Marc. 31.5.3, explicitly states that the *Greuthungi* were only able to cross because the Romans had withdrawn the troops and the crews of the fleet's boats to escort the Tervingi elsewhere.

THE GOTHS REBEL

The Danube forces were strong enough to keep out the Goths. What they were *not* sufficiently powerful to do was to admit one group, organise, disarm them and take them away, *and* keep the other group out. Soon food-supplies for the Goths broke down. This could have been expected. The 20,000–30,000-strong army that Valens assembled in the same region for his 367–9 Gothic war had required a huge logistical effort to support, which the Empire found difficult to maintain after three years of indecisive campaigning. The Balkan provinces were not prosperous. To be fed properly, even 40,000 Goths (of all ages and both sexes) would have required a well-organised and competently managed supply system. With the emperor far distant and with his gaze fixed upon Persia it is not surprising that such a system was not properly established and that that which was soon collapsed. Local officials made the most of the ensuing hardship and sold food to the Tervingi at absurd prices. The latter supposedly sold their children into slavery to buy dog-meat, at a rate of one dog for one child. The restless Goths were escorted away from the river by the local troops; in their absence, the Greuthungi crossed the Danube unopposed and fully armed. Soon afterwards, the Goths rose in open rebellion as a result of their mistreatment and after Lupicinus, the local Roman commander, bungled an attempt to kill their leaders at a banquet.[47] This latter event may have been on imperial orders;[48] it might have been a panic response to a situation fast getting out of hand. The mishandling of the Tervingian *receptio* illustrates graphically the problems of running the Roman Empire. With the emperor far away there was only too much opportunity for officials on the spot to leave jobs half-done and, more importantly, to abuse the situation for their own ends.

Joining Alatheus and Saphrax's *Greuthungi*, the Goths defeated Lupicinus and ravaged far and wide within the Balkan provinces.[49]

---

[47] Amm. Marc. 31.5.5–8.

[48] Heather (1991), pp. 131. Heather's view is that local responses to the Goths represent official strategy to deal with a barbarian group that the Empire had had no choice but to admit. The case is forcefully argued but I prefer to see the Empire as admitting the Goths from a position of strength, and to follow Ammianus' account in attributing the subsequent mismanagement to corruption and inefficiency.

[49] Amm. Marc. 31.5.9–10.

In 377 the Romans, with the aid of troops despatched from the Persian front, were able to box in the Goths north of the Haemus mountains, before attempting to defeat them in pitched battle. This encounter, at Ad Salices (in the modern Dobrudja), was drawn; the Goths formed their wagons into a laager and beat off the Roman attacks.[50] Both sides suffered heavily. Shortly afterwards, the Goths outflanked the blockading Romans with the assistance of some Huns and Alans who had also taken the chance to cross the Danube. Again the barbarians plundered widely.

THE BATTLE OF ADRIANOPLE AND AFTER

When, in 378, Valens was able to extricate himself and the eastern field army from the Persian war the stage was set for a major confrontation. Valens appealed for help to his nephew, Gratian. Gratian assembled a large force and moved east to help Valens, but was delayed en route by an Alamannic invasion, which he defeated.[51] Meanwhile, Valens, commanding his own large army, jealous of Gratian's success[52] and still without the great military triumph which was the stuff of imperial prestige, received information that the Goths at Adrianople (Edirne, Turkey) were significantly fewer than they actually were. He decided to engage Fritigern's warriors alone.[53] The Goths played for time. The leading elements of the Roman army, still largely strung out in column of march, attacked the Gothic laager. The remainder were drawn into the battle willy-nilly and when the Gothic cavalry surged out of ambush and into the rear of the Roman left flank Valens' defeat was sealed. The Goths rolled up the Roman line until those who had not fled were surrounded and driven in on themselves. Many died panicking in the crush. Valens was killed in unclear circumstances. The most popular story was that, wounded, he was taken to a nearby farmhouse, which the Goths then burnt over his head.[54] The tale's popularity might, however, have had less to do with its accuracy than with the didactic purposes to which it lent itself: the burning of a heretical emperor prefiguring his eternal

---

[50] Amm. Marc. 31.7.   [51] Amm. Marc. 31.10.
[52] Lenski (2002), pp. 355–67, sets out the numerous tensions, including religious differences between the Catholic Gratian and the Arian Valens, that existed between the two imperial courts.
[53] Amm. Marc. 31.12–13.   [54] Amm. Marc. 31.13.14; Soz. 6.40; Oros. 7.33.15.

torment in hell. The eastern field army was slaughtered. Estimates of the dead vary between 10,000 and 20,000.[55] We shall never know the precise figure but it is more significant to note who died than how many. The regiments that suffered worst at Adrianople were the best eastern Palatine and comitatensian units. These troops could be replaced in quantity but not quality. Crucially, many of the army's leading officers were also slain. Valens gave battle at Adrianople to gain prestige within the Empire, just as, for similar reasons, he had attacked and destabilised the Gothic realms nine years previously. His fate, like the whole Gothic crisis, resulted from the demands of internal Roman, rather than Romano-barbarian, politics.

Immediately after their triumph, the Goths again spread out to plunder. Defeated before the walls of Adrianople, they briefly threatened Constantinople, before being driven off by Roman reinforcements, including Arab allies who were, allegedly, too barbaric even for the barbarians.[56]

Ammianus ends his history in the aftermath of Adrianople, giving the battle a decisive appearance, but his reason for laying down his pen was that the reigning emperor, Theodosius I, now came to power. Few, if any, late antique authors engaged in the dangerous pastime of writing contemporary history and, whilst Ammianus was a pagan, Theodosius was a zealous Catholic. Ammianus compared Adrianople with Cannae (216 BC), Hannibal's great defeat of the Romans,[57] but this is less damning than is superficially the case. As Ammianus' audience knew, the point about Cannae was that, horrific disaster that it was, Rome revived and won the war. Rome recovered from Adrianople, too. Gratian arrived on the scene and in January 379 appointed Theodosius, a Spanish officer, as *augustus* in the east.[58] Meanwhile, such Goths as had already been moved into the Empire and enrolled in the army were ruthlessly massacred.[59] Three years of hard campaigning followed. The Danube provinces were sealed off and the Goths, prevented from spreading their raids further west or

---

[55] Heather (1991), pp. 146–7; (1996), pp. 134–5. Cp. Halsall (1999a), p. 138, n. 36.
[56] Amm. Marc. 31.16.5–6. There may be more than a touch of irony in Ammianus' account of the blood-drinking Arabs shocking the Goths into retreat: Halsall (2002b), pp. 97–9; Woods (1996); (2002).
[57] Amm. Marc. 31.13.19.
[58] He was the son of the Count Theodosius who settled the Romanus affair.
[59] Amm. Marc. 31.16.8. This is the last event recorded in Ammianus' narrative.

south, were gradually worn down.[60] No dramatic Roman victory occurred in the field but there was no doubt who was the winner of this war. At the beginning of 383 Theodosius celebrated victory over the Goths.[61] If Adrianople was Cannae repeated, then that made Theodosius Scipio Africanus reincarnate, something doubtless not lost on Ammianus' audience and patrons.

TRYING HARD TO RECREATE WHAT HAD YET TO BE CREATED: HISTORIANS AND THE 'TREATY OF 382'

It is generally thought that the war ended with a treaty. In very traditional views, this 'treaty of 382' represented a landmark in Roman history: the first *foedus* to establish a semi-autonomous non-Roman group on imperial territory.[62] The usual interpretation of the treaty's terms runs something like this: the Goths were given land to settle upon and farm; their tribal structure was left intact and the Goths continued to live by their own laws; in return they were to provide troops for the Empire whenever needed but these would serve under their own leaders, under the overall command of Roman generals; the treaty, however, recognised no overall Gothic leader.[63] Thus a semi-autonomous group, living partly without the structures of Roman law and administration, came into existence upon imperial soil: an important development indeed.

Unfortunately, as even those who argue for the dramatic significance of the '*foedus* of 382' admit, we know nothing of this 'treaty'.[64] Its supposed provisions have been reconstructed from a particular interpretation of the nature and subsequent history of Alaric's Goths and an assumption that later treaties were attempts by the Goths to improve upon the terms of the 382 *foedus*. Alas these later treaties, at least before that made between King Theoderic I of the Visigoths and the representatives of Valentinian III in 439, are usually as hypothetical as that of 382 and sometimes even more so. This must, therefore, be a flawed approach. In fact, not a single source, at least

---

[60] Burns (1994), pp. 43–91 for detailed account.

[61] Themistius, *Orations* 16, 'On the Peace'.

[62] Its significance is argued for by, to take a small selection of recent authors, Cesa (1982); (1984); Wolfram (1983). Heather downplays the treaty's importance as a turning point: Heather (1991), p. 158; (1996), p. 138.

[63] See, e.g. Heather (1991), pp. 158–65 (terms), 165–81 (discussion).

[64] Cesa (1984), p. 316.

before Jordanes in the mid-sixth century, even refers to this *foedus* with the Goths. Jordanes' narrative of Gothic history, furthermore, casts it in terms of a series of treaties with the Romans, finally resolved by Justinian's conquest of the Gothic kingdom of Italy in the 550s and the final 'treaty': the marriage of the imperial prince Germanus to the Gothic princess Matasuentha.[65] Contemporary sources, by contrast, are unambiguous in talking of the Goths' surrender. The only treaty they refer to is with the Gothic king Athanaric, who finally gave up his struggle in *Gothia* at the end of 380 and was received into the Empire, only to die in Constantinople in January 381.[66] This *foedus* has no bearing on the victors of Adrianople. Athanaric had no authority over them – indeed they were his opponents – and died too soon for this treaty to have any role in ending the Gothic war nearly two years later.

The one absolutely contemporary commentary on the end of the Gothic crisis is Themistius' sixteenth oration, 'A Thanksgiving for the Peace', delivered to Theodosius' court early in 383. Themistius makes it clear that the war had been hard and that the Gothic surrender was something of a relief. This, as Heather and Moncur state, was quite an admission by the standards of late Roman imperial rhetoric.[67] Nevertheless Themistius says explicitly that the Goths *had* surrendered. All contemporary and near contemporary sources talk in similar terms.[68] The counter to this point is usually that official Roman sources might want to make a negotiated treaty sound like an abject surrender. Nevertheless, to start from an assumption that an event took place, although not explicitly mentioned by any source written within 170 years of its putative occurrence, and then to explain away the sources' silence, and read vague references as allusions to the event, is not the soundest historical method. Some narratives were, furthermore, written half a century afterwards, when the Gothic problem had become much more serious. In such circumstances one might expect a certain interest in pointing out where things had gone wrong, in settling the Goths, in the same way as the

---

[65] For Gotho-Roman treaties, see, e.g. *Getica* 19.106, 21.112, 27.139, 28.145, 32.164, 34.177, 57.290.

[66] Oros. 7.34.6–7. Orosius mentions *foedera* with Athanaric and the Persians but not with the Goths in Thrace.

[67] Heather and Moncur (trans.) (2001), pp. 261–4.

[68] *Consularia Constantinopolitana* 420 (*s.a.* 382)

fifth-century historians enhance the significance of the defeat at Adrianople, or indeed in the way that Synesius of Cyrene lamented the settling of the Goths. However, no source adopts this tone with regard to the events of 382. The Goths surrendered to the might of the Roman Empire. In Themistius' oration, it seems difficult to square the idea that the orator had to dress up an embarrassing negotiated peace as an abject surrender with his evident desire to remove the Emperor Gratian from any share of the glory.[69] Surely referring to advice from the western *augustus* would have helped explain the disappointment. Gratian's help had been decisive. If, as seems fairly clear, in early 383 Theodosius' court wished to deny him any credit in ending the Gothic wars this was because, while there might have been less glory to go round, they wished to claim it all for themselves.

Other rhetorical compositions have also been used. One such is Synesius of Cyrene's *On Kingship*, a tirade against the importance of Goths in imperial circles probably associated with the employment of Alaric's troops, *c.*397.[70] Another is Pacatus' panegyric for Emperor Theodosius after his victory over the usurper Maximus in 388. These are fairly close to events too but neither makes any mention of a treaty, even though the whole point of Synesius' work is to criticise the presence of the Goths within the Empire. These sources do, however, comment on the role of the Goths and it is these remarks that have been the basis for the reconstruction of the terms of the 'treaty of 382'.

The circumstances are important. In the later phases of the war, the Roman strategy of blockade combined with the difficulties of the terrain to force the Goths to break up into smaller groups in order to find food: most interpreters seem agreed on this. Fritigern disappears from the record, either killed in a skirmish or precisely because he was now no more than one of many leaders. Thus the peace was made with a series of small groups rather than with a unified group. The war was ended by a series of *deditiones* rather than a single *foedus*.[71] This point is profoundly important for any understanding of the

---

[69] Heather and Moncur (trans.) (2001), pp. 257–9.

[70] Cameron, A. D. and Long (1993); Heather (1988a). Alternative (if probably less plausible) readings, however, put this in 400, connected with Gaïnas and Tribigild's rebellions.

[71] Cesa (1994a), p. 44. See also Burns (1994), p. 75, for similar points.

subsequent history of the Goths. The processes of peace-making are significant too. Heather points out that the war did not end with barbarian kings being thrown to the beasts or with vast numbers of Goths being sold in the slave markets of the east.[72] Yet nor did Theodosius meet with any Gothic leaders to sign the 'treaty'. He remained in Constantinople and sent Saturninus, a survivor of Adrianople, to clear up the situation.[73] This is quite different from Roman practice in dealing with sovereign groups, such as in Valens' treaty with Athanaric or Valentinian's with Macrianus. It was indeed a war that ended with a whimper rather than a bang, and any terms may have been different from, and better than, those granted to other barbarians, but that does not imply a single treaty between equal parties.

All this has a crucial impact upon the issue of Gothic sovereignty within the Empire. Even sophisticated interpreters of these events admit that no Gothic leader is acknowledged either in the treaty or in the events of the next decade and more.[74] Isidore of Seville, writing in the early seventh century had to backdate Alaric's 'kingship' to the early 380s in order to close this gap.[75] A treaty with a sovereign group with no acknowledged leaders seems most unlikely. Roman dealings with such bodies tended towards the recognition – sometimes the creation – of leaders, not their denial. This in itself poses a huge problem for the traditional view. Just as the peace was made with smaller groups of Goths, so the Goths must have been settled in small units in Thrace. Some, but not necessarily all, may have retained their social hierarchies.[76]

Gothic military service after Adrianople is problematic. The sources talk of Goths in the Roman army, Gothic farmers and the granting of land to the Goths.[77] These snippets have led historians to suppose that, when needed, the Goths supplied semi-regular allied contingents 'en masse'[78] to the Roman army. There is no clear

---

[72] Heather (2005), p. 184.   [73] Themistius, *Orations* 16.208b–209b.

[74] Heather (1991), pp. 180–1.   [75] See below, pp. 202–6.

[76] Cesa (1994a), pp. 44–5.

[77] Gothic soldiers: *Latin Panegyrics* 2.22.3, 2.32.4 (Pacatus' Panegyric for Theodosius); *Not. Dig.* orr. 5–6. Gothic farming/land-owning: *Latin Panegyrics* 2.22.3 (Pacatus' Panegyric for Theodosius); Themistius, *Orations* 34.22. Synesius, *Kingship* 25. Also implicit in Themistius, *Orations* 16.211d (as Heather (1991), p. 159).

[78] Peter Heather repeatedly uses this phrase: e.g. Heather (1991), p. 164; (1996), p. 139.

evidence to support this.[79] The context of Synesius' work and the fact that it post-dates the end of the Gothic war by over a decade, belonging to the period after Alaric's acquisition of military authority in the Balkans, make it an unreliable source for the events of 382. So too does its generally vague language. Synesius is saying that these people should never have been allowed into the Empire as they will (the threat lies in the future) cause trouble.[80] None of the references to Goths in the army automatically force one to see them as semi-regular allied contingents. There is as much evidence to support the notion that they were drafted into regular units. It may be best to adopt Liebeschuetz's suggestion that units described as *foederati* in the sources after Adrianople refer, not to allied contingents provided by autonomous or semi-autonomous barbarian groups, but to regular units recruited entirely from barbarian recruits.[81]

The Goths were accepted into the Empire and settled. There may have been new and unusual elements of this settlement. Rather than being sold off into slavery, or made tenants, they appear to have been granted land, probably in deserted areas, and to have paid taxes, perhaps, as Cesa says, as a sort of privileged *laeti*.[82] Possibly citizenship was envisaged, at least for those who served in the army.[83] It is difficult, and unnecessary, to view them as having been settled as one group in a particular area.[84] Some became farmers; others entered the army. In fact the recruitment problems after Adrianople meant the enlistment of large numbers of Goths.[85] Whole units and even armies could be thought of as Gothic. Gothic commanders rose to pre-eminence. But the '*foedus* of 382' did not settle a semi-independent people in Roman territory or mark a massive constitutional change in imperial history. That would be to go far beyond the evidence. The

---

[79] The only evidence is Jordanes, *Getica* 28.145, whose statement that the Goths served in the Roman army *velut unum corpus* (as though in a single body) is demonstrably untrue. Jordanes' whole work aimed at portraying the Goths as a unified people.

[80] Cameron, A. D. and Long (1993), p. 110.

[81] Liebeschuetz (1991), pp. 34–6; see, further, below, pp. 191–2. See also Cesa (1994a), pp. 89–90.

[82] Cesa (1994a), p. 45.

[83] Themistius, *Orations* 16.211d, with Sivan (1987), pp. 762–3 and nn. 17–18.

[84] Cesa (1994a), pp. 44–5, recognises this diversity in the circumstances and careers of the Goths settled in 382, but appears not to appreciate the difficulties that this poses for her reconstruction of later Gothic history.

[85] Liebeschuetz (1991), pp. 25, 26–31.

'*foedus* of 382' is a historian's construct. Once settled, we lose sight of the Tervingi on Roman soil.[86] When we next hear of Goths in the Roman Empire they are soldiers, like Alaric's followers, largely drawn from Gothic settlers to be sure, but not identifiable in any simple or straightforward way with the large group which crossed the Danube under Fritigern and Alaviv. In the silent years between 382 and 395 the nature of 'the Goths' altered profoundly.

---

[86] Cp. Sivan (1987), p. 765. The next mention of the Goths is Zosimus' garbled account of Theodosius' quashing of barbarian banditry in Macedonia in 391: Zos. 4.48–9. Claudian, *Against Rufinus* 1, refers to a rising of barbarians instigated by Rufinus, but it is all very garbled. Burns (1994), p. 102, suggests that a speech put in Alaric's mouth by Claudian (*Gothic War* 524; *Sixth Consulship of Honorius* 107–8) refers to the same incident (and would put Alaric in the frame as the bandits' leader) but, while possible, this is by no means clear.

7

THE CRISIS OF THE EMPIRE, 382–410

·

THE USURPATIONS OF MAGNUS MAXIMUS
AND EUGENIUS AND THE DEATH OF
THEODOSIUS, 383–395[1]

In 383 things went wrong for Emperor Gratian. The British army raised one of its commanders to the purple, a Spaniard called Magnus Maximus. Maximus crossed to Gaul and confronted Gratian at Paris. Abandoned by his troops, the emperor was killed, by a ruse, at Lyon (25 August).[2] The reasons for the break-up of Gratian's regime are unclear. The emperor had not been unsuccessful, winning military laurels against the *Alamanni* and playing his part in suppressing the Gothic revolt. He married his half-sister to Theodosius, evidently aware that the division of the Empire only worked when family links united the emperors. Gratian's management of imperial patronage seems to have been at stake, perhaps unsurprising given that at his death he was still only twenty-three. Contemporaries wrote that Gratian was intelligent and possessed many qualities but had never

---

[1] For other (usually rather different) narratives of the events of this chapter, see also Blockley (1998); Heather (1991), pp. 193–224; (2005), pp. 191–258; Wolfram (1988), pp. 139–71. Paschoud's extensive commentary to his edition and translation of books 5 and 6 of Zosimus' *New History* (Paschoud, ed. and trans. (1986); (1989)) is invaluable. Note throughout this chapter that Zosimus is heavily reliant on Eunapius and Olympiodorus. I have, however, only cited separately the fragments of these two authors that are not found in Zosimus' *New History*.

[2] Oros. 7.34.10; Soc. 5.11; Soz. 7.13; Theodoret, *Ecclesiastical History* 5.12; Zos. 4.35.2–6 (mistaking Lugdunum for Singidunum).

been taught how to rule, or shown himself willing to learn.[3] What this meant in practice might be illustrated by Gratian's showing undue preference to Alan troops, presumably raised from barbarians defeated during the Gothic crisis, thus alienating his regulars.[4] In the north-west, where the revolt broke out, unrest might have been caused by his increasingly frequent residence in Italy. In 380 the western court moved to Milan and the influence of the Gallic faction based around Gratian's tutor Ausonius appears to have ended.[5] The importance of imperial presence in Gaul has been mentioned. Also surely noticeable in the west was a cooling of relations between the imperial courts. In early 383 Theodosius made his son Arcadius co-emperor without Gratian's permission. The eastern court was at this point gradually writing Gratian out of recent history.[6] Gratian's style of rule, his removal from the strategically crucial north-west and his alienation from the Constantinopolitan court made the time ripe for revolt by Maximus, apparently an old colleague of Theodosius.

Maximus reigned over Britain, Gaul and Spain, from Trier, for five years, briefly being recognised as a colleague by Theodosius and Valentinian II. Eventually, having invaded Italy and forced Valentinian to flee to Constantinople, he incurred Theodosius' wrath. Theodosius defeated Maximus' troops twice in the Balkans and the usurper was killed at Aquileia. Although Maximus' family and immediate sup-porters were slain, there was no purge and the defeated armies were incorporated into Theodosius' forces. Valentinian II was reinstated but placed under the tutelage of his Frankish master of the soldiers, Arbogast, who had dispatched Victor, Maximus' son.[7]

In 392 the hapless Valentinian died mysteriously, aged only twenty-one. Arbogast claimed that he had killed himself; contem-poraries suspected he had been murdered. The general appointed a rhetorician named Eugenius to be Valentinian's successor. Theodosius assembled a huge army to confront the usurper, including large numbers of Gothic recruits. On 5–6 September 394 Arbogast and Eugenius were defeated in a terrible battle at the river Frigidus and

---

[3] Amm. Marc. 31.10.18; Eunapius, fr. 50.   [4] Zos. 4.35.2–3: Burns (1994), p. 94.

[5] Few of Ausonius' associates held office after 380/1. On these aristocrats and their careers, see Matthews (1975), pp. 56–87.

[6] Heather and Moncur (trans.) (2001), pp. 213–16.

[7] On these events: Oros. 7.35.1–6; Soc. 5.12, 5.14; Soz. 7.14; Theodoret, *Ecclesiastical History* 5.14–15; Zos. 4.42–7.

the western army was slaughtered. Theodosius entered Italy in triumph over western rebels for the second time in six years. Shortly afterwards, in January 395, he died at Milan, leaving the west to the younger of his two sons, Honorius, and the east to the elder, Arcadius.[8]

Theodosius' death produced crisis in the western Roman Empire. The fourth-century imperial system relied upon adult emperors who moved about the Empire, distributing and redistributing their patronage and demonstrating through military success their ability to defend both the Empire from the barbarians and, by implication, themselves from Roman rivals. Theodosius' death changed this situation decisively. The problems that had arisen in the west since Valentinian I's death were in no small measure attributable to the emperors' youth. Gratian acceded at the age of sixteen and, after Maximus' execution, Valentinian II became sole western *augustus* at seventeen. In such circumstances, domination by favourites and the related mismanagement of patronage are not difficult to understand.

Now the western Empire was ruled by a ten-year-old and the east by a seventeen-year-old. The governance of the whole Empire by youths had not happened since before the third-century civil wars. Gratian and Valentinian II's inexperience had been moderated to some extent by their adult relatives or colleagues. Quite apart from a child's inability to win battles, the problem lay in the domination of the emperor by Palatine factions, whose grip on power depended upon their retention of exclusive access to the imperial presence.[9] As Gratian's fate had shown, the end of evenly distributed patronage caused stress. A skilful military commander controlling the imperial person might appear to rule as effectively as an adult emperor, but there was a crucial legitimacy gap, all too able to be exploited by rivals. When the military commander was a non-Roman, this problem was exaggerated. Exacerbating all of these matters, however, was the fact that the western court remained in Italy at Milan, apart from a brief sojourn in Vienne in southern Gaul. The Gauls had been at the heart of Roman politics and the main western capital had been in Gaul, at Trier, since the mid-third century. For the first time in over a century they were cut off from an active role in, and easy

[8] On these events: Eunapius, frr. 58, 60; Oros. 7.35.10–23; Soc. 5.25–6; Soz. 7.22, 7.24, 7.29; Theodoret, *Ecclesiastical History* 5.24–5; Zos. 4.42–7.
[9] Lütkenhaus (1998), pp. 12–16.

access to, the centre of government.[10] The political history of the next two decades underlined all of these points as court factions in Italy and in Constantinople seized control over the young emperors. The incapability of both Honorius and Arcadius meant that they were unable to escape from this domination even when they reached maturity. Where they can be discerned, Honorius' individual actions were invariably ill-judged and Arcadius' early death in 408 only resulted in another minority, that of his son Theodosius II. Ironically, as has often been remarked upon, whilst the female scions of the Theodosian dynasty were strong-willed and decisive figures their male relatives were uniformly feeble, yet were the only family-members permitted to rule.[11]

Problems immediately arose as the general Stilicho, left in charge of Honorius, claimed to have been given authority over Arcadius too.[12] The eastern court, where the Palatine official Rufinus had established control, denied this, needless to say, and, combined with disputes over the strategically vital Balkan prefecture, this produced conflict. Within this context a Gothic commander called Alaric rose to pre-eminence.

ALARIC'S GOTHS

The origins of Alaric the Goth, probably the second-most famous barbarian of late antiquity (Attila the Hun surely claiming first place), are obscure. Claudian claims that he was born on Peuke, an island in the Danube.[13] There is little solid basis for the idea that he was born into a leading, let alone royal, Gothic family, beyond the alliterative similarity of his name and those of Alaviv and Alatheus, Tervingian and Greuthungian leaders respectively in 376.[14] His pre-existing leadership has also been suggested on the basis of the hierarchical tribal structure of the Goths[15] although there is no substantial

[10] Ward-Perkins (1998), p. 391, also perceives the importance of the change of imperial residence. I cannot, however, possibly see this move as representing the emperors being 'forced to scuttle back from the frontiers to cities which were safer'.

[11] On the women of the family, see Holum (1982); Oost (1968).

[12] Eunapius, fr. 62; Zos. 6.1–4. Stilicho's claim is made manifest in the poems by his propagandist Claudian, *Against Rufinus*, esp. 2, lines 5–6.

[13] *The Sixth Consulate of Honorius*, line 105.

[14] Wolfram (1975). Heather (1991), p. 31, n. 47, for critique of this notion.

[15] Heather (1991), pp. 196–7.

evidence for such a structure surviving under Roman rule in the
Balkans. The idea that he was a king at all before 400 is based upon
later sources and few scholars claim this any longer.[16] His first certain
appearance in history is as the commander of Gothic units under
Theodosius against Eugenius and Arbogast in 394. Zosimus and
Socrates Scholasticus (presumably following Eunapius) state that
Alaric had been given command of allied barbarian troops in this
campaign.[17] He was not alone in this sort of status. Gothic and
barbarian troop commanders abound at the end of the fourth
century: Gaïnas, Tribigild, and Sarus to name but three. Others still
commanded armed forces outside the imperial confines.

The nature of Alaric's forces has been much debated. Some see
them as the Gothic tribe or people who had entered the Empire in
376.[18] This is difficult to square with the sheer profusion of Gothic
groups around 400. Others have therefore advanced the opinion that
Alaric's force and those of the other Gothic leaders were warbands or
armies recruited by Rome, probably on a short-term basis, in the
aftermath of Adrianople. Although led by Goths these were polyglot
in composition.[19] A third, more radical view envisages the troops
commanded by Alaric (and the others) as Goths recruited into regular
auxiliary units of the Roman army of a new, if not unrecognisable,
type.[20] It has also been argued that this 'nation or army' debate is
incapable of resolution on the basis of the evidence as we have it.[21] It
is certainly difficult to resolve from descriptions of the Goths'
activities. The sources are patchy and cryptic and armies in this period
(as in most later eras) took their families with them when on the
move. Concerns over this had led the western army to mutiny and
proclaim Julian *augustus* in 361.[22] Barbarian recruits brought their
families along. Thus references to wagon trains (assumed to contain
women and children) do not demonstrate that the Goths were a
'people' any more than they prove what sort of army (Roman
regulars or federate barbarians) they were. Heather cites references to
Gothic carts (not said to contain women or children) as decisive in
showing that Alaric possessed a 'wagon train used to transport families

[16] See below, pp. 202–6.
[17] Soc. 7.10; Zos. 5.5.4. Above, p. 185, n. 86 for his possible involvement in a
rebellion during Theodosius' campaign against Maximus.
[18] Heather (1991).   [19] Liebeschuetz (1992).   [20] Burns (1994).
[21] Kulikowski (2002b).   [22] Amm. Marc. 20.4.10–11.

and goods. This seems to confirm that we are dealing with a sizeable social phenomenon.'[23] All armies have wagon trains. The sources similarly permit more than one interpretation of the nature of Alaric's force on the basis of their activities and demands.

I have tended towards the interpretation of Alaric's followers as a military force rather than a tribe or people on the move in search of lands to settle. Their emergence from formal units of the eastern army seems clear enough. Zosimus, although an often garbled source, makes a number of references to Gothic troops in what seem clearly to be regular regiments.[24] That the Goths served independently under their own leaders by the terms of the so-called 'treaty of 382' finds no clear support. Pacatus can be understood as referring to regulars just as easily as to irregular allies.[25] Alaric generally desired, and often received, Roman military rank. His career, as Peter Heather has remarked, is unusual but one cannot say that there was no point in his career when Alaric pursued a normal Roman military career.[26] Such a statement depends on controversial readings of the sources – *all* interpretations of the career of Alaric's Goths (including this one) depend upon controversial readings of the sources. If Alaric operated in Stilicho's service in 405–8 (this at least is fairly uncontroversial) then his career at that point is not abnormal. Furthermore, there were two periods (397–400 and 402–5) when Alaric's forces were simply posted somewhere and we hear little of them. This too might be considered normal. About half of Alaric's recorded activity before his final break with Honorius' government in 408 can be read as a fairly normal military career. What made Alaric untypical was the political grey area in which he found himself and, of course, his and his followers' Gothic origin, which posed problems as the result of political events at the Constantinopolitan court.

Even if his followers formed a tribe or people, they never dispersed, settled and farmed, though some authorities see this as their aim. Had they done so, either during the three years between 397 and 400 or during those between 402 and 405, they would have had to spread themselves across the countryside, amongst the land holdings of

---

[23] Heather (1991), p. 194 citing Claudian, *Against Rufinus* 2, lines 124 ff.; *Fourth Consulate of Honorius*, line 466; *Consulate of Stilicho* 1, lines 94–5; *On the Gothic War*, lines 604 ff. Claudian does refer to the capture of Gothic wives and children at *Gothic War*, lines 85 ff.

[24] Zos. 4.45.3, 5.13.2.   [25] Above, pp. 183–4.   [26] Heather (1991), pp. 199–200.

Roman farmers (these interpretations usually talk of about 20,000 Gothic warriors and their dependants, so over 10,000 family units). This would have involved considerably greater dispersion than the usual billeting of troops and made it easy for the Roman army, even in this period of recruitment problems, to mop them up. Furthermore, it would have been difficult for Alaric to maintain coherence within his group, or to call them away from their farms to an insecure future. The practicalities of so doing seem not to have troubled supporters of the 'people on the move' interpretation.

Other problems (in my view decisive) for the 'tribal' interpretation are posed by the very proliferation of Gothic groups within the Empire at this time – often described in exactly the same terms as Alaric's following – and also by Zosimus' reference to Alaric commanding 'only the barbarians Theodosius had given him' during his first campaign against Stilicho.[27] The latter reference seems to preclude Alaric's position at the head of his Goths stemming from a long-standing kingship over them, a constitutional position as head of semi-independent Gothic contingent based upon the mythical 'treaty of 382', or even a position near the top of an independent Gothic tribal hierarchy. Eastern writers refer to Alaric's force as his Goths or as his barbarians but there is little to choose between these descriptions and the same sources' accounts of Tribigild's army.[28] Zosimus apparently opposes barbarians to Roman troops in his account[29] but in so doing he seems only to be distinguishing Roman units from those composed of barbarians, with nothing implicit about the barbarians' irregular status. Indeed his reference to Tribigild's command of barbarian *alae* (cavalry regiments) suggests the opposite.[30] This would support the arguments of Burns and Liebeschuetz about the nature of Gothic 'federate' regiments after Adrianople.[31]

Zosimus describes Rufinus ordering Alaric to advance against Stilicho 'with his barbarians and men of all origins'.[32] Similarly, Stilicho planned to send Alaric's 'army of barbarians' alongside

[27] Zos. 5.5.4.   [28] Below, pp. 200–01.

[29] As Paschoud (ed. and trans.) (1986), p. 90, notes, he opposes *barbaroi* to *stratiotai*.

[30] Zos. 5.13.4, confirmed by Claudian, *Against Eutropius* 2, line 176.

[31] Burns (1994), pp. 92–111; Liebeschuetz (1991), pp. 34–6.

[32] Zos. 5.5.4. Zosimus conflates the campaigns of 395 and 397, associating Rufinus with both. This might cast doubt on his testimony.

Roman troops to fight Constantine 'III' in Gaul.[33] In Italy in 408, too, Alaric was joined by mutinous barbarians recruited from other bands and by Roman slaves.[34] This too must have made his force more ethnically mixed than the traditional interpretations allow.

However, the interpretation of Alaric's Goths as a warband of diverse background also requires special pleading. Claudian is unambiguous in referring in his tirades against Stilicho's enemies to the Goths as a barbarian people (*gens*) and especially as the descendants of those who crossed the Danube in 376.[35] Synesius, in *On Kingship*, makes similar equations. Whilst it is hard to make these statements support a direct equation between Alaric's forces and the 'treaty Goths' of 382, it is just as difficult to square them with an interpretation of Alaric's force as a polyglot warband or Roman army. One must therefore agree with Heather to the extent that what struck contemporaries about Alaric's troops, and what posed problems for Alaric, was not their diverse origins or their rebellious nature as Roman units but their very Gothicness. Alaric always commanded some non-Gothic troops and after 408, when dissatisfied barbarian recruits and others joined his army, his force became genuinely polyglot. Between 395 and 408, however, it seems best to see Alaric's troops as recruited predominantly from Goths. This allowed Claudian and Synesius to stress their non-Roman identity and decry the fact that they had been mistakenly allowed into the Empire. This implies nothing about the terms of the 382 settlement or those under which the individual Goths had joined the army. Alaric, like Tribigild, commanded an army mostly composed of Gothic units. They were therefore thought of by contemporaries as 'the Goths' and probably ought to be treated by us in the same way.

The Goths of the crisis of 376–82 had come from two hitherto distinct groups but, given that contemporary commentators never again use the names Tervingi and Greuthungi for them,[36] it is reasonable to argue that the two groups fused when they were settled. The formation of a Gothic identity therefore involved the decision by people to stress a hitherto very general level of ethnicity over one that had previously been more important.[37] Given the

---

[33] Zos. 5.31.5.   [34] Zos. 5.35.6.   [35] *Gothic War*, lines 490–1, 533.

[36] But see *Not. Dig.* or. 6, for a unit of *Tervingi* recruited before the later 380s.

[37] Heather (1996), p. 100, discussing Athanaric's response to the Greuthungian retreat from the Huns, refers to the judge's wariness about this influx of 'foreign Goths'.

absence of evidence for any Gothic polity within the Empire, this decision was more likely to have been made in the context of Gothic recruitment into the army. In the formation of this identity, other groups previously seen as separate might also have been incorporated. The army was quite accustomed to adopting barbarian identities. Further, the name *Visi*, later (as Visigoths) to become the usual eastern Roman appellation of the political unit that emerged from Alaric's army, is first attested in the *Notitia Dignitatum*.[38] Gothic identity might have been hardened in the campaigns of the following decades but it is worth remembering that it was in important senses a recent and somewhat artificial creation.

Whatever the precise details of their internal composition, between 395 and 418/19, and especially after 408, Alaric and his successors' Goths were usually employed, and acted on their own behalf, as an armed force. Within these parameters it seems best to treat them functionally as an army rather than as a people. That said, political events and the situation in which the group found itself, again especially after 408 (when paradoxically it probably became more mixed in origin), led to the Goths' increasing cohesion as something more. If Alaric only commanded a military force (with the usual baggage train and camp followers) in 395, by 418 his eventual successor Wallia was leading something more socially closely knit. Whether or not it can justifiably be called a people, it was something different.

ALARIC, STILICHO AND COURT POLITICS, 395–397

Alaric and his troops in the Balkans might never have earned their place in the history books had it not been for the problems caused by Theodosius' death and the youth of his successors. Soon after Theodosius died, Alaric took his troops from the army in Italy and back to the Balkans, where he rebelled and harried territory around Constantinople.[39] The Balkans had clearly been sinking into a state of some turmoil in the 390s, of which the infamous riot and massacre at Thessalonica in 390 might have been just one example.[40]

---

[38] *Not. Dig.* or. 5.
[39] On the events described in this paragraph, see: Claudian, *Against Rufinus* 2; Eunapius, fr. 64 ; Soc. 6.1; Soz. 8.1; Zos. 5.1–7.
[40] Kulikowski (2006), pp. 159–60, 165.

As a result Alaric became a focus for other discontents as well as his Goths. His may have been a ploy to blackmail the eastern court and it may have worked. What happened in 395 is unclear. Sources hostile to Rufinus – Claudian and Zosimus – imply that Rufinus paid Alaric off, and may even have used his forces to block Stilicho's attempt to use the Balkan trouble to impose his will on the east. Yet before the two could square up against each other, Arcadius (presumably acting as a mouthpiece for Rufinus) despatched an order for Stilicho to return to the eastern Empire those regiments that had marched west in 394. Burns argues that Stilicho must have been on the verge of defeat to have agreed to Arcadius' demand.[41] Heather points out that the eastern and western units that had fought each other so bloodily the previous year cannot have made a harmonious force.[42] Stymied in his operations against Alaric and in his efforts to attach Illyricum to the western Empire, Stilicho complied, but Rufinus paid a terrible price. Met by the emperor and Rufinus just outside Constantinople, Gaïnas, commanding the regiments ordered back east, fell upon the chief minister and killed him. If this was Stilicho's plot, however, it failed. Gaïnas was outmanoeuvred by Eutropius, a eunuch of the bedchamber, and rewarded only with his old command as *magister militum* in Thrace, which Burns suggests might have been purely nominal at this point, with no actual troops to command.[43] No wonder he felt resentment. Meanwhile, Alaric's forces moved to Greece, whether paid off by Rufinus and then, after his fall, finding themselves out in the cold, or moving there independently of any authority once it became clear that, especially after the return of the eastern field army, Constantinople was too well defended. Either way, they seem to have caused considerable trouble there for the next two years.

MILITARY WITHDRAWAL FROM THE NORTH

These years, and particularly Maximus' and Arbogast's revolts, were crucial for the history of Gaul and Britain. Theodosius recruited barbarian troops to defend the Balkan frontiers whilst he attacked Maximus and later stripped those borders for the civil war against Eugenius. Equally, Maximus, Arbogast and Stilicho withdrew regular regiments from the diocese of the Gauls, and might have similarly

---

[41] Burns (1994), p. 154.   [42] Heather (1991), p. 202.   [43] Burns (1994), p. 155.

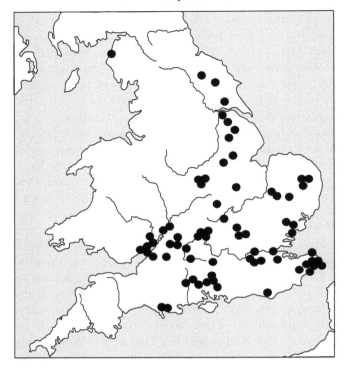

Map 13 Distribution of military metalwork in later fourth-century Britain

used barbarians to defend the frontiers. Britain in particular was
reorganised. Metalwork associated with the regular army is found
only across the lowland zones, the region covered by the spread of
villas, with only a handful of items being found on the line of
Hadrian's Wall (map 13).[44] This is very curious. Military metalwork
is often found in regions where the army was not stationed,
northern Germany for example, but it is strange to find it absent
from areas where the army *was* deployed. Other forms of metalwork
with no particular military association show a similar distribution;
the villa zone corresponds roughly to that covered by cereal agriculture and thus where chance finds are more possible. Yet the
highland zone's forts have frequently been well excavated and the
problem is only compounded by the fact that recent excavations

[44] Böhme (1986).

reveal that the Hadrian's Wall forts were occupied in this period and indeed beyond.[45] It might be that the highland zone and the northern frontier troops were entirely separated, in material cultural terms, from the lowland zone and its army. This is possible but unlikely when compared with the Gallic situation or the Saxon Shore. These distributions may imply that the regular army was withdrawn to a line roughly from the Severn estuary to the east Yorkshire wolds (fourth-century fortified posts along the Fosse way have, for example, been noted[46]), with defence in the highlands being given over to regional leaders (possibly former commanders of local *limitanei*), legitimising their political and military power. Magnus Maximus is found, as Maxen Gwledig, at the origin of many later Welsh dynasties and Roman titles were at least claimed by highland rulers.[47] Such a reorganisation might also explain the reoccupation of hillforts along the border between the two zones. Some areas of the west coast may have been given over to Irish settlers to defend.[48]

It may have been at this time that Saxon mercenaries were introduced into Britain, again to shore up the island's defences in Maximus' absence. This argument depends upon an identification of the 'proud tyrant' mentioned in Gildas' *On the Ruin and Conquest of Britain* with Maximus, rather than with a semi-legendary (at least) character called 'Vortigern' referred to in later sources.[49] The technical case for this identification is argued in detail in the Appendix. If the *tyrannus* who settled the Saxons was Maximus this makes much sense in the context of the apparent military reorganisations in Britain and against the background of Theodosius' deployment of barbarian garrisons to cover his back during his wars against the west.[50] In this reading the Saxon revolt would occur later, after the economy and socio-political structure of the diocese collapsed around 400, as described in chapter 11, and especially after the fall of Constantine 'III's' regime (see below), which is also plausible.

---

[45] Dark, K. R. (1992); Wilmott (1997).   [46] Johnson (1980), pp. 118–19.
[47] Alcock (1971), pp. 96–8.   [48] Rance (2001); below, p. 373.
[49] *DEB* 23. Woolf, A. (2003) has recently argued (on not entirely dissimilar grounds) that the *superbus tyrannus* might be Constantine 'III'.
[50] A curious comment (*HB* 31) assigns the reception of the Saxons to Gratian's reign (in AP 347, i.e. 374 AD). Nevertheless, little faith can be placed in the *Historia*'s account of late Roman history, which is usually very consistent in dating the arrival of the Saxons to 428.

However, the earliest material culture clearly derived from northern Germany, and thus associated with 'Saxon' incomers, dates to the second quarter of the fifth century. This objection can be overruled if one considers more closely the interpretation of material culture. We can leave aside the fact that some of the supposed traits associated with the Anglo-Saxons are probably not imports from *barbaricum*;[51] some material – artefactual, structural and ritual – is unmistakably of northern German origin and occurs from about the 430s.[52] It is equally demonstrable that most of the fourth-century material culture once associated with Anglo-Saxon settlers in Britain has been misinterpreted. 'Romano-Saxon Ware', once believed[53] to represent the work of Roman potters employed by Saxon federate settlers, is now seen simply as late Roman British pottery.[54] Fourth-century so-called 'federate metalwork' is official Roman metalwork with no necessary connection with barbarian federates.[55] However, we must view material culture as an active element in social change. Traditionally it simply reflects reality. Thus if Anglo-Saxon material appears in Britain in the 430s and not before, this means that Anglo-Saxon settlement began at that date. But, as we have seen, the barbarians expressed power and status in very Roman fashion and, when settled within the Empire (at least in the west), rarely if ever demonstrated their non-Roman origins through material culture. Why should we expect the Saxons to manifest their cultural difference from Rome when serving an effective imperial system from which they derived notions of status and prestige? The appearance of non-Roman material culture makes more sense in the context of a rebellion within a province where traditional power-structures were breaking down, such as would clearly exist by the 430s. This material culture, interestingly, appears north of the Thames (map 14), rather than in Kent (the area that, by the seventh or eighth century, had appropriated the origin myth based on Gildas). This also makes sense as the area for a military settlement of Saxons by Maximus, close to, but not on, either the frontier line or key lines of communication, just as the Goths were settled on the Garonne in 419.

---

[51] See below, pp. 360–1.   [52] Welch (1993).
[53] Myres (1986) for an extreme statement.
[54] Gillam (1979); Roberts, W. I. (1982).   [55] Haseloff (1973); (1981).

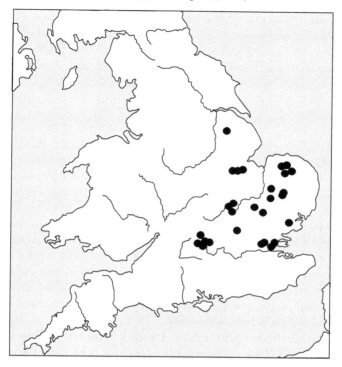

Map 14 Distribution of metalwork from Germany in earlier fifth-century Britain

The units withdrawn from the north-western provinces lost heavily in the battles with Theodosius' eastern troops, especially at the Frigidus. The weakened Rhine army suffered further when an attempt to cross the Rhine and campaign in Frankish territory met with disaster.[56] With the exception of these offensives against the Frankish kings Marcomer and Sunno it is difficult to see any effective re-establishment of imperial authority in northern Gaul after 388. There was hardly any time for governmental structures to be reorganised after Maximus' usurpation before troops were again withdrawn for Eugenius and Arbogast's rebellion. Thereafter the north was seemingly left as a political twilight zone. Stilicho's 395 campaign in the Rhineland was a flying visit, which did little more than bolster the frontier with treaties with the Frankish and

[56] Renatus Profuturus Frigeridus, at *LH* 2.9.

Alamannic rulers just across the river.[57] Doubtless there was no deliberate abandonment of northern Gaul[58] but before long, Stilicho too was withdrawing troops from the north-western provinces to face the threats from Radagaisus and Alaric and to pursue his ambitions with regard to the eastern Empire.

ALARIC'S INVASION OF ITALY, 397–405

In 397 Stilicho tried again to wrest territory from the east, in the Peloponnese, and was again fought to a standstill by Alaric, who apparently received the title of *magister militum* in Illyricum from the eastern court at about this time and took his troops there from Greece.[59] For the next few years Alaric and his men were quiet. One reason for the failure of Stilicho's operation was the declaration in favour of Constantinople by Gildo, the master of both services in Africa (and brother of the Firmus who had rebelled in the 370s). Gildo withheld the grain fleet and caused much alarm in Italy[60] but was defeated by a force led by his other brother Mascazel. Rather than leaving any further hostages to fortune, Stilicho had Mascazel drowned soon afterwards.[61]

Meanwhile, Eutropius achieved military success against Huns invading Asia Minor. Then trouble broke out. The details need not detain us but the main events are nevertheless important.[62] An uprising took place in Asia Minor and Tribigild, the Gothic officer sent to quell the disturbance, instead joined the rebels. After the Roman force sent to combat Tribigild was defeated Gaïnas made a deal with the rebel, joined forces with him and in July 399 blackmailed Arcadius into dismissing Eutropius. Arcadius exiled Eutropius and acceded to another change in the faction controlling the court. This time Gaïnas could take charge, but not for long. In July 400 the citizens of Constantinople rose up and slaughtered the Goths stationed in the city, perhaps a fifth of Gaïnas' army. Arcadius

---

[57] Claudian, *Fourth Consulate of Honorius*, lines 439–58.   [58] Bleckmann (1997).

[59] On the unravelling of Stilicho's two campaigns (395 and 397) from confused sources, see, above all, Cameron, A. D. (1970), pp. 474–7.

[60] *CTh* 14.15.3–4.

[61] On Gildo's revolt, see Claudian, *Gildonic War*; Oros. 36.2–13; Paulinus of Milan, *Life of Ambrose* 51; Zos. 5.11. Cameron, A. D. (1970), pp. 93–123. For useful recent discussion, see Blackhurst (2004).

[62] On these events, see: Eunapius, frr. 67–69; Soc. 6.6; Soz. 8.4; Zos. 5.11–22.

called upon yet another Gothic officer, Fravitta, then *magister militum per orientem* at Antioch, to lead the campaign against Gaïnas' remaining troops and at the beginning of January 401 Gaïnas' head was paraded through the streets of the eastern capital. Gaïnas had fled north and been killed by a Hunnic leader called Uldin. The appearance on the scene of the Huns as a power to be reckoned with is noteworthy.

These events are important because they must bear upon the fact that in late 401 Alaric left Illyricum and invaded the west.[63] Alaric had held a military command under Rufinus and Eutropius. After Eutropius' fall his position might have been secure, under a fellow Goth, Gaïnas, but after the uprising of July 400, and especially after Gaïnas' death, things surely began to look rather different. It is possible that in the change of regime he lost his command as *magister militum*. Burns argues that the east returned *Pannonia* to the west in 399/400, leaving Alaric in a political grey zone, without a command in an area now commanded by his former enemy, Stilicho.[64] This proposal is attractive but the evidence, the *Notitia Dignitatum*, is insecure.[65] Nevertheless the political changes in Constantinople presented Alaric with serious problems. The regime's anti-Gothic stance, emphasised by Fravitta's murder soon after his success, looked set to place Alaric and his Goths clearly on the wrong side of Roman ideology about barbarians and legitimate authority. Indeed, such ideology had been deployed by Synesius of Cyrene to criticise Alaric's position not long before.[66] The loss of his title would be serious for Alaric, ending his rights to food and payment for his men from the Illyrian territories within which he was stationed. It would also terminate, at least in Roman terms, the legitimacy of his command over his troops.

Alaric's attack on Italy in late 401 caught Stilicho on the hop.[67] Stilicho had been dealing with frontier issues in *Raetia*. Hurrying back, he confronted Alaric in two indecisive battles at Pollentia and at Verona (402). Stilicho had the better of these encounters and

[63] Modern authorities of all persuasions agree on this. E.g. Burns (1994), p. 178; Heather (1991), pp. 206–8; (1996), p. 146; Wolfram (1988), p. 150.

[64] Burns (1994), pp. 166–78.

[65] Kulikowski (2000a) for problems of using the *Not. Dig.* too precisely for the constitutional history of the Empire.

[66] Cameron, A. D. and Long (1993); Heather (1988a).

[67] Claudian, *Gothic War*, lines 267–404.

has often been criticised by historians enamoured of the Roman Empire for not finishing off Alaric. His decision to permit Alaric's withdrawal into *Pannonia* makes more sense if we see Alaric's force entering Stilicho's service, and Stilicho's victory being less total than Claudian would have us believe. The evidence is, nevertheless, unclear. Discussing the events of 405, Zosimus referred to an agreement reached between Stilicho and Alaric;[68] Alaric was clearly in western service at that point. This agreement probably dates back to the conclusion of the 402 campaign. On balance, it makes more sense to assume that Alaric – whose career, and that of his army, is obscure between 402 and 405 – was given an official title and stationed in *Pannonia*, probably by now returned to the western Empire, than to argue that he and his Goths spent three years there independently, without either Empire attempting to remove them and without this loss of strategically vital territory to barbarian control exciting any notice in the (admittedly sparse) contemporary sources.[69]

ALARIC, KING OF THE GOTHS?

Alaric's various titles during these turbulent years are of central importance to the emergence of non-Roman polities on imperial soil. Traditionally, in 'people on the move' theories, he was simply king of the Goths, although his elevation is associated with his rebellion in 395, or perhaps his move to *Illyricum* in 397, but he sometimes acquired additional Roman official titles.[70] That Alaric held Roman offices is indisputable even if the precise titles are sometimes unclear. Zosimus and Claudian specify that Rufinus sent Alaric against Stilicho, Zosimus stating plainly that the Roman troops were ordered to give his men free passage.[71] Alaric appears to have been rewarded with a military command in eastern *Illyricum*. Even Claudian's hostile writings make this clear.[72] Following his

---

[68] Zos. 5.26. See also Olympiodorus frr. 1.2, 5.2; Oros. 7.38.2; Zos. 5.29.

[69] A letter from Honorius to his brother in late 404 accuses the eastern court of failing to inform him of depredations in *Illyricum*. Liebeschuetz (1991), p. 65, points out that we know of no barbarians other than Alaric's in the region, but I fail to see why this could not refer to an incursion from *beyond* the frontier. The reference might rather be to the first rumblings of Radagaisus' attack; below, pp. 206–7.

[70] Wolfram (1979a), a heavily 'constitutional' reading of the sources.

[71] Zos. 5.5.   [72] *Gothic War*, lines 535–40.

defeat in 402 Alaric again seems to have been given a formal title. Orosius tellingly calls him a king of the Goths and a count of the Romans at the time of the sack of Rome.[73] Synesius' *On Kingship* was also written in a context where Alaric had received official Roman titles, something he criticises. Later, under his puppet emperor, Attalus, Alaric received further Roman offices, although he was unable to make much use of them.[74] Alaric's titles (and his desire for them) were important; they entitled him to receive food, supplies and equipment from designated military jurisdictions. However, Alaric was not in independent control of these territories. Stilicho sent a Roman official Jovius to accompany him in *Illyricum*.[75] Alaric seems to have been part of the usual imperial administrative system, with separate civil and military offices. He had no say in the raising of taxes or supplies to pay or feed his followers. This must only have added to the problems posed by regime changes in Constantinople.

But was Alaric a king of the Goths? T. S. Burns makes much of the fact that, writing 150 years later, Jordanes said that Alaric took the title of king in the year of the consulate of Stilicho and Aurelianus – 400.[76] If Jordanes is correct, Alaric's decision makes sense in the turbulent context of eastern court politics. Threatened with the loss of his command, Alaric could stand down in favour of an eventual replacement, though during the events of summer 400 to early 401 that might well have been a dangerous option (especially given Fravitta's murder). Otherwise, he could find another source of legitimation. Thus, according to Burns, he took the momentous step of declaring himself *rex* – king – of the Goths.[77] Emperors were sometimes referred to as kings, particularly in the east, where the word *basileus* was the usual word for emperor, but *rex* was never used *officially* as the title of a Roman emperor.[78] It had been something of a dirty word since the Romans had expelled their last king, Tarquin the Proud, many centuries before. A king could only rule a non-Roman people. Most of Alaric's troops were Goths like himself, even if enrolled into formal units. Thus king of the Goths was a suitable title.

This is an interesting and attractive proposition. However, it should be made clear that the evidence does not render it

[73] Oros. 2.3.3. [74] Below, p. 216. [75] Olympiodorus, fr. 1.2.
[76] Burns (1994), p. 176. Jordanes, *Getica* 29.147. [77] Burns (1994), p. 179.
[78] See Fanning (1992); (2002); Gillett (2002a).

indisputable. Jordanes states not that Alaric took the title of king in 400 but that, when Alaric was made king, he decided that the Goths should create their own kingdom and invaded Italy from *Pannonia* in the consulate of Aurelianus and Stilicho. In this, Jordanes seems to have the year wrong, as commentators agree on late 401 (consulship of Fravitta and Flavius Vincentius) for Alaric's entry into Italy. Jordanes does associate Alaric's elevation to the kingship with his invasion of Italy, and says that the Goths' creation of Alaric as king was based upon fear of the Roman court, plausible enough in 400/1, but Jordanes, alas, is rarely a very reliable witness.

Alaric is not often given any title in the Greek sources. Olympiodorus of Thebes calls him *phylarch* and *hegemon* of the Goths in his account of the first decade of the fifth century.[79] He uses both titles for Wallia, who settled the Goths in Aquitaine, and even mentions that the Goths proclaimed him *phylarch*.[80] Orosius, writing very soon after the event, renders these events as Wallia succeeding to the kingdom and being elected king.[81] Prudentius describes Alaric as *geticus tyrannus* in a reference to his attack on Italy.[82] As these references all relate to events after Burns' proposed date for Alaric's assumption of the royal title, this evidence might fit his theory, although Olympiodorus says nothing of the period before 400 and usually gives Alaric no title at all.

Olympiodorus refers to an earlier 'king [*rex*] of a part of the Goths'.[83] This can be read equally as posing problems for Burns' proposal or as adding weight to Olympiodorus' silence on Alaric's title. Eunapius, a contemporary, gives Alaric no title in discussion of the 390s.[84] Following him, Zosimus uses Alaric simply as a metonym for all the forces under his command, which are rarely described at all, except as barbarians. This is interesting but Zosimus, like Jordanes, is a source of uncertain value. Support for the position, however, comes from Priscus of Pannium later referring to the Goths of *Galatia* (Gaul) as having been named after Alaric, implying that they were his creation.[85] Claudian, writing during Stilicho's

---

[79] Olympiodorus frr. 6–7.　　[80] Olympiodorus, frr. 26, 30.　　[81] Oros. 7.43.10.

[82] Prudentius, *Against Symmachus* 2, line 696.

[83] Olympiodorus, fr. 26. This is usually assumed to be Sarus, though he is not named.

[84] Eunapius, fr. 64.1: 'a force of barbarians led by Alaric'; 64.2 'Alaric with his barbarians'.

[85] Priscus, fr. 59.

campaigns, and thus another contemporary – if hardly unbiased – witness, never gives Alaric a title. He links his followers with those who crossed the Danube, refers to the Goths as a *gens*, wheels out all the traditional stereotypes of fur-clad barbarians, and describes Alaric consulting with a Gothic *curia* (council). Nevertheless he never, even disparagingly, refers to Alaric as a king or as having taken such a title (unlike Prudentius), contrasting with his reference to Odotheus, leader of a Gothic attack on the Danube *limes* in 386, as a *rex*.[86] Orosius calls Alaric a king when referring, in typically rhetorical fashion, to the events of the first decade of the fifth century.[87] Once, however, he alludes to Alaric as king of the Goths and count of the Romans, further underlining the fact that Alaric's authority had (or Alaric always intended it to have) a basis in the Roman hierarchy.[88] Usually Orosius gives Alaric no title (unlike his discussions of Athanaric, who is always referred to as a king). After Alaric's death, however, he consistently refers to his three successors as kings and as having succeeded to the kingdom (*regnum*) or been created or elected king.[89]

Fifth-century annalistic sources present a similar picture. Prosper of Aquitaine (writing 433–55) refers simply to Goths under Alaric's command sacking Rome but says that the Goths entered Gaul under King Athaulf and that Wallia seized the kingdom. The *Gallic Chronicle of 452* similarly refers to Rome being sacked by Goths 'under the command of Alaric' but twice indirectly describes Galla Placidia's husband Athaulf as a king. The so-called *Consularia Italica* never calls Alaric a king or gives him any title, although Radagaisus, Gundegisel of the Vandals and the Visigothic kings from Theoderic I onwards are called *reges*. The anonymous *Narrative of the Emperors of the Valentinianic and Theodosian Houses*, written in the mid-fifth century,

---

[86] Claudian, *Fourth Consulate of Honorius*, lines 632 ff.

[87] Three references in book 7: 'king Alaric with his Goths' (*Alaricus rex cum Gothis suis*) during an attack on Stilicho's general policies and behaviour (Oros. 7.37.2); 'two Gothic peoples with their two very powerful kings' (*duo tunc Gothorum populi cum duobus potentissimis regibus suis*), where Alaric (unnamed) is contrasted as a heretical Christian with the pagan Radagaisus (Oros. 7.37.8); at the end of the account of Radagaisus' invasion the behaviour of the Romans during this pagan attack was to be punished by the invasion of the Christian king Alaric (Oros. 7.37.17).

[88] Oros. 2.3.3.

[89] Oros. 7.43.2 (*Athaulfus rex ... Alarico in regnum successerat*); 7.43.9 (*Segericus, rex a Gothis creatus*); 7.43.10 (*Vallia successit in regnum, ad hoc electus a Gothis*); 7.43.15 (*Vallia Gothorum rex*).

however, calls Alaric a king at the time of the sack of Rome. By Hydatius' time, in the third quarter of the fifth century, the tradition was established that a king had always ruled the Goths. In the second quarter of the sixth century, Marcellinus Comes pushed Alaric's kingship back to his first appearance in 395 and in the early seventh century Isidore of Seville completed the process by linking it to the Gothic submission in 382.[90] Olympiodorus also refers to succession and election after the deaths of Alaric, Athaulf and Wallia. The evidence is vague and allows multiple interpretations but, cumulatively and alongside Jordanes' comment, the silence of the contemporary or near-contemporary sources about Alaric's regal title before 400 (and usually thereafter too), combined with their reference to Gothic kings and forms of succession from Athaulf onwards, suggests that the title was not adopted in 395. Jordanes' statement might apply to the first time this expedient was used, in particular circumstances in 400/1. It would appear that it only (and gradually) became an important feature of western politics after that date. Athaulf was possibly the first to employ it regularly. Particular circumstances lay behind this development too. To see the title king as adopted intermittently but with increasing regularity in response to specific political developments permits a better understanding of the evolution of Gothic kingship inside the Empire than to assume that it was a constitutional position based upon (usually fictional) treaties from 395 onwards.

RADAGAISUS, 405–406

Another character occasionally described by contemporaries as 'king of the Goths' is Radagaisus,[91] who led a large force from the Danube to Italy in 405, possibly harrying *Illyricum* on the way.[92] Contemporaries impossibly described his army as 200,000 and even 400,000 strong: a measure of the panic that his appearance produced. Radagaisus' army must have been large: he could divide it into three, presumably for ease of supply. Stilicho assembled an army (described

[90] Prosper, *Chron.* AP 383 (= 410), AP 385 (= 412), AP 388 (= 415); *Chron. Gall. 452*, 67, 77; *Narrative of the Emperors of the Valentinianic and Theodosian Houses* 6; Hydatius, *Chron.* 35; Marcellinus, *Chron. s.a.* 395; Isidore, *History of the Goths* 12.

[91] Oros. 7.37.8, 15; *Chron. Gall. 452*, 50; *Consularia Italica* 535.

[92] *Chron. Gall. 452*, 50, 52; Olympiodorus, fr. 9; Oros. 7.37; Zos. 5.26. Honorius, *Letter to Arcadius*; above, n. 69.

as thirty *numeri* or units) with Hunnic and Alan allies[93] and, perhaps striking before Radagaisus could assemble his dispersed forces, surrounded the barbarians near Fiesole. Radagaisus was captured and executed (23 August 406),[94] and 12,000 of his troops were drafted into the Roman forces. Orosius says that there was little bloodshed so this might represent the bulk of the invading army, but we should remember that part of Orosius' purpose was to show how the Christian God helped his Roman followers to achieve bloodless victories.[95] It would still make the invading force very substantial. Stilicho's force has plausibly been estimated as about 15,000 men.[96] The armies were large and evenly matched.

Radagaisus' attack most plausibly resulted from the Romans' failure to maintain effective policy along and beyond the frontier.[97] Stilicho, like any Roman leader, especially one in his position, was more concerned with internal politics and seems to have paid little attention to two crucial issues: effective presence in the northwestern provinces and the maintenance of equilibrium among the barbarian groups beyond the *limes*. Claudian's panegyrics claim successful campaigns and the restoration of secure frontiers in Britain and along the Rhine.[98] However, Claudian repeatedly uses Britain and its potential assailants (Scots, Picts and Saxons) rhetorically when he wishes to stress his patrons' fame and might extending to the end of the world. His geography is utterly implausible (he refers, for example, to victories by Theodosius the Elder over Saxons in the Orkneys and over Picts in Thule, the island at the end of the world identified variously with the Shetlands, the outer Hebrides and Iceland[99]) and there is no time available in Stilicho's career for a Pictish war. Stilicho crossed the Alps but even Claudian admits that he left the Rhine defended more by the threat of Roman revenge than by any reorganisation.[100]

---

[93] Zos. 5.26.3; Oros. 7.37.12 also mentions Hunnic and Alan allies.

[94] *Consularia Italica* 535.   [95] Cp. Oros. 7.35.20.

[96] Burns (1994), p. 198, and n. 53.

[97] Burns (1994), p. 198 suggests a revolt of barbarian recruits. Here, however, his desire to wrestle with all of Rome's barbarian problems in the context of Roman *receptio* and military recruitment results in unnecessarily convoluted reasoning.

[98] Claudian, *Against Eutropius* 1, lines 390–6; *Fourth Consulate of Honorius*, lines 439–58; *Consulate of Stilicho* 2, lines 242–55.

[99] Claudian, *Fourth Consulship of Honorius*, lines 31–4.

[100] Claudian, *Fourth Consulship*, lines 439–58; *Gothic War*, lines 423–9.

Roman neglect of traditional areas of 'barbarian policy' allowed one barbarian group to acquire military primacy over its neighbours, as had happened during Roman civil wars before. For the first time since the 370s a dominant power, the Huns, emerged north of the Danube. Their warbands were even active north of the upper Rhine/Danube in 384.[101] This provided an alternative to Rome.[102] Uldin, the first named Hunnic leader appears as a powerful figure during Gaïnas' suppression and in Stilicho's army at Fiesole.[103] Within a few years other groups beyond the frontiers were entering the Empire. Some contemporaries adopted the imagery of the Huns pushing or driving other peoples before them into the Empire; the reality seems more complex.

Radagaisus' followers are usually called Goths, although Zosimus curiously describes them as Celts and Germans.[104] It seems reasonable to view Radagaisus as the leader of a Gothic political faction ousted during the Hunnic acquisition of supremacy. The Huns formed the focus for the dominant political identity in the area for the next half-century. Like Fritigern's Goths of 376, Radagaisus was compelled to take his supporters into the Empire. Either they would be settled on arrival at the border or, if this did not happen, perhaps a show of force and military success would compel the Empire to treat with them. Alternatively military success and booty would enable a return to *barbaricum* and political dominance. No attempt was made to treat with or settle Radagaisus' army at the frontier and Stilicho's counter-attack ended any other ambitions. Nevertheless, the writing should have been on the wall. Radagaisus' invasion was produced by stress caused by the Empire's failure to manage the symbiotic relationship between Roman and barbarian politics described in chapter 5.

In spite of the chaos caused by Radagaisus' invasion, Stilicho continued to fix his gaze on the eastern court. His failure to deal with the frontiers or to pay attention to the government of the north-western provinces had unsurprising results in the 'great invasion' of Gaul in 405/6 and, shortly afterwards, the raising of the standard of revolt in Britain. Nevertheless, Stilicho appears to have resumed his

[101] Ambrose, *Letters* 30.8 (Liebeschuetz, trans. (2005), p. 355; Beyenka, trans. (1954), p. 60).
[102] Wolfram (1997a), pp. 123–44, coins the term 'the Hunnic Alternative'.
[103] Zos. 5.22.1–2 (suppression of Gaïnas); Oros. 7.37.12 (Fiesole).
[104] Zos. 5.26.3.

plans to take all of the Balkan provinces from the east and in 405 Alaric was ordered to move from *Pannonia* to Epirus.[105] To understand events in the north-west we must return to the consequences of the military and governmental withdrawal there.

The capital of the Gallic prefecture was moved from Trier south to Arles. The date of this has been much debated and there is little decisive evidence either way, though it must have taken place between 395 and 418. An early date within that bracket is made likely by the closure of the Trier mint shortly after Eugenius' suppression.[106] After 388 Valentinian II's court was at Vienne, south of Lyon, possibly prefiguring this move. It has recently been argued plausibly that an intermediate stage took place, when the prefecture returned to Lyon, the old capital of Gaul.[107] By the time that the relevant part of the western portion of the *Notitia Dignitatum* was compiled, a number of other offices had been moved from the north to the south.[108] Most importantly of all, for the first time since the mid-third century, the emperor no longer resided in Gaul. He may have been seen as a usurper in Italy and the east, but Maximus was apparently popular in Gaul.[109] In Spain, Orosius praised him, saying that only his illegal seizure of the throne counted against him. Half a century later, Sidonius Apollinaris implied that he was the last emperor to have governed Gaul.[110] British tradition, from Gildas onwards and especially in the ninth-century *History of the Britons*, while less positive about Maximus himself, nevertheless saw him as the last Roman emperor.[111] From 395 the Gauls found themselves removed from the Empire's political core.

The extent of northern Gaulish and British society's dependence upon the presence of the Roman state and its effective management of patronage has already been noted.[112] Imperial offices and titles established the pecking order of the region's aristocracy, a group

---

[105] Olympiodorus, fr. 1.2; Zos. 5.26.

[106] Chastagnol (1973), followed by Kulikowski (2000b), argues for 408, in the face of Constantine's rebellion. Bleckmann (1997), pp. 575–85, sensibly doubts that the withdrawal was the result of any hard and fast strategic decision. The *terminus ante quem* of 418 is established by the date of the re-establishment of the Council of the Gauls, which met at Arles in the presence of the prefect. The closure of the Trier mint: Wightman (1970), p. 68.

[107] Drinkwater (1998), p. 274.   [108] E.g. *Not. Dig.* occ. 12.27.

[109] Sulpicius Severus, *Dialogues* 3.11.   [110] Sid. Ap. *Poems* 5, lines 353–7.

[111] *DEB* 13; *HB* 26.   [112] Above, pp. 79–86.

often not otherwise sharply differentiated from the remainder of the population. The legitimacy which rank and office provided and the backing of the state cemented their local predominance. The Empire's absence thus called the very fabric of local society into question. At this time we may detect archaeological evidence of a collapse, which must relate to the withdrawal of state presence, and which is described in more detail in chapter 11.[113] With time all this might have changed. The government might have re-established its control. However, for all its resources, time was one commodity the western Empire did not have. Events were rapidly overtaking the unfortunate young Emperor Honorius: events in the east; events in the core of the western Empire; events north of the Rhine and Danube; and events in the outer provinces. With Gaul denuded of troops and relying on the frontier kings' good will for its defence, north of the Loire there was a disaster waiting to happen.

THE GREAT INVASION AND CONSTANTINE 'III', 406–408

The disaster was doubtless brought closer by Alaric's and Radagaisus' attacks upon Italy, necessitating yet more troop-movements from the north-west, and also by Stilicho's politicking, further directing the attention of the western court away from the Rhine. It came closer still with the establishment beyond the Danube of the powerful Hunnic confederacy. For the peoples who lived between the Huns and the North Sea this was a testing time. Their politics and social structures were closely linked to relationships with the Empire, especially to imperial gifts.[114] Just over the frontier, amongst the Franks and Alamans whose leaders had recently had their power bolstered by Stilicho's treaties, things will not have changed drastically, but beyond them things were different. Society and politics here could have been as hard hit by the Empire's withdrawal from the Rhine as they were in the north-western provinces. Archaeological data suggest considerable social change and instability around 400, whereas the regions just beyond the frontier show more stability, as is discussed in chapter 12.[115] If political structures were under stress, as the invasion of Radagaisus also implies, the 'Hunnic alternative'[116] will have seemed attractive to some factions. As in 376,

---

[113] Below, pp. 346–68.   [114] Above, pp. 123–4, 150–2.
[115] Below, pp. 383–6, 399–403.   [116] Wolfram (1997a), pp. 123–44.

other groups were driven out and headed for the imperial border. Again the Roman Empire fell victim to a disaster of its own making. Its internal politics produced a crisis beyond the *limes*, with devastating results.

On 31 December 405 a huge body from the interior of *Germania* crossed the Rhine: Siling and Hasding Vandals, Sueves and Alans.[117] The date for this invasion is usually given as 31 December 406. Prosper of Aquitaine's *Chronicle* indeed says that, during the consulate of Arcadius (for the sixth time) and Probus (i.e. his year AP 379, or our 406 AD), 'the Alans and Vandals, having crossed the Rhine on the day before the kalends of January, entered Gaul'. This would imply a date of 31 December 406. Recently, Michael Kulikowski has argued that analysis of Prosper's style suggests that he probably meant the last day of the preceding year.[118] While Orosius says the attack took place two years before the sack of Rome,[119] thus in 408, fitting neither argument, Zosimus (though garbled) dates the rampages of these barbarians to the consulate of Arcadius and Probus (406). It seems unlikely that he would assign the ravaging of Gaul to a particular year if the barbarians only crossed the frontier (and so can barely have passed a few miles into the interior) on its last day. Kulikowski's argument also makes more sense of the relationship between this invasion and the British usurpations.[120]

Historians often state that the Rhine was frozen, though no contemporary source says as much. Such is the legacy of Roman ideas of barbarian ineptitude![121] The Franks in the area fought back furiously and even killed the Vandal king. Significantly no source mentions any defence by Roman troops, although Jerome mentions a long siege at Worms. Eventually, however, numbers told and the Franks were defeated. The Rhine frontier, such as it was, was breached and Gaul lay open to the ravages of what historians have termed the 'great invasion'. The invaders' route is unclear. Jerome's list of captured towns makes little sense as an itinerary and suggests

[117] For these events: Jerome, *Letters* 123; Oros. 7.38.3–4; Prosper, *Chron.* AP 379; Renatus Profuturus Frigeridus, *History*, at *LH* 2.9; Zos. 6.3.1.
[118] Kulikowski (2000b), pp. 328–9.   [119] Oros. 7.40.3–4.
[120] I am unconvinced by the attempt to reconcile Zosimus' statement that the British usurpations of 406 responded to the barbarian invasion with that invasion's dating to 31 Dec. 406, given by Paschoud (ed. and trans.) (1989), pp. 22–3.
[121] Kulikowski (2000b), p. 326, n. 8, traces this myth to Gibbon's *Decline and Fall*.

that the barbarians divided into several groups.[122] At this point the British army intervened.

After a decade of neglect, it is unsurprising, given what has been said about the importance of imperial government in maintaining social stability, that the Britons should have taken steps forcibly to reassert their links with the Empire. The barbarian attack is specified by Zosimus[123] as motivating the usurpations but this was probably only the final straw. In 406 (before the seventh consulate of Honorius (407), says Olympiodorus)[124] two Britons, Marcus and Gratian, were raised to the purple and assassinated in short succession before the army elected a soldier called Constantine, taking hope in the prestige of his name and perhaps aware that 100 years earlier their precursors in the British garrison had made the first, great Constantine emperor at York. To further this image, Constantine may have changed the names of his sons to Constans and Julian.[125] Constantine 'III' took what was left of the British field army to fight the invaders and may have succeeded in pinning them into the north of Gaul.[126] Constantine rapidly acquired control of most of Gaul, his forces heading first for Lyon before restoring the situation in the north and reopening the mint in Trier. For a while, the area around Arles appears to have remained under Honorius' authority, but Spain submitted to the usurper.[127] Stilicho's belated response to these events brought about his own downfall.

THE FALL OF STILICHO, 408

In 408 Stilicho sent another Gothic officer, Sarus (who Orosius[128] claimed had fought at Fiesole), to stop Constantine's advance.[129] After some success, Sarus was forced to retreat into Italy, losing his baggage to Alpine *bagaudae* in the process, and the area around Arles fell to Constantine. A further blow to Stilicho's plans was struck by

---

[122] See the map in Heather (2005), p. 207.   [123] Zos. 6.3.1.

[124] Olympiodorus, fr. 13.1.   [125] Drinkwater (1998), p. 272.

[126] Again, following Kulikowski (2000b), though the evidence is not decisive. Zos. 6.3.3 would support his argument.

[127] On Constantine's movements in Gaul, see Drinkwater (1998), pp. 275–9, *contra* Paschoud (ed. and trans.) (1989), pp. 25, 27–8, 31. Also Kulikowski (2000b), pp. 333–4, although with confusion about Gallic geography on p. 333; Lyon *is* in the Rhône valley.

[128] Oros. 7.37.12.   [129] Zos. 2.3–5.

a rumour that Alaric had died,[130] underlining the two generals' association at this point.

Alaric, probably appreciating that Stilicho's eastern campaign was now unlikely, moved from Epirus north to Noricum, from which point he could threaten Italy in his own right while also being in a position either to join Constantine, whose coins are found in neighbouring *Raetia*, or hold the Alpine passes against him. Alaric demanded 4,000 pounds of gold. Making the situation yet more complex, Arcadius died on 1 May 408, leaving a child, Theodosius II, as successor. Again, like any true imperial statesman, in spite of the looming catastrophe north of the Alps, Stilicho's first thought was of Roman politics. He decided to use the situation to ease the problems in the Balkans and make good his long-standing claim to be the guardian of Theodosius I's descendants in the east. A deal was struck with Alaric's army ('a pact of servitude' one Roman aristocrat called it), which was to cross Italy, pick up Roman contingents, and attack Constantine. The plan came to nothing. On 13 August 408 a faction centred on Olympius, Honorius' master of offices, raised the troops at Pavia, alleging that Stilicho's planned move to Constantinople with four legions to secure Theodosius II's succession was in fact a plot to depose Theodosius in favour of Stilicho's son Eucherius. The enraged army butchered Stilicho's supporters. Stilicho, isolated at Bologna, found his position exacerbated when Sarus, having gone over to Olympius, massacred his Hunnic bodyguards. Eventually, lured from the church in Ravenna where he had taken refuge, Stilicho was executed. Most of his family, regardless of age or sex, followed soon after.[131]

Stilicho's career and the crisis that produced his fall illustrate clearly how important the fourth-century style of government was and, in a sense, how little this was appreciated. When the chips were down, Stilicho, like many a fourth-century emperor, knew that internal Roman politics were more important than any barbarian menace. He realised that barbarians could not themselves overthrow the Empire; more serious military dangers came from within. This was indeed true but imperial management of the barbarian threat was about more than preventing attack. An emperor on the frontier could

---

[130] Zos. 5.27.2.

[131] For the events of this paragraph: *Consularia Italica* 538; Olympiodorus, frr. 5, 7.6; Zos. 5.27.2, 5.29.4, 5.24.9, 5.32.1–4, 5.33–5.

present himself as fulfilling his duty, was accessible to the provincial élites and able to distribute and redistribute his patronage, all reducing the threat of political disaffection. The 'legitimacy gap' left Stilicho, a commander who dominated an emperor but who was not emperor himself, more open to internal threat and thus he turned further away from traditional government.[132] Barbarian political instability and attacks on the provinces were not in themselves irremediable. The emperor's absence from the trans-Alpine territories had, however, created a volatile political situation which, when combined with barbarian unrest, critically loosened the bonds that tied the north-western provinces into the Empire.

ALARIC IN ITALY AND THE SACK OF ROME, 408–410

Olympius promulgated laws damning Stilicho and all his supporters and confiscating their property,[133] but the end of Stilicho's supremacy did not ameliorate the situation. In fact, Olympius' faction's rabid hostility exacerbated it. The families of Stilicho's barbarian recruits were massacred and the furious troops understandably abandoned Honorius.[134] Alaric was left, again, without a formal command or recognition, producing another crisis of legitimacy and compelling him to take his troops into Italy, where Stilicho's outraged non-Roman soldiers joined him. Even with these reinforcements, Alaric could not hope to take Ravenna. Marching on Rome, he took Portus and produced famine in the city. The senate bought Alaric off with 5,000 pounds of gold, 30,000 pounds of silver, 4,000 silk tunics, 3,000 scarlet coloured skins and 3,000 pounds of pepper.[135] It has often been remarked that these were not huge sums when compared with the wealth of the great Italian senatorial families but, in the context of the siege and being cut off from their estates, they might have impacted more seriously upon the Roman nobility.

A proper settlement with Alaric was not reached. Meanwhile, two of Honorius' relatives, Didymus and Verenianus, raised private armies and rebelled against Constantine in Spain but the latter's general Gerontius defeated, captured and eventually executed them.[136] Other

---

[132] Lütkenhaus (1998), pp. 12–16.   [133] *CTh* 9.42.21–2; Zos. 5.35.
[134] Zos. 5.35.5–6.   [135] Zos. 5.41.4.
[136] Olympiodorus, fr. 13.2; Oros. 7.40.5–8; Zos. 6.4–5.

members of the Theodosian house fled abroad. Constantine's son Constans, now *caesar*, appears to have been given Spain to rule. The Vandals, Sueves and Alans now broke out and invaded southern Gaul (if they had not done so already). Contemporaries wrote with feeling about the ravages of this horde. Probably the most famous phrase is that of Orientius: 'All Gaul burned as a single funeral pyre.'[137]

Constantine 'III' now made overtures to Honorius to receive recognition.[138] He evidently thought he had achieved this, too, as he apparently declared himself consul for 409 throughout his dominions.[139] He seems to have been mistaken.[140] The possibility of playing Constantine off against Alaric led Honorius' court to prevaricate. The situation was further complicated by another coup, replacing Olympius (forced to flee to *Dalmatia*) with a cabal of military and civilian officials led by Jovius, Alaric's former associate in *Illyricum*.[141] Alaric's demands also posed problems. Besides annual payments of grain and gold for his troops, he also wanted Histria and Venetia as well as *Dalmatia* and the Norican provinces. To make matters worse, Jovius claimed that Alaric also wanted the title of *magister utriusque militiae* (master of both the services – infantry and cavalry).[142] This had been Stilicho's title (brought with him from the east in 394); the Ravennate court had no wish to be reminded of Stilicho. The demand for *Histria* and *Venetia* was more problematic still. If Alaric controlled those provinces and thus the Alpine passes and usual defensive lines he would perpetually have Italy at his mercy. Alaric's demands might simply have been an opening bargaining strategy but Jovius and the court handled them with phenomenal ineptitude and tactlessness.[143] When Alaric made clear that he did not ask to be *magister utriusque militiae* and dropped the claim to *Histria* and *Venetia*, his demands were still refused, and he was compelled to attack Rome a second time.[144] Seizing Portus and threatening another famine he again forced the senate to yield. Feeling that taking the city would do little good in bargaining

---

[137] Orientius, *Commonitorium* 2, line 184. For analysis of literary responses, see Courcelle (1964); Roberts, M. (1992); Wood (1992).

[138] Olympiodorus, fr. 13.1; Zos. 5.43, 6.1.

[139] As declared on an inscription from Trier: *RICG* 1.193.

[140] The *Consularia Constantinopolitana* gives the year's consuls as Honorius and Theodosius, although the *Consularia Italica* names no consuls at all.

[141] Zos. 5.46–7.   [142] Zos. 5.48.3.   [143] Olympiodorus, fr. 8.1; Zos. 5.49.1, 5.51.

[144] Zos. 6.1.

with Honorius, he and the disenchanted senate raised a new emperor, Priscus Attalus, an experienced aristocrat sent by Honorius to treat with Alaric.[145]

Alaric got all he wanted from Attalus, becoming *magister peditum* (master of the infantry, the senior western military command),[146] and his chief supporters were rewarded with offices. None of this mattered much. Honorius still occupied Ravenna, unexpectedly reinforced by 4,000 eastern troops, his general Heraclianus held Africa and withheld the grain fleet, Sarus effectively raided Alaric's forces, and Constantine 'III' invaded in Italy, possibly in Honorius' support.[147] Heraclianus' actions were the most important. An emperor in Ravenna was pinned down under siege just as surely as Alaric was unable to take the city; Constantine soon withdrew, possibly after a defeat by Alaric's troops; Sarus' actions were little more than an irritant; but the absence of the African grain produced hunger in Rome and in Alaric's army. This matter needed resolving but Attalus' forces' half-hearted attempt to wrest Africa from Heraclianus was defeated.[148] When deposing Attalus and offering to negotiate with Honorius again failed to produce results, Alaric, driven to desperation, marched back to Rome. On 24 August 410 the starving city opened its gates and Alaric's soldiers marched in.[149] The damage was limited. Alaric ordered that anyone sheltering in a church was to be spared (something much cited by Christian apologists) but nevertheless the Goths looted the city for three days and the fall of the eternal city sent a shock around the Roman world.

Rome's fall had less striking political effects. Alaric, unable to treat with Honorius, remained in the political cold. Knowing that he could only change this situation by controlling the African grain supply, he decided to force a crossing to Africa, via Sicily, and

[145] Olympiodorus, fr. 10; Zos. 6.2. Cesa (1992–3) for the importance of the Italian senators in this usurpation.

[146] Olympiodorus, fr. 10.1, claims that Alaric was made *strategos hekateras dunameos* (= *magister utriusque militiae*). Zos. 6.7, however, claims that he shared command with Valens. As Zos. 6.10 refers to Valens as *hippou strategos* (= *magister equitum*), Alaric took the senior post of *magister peditum*. Alaric had Valens killed in 410, however, and might at this point have become master of both services.

[147] Olympiodorus, frr. 10.1–2, 11.1–2, 15.1–2; Zos. 6.8.2, 6.11.1.

[148] Olympiodorus, fr. 10.1.   [149] Olympiodorus, fr. 11; Oros. 7.39.1–40.3.

headed south through Campania and Lucania to Bruttium, where he died of a fever.[150]

Alaric's importance cannot be overestimated. Leading a force of barbarian recruits and perhaps other units, he wanted a formal Roman command and for some time achieved this; we should not overlook the years when Alaric and his forces are recorded as doing nothing other than occupying their station. In the end, though, he was caught in the rivalry between the eastern and western empires and in the fall-out from court intrigue. In order to maintain his position he was compelled to transform the nature of his command. In 401, when he lost his military office and was forced into rebellion, he seems to have proclaimed himself king. After 408, with no effective Roman rank (Heraclianus' retention of the grain fleet and Honorius' intransigence, meant that those he received from Attalus never produced the desired results) it might be that he maintained this title more consistently. He had become a king of the Goths and as such he died.

THE CRISIS AT THE PERIPHERIES

In 410 Honorius wrote to the citizens of *Brittia*, telling them to look after their own defence.[151] Traditionally, *Brittia* is held to be Britain but in 1975 John Matthews implied that Honorius' letter was actually addressed to the citizens of Bruttium in Italy.[152] The latter location makes some sense in the context of 410[153] and indeed in this passage Zosimus seems entirely concerned with Italian affairs.[154] Before mentioning *Brittia*, Zosimus talks of Alaric's attempts to ensure Aemilia and Liguria's loyalty to Attalus and his unsuccessful siege of Bologna. Following his statement about *Brittia*, he says that, after paying his troops with money sent by Heraclianus, Honorius felt secure, having won the support of armies everywhere. The proposition that *Brittia* is Bruttium has never been convincingly

---

[150] Jordanes, *Getica* 30.157; Olympiodorus, frr. 11.2, 11.4, 16. Jordanes, *Getica* 30.157–8, for a colourful if probably legendary account of Alaric's burial.
[151] Zos. 6.10.2.   [152] Matthews (1975), p. 320, n. 7. See also Bartholomew (1982).
[153] Olympiodorus, fr. 16.
[154] Bleckmann (1997), pp. 572–5, suggests that the error stems from Zosimus' (or his source's) confusion of Bolonia in Italy with Boulogne in northern Gaul (both called Bononia by the Romans). Woolf, A. (2003), pp. 346–7, leaves the issue open.

rejected even though Matthews himself later distanced himself from it.[155] Whatever the case, Zosimus states that at this time the Britons threw out the Empire's officials and ruled themselves.[156] An anonymous account of Honorius' reign written not long after it ended claims that Britain was lost forever during his rule.[157] The *Gallic Chronicle of 452* states that Britain was ravaged by Saxons in 410.[158] This is traditionally the context in which Britain's rulers invited Saxon mercenaries to help defend the province, although that seems more likely to have taken place earlier.[159]

Zosimus states that the citizens of Aremorica followed the Britons' example and threw out imperial officers.[160] Northern Gaul was certainly something of a political grey area, neither abandoned by the Empire nor effectively governed by it, although a Roman commander called Exuperantius was described as restoring Roman rule to Aremorica in 417.[161] This period saw the appearance of the *Bagaudae*. Originally seen as peasant rebels, the inevitable product of class conflict within the supposedly increasingly oppressive late Roman social structure (a structure which is unlikely to have existed in northern Gaul),[162] more recent work plausibly suggests that the *Bagaudae* were people who took over local leadership without imperial legitimation.[163] They were thus condemned as bandits or rebels whenever the Empire tried to make its writ run in the north, as during Exuperantius' campaign. They were also symptomatic of social and political instability, not helped by the flight of many aristocrats or by the apparently widespread executions that followed Jovinus' usurpation.[164] Northern Gaul, like Britain, was fast becoming a political vacuum. The archaeological record, discussed below in chapter 11, shows how this vacuum produced a

[155] In the 1990 reprint (p. 403), Matthews retracted the idea in the face of objections raised by E. A. Thompson (1977). However, the weight of Thompson's riposte lay more in vehemence than argument.

[156] Zos. 6.5.3.   [157] *Narrative of the Emperors of the Valentinianic and Theodosian Houses 6.*

[158] *Chron. Gall.* 452, 62.   [159] Above, pp. 197–8, and Appendix, below.

[160] Zos. 6.5.3.   [161] Rutilius Namatius, *On his Return*, pp. 226–7.

[162] E.g. Thompson, E. A. (1952); De Ste Croix (1981); the idea is resurrected by Dark, K. R. (1994), pp. 55–7, but rectified to some extent in Dark, K. R. (2002), p. 30. Above, pp. 81–6, for northern Gallic social structures.

[163] Van Dam (1985), pp. 16–20, 25–56; Drinkwater (1989); (1992); Minor (1996) for the spelling. Unlike Van Dam, I do not think that these were necessarily, in the context of northern Gaulish society at least, second-rank aristocrats.

[164] Below, pp. 222–4.

rapid and dramatic collapse of the material traces of traditional Roman society and culture.[165]

A similar picture may also have pertained in Africa. In the decades around 400 changes are detectable in many African cities, involving a radical reuse of space.[166] What this means is difficult to establish. The North Africans appear to have maintained their unusual Romanness in many ways and economically the region continued to prosper. The chronological link with the period of crisis is, however, striking and there had been several rebellions in the area led by Moorish princes but with provincial support. The changes in the cities possibly reveal similar developments to those shown in the regional rebellions. Perhaps, outside Carthage, the Africans began to feel themselves being cut off from the centre of Roman politics and began to turn away from some traditional manifestations of political participation and towards other expressions of Roman identity.

[165] Below, pp. 346–55, 357–68.   [166] Below, pp. 321–3.

8

THE TRIUMPH OF THE GENERALS, 410–455

·

THE SUPPRESSION OF THE USURPERS, 410–413

Alaric's death did not much improve matters for the court in Ravenna (map 15). Athaulf, his brother-in-law, succeeded him.[1] He had been master of the household cavalry in Attalus' regime but after Attalus' deposition by Alaric, in an attempt to negotiate with Honorius, Athaulf had no legitimate title by anyone's definition. In the circumstances it was unsurprising that he took the title king. He might not have intended it to be permanent. Despite having the emperor's sister, Galla Placidia, and the deposed Attalus in his train, Athaulf had no more success in negotiating with Honorius than Alaric had had. After two years' campaigning in Italy, causing serious damage but failing to achieve any significant success,[2] he took his doubtless dwindling forces across the Alps to Gaul, where the political situation presented greater opportunities.

Things had begun to go awry for Constantine 'III'. His general in Spain, Gerontius, had proclaimed a follower called Maximus emperor and attacked Constans, who fled.[3] Meanwhile, the barbarians

---

[1] *Chron. Gall. 452*, 69; Hydatius, *Chron.* 37; Olympiodorus, fr. 11.4; Oros. 7.43.2.

[2] *CTh* 11.28.12 (15 Nov. 418) reduces the tax assessment of Campania by 89 per cent on account of Gothic depredations but the extent of damage may be overestimated: below, pp. 328–32.

[3] Maximus is described as Gerontius' son at Olympiodorus, fr. 17.1, but elsewhere he is simply called a member of Gerontius' household. Olympiodorus, fr. 17.2; Oros. 7.42.4–5.

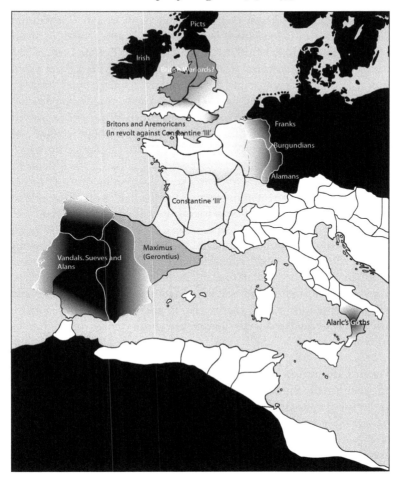

Map 15 The western Empire in 410, at the death of Alaric

who had crossed the Rhine in 405/6 entered Spain. At first the
Pyrenean passes had been held against them. Constantine, however,
replaced the local garrisons with recently raised troops – *Honoriaci* – and
while these took the opportunity to loot the locals, the Sueves, Vandals
and Alans were able to enter the peninsula. This took place in late 409.
Hydatius says that it could have been 28 September or a fortnight later

on 12 October, but it was certainly a Tuesday.[4] In 410 Constantine planned a two-pronged offensive, sending Constans to recover Spain while he invaded Italy.[5] Both failed. Constans was defeated and in late 410 or early 411 Gerontius' troops followed him into Gaul and killed him.[6] Constantine soon scuttled back to Arles,[7] where by about May 411 Gerontius had besieged him. The Italian army under the patrician Constantius and yet another Gothic officer called Wulfila now crossed into Gaul. Faced by these forces, Gerontius' Spanish troops rebelled and joined Constantius, who took over the siege of Constantine in Arles.[8] At this point the fragmentary sources make the narrative difficult to reconstruct. An attempted relief of Arles by Constantine's Frankish officer Edobech was beaten in battle. Edobech fled to the estate of one Ecdicius, believing him to be a friend, but Ecdicius murdered him. However, in the north of Gaul another emperor, Jovinus, had been declared with the support of the Burgundians and Alans (411). Jovinus and his allies marched on Arles alongside a large army of barbarians recruited from along the Rhine, perhaps by Constantine's officials. Constantius apparently felt unable to meet this second army in battle whilst Constantine feared capture by Jovinus' forces. Consequently Arles was surrendered and Constantine took refuge in a church, becoming a monk.

This seems the best way of reconciling Olympiodorus' and Renatus Profuturus Frigeridus' accounts.[9] Olympiodorus describes Edobech's relieving force being defeated, giving some details of the tactics used, and says that Constantius then took Arles and retreated. Renatus says that Constans had sent Edobech north to contain the barbarians, but the army that approaches Arles is led by Jovinus and associated with his usurpation rather than (as is Edobech's attack in Olympiodorus' story) with Constantine's reinforcement. This force is made up of barbarians, whereas Olympiodorus does not suggest that Edobech's army was non-Roman. At its approach Arles is surrendered and Constantius withdraws. These accounts cannot

---

[4] Hydatius, *Chron.* 34.

[5] Olympiodorus, fr. 15.1, 17.1; Oros. 7.40.7–10; Zos. 6.1.2, 6.4–5 (Zosimus based his account on Olympiodorus; as before, I have only used Blockley's numbering of the fragments where they are not to be found in Zosimus' work).

[6] Olympiodorus, fr. 17.2; Oros. 7.42.4; Prosper, *Chron.* AP 384 (= 411).

[7] Above, p. 216.   [8] Olympiodorus, fr. 17.

[9] Olympiodorus, fr. 17.2; Renatus Profuturus Frigeridus, at *LH* 9. Cesa (1994a), p. 150 for a similar reconstruction.

represent two versions of the same attack. Olympiodorus is quite clear about Constantius' victory but if Jovinus' army was defeated Constantius' withdrawal and abandonment of Gaul to the usurper are inexplicable.[10]

Constantine's tonsure did him little good. He and his son Julian were captured and taken to Italy. Promises of safety might have been given but once across the Alps both were beheaded.[11] Gerontius was hounded down, although Maximus escaped to the barbarians in Spain.[12]

After Constantius' withdrawal to Italy, Jovinus was left in peace for between one and two years.[13] It is doubtful that he controlled all Gaul. Constantius' prefect of the Gauls, Dardanus, seemingly held the south coast. The north-western regions that had expelled Constantine's officers in 409 might not have been under his effective authority either. In this light it is unsurprising that Jovinus was unable or unwilling to spread his authority any further to Britain or Spain, rendering the thesis that he spearheaded a Gallic aristocratic separatist movement difficult to sustain.[14] Athaulf intervened at this point. Attalus apparently advised him that he should support Jovinus so the Goths abandoned their fruitless Italian campaign, doubtless made even less attractive by Constantius' return, and crossed into Gaul (early 412).

The alliance was short-lived. Sarus, the old enemy of Alaric and Athaulf, decided to join Jovinus but, not entirely surprisingly, was killed and his force destroyed by Athaulf's Goths.[15] Jovinus, understandably alarmed by this turn of events, blamed Attalus for bringing the Goths in the first place. Clearly perceptions of the Gothic leader's role differed. Jovinus' Rhine barbarian allies appear to have served in

[10] See also Ehling (1996); Scharf (1993), pp. 1–2. Cesa (1994a), p. 150, points out that Jovinus struck coins at Trier, Lyon and Arles celebrating this 'victory'.

[11] Olympiodorus, fr. 17.2; Oros. 7.42.3; Renatus Profuturus Frigeridus (at *LH* 2.9).

[12] Oros. 7.42.5.

[13] Cesa (1992–3) points out that the *Ravenna Annals* record Jovinus' head being brought to Ravenna on 30 August 412 but most authorities associate his end with that of Heraclianus and move the date forward to 413 (*Consularia Italica* 541; Prosper, *Chron.* AP 386 [= 413]; cp. Hydatius, *Chron.* 46). Marcellinus, *Chron. s.a.* 412, would support the earlier date, as might the *Chron. Gall. 452*, 68–70. An acceptance of one or other date is important for the reconstruction of Athaulf's break with Ravenna. On balance 413 seems preferable.

[14] Scharf (1993). Scharf makes many excellent points but we simply do not have enough evidence about Jovinus to support his theory.

[15] Olympiodorus, fr. 18.

return for settlements or recognition in the north but Athaulf was angling for high imperial command and might only have seen Jovinus as a puppet like Attalus. The final straw was Jovinus' proclamation of his brother Sebastian as co-emperor, without Athaulf's approval. Athaulf changed sides, captured Jovinus and handed him over. Once he had Jovinus and his brothers in his control, Dardanus had them executed, apparently at Narbonne, and sent their heads to Ravenna to join those of Constantine 'III' and Julian.[16] The carnival of treachery, intrigue and usurpation that Honorius' reign had become continued, however, with the rebellion of Heraclianus in Africa. Realising the importance of his position and continued loyalty in the events of 408–10 Heraclianus clearly felt that he had been insufficiently rewarded. In 413 he landed in Italy with an army but was quickly defeated by Count Marinus. Simultaneously, Honorius permitted African landowners to resist forcibly the African army's billeting officers.[17] Heraclianus fled back to Carthage, where Marinus had him killed. His estate contained enough gold to fund the celebration of Constantius' consulate on his return to Ravenna.[18]

THE SUPREMACY OF CONSTANTIUS: THE EMPIRE ON THE
OFFENSIVE, 413–421[19]

Constantius' emergence during the warfare against Constantine 'III' ushered in a period of almost half a century when generals of Roman extraction held power in the west. They seem overall to have posed as much of a problem as non-Roman officers like Arbogast, Alaric and Gaïnas. Like many fourth-century soldier–emperors and numerous late Roman military leaders, before and after, Constantius was from the Balkans, born in Naissus (Niš, Serbia). The suppression of the usurpers removed the principal political and military threat to Honorius' regime and left Constantius free to take the offensive against the lesser danger posed by the non-Roman groups within imperial territory and to put the western Empire's house in order after the anarchy of the previous decade. Athaulf was asked to return

---

[16] *Chron. Gall. 452*, 69; Olympiodorus, fr. 20; Oros. 7.42.6.   [17] *CTh* 7.8.10.
[18] Heraclianus' revolt: *Chron. Gall. 452*, 75; *Consularia Italica* 541; *CTh* 9.40.21, 15.14.13; Hydatius, *Chron.* 43, 48; Marcellinus, *Chron. s.a.* 413; Olympiodorus, frr. 20.3, 23; Oros. 7.42.10–15; Prosper, *Chron.* AP 386 (= 413).
[19] On Constantius, see Lütkenhaus (1998).

Galla Placidia and, to help him make up his mind, Constantius withheld the Goths' promised grain rations.[20] Alternatively, the ending of the Goths' grain supply might have been unintentional, consequent upon Heraclianus' revolt.[21] This provoked only war. The Goths attacked Marseille but were beaten off by Count Boniface and Athaulf was wounded. Retreating thence, Athaulf took Narbonne, Toulouse and Bordeaux. Now in full revolt, he raised Attalus back to the purple and in summer 414 married Galla Placidia in a memorable ceremony of great pomp.[22] Athaulf apparently saw himself potentially as a new Stilicho, his marriage to Galla paralleling Stilicho's to Theodosius' niece, Serena.[23] Athaulf and Galla Placidia had a son, whom they called Theodosius, further emphasising the Gothic commander's ambitions, but the boy soon died. According to Orosius, who heard the story from an eye-witness whom he met chez Jerome in Bethlehem, Athaulf used to say that he had once thought of replacing *Romania* with *Gothia* but, realising that his Goths were incapable of living according to the law, without which a state cannot exist, he had thought better of it and decided instead to uphold the Roman Empire with Gothic arms.[24] This odd story has been variously interpreted, usually as a Gothic policy statement.[25] If anything, although Athaulf might have been articulating his 'Stilichoian' ambitions, he seems most likely to have been making a joke, interestingly playing on stereotypical Roman ideas about barbarians' inability to live according to the law.[26]

The Ravennate court did not see the funny side. Athaulf's actions produced anything but a harmonious concord between Goth and Roman. Constantius counter-attacked by blockading Narbonne and the Goths were driven from Gaul into Spain, although not before

[20] Olympiodorus, fr. 22. [21] Cesa (1992–3).
[22] On these events: Hydatius, *Chron.* 47, 49; Olympiodorus, fr. 24; Oros. 7.43.1–2; Prosper, *Chron.* AP 387 (= 414).
[23] Scharf (1993). Cesa (1992–3), p. 41, argues that the marriage was against all precedent. This ignores the marriages into the Theodosian house of the Frank Bauto and the Vandal Stilicho. The view of the marriage as unprecedented only stands if one stresses Athaulf's royal status. It seems far from clear at this stage that the title of king of the Goths was either formally recognised by the Romans or necessarily intended by the Goths to be permanent.
[24] Oros. 7.43.4–6.
[25] E.g. Matthews (2000b), an interpretation based upon later developments.
[26] Halsall (2002b), pp. 99–102.

sacking the cities which they had occupied.[27] Athaulf took Barcelona and established his headquarters there but was (415) assassinated by the appropriately named Dubius, in revenge for Athaulf's killing of his former master, described by Olympiodorus as a 'king of a part of the Goths'.[28] This is usually assumed to mean Sarus, whose brother Sergeric[29] now took over the command of the Goths, suggesting that the remnants of Sarus' forces had been incorporated into Athaulf's army. However, after a seven-day spree of vengeance-killings and humiliation of Galla Placidia, Sergeric was in turn murdered and replaced by Wallia. Some Goths now tried and failed to cross to Africa.[30] This has usually been interpreted as an attempt at a crossing by the whole Gothic force but Orosius is clear that it was only one band (*manus*).[31] The Goths found themselves again reduced to hunger by Constantius' blockade, to the point where the Vandals sold them grain at the absurd rate of one *solidus* for a *trula* (spoonful), leading the Vandals to nickname the Goths *truli* – 'spoonies'.[32] The Goths were, however, able to take their revenge, making a treaty with Constantius. Galla Placidia was returned to the Roman court, shortly to marry Constantius, much against her will according to Olympiodorus. Attalus attempted to flee but was caught, mutilated and exiled.[33] He had escaped lightly.

The Goths, furthermore, undertook to fight the other barbarians in Spain. The Spanish situation is complex, not least because of the paucity of sources. We are lucky in having several Spanish narratives but Orosius is notoriously vague and rhetorical at this closing point of his work. Hydatius wrote up to half a century after the event and the various anonymous chroniclers later still. Hydatius says that at some

---

[27] Paulinus of Pella, *Thanksgiving*, p. 254.

[28] Olympiodorus, fr. 26. Jordanes, *Getica* 163, says that Athaulf was killed by one Everulf, whom he used to mock for being short. If so, Athaulf's rather odd sense of humour again had unfortunate consequences. See also Hydatius, *Chron.* 52; Oros. 7.43.8–9; Prosper, *Chron.* AP 388 (= 415).

[29] Also rendered Sigeric or Singeric.   [30] Oros. 7.43.11–12.

[31] See Kulikowski (2001), p. 29; (2004), pp. 168–9.

[32] Olympiodorus, fr. 29.1. Gillett (2002b) decisively rejects the interpretation of this utterly straightforward passage by Germanist scholars (e.g. Wolfram (1988), p. 26) as showing that the Vandals called the Goths trolls. For useful comparisons with normal grain prices see Blockley (1983), p. 218, n. 62.

[33] Hydatius, *Chron.* 52; Olympiodorus, fr. 26.2, 30; Prosper, *Chron.* AP 389 (= 415) (treaty); Olympiodorus, fr. 33.1 (Galla's unwilling marriage); fr. 26.2; Oros. 7.42.10 (Attalus' mutilation).

point in 410 or 411, after visiting devastation upon the Spanish provinces, the barbarians settled down and divided the different provinces amongst themselves by lot (*sorte ... sibi diuidunt*).[34] The Sueves received part of *Gallaecia*, the Hasding Vandals the rest, the Alans *Lusitania* and *Carthaginiensis* and the Siling Vandals *Baetica*.[35] *Tarraconensis* evidently remained Roman, perhaps because it was Gerontius' base. From this it would seem that the Alans and the Silings had the whip hand, receiving the most important provinces within the partitioned area; indeed the Roman counter-offensive concentrated upon these groups. Orosius says that after their initial attack the barbarians settled down and, employing a shockingly critical rhetorical phrase that would be repeated many times in these years, that some Romans preferred to live in poor freedom under the barbarians than be subjected to Roman taxation.[36]

It has been suggested that this was a formal, treaty arrangement with Gerontius and Maximus' rebellious regime.[37] This suggestion makes a certain sense as a policy adopted by Gerontius to cover his back when marching against Constantine 'III', especially in the light of Magnus Maximus' and Theodosius' earlier strategies. Our evidence does not, however, support it.[38] For one thing, the date is imprecise and might be later than Gerontius' suppression. Furthermore, Hydatius states clearly that the barbarians divided up Spain themselves, not that they were granted provinces. Orosius' language, too, must imply independent barbarian control of territory, beyond Roman rule. Indeed the Latin sources are unambiguous in stating that the barbarians took land for themselves. Only Olympiodorus says that Gerontius made peace with the barbarians before attacking Constantine.[39] Closer inspection strengthens these doubts. Gerontius had little to fear from the provinces where the barbarians settled. There was scant danger of anyone attacking *Gallaecia* and *Lusitania* although *Baetica* and *Carthaginensis* might have needed holding against the loyalist Mediterranean fleet and troops in Africa. Furthermore, no source states that Gerontius received any aid from these barbarians. Olympiodorus mentions that the staunchest member of Gerontius'

[34] Hydatius, *Chron.* 40–1.   [35] Kulikowski (2004), pp. 166–7. See also Arce (2003).
[36] Oros. 7.41.7.   [37] E.g. Burns (1992), pp. 58–9.
[38] Kulikowski (2004), p. 165, and n. 62, roundly dismissing the possibility of a treaty.
[39] Olympiodorus, fr. 17.1.

household was an Alan but Alans seem to have been everywhere at this time (some were with the Goths and a third band, under the long-lived king Goar, supported Jovinus).[40] Gerontius' rebellion was launched only with Roman troops. On balance it seems that the barbarians seized land in Spain and that Gerontius recognised their occupation before moving to Gaul. Yet again, Roman politicians, even rebels, saw barbarians as less important than Roman rivals. This is very important as it implies that the Vandals', Sueves' and Alans' partition of most of Spain in 410–11 was the first outright barbarian seizure of political control over Roman territory to receive recognition (albeit from a usurper).

Now in Roman service, Wallia's Gothic army marched against the Alans and Siling Vandals in *Baetica* and *Lusitania* with dramatic success. Probably beginning in 417 and on through 418 the Silings were hounded with heavy losses. Moving west against the Alans in 418, Wallia's force killed their king, Addax, and drove the survivors north to take refuge with the Hasding Vandals in *Gallaecia*.[41] The plan might have been for a two-pronged attack, with the Goths advancing from the south and Roman troops moving west from *Tarraconensis* but, thinking the campaign as good as won, Constantius withdrew Wallia's Goths and settled them in southern Gaul.[42] This took place in 418 or more probably 419. There has been some debate on the date of the settlement. It is usually dated, following Hydatius, to 418, but Prosper places it in 419.[43] Prosper's chronology is probably to be preferred, being compiled closer to events.[44] The initial withdrawal may have taken place in 418 but with the settlement being carried though in 419 by Wallia's successor Theoderic I (sometimes called Theoderid). Contemporary sources specify Aquitaine as its location. Prosper gives the most detailed statement, that the Goths received *Aquitania* II and cities in neighbouring regions. Hydatius says that they were settled from Toulouse to the ocean. The *Chronicle of 452*,

---

[40] Olympiodorus, fr. 17.2.

[41] Gothic campaign in Spain: Hydatius, *Chron.* 52, 55, 59–60; Oros. 7.43.11.

[42] *Chron. Gall. 452*, 73; Hydatius, *Chron.* 61; Olympiodorus, fr. 26.2; Prosper, *Chron.* AP 392 (= 419).

[43] Schwarcz (2001), pp. 15–18; Wood (1992), p. 15. Some of Schwarcz's arguments about the precise layout of Hydatius' text are refuted by the manuscript research of Burgess (ed. and trans.) (1993) (see pp. 29, 43–4).

[44] See below, p. 237, n. 78. One defender of the 418 date still accepts Prosper over Hydatius when dating Athaulf's assassination: Kulikowski (2004), p. 168, n. 82.

wildly misdating the event, just states that Aquitaine was given over to the Goths, and Olympiodorus simply that the Goths received grain and 'a part of Gaul to farm'.[45] Thus the overall picture is of Gothic troops being transferred to stations along the Garonne valley from Toulouse to Bordeaux and up the coast to the Loire estuary.

The mechanisms of the Gothic settlement receive further analysis in chapter 13. Constantius' reasons for relocating the Goths to the Garonne have produced a wealth of speculation, the one point of consensus being that the Empire had the upper hand in the relationship. This was not a case of an imperial regime acceding to a request for land by a powerful barbarian group, as might (albeit improbably) have been the case in Spain. Thus the Empire's motives are the most important to reconstruct. Explanations have related the Gothic settlement to defence against the *Bagaudae* north of the Loire or marauding Saxon fleets.[46] Another proposal has been that the Goths were settled in Aquitaine to maintain equilibrium amongst the barbarians; Constantius ended the Spanish campaign early in order to keep the Sueves and Vandals as a counterpoint to the Goths and settled the Goths in order to have a counterbalance available against the Sueves and Vandals.[47]

Though all plausible to some extent, none of these explanations is entirely convincing. The idea that the Goths were settled to defend the rich provinces of Aquitaine against the *Bagaudae* requires us to see the latter as subversive peasant revolutionaries, a probably mistaken interpretation. Furthermore, Exuperantius waged a successful campaign against the *Bagaudae* in *Aremorica* in 417, whilst the Goths were fighting in Spain.[48] Moreover, in the situation in 418 the Empire did not need to maintain a balance amongst the barbarians. When Constantius withdrew the Goths, the barbarians in Spain were thoroughly defeated and further Roman offensives worsened their situation. The Sueves and Vandals did not require a counterweight and, if balance *were* required, it is odd that Constantius continued to

---

[45] The suggestion by Halsall (2003a), p. 44, n. 16, that the *Taifali* mentioned in Poitou by Gregory of Tours were settled alongside the Goths at this time, is probably (though not necessarily) rendered incorrect by the reference to a prefect of Sarmatians and Taifals at Poitiers in *Not. Dig.* occ. 42.

[46] *Bagaudae*: Thompson, E. A. (1956); Saxon fleets: Wallace-Hadrill, J. M. (1962), 25–48; barbarians in Spain: Burns (1992).

[47] Burns (1992); (1994), pp. 270–1.

[48] Rutilius Namatius, *On his Return*, pp. 226–7.

hound them. Furthermore, the barbarians on the Rhine were generally quiet or had been defeated with Jovinus, and the Burgundians had been formally settled around Worms in about 413. There seems, at this stage, to have been no significant barbarian menace that required any such balancing act, and Suevic and Vandal disarray precluded the need to defend southern Gaul against attack from them. Arguments referring to the recovery of the Sueves and Vandals in the 420s have no bearing on the decisions made in 416–18; at that point, as Orosius, writing at the time, makes clear, it seemed that the barbarian threat in Spain had been eliminated.[49]

The precise location of the settlement in Gaul receives mutually contradictory economic explanations. Some claim that *Aquitania* needed defending because of its prosperity, having as yet been little damaged by barbarian attacks.[50] Others, noting the Goths' harrying of the cities before their departure for Spain, say that, by contrast, the region's parlous economic situation made the local élites more likely to accept barbarian troops billeted on them and their estates.[51] This only shows the weakness of the evidence and the wide range of interpretations that it engenders. Saxon raids on this part of the Gallic coast are not yet mentioned as a threat, although they were a problem later in the century and might already have required response. Whether defence against seaborne raids was the only factor in determining the Goths' location, however, seems doubtful and a garrison at Toulouse would not be ideally placed to repel raids on the Atlantic coast.

Thus it has been proposed that, instead of defence against external threats, the main reasons behind Constantius' positioning of the Goths in south-western Gaul were internal Roman politics. Kulikowski argues forcefully that after repeated attempts at usurpation the government in Ravenna wished to station an army in a secure and hitherto loyal part of Gaul.[52] This is attractive but we know too little about Constantine, Jovinus and Attalus' Gallic supporters to make confident statements about which provinces had remained loyal and which had backed the rebellions. Indeed the only known Gallic official of Priscus Attalus is Paulinus of Pella, who came from Bordeaux in *Aquitania* II, where the Goths would shortly be

---

[49] For further discussion and rejection of the 'balancing act' interpretation, see Kulikowski (2004), pp. 170–2.

[50] Thompson (1956).   [51] Burns (1994), pp. 262–3.

[52] Kulikowski (2001), pp. 33–4.

stationed. Nevertheless the idea that an army in Gaul would help secure the region is surely correct.

Kulikowski also points out that at this stage the Goths might not have been regarded as a major threat.[53] Their campaigns had yielded little success. The sack of Rome, their most notable triumph, was brought about by treachery and did them little good, and despite some minor successes the Goths had proved incapable of defeating western imperial forces in any significant encounter. The draw at Pollentia was the closest they came. Constantius had twice forced them into dire straits by blockade and had moved them at will from Spain to Aquitaine. Ten years after the last major reinforcement of Alaric's group and with long marches, two harrowing blockades and consequent starvation, and hard warfare against Romans and other barbarians in the interim it is unlikely that the Gothic army can have been as numerous as it was after Stilicho's barbarian recruits and others joined it in 408. Nonetheless, even if now numbering 10,000 troops or fewer, the Goths were still numerically important and certainly battle-hardened.

The settlement enabled the Goths to defend the coast if needed and, more importantly, be moved quickly to trouble spots but it also lay away from the crucial lines of communication between Italy, Arles and Spain, or the important strategic corridor along the Rhône and Saône from Arles to the Moselle and Trier.[54] In this sense the location of the Gothic settlement would parallel the possible Saxon settlement in East Anglia. Even more so, however, it illustrates the Empire's retrenchment in the south of Gaul. The Gallic prefecture had by now moved to Arles. In 418 the emperor ordered an annual council to meet there, but it was a council only of the Seven Provinces.[55] Its first meeting very probably discussed and agreed upon the Gothic settlement. We know of no similar establishment for the provinces north of the Loire, though this absence of evidence is not decisive. The Seven Provinces conformed roughly to the area of Gaul enclosed by the Loire, although the diocesan frontier generally stopped somewhat short of that river. The Loire appears to have been viewed as the effective boundary of Roman Gaul, with a military zone of fluctuating extent on both sides of the river. The Loire was regarded as on the very limits of Roman government, as shown by a

---

[53] Kulikowski (2001), p. 32.   [54] Kulikowski (2001), p. 34.

[55] Honorius, *Letter to Agricola.*

famous passage in the fifth-century comedy *Querolus* where the eponymous hero is advised that if he wants to do whatever he likes, without feeling restricted by Roman law, he should go and live on the Loire.[56] Henceforth there was little effective government north of this line except through military intervention, which had drastic effects on northern Gaulish society. Seeing the Gothic settlement as the quartering of a field army held in reserve close to, but not on, the frontier makes its precise location appear less out of line with previous Roman policies than has often been appreciated. The Gothic army was stationed to secure the western Empire's left flank and support offensives like Exuperantius' launched from bases along the Loire to re-establish control in the north.

The barbarian settlements have been seen as strategically located across a belt of central Gaul in order to defend the base of Roman power in the south.[57] However, this argument makes the mistake of lumping the Gothic settlement together with those of the Burgundians and other groups over two decades later. This strategic policy might very well have existed in the 440s but in 418/19 we should probably see the Gothic settlement in *Aquitania* II as a much more temporary expedient.[58] There is little evidence that it was intended to be permanent, which ought to bear on discussions of the settlement's mechanics. Like many aspects of Gothic history, it has often been interpreted teleologically. We know that the 419 settlement in the end gave rise to the non-Roman kingdom of Toulouse, but it was not seen as doing so at the time. We do not know whether the Gothic leaders' royal title was recognised and the letter establishing the Council of the Seven Provinces makes it absolutely clear that *Aquitania* II and Novempopulana remained under Roman governors.[59] If full control had been restored over the north the Goths might well have been relocated. However, it seems that a formal treaty was signed. We cannot be sure of this,[60] but Sidonius

---

[56] *Querolus* 2 (29–34).

[57] Mathisen and Sivan (1998), pp. 6–7. Halsall (2005b) makes a similar argument, with the same problems, and overstates the case for the Gothic settlement being *on* the frontier.

[58] Bleckmann (1997), pp. 586–90, also makes this point. Wolfram (1983), p. 21, states that we do not know how permanent the settlement was intended to be.

[59] Honorius, *Letter to Agricola*.

[60] Even Wolfram (1983), pp. 21–2, who normally envisages formal treaties behind events, admits that we cannot be sure that a *foedus* was signed in 418/19.

Apollinaris, writing about the events of 439, states that the Roman official Avitus renewed the *foedus* and Prosper writes about a Gothic attack in the 430s as confounding the peace agreements.[61] Although both possibly referred to events in 426, there is no clear evidence of any formal cessation of hostilities between Goths and Romans between 425 and 439. References to the Goths as *foederati* or *symmachoi* only become common after 418/19. Nevertheless, this treaty founded no independent kingdom. Almost forty years after the supposed treaty of 382 the Goths had still not formed the quasi-independent state on Roman soil that that 'treaty' is assumed to have so crucially created.

The Gothic settlement was only one component of Constantius' strategy. Exuperantius' 417 campaign north of the Loire against the *Bagaudae* was another. The offensive in Spain continued. In 418, after the Goths' withdrawal, King Hermeric of the Sueves and Gunderic, king of the Hasding Vandals, fought each other and the Sueves were besieged in the mountains.[62] Later that year or in 420 Constantius' officers, Maurocellus and Astirius, *vicarius* and count of the Spains respectively, drove the Vandals away from their siege, killing some outside Braga.[63] The Vandal retreat out of mountainous *Gallaecia* into prosperous *Baetica* was probably not, however, the desired outcome. The Romans' attack on the Vandals, rather than leaving them to destroy the Sueves, might have been prompted by the fact that one or other party had raised Maximus back to the purple. Astirius was rewarded with the patriciate after capturing the usurper, who was paraded in chains in Honorius' thirtieth-year celebrations in 422.[64] The Goths were shortly afterwards called out on their first campaign under the new arrangement in order to continue this attack. Simultaneously, another general, Castinus, campaigned in northern Gaul against the Franks.[65] An entry in the *Anglo-Saxon Chronicle* states that the Romans

---

[61] Sid. Ap. *Poems*, 7, line 308; Prosper, *Chron.* AP 409 (= 436).

[62] Hydatius, *Chron.* 63.

[63] Hydatius, *Chron.* 66, may mean that the casualties were Roman, as Burgess (ed. and trans.) (1993) and Kulikowski (2000c), p. 126, and (2004), p. 173, argue (*Vandali suevorum obsidione dimissa instante Astirio Hispaniarum comite et sub vicario Maurocello aliquantis bracara in exitu suo occisis relicta Gallicia Beticam transierunt*).

[64] Kulikowski (2000c) for a different reconstruction.

[65] Renatus Profuturus Frigeridus (at *LH* 2.9). As Castinus was campaigning in Spain by late 421 or 422, this must have occurred in about 420.

now collected the treasure in Britain and withdrew to Gaul.[66] Little
weight can be placed upon this legendary fragment but the chronological coincidence (which is probably all it is) with Constantius'
re-establishment of imperial authority in the west, and particularly
Exuperantius' Aremorican campaign, is curious.

After his success in restoring the situation, Constantius was raised
to the purple in 421, although Honorius was unwilling to share power
and the arrangement was apparently not a happy one.[67] Nevertheless
at this point it must have looked, as Orosius thought when he finished
his *History* a few years previously, as though the crisis had passed
and that the western Empire was well on the way to full restoration
(map 16). The barbarians in Spain had been defeated,[68] the Goths
brought to heel and campaigns were already apparently returning
northern Gaul to the fold. A few more years of such well-directed and
energetic leadership would thoroughly re-establish the western
Empire even as far as Britain. The damage and dereliction revealed on
archaeological sites across the west would be visible only as one phase
in a more continuous history of occupation.

COMPETITION FOR AUTHORITY, 421–434

Constantius died of pleurisy in the eighth month of his reign, and
without his firm hand at the helm the promising situation soon
collapsed.[69] Even before his death things had started to deteriorate.
The usual factors played their part. Constantius' elevation had
annoyed Theodosius II, who refused to acknowledge the new
emperor. According to Olympiodorus, Constantius was planning a
campaign against the east when he died.[70] A political crisis and open
warfare broke out between the eastern Empire and the Sassanids in
420–1, which, it has been suggested, stemmed from the eastern
court's attempts to secure its eastern frontier independently of Persian

---

[66] *Anglo-Saxon Chronicle s.a.* 418.

[67] *Chron. Gall. 452,* 88; Olympiodorus, fr. 33.1; Prosper, *Chron.* AP 393 (= 420).

[68] Kulikowski (2000c), p. 133: 'throughout Letter 11* [of Consentius to Augustine]
Consentius is totally dismissive of any barbarian problem'. Kulikowski dates this
letter to 420/1.

[69] *Chron. Gall. 452,* 88; Olympiodorus, fr. 33.1, suggests at one point that
Constantius died in the seventh month of his reign, and at another that he died
after seven months of rule. At fr. 33.2 he says he died after six months.

[70] Olympiodorus, fr. 33.1–2.

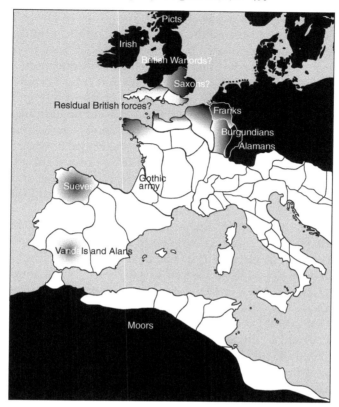

Map 16 The western Empire in 421, at the death of Constantius 'III'

alliance.[71] This would make sense in the context of a threatened war against Constantius. Roman internal politics again reared their ugly head, with all too predictable results.

Meanwhile Castinus had called out the Gothic army and was continuing the campaign against the Vandals in *Baetica*. However, he snatched defeat from the jaws of victory when, having reduced the Vandals to the point of surrender, he offered battle and was defeated, allegedly because of Gothic treason.[72] The defeat occurred after

[71] Rubin, Z. (1986). Rubin does not make the connection with Constantius' preparations for war against the east, apparently seeing defence against external aggression as the Romans' only military concern.
[72] Hydatius, *Chron.* 69; Prosper, *Chron.* AP 395 (= 422).

Constantius' death but it is likely that the campaign had been begun earlier, continuing Maurocellus' and Astirius' attack. Castinus' ill-advised commitment to open battle was possibly an attempt to win prestige for himself in the immediate aftermath of Constantius' death and perhaps gain a more favourable position. A rapid and decisive end to the campaign would have allowed him to return promptly and victoriously to the centre of the Empire. Also during this campaign, again probably related to the jostling for position after Constantius' death, Castinus fell out with his fellow commander Boniface, who stalked off to Africa.[73] After Constantius' demise Galla Placidia and her brother became very close – scandalously close according to some – but were induced by court intrigue to fall out and Galla and her children were exiled to Constantinople.[74]

Honorius died on 27 August 423, not long after celebrating his thirtieth year as *augustus* (his father had placed him on the throne before setting out against Eugenius and Arbogast), leaving as his heir his four-year-old nephew Valentinian, the son of Constantius and Galla Placidia.[75] Most contemporaries saw Honorius as a disastrous emperor and it is difficult to disagree. Perhaps the strongest argument in his defence is his stubbornness in refusing to treat with Alaric, which eventually drove the Gothic leader to his death. Be that as it may, Honorius' demise did the Empire few favours. No sooner was he dead than, with Valentinian absent in Constantinople, John, the chief palace notary (*primicerius notariorum*), seized the throne. Castinus apparently supported the usurpation; he was made consul for 424.[76] Exuperantius was lynched by his troops in Arles but in Africa Boniface, maintaining his opposition to Castinus, held the province for the Theodosians and defeated an army sent against him. This weakened John's forces and in 425 an expedition was sent from Constantinople by sea, under Ardabur, and by land under Candidianus and Ardabur's son Aspar. Help was brought to John by the general Aëtius and a large (allegedly 60,000-strong) force of Huns. Ardabur was blown off course and captured but managed to suborn John's commanders whilst the land forces took Aquileia and other cities. John, betrayed by his troops, was executed and Valentinian, still barely six, declared *augustus*. Aëtius' army arrived three days too

---

[73] Prosper, *Chron.* AP 395 (= 422).
[74] *Chron. Gall. 452*, 90; Olympiodorus, fr. 38.
[75] Olympiodorus, fr. 39.1–2.   [76] Prosper, *Chron.* AP 396 (= 423).

late to save John and fought a bloody but indecisive battle against Aspar. Aëtius, however, received clemency in return for persuading his Hunnic allies to return home.[77]

For the remainder of the 420s Aëtius appears to have striven to restore imperial authority, but the chronology of his campaigns is extremely confused. The brevity, vagueness and chronological imprecision of the sources makes it difficult to know for sure whether similar events placed in varying years in different sources are the same happenings or separate events. For example, Prosper records a Frankish campaign by Aëtius in the consulate of Felix and Taurus (428) whilst Hydatius records one in the year 470 of the Spanish era (= 432 AD). Some authorities see this as evidence of two wars but closer inspection suggests that it is the same campaign but with its date calculated according to two different systems.[78] Nevertheless, some outlines can be given, showing the general areas of activity. The reconstruction below streamlines Aëtius' career, preventing him from having to rush about all over the west, simultaneously fighting barbarian attacks and Roman civil wars, as he does in some modern accounts.[79]

In 426, in his first operation after Valentinian's elevation, Aëtius drove a Gothic force under Anaulf away from Arles.[80] In succeeding generations the Goths tended to threaten Arles, seat of Roman government in Gaul, in order to obtain some sort of concession.

[77] On the suppression of John's usurpation, see Olympiodorus, fr. 43.1–2.

[78] Two campaigns: Drinkwater and Elton (eds.) (1992) p. xviii; Heather (2000), p. 7. Prosper thought the campaign took place in the 401st year after Christ's passion and Hydatius believed it took place in the eighth Jubilee (400 years) after Christ's ascension, arguing for one campaign, 400/1 years after Christ's passion and ascension, but placed further apart according to two different chronological systems. Prosper used a different calculation for the date of Christ's passion from Hydatius, calculating this to the fifteenth year of Tiberius, whereas Hydatius, following Jerome, believed it took place after a three-year ministry beginning in Tiberius' fifteenth regnal year (Humphries (1996), pp. 159–60). Hence the discrepancy between the two, which applies to other duplicated campaigns. The consular date given by Prosper and his closer proximity to events probably permits us to prefer his date and to propose a single campaign in 427/8.

[79] On Aëtius' career, see, above all, Stickler (2002).

[80] This campaign is recorded by Prosper in 426, but in 430, with the commander named as 'Anaolsus' (presumably Anaulf), by Hydatius. However, see n. 78 for explanation of the difference between Hydatius' dating system and that used by Prosper. Thus, *pace* most modern commentators (e.g. Heather (1996), p. 185; (2000a), p. 7), there was probably only one campaign.

What they were aiming at on this occasion we do not know but especially when one looks at the Goths' actions in Gaul throughout the fifth century until 471, it is most likely that their campaign represented an attempt to become involved at the heart of Roman politics in the confusion caused by Honorius' death. Clearly the Goths were now too well established and important for a Roman victory in the field to permit their expulsion from Aquitaine or otherwise revise the terms of their stationing there. Whether the Goths were thoroughly pacified after Aëtius' victory is unknown. Sidonius' and Prosper's references to previous treaties in discussing the events of the 430s might refer to an agreement in 426.[81]

Aëtius also campaigned against the Franks near the Rhine in 427/8 and at this time St Germanus, bishop of Auxerre and former soldier, visited Britain, ostensibly to resolve a dispute between Pelagian heretics and Catholic Christians in Verulamium (St Albans).[82] Similar uses of heresy accusations are known from other parts of the Empire at this time.[83] The petition to Germanus was especially timely, as the Empire appeared to be restoring its presence in northern Gaul. Doubtless it seemed possible that Roman troops might soon cross the Channel to restore government to Britain.

That local power could still be maintained through traditional Roman means of legitimation in Britain is further suggested by the archaeological data. During the middle quarters of the fifth century, south of the Thames, a form of metalwork becomes common, called 'quoit brooch style' after one of the types of artefact upon which it is found (map 17).[84] This insular development of the styles used on late fourth- and early fifth-century official metalwork employs very similar decorative vocabulary. Although found on feminine artefacts, such as the brooches, perhaps suggesting a different gendering of power (Roman official art motifs were less commonly found on feminine items of apparel) it is also used, like earlier motifs, on elaborate belt-sets, the classic Roman masculine badges of office, and some weaponry. All this suggests that, south of the Thames, power was displayed through claiming links to the Empire and traditional sources of authority.[85]

---

[81] See above, n. 61.

[82] Constantius, *Life of Germanus* 12–18; Prosper, *Chron.* AP 401 (= 428).

[83] Van Dam (1986). Below, pp. 323, 341.   [84] Suzuki (2000).

[85] See below, p. 276, for further discussion.

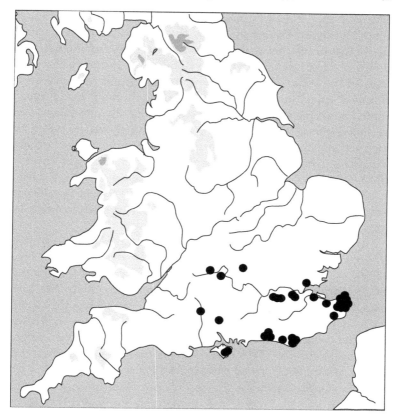

Map 17 Distribution of quoit brooch style metalwork

This contrasts interestingly with the regions north of the Thames where, already, artefacts of northern German origin were being employed.[86]

Meanwhile, the Vandals, recovering from their near destruction at Castinus' hands, raided widely. In 425–6 they are recorded as having sacked Seville and other cities, acquired a fleet, attacked the Balearic Islands, and even plundered *Mauretania* (presumably *Tingitania*). After capturing Seville in *c.*426–8, however, their king, Gunderic, died and was succeeded by his brother Gaiseric.[87] Civil strife seems now to have broken out between the Ravennate court, led by Felix, and

---

[86] Böhme (1986), pp. 542–58.   [87] Hydatius, *Chron.* 76–7, 79.

Galla Placidia's supporter Boniface in Africa, perhaps as a result of Aëtius' intrigues. Procopius claims that Galla Placidia was led to believe that Boniface was planning treason and ordered him to return to Italy. Aëtius, however, wrote to Boniface warning him that if he returned he would be killed. Unsurprisingly, Boniface stayed away and his absence thus confirmed the suspicions about his loyalty.[88] Three commanders were sent against him but all were killed, two through the treachery of the third, who was then executed. In their place a commander called Sigisvult was sent, with Gothic troops, perhaps implying that the Goths had indeed been brought to heel in 426.[89] Prosper of Aquitaine links this struggle with the Vandals' acquisition of ships.[90] He also says that both sides sought the alliance of the Vandals, and Boniface does appear to have recruited Vandal troops.

The Vandals' famous crossing to Africa in the May of some year between 427 and 429 should also be seen in this context.[91] Two references suggest that their ravages after the deaths of Constantius and Honorius produced a major campaign against them. Hydatius states that the Vandals were about to cross to Africa when they heard that a Suevic army under Heremigar was campaigning near Mérida, whereupon Gaiseric turned back and defeated the Sueves, before resuming his crossing.[92] However, Mérida is too far from the coast for Gaiseric just to have turned back and fought the battle to cover his rear. The *Gallic Chronicle of 452* records the death of 20,000 troops fighting the Vandals in Spain and, though (not unusually) it misdates the event, it nevertheless places it immediately before the Vandals' migration to Africa.[93] A further offensive had been organised by the Romans, using the Sueves as allies. Salvian possibly refers to this

---

[88] Procopius, *Wars* 3.3.16–31; Prosper, *Chron.* AP 400 (= 427), who confirms Boniface's refusal to come to Italy.

[89] The arrival of Goths, presumably in these imperial forces, is found in Possidius, *Life of Augustine* 17. See Mathisen (1999). Sigisvult's mission is another episode recorded under two dates by two different sources, in this case Prosper, *Chron.* (AP 400(= 427)) and *Chron. Gall. 452* (96 = *s.a.* 424). Mathisen (1999), p. 176, n. 12.

[90] *Chron.* AP 400 (= 427).

[91] Victor of Vita, *History of the Vandal Persecution* 1.2. The date of this crossing is far less secure than is often believed. See, e.g. Mathisen (1999), p. 177, n. 16.

[92] Hydatius, *Chron.* 80.

[93] *Chron. Gall. 452.* The *Chronicle's* chronological laxity makes it far from impossible that this is a misplaced reference to Castinus' defeat in 422.

campaign and defeat,[94] which seems to have destroyed the regular Roman military presence south of the Pyrenees. Defence and political organisation fell to local leaders, not always unsuccessfully. Immediately afterwards, the Vandals crossed to Africa. In the sixth century, Procopius and Jordanes claimed that Boniface invited the Vandals into Africa during his war against Felix.[95] This seems implausible, not least because he was soon fighting against their invasion. Possibly, in the face of repeated offensives against them, and knowing Africa's strategic importance, the Vandals felt that Spain was getting too 'hot' for them and so, under cover of their victories against Roman and pro-Roman forces, they moved to the crucial province of Africa. It is also possible that Aëtius gave them carte blanche to move, perhaps in negotiations after the destruction of the Spanish field army.[96]

Meanwhile, Sigisvult had apparently bloodlessly resolved the situation with regard to Boniface, who was reconciled with the Ravennate court. Boniface was free to move against Gaiseric's Vandals but was defeated. The intrigue in Ravenna had not ceased, though. Foiled in his plots against Boniface, Aëtius nevertheless engineered Felix's downfall and execution and returned to Italy to take up the senior military command, the master of both the services (*magister utriusque militiae*).[97] In around 430 he defeated the Alamannic *Juthungi* who had invaded north of the Alps and also fought against rebellious inhabitants of Noricum.[98] In the confusion of the previous decades it seems likely that the Alamans might have been drawn into the political vacuum north of the Alps in support of various local leaders. Aëtius also negotiated with the Sueves who, in the aftermath of the Roman defeat in Spain and the Vandal withdrawal, had taken the opportunity to attack the provincials of *Gallaecia*, where they had their base. A treaty was apparently patched up but Spain was now another area where barbarian warlords jostled with local leaders viewed with varying degrees of hostility by Ravenna, some formed into senates based upon the cities. For the time being, although

---

[94] *On the Governance of God* 7.6.11. It is also possible that Salvian was referring to Castinus' defeat.

[95] Jordanes, *Getica* 33.167; Procopius, *Wars* 3.3.22–6.

[96] Mathisen (1999), pp. 189–91, suggests Aëtius' responsibility and successfully clears Boniface's name.

[97] Hydatius, *Chron.* 84; Priscus, fr. 30.1; Prosper, *Chron.* AP 403 (= 430).

[98] *Chron. Gall. 452*, 106; Hydatius, *Chron.* 83, 85.

currently held in check, the Sueves had the greatest potential for
military and political domination. Like Britain, although to a lesser
degree, Spain became a political vacuum. As with Britain, however,
the Romans had made no firm decision to abandon the peninsula.
The comparison between Britain and Spain should be stressed. In
both areas the end of Roman rule came messily, without either a
rapid conquest or a neat treaty. However, the consequences were
very different. In Britain, the Roman social, political and economic
order collapsed rapidly and dramatically whereas in Spain this order
survived well beyond the end of the fifth century, as is discussed
below.[99]

In 432 Boniface rebelled against Aëtius. Placidia's old ally probably
feared being under the sway of her senior general. Aëtius' dominance
might also have alarmed the Constantinopolitan court, which had
despatched Aspar to help against the Vandals. He also covered
Boniface's back as his army landed in Italy. Boniface defeated Aëtius,
but died of wounds. After briefly retiring to his estates, Aëtius left
Italy only to return in 434 with another large army of Huns, with
whose support he drove out Boniface's son Sebastian and restored his
domination.[100] Also in 434 the Vandals, having beaten an eastern
Roman force under Aspar, were granted by treaty the Mauretanian
provinces and *Numidia*, the least prosperous portion of Roman North
Africa.[101]

AËTIUS, GAISERIC AND ATTILA, 434–453

Like countless Roman leaders before him, Aëtius had prioritised the
acquisition of supreme power within Roman politics over the threats
posed by the barbarians, inside and outside the former frontiers. The
thirteen years between Constantius' death and Aëtius' achievement
of unchallenged dominance had, however, profoundly changed
the political situation. By 434 Britain had been removed from any
formal links with the Empire for a quarter of a century. Although it
seems that the possibility was retained of reunification with the

[99] Below, pp. 338–46, 357–68.
[100] On these events, see: *Chron. Gall. 452*, 109–12, 115; *Consularia Italica 550*;
Hydatius, *Chron.* 89, Priscus, fr. 30.1; Prosper, *Chron.* AP 405 (= 432).
[101] *Chron. Gall. 452*, 108; Procopius, *Wars* 3.3.30–6; Prosper, *Chron.* AP 408 (= 435).
The story told by Olympiodorus, fr. 40, presumably belongs to this period.

Empire, even contemporaries thought that Britain had been lost for good.[102] The Rhine frontier had collapsed and although Frankish and Alamannic expansion had been checked, at least in part, the promising situation that pertained when Constantius died had evaporated. Northern Gaul again fell outside formal Roman administration and the regulation of power and patronage. Consequently it seems to have become a patchwork of territories ruled by unrecognised local chiefs, leaders whose authority was based upon claimed Roman titles, and barbarian warlords.[103] The Goths in *Aquitania* II and *Novempopulana* may or may not still have been in revolt. Spain presented a similar situation to northern Gaul and the Sueves had tightened their grip on *Gallaecia*. *Numidia* and the *Mauretanias* had been granted by treaty to the Vandals. Only Italy and the recently pacified provinces north of the Alps, the west's Balkan provinces, *Africa Proconsularis* and *Byzacena*, *Narbonensis*, *Viennensis*, and perhaps the frontier zone along the Loire remained under direct imperial control. Little territory had been formally, let alone definitively, abandoned but the effective circumscription of imperial administration obviously affected Aëtius' ability to raise troops or the taxes to pay for them. Recruitment was vital. Since 406 the western army had fought itself in Gaul in 408; it had fought another battle against the forces (also probably largely drawn from Roman units) of Constantine 'III' in 411 and inflicted heavy losses upon them; a bloody, indecisive battle had taken place against Aëtius' Huns in 425; the army had suffered heavy defeats at the hands of the Vandals in 422 and 427–9; and another severe engagement was fought between Aëtius and Boniface in 433. Other skirmishes and victorious encounters had produced yet further casualties. How could these losses be replaced? With perhaps two thirds of the western Empire outside his effective control, at least temporarily, it is hardly surprising that Aëtius came increasingly to rely upon barbarian allies recruited from outside the Empire. It is also unsurprising that the Empire was unable to displace the Goths from Aquitaine or that the manpower of the Gothic army became so important. A regular Roman army still existed and was plainly still effective[104] but it would need help if it were to re-establish the western Empire.

---

[102] *Narrative of the Emperors of the Valentinianic and Theodosian Houses* 6.
[103] This is the picture given by Salvian's *On the Governance of God*.
[104] Elton (1992), who perhaps overstates the case.

Nevertheless, Aëtius set about his task energetically. His first operations were in Gaul. He appears to have wanted to restore the Rhine frontier so in 435–6 he destroyed the Burgundian kingdom on the middle Rhine.[105] In this he was helped by a large number of Hunnic auxiliaries, some serving in his army, others perhaps used from outside the Empire, as allies. The death of the Burgundian Gundigar and the slaughter of his people by the Huns became the origin of the medieval Nibelungen saga.[106] This campaign might have re-established imperial authority in Trier. Aëtius' difficulties in 432–4 seem to have encouraged the Goths to launch another attack against Narbonne and Arles – points of crucial strategic importance for the western government – presumably in a bid to become more centrally involved in the regime.[107] If Aëtius was ever to restore imperial fortunes in Spain he needed to retain control over the southern Gaulish coast. After defeating the Goths and apparently leaving his general Litorius with a Hunnish army to follow this up by attacking Gothic territory, Aëtius returned to northern Gaul. There the confusion at the centre of the Empire had led to local leaders assuming control in their regions, especially in the west of this area, *Aremorica*. As before, the powers in Ravenna regarded this as rebellion and called the 'rebels' *Bagaudae*.[108] Aëtius' attempts to bring them to heel were forcibly resisted but by 439 had been successful. Once again, the movement of Roman forces into the north of Gaul had consequences in Britain. The *Life of Germanus* claims that the bishop returned to Britain at about this time to adjudicate in another dispute.[109] Alongside problems with chronology (it is difficult to find the time for this visit in what we know of Germanus' last, busy years), this episode mirrors his first visit so closely that historians have been inclined to dismiss it as a literary device.[110] However, the chronological coincidence between imperial campaigns in northern Gaul

---

[105] Burgundian campaign: *Chron. Gall. 452*, 118; Hydatius, *Chron.* 99; Prosper, *Chron.* AP 408 (=435).

[106] The ascription of the kingdom's destruction to Attila appears first in Paul the Deacon's late eighth-century *Book of the Bishops of Metz*. It is possible that the latter phase of this war, alluded to by Prosper (see n. 105) was led by Attila, perhaps as Aëtius' ally. On these myths, see Barnish (1992); Wood (2003), pp. 247–9.

[107] Hydatius, *Chron.* 101, 104; Prosper, *Chron.* AP 409 (=436).

[108] *Chron. Gall. 452*, 117, 119.   [109] Constantius, *Life of Germanus* 25–7.

[110] On this, see Wood (1984), pp. 14–17.

and British appeals to officials of the Empire is again striking. In 439, however, Litorius rashly engaged the Gothic army at Toulouse and, although the battle went well, was captured and executed.[111] An even more serious reverse was suffered in Africa where, profiting from the western government's concentration on Gallic campaigns, Gaiseric seized Carthage in a surprise attack. The sack of the city was apparently brutal.[112]

Litorius' death and the loss of Carthage completely changed the political situation, which had hitherto been looking most promising for Aëtius' regime (map 18). Aëtius was forced to make peace with the Gothic king Theoderic I in order to free himself to face the Vandals.[113] The Vandal threat also led to an apparent policy of retrenchment in Gaul although, as ever, this does not mean that any firm decision had been made permanently to abandon any imperial territory. This clearly stemmed from the manpower crisis mentioned earlier. The western Empire simply did not have enough troops to pursue operations on two fronts. Meanwhile the Sueves who had been brought to the brink of a peace settlement, albeit largely through the efforts of local Gallaecian nobles, took advantage of the situation to enter upon a period of domination in Iberia under their kings Hermeric and Rechila. Rechila captured Mérida in 439 and by 442 had taken Seville and spread his authority over *Baetica* and *Carthaginiensis*.[114] The only province outside his control, *Tarraconensis*, removed like Gaul from effective governmental authority, witnessed a rise of *Bagaudae*.[115] By the 440s northern Gaul too was reported to be again under the control of such unauthorised leaders.[116]

The treaty with the Goths is particularly significant. If the Goths had remained hostile since their rebellion after Honorius' death, government in *Aquitania* II and parts of Novempopulana must have been taken over by their king. The references to a *foedus* in Prosper's and Sidonius' accounts of the 430s might be to a treaty of *c.*426 rather than to the settlement of 419[117] and thus mean that conflict had not gone on uninterrupted since the early 420s. Even if this is the case, between

[111] Hydatius 108; Prosper, *Chron.* AP 412 (= 439).

[112] *Chron. Gall. 452*, 129; Hydatius, *Chron.* 107; Prosper, *Chron.* AP 412 (= 439); Victor of Vita, *History of the Vandal Persecution* 1.5; Modéran (2002a).

[113] Hydatius, *Chron.* 109.   [114] Hydatius, *Chron.* 91–2, 105–6, 111, 113.

[115] On Spanish *Bagaudae* see Kulikowski (2004), pp. 182–3; Orlandis (1987), pp. 38–40.

[116] *Chron. Gall. 452*, 133.   [117] As above, p. 233.

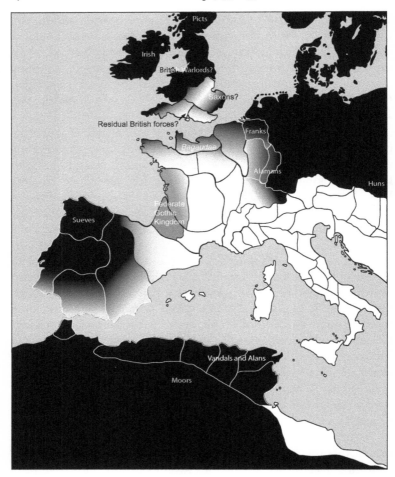

Map 18 The Western Empire, 439, after the Vandal sack of Carthage

436 and 439, and possibly during the confusion in Italy between 432 and 434, the Empire was in no position to impose governors or administrative officers in the Garonne valley. The treaty of 439 is perhaps the most important in the development of the Gothic kingdom. It might even be argued that it was the first definite formal treaty signed between the Empire and the group originally led by Alaric in which both sides acted as sovereign entities. It looks more like a bilateral agreement between two parties than any such agreement in Gothic history since 369. It was possibly the first to recognise the

Goths' rule by a king. Within a few years the Goths were following their own foreign policy, marrying one of Theoderic's daughters to Huneric, heir to the Vandal throne, and another to King Rechiar of the Sueves.[118] This ought to be less surprising given the Empire's recognition by treaty of the Vandals' seizure of land in Africa only five years previously. Now it seems incontrovertible that there was a sovereign or semi-sovereign Gothic polity within Rome's frontiers. Once again, though, we should not be forced into thinking that this situation was regarded as permanent by anyone. The treaty with the Vandals was held in place only by military balance,[119] and the Empire made more than one attempt forcibly to alter the situation.

The Goths remained quiet for the next decade and more, contributing troops to Spanish operations, but the Empire's situation was not dramatically ameliorated. In 440 Gaiseric attacked Sicily but met with resistance.[120] Misinformation that Boniface's son-in-law Sebastian was about to cross into Africa possibly slowed his campaign.[121] The next year an eastern fleet was dispatched to help defend Sicily but it ended up doing little to fight the Vandals and was a heavy burden on the Sicilians.[122] The eastern forces were held back rather than committed to battle because a war between Persia and the east was about to break out.[123] The east was also under pressure in the Balkans from the Huns, now a very powerful military and political force led by Bleda and his more famous brother, Attila. In 442, perhaps helped by a possibly Roman-inspired conspiracy against Gaiseric in Carthage, the Empire was able to conclude a treaty with the Vandals, recognising their possession of *Numidia*, *Byzacena* and *Proconsularis*.[124] This gave Gaiseric an enormous bargaining chip in his demands to be included in politics at the heart of the Empire. The Mauritanian provinces were apparently returned to Rome but there was currently little that the Empire could do to govern them effectively, given the Spanish situation. Another political vacuum was created, into which

---

[118] Hydatius, *Chron.* 132; Jordanes, *Getica* 36.184. On diplomacy in this period, see, above all, Gillett (2003).

[119] Ausbüttel (1991).

[120] Hydatius, *Chron.* 112; Prosper, *Chron.* AP 413 (= 440). Gautier (1932), pp. 222–5.

[121] Mathisen (1999) makes this suggestion.

[122] Prosper, *Chron.* AP 414 (= 441).   [123] Rubin, Z. (1986).

[124] Procopius, *Wars* 3.4.13–15 (seemingly relating to the treaty of 442); Prosper, *Chron.* AP 415 (= 442); Victor, *History of the Vandal Persecution* 1.13. Gautier (1932), pp. 226–7.

not only the Vandals but also the Moorish rulers expanded their power. It is unlikely that the imperial court (and perhaps Gaiseric too) had any intention of remaining bound by the treaty's terms if the opportunity of altering them presented itself. For now, though, Gaiseric turned to consolidating his rule in Africa. Something of a rule of terror was introduced with Roman landowners being dispossessed and the Catholic church persecuted.[125] A few years later, nevertheless, Valentinian further bound the Vandals into the regime by engaging his daughter Eudocia to Gaiseric's son Huneric and Gaiseric relaxed his persecution.[126] Huneric, of course, was already married to the daughter of Theoderic of the Goths. This posed problems for all, not least Theoderic's daughter.

The respite from Vandal attacks (we hear nothing of Vandal piracy for about ten years after 445) allowed Aëtius to secure his bastion in southern Gaul. At about this time, he moved what was left of the Burgundians south to settlements in Sapaudia (roughly between Lac Léman and Windisch)[127] and settled groups of Alans in Valence and in *Gallia Ulterior*, apparently near Auxerre.[128] The *Gallic Chronicle of 452*'s references to Gaul north of the Loire as 'Further Gaul' indicate graphically the effective retreat of Roman power to the south. The mechanisms of these settlements receive more detailed treatment in chapter 13. What needs to be made clear now is the difference between the Empire's situation in the early 440s and that in 418/19. By this stage it looks very much as though the policy in Gaul had involved a retreat to a line from the mouth of the Loire to the northern edges of the Alps, with federate groups settled along that frontier to help defend it. In the middle Loire, between the Gothic settlement and that of the Alans and Burgundians, the remnants of the Gallic field army was left to bear the brunt of campaigns to restore Roman rule to the north. Nevertheless, between 434 and 442 the Empire had formally admitted the loss of considerable swathes of territory in Gaul, Africa and possibly Spain too. The significance of this decade has not always been recognised yet it saw some very important developments.

---

[125] Victor, *History of the Vandal Persecution* 1.9–51.

[126] Oost (1968), pp. 260–1.

[127] The date of this is usually given as 443 but the evidence is uncertain: Shanzer and Wood (eds. and trans.) (2002), pp. 14–15. Kaiser (2004), pp. 38–45 and map at p. 33.

[128] *Chron. Gall. 452*, 127; Constantius, *Life of Germanus* 28.

Nothing daunted, Aëtius set about rebuilding Roman authority. There were two principal theatres of operations. The first was northern Gaul. Aëtius' settlement of the Alans seems to have been a means of quelling independent local leaders, the so-called *Bagaudae*. This impression is certainly given by Constantius' *Life of Germanus of Auxerre*, which links Aëtius' transfer of land in *Aremorica* with his exasperation with the region's inhabitants.[129] The *Gallic Chronicle of 452* also says that the Alans forcibly dispossessed the local landowners, some of whom violently resisted them.[130] As late as 448 the *Chronicle* refers to *Bagaudae* in the region, although in the context of one of their leaders fleeing to Attila's Huns, suggesting that the area was again being pacified. At the same time, Aëtius' troops campaigned against the Franks and defeated them at *Vicus Helena* (usually identified as Hélesmes in the département of Nord).[131] It seems clear that although Aëtius might have been concerned to secure his southern base, he still entertained hopes of restoring the Rhine frontier and effective government in northern Gaul, and was capable of campaigning against Frankish incursions. It was probably at this time, when Aëtius was again campaigning in the north, that the Britons appealed to him.[132]

The second theatre of operations was Spain. Again, the chief targets of this activity were local warlords who had established their own authority. As usual, legitimist sources refer to such leaders as *Bagaudae*.[133] As early as 441, perhaps with the Vandal withdrawal from Sicily, Asturius had been sent as *magister utriusque militiae* to *Tarraconensis*, the strategically vital north-eastern province including the Ebro valley, and had, according to Hydatius, slaughtered a large number of *Bagaudae* there. Two years later, while Aëtius was securing central Gaul, Asturius' son-in-law Merobaudes repeated the operation.[134] Despite evident success, however, Merobaudes was recalled to Rome. Nonetheless, the campaign to restore authority in Spain continued. In 445 the Vandals raided the Gallaecian coast.[135] This is so far from their African base and such an unlikely source of booty

---

[129] Constantius, *Life of St Germanus* 28.   [130] *Chron. Gall. 452*, 127.
[131] Sid. Ap. *Poems* 5, lines 212–54.   [132] *DEB* 20.
[133] Kulikowski (2004), p. 182, sees these people as representative of an upsurge of 'well-organised bandits'.
[134] On these campaigns: Hydatius, *Chron.* 117, 120.
[135] Hydatius, *Chron.* 123.

that one must suspect a Roman initiative behind this attack on Suevic territory, possibly associated with Eudocia's engagement to Huneric. The following year, the offensive against the Sueves was pursued when a third *magister utriusque militiae*, Vitus, led an army including Gothic federates through *Carthaginiensis* and *Baetica*.[136] This suggests that Merobaudes must have pacified *Tarraconensis*. All was going very well for the Empire until Vitus' operation provoked a Suevic counter-attack. Rechila defeated Vitus heavily. In the aftermath the Sueves restored their rule over *Baetica* and *Carthaginiensis* and the Spanish situation collapsed. Although Rechila died in August 448 by the next year his successor Rechiar was campaigning alongside a *Bagauda* with the suitably presumptuous name of Basilius (emperor) in the Ebro valley, as far as Saragossa. Federates (probably Goths) were massacred in a church in Tyriasso.[137] The repeated mention of *foederati* and Goths in the accounts of these campaigns shows that Roman military efforts in this sphere were largely reliant upon allied contingents. All the work of Asturius and Merobaudes was undone. Rechiar also raided in *Gallaecia* and into the Pyrenees and, perhaps more disturbingly, visited Theoderic in Gaul and married his daughter.[138] The aftermath of the treaty of 439 can be seen in the Goths' ability to conduct an independent 'foreign policy'. Rechiar's marriage alliance might have been aimed at stopping the Goths from providing troops for Roman campaigns in Spain. By 450 Aëtius' policy of 'government through punitive expedition'[139] was enjoying mixed success. In Spain it was in tatters but north of the Loire it might have been on the way towards re-establishing effective authority as far as the Rhine. At this point events, not without an element of farce about them, overtook Roman attempts at re-establishment.

The history of the Huns does not directly concern this volume except insofar as it impinged upon the west, and good accounts can be found elsewhere.[140] A brief résumé is nevertheless useful. In the first quarter of the fifth century the Huns had grown in power in the territory north of the Danube. As noted, Hunnic allied forces were playing an important role in Roman politics from the 420s.

---

[136] Hydatius, *Chron.* 126.   [137] Hydatius, *Chron.* 129, 132–4.

[138] Hydatius, *Chron.* 134.

[139] Halsall (1995a), p. 8, borrowing a phrase from Kapelle (1979), pp. 120–57.

[140] Bona (1991), pp. 46–80; Heather (2005), pp. 300–48; Maenchen-Helfen (1973), pp. 81–129; Thompson, E. A. (1996), esp. pp. 69–136; Wolfram (1997), pp. 123–44.

In 425 and 434 western imperial politics were resolved with the aid of Hunnic military forces. By the later 430s, when Attila and Bleda succeeded to the kingship, their military power was such that they could, like no previous barbarian group in that region, launch devastating attacks into the Roman Balkans, defeat the armies sent against them and make ever more imperious demands upon the courts in Constantinople and Ravenna.[141] As well as hounding the east and receiving enormous subsidies from Constantinople, Attila, having murdered his brother in 444, also overran western territory in Pannonia. The sources on the Huns are fraught with difficulties but some interesting points can be made. Priscus tells of how Attila extended his authority over a tribe called the Akatziri, who it seems lived on the eastern fringes of his territory, north of the Black Sea (the political centre of Attila's regime was north of the Danube in the western lands once occupied by the *Tervingi*).[142] He exploited rivalry between one of their kings and the others, apparently a common process, which he repeated elsewhere. As had so often happened before, the defeated parties fled to the Empire, leading to imperious Hunnic demands for their return. The power of the Hunnic 'Empire' had led to an ever more important alternative to Rome in barbarian politics. This situation was produced not only by the growing military strength of the Huns but also by the increasing inability of the Empire, especially the west, to intervene in barbarian politics. By the late 440s the power of the Huns appears to have reached well into the area east of the Rhine. As mentioned, the destruction of the Burgundians seems to have been partly accomplished by Huns from *barbaricum*. In *c.*450 a Frankish succession crisis brought about a situation where one claimant appealed to the Huns for help.[143] As ever, his rival turned to Rome and on this occasion he received the help required because of developments at a higher level.

By this time, especially as the eastern Romans sorted out their differences with Persia, resistance to Attila and his demands began to harden. If Attila was to continue to win military laurels, such as were evidently necessary for the maintenance of his regime, he would need to look elsewhere. He had already picked a quarrel with Valentinian III over some silver bowls that a former secretary of his, a

---

[141] On all this, see the memorable but sadly fragmentary account of Priscus (frr. 2–19), who went on an embassy to Attila in the late 440s (frr. 10–14).
[142] Priscus, fr. 11.2.   [143] Priscus, fr. 20.3.

Roman called Constantius, had stolen and sold in Rome.[144] His pretexts were, allegedly, furthered from the most unlikely quarter. Valentinian's elder sister, Honoria, had been caught having an affair with the head of her household. Her lover was executed and her brother betrothed her to a man called Herculanus, universally admired and feared by no one. Smarting at this treatment, Honoria sent one of her household eunuchs, called Hyacinthus, to Attila with her ring and the message that she was willing to marry the Hunnic king. Delighted at this proposal, Attila demanded his bride and half of the western Empire as a dowry.[145] Neither, needless to say, was forthcoming.

Assembling his forces, in 451 Attila marched west, where he joined the Frankish prince who had sided with him.[146] Crossing the Rhine, he destroyed several, presumably defenceless, cities including Metz. Only when he reached the Loire could the Romans resist him, Orléans crucially holding out against his forces. Meanwhile Aëtius had been frantically mustering the factions in Gaul to oppose Attila's army. The Goths were brought into the fold by the Gallic nobleman Avitus, having possibly strayed from earlier obligations, as a result of Theoderic's marriage alliance with Rechiar of the Sueves.[147] Aëtius' cause might not have been helped by Valentinian's decision to marry his daughter to Gaiseric's son, Huneric. Gaiseric, on accepting this betrothal, had mutilated Theoderic's daughter, Huneric's current fiancée, and sent her back to Gaul.[148] This is unlikely to have endeared Valentinian to Theoderic but Gaiseric is said to have allied with Attila and this might have induced the Goth to fight his rival's ally. Yet the Vandals seem to have been incorporated into the imperial regime at this point and it may be easiest to assume that Jordanes, our source, was (as so often) mistaken. Most probably, simple pragmatism governed Theoderic's decision to help counter

---

[144] Priscus, fr. 11.2.

[145] Priscus, frr. 17, 20.3, 22.1. Bury (1919); Holum (1982), pp. 1–3; Oost (1968), pp. 282–5. Holum uses the date of 434 for Honoria's indiscretion, following Marcellinus, *Chron.*, but Bury argued convincingly that this was an error, Marcellinus placing the event in the wrong indiction (though see Croke, ed. and trans. (1995), pp. 80–1, for an attempt to reinstate the date of 434).

[146] On the campaign of 451, see: *Chron. Gall. 452*, 139; Hydatius, *Chron.* 142, 144–5; Jordanes, *Getica* 36.191–40.213; *LH* 2.5–7; Priscus, fr. 21; Prosper, *Chron.* AP 434 (= 451).

[147] Sid. Ap. *Poems* 7, lines 332–53.   [148] Jordanes, *Getica* 36.184.

Attila; ultimately, the Goths always acted as Gallic aristocrats.[149] Aëtius was also reinforced by the ousted Frankish faction and by the Alans settled north of the Loire. The warbands of the northern Gallic petty chieftains (hitherto called *Bagaudae*; now, at this moment of peril simply referred to as Aremoricans) also joined his army, which seems to have been a hotchpotch of all sorts of late Roman units, possibly including former Rhine *limitanei* and even the remnants of the old British field army.[150] Nonetheless this force was enough to induce Attila to fall back from Orléans until he turned at bay halfway between Troyes and Châlons-sur-Marne. Listed by J. F. C. Fuller as one of the 'decisive battles of the western world',[151] the 'battle of the Catalaunian Fields', or of the *Campus Mauriacus* as contemporaries more often called it, was a cataclysmic affair. Jordanes' account of the fight, written almost exactly 100 years later although possibly based upon earlier sources, is eternally memorable and equally difficult to rely upon in detail. Nonetheless, the ferocity and bloodiness of the fighting impressed contemporaries. Prosper of Aquitaine, writing within four years of the battle, recorded an incalculable slaughter; Hydatius, penning his version not long afterwards, attempted to calculate the dead and estimated them (impossibly) at 300,000; the *Gallic Chronicle of 511* wrote of innumerable cadavers. Theoderic of the Goths died at the head of his contingent. Only nightfall stopped the carnage but although the battle was indecisive Attila had clearly had the worse of the exchange and continued his withdrawal to *Pannonia*. In many readings this was the crowning achievement of Aëtius' career but his army was too battered to pursue and Thorismud, Theoderic's heir, withdrew to Toulouse to ensure his inheritance.[152]

However bruised, Attila had not been defeated. In 452 he assembled another army and attacked Italy.[153] After his losses in 451 and the disintegration of his polyglot army, Aëtius was unable to defend the peninsula. The Huns stormed Aquileia and destroyed Milan and other cities but, marching upon Rome, Attila suddenly stopped and

---

[149] Below, pp. 273–4.
[150] Scharf (1999). A garbled list of allies is given by Jordanes, *Getica* 36.191.
[151] Fuller (1954).   [152] *Consularia Italica* 567; Jordanes, *Getica* 41.214–16.
[153] On the Italian campaign of 452, see *Chron. Gall. 452*, 141; *Consularia Italica* 568; Hydatius, *Chron.* 146; Jordanes, *Getica* 42.219–24; Priscus, fr. 22; Prosper, *Chron.* AP 425 (= 452).

withdrew. In papal legend this was because Pope Leo I led an embassy that induced the Hunnish king to abandon his plan to destroy Rome.[154] Another account speaks of the Hunnic aristocracy's fears (based upon Alaric's death soon after the sack of 410) that there was a curse on anyone who took Rome. Leo certainly entreated Attila to withdraw but his success more likely resulted at least partly from the factor that had really killed Alaric: disease. Italy was a graveyard for late antique and early medieval armies and it may be that malaria or dysentery was afflicting the Hunnic army just as they decimated so many later ones. Perhaps even more to the point, in a rare instance of co-operation, an eastern Roman army, confusingly commanded by another general called Aëtius, crossed the Danube and raided the heartland of Attila's kingdom.[155] Attila and his army retreated beyond the Danube. In 453, after drinking to excess as he celebrated yet another marriage, he suffered a nosebleed and died in his sleep.[156] Farce was not restricted to the Romans in the fifth century. Within a few years the 'Hunnic Empire' had completely fallen apart. The subject peoples had risen up against Hunnic domination and defeated Attila's heirs in a massive battle on the river Nedao.[157] The Hunnish remnants, in a move reminiscent of that which followed their first appearance north of the Danube in the 370s, eventually petitioned to be allowed to enter the eastern Roman Empire, were admitted and settled.

THE DEATHS OF AËTIUS AND VALENTINIAN AND THE SECOND SACK OF ROME, 453–455

The most serious concerted military threat to be launched against the western Empire, and certainly the only such expedition apparently carried out with the avowed aim of its subjugation, probably since the second Punic war, had been beaten off. Aëtius, the hero of the hour did not long survive it. With typical energy, in 453 he resumed his efforts to restore Roman authority in Spain. A new count of the Spains was appointed, Mansuetus, and he and another count, Fronto,

---

[154] *Book of the Popes* 47.   [155] Hydatius, *Chron.* 146.

[156] Hydatius, *Chron.* 146; Jordanes, *Getica* 49.254–5; Priscus, frr. 21, 22.2; Prosper, *Chron.* AP 426 (= 453).

[157] On these events, see, e.g. Heather (2005), pp. 351–84; Maenchen-Helfen (1973), pp. 143–68; Thompson (1996), pp. 167–76.

signed a peace treaty with the Sueves.[158] Under its terms it would appear that parts of *Carthaginensis* were returned to Roman rule. With the Suevic threat nullified, Aëtius sent Frederic, the brother of the new Gothic king, Theoderic II (who had killed his other brother Thorismud to become king in 452), with the Gothic army to *Tarraconensis*, where he slaughtered the *Bagaudae*.[159] In 454 Aëtius became yet another victim of palace intrigue and was cut down by Valentinian III himself with the aid one of the chief palace eunuchs.[160] His failure to stop Attila's 452 attack on Italy had likely undermined his position. The indecision of the *Campus Mauriacus* had indeed cost him dearly. A purge of Aëtius' officials followed. Valentinian was shrewd enough to realise the influence his murdered general had on the barbarians and sent envoys to them all, including the Sueves, to ensure they remained peaceful (map 19). This did not spare him from threats closer to home. In 455 another plot induced two of Aëtius' bodyguards to avenge their master's death. Whilst riding and practising his archery on the *Campus Martius* Valentinian had his head hacked into by these aggrieved troopers, who rode off with impunity.[161] Aëtius is often described as leading a Hunnic bodyguard but it is interesting to note that his avengers both had Gothic names: Optila and Thraustila. Many of the Huns known to us, not least Attila and his brother Bleda, bear Gothic names.[162]

The aftermath of Valentinian's murder was dramatic. The Sueves abandoned their treaty and plundered *Gallaecia* but, more importantly, Gaiseric, bound by treaty to Valentinian, decided to attack Italy to seize his son's fiancée.[163] In Rome, the author of the plot against Valentinian III, Petronius Maximus, bribed his way to the throne but within three months of his accession Gaiseric's fleet appeared off Ostia. Panicking, Petronius fled but was torn to pieces by an angry mob and, after they had been paraded through the capital's streets on spears, the remnants of his body were thrown into the Tiber. That did not save the Eternal City, which the Vandals plundered far more seriously than had Alaric in 410. They carried off everything of any

---

[158] Hydatius, *Chron.* 147.   [159] Hydatius, *Chron.* 148, 150.

[160] Hydatius, *Chron.* 152; Marcellinus, *Chron. s.a.* 454; Priscus, fr. 30; Prosper, *Chron.* AP 427 (= 454).

[161] Hydatius, *Chron.* 154; Marcellinus, *Chron. s.a.* 455; Priscus, fr. 30; Prosper, *Chron.* AP 428 (= 455).

[162] Maenchen-Helfen (1973), pp. 386–90.

[163] On these events, see Hydatius, *Chron.* 155–61; Priscus, fr. 30.

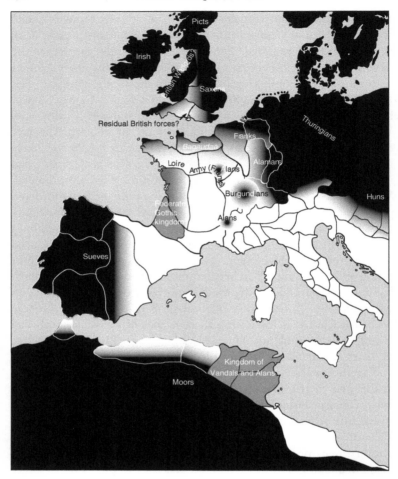

Map 19 The Western Empire, 455, on the eve of the assassination of Valentinian III

value that had not been nailed down, and some things that had been. The booty included Valentinian's two daughters and widow, whom some suspected of inviting in Gaiseric. Gaiseric was able to marry his son to the Theodosian princess and associate himself with the imperial dynasty. This was important not least because the last eastern emperor of the dynasty, Theodosius II, had died from a riding accident in 450. From now on, in Gaiseric's view and possibly that of many others, the legitimate heirs to the western Roman Empire would be any male offspring of Huneric and Eudocia.

9

THE PARTING OF GAUL AND ITALY, 455–480

Writing 275 years later, Bede wrote that Valentinian III's murder brought the Roman Empire to an end,[1] and the western Empire's last two decades can indeed make a sorry tale. The task before any emperor was ever more difficult, yet several occupants of the throne were capable men and possibilities existed to stabilise the situation or even reverse the process of the past fifty years. Contemporaries do not seem to have thought the Empire was finished. In a memorable scene towards the end of the 1968 British farce *Carry on up the Khyber*, the governor of a besieged town in the Raj holds a dinner-party for his associates. Despite rifle- and shellfire bringing the ceiling, plaster and paintings down around them, the party continues to maintain 'stiff upper lip'. Affecting not to notice their situation, host and guests continue to behave according to all the most ludicrous rules of Victorian etiquette. The late Roman Gallic aristocracy often appear similarly ridiculous. The flourishing of Gallic letters in this period might be seen, in many ways plausibly enough, as a manifestation of a desire to look as much as possible like Roman aristocrats of old while political changes were bringing the world where such noblemen

---

[1] *HE* 1.21. Bede was adapting Marcellinus, *Chron. s.a.* 454, which said that the death of Aëtius marked the end of the Empire. Marcellinus also placed this judgement on Romulus' deposition in 476 (below, pp. 280–2).

belonged crashing down around their ears. Bede's judgement looks reasonable enough with the benefit of hindsight and some of these Gallic aristocrats can seem to be wilfully refusing to read the writing on the wall. If we remember, as historians often seem not to, that twenty-one years took as long to pass then as they do now, and indeed represented the best part of a generation in late antiquity, then any writing on the wall was probably far less clear to contemporaries in the late 450s and 460s and open to rather more readings. The golden age of Gallic writing was a response to changing situations, to be sure, but restored to a historical context where the End of the Roman Empire was neither inevitable nor taken for granted, it takes on a subtly different aspect.

The sack of Rome and Petronius' death presented the Gallic aristocracy with an opportunity to turn back the political tide of the previous sixty years. Since Gratian's move to Milan they had been progressively cut off from access to court, and power had passed to the Italian nobility, who exerted ever-greater control over imperial politics, culminating in the seizure of the throne by an Italian senator.[2] The Council of the Seven Provinces, established in 418, had presumably been intended to combat feelings of separation but, as it turned out, it seems rather to have given them a rallying point. Petronius had sent Avitus, a member of a Gallic senatorial family,[3] to negotiate with Theoderic II of the Visigoths (whom we shall henceforth call by that name to differentiate them from the newly emerging Ostrogoths in the Balkans, while noting that neither group called themselves by these names[4]) to ensure that the Goths supported the usurper. Avitus apparently succeeded, but while at the Gothic court he learnt of Petronius' murder. A hastily convened meeting declared Avitus emperor, and the Gallic nobility soon afterwards gave their support at an assembly at Beaucaire. Avitus entered Arles at the head of the Gothic army, with Theoderic and his brother Frederic alongside him.[5] The force then entered Italy and put Avitus

---

[2] Gauls still travelled to Italy to hold office, but opportunities were becoming scarcer: Mathisen (1992); (1993), pp. 21–2.

[3] Possibly Petronius' brother-in-law, though the evidence for this is circumstantial: Mommaerts and Kelley (1992).

[4] The term *Vesi* is sometimes used for the Gallic Goths (Sid. Ap. *Poems* 7, line 431) and the personal name Ostrogotha appears among the Italian Goths.

[5] Marius of Avenches, *Chron. s.a.* 455; Hydatius, *Chron.* 156; Sid. Ap. *Poems* 7, lines 357–602.

on the throne. In attendance upon Avitus was his son-in-law, Sidonius Apollinaris, whose writings form one of the most important sources for later fifth-century Gaul. Avitus' Gallic supporters came from families with long traditions of fighting for the restoration of the fourth-century style of Empire, ruled from Gaul with the Gallic aristocracy's prominent involvement. Sidonius' grandfather had served Constantine 'III' as praetorian prefect and another of Avitus' supporters was Consentius of Narbonne, Jovinus' grandson.[6]

According to Procopius, when Valentinian murdered Aëtius, one of his officers, Marcellinus, rebelled against the Empire in Dalmatia.[7] An obscure sentence in Sidonius' panegyric for the new emperor, referring to Avitus quietening *Pannonia* with a simple march, might imply that he brought Marcellinus back into the fold.[8] Certainly the general is loyal when we next hear of him. However, there are problems with Procopius' evidence and Marcellinus might not have struck out on his own until 461.[9] The Vandal problem was the most important one facing Avitus. Gaiseric had attacked Sicily, claiming the right to a dowry for Eudocia. The Italian army, under Majorian and Ricimer fought back vigorously. By subterfuge according to Hydatius, a Vandal force was destroyed in Corsica on its way to attack Gaul. Priscus appears to mention the shipwreck of a Vandal fleet. Avitus felt confident enough to remind Gaiseric of his treaty obligations, and threaten attack if he persisted in ignoring them.[10] Perhaps taking heart from the Vandals' setbacks, Avitus withdrew his Visigothic army from Italy, paying them with precious metal obtained by stripping statues and other ornaments from public buildings.[11] Rather than simply sending Theoderic's troops home, Avitus was actively taking steps to restore the situation in Spain as the necessary precursor for an attack on Africa.

The Sueves had continued to attack Roman territory by raiding *Carthaginiensis*. Avitus despatched Count Fronto on an embassy to Rechiar and, further underlining the Visigoths' autonomy, Theoderic II also sent envoys. Rechiar dismissed both parties and proceeded to attack *Tarraconensis*.[12] A successful Suevic conquest would have given them control over the entire peninsula; Frederic's

---

[6] Mathisen (1979a).   [7] Procopius, *Wars* 3.6.1–2, 3.6.5–25 (= Priscus, fr.53.3).
[8] Sid. Ap. *Poems* 7, line 590.   [9] Kulikowski (2002b).
[10] On the Vandal attacks: Hydatius, *Chron.* 169; Priscus, fr. 31.1–2.
[11] Priscus, fr. 32.   [12] Hydatius, *Chron.* 163.

453 campaign appears to have destroyed the area's independent Roman leaders. At this point seven shiploads of Heruls attacked the Gallaecian coast and, though driven off, caused considerable damage.[13] Exactly who these Heruls were is mysterious. Herul groups could be found in diverse parts of Europe at this time: north of the Danube, for instance, or in the Roman army.[14] Sidonius Apollinaris lists Heruls amongst the threats to Gaul that Aëtius had had to confront and later refers to Herul pirates in attendance at the Gothic court in 476.[15] This seaborne group may have been based somewhere in northern *Germania Magna*, although the Spanish coast seems very far from their homelands. It must at least be a possibility that their raid constituted part of the Romano-Visigothic offensive against the Sueves. Rechiar invaded *Tarraconensis* again and carried off large numbers of captives.[16] This seems to have provoked Avitus to dispatch Theoderic's Gothic army against him.[17] Marching into Spain, the Visigoths, alongside a Burgundian contingent, met the Sueves in a decisive battle near Astorga (5 October 456). The Burgundians had recently suffered defeat at the hands of some Gepids[18] and might consequently have been keen to take part in imperial policies. The Suevic army was utterly defeated and Rechiar fled to Oporto whilst the Visigoths invaded *Gallaecia* and sacked Braga, his capital. Soon afterwards, Rechiar was captured and in December Theoderic had his brother-in-law executed. Many other Sueves who had surrendered to the Visigoths were also killed.[19] 'The kingdom of the Sueves was destroyed and put to an end' said Hydatius, inaccurately.[20] Quite who would replace it as the dominant power south of the Pyrenees, and whether imperial rule would be restored was unclear. For now anarchy reigned in Spain. Not the least reason for this was a change of circumstances in Italy.

---

[13] Hydatius 164.　　[14] Pohl (2002), pp. 122–3.

[15] Sid. Ap. *Poems* 7, line 236; *Letters* 8.9.　　[16] Hydatius, *Chron.* 165.

[17] For discussion, see Kulikowski (2004), pp. 186–9.

[18] *Consularia Italica* 574. The circumstances are unclear. Kaiser (2004), p. 48.

[19] Hydatius, *Chron.* 166–8; Jordanes, *Getica* 44.231–2.

[20] Hydatius, *Chron.* 168. The Suevic kingdom lived on to 585. Hydatius' mistake, which must have been apparent to him within a few years, is one reason to believe that his composition of the *Chronicle* began at the time of Theoderic's Gothic invasion. Burgess (ed. and trans.) (1993), p. 6. Gillett (2003), pp. 47–8, sees a first draft of the work ending at this point.

The Vandal raids, predictably enough, had caused famine in Italy and resentment against the new Gallic emperor. Hardly had the Visigothic army departed than the Italian army's generals Ricimer and Majorian took advantage of its absence and the onset of winter (rendering Vandal raids unlikely) to rebel.[21] Avitus' *patricius*, Remistus, was murdered in the palace at Ravenna and, according to Hydatius, news came to Theoderic in Spain that the emperor had retreated to Arles.[22] Avitus' move to Arles, if correctly reported, might have been connected with measures against the Vandals in Corsica and the trouble in Italy might then have broken out during his absence, culminating in Remistus' assassination by Ricimer and Majorian, rather than Avitus' retreat northwards being produced by Roman rioters and rebels in the Italian army as Priscus describes. Returning to Italy, Avitus confronted his opponents at Piacenza (17 October 456) but was defeated (Remistus' replacement, Missianus, being killed), captured and ordained bishop of the city.[23] Within a month he was dead. Most people suspected foul play. Avitus had the makings of a good emperor, having been a successful diplomat and military subordinate. He had, furthermore, vigorously set about restoring Roman government in the west. His regime scored success against the Vandals and heavily defeated the Sueves. It had incorporated the Visigoths and Burgundians and made good use of their manpower. Its rapid failure illustrates how the political situation had changed. The Vandal presence in Africa placed Italy in the front line. No longer could an emperor leave Italy to its own devices and govern from strategically more important frontier regions. Whenever the Vandals felt they were obtaining insufficient rewards from a regime, Italy and Rome were open to armed attack and could be starved by the retention of the grain fleet. While the Gauls wanted a return to the fourth-century situation, the Italian aristocracy had now been at the centre of politics for three generations and was unlikely to relinquish that position. Strategic demands meant that an army was now needed in Italy and could be manipulated by Italian political

---

[21] Priscus, fr. 32. The precise details of Avitus' fall are difficult to unravel. To some extent, I have followed Stein (1959) 1, p. 372.

[22] Remistus' murder: *Consularia Italica* 579; withdrawal to Arles: Hydatius, *Chron.* 170.

[23] *Consularia Italica* 580; Hydatius, *Chron.* 176; Marius of Avenches, *Chron. s.a.* 456; Priscus, fr. 32; Gregory of Tours, *LH* 2.11, relates Avitus' downfall to his general theme in that book, the relationship between legitimate authority and sexual propriety, claiming that Avitus was deposed because of his adulteries.

factions. The manpower shortage was aggravated as Spain drifted further out of the emperor's grasp, producing a heavier reliance upon Visigothic forces, whose kings increasingly followed their own foreign policy. The Visigoths were thus another internal pressure group with its own armed force that had to be incorporated into any regime. Managing the Empire, let alone overseeing the recovery of territory, would require immense tact and skill.

MAJORIAN, 456–461

Fortunately for the western Empire, the man who emerged as emperor in the aftermath of Avitus' downfall possessed tact and skill in abundance. Majorian was a young commander of possibly Egyptian descent whose father had served Aëtius, controlling his finances.[24] Majorian had fought with distinction under the Patrician in northern Gaul in the later 440s.[25] At the end of 456 he was faced with problems on all sides. Vandal raids would likely resume as soon as the weather improved. The differences between Gaul and Italy were further underlined by Avitus' fall, on the news of which the Burgundians, newly returned from Spain, rebelled and seized land near Lyon.[26] The Lyonnais do not appear to have welcomed Majorian's accession. Inscriptions show that they did not recognise his consulate in 457.[27] Indeed they seem to have been in league with the Burgundians. Meanwhile, another rebellion appears to have taken place in Narbonne, led by an obscure figure called Marcellus but focused upon Avitus' supporters.[28] In Spain a Gothic army loyal to Avitus was plundering widely, various factions were competing for control of the remnants of the Suevic kingdom and there were further outbreaks of brigandage.[29] The situation did not look hopeful.

---

[24] Priscus, fr. 30.1 says that an unidentified Maximian was the son of a Domninus who had served under Aëtius. Blockley (ed. and trans.) (1983), p. 393, argues that, although *PLRE* 2, p. 739 (Maximianus 5), rejects the identification, Priscus' Maximian is an error for Majorian, which makes more sense of the passage. Sid. Ap. *Poems* 5, lines 116–25, confirms that Majorian's father had served Aëtius.

[25] Sid. Ap. *Poems* 5, lines 197–274.

[26] Marius of Avenches, *Chron. s.a.* 456, records the division of land between the Burgundians and the Gallic senators. *Consularia Italica* 583 for the Burgundians' return from Spain after Rechiar's death.

[27] *CIL* 13.2363.   [28] Mathisen (1979a) for discussion.

[29] Hydatius, *Chron.* 171–6; Jordanes, *Getica* 44.233–4. Kulikowski (2004), pp. 189–90.

The year after Avitus' death was one of uncertainty. The eastern emperor, Marcian, died at about the same time as Avitus, producing a succession crisis. His successor Leo appointed Majorian as master of both services in February. Although the Italian army proclaimed Majorian emperor in April 457, presumably with Leo's approval, it does not seem that he received formal recognition until December.[30] In the meantime, apparently still using the title of master of both services, Majorian beat off an Alamannic attack on *Raetia* and in early 458, after his elevation, a Vandal attack on Campania.[31] Having secured Italy and his throne, he attended to the Gallic situation.[32] The 'conspiracy' in Narbonne was rapidly quelled, apparently without force. The leading members of the faction that supported Marcellus were removed from their offices (some were Avitus' appointees) but permitted to retain their titles and estates. Avitus' commander of the Gallic army, Agrippinus, was replaced by a Gallic officer called Aegidius, who had possibly been campaigning on the middle Rhine.[33] As with the civilian officials, he was permitted to retain rank and lands but resentment clearly festered. The Frank Childeric was possibly another of Avitus' commanders in Gaul removed from office. Gregory of Tours records a story of how Childeric was driven out by his Franks and for eight years replaced as their king by Aegidius.[34] Although this is only one interpretation of the fragmentary sources, an eight-year period ending with Aegidius' death would allow us to associate Childeric's expulsion with Majorian's accession and appointment of Aegidius.[35] Aegidius retook Lyon and before the end of 458 Majorian himself had crossed the Alps and arrived in the city.

It was the first time since Valentinian II's reign that an emperor had left Italy to come to Gaul. Sidonius Apollinaris delivered a fulsome panegyric to the young emperor, claiming that Gaul had been ignored by the 'cloistered emperors' since 388 – he tactfully

---

[30] *Consularia Italica* 582–3; *Nov. Maj.* 1.   [31] Sid. Ap. *Poems* 5, lines 373–440.

[32] Mathisen (1979a) for excellent analysis of Majorian's policy in Gaul.

[33] Stein (1959), I, p. 378; Harries (1994), p. 86. The evidence is slender. The eighth-century *LHF* (ch. 8) refers to the Franks' capture of Cologne. A date after 459 for this siege is only sustained by the argument that Aegidius seems to have spent his remaining years fighting on other fronts. This is insufficient.

[34] *LH* 2.12.

[35] Halsall (2001) for this interpretation. Jarnut (1994) for a slightly different reconstruction.

omitted any reference to his father-in-law Avitus, in whose downfall (and possibly death) Majorian was involved.[36] Majorian appears to have assembled leading Gallic senators in Lyon and won them over to his regime. He sensibly introduced as his officers in Gaul members of the Gallic aristocracy who had close links with Italy.[37] The Gauls were restored to a position in the administration of the Empire, yet without alienating the Italians. One such appointee was Magnus, installed in place of Avitus' supporter Paeonius as vicar of the Seven Provinces in Narbonne. Magnus' first task was to help defend the region against the Visigoths.

Theoderic II was in *Lusitania* when, apparently at Easter 457, he heard of Avitus' death.[38] This caught the Visigothic king very much on the back foot. He and his troops were far from the political centre-stage. Their candidate for the throne had been removed and looked likely to be replaced by an Italian commander. The situation in Spain was very confused. The Suevic remnants had raised two candidates for the kingship, Maldras and Framtane, whilst a Goth called Aioulf also made a bid for their throne.[39] Theoderic broke up his army, described by Hydatius as composed of 'a multitude of various nations', probably for ease of supply, and allowed parts of it to ravage within Spain, presumably to prevent any resurgence of Suevic power.[40] With the remainder he returned to Gaul. There his movements are obscure but by 459 he seems to have been defeated by Majorian's forces under Aegidius at Narbonne and made peace with the new emperor.[41]

At this stage things were going well. Having established a regime that incorporated the Visigothic king and his troops and involved the leading Gallic aristocrats, without alienating Avitus' supporters or the Italian senators, Majorian was free to move against the Vandals. The restoration of direct rule over Africa had to be any emperor's ultimate goal. With this, Italy would be removed from danger and troops there could be redeployed to revive Roman government elsewhere. The situation in Spain permitted the possibility of an advance to the ports there and a short crossing to *Mauretania* (thus with a better chance of evading the Vandal fleet). The Sueves had staged something of a revival and Maldras had emerged as their

---

[36] Sid. Ap. *Poems* 5, lines 353–60. Mathisen (1979b).   [37] Mathisen (1979a).

[38] Hydatius, *Chron.* 179.   [39] Hydatius, *Chron.* 180–1.

[40] Hydatius, *Chron.* 179.   [41] Hydatius, *Chron.* 192.

only king, raiding into *Gallaecia* and *Lusitania*.[42] However, Theoderic
still had forces in the far south.[43] Again it seems that the Heruls
were incorporated in his plans, for a Herul fleet is mentioned as
raiding *Gallaecia* on its way to *Baetica*, presumably to join the Visigoths there. In May 460 Majorian crossed the Pyrenees.[44] A new
master of the soldiers in Spain, Nepotianus, was appointed to
command alongside Theoderic's general Sunieric and ships were
assembled at Cartagena. At the same time, the Roman general in
Dalmatia, Marcellinus, was moved to command forces in Sicily,
perhaps with another prong to the attack in mind, or to act as a
diversion.[45] Gaiseric was sufficiently alarmed to send an envoy to
Majorian asking for peace. The emperor would not be deterred, so
Gaiseric took other precautions. According to Priscus he poisoned
the wells in *Mauretania*, through which the Roman army would
have to march to reach the core of his kingdom.[46] He also sent out his
navy and, in a surprise raid, destroyed or carried off the Roman
fleet at Cartagena.[47] Some suspected treason. Majorian had no choice
but to make peace. Priscus says that this was done 'on shameful
terms', though what these were is unclear. Possibly the Vandals were
granted possession of the *Mauretanias*. It was the end of Majorian's
planned African offensive and, as it turned out, his regime. Sunieric
and Nepotianus were sent with their troops to attack the Sueves in
Gallaecia instead and Majorian withdrew to Italy.[48] Once he was
back across the Alps and out of Gaul, which he appears to have
made loyal, Majorian was seized by Ricimer at Tortona and executed
(2 August 461).[49] Contemporaries blamed a jealous palace faction.

It is difficult to know for sure why Majorian was murdered. He
had proved an excellent emperor until the failure of his Vandal
campaign. The blame is usually placed upon Ricimer's fear of an
emperor who might remove him from his 'king-making' position
in Italy. This does not seem entirely plausible. Although Majorian

---

[42] Hydatius, *Chron.* 190.   [43] Hydatius, *Chron.* 185, 188.

[44] Hydatius, *Chron.* 195. Kulikowski (2004), pp. 190–2.

[45] On these preparations, see Hydatius, *Chron.* 192, 195; Priscus, fr. 38.

[46] Priscus, fr. 36.

[47] Hydatius, *Chron.* 195; Marius of Avenches, *Chron. s.a.* 460; Priscus, fr. 36.

[48] Hydatius, *Chron.* 196.

[49] *Chron. Gall. 511, s.a.* 461; *Consularia Italica* 588; Hydatius, *Chron.* 205; Marius of
Avenches, *Chron. s.a.* 461; Priscus, fr. 36.2. Gautier's ((1932), p. 249) marvellous
Franglais sums up the event's significance: 'L'Empire d'Occident est knock out.'

referred to him as 'our father' in one of his 'novels' (new laws added to the Theodosian code),[50] Ricimer had not yet become a king-maker and Majorian's reliance upon him might, if anything, have been increased after the fiasco at Cartagena. A successful African campaign would have allowed the Italian army to be relocated to other theatres, possibly weakening Ricimer's role but, as far as can be told, he had not opposed the operation. It seems more likely that Majorian's downfall is to be ascribed to the ever-increasing importance of faction in the dwindling western Empire. His absence in Gaul, however skilfully managed, appears to have caused some Italian senators to fear the dominance of the Gallic aristocrats and, in Ricimer's case, that of the Visigothic and Dalmatian armies. After Majorian's death, Marcellinus was compelled to quit Sicily when Ricimer suborned his Hunnic troops. It was clearly becoming almost impossible to balance the factional interests within western Roman politics. Once Majorian was back in Italy, therefore, he was killed and, after an interregnum of a few months, replaced (19 November 461) with a Lucanian aristocrat called Libius Severus, about whose previous career nothing is known.[51]

THE SUPREMACY OF RICIMER, 461–472

Whatever the aim was behind Majorian's murder, its outcome cannot have been planned. Immediately afterwards, Theoderic II seized the opportunity to dismiss Nepotianus from command in Spain and replace him with Arborius.[52] For the next seven years we hear little from Spain, except (because our source is bishop Hydatius, who lived in the area) of Suevic raiding in *Gallaecia* and *Lusitania*, at times under the leadership of more than one king, and of embassies between the Sueves and the Goths.[53] Gothic garrisons remained in places like Mérida but we are poorly informed of any actions that they might have undertaken.

Majorian's commander on the Loire, Aegidius, refused to accept Severus as emperor.[54] It is possible that, to legitimise his position, he took the title king of the Franks. Gregory of Tours records that he replaced Childeric as king of the Franks for eight years.[55] The Roman

[50] *Nov. Maj.* 1 (11 Jan. 458).   [51] Cassiodorus, *Chron.* 1274.
[52] Hydatius, *Chron.* 208. *Pace* Burgess (1992), p. 25.   [53] Hydatius, *Chron.* 209–47.
[54] Priscus, fr. 39.1.   [55] *LH* 2.12.

field army on the Loire had clearly been confronting its manpower problems by recruiting heavily among the Franks. This made much sense but, just as the Balkan army in the 390s had been recruited overwhelmingly from Goths, so that it could be referred to in some circumstances simply as 'the Goths', the Gallic field army now included so many Franks that it could be called 'the Franks'. If Gregory is correct (and the interpretation presented here is far from being the only one possible), Aegidius' move might have been inspired by Alaric's adoption of the title king of the Goths during his rebellion against the government in Rome. Like Alaric, Aegidius wanted to be incorporated within Roman imperial structures and found himself out in the cold as a result of palatine intrigue. Significantly unlike Alaric, however, Aegidius was of Roman origin. Whether he claimed to be a Frank, as well as their king, we do not know. Either way, his apparent assumption of the title king of the Franks was an important index of how things had changed since Alaric's elevation.

In Dalmatia, Marcellinus too refused to acknowledge Severus and so did Gaiseric in Carthage.[56] The Vandal king wished a certain Olybrius, married to Valentinian III's daughter Placidia and thus the brother-in-law of his son Huneric, to be made emperor.[57] We can see how important their links to the imperial family were to the Vandals and how they (like all the other factions) desired to be at the core of imperial politics. Under this pretext, they attacked Sicily, more or less defenceless since Marcellinus' withdrawal. Ignoring garrisoned towns, they plundered widely in the undefended areas.[58] For the next few years of what Gautier called 'the Fourth Punic War'[59] the Vandal fleet raided the Roman coasts of the Mediterranean with absolute impunity. Sardinia and Sicily were taken over. Emperor Leo at least managed to persuade Gaiseric to release Placidia and Valentinian III's widow Eudoxia.[60]

Majorian's assassination meant that, for the second time, Theoderic II had been caught on the hop by events in Italy. Had he wished to intervene, he was prevented by the fact that his troops were in Spain and largely dispersed. The Gauls, however, appear to have given up the idea of creating their own emperor, so – apart from Aegidius – Severus had no Gallic rival. However, we should

[56] Priscus, fr. 39,1.   [57] Priscus, fr. 38.   [58] Priscus, frr. 38.1, 39.1.
[59] Gautier (1932), p. 216.   [60] Hydatius 211; Priscus, fr. 38.1.

probably not assume that Theoderic would automatically have wished to use the change of emperor to further 'Gothic aims'. Theoderic was probably only the second Gothic ruler (at most) to have been born in Gaul and given a Roman education.[61] If the thesis presented here, that the Gothic kingdom did not formally come into existence until 439, is correct, then it was a new and precarious-looking entity. Theoderic might not have wished to threaten its existence unduly.

Indeed, within Severus' new regime, Theoderic was in a strong position. The Gallic army on the Loire under Aegidius was in revolt and the Roman troops in Spain were effectively under Theoderic's command (he had, after all, recently dismissed their general). The new emperor probably had no forces north of the Alps other than the Goths and Burgundians and by 464 his Italian troops were engaged in defeating an Alan invasion, killing their king, Beorgor.[62] Thus, probably in return for his military support against Aegidius, Theoderic was granted Narbonne in 462. The person responsible for handing over the city was the Agrippinus whom Aegidius had replaced as master of the soldiers.[63] This dramatically altered the strategic situation. The emperor's troops could no longer move directly into the Spanish theatre of operations without crossing Gothic territory. The Goths had therefore to be sufficiently incorporated into the government and its strategies to accord with such a move, or military operations in Spain would have to be left to the Goths themselves. The latter option would, of course, run the risk of the Goths using the situation to spread *their* influence in Spain rather than the emperor's. This also altered the possibilities of action in Africa. The route through Spain to a short crossing of the Mediterranean at the Straits of Gibraltar was closed. Military intervention in North Africa would now have to come directly from Italy and Sicily, and thus be a more heavily naval operation. The king of the Burgundians, Gundioc, was seemingly named as Aegidius' replacement as master of the soldiers in Gaul.[64] He possibly also married Ricimer's sister, although the precise relationship between him, Ricimer and Ricimer's successor Gundobad is unclear.[65] He took

[61] M. Kulikowski, paper delivered at Thirty-ninth Congress of Medieval Studies, Kalamazoo, May 2004.
[62] *Consularia Italica* 593; Jordanes, *Getica* 45.235; Marcellinus, *Chron. s.a.* 464.
[63] Hydatius, *Chron.* 212.   [64] Hilary, *Letter to Leontius.*   [65] Wood (2003), p. 252.

the opportunity to extend his realm into the Rhône valley and retook Lyon.

Severus forces' campaigns against Aegidius on the Loire were not especially successful. In 463 Aegidius and his 'Franks' defeated the Goths near Orléans and killed Theoderic's brother Frederic.[66] Encouraged by this, Aegidius tried to open negotiations with Gaiseric, presumably with a view to joint operations against Ricimer and Severus.[67] The next year, however, he was killed, either in an ambush or by poison.[68] His demise brought Childeric the Frank back to command on the Loire after his eight years of exile, and indeed might have been associated with Childeric's return.[69]

Childeric, effectively the first Merovingian ruler in Gaul, is best known from his grave, discovered in Tournai in 1653.[70] This, probably originally covered by a large mound, contained enormous quantities of gold, adorning weaponry, items of clothing and horse-harness. Much of this was decorated in a gold and garnet style of Mediterranean origin but probably associated with the army and thus, by association, 'barbarians'. Childeric manifested the roots of his power. As befitted a commander who possibly began his career in Aëtius' service, his grave also contained the golden brooch that fastened his *paludamentum* (military cloak) and which proclaimed his status in the Roman army, and a seal ring. This latter, ultimately what identifies the grave as Childeric's, was another truly Roman item, although it nevertheless gives his title as *rex*, king.

The location of Childeric's tomb has led to the idea that the Merovingians' power originated in the north but moved slowly southwards, eventually reaching the Paris basin under his son, Clovis. Clovis, it is thought, triumphed over Aegidius' son, Syagrius, at a battle near Soissons in 486 and pushed the bounds of the Frankish kingdom to the Loire.[71] This interpretation tends to see the Frankish settlement of Gaul as a military conquest with a front

---

[66] *Chron. Gall. 511, s.a.* 463; Hydatius, *Chron.* 214; Marius of Avenches, *Chron. s.a.* 463.
[67] Hydatius, *Chron.* 220.   [68] Hydatius, *Chron.* 224.
[69] Halsall (2001). If the information preserved in *LH* 2.18 about Childeric's victory near Angers relates to Aegidius' 463 victory over Frederic then he might already have been in a subordinate position. Jarnut (1994) uses this as the *terminus ante quem* for Childeric's return from exile.
[70] Childeric's grave: Brulet (1997); Halsall (1995b), pp. 31–2 for very brief introduction; James (1988), pp. 58–64; Périn and Feffer (1987), pp. 119–33.
[71] For the battle at Soissons, see *LH* 2.27.

line moving neatly and steadily southwards.[72] This reading of the historical sources has been used to interpret the archaeological evidence and, conversely, excavated data have been employed to support the traditional narrative. Thus furnished inhumations regarded as Frankish have been dated according to the schema of a straightforward conquest not reaching the Paris basin until Clovis' reign. Simultaneously, in an entirely circular argument, the date of these burials has been used to support the notion that Frankish political overlordship only became effective in the Paris basin under Clovis![73]

However, only Childeric's tomb associates him with the far north. The written sources all link him with the Loire valley and the Paris basin. The *Life of Genovefa* mentions that Paris was besieged for ten years (probably meaning an annual blockade during the campaigning season) by the Franks, whose king paid heed to the appeals of the Parisienne holy woman.[74] A letter of Bishop Remigius of Reims to Childeric's son and successor, Clovis, congratulates the young king on taking over from his relatives the rule of *Belgica Secunda*, the province centred on Reims in the northern Paris basin.[75] The fragmentary records known as the Angers Annals, preserved in Gregory of Tours' *Histories*, also link Childeric with campaigns on the Loire.[76] Even the often-expressed idea that Aegidius left his northern command, a Roman enclave or even 'kingdom of Soissons', directly to his son, Syagrius, finds no clear support in the sources. The written evidence suggests fairly clearly that Childeric was the main power north of the Loire from the murder of Aegidius until his own death some time probably in the 480s.[77] This gave further unity to the Loire army as 'the Franks'.

Nevertheless, he was not the only military leader in the region. A Count Paul appears to have been acting in concert with his forces on the Loire.[78] Sometimes also seen as Aegidius' successor as master of the soldiers (unlikely as Gundioc held that office), Paul seems more likely to have been a former officer of Aegidius, now serving Childeric. Paul and Childeric were engaged in fighting against

[72] Verlinden (1954); For the continuation of this approach, see, Périn (1998); Dierkens and Périn (2003).
[73] James (1988), pp. 76–7, for critique.   [74] *Life of Genovefa* 6.25; 7.34.
[75] Remigius, *Letter to Clovis*.   [76] *LH* 2.18–19.
[77] Here I follow the argument of James (1988), pp. 67–77.   [78] *LH* 2.18.

Saxons on the Loire led by a certain 'Adovacrius' (Eadwacer), often, though almost certainly incorrectly,[79] identified with Odoacer, the future king of Italy. These Saxons had probably come by sea from Britain, perhaps as losers in the obscure political struggles there (and thus as precursors to Riothamus' move to Gaul later in the decade) although the Visigothic navy was defending the coast of Aquitaine against Saxon raiders in the 460s.[80] They are described as having bases on islands, but whether these are in the Loire, such as were used by the Vikings later on, or off the coast of Gaul is also unclear.[81] It is also possible, from the account of the Angers Annals, that the Saxons were in Gothic service. They first appear after Aegidius' death taking hostages from towns like Angers[82] and war broke out 'between the Saxons and the Romans' after the battle of Bourg-de-Déols, probably dated to 470–1.[83] This would fit the chronology of Euric's wars.

The far north of Gaul also had its war-leaders. Trier, for example, was ruled by a Count Arbogast, descended from the master of the soldiers of that name.[84] Franks had driven Aegidius' allies from Cologne in the 450s or 460s, perhaps as part of the rivalry between Aegidius and Childeric.[85] Frankish kings extended their power southwards into the far north of Gaul, Alamannic leaders were drawn into the political vacuum as far west as Troyes and, as mentioned, Paris appears to have maintained some sort of independence.[86] Aegidius' son Syagrius is described by Gregory of Tours as a 'king of the Romans' with a base at Soissons but it seems more likely that Syagrius made a bid for the command of the former Loire army after Childeric's death.[87] Nevertheless, with this as the core of his forces,[88] it is plausible that Childeric dominated the region and these lesser leaders.

The nonentity Libius Severus died on 15 August 465. For nearly two years afterwards the western throne remained vacant.

---

[79] MacGeorge (2003), pp. 103–6.   [80] Sid. Ap. *Letters* 8.6.13–15.   [81] *LH* 2.19.

[82] Tallying perhaps with Hydatius' statement (224) that after Aegidius' death the Goths invaded the territories he had defended.

[83] See below, p. 277.   [84] Sid. Ap. *Letters* 4.17; *Austrasian Letters* 22.

[85] *LHF* 8 – a late source.

[86] Alamans in Troyes: *Life of Lupus of Troyes* 10; Paris: *Life of Genovefa*, e.g. 3.10, 7.34–40.

[87] *LH* 2.27. James (1988), pp. 70–1; Halsall (2001), pp. 127–8.

[88] Procopius, *Wars* 5.12.9, 5.12.13–19. See further below, pp. 303–4.

Eventually Emperor Leo intervened and appointed an eminent eastern aristocrat called Anthemius as *caesar* in the west. Anthemius was an experienced soldier, having commanded with success in the Balkans, was descended from the Constantinian dynasty and connected to the Theodosian, being the son-in-law of the emperor Marcian (who had married into that family). Leo's motives for sending him west might have involved the removal of a potential rival in Constantinople as well as the recognition of his abilities. He came at the head of an army of eastern troops and with a supporting fleet under the Dalmatian warlord Marcellinus. Ricimer was placated by the offer of Anthemius' daughter Alypia in marriage. The *caesar* was proclaimed *augustus* outside Rome on 14 April 467.[89] Once again the throne of the west had an able incumbent.

As ever, the most pressing problem was the Vandal threat. Ricimer and Severus' cession of Narbonne to the Goths had reduced the strategic possibilities of dealing with Gaiseric. The best options were naval attacks across the central Mediterranean or a land-based invasion from Libya, in eastern Roman territory. For both reasons it is unsurprising that Anthemius, himself an eastern appointee, turned to the east for help. In 468 a huge fleet was assembled to transport a large army to Africa. Command was given to the eastern General Basiliscus, Emperor Leo's brother-in-law. At the same time a force under Heraclius was to march overland into Vandal territory and Marcellinus was directed to Sardinia with a western fleet. The Goths attacked the Sueves in *Lusitania*[90] and this too might have been part of the offensive. Majorian's attack had come via Spain and the Gothic campaign might have been intended either as another prong of the invasion or as a distraction to keep Gaiseric guessing. The cost of assembling this force was enormous (64,000 pounds of gold and 700,000 of silver according to Candidus the Isaurian)[91] but the rewards for success would be immeasurable. The wealth of the African provinces would replenish the western imperial coffers and increase the rewards to local leaders for continuing to support the Empire.

---

[89] *Consularia Italica* 598.
[90] Hydatius, *Chron.* 240, the first military offensive by the Goths in Spain mentioned by Hydatius since Majorian's Vandal expedition.
[91] Candidus, fr. 2.

Heraclius rapidly evicted the Vandals from *Tripolitania*, Marcellinus retook Sardinia and, transferring his forces to Sicily, drove Gaiseric's warriors thence too, while Basiliscus defeated a Vandal squadron near the island. Contemporaries said that if Basiliscus had acted decisively at this point the war would have been rapidly and victoriously concluded.[92] Alas he did not. Gaiseric negotiated a five-day truce and in the interim assembled a fleet, with fireships. Letting the latter drift into the eastern Roman armada the Vandal ships stormed into the confusion caused and utterly destroyed their opponents. In spite of individual acts of fruitless heroism it was a disaster for the Romans. Profiting from the defeat, the Vandals retook their lost territory in Sardinia and Sicily. Marcellinus was assassinated by his fellow generals.[93] It seems likely that Ricimer was behind this. He would have no rival in Italy, and especially not one backed by Constantinople.

Nonetheless, Ricimer still had one very able rival in Italy, with eastern backing: the emperor himself. The defeat of his great Vandal campaign did not – as is often thought – spell immediate doom for Anthemius' regime.[94] Eastern forces had sustained the heaviest losses. Whilst this ended the possibility of further aid from Constantinople, the western units had been successful in their efforts and at this point there may have been the highest concentration of troops in Italy for some time.

Anthemius' other task was to ensure that Gaul was securely bound into the Empire. Sometime after Anthemius' accession, probably in summer 467,[95] Theoderic II had been killed by his brother Euric. Euric seems to have spent the first years of his reign, like his brother, firmly rooted within western Roman politics. It is often stated that Euric was dangerously expansionist and only waiting for his chance 'to create a nation-state'.[96] There is, as Andrew Gillett has demonstrated,[97] very little evidence to support this notion. Since 439, if not before, the Gothic kings had consistently acted in line with the Gallic aristocracy. They wished to be at the heart of imperial politics, either with a Gallic emperor on the throne or, if not, receiving the Italian emperor's patronage in return for their

---

[92] For this campaign, see Priscus, fr. 53.
[93] Marcellinus, *Chron. s.a.* 468; Priscus, fr. 53.3 (= Procopius, *Wars* 3.6.25).
[94] As Heather (2005), p. 406.   [95] Gillett (1999).
[96] Harries (1994), p. 222. Cp. Heather (1996), p. 189.   [97] Gillett (1999).

support. Of course the Goths' military resources and the fact that they had their own patronage to dispense meant that they were *not* an element just like any other but the point stands. In 455, when the Gallic aristocracy had raised their own emperor, the Goths had backed them; in 457, like other Gallic nobles, they began by resisting Majorian but were then won round; in 461 they supported Libius Severus, faute de mieux, alongside other southern Gallic factions; and in 467, again like the Gauls, they rallied to Anthemius. The first military actions undertaken by the Goths in Euric's reign were against the Sueves in 468 and, as noted, this might have been part of Anthemius' great Vandal offensive.

In 469 the praetorian prefect of Gaul, Arvandus, was hauled to Rome on a charge of treason.[98] He was alleged to have incited Euric to rebel against Anthemius and carve up Gaul with the Burgundians according to the Law of Nations. There is no evidence that Euric had, or wanted, any part of this scheme. Until the end of the 460s Euric appears to have maintained his elder brother's extremely cautious policy of never going against the grain of Gallic aristocratic politics. Since 439, increasingly, southern Gallic aristocrats like Sidonius and many of his circle had been close associates of the Goths, serving them in numerous offices, a fact that must further have restrained Gothic policies that contradicted those of the Gallic nobility. Clearly the Goths were extremely wary of risking their young kingdom's existence and saw it very much as a part of the Empire.

Presiding over the bench at Arvandus' trial should have been the prefect of the city. On this occasion, however, the prefect had absented himself from town, for he was Arvandus' former friend Sidonius Apollinaris. Sidonius' embarrassment was completed by the fact that all three of Arvandus' Gallic accusers were associates of his, including two relatives. Sidonius had come to Rome in 467 and delivered a panegyric to the new emperor,[99] for which he was rewarded with the urban prefecture in early 468.[100] Indeed Anthemius seems to have tried to make sure that imperial offices were well disbursed in Gaul. These actions might have been what led some of the Gallic aristocracy to fight so hard for the Empire.

---

[98] Sid. Ap. *Letters* 1.7. Teitler (1992) portrays Arvandus as a 'quisling' (p. 317). This seems unsubtle.

[99] Sid. Ap. *Poems* 1–2.   [100] Harries (1994), pp. 141–66.

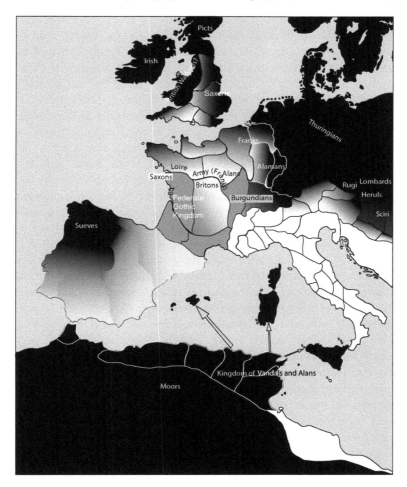

Map 20 The western Empire in 470

In 470, however, two years after the débâcle of the Vandal campaign, further underlining the fact that the failure of that offensive had not immediately ruined his regime, Anthemius quarrelled with Ricimer (map 20).[101] An attempt had been made to poison the emperor and a certain Romanus had consequently been executed on a charge of sorcery. Unfortunately Romanus had been a friend of Ricimer's. Ricimer took himself off to Milan with 6,000

[101] Priscus, fr. 62.

men, whilst Anthemius held Rome with his troops. For the time being, the two spent more time hurling abuse at each other than in military manoeuvring. The two sides were too evenly balanced to make an attack likely to succeed and Bishop Epiphanius of Pavia tried to mediate. Anthemius declared how sorry he was to have married his daughter off to a skin-clad barbarian, while Ricimer riposted by referring to the emperor as a Galatian or a 'Greekling' (*Graeculus*).[102] While these two engaged in the lunge and parry of rapier-like wit, trouble broke out in Gaul.

One cause of Arvandus' ill-advised letter to Euric was the appearance on the Loire of an army of Britons led by an enigmatic figure called Riothamus. Riothamus is alleged to have commanded an army of 12,000 men, doubtless an exaggeration but clearly indicating a substantial force.[103] The reasons for Riothamus' appearance are mysterious. Probably representing the last British commander, in the line going back to Constantine I, to take his forces across the Channel in an attempt to find a place within the Empire's political structures, it is likely that Riothamus was a loser in insular politics. By the late 460s Roman armies had not come close to the Channel for twenty years and non-Roman forces in the island, the Saxons, were probably gaining the upper hand. In these circumstances, perhaps Riothamus chose to cut his losses and take his troops to Gaul, into Anthemius' service. 'Quoit brooch style'[104] died out around the time of Riothamus' departure. Clearly, it would be flawed, seeing material culture as a passive reflection of reality, to link this metalwork directly with Riothamus' men, and its disappearance simply with their departure. Nevertheless it seems reasonable to see the end of quoit brooch style as a part of the same processes that led to Riothamus' decision to move to Gaul.

Relations between the Gothic and imperial courts were possibly already deteriorating. Perhaps Euric was alarmed by the presence of another military commander in Gaul, allied with the emperor. With the Burgundians closely associated with Ricimer's regime (one possible heir to their throne, Gundobad, was one of Ricimer's senior officers) it might have looked as though the Goths were

---

[102] Ennodius, *Life of Epiphanius* 51–74.
[103] On Riothamus and his intervention in Gaul, see: Jordanes, *Getica* 45.237; *LH* 2.18; Sid. Ap. *Letters*, 3.9.
[104] Above, pp. 238–9.

about to be squeezed out. As early as 468, this was clearly a fear that Arvandus could play on.

In 471, again showing how far from powerless Anthemius was, three years after the Vandal defeat supposedly so ruinous to his government, the imperial army crossed the Alps under the command of one of Anthemius' sons, Anthemiolus.[105] This campaign against Euric might well have been planned in conjunction with Riothamus' force on the Loire.[106] Anthemiolus came not only with troops, however, but also with diplomatic proposals. Anthemius proposed that Euric could acquire Clermont in return for ceding Septimania, the area around Narbonne, back to the Empire.[107] If Euric had accepted, this would have improved the Empire's strategic position considerably, reopening the routes into *Tarraconensis* and the possibilities of direct intervention in Spain. Possession of Spain not only allowed the short crossing to Africa; it was also a prosperous province that, once reconquered, was easily defensible. The often-overlooked importance of Spain to imperial strategy is further underlined by the fact that as late as 471 the emperor was still trying to find ways of retaking it. It all came to nothing, though, as Euric rejected the proposals. Accepting the fight on two fronts, he crossed the Rhône, defeating and killing Anthemiolus and his fellow generals.[108] A Gothic force met Riothamus' army at Bourg-de-Déols, inflicted a decisive defeat on them, and drove the remnants to seek safety amongst the Burgundians. Euric's troops took Bourges. The threat of Burgundian intervention meant that he did not expand his territory beyond the Rhône.

These defeats gave Ricimer the opportunity he had been waiting for to dispose of his 'little Greek'. Anthemius' forces were crucially reduced and Ricimer besieged him in Rome.[109] The siege went on for months, as the citizens and Anthemius' remaining units put up a vigorous defence. Four months into the siege, Ricimer at last declared Olybrius, brother-in-law to the heir to the Vandal throne, emperor.[110] Doubtless this was a move to placate Gaiseric, whose

[105] *Chron. Gall. 511*, 13.
[106] I follow Gillett's (1999), p. 25, n. 85, chronology in placing Euric's battle against Riothamus in 470/1 rather than 469, and thus linking it to Anthemiolus' offensive.
[107] Sid. Ap. *Letters* 3.1.4.   [108] *Chron. Gall. 511*, 13.
[109] For the end of Anthemius' regime, see Cassiodorus, *Chron. 1293*; *Chron. Gall. 511*, 15; *Consularia Italica* 606; Priscus, fr. 64.
[110] Olybrius may have declared his opposition to the east, backers of Anthemius, on his coinage: López Sánchez (2002).

forces had been harrying the Mediterranean coastline since Basiliscus' defeat, and cover Ricimer's back. At about this time, according to Jordanes, Videmer, a leader of the Ostrogoths, a people newly forged from the wreckage of the Hunnic realm, invaded Italy.[111] This, *pace* Jordanes' claims of an amicable division of spheres of influence by two Ostrogothic brothers, Thiudimer and Videmer, is more likely to have stemmed from internal wrangling. In the aftermath, like many another loser in barbarian politics, Videmer entered the heart of the Empire and possibly offered his services to Anthemius or his opponents, but died soon after.[112] In the eighth century, Paul the Deacon wrote that a certain Bilimer, 'rector of the Gauls', tried to raise the siege of Rome but was killed in battle by Ricimer.[113] This Bilimer might possibly be identified with Videmer, his title reflecting an offer of that of *magister militum per Gallias* to the Ostrogothic leader.[114] After more months of siege and starvation Rome surrendered. Anthemius tried to escape by disguising himself as a beggar outside the church of Santa Maria in Trastevere, but he was recognised, captured and beheaded by the Burgundian Gundobad (11 July 472).[115] Ricimer did not live long to relish his triumph over the 'Galatian' emperor. On 18 or 19 August 472 he coughed up blood and died, presumably of some sort of haemorrhage.[116] Olybrius named Gundobad as his new patrician but died himself shortly afterwards.[117]

EPHEMERAL EMPERORS, 472–480

With Anthemius' death contemporaries appear to have realised that the Empire was dying. By this time, outside Italy, the western emperor controlled only some territories in the south-east of Gaul, *Noricum* and Dalmatia. Anthemiolus' defeat and the fighting between

---

[111] Jordanes, *Getica* 56.283–4; *Romana* 347. *PLRE* 2, 'Videmer 1', p. 1164.

[112] Heather (1991), pp. 241, 250–1.   [113] Paul the Deacon, *Roman History* 15.4.

[114] Stein (1959) 1, p. 394. *PLRE* 2, p. 230, doubts the identification as the Videmers, père et fils, were (according to Jordanes) still alive under Glycerius. However, neither Jordanes' nor Paul's work is of sufficient reliability to permit such confidence.

[115] *Consularia Italica* 606.

[116] *Consularia Italica* 607; Cassiodorus, *Chron.* 1293, calculates this, nearly correctly, as forty days after Anthemius' murder (which he does not date).

[117] *Consularia Italica* 609 – date recorded as 23 Sept. or 2 Nov.

Ricimer and Anthemius had reduced the Italian army's capacity for offensive warfare to insignificance. Euric continued his Gaulish campaigns, regularly besieging Clermont, where Sidonius Apollinaris was now bishop.[118]

In Italy another interregnum ensued until in March 473 Gundobad proclaimed Glycerius, the count of the domestics, as successor to Olybrius.[119] Glycerius' regime was short-lived. He might have appointed the son of the Ostrogothic leader Videmer, also called Videmer, as *magister militum* in Gaul.[120] Videmer led his men to Gaul, where his force seems to have been absorbed into Euric's Goths, either through alliance or after a defeat.[121] If this *was* an attempt to intervene in Gaul, its dismal failure finished the regime. Soon afterwards, in 474, Glycerius had to abdicate and become bishop of Salona when Julius Nepos, nephew of the general Marcellinus, landed in Italy with the Dalmatian army and the backing of the new eastern emperor, Zeno.[122] Zeno had also, after Vandal raids on the eastern Mediterranean, formally concluded a treaty leaving Gaiseric in control of all of his territorial acquisitions.[123] The only Vandal concession was to end the persecution of Catholics and to release any Roman prisoners in the royal household, permitting Zeno's representatives to ransom as many other captives as possible. This put an end to the 'fourth Punic war', the only one won by the 'Carthaginians'. Glycerius' patrician Gundobad, having backed a losing candidate, left Italy to secure his place as a king of the Burgundians.[124] It may be emblematic of the situation at this date that it was preferable to rule a Gallic kingdom than to be the power behind the western imperial throne. Alternatively, and perhaps

---

[118] See Harries (1994), pp. 222–38.

[119] Cassiodorus, *Chron.* 1295; *Consularia Italica* 611; Priscus, fr. 65.

[120] Jordanes, *Getica* 56.284; *Romana* 347. See above for possible linkage to Bilimer's title of 'rector of the Gauls' in Paul the Deacon's work.

[121] Jordanes is generally reluctant to admit inter-Gothic fighting, and a defeat for Videmer is implied at *Romana* 347, though the implication is that this took place in Italy. Videmer is very likely the Vittamer who received two letters from Ruricius of Limoges in Gaul: Ruricius, *Letters* 2.61, 2.63.

[122] Anonymous Valesianus 7.36; *Consularia Italica* 613–14; Marcellinus, *Chron. s.a.* 474.2; Priscus, fr. 65. This too might have been the context for Videmer's defeat and move or flight to Gaul; the evidence is too vague to permit certainty.

[123] Malchus, fr. 5.

[124] Wood (2003), pp. 252–3 for analysis, though stating erroneously that Gundobad had killed Olybrius.

more plausibly, Gundobad's decision represented another instance where a barbarian general without official command turned to kingship of a people as an alternative source of legitimacy.

Freed from the threat of Vandal attack, Nepos might have had ambitions to restore imperial prestige. A Gothic attack on Italy might have been repelled[125] and a new patrician and *praesental* master of soldiers appointed: Ecdicius, Sidonius Apollinaris' brother-in-law, who conducted a spirited defence of Clermont against Euric's troops.[126] Meanwhile, the Burgundians returned to the imperial fold. There was by now, however, little that could be done. Ecdicius was forced to flee, Euric's forces conquered Provence and were only induced to return it when the Burgundians and three Gallic bishops, negotiating on Nepos' behalf, granted them Clermont instead, much to Sidonius' dismay; he was led off into brief captivity.[127]

In 475 Nepos found that he had been unable to win support in Italy and the Italian army rebelled under Ecdicius' successor, an interesting character called Orestes, a Pannonian who had served at Attila's court.[128] Nepos fled back to Dalmatia whilst Orestes' young son, Romulus, was installed on the throne of what was left of the western Empire (by now only Italy and southern Provence as the provinces north of the Alps were effectively under the control of *Alamanni* and *Rugi* and Nepos still held Dalmatia). Even the management of this rump proved too difficult with the resources available and within a year the Italian army mutinied, under its commander Odoacer (August 476). After a brief confrontation, Orestes was killed at Piacenza and Romulus 'Augustulus' (Little Emperor) placed under honourable house arrest, with an annual pension, in Campania, where he and his mother may have founded a monastery and where he was apparently still living in the early sixth century.[129]

---

[125] *Chron. Gall. 511*, 16. Stein (1959), 1, pp. 395–6, and n. 178. The episode is difficult to date exactly, or interpret from this evidence.

[126] Sid. Ap. *Letters* 3.3; The episode is exaggerated somewhat in *LH* 2.24.

[127] Harries (1994), pp. 238–42. Sid. Ap. *Letters* 8.3, 8.9.

[128] Fall of Nepos: Anonymous Valesianus 7.36; *Consularia Italica* 617; Jordanes, *Getica* 45.241; Marcellinus, *Chron. s.a.* 475.2. Orestes' background: Anonymous Valesianus 8.38; Priscus, frr. 11, 15.2.

[129] Fall of Orestes and Romulus: Anonymous Valesianus 8.37–8; Cassiodorus, *Chron.* 1303; *Consularia Italica* 619–20; Jordanes, *Getica* 46.242; Marcellinus, *Chron. s.a.* 476.2. Romulus' survival: Cassiodorus, *Variae* 3.35; Nathan (1992). On the monastic foundation at Lucullanum, see Cooper (1999); Wood (1999).

Meanwhile, Euric's Goths gobbled up what was left of Roman Provence.[130] Odoacer sent ambassadors to Zeno saying that there was no need for a western emperor as Zeno could rule the whole Roman world. All Odoacer asked for was patrician rank. Since Romulus had never been recognised in Constantinople and, as far as the eastern court was concerned, the western emperor was still alive and well and living in Dalmatia, Zeno's response was sharp. He reprimanded the Roman senate for having killed one emperor sent by the east (Anthemius) and exiled another (Julius Nepos) and urged them to accept Julius back. If Julius wished to bestow the patriciate upon Odoacer, that was for him to decide.[131] Odoacer had no wish to see Julius return and so, rebuked by the imperial court and left with no other means of legitimation, he did what more than one military commander had done before in that situation; he declared himself king.

One can argue that the events of 476 were of minor significance.[132] In the twenty-one years since Valentinian III's murder, the throne had been vacant for about three years in total, during which the eastern emperor had technically ruled the whole Empire. Odoacer's position was not novel and the western throne was not vacant in any case: Nepos still reigned in Dalmatia. For all these reasons it is perfectly reasonable to claim that no one would immediately have realised that no more emperors would reign in Italy. Yet, as Jill Harries has pointed out, people *did* notice.[133] Sidonius Apollinaris thought that the Empire had fallen in 476. His references to the 'dwindled Tiber' are also evidence of his awareness of the political situation.[134] The significance of the events of 476 might have been noticed at the time because people had perhaps realised since the early 470s that the Empire was on its last legs. One reason why was that the Empire had not died quietly. The west did not drift hopelessly towards its inevitable fate. It went down kicking, gouging and screaming. Most of the leaders who gained control of the core of the Empire fought tooth and nail to restore imperial power. The accessions of Avitus, Majorian and Anthemius were all followed by

---

[130] *Chron. Gall. 511*, 20: the date is difficult to establish.
[131] Malchus, fr. 14, for this exchange.
[132] Croke (1983); Garnsey and Humfress (2001), pp. 2–3.
[133] Harries (1994), pp. v, 241.   [134] Sid. Ap. *Letters* 8.9.6; cp. 8.2.1.

vigorous military campaigns. Anthemius was still attempting to restore imperial ability to intervene in Spain as late as 471 and even Glycerius might have despatched an army (Videmer's) to Gaul. For those reasons, Nepos' failure to put together any real offensive in 475 was surely remarked upon. Given the comparison with previous events, the Empire's powerlessness to project its authority outside Italy after 471 must have finally spelt out to people that Rome had no capacity to maintain local or regional power. Some new decorative styles appeared on metalwork in the last quarter of the fifth century, with origins in non-Roman territory in northern *Germania* and Scandinavia. Elsewhere, at the same time, archaeological material reveals the display of a costume which, although probably originating in the Mediterranean, had become associated with the army and, therefore, with 'barbarians'.[135] The fact that consciously barbarian means of displaying wealth and power replaced styles of clearly imperial derivation in areas like Britain is significant. Perhaps more so is the fact that, as discussed further in chapter 11, the new material cultural horizons appear at the start of the final quarter of the fifth century, precisely the time that the Empire came to its political end. The Fall of Rome was not an intellectual fiction unnoticed by contemporaries.

Four years after Romulus' deposition, in 480, evidently while plotting a campaign to restore his authority in Italy, Julius Nepos was murdered by two retainers (apparently at the instigation of the bishop of Salona, that same Glycerius whom he had deposed and driven into the church six years previously) and Odoacer took over Dalmatia.[136] With his assassination, the Empire in the west finally came to an end. It is, as has often been noted, more than a little ironic that its last two rulers shared names with the first king of Rome (Romulus) and, if not the first emperor, then the founder of the first imperial dynasty (Julius). The most ironic thing of all, however, is that during the preceding century it is almost impossible to identify a single figure who had actually tried to cause its demise. All the decisive acts in bringing down the Empire were carried out by people attempting to create a better position for themselves within the sorts of imperial structures that had

---

[135] Von Rummel (2005). Below, pp. 336–7, 344–6, 352–3.
[136] Anonymous Valesianus 7.36; Malchus, *testimonia.* 1 (Glycerius' involvement).

existed in the fourth century. In a famous dictum, André Piganiol wrote that 'Roman civilisation did not die a natural death; it was assassinated.'[137] Neither alternative seems correct. The Roman Empire was not murdered and nor did it die a natural death; it accidentally committed suicide.

---

[137] Piganiol (1947), p. 422: 'La civilisation Romaine n'est pas morte de sa belle mort; elle est assassinée.'

10

KINGDOMS OF THE EMPIRE, 476–550

———— . ————

With Nepos' murder, the thread connecting the period's narrative history is broken. Henceforth we must consider the history of different regions in turn. This book closes with the collapse of many of the first generation of barbarian realms: the Thuringians in *c.*532, the Burgundians and Vandals in 534 and the Ostrogoths in 555. The latter two kingdoms were destroyed by Emperor Justinian's eastern Roman armies. Justinian also attacked the Visigoths who, although they survived, were plunged into a period of crisis. Our narrative in this chapter generally stops with the onset of the political instability that led to Justinian's invasions. The Frankish kingdom, which destroyed those of the Burgundians and Thuringians, was involved in Justinian's wars but never suffered invasion. Here our story takes us to the death of Chlothar I, the first Merovingian to rule all Gaul except for Brittany and the Visigothic enclave around Narbonne. In a fashion reminiscent of the art styles emerging in northern Europe at the end of the period covered by this chapter, these individual stories will interlace with each other and with the narrative of Justinian's campaigns given in chapter 15.

ITALY: TWO NATIONS UNDER A GOTH?[1]

In the heart of the former Empire, Odoacer's reign is generally characterised by stability and the continuation of the late imperial

---

[1] For recent general studies of Ostrogothic Italy, see: Ausbüttel (2003); Burns (1984), pp. 67–201; Giese (2004), pp. 74–119; Heather (1996), pp. 221–58; (2003);

order.[2] His army was largely non-Roman but that made little difference from the previous state of affairs. Indeed, given the adoption of barbarian ethnicities by the late imperial army, like the dominance of military forces claiming non-Roman identity throughout the post-imperial west, it can be seen simply as the outcome of a process that had been steadily ongoing since the fourth century. Odoacer ruled Italy well for twelve years. His relationship with the eastern court was never easy, however, and in 486/7 the Emperor Zeno, who had heard that Odoacer was plotting with his enemy, an Isaurian called Illus, stirred up the Rugians of *Noricum* against Odoacer.[3] Odoacer destroyed the Rugians and evacuated the Roman population of *Noricum*, provocatively sending the trophies of his victory to Zeno. Zeno avenged himself and solved another of his problems by unleashing the Ostrogoths upon Italy.

The background to the Ostrogothic invasion of Italy is complex and excellent analyses can be found elsewhere.[4] A brief summary will suffice. The Ostrogoths emerged in the aftermath of the collapse of Attila's realm. The Goths' reappearance should not be understood as demonstrating their incomplete assimilation into the Hunnic empire. Rather it shows how, when the political domination of one group was broken, rival factions coalesced, using alternative identities. The hierarchy of ethnicities was reordered so that the Gothic layer was promoted and the Hunnic eventually discarded. The Ostrogoths, however, did not establish dominance in the Danube basin. A plethora of groups arose from the wreckage of Attila's short-lived 'empire': *Rugi*, *Skiri*, Gepids, Heruls and so on. Thirty or more years passed after the fall of the Tervingian confederacy in the 370s before the Huns established their pre-eminence.[5] The Hunnic realm's demise was followed by an even longer 'interregnum' before ultimately, in the 570s, the Avars created a hegemony that lasted over 200 years.[6] None of the rival groups managed to acquire lasting overlordship as military defeat rapidly brought down those who had temporarily achieved dominance. The Ostrogoths, in

Moorhead (1992); (2005a); Pohl (2002), pp. 133–47; Wolfram (1988), pp. 284–332; (1997), pp. 194–223.

[2] Cesa (1994b); Jones, A. H. M. (1962); Moorhead (2005a), pp. 142–3; Wolfram (1997), pp. 183–93.

[3] Eugippius, *Life of Severinus* 44.4–5; John of Antioch, fr. 214.7.

[4] Above all, Heather (1991), pp. 227–308.   [5] Above, pp. 250–1.

[6] On the Avars, the classic work is Pohl (1988).

spite of Cassiodorus' and Jordanes' propaganda, do not seem to have been particularly successful in this competition.[7] Like Fritigern's Goths a hundred years before, they crossed the Danube into the orbit of the eastern Empire.

A new family emerged in command of the Ostrogoths: the Amals. Their later claims to have ruled the Goths since remote pre-history, as represented by the writings of Cassiodorus and Jordanes, represent sixth-century attempts to give the family a more respectable pedigree.[8] The Amals, eventually under Theoderic, son of Videmer's brother Thiudimer, were one of several Gothic factions, their key rivals confusingly being led by another Theoderic, son of Triarius, known as Theoderic Strabo ('the Squinter'). With the collapse of the Danube frontier earlier in the fifth century, the Goths became an important element in eastern Roman politics and the military. A little like Alaric's Goths eighty years previously – although there can be little doubt that the Ostrogoths were an entirely non-Roman political and military body – they suffered from lying on the wrong side of the Roman–barbarian demarcation line. When not in imperial favour all the old stereotypes could be deployed against them. Perhaps even more so than Alaric's Goths, they depended upon their leader being able to secure recognition from the imperial court.

However, they were not competing only amongst themselves, but also with another group of 'internal barbarians', the Isaurians from southern Asia Minor. Between 473 and 488 a complex merry-go-round of alliances, treachery, murder and intrigue constantly shifted the balance of power.[9] The emperor sometimes needed Gothic support against other factions, but could not allow them to become too powerful. The Emperor Zeno, himself Isaurian but faced with rebellions by his own people, who wished to dominate the Constantinopolitan court, played the two Theoderics off against each other with some skill until in 483–4 he overplayed his hand. Strabo was killed in an accident, falling from his horse onto a spear,[10] and in the aftermath Zeno encouraged Theoderic the Amal (whom he rewarded with considerable honours, including the consulate) to

---

[7] Heather (1996), p. 152.

[8] Heather (1988b); (1991), pp. 34–67; (1996), pp. 113–17.

[9] Heather (1991), pp. 264–308, for the best modern account.

[10] John of Antioch, fr. 211.5.

murder the Squinter's son Recitach.[11] Rather than removing one of the problematic factions, however, this simply led to Recitach's Goths joining the Amal. Given the heavy weight upon imperial politics of Roman ethnographic ideology, it is difficult to see that the Thracian Goths had much alternative. Instead of two competing Gothic groups, Zeno was confronted by one large and very powerful force. This situation was not improved when Zeno used Theoderic's Goths to reduce his Isaurian rival Illus in Asia Minor. Now dominant, Theoderic wanted a yet better deal and conflict soon broke out. This resulted in stalemate. The Goths threatened Constantinople and ravaged the Balkans but could not take the capital, whilst Zeno, secure behind the city's famous triple line of walls and, after Illus' suppression, able to devote more resources to confronting the Goths, was unlikely to drive the latter completely from his territories. A solution was required and that found, and apparently agreeable to both parties, was for Theoderic's Ostrogoths to move to Italy and dispose of the 'tyrant' Odoacer. In 488 the Ostrogoths took the long road west.

On 30 August 489 at the bridge over the Isonzo, not far from the site of Theodosius' victory over Maximus at the Frigidus ninety-five years previously, almost to the day, Theoderic defeated Odoacer's army.[12] The war was not brought to as speedy a conclusion as Theodosius' campaign, dragging on for a further three and a half years.[13] Theoderic was besieged in Pavia in 490 before defeating Odoacer's army with the help of a Visigothic force from Gaul, and some of his Rugians briefly went over to Odoacer in the following year before rejoining the Gothic king. They were not the only ones to change sides more than once in the conflict. Eventually Theoderic eliminated Odoacer's field armies and besieged him in Ravenna. In March 493, after negotiations started by Bishop Johannes of Ravenna, Theoderic entered the city. Ten days later, at a banquet, he personally cut the sexagenarian king of Italy in half.[14] Odoacer's remaining followers were butchered in the aftermath and Theoderic was master of Italy.

[11] John of Antioch, fr.214.3.
[12] Anonymous Valesianus 10.50; Cassiodorus, *Chron.* 1320; *Consularia Italica* 639.
[13] Anonymous Valesianus 10.51–6; Cassiodorus, *Chron.* 1321–31; *Consularia Italica* 640–9; Ennodius, *Life of Epiphanius* 109–19. Heather (1996), pp. 219–20; Wolfram (1988), pp. 281–4.
[14] John of Antioch, fr. 214a.

Theoderic ruled Italy for thirty-three years, creating a Romano-Gothic realm which has justifiably attracted the fascination of historians. He did not at first receive recognition from Constantinople, this probably only being granted in 497–8.[15] Theoderic set about making himself dominant not only in Italy but also across the west. Even before Odoacer's defeat, Theoderic's Goths defeated the Vandals in Sicily and imposed an unfavourable treaty upon them.[16] In 500 Theoderic married his sister, Amalafrida, to the Vandal king Thrasamund in a deal that probably subjected the Vandals to his hegemony.[17] In 504–5 he extended his dominions in the Balkans, defeating the Gepids and taking the former province of *Pannonia* II (including the old imperial capital on the Danube, Sirmium).[18] This also involved the tacit annexation of imperial territory, helping to bring about an alliance between Constantinople and the Franks. Theoderic created ties with the other kings of the west by diplomatic marriages. He married Audofleda, the sister of Clovis, the ruler of the Franks; his daughters Thiudegotho and Areagni (renamed Ostrogotha) married Alaric II of the Visigoths and Sigismund of the Burgundians respectively, while his niece Amalaberga married King Hermanfrid of the Thuringians, the latter possibly turning to Theoderic for protection after a defeat by the Franks.[19] While Theoderic had married a Merovingian, the marriages of the Gothic princesses, as has often been remarked, created a diplomatic ring around the Franks (map 21).

In 507 Theoderic's diplomacy failed to prevent the defeat and death of his ally Alaric II at Clovis' hands[20] and the loss of most of Visigothic Gaul to the Franks and Burgundians. The Franks' eastern Roman allies sent a fleet to ravage the Italian coast.[21] Nevertheless the Ostrogoths did not lose out. Theoderic's armies took Provence, defeating the Burgundians in 508, and by 513 had secured the Visigothic territories. Theoderic acted as regent for his grandson

---

[15] Anonymous Valesianus 12.64; Heather (1996), pp. 220–1; Wolfram (1988), p. 284.

[16] Below, p. 294.   [17] Below, pp. 294–5.

[18] Cassiodorus, *Chron.* 1343; *Variae* 8.10; Ennodius, *Panegyric to Theoderic* 12.60–9; Jordanes, *Getica* 58.300–1; *Romana* 387. Ausbüttel (2003), pp. 115–16; Heather (1996), p. 231; Moorhead (1992), pp. 174–5; Wolfram (1988), pp. 320–1.

[19] Anonymous Valesianus 12.63, 12.68, 12.70 (getting Thiudegotho and Ostrogotha the wrong way round); Cassiodorus, *Variae* 4.1, 5.43; Jordanes, *Getica* 58.297–9; *LH* 3.4–5, 3.31.

[20] Below, pp. 306–7.   [21] Marcellinus, *Chron. s.a.* 508.

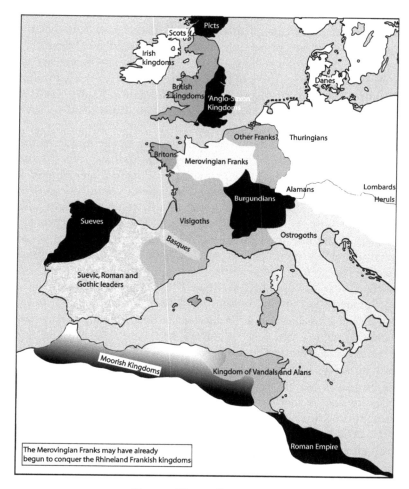

Map 21 Western Europe, 506

Athalaric.[22] This effectively put the Visigothic kingdom under his control. This did not equate with ruling Spain, however. The extent of Gothic dominance in the Iberian peninsula in the first decades of the sixth century was probably not great.[23] Numerous local polities existed, based upon the Roman cities, over which the Visigoths exercised little more than a loose hegemony. The Burgundians now

[22] Below, pp. 298–9.   [23] Kulikowski (2004), pp. 203–9, 256–66.

had much to fear from their powerful Frankish neighbours and recent allies, and the marriage alliance with Theoderic may have been a move to seek his protection.[24] If this betokened Ostrogothic supremacy, it was short-lived. Clovis' death brought insecurity to Merovingian politics; three of his four sons were very young and this doubtless lessened the danger of Frankish aggression. By 516, on Gundobad's death, the Ostrogoths and Burgundians seem to have come close to war.[25]

Theoderic's political domination of the west by the middle of the second decade of the sixth century appears to have affected the presentation of his rule.[26] He increasingly adopted a quasi-imperial style. Theoderic had not been above this type of posturing earlier in his reign but it became more noticeable in the latter stages, and associated with a change in ideology. Theoderic increasingly emphasised his neo-imperial status. When his armies took Provence he installed his own 'prefect of the Gauls' and used traditional Roman vocabulary to describe this acquisition of territory.[27] A 'prefect' was also installed in Spain.[28] By 513 he seems to have encouraged the Pope to appoint the bishop of Arles, Caesarius, as papal *vicarius* of all of Gaul.[29] Caesarius visited the king in Ravenna before receiving his new title from the Pope. As early as 508 Theoderic had written to Emperor Anastasius in terms suggesting that he viewed his realm as very nearly the equal of the eastern Empire and certainly the only Roman state in the west.[30] A couple of years later, a member of the senatorial Decii family erected an inscription which even referred to Theoderic as *augustus*.[31] As Theoderic's control of government became more secure his ideology changed accordingly, claiming simply that the Goths' valour and strength justified their rule.[32]

---

[24] Heather (1996), p. 233.

[25] Avitus, *Letters* 94; Cassiodorus, *Variae* 3.41 (and possibly 3.42) suggests tension on the Burgundian frontier. Shanzer (1998a).

[26] For discussions of Theoderic's ideology, see Amory (1997); Heather (1995b); McCormick (1986), pp. 267–84; Reydellet (1995).

[27] Cassiodorus, *Variae* 3.17 (also 3.16); below, p. 490.

[28] *Chronicle of Saragossa, s.a.* 529.

[29] Caesarius of Arles, *Letters* 7b.11; *Life of Caesarius* 1.36–42. Klingshirn (1994), pp. 130–2.

[30] Cassiodorus, *Variae* 1.1; Heather (1996), p. 229, for discussion.

[31] *CIL* 10.6850–2. McCormick (1986), p. 278–80.

[32] For the role of Theoderic's ideology in governing Italy, see below, pp. 332–4.

In his last years, Theoderic faced serious problems, some brought about in no small part by the success of his policies.[33] In Constantinople Anastasius' death brought to the throne a Balkan soldier called Justin. Justin was at first very conciliatory towards Theoderic but from about 520 onwards, perhaps under the influence of his nephew, Justinian, imperial views began to harden. Possibly in response to Theoderic's increasingly imperial pretensions, an ideology emerged that stressed the loss of the west – the first references to the 'fall of the Roman Empire' belong to this period.[34] The denial that the west was still part of the Roman world struck directly at the legitimacy of barbarian kings like Theoderic and provided a focus for opposition to the Ostrogothic ruler at home and abroad. Within Italy this was not helped by Theoderic's failure to produce a male heir. His daughter Amalasuentha had married a Visigoth called Eutharic, presumably to help consolidate the pan-Gothic realm, and Justin had recognised Eutharic, sharing the consulate with him in 519 and adopting him as his son in arms.[35] Eutharic died in 522/3, however, and this brought a number of tensions to the fore. It made the succession problematic. Other people might have manoeuvred for power but the principal candidates were Theoderic's nephew, Theodehad, and his four-year-old grandson Athalaric. The results of Theoderic's declaration in favour of Athalaric reveal the dynamics of his kingdom.

Boethius and Symmachus, leading senators, were tried and executed. Their associate, Albinus, was accused of having written to the emperor about the royal succession, a reckless act at best and probably treasonable. Boethius rashly declared that if Albinus was guilty then so were he and the entire senate. He was thrown into prison as a result, where he wrote his *Consolation of Philosophy*, a classic revealing Boethius as capable of rather more considered thought than that behind the comment which had landed him in jail. After a year, in 524, he was cudgelled to death.[36] Symmachus was executed the following year and in 526 Pope John died in prison,

---

[33] Ausbüttel (2003), pp. 129–48; Heather (1996), pp. 248–58; Moorhead (1983); (1992), pp. 212–51.

[34] Jordanes, *Getica* 46.243–47.245; Eugippius, *Life of Severinus* 20.1; Marcellinus *Chron. s.a.* 476. Amory (1997), pp. 135–47; Croke (1983).

[35] Cassiodorus, *Variae* 8.1.

[36] Anonymous Valesianus 14.85–7; Boethius, *Consolation of Philosophy* 1.4; *Book of the Popes* 55.

where he had been thrown for allegedly plotting with Constantinople (his embassy to the eastern court, to intercede for Arians in the Empire, had failed to bring the results Theoderic desired).[37]

To preserve their involvement in politics, as demanded by their culture and indeed as had become customary for Italian senators during the fifth century, it was necessary for aristocrats to maintain access to court and the patronage dispensed from there. Boethius and his associates had acquired pre-eminence at court in Theoderic's last years, doubtless causing resentment among other factions, yet the latter half of Theoderic's reign had shown that such dominance could not be assured. Growing awareness after 523 that a succession crisis was looming would have exacerbated not only Boethius and his allies' wariness of losing their access to power when Theoderic died, but also presented their opponents with a chance to bring about their fall. Boethius appears to have had links with Theodehad and, as events seemed to show that his faction would be excluded from power after Theoderic's death, it is possible that a desperate gamble was made, with fatal results. Their enemies seized their chance to bring down the dominant faction, and Theoderic demonstrated his absolute control over patronage a final time. The dependence of aristocrats upon royal favour was such that the demise of Symmachus and Boethius produced few shock waves, although it blotted the Gothic king's reputation somewhat and allowed propagandists to besmirch his name.[38] The deaths of Boethius and the others do not constitute an anti-Roman 'purge'. They rather show how secure was Theoderic's grasp on power at the end of his reign, as he executed very powerful Roman nobles with, to all intents and purposes, impunity.

Theoderic's failures should not be forgotten. His general in Spain, Theudis, a member of a powerful family that later ruled the Ostrogoths and the Visigoths, seems to have been effectively independent, refusing to come to Ravenna.[39] Nevertheless, within Italy, Theoderic appears to have created a stable realm wherein local society was closely integrated into the central government.[40] The

[37] *Book of the Popes* 55.

[38] Moorhead (1978); Anonymous Valesianus 14.79–16.96. Procopius, *Wars* 5.1.32–9 says the executions of Boethius and Symmachus were Theoderic's only unjust acts.

[39] Procopius, *Wars* 5.12.50–4.   [40] Below, pp. 332–8.

extent of his success can be gauged by the aftermath of his death in 526. Although Spain and Italy rapidly separated, under his two grandsons, the Italian realm held together very well in the face of a prolonged succession crisis.[41]

THE VANDALS IN AFRICA[42]

After bringing his war against the Roman Empire to a successful conclusion, the greatest Vandal king, Gaiseric, died within a year of Romulus' deposition, on 24 January 477. He was succeeded by his eldest surviving son, Huneric, the husband of Eudocia (who had managed to escape to Jerusalem in 471/2, where she died). Huneric, as Courtois said, has had a bad press amongst historians.[43] This results essentially from his persecution of the Catholic church. This produced the best known of all the sources from Vandal Africa, Victor of Vita's *History of the Vandal Persecution*.[44] Most of the literary output from his reign dwelt upon his assault on the Catholics. The extent of persecution during Huneric's reign can be debated. It was of comparatively short duration and the number of deaths was probably low but one should not underestimate the suffering and misery that it caused whilst in operation. Huneric's wrath was not limited to Catholics. He also persecuted the Manichaeans within his realm. Indeed, Huneric appears to have devoted his reign to establishing internal security within the kingdom. He eliminated potential rivals for the throne, chiefly his brother Theuderic and his children, and he adopted titles closely modelled upon those used by the emperors: *dominus* (master) for example.[45]

When Huneric died in late 484 he was succeeded by Gunthamund, his nephew, Gaiseric having instigated a system whereby the eldest eligible royal male acceded.[46] This was designed to ensure that an adult always occupied the Vandal throne, avoiding minorities and, theoretically, making sure of the king's ability to conduct military and diplomatic affairs in person. Little is known about Gunthamund.

[41] See below, p. 510.
[42] Clover (1993); Courtois (1955); Diesner (1966), pp. 75–97; Liebeschuetz (2003); Merrills (2004a); Pohl (2002), pp. 80–6; (2004); Wolfram (1997a), pp. 159–82.
[43] Courtois (1955), p. 262. Merrills (2004b) proposes that the bleak received image may be badly distorted.
[44] Victor of Vita, *History of the Vandal Persecution*, books 2–3.
[45] McCormick (1986), pp. 261–6.   [46] Jordanes, *Getica* 33.169.

He recalled the Catholic bishops from exile and relaxed Huneric's persecution.[47] Like Huneric he appears to have kept a tight rein on domestic politics, imprisoning the poet Dracontius and his family when the latter was accused of praising another ruler, possibly Huneric, whose anti-Catholic policies might now have been an embarrassment.[48] He seems to have lost most of the Vandal possessions in Sicily by 491 in spite of possibly winning a minor action against the Goths.[49] In the latter part of his reign, Moorish attacks seem to have increased around the frontiers of the kingdom, although Gunthamund is alleged by Dracontius to have won victories against them too.[50] An inscription records the burial on 10 May 495 of an unnamed bishop from *Mauretania Caesariensis* who (after many trials and exile under the Vandals) had been killed in battle against the Moors.[51]

Gunthamund died in 496 and was succeeded by his brother Thrasamund, 'the most sympathetic of the Vandal kings', according to Courtois.[52] Thrasamund enjoyed a long reign (496–523) and appears, like his predecessors, to have played the emperor within his realm. The *Latin Anthology* contains several poems praising him and his public building projects.[53] A devout Arian, he wished to debate theology with Fulgentius of Ruspe, recalling the latter from exile in Sardinia.[54] He nevertheless banned the Catholics from consecrating new bishops, in the hope that the Catholic episcopate would simply die out as a consequence. The bishops refused and as a result many, including Victor, the primate of *Byzacena*, were arrested and exiled in Sardinia.[55] Thrasamund was a little more active in foreign affairs than his brother had been, if no more successful. He apparently gave some succour to Alaric II's elder son Gesalic in his efforts to secure the Visigothic throne against his young half brother, Amalaric. Amalaric was backed by his grandfather, Theoderic of Italy, who

---

[47] Victor of Tunnuna, *Chron. s.a.* 479.2.

[48] This has traditionally been supposed to have been a foreign monarch, probably the emperor. However, Merrills (2004b) argues very convincingly that it was more likely to have been Gunthamund's predecessor Huneric; Dracontius had backed the wrong horse in Vandal politics.

[49] Dracontius, *Apology* lines 213–14. Modéran (2003b), p. 552, doubts this reading.

[50] Dracontius, *Apology*, line 214. Modéran (2003b), pp. 551–2.

[51] *CIL* 8.9286; Courtois (1955), p. 378, no. 94.   [52] Courtois (1955), p. 267.

[53] Courtois (1955), p. 267.   [54] *Life of Fulgentius of Ruspe* 20–1.

[55] *Life of Fulgentius* 13; Victor of Tunnuna, *Chron. s.a.* 497.4.

sharply warned the Vandals to stay out of 'pan-Gothic' politics.[56] Thrasamund married Amalafrida, Theoderic's sister and the mother of Theodehad (king of the Ostrogoths, 534–6). Although this ensured that the Vandals retained the western tip of Sicily around Marsala, there was a price to pay. Amalafrida arrived in Carthage with a 5,000-strong Gothic escort.[57] If the number is any way accurate, this was a sizeable force by sixth-century standards, allowing Theoderic to intervene in Vandal affairs should he so wish. Certainly it was an effective counter to that common Vandal tactic, the retention of African grain and probably made Thrasamund a subordinate of the Gothic king.[58] Towards the end of his reign, Thrasamund's forces suffered a severe defeat at the hands of a Moorish rebellion in the south of the kingdom.[59] Alliance with Saharan nomads may have made the Moorish kingdoms' threat yet more formidable.

Thrasamund's death in 523 brought about the long-deferred accession of Huneric and Eudocia's son, Hilderic. The weaknesses of Gaiseric's succession system now became apparent. Hilderic's mother had fled Africa fifty-one years before his accession and the new king could have been in his mid-sixties. The age of the later Vandal kings doubtless explains their lack of vigour in dealing with the problems that beset their realm. Had Hilderic succeeded his father in 484, shortly after Nepos' murder, the Vandals might have been able to make much of his Theodosian ancestry and perhaps even bid for power in Italy. There was less such capital to be made in 523 and the king is usually depicted as lacking the energy to make anything of that which did exist. This might not be entirely fair. Hilderic had converted to Catholicism, something that might have resulted in greater integration of the Vandals and Africans. Despite promising Thrasamund not to grant freedom of worship to the Catholics, he did so as soon as he ascended the throne.[60] This doubtless improved relations with Constantinople. Nonetheless Hilderic did little to promote any further religious unity within the kingdom. His murder of Amalafrida (allegedly for plotting against him) and her Gothic guard might have been a more vigorous

---

[56] Cassiodorus, *Variae* 5.43–4.   [57] Procopius, *Wars* 3.8.11–14.
[58] Heather (1996), p. 231.
[59] Procopius, *Wars* 3.8.15–29. Procopius' account of the Moors' use of camels is heavily influenced by Herodotus. Modéran (1991); (2003b), p. 550.
[60] Victor of Tunnuna, *Chron. s.a.* 523.2.

move, casting off Ostrogothic domination and aligning himself with the aggressive Constantinopolitan regime.[61] This might suggest a policy based on his Theodosian descent and have facilitated the probably groundless allegations that later circulated that he was planning to give the Vandal kingdom over to Emperor Justin I.[62]

Hilderic was, however, too old to win military laurels for himself. The Moorish kings, who had been encroaching on Vandal territory since Gunthamund's time, needed to be tackled. This was all the more urgent as they had recently united under the leadership of one Guenfan.[63] The Moors inflicted a serious defeat upon Hilderic's armies, under his general Hildimer, in the mountains of *Byzacena*, well inside the Vandal kingdom.[64] The date is unknown but seemingly towards the end of Hilderic's reign. Hilderic also despatched his cousin, Thrasamund's nephew Gelimer, against the Moors. Gelimer won some successes but then, on the basis of this and of Hildimer's defeat and its weakening of Hilderic's prestige, took the opportunity to enrol the support of some of the Moors, take his victorious army back to Carthage and depose Hilderic.[65] Hilderic and his children, alongside another relative and commander Hoamer ('the Achilles of the Vandals', says Procopius[66]), were imprisoned. This coup provoked the military intervention of the Emperor Justinian.[67]

THE VISIGOTHS FROM GAUL TO SPAIN[68]

Although he completed the conquest of Aquitaine and Provence, after the demise of the western Empire in 476, Euric of the Visigoths was unable to establish any real hegemony. Gundobad's

---

[61] Procopius, *Wars* 3.9.4–5; Victor of Tunnuna, *Chron. s.a.* 523.1.

[62] Procopius, *Wars* 3.9.5, 3.9.8. Cp. John Malalas, *Chron.* 18.57.

[63] Courtois (1955), p. 343; Modéran (2003b), pp. 314–34.

[64] Procopius, *Wars* 3.9.3.

[65] John Malalas, *Chron.* 18.57; Procopius, *Wars* 3.9.6–10; Victor of Tunnuna, *Chron. s.a.* 531.

[66] Procopius, *Wars* 3.9.2. Hoamer was seemingly Hilderic's nephew and thus had a better claim to the succession than Gelimer. Given the Vandal army's generally dismal record in its last years, the value of the title 'Achilles of the Vandals' might have been relative rather than absolute.

[67] Below, pp. 499–501.

[68] Giese (2004), pp. 41–62; Heather (1996), pp. 181–210; Mathisen and Sivan (1999); Pohl (2002), pp. 58–66; Wolfram (1988), pp. 172–246; (1997), pp. 145–58.

Burgundians and the Franks in the Paris basin were powerful foes and Euric ceased to expand his realms in Gaul. He died in 484 and was succeeded by his son Alaric II. This was the first succession of son to father amongst the Visigoths since 451, and the first since that date not to involve the murder of the previous king. Indeed, of the first nine Visigothic kings (including Alaric I) Alaric II was only the fourth not to accede by killing his predecessor.

Alaric attempted no further expansion against the Franks or the Burgundians, although his troops decisively helped Theoderic's conquest of Italy in 490.[69] Instead Gothic forces turned south into Spain. There had been Gothic garrisons in Spanish cities since the middle of the fifth century as a result of campaigns under or in alliance with the Empire.[70] These did not amount to extensive lordship, however. The evidence for the increase in Gothic activity in Spain is slender and comes from sketchy sources such as the fragmentary *Chronicle of Saragossa*. This records that in 494 the Goths entered Spain. As there had been Goths in Spain for some time it has long been thought that this bald chronicle entry must mean something special. Three years later the same source records that the Goths received dwellings in Spain. Rather than, as has sometimes been supposed, representing a mass movement of the Goths, this account seems instead to represent the final Gothic conquest of *Tarraconensis*. Although Frederic had destroyed the *Bagaudae* in the Ebro valley in 453, the province does not appear to have been brought under the lasting governance of any group thereafter.[71] It is likely that there were Gothic garrisons in the region but they were not the only contenders for power. The *Chronicle of Saragossa* records under 496 that Burdunelus assumed a tyranny in Spain. Captured by the Goths in 497 (the same year as the *Chronicle* records that the Goths received dwellings), he was allegedly executed by being burnt inside a bronze bull.[72] In 506, according to the same source, another tyrant, Peter, was captured in Tortosa when the Goths took that city. These 'tyrants' are clearly the Goths' rivals for authority in the

---

[69] Anonymous Valesianus 11.53.   [70] See above, pp. 264, 266.

[71] *Chron. Gall.* 511, 16, records Gothic campaigns in the region in the 470s.

[72] This is very odd and seems unlikely to be accurate. The form of execution was known and associated with tyrants because of the story of Phalaris, a Sicilian tyrant who executed captives in this fashion before suffering the same fate himself: Cicero, *On Duties* 2.26.

area and possibly represent a direct continuation of the type of lordship earlier dismissed as 'bagaudic'.

North of the Pyrenees, again according to fragmentary annalistic sources, the Franks attacked Visigothic Aquitaine from the 490s, reaching Saintes and even Bordeaux.[73] Gregory of Tours records that Clovis of the Franks was able to force Alaric II to hand over his defeated rival, Syagrius, for execution.[74] Given the insecure chronology of Clovis' reign, it is not impossible that the diplomatic pressure that led to Alaric giving Syagrius up was associated with these attacks.[75] Again probably because of these raids, Alaric II and Clovis met on an island in the Loire, near Amboise, and signed a treaty.[76] It has been assumed that the Goths paid such a large tribute to the Franks as a result of this treaty that Gothic coinage had to be debased.[77] This seems unlikely. Gregory of Tours does not state that the Goths paid any tribute, giving the impression that the treaty of Amboise was very much between equal parties. The peace did not hold, however, and in 507 the Franks invaded Aquitaine again. Alaric II's army met them at a place called *campus vogladensis*, usually located at Vouillé although it has been argued that Voulon is more probable.[78] The Visigoths were defeated and Alaric himself killed.[79]

This produced a crisis within the Visigothic realm. Alaric II left two sons, an adult called Gesalic (the son of a concubine) and a child, Amalaric. Gesalic seems to have taken control of the kingdom but in 510 Theoderic's general Ibba attacked him in his grandson, Amalaric's name. Gesalic was driven to Africa, but Theoderic's hegemony ensured that he received little support. Returning to Spain he was again defeated, forced into Burgundian territory and soon afterwards murdered.[80] Theoderic now seized control of the Visigothic kingdom as regent for Amalaric, apparently appointing a

---

[73] *Consularia Italica* 650–3.   [74] *LH* 2.27.

[75] The traditional date for Clovis' defeat of Syagrius is 486, but this date is insecure: Halsall (2001). Although Gregory implies that Syagrius' betrayal and execution took place shortly after his defeat this need not necessarily have been the case.

[76] *LH* 2.35. The event is, as ever, undated but usually placed *c.*502.

[77] Avitus, *Letters* 87, claims the coinage was debased. James (1988), p. 86.

[78] Gerberding (1987), p. 41.

[79] *Chron. Gall. 511*, 15; *Chronicle of Saragossa, s.a.* 507; Isidore, *History of the Goths* 36; *LH* 2.37; Venantius, *Miracles of Hilary* 20–1.

[80] On these events, see: Cassiodorus, *Variae* 5.43–4; *Chron. Gall. 511*, 15; *Chronicle of Saragossa, s.a.* 508–11; Isidore, *History of the Goths* 37–8.

prefect for Spain, called Stephen.[81] His commanders, presumably including his general Theudis, effectively governed Visigothic territory and appear, from a comment in Gregory of Tours' *Histories*,[82] to have retaken some of the Frankish conquests in Aquitaine. Theudis seems to have ruled to all intents and purposes independently of Theoderic.[83] Nevertheless, when Amalaric came of age he took the throne. Trouble followed. He had married a daughter of Clovis but, allegedly refusing to convert to Arianism, she was so mistreated that, according to Gregory, she summoned her brothers to avenge her.[84] In 531 the Frankish kings assembled their armies and marched south, defeating Amalaric near Narbonne. Amalaric was killed in flight. The fragmentary *Chronicle of Saragossa* says he was killed by a Frank called Besso, who threw a spear called an *ango* at him.[85] The Franks were unable to make any permanent inroads into Septimania, the area around Narbonne, which, safe behind encircling mountains, remained in Gothic hands. Theudis seized the throne in the aftermath and maintained his rule, interestingly, with the aid of an army raised from the slaves of his Hispano-Roman wife.[86] In 541 Theudis and his general Theudegisel, or Theudisculus ('Little Theudis'), defeated a Frankish attempt at conquest when his troops closed the Pyrenean passes behind Childebert I's invading troops and trapped the latter.[87] Theudis ruled energetically, issuing laws in Roman tradition, until 548.[88] Nevertheless, although Visigothic power seems to have spread south, it remains unlikely that the Visigoths exerted more than hegemony over the Roman cities of the southern peninsula. Indeed it was an attempt to exact more control that produced another crisis for the Gothic kingdom and an eastern Roman invasion.[89]

---

[81] *Chronicle of Saragossa, s.a.* 529.   [82] *LH* 3.21.

[83] Above, pp. 292–3.   [84] *LH* 3.10. Isidore, *History of the Goths* 40.

[85] *Chronicle of Saragossa, s.a.* 531. Gregory confirms that a thrown spear slew the Gothic king: *LH* 3.10.

[86] Procopius, *Wars* 5.12.50–4.

[87] Isidore, *History of the Goths*, 41. *LH* 3.29 records the campaign as a Frankish victory. Gregory seems to have known little beyond a miracle story concerning the tunic of St Vincent. Nevertheless, historians' general preference for Isidore's version (in spite of his greater distance from events) may stem simply from Isidore's more modern, 'rational'-looking story. The *Chronicle of Saragossa, s.a.* 541, (possibly closest to events) states that the Franks caused great damage.

[88] Zeumer (1898).   [89] Below, pp. 505–7.

Little can be said of the other principal power in the Iberian peninsula, the Sueves.[90] After Hydatius laid down his pen in 468 the Suevic kingdom enters a period of absolute historical darkness, from which it only emerges at the very end of the period covered by this book. At that point a Pannonian called Martin became bishop of Braga and wrote a tract about the conversion of rustics. He also called a council of bishops at Braga, allowing us to suggest that the Suevic kingdom maintained some of the infrastructure of Roman *Gallaecia*.[91]

THE BURGUNDIAN KINGDOM[92]

The Burgundian king Gundobad, patrician and associate of Ricimer, was possibly one of those who had noticed the significance of the events following the collapse of Anthemius' regime.[93] Abandoning Glycerius, he returned to Burgundy in 473, where he became king, although how, when and his precise relationship to Chilperic I are all unclear. The political history of the Burgundian kingdom is hampered by the absence of contemporary annalistic records. The nature of the best source for the kingdom, the writings of Bishop Avitus of Vienne, is such that political historical details are often, at best, only inferred. Political authority within the realm appears frequently to have been divided (as between Chilperic I and his brother Gundioc), although not, it seems, on strictly territorial lines, and Gundobad needed to share power with three relatives: Chilperic II, Godemar and Godegisel.[94] Relations between the four were not harmonious. Nothing is known of Godemar's fate, but Gundobad killed Chilperic and around 500 Godegisel allied with Clovis against Gundobad.[95] Gundobad was defeated and agreed to pay the Franks tribute. With Godegisel's allies bought off, Gundobad rallied his forces and defeated and

---

[90] Thompson, E. A. (1982), pp. 161–87.

[91] Castellanos and Martín Viso (2005), pp. 5–10.

[92] Favrod (1997); Kaiser (2004); Perrin (1968). In English, the best accounts are the succinct but sophisticated analyses in Shanzer and Wood (eds. and trans.) (2002), pp. 13–27, and Wood (2003). See also Wolfram (1997), pp. 248–59.

[93] Above, pp. 278–9.

[94] Wood (2003), p. 253. The latter two were his brothers. The two Chilperics, 'I' and 'II', may in fact be one and the same!

[95] *LH* 2.32; Marius of Avenches, *Chron. s.a.* 500.

killed his brother. Numerous Burgundian and Gallo-Roman aristocrats who had backed the wrong side were executed in the aftermath of this war, and their estates presumably confiscated. This has important implications for the study of Burgundian settlement.[96] Godegisel's disposal left Gundobad free to promote his own son Sigismund to the throne.

The Burgundian royal family seems not to have had an exclusive allegiance to either Catholic or Arian Christianity, although, insofar as a pattern can be detected it seems that the men of the family were Arian and the women Catholic.[97] This, and the Burgundians' generally good relations with the Gallic church, might relate to the divided kingship and the unharmonious relationships between the kings. Different rulers might have been keen not to deter their Gallo-Roman followers (and so strengthen the hand of their rivals) by pursuing hard-line Arian policies and, by having Catholic relatives, left an avenue open for Catholics to the royal presence. Meanwhile their own Arianism meant that their Burgundian followers were not alienated. We might see in a similar vein the Burgundians' continued desire for imperial backing for their rule. Gundioc and Chilperic had employed the titles of patrician and *magister militum* within their realms, and Gundobad had held these ranks in Italy.[98] Before Gundobad's death, his son Sigismund petitioned Emperor Anastasius to be granted the title of *magister*.[99] By 515 he had been given the patriciate as well (possibly implying that his title, like his father's, was *magister utriusque militiae praesentalis* – master of the soldiers in the imperial presence). Arguably the rulers of no other post-imperial western kingdom were as keen on obtaining imperial titles to legitimise their authority. In letters to Anastasius, Sigismund gave the impression that he still regarded his realm as part of the Empire.[100] The reason might be that the Burgundian kingdom appears to have been based upon a close alliance between the kings and the local senatorial nobility from the start.[101]

---

[96] Below, pp. 442–3.

[97] Kaiser (2004), pp. 152–7; Wood (2003), pp. 263–4.

[98] Gundioc: above, p. 268; Chilperic: *Lives of the Fathers of the Jura* 2.10 (92); Sid. Ap. *Letters* 5.6.2. Gundobad: above, pp. 278–9.

[99] Avitus, *Letters* 93. Theoderic of Italy appears to have tried to prevent this: Avitus, *Letters* 94.

[100] Avitus, *Letters* 93–4.   [101] Above, pp. 262–3.

Although he had been dealt with (rashly) as an inferior by Theoderic of Italy, Gundobad joined Clovis in the latter's attack on the Visigothic kingdom. The Burgundians did not participate in the Vouillé campaign but after Alaric II's defeat their armies seized Gothic territory in Provence and raided as far as Toulouse and Barcelona. They were unable to take Arles, however, as Ostrogothic troops intervened and drove them back.[102] They may, nevertheless, have briefly captured Marseille or, perhaps with more likelihood, retained some sort of an interest in the city and its revenues.[103] The latter alternative, envisaging some sort of condominium and partition of the toll income and trade from the port (such as existed between later Frankish kings) might be strengthened by the good relations between the Ostrogoths and the Burgundians which prevailed from some time after the war of 507–8. Theoderic seems to have brought the Burgundians into his network of alliances and married his daughter to Sigismund. Gesalic, the losing candidate for the Visigothic throne, was killed in Burgundian territory.[104]

Sigismund's reign was disastrous. Internally, he was beset with a crisis when he backed the incestuous marriage of one of his court officials, provoking the Burgundian church to go on strike.[105] Although the situation was resolved, the episode tarnished Sigismund's image as first Catholic king of the Burgundians. Matters were not improved when he had his own son, Sigistrix,[106] strangled.[107] As Sigistrix was Theoderic's grandson, who seems to have considered him as a possible successor, this move might, like Hilderic's imprisonment and murder of Sigistrix's great-aunt Amalafrida, be read as an attempt to move out of the orbit of the Ostrogothic king,[108] though there is no clear evidence that the Burgundians were ever very subordinate to Theoderic.[109] There are other parallels with Hilderic, also a Catholic. Sigismund had long courted favour with the Constantinopolitan court and might have been swayed by the hardening of imperial attitudes towards the Ostrogoths. Sadly for Sigismund, this move seems only to have

---

[102] On this campaign: Cassiodorus, *Chron.* 1349; *Variae*, 1.24, 3.16–17, 8.10; *Chron. Gall. 511*, 15; *Life of Caesarius* 1.28–32.

[103] Avitus, *Letters* 79. Shanzer and Wood (eds. and trans.) (2002), pp. 17, 237–8.

[104] Above, p. 298, n. 80.

[105] Shanzer and Wood (eds. and trans.) (2002), pp. 23–4; Wood (1999), pp. 299–300.

[106] Sigeric in some sources.   [107] *LH* 3.5.

[108] As Heather (1996), p. 248.   [109] Above, pp. 289–90.

brought about an opportunistic Frankish attack. The nearest Merovingian king to Burgundy, Chlodomer of Orléans, invaded, possibly in alliance with the Ostrogoths.[110] The latter seem to have seized Burgundian territory in the south at this time and any Burgundian interest in Marseille was probably lost. Sigismund was captured by Chlodomer and executed. Nevertheless, his younger brother Godemar[111] rallied the Burgundians and defeated the Franks the following year, killing Chlodomer in the process. Little is known of Godemar's reign. Another Frankish invasion appears to have reduced the realm to tributary status and in 534, as internal crises removed any possibility of Ostrogothic support, the Franks wiped the Burgundian kingdom off the map for good.[112] Godemar's fate is unknown but unlikely to have been peaceful.

GAUL: CLOVIS AND THE TRIUMPH OF THE MEROVINGIANS[113]

The power of the Merovingian dynasty, which destroyed the Burgundians, had grown out of the last Roman field armies on the Loire. On these foundations, the Paris basin appears to have been partly under Merovingian control from Childeric's reign. The traditional view of a steady southward movement of Frankish authority is very problematic.[114] One basis for this reconstruction is the idea that Clovis only took control of the Paris basin after a victory over Syagrius, 'king of the Romans' in the fifth year of his reign, usually assumed to be 486. The date of Clovis' accession is however less well known than often supposed and could have taken place at any time after 474, perhaps even as late as 491.[115] While there is no reason to doubt Syagrius' existence, the reality of his 'kingdom of the Romans', which is given concrete form in historical atlases, has been, and should be, questioned.[116] It seems

---

[110] *LH* 3.6; Wood (1988).
[111] The fact that Gundobad named his second son after one of his brothers suggests, perhaps, that this brother had died peacefully!
[112] *LH* 3.11.
[113] Numerous general works on the Merovingian realm exist. Recent surveys include: Ewig (2001); Hartmann (2003); Geary (1988); James (1988); Lebecq (1990); Wood (1994a). James (1982a) is an excellent thematic treatment.
[114] Above, pp. 269–70.
[115] Halsall (2001).   [116] James (1988), pp. 59–77.

more reasonable to place the conflict between Clovis and Syagrius, sons respectively of Childeric and Aegidius, the rival commanders of the Loire army in the 450s and 460s, in the context of continued competition for the control of that force.[117] Clovis won, partly by bringing in support from his relatives, who ruled the Frankish kingdoms in the north of what had been Belgica and Germania, and eventually pressurised Alaric II of the Visigoths, into handing Syagrius over for execution.[118]

The sources for Clovis' reign are thin. The most detailed narrative is that provided by Gregory of Tours but this is extremely stylised.[119] The bishop knew remarkably little about Clovis and wove disparate scraps into a moral tale presenting him as a model ruler, a latter day Old Testament figure, walking righteously in the sight of God and smiting his enemies. Apart from that we have a few letters to the king and one from his *scriptorium* to the bishops of Aquitaine. These give a rather different view of Clovis from that presented by the bishop of Tours.[120] Clovis, perhaps like his father, comes across as a very Roman figure, which should probably not surprise us. In a typically bizarre story by Procopius, the Franks make an alliance with the *Arborychoi*, who Procopius says used to defend Gaul.[121] It seems most likely that the *Arborychoi*, whose name seems to be a corruption of *Armorici* or *Armoricani*, are the Roman forces on the Loire. However garbled, this appears to be further evidence that the power base of the Merovingians originated in the Loire army.

Warfare continued against the Goths on the Loire frontier and further south, with attacks on Bordeaux and Saintes in the 490s.[122] In 500 Clovis, in the first securely datable action of his reign, intervened in the Burgundian civil war between Gundobad and Godegisel and received tribute as the price of his withdrawal.[123] His marriage to the Burgundian princess Chlothild probably took place before this. Slightly later, although the chronology is impossible to establish, he made peace with Alaric II.[124] Clovis was active militarily on his other frontiers, attacking and defeating the Alamans to the east.[125] As ever the chronology is fraught with

[117] Halsall (2001) for further discussion.   [118] *LH* 2.27.
[119] Carozzi (1992); Halsall (2001); Wood (1985).   [120] Daly (1994).
[121] Procopius, *Wars* 5.12.12–19.   [122] Above, p. 298, n. 73.
[123] Above, p. 300.   [124] Above, p. 298.
[125] Cassiodorus, *Variae* 2.41; *LH* 2.30.

difficulties. A comment in Gregory's *Histories* dates his war against the Alamans to the fifteenth year of Clovis' reign, traditionally placed in 496 on the basis of the conventional dating of Clovis' succession to 481. This regnal year has been interpolated into Gregory's account and, since we do not know the date of Clovis' accession, we cannot know when his fifteenth regnal year was in any case. A letter of Theoderic the Great to Clovis, referring to his recent defeat of the Alamans, is datable to 506 and would imply that, although ongoing conflict with the *Alamanni* should not be excluded, Clovis had secured his southern borders against the more militarily powerful Goths and Burgundians before turning on the Alamans. He had also forced the Thuringians, who had emerged as the main power on the Elbe, to submit.[126] By 507 Frankish dominance in Gaul was securely established.

In the early part of his reign Clovis may have made strenuous efforts to win support from his Gallo-Roman subjects. Procopius' story of the alliance with the *Arborychoi* may reflect this. Another odd and, in itself, unreliable story recounts that he married a daughter to a Roman senator.[127] If these snippets of admittedly dubious information reflect a process of integration with the Gallo-Romans, it would parallel Theoderic's contemporary policy and accompanying ideology of *civilitas*, assigning different roles to the two ethnic groups within his kingdom. The Franks would be the army and the Romans the taxpayers and administrators.[128] This is the situation that appears in the much better-documented second half of the sixth century. Earlier in his reign, Theoderic also had to incorporate other, potentially rival Gothic leaders in his regime. It was every bit as necessary for Clovis to do the same with Frankish chieftains. Like Theoderic's, Clovis' family were newcomers on the political scene. They are known as the Merovingians, meaning descendants of Merovech. Merovech was Childeric's father and, writing in the last quarter of the sixth century, Gregory of Tours had to admit that people only *claimed* (*adserunt*) that Merovech was the son of Chlodio, the previous king.[129] All this underlines that this dynasty had no deep roots. There were at least three Frankish

---

[126] *LH* 2.27.
[127] Paul the Deacon, *Book of the Bishops of Metz*, p. 264.
[128] Halsall (2003a), pp. 32–3, 46–50.
[129] *LH* 2.9. Chlodio is attested (as Chloio) by Sid. Ap. *Poems* 5, line 212.

kingdoms in the north of Gaul, which had expanded from the areas of fourth-century Frankish settlement in Toxandria into the former Roman provinces.[130] These were ruled by kings with every bit as much Frankish pedigree as Clovis. Some were relatives, though we have no way of knowing whether Childeric and Clovis were senior members of a ruling house, as is usually assumed, or scions of a cadet branch. The latter might be strengthened by the refusal of at least one northern king to help in Clovis' wars.[131] In the second quarter of the sixth century, other Frankish leaders with blood-connections to Clovis' family or other claims to seniority within Frankish politics, are known.[132] The Merovingians' position was not assured, underlining the importance of good relations with northern Gallo-Roman leaders and of the command of the former Loire army.

At some point between 496 and 507, and probably closer to the latter date, Clovis adopted Catholic Christianity, being baptised in Reims by St Remigius.[133] Gregory of Tours depicts him as converting directly from paganism but he had his own reasons for wanting Clovis, his model ruler, to move directly from outright heathenism to unsullied Catholic Christianity. A letter to the king from Avitus of Vienne makes it clear that Clovis had at least dallied with Arianism.[134] Even Gregory lets slip that his sister Lanthechild was an Arian and was baptised with her brother. Given how widespread Arianism was amongst the Germanic-speaking barbarians, this should not surprise us. Though we should not rule out personal piety, Clovis' conversion was, as has long been recognised, an astute political move. It enabled the Franks to ally with the Catholic Empire in Constantinople and gave their kings an advantage over their Arian Visigothic and Burgundian rivals. Indeed it might have been the only way that Clovis could try to pry the southern nobility away from their loyalty to their kings.

The balance of power within Gaul changed dramatically in 507. With the support of the Burgundians and Sigibert the Lame, ruler of the Frankish kingdom on the middle Rhine, Clovis attacked the Visigoths. The Frankish army crossed the Loire and Clovis wooed the Aquitanian church by instructing his troops not to

---

[130] *LH* 2.40–2.   [131] *LH* 2.41.   [132] *LH* 3.14, 3.23.

[133] *LH* 2.31. On the dating, see Shanzer (1998b); Spencer (1994); Wood (1985).

[134] Avitus, *Letters* 46.

forage on church estates, indeed executing troops who broke this command.[135] His letter to the Aquitanian bishops outlining this stance survives.[136] Clovis' army put the Goths to flight and Alaric II was killed, allegedly by Clovis himself.[137] The Franks took most of the rest of Aquitaine, although the conquest was more drawn out than appears in the traditional accounts based upon Gregory of Tours' *Histories*. Gregory had reasons to depict the outright triumph of a Catholic convert over the Arian Goths.

The incorporation of Aquitaine enabled Clovis to move against leaders with competing claims to authority over the Franks.[138] He waged a series of campaigns against the northern Frankish kings.[139] Portraying the Frankish king as a cunning, latter-day David, Gregory details how he suborned their aristocrats and had them murdered, one by one, until he was the sole remaining ruler.

In 511 Clovis convened a council of bishops at Orléans where he legislated to order and protect the church within his new kingdom. It may be that the first Frankish law code, the *Pactus Legis Salicae* (the *Compact of Salic Law*) was promulgated at this gathering. The date of this law is usually placed before 507. One basis for this supposition is a clause referring to pagan sacrificial animals.[140] However, although the final compilation may have been issued at a specific date, it seems very likely to have included edicts from a long period of time, perhaps going well back into the fifth century and possibly including subjects that would be surprising if composed at a council of bishops![141] Another support for a date before 507 is the clause stating that it applies between the Loire and the Ardennes.[142] However, this does not necessarily imply that only that region was subject to the Franks, not least because the law envisages that the Franks could recover people wrongly sold into slavery beyond these limits. The formerly Gothic kingdom south of the Loire had its own code, in Alaric's Breviary and Clovis might

---

[135] *LH* 2.37.   [136] Clovis, *Letter to the Bishops of Aquitaine*.
[137] Above, n. 79, for references to the battle.
[138] The effects of Vouillé on the kingdom's social structures are examined below, pp. 356–7.
[139] *LH* 2.40–2. The chronology is vague, as Gregory's account is so stylised. Relative chronological indications nevertheless suggest that at least some of these campaigns took place after 507. I am grateful to Adrian Smith for aiding my understanding of these episodes.
[140] *PLS* 2.15.   [141] Collins (1998).   [142] *PLS* 47.1.

have felt no need to legislate for that region. Furthermore, the signatories to the Council of Orléans include none of the bishops from what became the kingdom of Austrasia, beyond the Ardennes. This might suggest that the recently conquered Frankish territories on the middle Rhine had retained some political independence. The region was ruled after Clovis' death by his eldest son, Theuderic, who, significantly older than Chlothild's sons, his half-brothers, had been given the area to rule as a sub-kingdom even before his father's demise.[143] If so this would explain Salic Law's restriction to the area west of the Ardennes. Clovis was legislating for the Frankish areas under his rule, north of the Loire. Indeed the bulk of those present at Orléans (twenty out of thirty-two) were bishops of sees between the Loire and the Ardennes and it might be that Salic Law was the secular counterpart to the ecclesiastical legislation promulgated at that gathering. One objection to this thesis would be the absence of any manuscript evidence linking Salic Law with the council's acts, but the earliest manuscript of Salic Law dates to two centuries after its probable promulgation so there was time for the two bodies of legislation to become separated.

Clovis died within a year of the Council of Orléans, and his four sons divided the kingdom between themselves.[144] This was long thought to represent the application of Frankish partible inheritance, whereby all sons received equal shares, to the matters of royal succession. However, in an important article, Ian Wood showed that for the first century and more of Merovingian rule, divided inheritance was never automatic.[145] Instead it resulted from the constellations of power politics surrounding a king's death. The situation in 511 was no different. Clovis' formidable widow, Chlothild, controlled Paris and the royal treasury and forced Theuderic to divide the kingdom with his young half-brothers, Chlodomer, Childebert and Chlothar. If Theuderic was already king in Austrasia this makes Chlothild's achievement all the more impressive and makes sense of the partition itself, which seems only to apply to the Frankish territories outside Austrasia. Theuderic retained the lands east of the Ardennes together with the Auvergne and a share of Aquitaine, which he had conquered in the aftermath

[143] Halsall (1995a), p. 9, for this suggestion.
[144] *LH* 3.1.   [145] Wood (1977).

of Vouillé. His capital was at Reims, a great city of Roman Gaul and site of his father's baptism. Childebert, Chlodomer and Chlothar based their realms on Paris, Orléans and Soissons respectively,[146] equally cities associated with the key events of their father's reign.

Clovis' sons plotted against each other but on the whole continued their father's work. At some point the Danes attacked Theuderic's realm and were beaten off by his son Theudebert.[147] This represents the Danes' entrance into history and the combat was doubtless part of a struggle for dominance in the North Sea and especially its mainland European littoral.[148] This era is dimly lit historically, however. Gregory of Tours appears to have known little, in spite of this being the period of his parents' lifetimes. Clovis' sons continued to wage expansionist warfare. Attacks on Burgundy resulted in Chlodomer's death, but Burgundian subjection to Frankish domination.[149] The threat of Ostrogothic intervention might have restrained the Franks until 534 when, in the context of the Ostrogothic internal crises after Athalaric's death, they conquered the Burgundian kingdom.[150] In the north, Theuderic and Chlothar attacked and destroyed the Thuringian realm, something else probably made possible by the collapse of Ostrogothic power after 526.[151] The defeat of the Danes and Thuringians led to Frankish hegemony throughout the former *Germania Magna*. The Saxons too were brought to heel; in 555 they are recorded as refusing to pay their accustomed tribute to the kings of Austrasia,[152] suggesting that the Franks had established dominance over them some time before. In the south, Frankish attacks were launched against the Visigoths, with varying success, in 531 and 541.[153] Theuderic died in 534 and was succeeded by his son Theudebert.[154] Theudebert and his son and successor Theudebald intervened in the Gothic wars that had broken out in 535, and acquired territory in northern Italy[155] as well as establishing Frankish hegemony over the formerly Ostrogothic

---

[146] *LH* 4.22. [147] *LH*. 3.3. [148] Storms (1970); Wood (1983).
[149] Above, pp. 302–3. [150] Above, p. 303.
[151] *LH* 3.4, 3.7–8. Below, pp. 501–5. [152] *LH* 4.14.
[153] Above, p. 299. [154] *LH* 3.23. On Theudebert, see Collins (1983).
[155] Below, pp. 502–3.

territories north of the Alps, completing Merovingian dominance west of the Elbe.

Royal succession continued to be far from smooth. Chlodomer's children were murdered by their uncles and, when Theuderic died, Childebert seems to have tried to prevent Theudebert's accession.[156] Fortunately for Theudebert, he controlled his father's treasury and was old enough to rally support amongst the Austrasian aristocracy. From this point onwards, armed conflict between the different Frankish kingdoms became more common; Theudebert and Childebert allied against Chlothar for example. These 'civil wars', as Gregory of Tours despairingly referred to them, need not have been as deleterious to Merovingian power as might at first be thought. Divided kingship gave the Frankish kings opportunities for warfare and booty within Gaul as well as beyond its frontiers. This was as well as Visigothic resistance hardened after 560 and the Lombards established dominion in Italy from 568. Divided kingship also meant that the kings were able to distribute and redistribute their patronage more effectively within their smaller kingdoms and political opposition, which in other realms crystallised around powerful magnates and possible rivals for the throne, focused on other members of the same family.[157] Clovis' sons, especially Theuderic, seem to have continued his policy of eliminating any contenders for political authority.[158] By the end of the period covered by this volume, the Frankish aristocracy was dependent upon royal favour and patronage for its local pre-eminence and the more independently powerful Aquitanian nobility was also bound, by competition for offices and other rewards, into the structures of the kingdom. When Chlothar I succeeded to the kingdom of Paris, on the death of his childless brother Childebert in 558, thus becoming the first Merovingian to rule all of Gaul (he had acquired Austrasia in 548, when Theudebald died without heirs), the Franks had become the dominant power in the west (map 22). Furthermore, the Merovingians' adroit policies meant that the ties binding local communities into their realm were fast becoming stronger than those created in any other post-imperial western European kingdom.[159]

---

[156] *LH* 3.18, 3.23.   [157] James (1982a), pp. 134–5; Wood (1994a), p. 101.
[158] E.g. *LH* 3.14, 3.23.   [159] See further below, pp. 356–7.

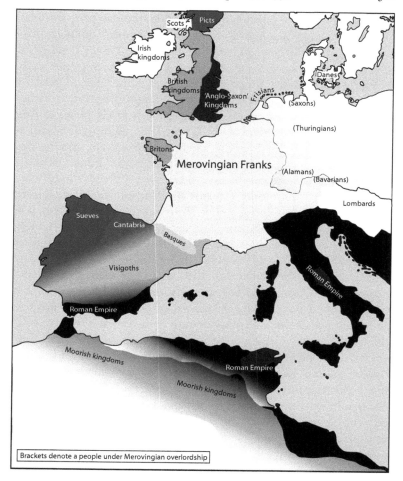

Map 22 Western Europe, 560

WHERE NO NARRATIVE IS POSSIBLE: BRITAIN[160]

There are no reliable written sources for British history between the middle of the fifth century and the end of the sixth. Gildas' last chronological fixed point is the appeal to Aëtius, dated to between

---

[160] Good recent reviews of this period of British history, inevitably to be explored mainly through archaeology, include Charles-Edwards (2003); Dark, K.R. (1994); Davies (2005); Hamerow (2005); Hills (2003); James (2001); Kirby (2000); Woolf, A. (2003); Yorke (1990); (2003).

446 and 453. It is not possible to see the post-Roman part of Gildas'
'historical section' as constituting a straightforward unilinear narrative beginning in 383 and ending in the mid-sixth century.[161]
Nevertheless, however one reads it, even following the early
chronology for Gildas proposed here, it is impossible to put the
battle of Badon or the date of Gildas' composition much earlier
than about 470–90. Alternative interpretations rarely give the date
of the *DEB* as later than 550. Within this eighty-year bracket
(470x550) we have a situation wherein the west of Britain was
already ruled by a series of apparently powerful kings, none of
whom amounted to much in Gildas' eyes. These kings were
Constantine in Dumnonia (Cornwall), Vortiporius, Cuneglassus,
Maglocunus and Aurelius Caninus (Aurelius the Dog, possibly one
of the grandsons of Ambrosius Aurelianus referred to disparagingly
by Gildas).[162] It has proved impossible to date any of these figures
by reference to sources external to Gildas' work.[163] Even the
identification of the territories ruled by these men is, with the
exception of Constantine's, extremely difficult. Maglocunus has
been identified with a King Maelgwn of Gwynedd. The name is
the same and Gildas calls Maglocunus 'Dragon of the Island',[164]
which scholars have thought to refer to Anglesey. The identification may not be correct. Gildas refers to Britain as 'the island' so
'Dragon of the Island' might not refer to anywhere more specific.[165] Vortiporius has been assumed to be the Vortipor/Vorticor
commemorated on an inscription from Castell Dwyran (Dyfed),
and who appears in Welsh genealogies.[166] This association seems
fairly plausible, although far from completely certain. Cuneglassus
has been linked with Dinarth on the basis of one of Gildas' characteristically vague and allusive remarks about Cuneglassus being
chariot-driver in the den of the bear (Dinarth might mean 'Bear's
Fort').[167] Aurelius' kingdom cannot be located. Gildas also states
that access to some of the religious sites of Britain, such as
the martyr's shrine at St Albans, is denied by Saxon political

---

[161] See Appendix.   [162] *DEB* 28–36.   [163] Dumville (1984a).
[164] *DEB* 33.1.   [165] Daniell (1994).
[166] *DEB* 31.1. Full discussion of this stone, and references, can be found on the
database of the Celtic Inscribed Stones Project: http://www.ucl.ac.uk/
archaeology/cisp/database/. The stone's reference is CDWYR/1.
[167] *DEB* 32.1.

domination.[168] His generally vague account nevertheless gives the impression of substantial realms apparently with fairly complex instruments of government. He also alludes to anointing as a means of king-making.[169] This predates the employment of such ritual in Visigothic Spain, making the western British rulers the first to use this Old Testament mechanism to legitimise royal government.

In recent years it has become customary to interpret the period following the end of Roman rule in Britain, especially lowland Britain, as seeing the fragmentation of the former provinces into myriad small kingdoms.[170] Even the existence of kingdoms has been doubted. It is frequently proposed that true kingship was not established until the decades around 600.[171] The sixth century in the Anglo-Saxon territories has been argued to have been a period when society was 'tribal'. The basis for this interpretation is complex and the result of a great deal of painstaking work. There is no room for an extended critique but the main tenets of the argument are as follows. A probably seventh-century document called the *Tribal Hidage* lists territorial units, valuing them at a number of hides, presumably for the purposes of assessing tax or tribute.[172] Whether, as has been variously argued, this list is Mercian or Northumbrian matters little for our purposes. What is important is that the different units named in the list have been argued to be kingdoms. On this basis it is proposed that seventh-century Anglo-Saxon England was made up of numerous small kingdoms. By the eighth century most had disappeared from the record, subsumed within larger kingdoms, mainly Mercia, so it is assumed that this process of the absorption of the small kingdoms by the large can be pushed back into a fifth- and sixth-century 'Dark Age' and the number of kingdoms once in existence increased proportionately. Place-name studies and other research into early Anglo-Saxon territorial organisation have revealed other units, also believed to represent these tiny lost kingdoms.[173]

Archaeological evidence is also thought to show a society in which kingship had not yet emerged. Cemeteries with grave-goods are

---

[168] *DEB* 10.2.   [169] *DEB* 21.4.   [170] The classic statement is Bassett (1989).

[171] Hamerow (2005), for example, sees this period as crucial. See also Arnold (1988); Carver (1989); Hodges (1989), pp. 10–42. Behr (2000) for a different approach.

[172] On the *Tribal Hidage*, see Dumville (1989a).

[173] Bassett (1989) contains case studies.

supposed to indicate a social structure wherein kinship was more important than position in a rigid social hierarchy.[174] This lack of social stratification and the insecurity of local power are thought to be antithetical to the existence of complex or extensive political organisation. In the period's settlements, although not very many are securely dated to the era covered by this book, there seems to be similarly little evidence of any vertical hierarchy of power and wealth.[175]

There are, however, problems with this thinking. We may begin with the *Tribal Hidage*. Some units listed – Kent, Sussex, Wessex, Essex and East Anglia – certainly were independent kingdoms. Others, like the Hwicce of Worcestershire and Gloucestershire, are attested in the charter record as ruled by a king, although he is always subordinate to the ruler of Mercia and whether the Hwicce were ever independent is debatable. As for the others, it is by no means established that they were ever anything other than administrative units.[176] Similarly, we need not doubt the reality of the territories revealed through study of the landscape, place-names and charters, but equally we need not assume that these were ever kingdoms as opposed to estates, other sorts of lordships, administrative units or communities. Furthermore, the comparatively well-documented political history between 600 and 850 reveals few if any instances of Anglo-Saxon kingdoms being conquered and absorbed by their enemies. In fact the number of polities remains fairly stable between four and seven (the 'heptarchy' – rule of seven – of traditional Anglo-Saxon histories). We need not postulate that the number of fifth- and sixth-century political units was necessarily any larger. Continental parallels from this period, revealing the fragmentation of large polities as well as the expansion through conquest of others, suggest that there could even have been fewer kingdoms in the immediately post-imperial period than there were in 'middle Saxon' England. Indeed mainland European comparisons show that the norm in post-imperial Europe, often outside the bounds of the former Empire as well as within them, was for large, not small, kingdoms.

---

[174] Hamerow (2005), pp. 270–3; Hines (2003), pp. 76–83, for surveys. Stoodley (1999).

[175] Hamerow (2005), pp. 273–6; Hamerow (2002) for more detail.

[176] See Dumville (1989b) for the Middle Angles.

That leaves the archaeological data. The conclusions relating the furnished burial ritual to the absence of a securely stratified local society are plausible enough.[177] The move from this to the assumption that there were no meaningful kingdoms is highly questionable. Northern Gaulish archaeological evidence is quite similar. There too the cemetery evidence suggests a society where local authority was insecure and where gender and age were important structuring principles.[178] In Gaul as well rural settlements do not reveal important differences in wealth. Yet there we know from written sources that a large, powerful kingdom had come into being by the end of the fifth century, one larger than any of the Middle Saxon 'heptarchic' kingdoms. The Frankish realm, as we learn from sources written in Aquitaine, maintained a taxation system and used written instruments of government. Thus the archaeological signature of later fifth- and sixth-century society in lowland Britain is not necessarily that of a 'tribal' and politically fragmented society. The coexistence of large political units and insecure local power should not surprise us, for reasons discussed in the next chapter. Another implication of the northern Gaulish comparison is that we should not assume that the absence of written records means that writing was not employed in the government of these kings. There are hardly any such records from fifth- and sixth-century northern Gaul either, although we know that these must have existed.

The insularity of early Anglo-Saxon studies means not only that valuable mainland parallels have been ignored but also that comparison with the British west has been neglected. The archaeology of the more westerly highland regions shows high-status sites (discussed in the next chapter) suggesting considerable political authority.[179] Taken in conjunction with Gildas' comments it would seem that the western kings were powerful rulers. In this context it is interesting to wonder how a comparatively unstructured 'tribal' society, fragmented into political units no bigger than a particular valley, would have fared in trying to stave off conquest and domination by these kings, let alone in taking control over lowland territory. It may very well be that the western kings were the politically dominant figures in later fifth- and sixth-century Britain. In addition to the control of manpower and the trade with the

---

[177] See below, pp. 366, 388.   [178] Below, pp. 356–7.
[179] Below, pp. 359–60.

Mediterranean world, at this point they controlled all of the regions that produced valuable metals like silver and tin. This does not force us to postulate tiny tribal communities in the lowlands of the former province. Study of economic networks there also suggests the existence of larger-scale and more complex social groupings than the model of complete fragmentation would imply.[180]

It is not possible to obtain any more detailed idea of the political history of these decades. It is of course into this period, the darkest part of the so-called Dark Ages – all the darker if one supposes that Gildas might have been writing in the 490s – that the legendary 'King Arthur' is supposed to fit. We cannot discuss the historicity of Arthur here.[181] Suffice it to say that the evidence for his existence is all late and unreliable. The earliest securely datable reference to Arthur is in the *Historia Brittonum* of the 830s but even here, as well as featuring in a confused but historical-looking battle list (the Twelve Battles of Arthur), he already occurs in entirely mythical contexts.[182] Nevertheless absence of evidence is not evidence of absence. That we know nothing of the historical Arthur does not imply that there can have been no such figure. Non-existence is as difficult to prove as existence. If we suppose a complete breakdown into tiny tribal units it is hard to see any political context for a great military leader. Although the 'proto-Arthur' could simply have been a successful warrior from one such 'tribe' it is not easy to understand how this could have provided the basis for later legend, even in its early ninth-century guise. However, if we see post-Roman Britain as divided into competing kingdoms as large as those attested in the immediately succeeding centuries then a more plausible context for 'Arthur' is restored. In the end, however, we should admit that 'King Arthur' remains one of history's most tantalising 'unprovables' and leave it at that.

One possibility (it can be no more than that) concerns the distribution of ethnic names in post-imperial Britain. Bede[183] says that the Jutish settlers came to Kent, the Isle of Wight and the part of Hampshire opposite it whilst the Saxons settled the areas known in

---

[180] Below, pp. 362–3.

[181] Gidlow (2004) and Higham (2002) offer opposing views on the historicity of Arthur. Both present reasoned and coherent arguments even if, inevitably, neither is ultimately convincing. James (2001), pp. 99–101, is judicious.

[182] *HB* 56, 73. Padel (1994).   [183] *HE* 1.15.

his day as Essex, Sussex and Wessex. Finally, says he, settlers from the Angles (or English) founded Mercia, East Anglia and Northumbria. It has long been noted that Bede's account has more to do with the ethnic traditions of his own day, the early eighth century, than with the actual geographical origins of the settlers who founded and inhabited these kingdoms.[184] Nevertheless, there seems to be a fifth-century material cultural division roughly along the Thames, between the area of quoit brooch style (which also covers Essex) and that where styles from northern Germany (and cremation) became common. This would roughly equate with the division between the eastern part of the area covered by Bede's 'Saxon' and 'Jutish' kingdoms and those occupied by his 'Anglian' ones. Given that 'Saxon' was the generic Roman term for northern Germanic barbarians, and has remained such in Welsh (Saes) and Gaelic (Sassenach), we might wonder whether it was a more appropriate ethnic identity to be claimed by the rulers and inhabitants of a hybrid Romano-British/barbarian polity growing out of the shadowy Roman successor state south of the Thames whose existence is suggested by the quoit brooch style.

The problem with this suggestion is, of course, the presence in this quoit brooch area of 'Jutish' regions. Yet, as mentioned above, large immediately post-imperial polities might have fragmented by the time that we can discover anything reliable about Anglo-Saxon political history, in the late sixth century. Bede had access to a source that listed kings who had had overlordship over Kent, which he incorporated into his famous list of kings with *imperium*.[185] Before Æthelberht of Kent, important to Bede, naturally, as the first English king to adopt Catholic Christianity, are two rulers of whom little is known. Immediately preceding Æthelberht is Ceawlin of Wessex. Ceawlin is mentioned in the *Anglo-Saxon Chronicle* as having defeated Æthelberht and driven him into Kent at a battle which it places, probably too early, in 568, confirming his overlordship over Kent. The king before Ceawlin is Ælle of Sussex. Ælle is placed by the *Chronicle* in the late fifth century but the *Chronicle*'s account of that century is entirely artificial, beginning with the foundation of Kent, moving on to Ælle's founding of Sussex before culminating in the creation of Wessex by King

---

[184] James (2001), pp. 107–15.   [185] *HE* 2.5.

Alfred's ancestors.[186] It seems much more likely that Ælle was the ruler who dominated the southern kingdoms before Ceawlin, thus at some point in the third or even fourth quarter of the sixth century. All this suggests that, in the late sixth century, political control over the kingdoms south of the Thames was still competed for by rulers from Kent, Sussex and Wessex. This might stem from an earlier political unity. The supposed presence of Jutes in Wight and Hampshire, and the clear competition for Wight in the genealogies of Wessex and Kent, support this notion. Æthelberht established his supremacy, if the *Chronicle* can be trusted for the 590s, during a period of West Saxon internal weakness, backing this up with the introduction of an archbishop from Rome. It might be that it was at this time that the Jutish ethnic identity of Kent was promoted and the Hengest and Horsa origin legend appropriated.

Another change following the abandonment of quoit brooch style presents an alternative possibility to that just made. In the late fifth and early sixth centuries the general boundary between the regions defined by different forms of material culture shifted north from the Thames valley to the rivers flowing into the Wash. These material cultural zones usually relate to female costume. Here the artistic style, Style I,[187] was shared throughout lowland Britain. Variants in female costume might reflect no more than regional fashion, and the dress in which a woman was buried could relate to her age.[188] Nevertheless, it is possible that, in demonstrating social categories and beliefs relating to correct social roles, such costume might have manifested some form of ethnic identity or political allegiance. In making this statement we must remember that the communities formed by such ethnic/political allegiances were ones of belief and not of shared biological descent or geographical origins. If we accept this proposition then there might have been a large political unit in the south of sixth-century Britain. Perhaps this broke up in the latter part of the sixth century – Bede, for example, states that the king of the East Angles was under the sway of Æthelberht of Kent – leading different components to adopt different ethnic identities: Saxon, Jute and Angle.

---

[186] Yorke (1989) for how the *Chronicle*'s compilers adapted the Kentish origin story to give Alfred's ancestors an origin myth as good as that of their by now subject kingdom.

[187] Below, p. 362.   [188] Clark, D. F. (2000); Stoodley (1999).

It is notable that even Northumbria could be drawn into this political sphere. Edwin of Northumbria was thought to have dominance over all of the English in the 620s, for example.[189] The stability of the number of English realms and the refusal of victorious kings to conquer defeated English kingdoms are interesting. Although some British territories were conquered and annexed, especially in the north,[190] it seems that the English soon applied the same ideas of overlordship to non-English polities. This perhaps suggests that the English had adopted a late Roman attitude to enemies beyond their frontiers, establishing overlordship and replacing troublesome enemies with more biddable clients rather than attempting outright conquest. These points strengthen the possibility that post-imperial politics in Britain were played out in large arenas. Such unverifiable suggestions are, alas, as far as we can take political history in late fifth- and sixth-century Britain.

---

[189] *HE* 2.9.

[190] *HB* 63 for the conquest of Elmet, with *HE* 4.23 for possible explanation. The conquest of Rheged is implicit in Bede, *Life of Cuthbert* 28. English occupation of Stirling is made clear in *HB* 64. By the later seventh century, however, the English appear to have reduced defeated Welsh and Picts to tributary status and occasionally introduced subordinate kings of English stock, rather than seeking complete absorption. James (2001), pp. 129–46.

II

PROVINCIAL SOCIETY IN THE
LONG FIFTH CENTURY

·

Fifth-century evidence exists in diverse forms in different places and the varying survival of data itself indicates how well a region weathered the storms of the century. The bulk of the written material comes from southern Gaul, Italy, Africa and to a lesser extent Spain. Northern Gaul and Britain, however, are more or less documentary blanks. The visibility of archaeological evidence tends to follow the same pattern, although the quality of investigation has until recently not been very even. This only underlines the point. Significant traces of fifth-century settlement have been found in those areas that produced the bulk of the written data, even when the theory and practice of excavation remained elementary. On the other hand, where the documentary record is sparsest the archaeological evidence has been the most intractable. In Britain, for example, a considerable corpus of such material exists, but it has required much greater technical expertise for its recovery. The nature and survival of evidence are not haphazard but speak eloquently about the diverse experiences of the fall of Rome.

THE MATERIAL BASE: SOCIETY AND ECONOMY[1]

Africa[2]

From the end of the fourth century and the beginning of the fifth, North African towns underwent significant changes, not least in the use of public space.[3] Many *fora* were abandoned or given over to new uses. In Belalis Maior (Henchir el-Fouar) a dirt layer, with some burials, covered the forum while that at Bulla Regia (Hammam Derradj, Tunisia) also fell into disrepair, although other public buildings continued in use. These changes corresponded to a rise in the importance of the towns' Christian areas. At Augustine's see of Hippo Regius (Annaba/Bône, Algeria) the forum became a cemetery, probably associated with the lavishly furnished Christian quarter nearby. In the far west of the Vandal kingdom, Iol Caesarea's (Cherchel, Algeria) forum retained its importance because it became a Christian centre[4] and a church was built on the forum at Diana Veteranorum (Zana, Algeria). At Sabratha (Tripolitania; Libya) the forum survived as a public square adjoining a church built around 400. Most towns whose *fora* fell out of use in their original form saw the rise of well-appointed churches. Nevertheless other forms of public building continued. At Sitifis (Sétif, Algeria), for example, the bath complex fell into disuse by the early fifth century, perhaps as a result of an earthquake, but *c.*425 a new, smaller one was constructed, which remained in use until 600. Even though their *fora* were dilapidated, the public baths continued at Bulla Regia and Belalis Maior.

---

[1] On these issues the reader is now referred to the massive and magisterial study by Chris Wickham (2005), which appeared too late for me to make much use of here. Wickham makes much greater use of the pottery evidence than I do. The differing chronological spans of our work means that I have attached greater weight to change within the period 350–550. On other types of evidence surveyed in this chapter, see Chavarría Arnau and Lewit (2004) for rural settlement, and, for towns, Lavan (2001); Liebeschuetz (2001).

[2] Merrills (2004a); von Rummel (2003) for excellent overviews of the current state of play. There has been a recent upsurge of interest in Vandal Africa in the English-speaking world. See, e.g. Merrills (ed.) 2004.

[3] For useful surveys of this evidence, see: Potter (1995), pp. 64–79; Roskams (1996a), (1996b); (forthcoming); von Rummel (forthcoming). I am very grateful to Steve Roskams and Philipp von Rummel for allowing me to cite their articles in advance of publication.

[4] Bensseddik and Potter (1993).

Carthage continued to flourish but with similar changes in spatial organisation, sometimes difficult to unravel.[5] The Vandal sack was serious but appears not to have affected the city's overall prosperity. Some public buildings went into decay (sometimes hastened by the Vandal attack). The city's circular harbour (originally built to house Carthaginian war-galleys but turned into a religious site under Rome) became a refuse dump in the fifth century, whence tons of late antique pottery have been recovered. The basilica on the Byrsa (the hill at the centre of Carthage) was largely (though not entirely) abandoned and the impressive Antonine Baths became derelict, although another thermal complex continued in use. In connection with these developments, a gradual increase in the number of cisterns within the city suggests a decline in the system of water supply via aqueduct. Private residential and economic areas could flourish, if in uneven and ramshackle fashion. On the fringes some houses fell into disrepair; elsewhere well-appointed dwellings were occupied until the sixth century. Near the harbour, economic activities continued undisturbed. Burials began to take place within formerly urban areas, as in other cities. Nevertheless, around 500, North African poets could still discuss such functioning civic amenities as the baths and the circus in ways that would have been recognisable to their fourth-century predecessors.[6]

The different fortunes of the various forms of public building interestingly illustrate North African society's response to the breakdown of direct rule from Rome around 400. The abandonment of *fora* must imply the decline of the towns' importance as centres of municipal government. This had been vital to African society in the fourth century, with local politics frequently being played out by reference to the legitimacy provided by offices. Once the Empire ceased to be effective in the region, it is no surprise that municipal government collapsed. Private buildings commonly encroached upon formerly public spaces (*fora* and streets) and many public buildings became derelict. The custom of erecting public inscriptions on buildings died out very rapidly after the Empire's loss of Africa. This sort of activity was no longer politically useful. On the other hand, the imperial cult remained (see below). The continued importance of the baths, by contrast, shows that features

[5] Roskams (forthcoming).   [6] Clover (1978); (1982).

of Roman social and cultural life remained important even as old-style politics declined.

The growth of church-building in formerly public spaces demonstrates the other area in which Rome persisted beyond the end of effective imperial governance: Christianity. It is interesting that the Donatist schism fizzled out more or less as soon as Roman rule ended.[7] The Roman state had been induced to outlaw the schismatics and to use force against them. Nevertheless it seems unlikely – certainly surprising – that such a policy could have such widespread and rapid success. The controversy, and the competition for legitimacy, had been played out with reference to the Empire and its structures. Again, once these ceased to be an effective presence in the area there was little to be gained from this form of competition for authority. Furthermore, the Vandals were Arians, despised equally by Donatists and their opponents. The Vandal court's Arianism can be seen in some ways as replacing imperial Catholicism: some could adopt the regime's belief as a means of increasing local authority; their opponents could refuse the legitimacy of this strategy by stressing the unorthodoxy of their position. The means by which doctrinal dispute could be employed in local politics found a new focus.

Rural settlement was similarly diverse. Fairly plentiful data has been gathered through field surveys, such as in the Kasserine valley, the Segermes region of northern Tunisia and around Cherchel, providing information from contrasting regions within the Vandal kingdom.[8] Some processes apparently beginning in the late Roman period, like the fortification of farmsteads, continued under the Vandals. Villas were still built and furnished. Some mosaics hitherto considered to be fourth-century (largely on the basis of the Vandals' unenviable reputation) are now recognised as belonging to the Vandal period. At Nador, near Cherchel, one of the few rural sites excavated to modern standards, a villa of twenty-three rooms was converted into one of fifty-seven in the early fifth century.[9] Whether this was associated with changing land-owning patterns, as with the 'communal' use of Spanish *villae* at this time is unknown, but plausible. From around 400 political events left the western regions of North Africa increasingly in a political grey area,[10] possibly

---

[7] Markus (1964).   [8] Leveau (1984); Dietz, Sebaï and Ben Hassen (1995).
[9] Potter (1995), p. 78; Roskams (1996a), p. 51.
[10] Above, p. 219; below, pp. 405–11.

compelling large landowners to abandon estates in the area or preventing their effective management. On the other hand, though, Nador's fifth-century phase saw a doubling of the number of olive presses, which more plausibly implies an intensification of production.[11] This would match the impression given by other evidence (see below). The picture is not universal, however. Decline in the rural settlement pattern seems to have set in during the fifth century in southern Tunisia.

Burial customs continued late Roman practices and a plentiful corpus of funerary inscriptions, many in mosaic form, yields precious information on late antique North African society. A handful of grave-goods has been found, mostly clothing fasteners, which have been argued to be Vandal, although this is disputed.[12] Whatever the nature of the goods, the burials do not suggest radical change in the methods of disposing of the dead. They simply use more archaeologically visible dress adjuncts in the normal inhumation ritual. The most important development was the appearance of burials within formerly public areas of towns, such as the *fora*, noted above.

Economically the period appears to have been prosperous. Although there were changes, production of *garum* and olive oil persisted. The written sources (the *Albertini Tablets*, a collection of private documents written on wood, discovered in 1928, and the poetry collected in the *Latin Anthology*) stress the importance of oil in particular, something backed up by the evidence of olive presses. The manufacture of African Red Slip, the classic index of North African exports, continued without any break. No change in production or in the forms or decoration of the pottery can be traced to the Vandal period, which, at least during the fifth century, possibly represented something of a boom for North Africa. Products hitherto taken as part of the *annona*, especially, to supply Rome with grain, could now be commercially exported. Whether or not African grain reached Rome, imported North African pottery continues to dominate Roman finds assemblages throughout the fifth century. In Rome, ARS still accounted for 90 per cent of imported finewares in the later fifth century and African amphorae formed 30–40 per cent of the total throughout the century.[13] African exports nevertheless seem to switch focus to some extent

---

[11] Roskams (1996a), p. 51.   [12] Eger (2001).
[13] Von Rummel (2003), p. 17; (forthcoming).

from Italy and southern Gaul to Spain. Simultaneously, the numbers of imported eastern Mediterranean amphorae in Carthage increased and Procopius refers to large numbers of eastern merchants in the city. The feared Vandal war-fleet might largely have been made up of impressed merchantmen rather than true naval galleys; Gaiseric was usually reluctant to face the Roman fleet in open battle.[14] His raids around the Mediterranean must also have brought wealth into North Africa. The Vandal kings reformed their coinage and small-denomination Vandal copper coins are found widely distributed across the Mediterranean.[15] This reform appears to have been the first genuine stabilisation of the low-denomination currency since the third century.

However, change also took place. The disjunction between coastal and inland regions noted in the late fourth century was apparently accentuated, inland areas showing little evidence of imported pottery.[16] It might, however, be that goods were transported from the coast in archaeologically invisible containers such as skins, as suggested by some *ostraka* (small texts inscribed on pottery sherds) from Carthage. There was an apparent move from town to countryside in pottery production and written sources suggest that aristocratic estates were becoming autonomous. The changes at Nador could relate to this sort of intensification of production. All these developments are doubtless connected with the end of the Roman state's presence. Without support of the state, which needed to extract surplus as part of the *annona*, transportation costs for private producers will have risen, emphasising the separation of coast from hinterland. At the same time rural landowners could now control this production for their own benefit, dealing another blow to the cities, the nodes of the old state-controlled surplus-extraction and transport, and to municipal government (a similar process may have taken place in southern Italy). The Segermes region survey shows continuity of rural settlements through to the sixth century but the town at the centre of the region reveals typical development, with the theatre turned into a rubbish dump and burials taking place in the forum.

---

[14] MacGeorge (2003), pp. 308–11.
[15] Hendy (1995) is a useful overview of Vandal coinage.
[16] Von Rummel (2003), p. 17.

Written sources underline the general impression of continuity, in spite of their usually hostile tone. Even Victor of Vita's writings reveal the continuation of most key Roman governmental institutions, a picture confirmed by the *Albertini Tablets*, which show that Roman Law was effective even on the kingdom's southern edges.[17] Latin education persisted, producing the hostile tirades of churchmen and the poetry of the period in like measure,[18] and providing the background for post-Vandal African Latin writers such as Corippus and Fulgentius the Mythographer.[19] One interesting feature of Roman–Vandal continuity concerns the imperial cult, whose persistence had made North Africa distinctive in the late Empire. Local aristocrats continued to hold office as *duumviri* or *flamines* (priests) of the cult in spite of their, and the Empire's, Christianity. This continued, perhaps even more oddly, under the Vandals.[20] Whether the king adopted the role of the emperor, or whether this was, even more so than before, a mark of local standing more than anything else, or indeed whether it signified a continuing acceptance of the Empire's legitimacy, is unclear. The Vandal kings certainly saw their dynastic ties with the Theodosian dynasty as hugely important. Given the decline of municipal politics it seems likely that these titles had become inherited family distinctions.

Where did the Vandals fit into this picture? Although some objects in burials are believed to be of Vandal provenance, the most sophisticated analysis argues plausibly that 'Vandal costume' in fact manifests general late Roman Mediterranean military or hunting dress. Associated with the military and political élite, the Vandals, this could be described as 'barbarian costume' by hostile Catholic writers like Victor of Vita.[21] If the handful of graves revealing this costume is associated with the Vandals then the fact that this costume was deposited in public ritual, usually in churches in the cities of the realm, surely illustrates that the family of the deceased was staking a claim to a particular ethnic identity and the social and political advantages it brought. It is clear from Victor's writings that some North Africans took service with the Vandals and adopted

---

[17] Conant (2004).   [18] George (2004) for the poetry of Vandal Africa.

[19] Hays (2004).   [20] Clover (1982); (1989).

[21] Victor of Vita, *History of the Vandal Persecution* 2.8; von Rummel (2002); (2005).

this costume. Indeed it is likely, reading between the lines of the hostile sources, that the Vandals' separation from and unpopularity amongst the indigenous population has been greatly overestimated. It may indeed be that the very vehemence of the Catholic sources stems from the Vandal rulers' success in encouraging Roman Africans to subscribe to their regime and their religious doctrine.[22] Local politics might well have followed a familiar North African course, as discussed above. Those who were less successful in obtaining royal patronage, vociferously denounced the regime and were ready to side with the Empire (and its religious beliefs) if the opportunity arose.

It has been pointed out that, from archaeological evidence, we would have no idea at all that the Vandals had invaded North Africa.[23] It has equally been argued that explanations have tended to stress political and religious history at the expense of broader social concerns.[24] This is a somewhat simplistic diagnosis. To be sure, it is mistaken to point to the chronological coincidence between change in the archaeological record and high political events and assume that the latter explain the former. The Vandals' appearance or the end of Donatism do not in and of themselves explain the transformations. Nonetheless the changes visible in North African society and economics in the fifth century relate intimately to the Roman Empire's demise and the Vandal take-over. These were not superficial events, only affecting the ruling strata. The changes at the high political level – the collapse of effective imperial government in the region – removed earlier means of ensuring standing in local society, compelling local élites to adopt new strategies. Imperial patronage was no longer available, municipal government atrophied and the Donatist/Catholic controversy evaporated. In their place came Vandal royal patronage and the Catholic/Arian rivalry, and new economic opportunities opened up for maximising the rewards of local land holding. All this profoundly affected social structure, local political relationships and the settlement pattern and all were directly connected to the high politics of the century.

---

[22] Jonathan Conant, paper given at Eleventh International Medieval Congress, Leeds, July 2004.
[23] Von Rummel (2003), p. 19.   [24] Roskams (1996a), p. 49.

Italy[25]

The key to understanding Italian developments is the shrinkage of political horizons in the fifth century. In many ways this continued a trend visible since the third century and Italy's reduction to provincial taxation-status, but the gradual loss of the provinces reduced the Italian nobility's political options and accentuated the development. As these opportunities shrank to encompass only the peninsula, the economic consequences of the loss of the rest of the Empire affected local society and politics. Evidence throughout Italy suggests that the general contraction of the settlement pattern that had begun in the third century persisted. The numbers of occupied sites continued to decline.[26] In Tuscany the decades around 500 witnessed the final collapse of the old organisation of rural production.[27] Villas were occupied to a lesser extent than before and it has been claimed (probably excessively) that most were dilapidated by the fifth century.[28] Some were rebuilt in this period and there could still be considerable investment in *villae*. The documentary evidence indicates that the senatorial nobility continued to enjoy considerable wealth. There are, however, important pointers to future developments. Certain villas incorporated defensive or defensible aspects. Some, such as the towers at San Vincenzo al Volturno (Molise) or San Giovanni di Ruoti (Basilicata) are probably best regarded as status symbols, points that could be seen from far and wide and provide views over one's estates, but they were also defensible. Other fifth-century sites, such as Monte Barro and Castelseprio in Lombardy, are clearly fortified, as are two sites near Ravenna associated with Theoderic: Palazzolo and Galeata. Others still, meanwhile, incorporated churches within their complexes. That at San Giusto, with its church and baptistery, has been interpreted as the seat of a bishop.[29]

Political developments were important in determining the fates of particular regions. The loss of the provinces meant that Rome

---

[25] Humphries (2000a) and Potter (1987), pp. 192–209 are valuable surveys. The comprehensive Christie (2006) came to hand just as this volume was finished. For historical overviews, see above, p. 285, n. 1.

[26] For general survey, see Christie (1996); Francovich and Hodges (2004), pp. 37–51; Sfameni (2004). See also case studies in Brogiolo (ed.) (1996b).

[27] Valenti (1996), p. 97.   [28] Francovich and Hodges (2004), pp. 37–8.

[29] Volpe (ed.) (1998).

had to draw its supplies much more heavily from the south of Italy. The production of wine underwent something of a boom there. The fifth-century phase at San Giusto, for example, contained facilities for the production of 36,000 litres of wine.[30] This, it has been argued, led to the dominance of the class of wealthy *possessores*, who benefited from the trade associated with involvement in the provisioning of Rome.[31] Similarly, Ravenna's elevation brought prosperity to Histria, which became 'the Campania of Ravenna', providing the new capital with oil, wine and cereals.[32]

The fate of Italian towns similarly suggests mixed fortunes but with an overall tendency towards survival and stability. There was some contraction and dereliction, even in Rome, and towns were abandoned (as at Iuvanum, south of Chieti). One of the most important features of Italian urban history at this time is the reordering of the spatial hierarchy. Many *fora* fell into disrepair, were abandoned or turned over to other uses.[33] Paestum's had refuse pits and stalls cut through the paving, that at Luni was abandoned, and Ordona's became a cemetery. The forum at Verona was used for agriculture and even in Rome, the *basilica Aemilia* was burnt down early in the fifth century and not restored. Elsewhere, theatres suffered similar fates.[34] In the south, hand in hand with the prosperity of the *possessores* was the final decline of the cities, which lost out in the struggle to harness the surplus of the countryside (perhaps as in parts of Africa). There, as throughout the peninsula, burials appeared within the towns.[35] This southern Italian urban decline did not imply any lack of regional prosperity. Here (and in the African hinterland) we have a situation which differs from the general rule, attested further north in Europe, that the continuation of Roman rural settlement patterns tends to match the level of urban survival. However, the reasons seem clear and it is worth stating that the evidence of urban occupation remains more substantial than that in the north-western provinces.

The opposite of this decay in public structures was the increased importance of Christian building and topography. At Brescia, for example, whereas the eastern side of the town, near the forum, shows decay, the areas close to the Christian centres continued to be occupied. Private investment in public building had long begun to

---

[30] Volpe (ed.) (1998), p. 289.   [31] Noyé (1996).   [32] Humphries (2000a), p. 546.
[33] On this, see Potter (1995), pp. 90–8.   [34] Barker (1995), p. 237.
[35] Noyé (1996).

dry up and by the early fifth century only in Rome can we find continued evidence of such private patronage. A clear indication of the trend is the fact that, after Attila sacked Aquileia in 452,[36] the rebuilt city enclosed the cathedral within its walls but left the old forum outside.[37]

Nevertheless, some traditions of public munificence continued under Odoacer and Theoderic. In Rome, senators placed inscriptions in the Coliseum up until the end of the fifth century and in Faenza, for example, the curator of the private estates (*curator rei privatae*) remained responsible for building work under the Ostrogoths.[38] The most obvious, but unsurprising, exception is Ravenna. The court's move there in 402 resulted in heavy investment in new works and in the refurbishment of the city's walls. The court's presence might have had beneficial effects on the other towns in the region, arresting the general process of decay.[39]

Italy manifested the reduction in her political horizons economically too. Sometimes, as in the south and perhaps in Histria, this was to the advantage of local areas. Imports declined. Although African pottery continued to find its way to Italy until the end of the sixth century, it declined in absolute volume (if not in its share of the market). It has been estimated that African imported pottery in the period 470–550 was only about a third of that of the early to mid-fifth century.[40] In the Biferno valley on Italy's east coast African and eastern Mediterranean imported ceramics declined after about 450 and had ceased to appear by the sixth century.[41] It is clear that, throughout the period, inland areas found it ever more difficult to gain access to imported wares. Coarse wares predominated, although some local potters tried to imitate African designs, showing that demand for such goods had not dried up.[42]

One exception to this trend concerns military equipment. A type of helmet known as a Spangenhelm ('clasp-helmet', because the bowl of the helmet is made up of a series of plates clasped together by a framework of metal bands) originated in Ostrogothic Italy (though some writers have questioned this provenance).[43] These are usually very lavishly decorated and about thirty examples have been

---

[36] Above, pp. 253–4. [37] Humphries (2000a), p. 540.
[38] Ward-Perkins (1984). [39] Gelichi (1996), p. 69.
[40] Francovich and Hodges (2004), p. 58, citing the opinion of John Hayes.
[41] Barker (1995), p. 240. [42] Humphries (2000a), p. 547. [43] Böhner (1994).

found across the post-imperial west and the Balkans, as far north as Scandinavia and, possibly, Scotland.[44] It seems that the export of these prestige items was associated with Theoderic's foreign policy, as gifts bestowed upon allies, and then redistributed to their followers. The distribution of these helmets interestingly skirts around the Frankish territories, which might superficially tie in with Theoderic's policies, but little weight can be placed upon this. The Merovingian burial ritual did not generally encompass the interment of armour, so the absence of Ostrogothic Spangenhelme from the heart of Frankish territory is probably not significant.

As mentioned, the Italian nobility continued to be very wealthy but the short-term advantages brought by their hold on imperial politics after 380 were eventually outweighed by the consequences of the western Empire's fragmentation. Many lost estates and incomes in Spain, southern Gaul, Africa and beyond. As the number of offices available to the Italian élite declined, competition was presumably heightened. The fact that such posts were increasingly to be held *within* Italy, alongside the presence of the Italian army as another powerful faction, made the peninsula a political hothouse. The loss of foreign estates might have attenuated the difference between the senatorial nobility and lesser aristocrats. One feature of this period was the increasing importance of local élites, some of whom competed with the old nobility for high office, while others remained focused upon dominating their locality. The triumph of the southern aristocracy over the towns has been noted and there are signs of a growing militarisation throughout the fifth century with the fortification of villas and the involvement of aristocrats in regional defence. The localisation of power might have involved a change in the relationships between villa owners (remembering that the villas tend to be rather smaller and less lavishly appointed than their precursors) and the other members of their communities. In the fifth-century phase at San Giovanni di Ruoti, the excavators noted a change in refuse disposal patterns, which seemed to imply feasting around long benches rather than traditional Roman banqueting. Instead of reading this ethnically and ascribing the change to the villa's occupants' 'Germanic' nature, we might more interestingly consider that the distribution of food and drink in feasts was, as elsewhere in the post-imperial west, an important

---

[44] Below, pp. 378–9.

component of the gift-giving that served to underpin local pre-eminence.

Integration and ethnicity in Ostrogothic Italy has been much debated.[45] Italy is a difficult place to govern and there were, in the Roman and Gothic nobilities, people with considerable power and legitimate claims to rule. Some Gothic noble families were no less throneworthy than the Amals. Distributed, of necessity, in garrisons across the peninsula, they could pose enormous problems. Equally, the Italian aristocracy's wealth and local influence could not lightly be ignored. After a century of close involvement with government, they were accustomed to a leading political role. These problems were accentuated by increasing regionalism. Theoderic had to incorporate these groups into his regime and thus bind Italy's disparate regions into one kingdom[46] and to do this the king made excellent use of ideology. Theoderic famously instituted a bi-ethnic realm in which, broadly speaking, the Goths formed the army while the Romans staffed the bureaucracy and paid taxes. In many ways, this did no more than continue the state of affairs during the last decades of the western Empire in Italy, similarly defended by an army that had increasingly adopted barbarian identities and indeed was very largely composed of non-Roman mercenaries. Justifying this situation was what has been called, on the basis of Cassiodorus' terminology in his *Variae*, the *civilitas* ideology.[47] As the name implies, this played upon the maintenance of the civility that divided Roman from barbarian; in Theoderic's ideology the Ostrogoths were rarely called barbarians. Goths and Romans both had a role to play, the former defending civilisation and the latter maintaining it through traditional patterns of service.

During the first decades of his rule, Theoderic made much use of the Roman senatorial nobility. Members of great senatorial dynasties like the Anicii and the Decii were employed in the bureaucracy's higher echelons.[48] One of the Anicii, Boethius, held high office alongside a number of his relatives and associates. Throughout the reign Gothic noblemen were given military and

---

[45] See, e.g. Amory (1997); Heather (2003); Moorhead (1992), pp. 66–113; Wolfram (1988), pp. 290–306.

[46] I base my comments on the excellent and thoroughly convincing analysis of Heather (1995b); repeated in Heather (1996), pp. 236–48.

[47] Amory (1997); Reydellet (1995).   [48] Moorhead (1984).

other governmental roles. However, Theoderic's ideology stressed that all legitimate power originated with him, gradually eroding any idea that an acceptable claim to leadership might exist independently of his authorisation. At periodic assemblies of the Goths – his army – monetary donatives were paid, he rewarded those who had served well and punished those who had not.[49] On these occasions royal patronage was publicly distributed and redistributed and the Goths subjected to the regime's ideology, not simply its words, but in terms of artistic and architectural display.[50] By appointing his own men to regional office, Theoderic eroded the claims of rival families, forcing them to compete for his favour in order to maintain the legitimacy of their local dominance. He may simultaneously have made increasing use of lower rungs within the Italian aristocracy (as noted, becoming more significant in this period) to undermine the great senatorial dynasties' pre-eminence.[51] Theoderic's best-known Roman administrator, Cassiodorus, was from a recently ennobled family. Theoderic had played senators off against each other earlier in the reign, Symmachus being employed to try other senators accused of witchcraft, for example.[52]

Theoderic's policy was successful. Never excluded from service (Boethius was *magister officiorum* at the time of his downfall) the great senatorial families nevertheless had to compete for royal favour with lesser aristocrats. Accustomed to traditions of service (*negotium*) and involvement at the heart of politics, this could produce resentment, but no serious threat to his rule. In the latter half of the reign, although the evidence cannot be decisive, Theoderic may even have employed them less often. Potentially dangerous Gothic leaders were eliminated, a certain Pitzias being killed in 514, for example.[53] As Theoderic's control of government became more secure his ideology gradually stressed *civilitas* less.[54] Instead, by the time Cassiodorus returned to writing letters for the king, it stressed the valour of the Gothic *gens* under its ancient and noble ruling house, a view

---

[49] Cassiodorus, *Variae* 5.26–7. Heather (1995b), esp. pp. 161–2, for discussion.

[50] On which Wharton (1995), pp. 105–47, is interesting.

[51] Moorhead (1992), pp. 147–58. A crucial gap in Cassiodorus' *Variae* leads to considerable unevenness in our knowledge of Theoderic's officers. Nevertheless, in line with the gradual changes in Theoderic's other policies, this seems very plausible.

[52] Cassiodorus, *Variae* 4.22–3. See also *Variae* 1.23.   [53] *Consularia Italica* 669.

[54] Amory (1997), pp. 59–71.

adumbrated in Cassiodorus' *Chronicle*, written for Eutharic's consulate in 519. In this work Gothic history is set alongside Roman, and Gothic victories against the Empire are celebrated.

In this view the Goths ruled Italy, not through working harmoniously alongside the Romans to maintain the legitimate Roman order, but because of their valour and strength. They were a people with as long, indeed a longer pedigree than the Romans, whose history represented their move from the edges of the world and ultra-barbarism, whence they drew their vigour, to their destiny, governing the heart of the civilised world. This apparently was the picture that Cassiodorus intended to create in his lost history of the Goths, as glimpsed through its epitome (and ideological reworking) by Jordanes. The Amals, furthermore, had always ruled the Goths, having been their first family since time immemorial. As Peter Heather has said, any Goth above the age of fifty would have seen this for the nonsense it was,[55] but such was the need for royal legitimation in maintaining local leadership they were prepared to grin and bear it, and buy into the regime and its ideology.

The functional bipartite division between Goths and Romans may have begun to break down in Theoderic's later years, as some Roman aristocrats began to adopt Gothic characteristics. One, Cyprian, learnt Gothic and had his sons trained in military matters at court.[56] Should such young Romans have gone into the army it is likely that, as they did in parts of Gaul, they would have eventually adopted a non-Roman identity. Amory has claimed that it was simply military service that made one a Goth, using Cyprian and his sons as a support for his thesis that identities were fluid and based around one's role within the kingdom.[57] Peter Heather counters vigorously, drawing attention to weaknesses in Amory's work.[58] We can, however, reconcile the two viewpoints to some degree by remembering, first, the dynamism of social relationships and, second, the brevity of Ostrogothic rule in Italy (this was the shortest-lived barbarian kingdom). Italo-Roman aristocrats were, increasingly, coming to undertake military responsibilities. Some held army commands (Cassiodorus was one such) and local garrisons

---

[55] Heather (1996), p. 239.
[56] For Cyprian and his career, see Amory (1997), pp. 369–71, or *PLRE* 2, pp. 332–3 (Cyprianus 3).
[57] Amory (1997).   [58] Heather (2003).

could be made up of Italians.[59] However, as Heather says, this did not automatically or immediately make them Goths. The field army might have been a separate affair (possibly continuing the later imperial distinction between field armies and garrison troops[60]) but this is by no means clear.[61]

The careers adduced and interpreted so differently by Amory and Heather are mostly those of high-ranking individuals. Little or no information exists about the lower social orders. Theoderic famously said that while a rich Goth acted the Roman, the poor Roman aped the Goth.[62] The Goths might have been augmented by lower-class Italo-Roman recruits, especially those making 'sideways moves' from garrisons to the field armies. Amongst the aristocracy the situation was probably always going to be rather different but they were beginning, like the Gallic nobility, to take up military roles. With time, this would undoubtedly have broken down the barriers between Goths and Romans. There were probably also regional variations, as in Gaul. Further from royal power (especially the south) it might have been possible to adopt military roles and remain Roman, as it was in post-imperial Aquitaine. Elsewhere, especially closer to the heart of Ostrogothic rule, the importance of royal patronage and the greater benefits of involvement in military service might have led the aristocracy to abandon its Roman identity and become Gothic, just as northern Gallic local leaders became Frankish and as Hispano-Roman aristocrats became Visigoths. Cyprian's career and his sons' education illustrate an early stage in this kind of process but do not mean that he had become Gothic. Such examples do not show that identity was a matter of career choice in Ostrogothic Italy but they do illustrate that ethnic boundaries were not immutable and were breaking down.

We can only see the beginnings of a process in the Ostrogothic evidence. How it might have turned out might be suggested by

---

[59] E.g. Cassiodorus, *Variae* 1.11, 1.40, 5.23, 9.25.9 (Cassiodorus' command).

[60] After all, most units with barbarian identities were found in the field armies.

[61] Wolfram (1988), pp. 316–17 claims that the troops (*milites*) commanded by Servatus, the *dux* of *Raetia* (at *Variae* 1.11) 'cannot have been Goths'. Heather (2003), p. 118, n. 89, says that Servatus is 'said to have led *limitanei* (i.e. inferior quality troops)'. This is not the case; this and Wolfram's claim are both interpretations rather than statements in the source. They are plausible and attractive suggestions but the documents cited do not provide *prima facie* support.

[62] Anonymous Valesianus 12.61.

comparison with Frankish Gaul but in Italy this process was cut short by Theoderic's death. His demise and his heirs' insecurity led to something of a return to the earlier *civilitas* ideology and to a hardening of the functional distinctions between Goths and Romans.[63] The process of change thus lasted only a generation, making it unsurprising that clear and decisive examples of Romans becoming Goths are difficult to find. The evidence does, nevertheless, show that the dynamics of social and ethnic realignment were the same in Italy as elsewhere in the post-imperial west.

Archaeologically, the presence of the Goths in Italy is represented by a series of inhumations wherein the deceased were interred with grave-goods, including a particular range of artefacts, usually dress adornments (map 23).[64] Most famous are eagle brooches and buckles with a square plaque inlaid with garnet, stones and coloured glass to produce a multi-coloured effect. These items, and the costume with which they were associated, have usually been

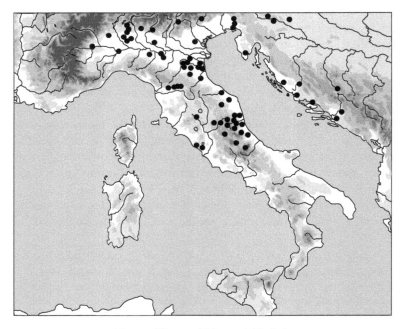

Map 23 'Ostrogothic' material in Italy

[63] Amory (1997), pp. 71–2.   [64] Bierbrauer (1994b) for well-illustrated survey.

related to Gothic identity, and their presence used to map Gothic settlement.[65] This is an increasingly problematic reading. In recent years it has become accepted that the 'polychrome' styles of artefact in these burials had become a general feature of costume right across the Mediterranean, rather than (as was previously believed) being exclusively of Danubian origin.[66] It is therefore a costume which, if it was adopted by the Goths, was probably adopted *within* the Empire. It is possible that this style might have been associated with the army and thus acquired barbarian overtones, but this would necessitate a significantly different reading of its symbolic and social value in Ostrogothic Italy. Furthermore, these graves are not very numerous. Although about fifty sites in Italy and Dalmatia have yielded such grave-goods, there are generally only one or such two burials per site. Some are found in urban cemeteries, at, for example, Rome, Ravenna, Aquileia and Milan and not infrequently associated with churches. If the costume had become identified with Gothic identity, it must still be the case that not all Goths were buried in this fashion. Thus the rite cannot simply reflect Gothic settlement. Burial with grave-goods, sometimes including weapons, was, moreover, known in northern Italy before the Ostrogothic settlement.[67] Inhumation with goods cannot alone distinguish a tomb's occupant as a newcomer. We need to ask why some people were buried like this but the vast majority was not.

The display of artefacts with possible associations with the Gothic holders of political and military power in the period immediately following the Empire's fall must be significant. The doubtless numerous barbarian troops in Italy during the fifth century had not chosen to display their ethnic identity through material culture. That the Goths did so in *their* burial ritual must therefore be a graphic index of how imperial collapse impacted upon social relationships even in the heart of the former Empire. Furnished inhumation was a public display. In suburban church burials we might assume that the audience comprised the politically powerful; elsewhere, as for example with the possible lavish burial of a woman at Domagnano in the modern territory of San Marino,[68] it might

---

[65] See, e.g. Heather (1996), p. 238; Moorhead (1992), pp. 68–9.
[66] See, e.g. Kazanski, Mastykova and Périn (2002); von Rummel (2005), pp. 258–69.
[67] See Gastaldo (1998); Massa (1996).
[68] The find might represent a hoard. Bierbrauer (1994b), pp. 194–202.

represent other local landowners and perhaps lesser people. The fact that women as well as men were buried like this argues for a particular gendering of power and shows that the deaths of all members of these kindreds could be marked by such displays. The families employing the ritual made clear the basis of their pre-eminence in association with the new powers in the peninsula. We might link this to the competition for royal patronage within local communities and among the political élite. Alongside the style's Mediterranean origins, it surely implies, therefore, that people adopting this costume in public rituals were not necessarily (possibly even unlikely to have been) incomers of Danubian origin. The fact that, as yet, this ritual was not used by numerous competing families within communities might suggest that their power was funda-mentally secure. Nevertheless these displays speak of some of the tensions involved in establishing new power-structures. Alas the evidence is so sketchy, many graves being discovered long ago in obscure and even dubious circumstances, that we cannot pursue this social analysis through the goods' associations with adults and children, men and women. Unfortunately, the artefacts' chronology can never be fine enough to examine whether these sorts of display were more or less common during Theoderic's later reign, when his ideology became more self-assured. Nonetheless, speaking to small communities, they can be understood as further indices of Italy's contracting political horizons and increasing regionalisation.

Spain[69]

Shrinking horizons are visible in Spain too, if in different ways. In an important sense, Spanish towns generally appear to have survived the problems of the fifth century fairly well.[70] Physically, there was contraction, decay and even abandonment. At Tarragona the upper town's forum had some of its paving torn up and a rubbish dump appeared on the site in the 440s.[71] There was dereliction at Mérida, possibly linked with the Suevic attack of 429. Clunia (Peñalba de Castro), Termes (Montejo de Liceras), Complutum (Alcalá de Henares) and Conimbriga (Coímbra) were reduced to small villages.

---

[69] Collins (2004), pp. 174–222, is a good English introduction to Visigothic Spanish archaeology. See also Keay (1988), pp. 202–17; Kulikowski (2004).
[70] Gutiérrez Lloret (1996) for survey.   [71] Keay (1996).

As in other parts of Europe, intra-mural burials and the turning of areas over to horticulture are all attested. Nevertheless, evidence of continuing urban occupation is clear, and some towns' cores seem to have been maintained in (however vaguely) recognisably Roman fashion. Evidence exists of civic munificence. A famous inscription records work on the bridge over the Ebro at Mérida, on the initiative of the local bishop and a Gothic count.[72] The inscription's mid-fifth-century date, earlier than the Goths' take-over of the region, may indicate the piecemeal establishment of Gothic political control, building out from individual strategic centres rather than following a straightforward pattern of territorial expansion. Alternatively, Gothic commanders, independent of the kingdom of Toulouse, may have controlled southern Spanish towns, perhaps in conjunction with local secular and ecclesiastical élites. Either alternative is plausible in the political context following the Suevic kingdom's military defeat in 456. The *Lives of the Fathers of Mérida* record building sponsored by the bishops at the end of our period.[73] Towns, whatever their physical state, generally remained the foci for local society and politics, and this is very important.[74]

A similarly good rate of fifth-century survival is attested for rural settlements.[75] Surveys such as that of the *Ager Tarraconensis* suggest general continuity in the settlement pattern.[76] In most areas archaeology shows the ongoing occupation of villas and even the construction of new ones, sometimes on a grand scale early in the century. As in Italy, there is regional evidence of contraction in the villa pattern but of significant investment in those that remained.[77] This picture does not apply to the whole century, however. At its end and early in the sixth century, as in Italy, many villas were abandoned, though others continued and even (at Vilauba) expanded in the sixth century. Their fate is difficult to ascertain. In the current state of the evidence, it seems that they commonly became the focus of small hamlets. This is all the more likely in that many Spanish villas seem to have developed churches as part of their

---

[72] Kulikowski (2004), pp. 205, 210.   [73] *Lives of the Fathers of Mérida* 5.3.
[74] Kulikowski (2001); (2004).
[75] For rural settlements, see Chavarría Arnau (2004); (2005); García Moreno (1991); (1999).
[76] Carreté, Keay and Millett (1995).   [77] Reynolds, P. (1993), pp. 9–10.

complexes in the fourth and fifth centuries.[78] That these villa churches were becoming foci for local communities was one concern raised during the Priscillianist controversy of the late fourth and fifth centuries.[79] In northern Spain, hillforts (perhaps reoccupied earlier in the late Roman era) became centres for some local communities and their politics.[80] Interestingly, in the area of Zamora, these occupy a distinctly different area from that covered by the surviving villas, which should imply something about the different social structures, and their varying means of coping with the end of Roman rule, between the uplands and the lower-lying basin. These differences might resemble those between lowland and highland Britain.[81]

Economically, too, Spain weathered the fifth century relatively well, its different economic zones continuing to exist. Fineware production in the central peninsula endured throughout the century, although it showed late fifth-century traces of decline in the forms produced.[82] Coastal areas maintained their Mediterranean economic links, especially with North Africa, and the production of *garum* continued.[83] Nevertheless, the Empire's demise produced inevitable stresses and strains. Some change seems to have taken place in the middle quarters of the sixth century. Terra Sigillata Hispanica Tardía declines by this time so that it is difficult to date and its value as a chronological indicator is weakened (leading to debate on the date of the last occupation of the villas). The demise of this industry might be part of a more general pattern of economic downturn that encompassed the end of the villas.

Perhaps more than in any other region of the post-imperial west, aristocrats continued to see cities as the focus of political activity. It has been argued that it is difficult to see a powerful Spanish landowning aristocracy in the era's political narratives.[84] Obviously this

---

[78] Bowes (2001).

[79] Priscillian has the dubious distinction of being the first person executed for heresy, under Magnus Maximus. He appears to have been doctrinally orthodox but Spanish and Gallic bishops considered him a threat to their authority as he apparently sponsored rural asceticism and lay preaching. Burrus (1995). Van Dam (1985), pp. 88–114; (1986).

[80] Martín Viso (2002).   [81] Below, pp. 357–68.

[82] Manares (1980); Perez-Rodriguez and Rosario García Rozas (1989).

[83] Étienne and Mayet (1993–4); Reynolds, P. (1993).

[84] Kulikowski (2001), p. 155. See, for a slightly different view, Castellanos (1996).

does not imply that the basis of power was not land-owning. It does underline that in much of the peninsula, especially the east and the south, politics was played out in the towns and that offices based upon urban institutions were important in legitimising authority. Even in the far north, a *curialis* is mentioned in the *Life of St Aemilianus*.[85] Cities (and some of the hilltop sites just discussed) provided foci for military resistance to the Sueves and later the Goths. It was difficult even for powerful Visigothic kings to enforce their will on urban communities.[86] It might be that, just as it has been suggested that Honorius' cousins Didymus and Verenianus had to raise their armed forces from their land holdings because the cities supported Constantine 'III',[87] Theudis might have had to rely on the 2,000 troops he raised from his wife's estates as a similar counterbalance to the cities as well as the Gothic nobles.[88] In the far north of Spain, a shadowy 'senate of Cantabria' is mentioned and it is likely that the citizens of Cordoba, who gave King Agila a bloody nose in the 550s, were organised around a similar institution.[89] Elsewhere, where there were no former *civitates* or *municipia*, such local politics were based around other nucleated settlements, or the hillforts mentioned above.

Bishops were key figures in these politics. Much of the peninsula's territorial organisation was based around ecclesiastical units and bishops were useful points between local society and central government, although at this date there was little central government in Spain away from the cores of the Suevic kingdom in the north-west and the Gothic realm in the north-east. With the importance of religious officials, it is not surprising that heresy and orthodoxy featured in the hothouse urban politics. Accusations of Priscillianism were effective tools in the denigration of opponents, as in a famous case in *Tarraconensis* in the second decade of the fifth century.[90]

Tension and social change is suggested on the fringes of the region of villa estates by the appearance of the 'Duero valley culture'

---

[85] Braulio of Saragossa, *Life of Aemilianus* 16.23.   [86] Collins (1980).
[87] Kulikowski (2001).   [88] Procopius, *Wars* 5.12.50–4.
[89] Senate of Cantabria: Braulio of Saragossa, *Life of Aemilianus* 11.18, 15.22, 17.24, 26.33. Cordoba: Isidore, *History of the Goths* 45.
[90] This episode, which came to light with the discovery of some hitherto unrecognised letters of Augustine, has been thoroughly studied. E.g. Arce (2003); Kulikowski (2002c); Van Dam (1986).

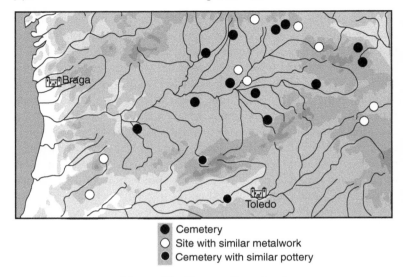

Map 24 The 'Duero valley culture'

(map 24).[91] These cemeteries and individual burials date from the end of the fourth century and on into the fifth. They are essentially typical late Roman inhumations but the dead were buried with more numerous grave-goods, not only costume accessories (mainly belt-sets) but also some weapons (large knives and spearheads) and horse-furniture, as well as occasional agricultural implements. They can be found in association with villas (as at La Olmeda). Like contemporary northern Gaulish burials,[92] these graves have been associated with incoming 'Germanic' settlers, notably *laeti*. This view is founded upon the vague similarity between these graves and those in the north of Gaul. However, no material culture in these burials can even tendentiously be argued to come from *barbaricum*. Indeed it is quite unlike that found in northern Gallic so-called federate graves, in the precise types and decoration of common artefacts, like buckles, and in the sorts of material buried. Weaponry is much less common in Spain, and horse-furniture and agricultural implements practically unknown in the Gallic inhumations. Other interpretations link these graves with a *limes hispanicus*, an internal

[91] Blazquez (1974); (1980); Fuentes Domínguez (1989); García Moreno (1990).
[92] Above, pp. 153–9.

frontier against the semi-barbarian tribes of the north-west, or with
local landlords' private armies.[93] There is little or no evidence for an
internal Spanish frontier and the discovery of burials like these
further away from the Duero valley in the decades since this
'culture' was first remarked upon renders this 'frontier' interpretation unlikely.

These burials are difficult to explain. We must consider their ritual
context. People used the interment of their dead to display items that
symbolised social status. The artefacts' symbolism is often difficult to
unravel. The belt-sets are classic indices of late Roman social status.
The weaponry could indicate hunting or a military role (unlike those
in the Gallic graves, the Duero weapons are rarely susceptible of
classification into military, hunting, or everyday utilitarian items). In
either interpretation, however, a claim to status might be made.
Hunting was an aristocratic pastime demonstrating leadership qualities. The horse-furniture might underline this aspect, although it
could equally have military symbolism. It has also been related to the
importance of horse-breeding in the region. But what of the agricultural items? Their symbolic value is difficult to unravel, although it
possibly related to claims to land, recently cleared or turned to
agricultural use.

These graves' occurrence in clusters within cemeteries suggests
that this ritual was employed by several families with possibly
competing claims. Unlike the Gaulish situation, however, their
appearance is not associated with the decay of villas or general
economic collapse. The villas survive but are often apparently
converted from private to more communal settlements. The most
satisfactory interpretation of these graves in the Duero area currently
appears to be that they are to be associated with a crisis in local
society. The region's villas seem to represent a late burst of economic prosperity.[94] Perhaps, with the fifth-century crises, possibly
absentee aristocrats could no longer make effective their claims to
land-ownership, and the communities on their estates thus took
over the buildings of their *villae*. Individual families competed to
fill the vacuum left by the aristocrats' absence. Alternatively, the
period's changes might have eroded the aristocrats' primacy, compelling them to live as part of their communities, maintaining local

[93] Palol (1977).   [94] Above, p. 88.

leadership through more costly rituals of display and gift-giving. The death of important male members of these families imposed stress upon the web of local social relations, so the rituals around the death of family members became an important focus for the competition for power. It is worth pointing out that these burials appear in the lowlands at the time that hillforts become more important in the nearby uplands. It is nevertheless important to note that the symbols used to display power and leadership continue to be located within established Roman traditions. As these graves are discovered with greater frequency this interpretation will require reconsideration in different local contexts, and the interpretation and recovery of good quality data is a pressing need. Nevertheless this social interpretation fits the evidence more satisfactorily than the appeal to 'Germanic' settlers.

Towards the end of our period burials appear on Spanish cemeteries, which have been associated with the Visigoths (map 25). Some new artefact-types appear, as in Italy including eagle-brooches and distinctive plaque-buckles, as well as bow-brooches whose

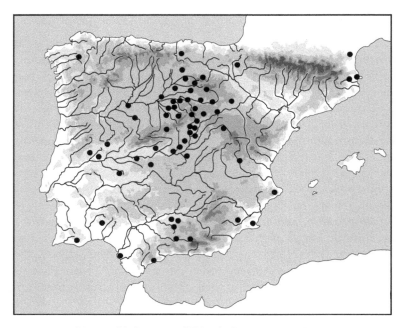

Map 25 Sixth-century 'Visigothic' cemeteries in Spain

typological origins may lie in the Černjachov culture.[95] As in Italy, this material and the costume it adorned, although generally Mediterranean, became associated with Gothic political identity. The problem is somewhat different from that in Italy, however. These graves appear in larger numbers on rural cemeteries; they do not immediately suggest the burials of local élites. They have traditionally been associated with Visigothic settlers and this interpretation remains dominant, however nuanced.[96] There are, however, very serious problems with it.[97] The numbers of such furnished graves are very low, especially if broken down by generation. At the famous site of El Carpio de Tajo near Toledo, the number of graves with 'Gothic' goods represents only about a dozen people per generation (there are ninety furnished burials from a cemetery estimated to have been used for two centuries). Clearly, as in Italy, not all Goths were buried like this and, more to the point, burials with these goods were a new phenomenon. The Goths had not employed this ritual in Gaul. Thus the fact that only a selection of the population used it and only did so from a particular moment requires explanation. So too does the burials' distribution, which, in the sixth century, spans a band of north-central Spain. This does not represent the whole area of Gothic settlement (although the burials have sometimes been used to demonstrate this).

These burials need to be studied in a broader context. Further north, in the foothills of the Pyrenees, cemeteries with different types of grave-goods, notably more weaponry, have also been located.[98] The distribution of the 'Gothic' graves also overlaps with that of the 'Duero valley civilisation'. It is clear that the strategy of displaying, and thus maintaining or enhancing, local status through the interment of a family's dead with grave-goods, was not uncommon in western-central Iberia in this period. The appearance of the new artefact-types in burials from about 525 may well relate to the use of appeals to the Gothic rulers and the claiming of Gothic identity as a local political strategy. This might make sense in the

---

[95] Palol and Ripoll (1999), pp. 235–78; Ripoll (1994); (1998a), esp. pp. 43–66, for discussion of the material and dating.

[96] Heather (1996), pp. 202–7; Ripoll (1998b); (1999a); (1999b).

[97] Collins (2004), pp. 174–86, is refreshingly critical. See also Kulikowski (2004), pp. 267–71.

[98] These have been the subject of much work by Agostin Azkarate Garai-Olaun. In English, see Azkarate Garai-Olaun (1992).

period of economic change referred to above. At this time, the region's villas were finally falling out of use, doubtless leading to local stress, and the Gothic kings were tentatively spreading their power out from the north-east, ultimately to establish their capital at Toledo by the mid-century. It is also interesting that the 'Gothic' burials tend to cluster around the fringes of the Suevic kingdom and of the later Byzantine enclave in the south. We might expect that claims to Gothic identity were of more value on the political margins. 'Gothic' material might have been employed as part of a political discourse. The fact that limited numbers of artefacts were placed in the burials does not necessarily argue for their subjects' poverty. Rather, this and the fact that few families within local communities (perhaps only one or two at El Carpio de Tajo) used this display, suggest that competition for local authority was relatively muted. In the Pyrenean foothills it may have been more intense and, rather than appealing to Visigothic identity and thus a link with the kings, the families competing for authority made clear reference to military power (in weapons) in their funerary displays.[99] Study of the Zamora region has linked the employment of Gothic material culture in the basin to a particular social situation, more keyed into links with the Visigothic kingdom than that in the mountains.[100] The central Spanish funerary rituals once again show, in some ways, how political horizons contracted to the local community but at the same time they show how involvement in the wider politics of the kingdom could be an important political tool.

Gaul[101]

As throughout its history, Roman Gaul can be divided into several regions. We shall continue with the crude separation of 'northern' from 'southern' Gaul, dividing the two along the Loire, but there

---

[99] See also the discussion of the Basques, below, pp. 479–80.

[100] Martín Viso (2002), pp. 19–37: an excellent analysis. I do not, however, agree that the social structures of the areas bound into the kingdom were more complex than in those remaining outside.

[101] Surveys of Merovingian archaeology: James (1988), pp. 200–29 is the best in English; see also Hartmann (2003), pp. 171–99; Périn and Feffer (1987), vol. 2; Salin (1950–9), though now very dated, remains comprehensive; Wieczorek, Périn, von Welck and Menghin (eds.) (1997) is the most thorough replacement. See above, p. 303, n. 113, for surveys of early Merovingian history.

were clear variations even within these general regions. The area between the Loire and the Île de France should be thought of as an intermediate zone and the region around Trier is also distinctive. Southern Gaulish towns present a picture similar to those of Spain and northern Italy. Arles, predictably, saw a late burst of building when the capital of the Gauls was transferred there.[102] At Marseille archaeology uncovers the beginnings of a much more significant revival, culminating in the port, very much subordinate to Arles during the Roman period, becoming the most important in Gaul.[103] Excavations at Bordeaux have also revealed fifth-century prosperity, associated with the continuing importance of the trade route from the Mediterranean, round Spain and across the Bay of Biscay to western Britain.[104] Otherwise, cities illustrate the general pattern of survival in reduced form encountered elsewhere. Another continuing trend, indeed exaggerated in the fifth century, was the Christianisation of the cities. It has been argued that the fifth century was a golden age of southern Gallic urban church building,[105] which seems a fair comment. Written sources refer to such projects and excavation in towns like Lyon and Geneva provides archaeological confirmation.

Further north the picture is more variegated but is, on the whole, one of much more serious decline. There were, of course, exceptions. At Trier, the former capital, traces of occupation cluster around key late Roman buildings,[106] some apparently turned into strongpoints, sensibly enough given the impractical length of the city's walled circuit. Other northern towns underwent more drastic decline. Evidence from this period is difficult to find within the city walls at Metz, although this might partly stem from a shift of settlement to the south-west around the amphitheatre, which could, like that at Trier and elsewhere, serve as a redoubt. The amphitheatre has yielded late antique evidence, though mostly of ecclesiastical or funerary nature.[107] Some towns fared worse still, and were abandoned. North of the Seine, although many cities continued to function as regional centres, at least in the ecclesiastical sphere,

---

[102] Loseby (1996).   [103] Loseby (1992); (1998a).   [104] Sivan (1992).
[105] Rouche (1979).
[106] Cüppers (ed.) (1984); Dierkens and Périn (2000), pp. 278–80; Kuhnen (1997); Wieczorek, Périn, von Welck and Menghin (eds.) (1997), pp. 856–66.
[107] Halsall (1995a), pp. 228–31; (1996).

whether any can truly be called urban is doubtful. Paris and the towns between the Seine and the Loire survived better. Archaeological evidence suggests continued occupation at Paris, though of a very much reduced area, and the early sixth-century *Life of Saint Genovefa* (Geneviève) depicts the continuation of communal life there in the mid- and later fifth century.[108] The Loire valley towns also appear to have maintained their municipal institutions. Collections of *formulae* (models to be used as the basis for legal documents) attest the survival of town archives.[109]

Rural settlement patterns follow the fates of the towns.[110] In the south, they underwent contraction and change but nevertheless persisted. In Poitou villas survived as such throughout the period. Around Bordeaux and Toulouse, they continued to be occupied and furnished with elaborate new mosaics, as at Lalonquette.[111] In Provence such high-status sites remained, and this period saw the construction of a well-known series of rural baptisteries, attesting the land-owning classes' continued power and prosperity. Simultaneously, however, there was decay and abandonment, and the occupation of other types of site, not least caves and defended hilltop settlements.[112]

In the north, decline was much more serious. Again, it is important to acknowledge regional differences.[113] Between the Loire and the Seine, increasing evidence is emerging of the continuing occupation of *villae* into the mid-fifth century. Equally, the large villas around Trier reveal traces of inhabitation.[114] Elsewhere, though, the picture is of collapse at the end of the fourth century. In most of northern Gaul the villa system declined drastically in the third century, so we should perhaps expect that the late fourth-century

---

[108] Paris: *Life of Genovefa*. Dierkens and Périn (2000), pp. 286–7; Périn (1997); (2002a); Velay (1992), pp. 83–107; Wieczorek, Périn, von Welck and Menghin (eds.) (1997), pp. 853–6.

[109] E.g. *Angers Formulary*. Loseby (1998b), pp. 247–9; Wood (1990a), pp. 64–5.

[110] Good surveys of Merovingian settlement archaeology: Lorren and Périn (1997); Périn (2002b); (2004); Wieczorek, Périn, von Welck and Menghin (eds.) (1997), pp. 745–73.

[111] Dyson (2003), p. 91.   [112] Klingshirn (1994), pp. 202–6.

[113] The best study of the far north remains Van Ossel (1992). See also Bender (2001); Halsall (1995a), pp. 178–88; Louis (2004).

[114] Van Ossel (1992) for the most thorough survey of the fate of villas in northern Gaul.

crisis should have finished it off. On most sites it is difficult to see much activity, or that the site was still functioning as a villa, by about 425. Even where there is better survival, south of the Seine and around Trier, *villae* appear to have been abandoned by the second half of the century. The settlements that replaced the villas are detectable only with difficulty. This results from several factors. Technical excavation problems play a big part, as does the long-standing lack of archaeological interest in the post-imperial era. It is also likely that settlement might have shifted only a little way but still have lain outside the excavated area. Mostly, though, fifth- and sixth-century traces of north Gallic settlement appear to be par-ticularly ephemeral. The evidence we have is of small wooden buildings accompanied by sunken-featured huts. More substantial traces of settlement only regularly become visible in the later sixth century, though one or two can be traced to earlier periods.

The Gaulish economy was similarly fractured. Before the fifth century, Gaul constituted at least two economic zones.[115] The fifth century's political events exacerbated this division.[116] The south continued to import goods from Africa and Spain, and the trade route that passed via Bordeaux continued to function.[117] The production of southern Gallic 'palaeochristian' wares persisted without any noticeable break.[118] In the north, things were different. Wheel-turned pottery in the Argonne Ware tradition continued.[119] The number of forms and decorative motifs was reduced to a minimum, however, meaning that such pottery is datable with difficulty. This reduction in variation indicates the industry's downturn, underlined by the shrinkage in the areas across which such wares were exchanged, and the loss of the trans-Rhenan hinterland. The dis-tances over which fifth- and sixth-century wheel-thrown ceramics were distributed nevertheless remained extensive. Some sort of exchange was therefore possible across quite large areas,[120] but the demand for these plain and unsophisticated pots possibly speaks

---

[115] Above, pp. 85–6.
[116] Wickham (2005), pp. 758–9, 794–805, and references.
[117] Hitchner (1992).   [118] Loseby (2005), p. 620; Reynolds, P. (1995), pp. 36–7.
[119] Wieczorek, Périn, von Welck and Menghin (eds.) (1997), pp. 581–93 for introduction.
[120] Indeed by the end of the period covered by this book, economic down-turns elsewhere meant that these regions were larger than those across which any other western European wares were distributed.

louder for an inability to produce such items locally, supporting gloomier readings of the pottery evidence. Other industries and manufactures were hit as badly or worse. Rhenish glass production continued on similarly reduced scale but the collapse of the villas and the towns put paid to tile manufacture and other crafts related to the up-keep and decoration of Roman-style stone buildings. There is, in northern Gaul, little evidence of craft specialisation. Coinage ceased to be struck at Trier early in the fifth century but a difference between the Loire–Seine area and that further north again becomes apparent. Silver imitations of imperial coinage were struck in the former area until the middle third of the fifth century, suggesting greater continued prosperity. After that, however, this too disappears.

The distribution of the furnished graves discussed in chapter 5 closely follows the areas where towns and villas declined most seriously around 400.[121] The southern half of northern Gaul and the region around Trier, where continuity was greater, have few or no such burials. Their appearance is symptomatic of the stress in northern Gallic society after Maximus' suppression, and perhaps earlier.[122] Without the underpinning of the Roman government and its patronage, a family's local pre-eminence was questioned by a member's death. This is clearest with adult males, figures of local pre-eminence. It is also relevant to the deaths of women, whose behaviour underpinned male status and who were, through marriage, the links between families, and to those of children, potential heirs. In these circumstances, the family had to make a public statement of its standing, and did so through the ritual of furnished burial. The artefacts used included most frequently the official belt-sets that were the obvious mark of imperial service, but they also comprised weaponry, symbols either of military service or the control of armed force, or of hunting. Vessels, presumably containing food and drink were deposited, very probably associated with funerary feasting. Gifts of food and drink were common means of cementing alliances. Some pottery is decorated in such a way as to underline the deceased's aristocratic status, as with the bowl from Saint-Rimay decorated with boar-hunting scenes.[123] Other items displayed wealth. The female dead were decked out in their finest jewellery, again demonstrating

[121] Above, pp. 153–9. Halsall (1992); (2000).   [122] See above, pp. 209–10.
[123] Böhme (1974), p. 107.

the family's ability to bury them with the greatest appropriate pomp, but also showing, through their costume, surely related to marital status, their virtue and the extent to which they met the demands placed upon the comportment of women.

Some other points require reiteration. These graves occur in small clusters and, although usually those of adults, particularly males – presumably because of the stress their deaths would cause – they include children as well. This suggests that only leading families employed this rite, to reinforce their status (as with the Ostrogothic burials discussed above). Other families do not as yet seem to have competed in this display. The artefacts' symbolism seems, further-more, to relate entirely to issues of leadership and standing in a 'vertical' social hierarchy. Finally, and especially important given the 'Germanic' identification usually placed upon these graves, this symbolism is entirely Roman. Status is displayed through claims to connection with the Empire and its authority. It is, for the reasons outlined in chapter 7, unsurprising that these families felt their position under threat.

The settlement pattern also reveals the gradual retreat of power to very local arenas. Metz, for example, shows traces of abandonment before the region's smaller towns, and the *villae* were occupied the longest.[124] As the social structure came under pressure the local élites, whose position was not based upon the command of overwhelming socio-economic resources independent of imperial patronage, became less secure. They could not remove themselves from the local arena. Instead their authority had to be cemented by displays of status to their communities, as in the furnished burial ritual, and through gift-giving, another focus of the funeral. In this context it is no surprise that there was insufficient control of surplus for the maintenance of craft specialists or organised production. Thus the pottery industry declined and tile-making and stone-quarrying died out, in turn making the upkeep of stone structures more difficult and contributing further to the dramatic end of traditional Roman settlements. The appearance of furnished inhumations must consequently be seen in its full context: the collapse of socio-economic structures in the region. Political hori-zons shrank more in the north of Gaul than anywhere else in the post-imperial west outside lowland Britain.

[124] Halsall (1995a), pp. 175–241.

The end of regular, official coin issues makes archaeological dating more difficult in northern Gaul, as does the contraction of the pottery industry. As forms and decorations become much more standardised, typological variation and change are harder to detect. Since decorated finewares form another key element of fine archaeological chronologies, this contributes to the difficulties of dating mid-fifth-century material. That said, imperial coinage occasionally reached the region and some unofficial coins were struck there.[125] Furnished graves, although becoming rarer, provide a series of 'sealed contexts', important for the construction of artefact typologies. Yet the mid-fifth century remains archaeologically extremely ephemeral. This is unlikely to be pure chance. The patterns of evidential survival, written and archaeological, are not random. The generally indistinguishable nature of material culture from the middle generations of the fifth century must itself indicate social and political change. The late fourth- and early fifth-century furnished burials employ Roman symbols of status and office. Since the start of the fifth century, certainly from Jovinus' suppression, the Empire had been unable to make its writ run in the region. Military campaigns had penetrated into the area in 417, 428, 448 and 451 but after Attila's defeat even these ceased. The effectiveness of basing claims to authority upon involvement with the Empire was directly linked to the ability of that Empire to make itself felt in the region. As this became ever more clearly limited then those bases of power were increasingly questionable. If authority was no longer effectively expressed through the traditional symbols, then what could replace it? No alternative power had established itself firmly in the region. Several competing sources of authority existed, some derived from Roman authority, others not. The near invisibility of this period in material cultural terms is thus surely to be expected.

So is the fact that the archaeological record should witness the end of the Empire in 476. At this time a new archaeological horizon appears, often in the form of lavishly furnished burials, most famously that of Childeric I in Tournai.[126] These graves deploy material culture, which, though sometimes referring back to Roman authority and frequently taking the same form as imperial badges of power (i.e. belt-sets), is largely of a new form. It belongs to the type that we have already encountered in Italy and Spain; derived from

---

[125] King, C. E. (1992).   [126] Above, p. 269.

fifth-century Mediterranean fashions it seems to have become associated with the army.[127] In Gaul the army had increasingly become dominated by barbarians: Franks, Goths, Burgundians and others. It does not seem implausible, therefore, to view the increasing popularity of the style, and especially its deployment in public ritual contexts like funerals, as associated with the political domination of northern Gaul by Franks and Alamans. That this material appeared when the Western Empire finally ended as a political institution illustrates graphically the fact that this 'high political' event was noticed 'on the ground'. When the Empire's ability to back up local claims to leadership ended once and for all, new means of expressing power could be found and employed. From the last quarter of the fifth century we move into a new archaeological phase.

Written sources also record differences in the extent of the Roman social system's survival. In the south the senatorial order retained its power. The fifth century was the golden age of literary production by these circles of nobles. This was itself partly a reaction to changed circumstances. Aristocrats had to compensate for Rome's political rejection by stressing the cultural retention of Rome and its values. Sidonius' letters are replete with discussions of how individuals represent Rome or continue Roman life even in these circumstances. Consequently the southern Gallic nobility maintained its traditional culture of *otium* and *negotium*, leisure and service and its social, economic and cultural distinction from the remainder of the population. Many entered the church, another institution where Rome could be argued to continue even whilst its aristocracy increasingly distanced itself from the political entity of the shrivelling Empire. Thus the Roman Gaulish social system was perpetuated through the fifth century south of the Loire, something also manifest in the survival of settlement patterns and economy.

North of the Loire the picture is much more confused. Again, the written evidence follows broadly the same contours as the archaeological. In Trier and its immediate environs, for example the local nobility survived, self-consciously referring to themselves as senators. Trier contains more post-imperial inscriptions than any other Gallic city.[128] Over 800 are currently known, about a third of the Gallic total. Outside Trier, northern Gaul yields barely a few

---

[127] Above, pp. 336–8, 344–6.   [128] Handley (2001a); (2003).

dozen. This self-consciously Roman mode of commemoration matches the names and titles employed. Roman names predominate, and some continue to deploy late Roman honorifics, such as the clarissimate.[129] In the seventh century the Trier aristocracy were still called senators.[130]

However, in most of the north the Roman social order broke down. Ever since early Roman times, outside the Triererland, the northern Gallic aristocracy had been less wealthy than its southern neighbours. Its power was probably based heavily upon the presence of the imperial state,[131] and when that was removed its authority was threatened. This picture is revealed by the archaeological data but finds support in the written record. Here we must refer to Salvian's celebrated and much debated account of what was wrong with Roman society, usually assumed to refer to northern Gaul.[132] Salvian discusses different means of maintaining authority, giving a fascinating insight into the options for survival available to Gallic aristocrats in these political circumstances. Some, says he, wielded tyrannical power in the name of Rome. 'As many *curiales* are there tyrants' he declaims, famously.[133] Such figures collected taxes in the name of Rome but unjustly and unevenly, forcing those unable to pay to sell up and enter into a relationship of dependency upon them.[134] To escape this 'slavery' in Rome, Salvian says, others flee to the barbarians or the *Bagaudae*.[135] Only Salvian's reference to these latter people, who are not mentioned in accounts of Gallic history south of the Loire, really allows us to localise his account in the north. Salvian himself was from the Trier area but, like many others, fled south during the early fifth-century chaos and his tirades against rapacious Roman landlords might be based upon the activities of the senators of Trier. Whilst some aristocrats continued to use or abuse Roman titles and the rights brought by involvement in imperial government, others had acquired positions of leadership and authority independent of such legitimation: the *Bagaudae*.[136] A third alternative in Salvian's account is to turn to barbarian leaders.[137]

[129] *RICG 1*, no. 192.   [130] Bobolen, *Life of Germanus of Grandval* 1.
[131] Above, pp. 81–6.   [132] *Governance of God* 3.10, 5.3–9.
[133] *Governance of God* 5.4.18.
[134] Whether Salvian's victimised *pauperes* were the poor, as we would understand it, or just the poorer aristocrats is an interesting problem.
[135] *Governance of God* 5.5.22, 5.6.
[136] Above, p. 218.   [137] *Governance of God* 5.5.21.

As time went by this proved to be the option with the best long-term chances of success.

The only northern Gallic aristocrat about whom much can be said concerning the material bases of his power is the bishop of Reims, St Remigius, who died in the early sixth century at a ripe old age. His will survives, presumably kept by the church at Reims as a relic, and lists his bequests.[138] It might be argued to demonstrate a considerable continuity of the Roman aristocracy and its power-bases in the region. Alas it is difficult to generalise from. Remigius was a bishop and the extent of his land holdings is likely to have been connected with that fact. He was, moreover, no ordinary bishop, but the metropolitan of *Belgica Secunda*, the diocese at the core of the Frankish kingdom. As such he baptised Clovis.[139] This importance and the connection with the Merovingian royal house very likely had a bearing upon his wealth. Yet even so, whilst attesting considerable property, Remigius' will does not demonstrate the colossal riches of a late Roman senator or even of a later Merovingian nobleman. Remigius names over eighty dependants, slaves and tenant farmers, in his will. Some of these he freed, whereas others he simply gave to his chosen heirs. This seems to be a full list. By way of comparison, an early eighth-century Merovingian nobleman called Weroald, probably from an important political faction but by no means in the 'premier league' of wealthy Frankish aristocrats, bequeathed to Wissembourg Abbey twenty-six unfree dependants and an unknown number (but at least twenty) of unnamed children.[140] The total in this one gift, a fraction of all of Weroald's wealth, almost matches the number in Remigius' will. Other seventh-century Gaulish wills dispose of far greater property than did Remigius.[141] The wealth of the northern Gallic élite had always been less than that of its southern counterparts. There are good reasons to suppose that political circumstances meant that the north was worse affected by the fifth-century changes than the south. Nevertheless, even if it was not, it is not difficult to see how the northern Gallic aristocracy's position was reduced to crisis point.

---

[138] Remigius, *Testament*. Castellanos (2000).   [139] Above, p. 306.
[140] Wissembourg Cartulary, no. 38.
[141] Most famously the *Testament* of Bishop Bertramn of Le Mans.

Clovis' 507 campaign dramatically changed the nature of Gaulish society and politics.[142] With the Frankish king now undisputed master of Gaul, the Aquitanian nobility again found themselves cut off from the centres of politics, located in the north (the chief Merovingian urban residences were, at this stage, Paris, Reims and Soissons). The evolution of the Gothic kingdom in Toulouse had enabled them to negotiate the political changes after 380 that had cut them off from the heart of imperial politics. Now no ruler resided in their region, which was administered by royal officers sent from the north. The latter owed their position to royal favour and were apparently not members of independently wealthy dynasties.[143] Gregory of Tours, a member of a southern noble family but no stranger to northern Gaul, almost never knew their descent or geographical origins (his usual criteria for nobility). Yet these 'Franks' could remove the Aquitanian nobles from involvement in politics and government and end their culture of *otium* and *negotium*. Consequently, whilst their learning and family status provided some means of combating these officials' political dominance, the Aquitanians had to compete for royal patronage and service in the Frankish administration and military if they were to maintain their position and status. This made Frankish royal power in Aquitaine considerable. The conquest of Burgundy raised similar problems for its regional nobility but ones alleviated by the existence of a Frankish kingdom of Burgundy and of royal centres at places like Chalons-sur-Saône.

The incorporation of Aquitaine also changed the nature of Merovingian rule in the north. The new offices in the south dramatically increased royal resources of patronage. Successful warriors could be raised to commands and rewarded with titles and gifts. Patronage enabled Clovis to create a class of service aristocrats that he could use to undermine other, more independently wealthy nobles and force them into equal dependence upon royal favour.[144] This is illustrated archaeologically by the fact that by about 525 burial with grave-goods had become common in large

---

[142] Above, pp. 306–7.
[143] Halsall (1995a), pp. 33–9, 251–61; Wickham (2005), pp. 178–203, for counter (but, to my mind, allowing evidence from after 600 to intrude too much into the analysis). Bergenruen (1958); Grahn-Hoek (1976); Irsigler (1969).
[144] See previous note.

cemeteries.[145] Although local aristocrats may have founded some such sites, the public ritual of display through furnished burial was, instead of being restricted to a few leading families, now employed across the community. The grave-goods, rather than being found with small family clusters of men, women and children, were now distributed according to age and gender.[146] The cemeteries themselves appear to be governed by communal norms. The people who received most grave-goods were those whose deaths would create most tension in local social relations: adult males who had died before their sons could establish a right to succeed to their local position; young women, either the mothers of small children or those of marriageable age, the linchpins of local politics. Analysis suggests that competition for local authority was fierce, maintained through a constant cycle of public gift-giving rituals (of which burial was only one, if one of the most important and certainly the most archaeologically visible). Power was expensive and up for grabs and élites were kept in their communities by the demands of this competition. The most effective way out was through participation in the kingdom, and receiving royal patronage. Nevertheless, the importance of such backing in local politics gave the kings all the aces. In Merovingian Gaul we can see very clearly how the kings used their patronage to reduce local leaders to political dependence upon them. Here, by the close of our period, unlike anywhere else in the post-imperial west, the royal dynasty was well on the way to establishing a monopoly over political legitimacy.

Britain[147]

Our survey ends in Britain, which undoubtedly experienced the most drastic change. Britain resembles the worst affected areas of northern Gaul and, in the continuum of the different fates suffered by the western provinces, represents the opposite extreme from that manifested by Italy. It is clear that British villas were generally

---

[145] Most of the surveys cited above, n. 101, dwell heavily upon this data. For brief (if now dated) description, see Halsall (1995b), pp. 9–13. For more detail, see Effros (2003).

[146] Halsall (1995a), pp. 75–163, 253–61. Interpretation refined in Halsall (1998); (2003b).

[147] For good, recent surveys, see Esmonde Cleary (1989), pp. 162–205; Hamerow (2005); Hines (2003); Richards (1995).

abandoned as such by the early fifth century. Excavation sometimes reveals continued occupation in the immediate vicinity, or of a part of the complex in different form, but the underlying fact remains. As aristocratic foci for the expenditure of surplus extracted from rural producers, these settlements ceased to exist.

Urban life ended at the same time.[148] Excavation has revealed shadowy occupation at some sites, leading some to proclaim the continuity of the Roman system.[149] This misunderstands the nature of urbanism. The occupation unearthed is small-scale, undistinguishable from rural agricultural settlements. In most Roman British towns deep layers of 'dark earth' cover the last Roman levels. This is most plausibly associated with dereliction and abandonment but it has been claimed that 'dark earth' is the accumulated debris of rotted down timber buildings and their thatched roofs.[150] Analogy is sought in the Viking period site at Birka on Lake Mälar (Sweden), where the settlement was represented by 'dark earth', similarly without clearly defined occupation thresholds or building plans.[151] However, the Birka 'dark earth' is rich in finds whereas that covering the late Roman deposits on British towns (and increasingly known from mainland European towns) mainly yields sherds of residual Roman pottery. Urbanism is a relationship between different components of society, settlement pattern and economic networks, not a simple matter of large numbers of people living together. If urbanism is revealed by 'dark earth', we must explain how it managed to remain artefactually invisible. What were the inhabitants of the town providing for the population of the hinterland? They surely provided something in order to remove themselves from subsistence agriculture. Markets, specialised production, even administrative or jurisdictional services, leave material traces. If these 'towns' existed on the extraction of surplus from their hinterland – though that is insufficient to constitute a truly urban relationship – again we would expect evidence of it. The 'dark earth' deposits' sterility is telling evidence against the hypothesis of continued fifth-century British urbanism. Similarly, the sunken-featured

---

[148] Esmonde Cleary (1989), pp. 144–54: to my mind still the most persuasive analysis.
[149] Principally in the work of Ken Dark (1994); (2002).
[150] Dark, K. R. (1994), pp. 15–19; (2002), pp. 50–3, *pace* Watson (1998).
[151] For introduction to Birka, see Clarke and Ambrosiani (1995), pp. 71–6.

buildings from towns like Canterbury and Colchester, or the agricultural reuse of 'Insula XXVII' at St Albans, point to people living in towns but not to urban life.

There are more interesting traces of continuing high-status roles for towns in the west. Lengthy excavations at Wroxeter have uncovered nebulous remains of post-imperial occupation in the civic baths complex.[152] The technical complexity of the Wroxeter excavations once led people to argue for a 'Wroxeter factor': post-Roman occupation was so ephemeral that only long-term detailed investigation could reveal it. It might be supposed to have existed, but to have been missed, at other Roman towns, explored through short-term rescue excavations. In some senses this might be correct. Fifth-century reuse of Roman urban buildings has doubtless gone unrecognised. However, the point remains that we should expect something more from a truly urban site. In parts of Europe where, and when, excavation techniques lagged behind those used at Wroxeter, archaeologists still picked up artefactual remains of post-Roman occupation – pottery and metalwork – even where associated occupation layers were not noted. The site's excavators have argued that Wroxeter continued as an urban centre, a central place for, and extracting tax from, its surrounding hinterland until the seventh century. It is difficult to see how this can have been the case when its inhabitants remained archaeologically all but invisible. Wroxeter, like the 'dark earth' deposits yielded little or nothing by way of material culture. As the archaeological 'signature' of an urban settlement this is most implausible. The Wroxeter baths basilica can very plausibly be understood as a high-status site belonging to a powerful local ruler established in the ruins of a Roman town. That is interesting in itself but, at least in our current state of knowledge, it is unlikely to have been something that we could call a town.[153]

Further west and north there are manifestations of the same trend. The fifth and sixth centuries saw a flourishing of reoccupied Iron Age hillforts in the western highlands, something that might have begun in the fourth century.[154] Usually univallate (with one bank

---

[152] White and Barker (1998).

[153] Loseby (2000b), pp. 332–5, for telling critique of the maximal interpretation of Wroxeter.

[154] Above, pp. 315–16. Alcock (1972); (1987), pp. 5–219; (1992); (2003), pp. 179–211; Dark, K. R. (1994), pp. 40–4, 164–9; Snyder (1998), pp. 176–202.

and ditch), even where the original fort was endowed with a series of such defences, they yield evidence of craft specialisation and the import of Mediterranean finewares. Along Hadrian's Wall increasing evidence has been uncovered showing several forts continuing into the sixth century as high-status settlements.[155] The distribution of these important new settlements is significant.

There were new lowland sites too, but they are rather different. Fifth-century rural settlements are defined by a new architectural repertoire. The first such buildings to be discovered were sunken-featured *Grubenhäuser*.[156] Similar to, though not quite the same as, those in northern Gaul, they show links with the Anglo-Saxons' continental homelands and are essentially tent-like structures erected over a rectangular pit, sometimes floored over but sometimes with occupation taking place in the pit itself. In Britain and France, it was long believed that the population actually lived in these huts but, with better excavation techniques, the traces of posts supporting the walls of larger buildings – halls – were uncovered.[157] Characteristically one such post-built hall was associated with several ancillary sunken-featured buildings. Unlike the *Grubenhäuser*, whose northern European links are clear (although more problematic than often acknowledged), the origins of the post-built hall are more debatable. These structures' similarities with those in northern Germany are less striking. In the 1980s it was suggested that the halls represented the recreation in wood of traditional rectangular Romano-British houses, or that the lowland British hall was a hybrid of native and imported features.[158] These fifth-century settlements are not very like those of the fourth-century Saxon homelands, where the principal dwellings are *Wohnstahlhäuser* (longhouses), completely absent from Britain. However, the fifth-century phases of northern German settlements also saw the abandonment of the longhouse and the replacement of earlier settlement layouts with plans resembling those of post-imperial Britain.[159] Other arguments interpreting the halls as straightforward Saxon imports have been less convincing and

---

[155] Dark, K. R. (1992).
[156] Tipper (2004) for recent overview. Hamerow (2002), pp. 31–5 for introduction.
[157] Hamerow (2003), pp. 46–50.
[158] Dixon (1982); James, Marshall and Millett (1985).
[159] Hamerow (2003), pp. 48, 50.

whether migration was the only factor producing analogous change around the North Sea in the fifth century is debatable.[160]

In the lowlands, as slightly earlier in Gaul, furnished inhumation appears. Again, the earliest such burials have nothing un-Roman about them, employing Roman material culture.[161] However, by the second quarter of the fifth century, north of the Thames a number of graves are found with artefacts undeniably originating in the Anglo-Saxons' north German homelands.[162] Although these objects probably indicate Saxon settlement, as with the Gallic graves we should not see burial with grave-goods, in itself, as indicating the presence of immigrant barbarians.[163] As in Gaul, furnished inhumation is not very common during much of the fifth century and frequently occurs in small clusters of graves. South of the Thames, quoit brooch style metalwork suggests how power in the far south was still manifested through deploying recognisably Roman symbols.[164]

However, north of the Thames, where northern German metalwork is found, cremation was also introduced from the Anglo-Saxon homelands.[165] Some Romano-Britons possibly threw in their lot with the powerful barbarians and adopted their culture but a decision to change the fundamental means of disposing of the dead is significant. Either this shows the weakness of lowland Romano-British political and cultural identity in the conditions of the fifth century, plausible given the extent of the collapse of Romano-British social and economic structures, or it indicates the relative numbers of the new settlers. Probably both factors were involved. In the non-Roman metalwork styles used and the spread of cremation, lowland Britain north of the Thames reveals the clearest fifth-century archaeological evidence of the migration of people.

---

[160] See further below, pp. 386–92.

[161] E.g. burials at Dorchester-on-Thames: Kirk and Leeds (1954), Gloucester: Hills and Hurst (1989); Winchester: Clark, G. (1979), pp. 377–403. Note the westerly distribution of these graves. The publications of these graves tend to assume that they are 'intrusive' but without *prima facie* evidence.

[162] Böhme (1986), pp. 527–8; Hamerow (2005), pp. 264–7; Welch (1993). Welch (1992), pp. 54–87, for a useful introduction to Anglo-Saxon burial practice. Hills (2003), pp. 95–9, for judicious discussion of the relationship between burial and migration.

[163] See further below, pp. 386–92.   [164] Above, pp. 238–9.

[165] Hills (2003), p. 96; Richards (1995), pp. 57–63; Welch (1992), pp. 55–6.

In the last quarter of the fifth century metalwork appears, decorated with what is known as Salin's Style I, after a Norwegian archaeologist who created a typology of post-Roman metalwork styles from Scandinavia, northern Germany and Britain. Style I derives ultimately from Roman official metalwork but in itself it is indisputably of northern German and Scandinavian origin.[166] Unlike quoit brooch style it is found overwhelmingly on feminine dress adornments, surely implying an importance given to gender in this period of transformation. The demise of the Roman-inspired quoit brooch style and the appearance of an undeniably non-Roman style graphically indicate the changes that took place in western Europe at that time.[167]

As in northern Gaul, the economy fragmented and reduced considerably in scale. The difference between eastern and western, lowland and highland, areas is repeated. Mediterranean finewares continued to be imported into the regions bordering the Irish Sea and are found on the high-status sites discussed earlier.[168] These did not reach the lowlands. There, ceramic industries declined drastically. Most lowland British pottery was now hand-made, frequently using motifs originating in the Anglo-Saxon homelands.[169] Much of it is, however, funerary. Its decoration and archaeological occurrence in sealed contexts means that it is more easily datable than might otherwise be the case. This is not so with other ceramic forms. It is now becoming apparent that, as in Gaul, the late Roman pottery industry struggled on in attenuated form.[170] Formal and decorative variety was much reduced, demonstrating considerable decline in the scale and complexity of the operation and making the detection of fifth-century wares a matter for considerable technical expertise. Nonetheless, in at least some areas further west and north, pottery was apparently made and distributed over more than purely local regions. These distribution areas are smaller than those in Gaul but still more significant than was once supposed. Although, clearly, the scale and complexity of fifth-century pottery-making cannot be compared with that of the fourth century, it may be an overstatement to claim that pottery industries 'died' around 400. As with the

---

[166] Haseloff (1981).   [167] See further above, pp. 281–3.
[168] Campbell (1996); Dark, K. R. (2000), pp. 125–32; Dark (ed.) (1996); Lane (1994); Thomas, C. (1982).
[169] Myres (1977).   [170] Whyman (2001).

Gallic distributions, though, there might be a less sanguine reading of local communities' need to import this undistinguished material. The spread of quoit brooch style metalwork across a fairly broad band of territory might force a similar modification of the 'extreme meltdown' position.[171] It is not as complex as the fourth-century official metalwork from which it descends but it attests craft-specialisation and the ability to distribute such work.[172]

Overall a distinction between east and west, between what had been the civilian and military zones of Roman Britain, is repeated across a number of forms of data. As elsewhere, the distribution maps of different types of evidence follow the same contours. This includes the written data. Famously, the fifth and sixth centuries of British history are a true Dark Age. Nevertheless the three insular written sources from this period, Patrick's *Confession* and *Letter to Coroticus* and Gildas' *On the Ruin of Britain*, all originate, in one sense or another, in western or northern Roman Britain. Patrick was from a curial family whose geographical origins are unidentifiable but certainly bordered on Britain's west coast. Gildas' work is a constant source of debate but it seems agreed that he did not write in the south or east of the civil zone.[173] This all demonstrates that the highland areas had weathered the crisis around 400 rather better than the lowlands.

The western hillforts represent local potentates' ability to control manpower (to build or refurbish large fortifications) and craft-specialists.[174] Overseeing the distribution of whatever resources were traded with the Mediterranean merchants who sailed into the Irish Sea, in return they had access to prestigious commodities from the Mediterranean and a window onto that world.[175] In this context it is unsurprising that an inscription from Penmachno is dated by reference to the last western consul.[176] Western Britain may have been the only part of the old Empire where political horizons expanded. Western British high-status settlements, and probably the site at Wroxeter and those along the line of the Wall,

---

[171] Though one must remember that much of this material was deposited later than its period of manufacture.

[172] See above, pp. 238–9.

[173] See, recently (albeit controversially), Higham (1994).

[174] Dark, K. R. (2000), pp. 132–5; Griffiths (1994).

[175] Above, nn. 154, 168.

[176] http://www.ucl.ac.uk/archaeology/cisp/database/ Stone reference: PMCH2/1

demonstrate a disjunction between the rural producer of surplus and its aristocratic consumer. The latter could extract surplus and invest it in separate settlements that displayed power and prestige. A hillfort was important not just defensively; it could be seen from afar, making a clear and permanent mark on the landscape. Surplus could be controlled and traded for the benefit of the ruling stratum.

Quite a high number of high-status sites existed in western Britain. How they related to each other is debatable. They have tentatively but plausibly been placed in a hierarchy from major sites to lesser, dependent ones.[177] This reconstruction sees rulers controlling their realms via the defended strongholds of lesser aristocrats, perhaps office holders. In the former military zone, epitaphs continue to use Roman official titles. Inscriptions, indeed, are something else absent from the lowlands in this period.[178] Although Roman epigraphy was always skewed towards the military zone, it is possible that this form of commemoration was employed, precisely *because* it had been associated with the Roman army, to underpin new, martial forms of leadership. The Coroticus whose slaving raids upon Ireland provoked a letter from Patrick was a western British potentate.[179] Frequently localised in Strathclyde, in reality we have no idea where his kingdom was. This evidence also reveals the political use of literacy. In this context of significant and secure political leadership, the reality of which is borne out by Gildas' tirade, it is unsurprising that written works should circulate and survive.

In the lowlands, the picture is quite different. Social interaction contracted to local communities. It is important to note that the region that has revealed post-imperial furnished inhumations is more or less the same as that covered by the distribution of villas (map 26). There are exceptions; villas spread slightly further to the west in Somerset and even what is now Gwent. By contrast there is a sprinkling of cemeteries north along the eastern side of Northumbria, where there were no villas. Nevertheless, the overall similarity is striking. Both distributions show the same gaps, notably around the north of London, further questioning the idea that burials with

---

[177] Campbell (1996).
[178] Handley (1998); (2001b); Thomas, C. (1994). http://www.ucl.ac.uk/archaeology/cisp/ for database.
[179] Patrick, *Letter to Coroticus.*

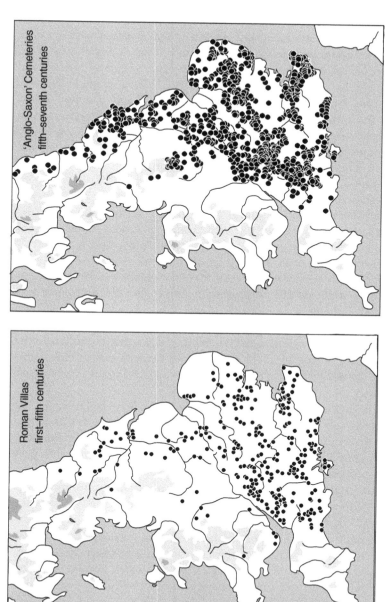

Map 26 The distribution of Roman villas and Anglo-Saxon cemeteries in Britain

grave-goods are symptomatic of barbarian settlement. Furthermore, Anglo-Saxon settlement and political control spread over a rather broader zone, especially in the Midlands, than is covered by these graves. This distribution is found with many classes of artefact and covers most of England's arable country.[180] While inevitably skewing the stray finds of individual artefacts, one cannot explain the distribution of discoveries of types of site, like cemeteries, by such a chance factor. If the cemeteries simply mark Anglo-Saxon ethnic communities, why are they not found in other types of ecological zone? The villas are distributed thus essentially because of the economic and landholding relationships made possible by arable or mixed arable–pastoral farming. We should view the cemeteries as associated with the demise of these sorts of relationships. It is also worth stressing that the general distribution of such burials remains generally constant throughout the early Anglo-Saxon period.[181] Although some gaps are filled in, there is no noticeable westwards drift, such as one might expect if these burials were linked to Anglo-Saxon settlement and political domination (the distribution of furnished cemeteries in northern Gaul also expands in the seventh century, without conquest being invoked[182]). It seems best to see furnished inhumation, as elsewhere, in social terms and link it to the end of the villa system. In the lowlands no archaeologically visible high-status sites replace the villas before the late sixth or even seventh century.[183]

The lowland British aristocracy had been closely linked to the Empire and its patronage, maintaining their social position and fourth-century Britain's stability and prosperity. With its removal, aristocrats had to compete with local rivals for power and their pre-eminence was maintained with difficulty. Analysis of Anglo-Saxon cemeteries reveals analogous distributions according to age and gender to those found in northern Gaul, necessitating a similar overall interpretation.[184] Unlike in the highlands, any surplus extracted was quickly spent in the locality, in gifts and counter-gifts. It is no surprise that craft-specialisation and industry declined or that large expensively maintained villas and town houses, or towns themselves – centres for the interaction of a political class that could

[180] Cp. above, pp. 196–7.   [181] Dark, K. R. (1994), p. 219, fig. 51.
[182] See Halsall (1995a), p. 185.   [183] Hamerow (2005), pp. 275–6.
[184] Above, p. 357, n. 146. Hines (1995); Richards (1995).

remove itself from local competitions for power – should have withered. Locally powerful families might have retained their position through the fifth century but the price was high, not least in the exclusion from wider arenas of political action, such as they had been used to under the Empire.

This competition for power, and the contraction of the arenas of competition should not, however, lull us into thinking that political units were necessarily small.[185] As in Gaul, the best means of maintaining local power and of participation in wider politics was to obtain the backing of an outside authority. This could centre on the remains of the army south of the Thames, or the incoming barbarian warbands, or the clearly powerful highland kings. The Severn estuary, in that region where villas had tended to be larger,[186] also seems to be the centre of the production and distribution of some classes of material, possibly revealing another political unit.[187] In later traditions referring to this period, the idea seemed acceptable that upland kings, like the probably mythical Vortigern,[188] should have held sway over the south-east. That local power struggles were resolved by reference to outsiders is repeatedly underlined in the fragmentary sources for fifth-century Britain. We can see the appeals to St Germanus in this light.[189] It is unlikely that Pelagianism had a long history as a British doctrine.[190] Pelagius, its founder, was British but he had written and promulgated his views in the Mediterranean, where indeed the whole debate about his teachings took place. What seems instead to have been at stake in Verulamium was the denigration of rivals through accusations of a recently declared heresy. In an area like Britain, with, as far as we can tell, little effective central government, competition for local power was intense. In such competition the accusation of heresy was a useful tool. Because of Pelagius' British connections, accusations of Pelagianism were perhaps particularly effective, and the appeal to a famous holy man an efficacious means of securing a judgement condemning one's opponents. There was apparently a precursor to this move in Victorinus of Rouen's visit to Britain in the 390s, when Roman society in the island was beginning to break down. This situation and strategy are attested elsewhere in

---

[185] Above, pp. 313–19.   [186] Above, pp. 80–1.
[187] Dark, K. R. (2000), pp. 132–4; Hines (2003), p. 95.   [188] See the Appendix.
[189] Constantius, *Life of Germanus* 13–18, 25–7. Above, pp. 238, 244–5.
[190] Markus (1986), *contra* Myres (1960).

the fifth-century west as traditional Roman social structures were called into question.[191] A similar appeal to outsiders can be seen in Gildas' account of the letter to Aëtius.

SURVIVAL STRATEGIES

This survey reveals the different options for survival available to aristocrats in this period. A number of factors weighed in different ways upon their considerations. The first was material. They had to retain their leadership of communities that were sometimes very local indeed. Elsewhere, where political change called the land-owning class's social and economic dominance less into question, the concern was more to retain a leading role within their stratum. Elsewhere again, the aim was to retain power at a yet higher level, that of the Empire itself. Another driving force behind the options chosen by aristocrats, particularly where they were concerned with regional or even imperial political stages, was cultural. Roman aristocratic culture was based upon a mix of *otium* and *negotium*. This bipartite existence had to be maintained.

In Britain and much of northern Gaul, the withering of imperial presence threatened the very basis of aristocratic power. Élites retreated to the cores of their estates and bought continued pre-eminence through comparatively costly strategies of ritual display, gift and counter-gift. As their resources were spent on securing power, and perhaps on the increasingly necessary maintenance of an armed following, there was little or nothing left for the upkeep of towns and lavish villas and no ability to remove themselves from local politics without external backing. In other regions, such as southern Gaul, Spain, Africa and Italy, the bases of aristocratic power were more secure.

It is abundantly clear that it was not easy to respond to the Empire's political decay simply by setting out to rule independently. The Empire was so deeply ingrained into ideas of all aspects of social and political action that the simple 'rejection' of Rome was not an option.[192] The Empire came close several times to restoring its authority in the west and, when on the offensive, it showed

---

[191] Van Dam (1986). See above, p. 341.

[192] This, alas, is an idea that has recently gained much popularity: Jones, M. E. (1996).

remarkably little tolerance for those who, it felt, had usurped its authority. For much of the earlier fifth century, the regional élites' response to the weakening of imperial presence was clearly to try to re-establish the Empire on the fourth-century model. Constantine 'III' and the other British usurpers, Jovinus and his brother, and Avitus can all be seen in this light – as attempts to return imperial authority and patronage to Gaul. Sidonius Apollinaris' career shows that some aristocrats continued to seek patronage from the emperors in Italy.

Appeal to Roman sources of authority therefore remained common through the fifth century and beyond. Even when an area was formally recognised as being under independent rule, or when individuals or groups filled the vacuum left by the retreat of imperial power, Roman titles and symbols were important. In the late fourth-century northern Gaulish graves, the vocabulary of authority used in these ritual displays was entirely Roman. One of post-Roman Britain's shadowy political groupings, south of the Thames, created its own badges of office derived from those of the Empire. The nobles of Spain grouped themselves into cabals, sometimes referred to as senates, as with the senate of Cantabria known from sixth-century sources. A Moorish ruler called himself *imperator* and a Welsh leader took the title *protector*.[193]

It must increasingly have been apparent that the Empire was unable to guarantee the position of those leaders who based their power upon Roman titles. The effectiveness of claiming Roman authority diminished the longer that Roman arms were absent. Yet at the same time, no one knew that the Empire was never going to make a recovery, until the 470s. Simultaneously, the barbarians had no developed political vocabulary independent of that based upon Rome.[194] It is therefore no shock either that much of the fifth century is so invisible archaeologically or that new forms of material culture and decorative systems emerge when the western Empire finally ceased to exist.

The other option available was of course to turn to the barbarians. This was increasingly attractive for numerous reasons. For one thing, barbarian military power became more important as the fifth

[193] Moors: below, pp. 408–9. The title *protector* is found on the Castell Dwyran stone: above, p. 312.

[194] Above, pp. 121–5.

century wore on. From the 420s, as the Empire lost control over its tax base and manpower reserves, allied barbarian contingents or whole armies became ever more important even to the Empire itself. Non-Roman leaders were very often the only sources of military backing for local power, especially in areas like northern Gaul and Britain.

The precise options available to local élites as the Empire fell apart, and indeed their freedom to choose between them, were profoundly influenced by the way in which the Empire and its ideology permeated other ideas about social structure. We shall consider this further in chapter 14.

12

BEYOND THE OLD FRONTIER

The regions beyond the *limes* tend to drop out of studies of 'the Migrations' as soon as the barbarians have moved. This however, prevents a proper understanding of the causes and processes of migration and change. This chapter surveys developments beyond the old frontiers during the fifth and early sixth centuries, which shed important light on the interlinked nature of society and politics inside and outside the Empire and upon the dynamics shaping late antique history.

WEST OF THE IRISH SEA[1]

Revolutionary changes took place in Irish society between the fourth and the early seventh centuries. By the end of that period the structures that appear to have persisted for centuries had been swept away by transformations that left untouched almost no area of Irish society, politics, economics and religion.[2] The most obvious change was the introduction of Christianity.[3] This might have begun in the fourth century – St Patrick is more difficult to place chronologically than is often believed.[4] The Roman church was certainly interested

---

[1] Surveys: Charles-Edwards (2003), pp. 24–34; Davies (2005), pp. 240–6; Mytum (1992); Ó Cróinín (1995), pp. 14–62; Warner (1988).

[2] Mytum (1992), pp. 43–52, for summary.

[3] Stancliffe (2005) for recent overview.

[4] Ó Cróinín (1995), pp. 23–7. The early Irish annals' reference to the death of one of Patrick's alleged students in 535/7 does not seem decisive. Also Dolley (1976).

in preaching to the Irish during the early fifth century and although its spread was slow Christianity surely played a vital role in underpinning the ongoing changes. It cannot, however, be seen as the sole explanation for these transformations, which are archaeologically visible in places that had not been converted as well as in those that had and may well begin before any significant Christian impact. Furthermore, to assume that the introduction of Christianity would act as a *deus ex machina* to instigate all of these developments is simplistic.[5] It is more plausible that its adoption was of use in dealing with or providing a focus for changes already taking place.

Ireland's relationships with the Roman world were changing in the later fourth and fifth centuries.[6] The church's interest in Ireland is another sign of Rome's impact, which nevertheless, remained less than in other regions bordering the Empire and its role in explaining the period's changes is debatable. However, political and cultural contacts doubtless helped provide a context for the movement of the Irish to Britain. This is a thorny topic.[7] The date and scale of migration is difficult to determine. There are no reliable written sources and archaeological evidence, such as the pottery sometimes adduced as evidence for migration to Cornwall, is often questionable.[8] Some cultural traits supposedly diagnostic of popular movement did not appear, either in Ireland or in western Britain, until after the presumed period of migration. The Irish figures found in Welsh genealogies are difficult to pin down chronologically, although surely representing authentic traditions about Irish settlement. Place-names, similarly demonstrating population movement, are impossible to date precisely. Irish people moved to what is now Wales and Argyll,[9] becoming a significant element in the politics of some regions, most

---

[5] Mytum (1992), in spite of claims to the contrary, does not significantly advance the explanation beyond the traditional ascriptions of change to Christianisation given by writers like De Paor and De Paor (1958). His processualist approach necessitates his invocation of an external stimulus as the sole agent of change. See above, pp. 26–7.

[6] Above, pp. 113–14.   [7] Thomas (1994), pp. 41–9.

[8] Grass-tempered ware: Cp. Alcock (1971), pp. 268–9; Thomas, C. (1973). The pottery evidence has gone from Thomas, C. (1994), pp. 41–9, 183–96, 209–21. By this date, Thomas preferred the notion of a secondary Irish settlement of Cornwall from Dyfed. Rahtz (1976).

[9] As mentioned above, p. 112, n. 1, it might be that the Scottish settlement in Argyll, later known as the kingdom of Dal Riada, predates the end of the Roman Empire.

notably in the west of what became Scotland and in Dyfed, but the precise date at which they did so is vexed.

One evidential form manifesting close cultural relations across the Irish Sea and the movement of people is epigraphy. Stone monuments inscribed with the names of individuals and, at this date, generally set upright are known especially from west Wales and in other regions of probable settlement, like Cornwall.[10] Many of those commemorated bear Irish names and a number of stones have parallel inscriptions in Latin and in Ogam. The latter, wherein letters were denoted by straight lines perpendicular or at an angle to the edge of the stone (or to a long incised line), was an Irish alphabet derived from Latin at some point in the late Roman period: another index of possibly increasing socio-cultural (if not necessarily economic) interaction between Ireland and the Empire. The Ogam series is believed to commence around 400 or perhaps in the late fourth century. This might suggest that, as often mooted, Irish military colonists were given responsibility for the defence of stretches of the west coast in the late fourth century, perhaps under Magnus Maximus.[11] This would be a further aspect of his defensive reorganisation of the British diocese.[12] In south Wales, these settlers might have formed a first wave, which became a focus for a later, sixth-century migratory phase.

The movements to Britain might have been part and parcel of the changes within Ireland. When Irish politics emerge into the half-light provided by credible written sources relating to the late sixth century, it seems clear that an earlier system of large-scale provincial kingships was being replaced by a new order.[13] The collapse of the great semi-legendary realms, like that of Ulster, seems to belong to the fourth century, although the myths link these kingdoms with much older sites. Exiles from these struggles could have been those who settled the west of Britain in the late fourth century. Later traditions certainly ascribed the settlement of such regions to the expulsion of their rulers from Ireland. In what Ó Cróinín calls the 'maelstrom' of the fifth and sixth centuries a number of dynasties lost their power and, as in other regions of the *barbaricum*, they may consequently have left for the

---

[10] Thomas (1994). But see also Handley (2003); http://www.ucl.ac.uk/archaeology/ cisp/database/.

[11] Rance (2001), with care.   [12] Above, pp. 195–8; Appendix.

[13] Ó Cróinín (1995), pp. 41–62 for excellent overview.

formerly imperial territories. If there were already Irish settlers in Great Britain, the links between them and their homelands would facilitate such moves.[14]

One of the most significant changes to Irish settlement archaeology was the appearance of small ringforts (raths, cashels or crannogs). This vitally important class of site has contributed enormously to our understanding of early medieval Irish society and economy.[15] A couple of such sites were built in the late third or early fourth century, and a slightly larger number in the later fourth but their construction really began in significant numbers in the fifth century. The trend continued through the sixth before an explosion in numbers in the seventh.[16] Though defended with palisade and ditch their purpose cannot be primarily defensive, as they would not have kept out any significant or determined attacking force. Indeed some may well have been cattle corrals. Instead they seem to mark a trend towards the marking out of property and perhaps social status and as such are a graphic index of profound social change. Researchers have long seen them as a manifestation of the society based around kin-networks, clientship and precisely defined social rank described in the early Irish laws.[17]

Dramatic changes in Ireland appear to have begun in the fourth century. As noted above, there is evidence of an upsurge in land-clearance from c.300.[18] These transformations did not really work themselves out until the seventh century, however. By that stage Ireland was incorporated into European trading networks and having a significant effect upon western religion and culture, but that lies beyond the scope of this volume. Whether the chronological correspondence between these changes' beginnings and the crisis of the western Empire is more than coincidence is hard to establish. In our present state of knowledge it is difficult to characterise the relationships between the 'fall of Rome' and change in Irish society. One might, from the changing and possibly more politically important

---

[14] Below, pp. 419–22.

[15] Proudfoot (1977) was the first to carry out a systematic survey of such information. See more recently Edwards (1990), pp. 6–33; Mytum (1992) *passim*; Stout (1997); (2000).

[16] Stout (1997), pp. 22–31. These figures are based upon carbon[14] and dendro-chronological dates and thus not dependent upon the varying archaeological visibility or ease of dating of artefacts.

[17] E.g. Warner (1988).   [18] Above, p. 113.

contacts between Ireland and the Empire, see Ireland as structurally similar to the 'middle band' of territories within Germanic-speaking *barbaricum*,[19] the rupture in these contacts causing dramatic transformation and the migration of political factions into formerly imperial territory. However, one might equally argue that the connections between Ireland and the Empire were not sufficiently close for a sudden break to have produced dramatic change, though this might remain a contributory factor. Changing links between Ireland and the Empire in the late Roman period may have begun a phase of social, economic and political change in the island, which continued regardless of Roman politics. It may be wisest to seek an internal, Irish explanation for the fourth- to seventh-century developments and envisage contacts with Rome and the introduction of Christianity as strategies within, and components rather than causes, of those changes. Irish migration to Britain may have belonged essentially to the sixth century, after the Empire's collapse, driven essentially by Irish political developments without much of a 'pull factor' from formerly Roman Britain. In this reading, Ireland would resemble barbarian territories like those in Scandinavia.[20] A similar picture to this can be traced in northern Britain.

NORTH OF HADRIAN'S WALL[21]

This crucial period is difficult to examine in northern Britain. Apart from the references in Gildas' works and some other vague allusions, many if not most of which are severely tainted by the Romans' tendency to use the *Picti* as a convenient rhetorical reference point for 'the end of the world', we have no documentary evidence. There is no securely dated reference to Pictish attacks on the diocese after the 380s. Gildas' citation of the letter to Aëtius specifies no barbarian attackers; only its position within the account allows us to assume it refers to Picts, and that might result from the rhetorical demands of the text.[22] Given the paucity of sources this is hardly an obstacle, but it

---

[19] Below, pp. 383–99. [20] Below, pp. 379–83.
[21] Foster (1996) is the best introduction: admirably clear and concise. See also Foster (1992).
[22] Below, pp. 519–25 for the problems of establishing any chronology from the *DEB*'s historical section, and pp. 524–5 for the rhetorical device of three appeals to Rome.

is clear that the Picts had no success at all in establishing themselves in former Roman territory – unlike the Saxons, Franks, *Alamanni* or even the Irish. Even in the territories immediately north of Hadrian's Wall, the English had become dominant by the seventh century.[23] It is clear that the British rulers of the highland zone were powers to be reckoned with, probably because of a transfer of local authority under Roman rule, further softening the effects of the end of imperial government.[24]

One reason for this might have been internal instability in the 'Pictish' regions and here it is worth stressing that there does seem to be a difference between the areas north and south of the Clyde–Forth line. To the south, evidence of change can be found in written and archaeological sources. At about the time when, it is suggested here, the Roman frontier was withdrawn from the Wall, in the 380s,[25] the hillfort of Traprain Law had its fortifications refurbished.[26] A famous treasure was deposited there, probably the result of raiding, but before long the site was abandoned again. The withdrawal of the Roman frontier would have had important implications for the inhabitants of the region immediately to the north. These, as we have seen, had quite close ties with the Empire and a stable society as a result. The removal of the frontier would have caused considerable instability, and probably the raiding described by Gildas. It was proposed in chapter 4 that the lands of the southernmost confederation of *Picti* began at the Wall. In the stress of the late fourth and fifth century it is likely that this confederacy fragmented. This led to the reappearance of groups like the *Votadini*, whose name resurfaces in the regional name of *Manau Gododdin* in this period. Like the *Angli* and Frisians, who had apparently been incorporated within the Saxon confederation, this ethnic identity had been overlaid by a higher-level, confederate identity, especially in dealings with the Romans. In the political turmoil surrounding the break-up of the larger group, it now came back to the surface. Other 'British' polities appear in Strathclyde and further south in Cumbria, apparently straddling Hadrian's Wall (Rheged) by the time our earliest post-imperial historical sources appear.

---

[23] For introduction to this region, see Lowe (1999). See further below, p. 377.
[24] Above, pp. 196–7.   [25] Above, pp. 196–7.
[26] Close-Brooks (1983); Feachem (1955–6).

On the east coast, by the close of our period, that other symptom of social stress and local instability, furnished inhumation, had also appeared. This is usually associated with 'Anglian' settlement and indeed Anglian became another of the competing political identities within the region. The formation of these *Angli* in the areas north of Hadrian's Wall is, however, likely to have been a much more interesting and complex process than the traditional, simple view of English migration, conquest and settlement allows. It is likely that this was another consequence of the break-up of the southern 'Pictish' confederacy. All this doubtless prevented the southern *Picti* from being drawn into political vacuums such as existed along the Rhine or in North Africa. Their failure to make much of a lasting inroad into the former provinces of Britain is thus unsurprising.

North of the Clyde–Forth, things seem to have been rather different. Fifth-century archaeological evidence is difficult to find.[27] Nevertheless, by the close of our period it is clear that important changes were under way, although these do not seem to have been complete until the seventh century. They are most visible in the settlement pattern. By the end of the fifth and the earlier sixth century a trend had set in towards occupation and investment in the fortification of hillforts. Some such sites are known from the fourth century, as at Burghead in Moray,[28] but the real upsurge in the use of such sites does not appear to have occurred until the fifth century and, usually, later. These hillforts are generally univallate, although some have a cellular plan, with a series of enclosures. There seem to have been transformations in the nature of other settlements at about this time, although the chronology is vague and, again, many changes do not appear to have been fully worked through until the seventh century or perhaps even later.[29] The trend seems, overall, to be towards status in the settlement pattern being concentrated in defended works placed on high points in a somewhat marginal relationship to the main farmed areas. This can be plausibly explained by a removal of political power from the immediate locality and kin-network, although whether this means a shift from kinship to clientship is doubtful – at least when stated that simply.[30] Shifts in burial practice are known, such as the custom of interment under barrows and ultimately the appearance of 'Class 1' symbol stones,

[27] Foster (1992), p. 219.   [28] Alcock (2003), pp. 192–7; Foster (1996), p. 43.
[29] Foster (1992), pp. 221–8.   [30] Driscoll (1988a); (1988b). Above, p. 117.

probably as grave markers, although both are difficult to date.[31] In the context of an apparent increase in investment in above-ground markers, the evident absence of grave-goods is probably significant, further suggesting the steady establishment of a secure aristocracy in the areas north of the Forth. The Romans' general lack of interest in the far north of Britain and its politics probably meant that the withdrawal of the frontier and the crisis of the Empire produced no significant results north of the Forth, and the competition between rival chieftains for authority there continued as before. Eventually, by the seventh century, this resulted in the creation of large 'Pictish' and Scottish polities. The end of any significant involvement by the Empire in northern British politics from the late fourth century might have played some part in starting the series of events which eventually led to this situation but, overall, the fall of the west does not seem to have made very much difference to the inhabitants of the regions north of the Clyde and Forth. The northern confederation of *Picti* appears to have endured and by the time we have written sources again, in the seventh century, this group seems to have become that referred to as the kingdom of the Picts.

The differences between the highland regions of the former diocese of *Britanniae*, on the one hand, and Britain north of the Wall and Ireland, on the other, can be seen in the distribution of imported pottery. Pottery from the Mediterranean is found on high-status sites around the Irish Sea (especially around the Severn Estuary) in the fifth and sixth centuries.[32] These wares (known to British archaeologists as 'A Ware' [=ARS and other Red Slip wares] and 'B Ware' [amphorae]) do not reach northern Britain, which appears only to be incorporated into long-distance trading networks from the seventh century.[33] This again would suggest that whatever transformations were taking place amongst the 'Picts' and their neighbours were not completed until after the close of our period. A possible fragment of an Ostrogothic *Spangenhelm* has been found in Dumfriesshire.[34] If this reached Scotland about the time of its manufacture it might suggest involvement in a different, North Sea political network. Ostrogothic 'foreign policy' probably encompassed the Danes and others who

---

[31] The barrow burials might appear from the fourth century, and the symbol stones from the fifth, though the latter could be significantly later: Foster (1992), p. 228–33. Driscoll (1988a); (1988b).

[32] Above, p. 362.   [33] Campbell (1996).   [34] Underwood (1999), p. 104.

might compete in that region with the Franks and this helmet fragment could represent a diplomatic gift, if more likely from northern *Germania* than directly from Italy.[35] However, we have no idea how, when or in what form this decorated metal strip found its way to Scotland, and even its identification as a helmet fragment has been questioned. Comparative economic isolation would also imply that the demise of the western Empire had less immediately drastic effects upon society and politics north of the Forth than in most other areas of *barbaricum*. The closest similarities might be sought in Scandinavia, but even there the end of the west had more archaeologically visible consequences. The reasons for this surely stem from the limited contacts between the Empire and the north.

EAST OF THE RHINE

In addition to describing the visible changes that took place in society east of the old Rhine frontier, we must also look at the creation of two new peoples, the Thuringians and the Bavarians, whose appearance is important to our comprehension of the politics of the migrations. We also need to step briefly outside the confines of the former *barbaricum* to look at changes around the North Sea. Only a broad, geographical perspective will allow us to understand the changes visible in the archaeology of fifth-century northern Germany.

Scandinavia[36]

We may begin in the far north, in Scandinavia. The changes that took place here during the fifth and sixth centuries are different from, and sometimes less dramatic than, those that occurred elsewhere in *barbaricum* east of the Rhine but they are very interesting. In Denmark[37] the settlement of Vorbasse saw significant change at this time. The settlement moved during the fifth century and changed its organisation, becoming a 'row settlement', with the settlement's houses arranged end to end. Norre-Snede also moved in the fifth century but it had shifted in the fourth century too. Overall the impression is of

[35] Below, pp. 381–2.
[36] There is no satisfactory recent survey in English. Myhre (2003), pp. 81–3, is brief and very traditional; Hedeager (2005) is idiosyncratic.
[37] The most interesting discussion of Denmark in this period is Hedeager (1992). See also *inter alia*, Axboe (1995); (1999); Näsman (1999).

stability, an impression underlined by other evidential forms. The bog-deposits change, becoming more votive in character. Their contents are more merely representative than they had been before and are local products rather than booty captured from invaders. Within the region's cemeteries, graves seem to be generally nonde-script. There are far fewer inhumations with weapons in the fifth century than there had been in the fourth. This is an interesting inverse proof of the point that lavish burial is generally congruent with social instability. The lack of investment in public, ritual displays to local audiences in Denmark goes hand in hand with the other data suggesting a more powerful and stable élite.

Some of the most interesting changes take place at the Gudme-Lundeborg complex on Fyn.[38] Around 400 the supply of imports from the Roman Empire began to dry up, which should not surprise us given the political history outlined in chapter 7. As the distribution of such prestigious items was seemingly one of the supports for authority in the region, this should have produced a certain amount of stress in the local political system. It might well have done so, but the local rulers responded imaginatively. The site continues to show evidence of various forms of craft-specialisation, presumably linked to the distribution of prestige goods as gifts to maintain the loyalty of more local chieftains. The decoration of some of the objects, as well as their intrinsic value in precious metals, also points to very interesting developments. In the fifth-century and later, Gudme has revealed astonishing quantities of gold. Many of the finds are bracteates, Scandinavian imitations of earlier Roman coinage, and what are known as goldgubber, small gold plates. Very many of these items are decorated with scenes from Scandinavian mythology, which can be identified with the aid of later texts and the runic inscriptions on some of the objects.[39] We should not read these scenes in too precise a way on the basis of central medieval Scandinavian sources.[40] Nevertheless, they clearly reveal that the manufacture and distribution of these artefacts had some religious function, surely implying that the region's leaders had adopted a new religious role. This might have played a part in binding dispersed communities into a single political unit.[41] The deposition of such artefacts within buildings inside

---

[38] Nielsen, Randsborg and Thrane (eds.) (1994).
[39] On bracteates, see Magnus (1997).   [40] Above, pp. 122–3.
[41] Above, p. 124.

settlements also implies a different, more socially selective, audience for the ritual. On the whole, the picture in Denmark is of continuing political development and political complexity. The Danes, as a people, might have been formed at this time, perhaps originating on the Baltic islands like Sjaelland, Fyn and Lolland and extending their power to Jutland. Some material culture, such as the 'swastika brooch' has been linked with this process. The losers might have been the Heruls of the Jutland peninsula, who are found raiding the coasts of Aquitaine and even Spain, taking service with the Goths in Gaul while other groups washed up on the Danube frontier.[42] It is thus perhaps no coincidence that in the early sixth century the first known Danish king, Chlochilaich (presumably the Hygelac of *Beowulf*), appears in contemporary written sources.[43] Chlochilaich attacked the north of the Merovingian territories in what has been interpreted as a conflict for control of the North Sea and even, perhaps, a component of Theoderic of Italy's 'foreign policy'.[44] This would be further evidence for the ways in which the regions surrounding the North Sea were intimately interlinked, as discussed below.

Some similar changes appear to be notable in what is now southern Sweden, in Scania. Hoards of the same sorts of gold object are deposited within settlements, equally suggesting a change in the nature of local leadership. In Norway local power is suggested by the continuing importance of the boathouses, associated with clusters of other signs of authority.[45] Although weapons are rare in Norwegian burials (as elsewhere in Scandinavia), the burials (cremations and inhumations) can be well provided with other objects. The end of Rome does not seem to have had a significant effect here, except perhaps in the area of art-styles.

Contacts continued between Scandinavia and the Danubian regions and thus the eastern Roman Empire.[46] The nature of these contacts may have been rather different, and more restricted to high-status gifts, than was the case with the fourth-century trading links.

---

[42] See above, p. 260. Hedeager (2005), pp. 503–4, for outline.

[43] *LH* 3.3; Cp. *Beowulf*, esp. lines 1202–13. His appearance in later Anglo-Saxon poetic epic might suggest that he was an even more significant figure in Scandinavian politics.

[44] Storms (1970); Wood (1983) for different but not entirely incompatible interpretations.

[45] Myhre (1997).   [46] Näsman (1998).

Nevertheless the movement of gold and other prestigious items was probably another way by which the élites maintained their power.

The changes of the period might be revealed by an examination of the art-styles employed on Scandinavian objects.[47] At the end of the fourth century a style known as Nydam style (after the bog-deposit containing the famous ship) was introduced. Nydam style is a distinctive local development but nevertheless it clearly owes its origins to official Roman metalwork. This is important in that, while it reveals the long-standing influence of Roman motifs on the 'grammar' of display and power in the northern *barbaricum* it also shows a conscious attempt to adapt and modify those motifs. As has been mentioned in discussion of lowland Britain, Style I appears around 475. This Scandinavian style, though recognisably growing out of Nydam style, is notably different, with its motifs and execution showing a radical shift away from the Roman styles. Again, this would seem to reveal that the significance of the end of the Empire was appreciated far outside the imperial borders as well as within them.

Changes appear across the region around the end of the period covered by this book. One aspect of these changes may have been an end of exchange links with central Europe[48] and, perhaps, a shift towards western trading-routes (Chlochilaich's raid might have been associated with this). In Denmark, the forms of evidence undergo significant shifts around the middle of the sixth century.[49] The trading site at Lundeborg generally fell out of use in the early sixth century. In some areas grave-goods become more common again (for example in Bornholm and Gotland). The last bog-deposits end around 500 and artefacts take on different forms and designs, bringing in the Vendel period in Sweden[50] and what has been, curiously, known since the end of the nineteenth century as the Merovingian period in Norway. The precise chronology of these changes is still debated but seems to have taken place in the middle quarters of the century. At the same time, Style I began to be replaced by the rather different Style II, which has been claimed to have some Byzantine influence in its origins. Style II has been argued to relate to a new warrior élite. In some areas such as the island of Gotland off Sweden, these changes

---

[47] Haseloff (1981); Kristoffersen (1999).   [48] Näsman (1999), p. 4.
[49] Näsman (1999), p. 7, fig. 5.
[50] Lamm and Nordstrom (eds.) (1983) for introduction.

brought with them interesting renegotiations of local social structures.[51] From the sixth century, Norway saw a significant expansion of the settlement pattern.[52] These sixth-century changes seem to be a suitable place to end our survey of Scandinavian developments. The end of the Roman Empire did not produce dramatic transformations and does not seem drastically to have affected the general trajectory of social change, but had significant and interesting results nevertheless.

The Saxons: settlements and cemeteries in north-west Germany[53]

Important changes took place in the settlement pattern of north-west Germany in the fifth century. The settlements themselves changed in form.[54] Previously the pattern had been for long *Wohnstallhäuser* with associated lesser buildings (SFBs and granaries). This changed, with the abandonment of many long-houses and their replacement with shorter, post-built houses that did not incorporate cattle byres. This can be seen at the Terp site of Feddersen Wierde, where the fifth-century phase also lost the carefully planned nature of its fourth-century predecessor. The important *Herrenhaus* was abandoned and there seems to have been a change in the settlement's economic base. It might be that there was a shift to a greater emphasis on craftworking as climatic changes rendered the surrounding salt-marshes less suitable for farming. At Flögeln, again, the fifth-century settlement is more scattered and less orderly, before being abandoned in the sixth century. Wijster, the large planned settlement whose well-being appears to have been linked to the Roman *limes*, was deserted by the second quarter of the fifth century, although it is important to note that its cemetery continued in use. Many settlements were abandoned at this time although those in the Geest region (the flat lands inland from the coast) continue into the sixth century before a second phase of abandonment.

The desertion of settlements in this region is a matter of important debate, relating to the migration of the inhabitants of the region to

---

[51] Rundkvist (2003)   [52] Myrhe (1992), p. 308.

[53] Capelle (1998) is a good introduction. Häßler (1991), pp. 285–320. Springer (2004) is disappointing on this period. For detail, see the essays collected in the volumes of *SzSf.* In English, Hamerow (2002), *passim*, is very useful, as are Dörfler (2003), Meier (2003) and Siegmund (2003).

[54] A valuable overview of the settlement data in English with references, can be found in Hamerow (2002), esp. pp. 53–85.

Britain in the fifth century.[55] Many settlements, like Feddersen
Wierde, were abandoned in the earlier fifth century. This was not
only true in the coastal regions where climatic change and attendant
flooding made the management of the marsh areas more difficult.
The picture is also suggested both in the Elbe–Weser region and in
Schleswig-Holstein as well as along the Frisian coast. Nor does the
evidence come solely from settlement archaeology. Were that the
case it would be possible to argue that settlements had simply moved
elsewhere. Palaeobotanical evidence suggests a reduction in the
extent of exploited land and an upsurge in reforestation. This should
imply some sort of serious population decline. The reality of this
picture will be further considered below, as will the issue of whether,
and in what way, it might relate to migration to Britain.

In the cemeteries of the region, too, changes occurred around 400.
As in northern Gaul, but slightly later (which, as discussed in chapter
5, is important for the 'ethnic' interpretation of the Gallic graves)
lavish inhumations appear, wherein the males are interred with
weaponry and the females with jewellery.[56] The extent to which this
represents a revolutionary change in funeral display in the region can
be debated. It has been argued persuasively that in the cremation
ritual the dead were laid out in a similar fashion, with their funerary
costume before the pyre was erected over them and the body burnt.
Nevertheless the change to inhumation remains significant for a
number of reasons. The first is that these graves make a clear ritual
display of difference from the remainder of the community. Second,
the rite used is probably Roman in origin.[57] Again, as with the frequent use of metalwork with Roman associations, the point of the
display was to claim the status and kudos of a link with the Empire,
the font of all ideas of power and legitimacy. Third, grave-goods seem
to be more lavish overall in these inhumation graves. Taken alongside
the evidence from the settlements, which likewise shows a breakdown in the established hierarchies of the fourth century, these
developments suggest a profound crisis. Locally prominent families

---

[55] Hamerow (2002), pp. 104–13, for survey.
[56] Böhme (1974), pp. 218–65, with Tafeln 1–58, remains an excellent, lavishly
illustrated, description.
[57] As argued by Böhme (1974), something else making the 'Germanic'
interpretation of the north Gallic inhumations utterly illogical. See recently
Kleemann (1999), with useful discussion of the historiography, and Bemmann
(1999) for comparison with Scandinavian inhumations.

responded by more ostentatious uses of funerary ritual to display, and thus try to maintain, their standing. Some extreme examples of this are the burials at Fallward, not far from Feddersen Wierde, where a boat was buried, containing a wooden bed and chair, both decorated with the motifs used on imperial metalwork.[58]

Many cemeteries seem to have been abandoned in the mid-fifth century. Given the desertion of settlements at this time this is perhaps not unexpected. However, it has recently been pointed out that the abandonment of cemeteries might be more apparent than real. A study of the survival of evidence at one of the region's largest and best-known cemeteries, Liebenau, suggests that under normal conditions two thirds of the burial evidence from the area in this period would have been lost simply due to preservation factors.[59]

Later in the fifth and in the course of the sixth century the region reveals cemeteries of furnished inhumations similar to the type by then common throughout northern Europe.[60] Nevertheless, there are local peculiarities, so that archaeologists are reluctant to refer to these cemeteries as *Reihengräberfelder* (row-grave-cemeteries). They are less neatly arranged and follow less clear patterns of development through time. As in the former provinces, these probably speak of local power structures that were more open to intense competition than had hitherto been the case. Close analysis of the cemeteries reveals that, as in other regions of the post-imperial west (though again with significant regional peculiarities) the grave-goods custom was structured heavily around age and gender. It has been pointed out that lavish burials of the late fifth and early sixth centuries are largely absent in the Saxon regions. This represents something of a contrast with the period around 400 and Siegmund argues that it shows that society was less differentiated in this region than in areas further south. This argument is unsatisfying for several reasons. One must remember that the later fifth-century inhumation graves of the region are distinguished in rite and in relative lavishness of furnishing from the more numerous cremation burials. One should also reject the idea that differences in the lavishness of grave-furnishing passively reflect rigid stratification in living society.[61] As has been argued above, furnished inhumation is an index of insecure status. Finally, we should not assume that the same artefacts (Siegmund mentions

[58] Schön (1999).   [59] Siegmund (2003), pp. 81–3, and refs.
[60] Siegmund (2003), pp. 88–9, and refs.   [61] Above, p. 28.

swords with gold grips and pommels and ostentatious Ostrogothic *Spangenhelme*) had the same symbolic value in all areas. The clear distinction in rite from the overwhelming majority of the population might combine with the relative lack of investment in lavish grave-goods (something that changed significantly shortly after the close of our period) to argue that the local élite in Saxony was relatively *secure* in its position. It still needed to display its difference from the remainder of the population in burial ritual, but this ritual does not seem to have been the locus for particularly fierce competition.

Unlike the Danish peninsula, the evidence from north-western Germany reveals important and dramatic change in the fifth century, which is suggestive of profound social reorganisation. It would appear that a crisis occurred around 400, leading the local élite to demonstrate its local standing in new ways. By the second half of the century, however, in spite of continuing change in the settlement pattern, this crisis seems to have been weathered to some degree. Understanding this requires us to consider two further related issues. The first is the issue of the migration to Britain and its effects upon the society of northern Germany, taking us briefly beyond *barbaricum*. The second is the emergence of the Thuringian kingdom as a new political unit on the Elbe valley.

Change around the North Sea and the Anglo-Saxon migration[62]

With the important exception of Denmark, study of the regions bordering on the North Sea – northern Germany, lowland Britain and northern Gaul – reveals similar important and interconnected developments. The changes visible in the Saxon homelands have generally been interpreted and explained in the light of the migration to Britain. The historicity of this migration cannot be denied; it is the one case of late antique migration that would be unequivocally attested by the archaeological record even without written sources. It is sometimes claimed that belief in this migration is based upon the domination of the archaeological agenda by a 'prescriptive framework' set out by the historical sources, such as Bede's *Ecclesiastical History*.[63] In purely archaeological terms (thus leaving aside linguistic shifts), one cannot convincingly account for the material

---

[62] For a judicious discussion of these problems, see Hills (2003).
[63] Lucy (1997), p. 151. Cp. Lucy (2002), pp. 73–6.

cultural change visible in fifth-century England without invoking some movement of people from northern Germany.[64] Giving the migrants the historically attested names of Saxons or Angles makes little or no difference to this fact.

The north German cremation ritual was introduced into eastern England, as well as a series of artefacts that have their origins in the same area.[65] New forms of settlement have also been associated with incoming Anglo-Saxons and the change of the region's language must also reflect population movement to some extent. What concerns us here, therefore, is not the reality of migration but whether it alone explains these transformations.[66] Migrations do not necessarily leave archaeological traces. The movement of countless people from *barbaricum* into the Empire during the first to fourth centuries left almost no material record at all.[67] Something beyond the mere fact of migration must be adduced to explain such cultural changes. Appeal has frequently, therefore, been made to the *scale* of the migration. To address this issue we must place the archaeology of the Saxon homelands in broader context, which is rarely done. Usually the only comparisons made are between eastern England and the North Sea coastal areas of Germany, the Netherlands and southern Denmark, in other words the origin and destination of the Saxon migrants, somewhat prejudging the issue. Alternatively, the abandonment of the 'migration hypothesis' by younger generations of British archaeologists has frequently turned into an excuse for not considering mainland Europe at all.[68] We come closer to a rounded appreciation of the significance, causes and effects of Saxon migration if, first of all, we see the North Sea as *connecting* diverse regions and, in association with that point, situate the archaeologically visible changes and the migration itself in the wider context of Romano-barbarian relationships.

The previous chapter demonstrated that the changes in imperial rule around 400 AD brought rapid and dramatic change to the north-western provinces. In Britain and the far north of Gaul villas

---

[64] Scull (1995), p. 73.   [65] Above, pp. 197–8.
[66] See further below, pp. 418–19.   [67] Above, pp. 159–61.
[68] There is, as far as I can see, only one (simplistic) reference (on p. 149) to the archaeology of mainland Europe made by those contributors to Lucy and Reynolds (eds.) (2002) aged under forty at the time of publication: a diametric contrast with all those aged over forty.

were abandoned. Some survived to the mid-fifth century but most were derelict by the end of the first quarter of the century. The great bulk of Roman cemeteries, too, were abandoned. Towns were deserted in Britain and in northern Gaul they contracted to a shadow of their former selves. Meanwhile, industry and craft-specialisation declined. Traces of fifth- and early sixth-century occupation of settlements are often nebulous. In this context there appeared, first in northern Gaul, a new form of inhumation rite, which displayed to a local audience symbols of the deceased family's local pre-eminence. In this light, the changes visible in the Saxon homelands can, and probably should, be seen as part of the same large-scale process. Many settlement sites were deserted and their successors are not visible for a considerable time – perhaps until the seventh century. Cemeteries are frequently abandoned and a response to the crisis is seen in furnished inhumations. Even changes in the forms of settlements are matched around the North Sea in these regions. The shorter, post-built hall appears in Britain, Gaul and Saxony, accompanied by the ubiquitous *Grubenhäuser*. Environmental data suggest a contraction in the occupied areas but this contraction began at various dates between the early fifth and the end of the sixth century. This pattern is matched in Britain where diverse patterns are recorded, including reforestation from various times after the collapse of Roman government.[69]

The similarity in the pictures emerging from northern Gaul and Britain should be placed alongside the comments made above about the caution necessary in assuming that settlement and cemetery abandonment equals depopulation and migration. A great many rural settlements were abandoned in the north-west of the Empire at this time and show no clear signs of reoccupation until the late sixth or seventh century, yet no one has adduced large-scale emigration or depopulation as explanations.[70] Climate changes made the coastal regions of northern Germany more difficult to work but it is by no means clear that the obvious response to such change was to undertake a long and hazardous journey to the coasts of eastern England, where similar changes were taking place. A simple move inland would be easier. It has been claimed that occupants of the coastal marshes would have found it difficult to transplant themselves to the Geest because a whole new way of life would have had to be

---

[69] Dark, S. P. (1996).   [70] Siegmund (2003), p. 83, for a similar point.

learnt. This argument, however, applies *a fortiori* to migration to Britain.

In the former provinces these changes have been explained as a consequence of the intimate connection between the local élite and the structures of the Roman Empire. To understand the Saxon changes we must remember the relationships between the *barbaricum* and Rome. The Saxon regions were closely linked to the Empire. Roman material culture played a very important role in social display in the region. As in Denmark, access to Roman items was probably more restricted here than in the Frankish regions next to the *limes*,[71] and its control important in underlining political power. Denmark, however, had some advantages over the north of Germany. Access to the Baltic meant a position on the trade-routes leading to the Black Sea and the eastern Empire and thus some continuing access to Roman gold and prestige items. It might also be that contact with the Empire was somewhat more limited leading to the development of other means of cementing authority. We might suggest, therefore, that the Saxon regions would feel the effects of the breakdown of Roman frontier management more critically either than the regions further away from the *limes* or those just over the frontier, where political authority seems to have been steadily growing in the later fourth century, bolstered by Roman treaties. The Saxons, like the Vandals, Burgundians, Heruls and probably the Sueves, as well as other groups that moved the furthest in the fifth century (we can possibly include the Lombards in this group), came from this crucial region just behind the frontier peoples.

As with these other groups, migration was linked to internal conflict. The archaeologically visible crisis in Saxony in the early fifth century might plausibly be linked to the break-up of the Saxon confederacy. In the migration period the Frisians, Jutes and Angles reappear in the written sources for the first time since early imperial times, in particular in connection with the migration to England.[72] Political instability in northern Germany caused by the collapse of effective imperial rule led some groups to form new political units, using as their foci levels of ethnicity hitherto subordinated to Saxon identity. Some groups, like the Angles, might have used migration to

---

[71] See also above, pp. 127–8.

[72] Angles and Frisians: Procopius, *Wars* 8.20.7. Jutes (probably): *Austrasian Letters* 20 (*Eucii*).

further their political ambitions, whilst others might have been the losers in barbarian politics, moving to the Empire in the traditional way to seek service with whatever authorities remained there. The Saxons in the south of England might have taken this route. As noted in chapter 10, the regions later thought of as Saxon are also those where metalwork descended largely from Roman imperial prototypes survived until the later fifth century. Indeed, political distinction between Saxons and Angles in post-imperial Britain could have been produced by insular political considerations.[73] Another group of Saxons took themselves off to join the Lombards in their move towards the Danube and, ultimately, Italy.[74] The break-up of the old confederacy might also be manifest in the way in which other cultural influences come to dominate the Saxon regions in the later fifth and sixth centuries. Some came from the south and the powerful Frankish kingdom, others from the new Thuringian realm on the Elbe and others from the north, Denmark. However, it is not possible to link this break-up with the acephalous situation recorded in eighth-century Saxony. Political development rarely operated along neat unilinear trajectories and archaeology suggests further important change in the area in the later sixth century. A Saxon 'duke' is mentioned at that time, though with uncertain reliability,[75] and there were periods of Frankish domination as well as independence from the Merovingians. The eighth-century situation could quite possibly have been a recent development.

It is important to note, however, in addition to this 'push' factor from within *barbaricum*, the 'pull' factor that was the political vacuum that the crisis of the Empire had produced in lowland Britain, where Saxon settlement may already have taken place.[76] In the previous chapter we saw that appeal to outside sources of political and military power was, increasingly, the most effective means of cementing local power in the north-western provinces during the fifth century. Thus the Franks and Alamans were drawn across the Rhine into northern Gaul. Similarly in Britain non-Roman warlords will have been sucked into the power vacuum. Analysis of the Saxon situation calls into question the recent revival of the traditional thesis attributing fifth-century invasions to the pressure of the Huns.[77]

---

[73] Above, pp. 316–18.   [74] *LH* 4.42.   [75] *LHF* 41. Scheibelreiter (1994).
[76] Above, pp. 197–9; Appendix.
[77] Heather (1995a), developed at length in Heather (2005).

The Huns were certainly a factor in some migrations but they played little or no part in migration from northern Germany to Britain.[78] Yet this movement can be shown to have been governed by the same general factors as produced other migrations or invasions. There must therefore have been forces at work other than Hunnic intervention.[79] The mechanisms for the incorporation of the Saxons into lowland Britain would only have been strengthened by the late fourth-century military settlement of Saxons, suggested above.[80]

The dramatic extent of the results of Roman authority's collapse in Britain also explains the degree of cultural change, as discussed in the previous chapter. We need not therefore evoke the numbers of migrants in order to explain such change. As the numbers of immigrants from northern Germany into Britain is never going to be susceptible of proof and as the number of migrants, even in relative rather than absolute terms, is, in comparative perspective, rarely a determinant of the degree of cultural change produced by migration, the debate on the numbers of Anglo-Saxons in post-imperial Britain must be unprofitable. There might have been more Anglo-Saxon migrants in post-imperial Britain than, for example, Goths in Aquitaine. The degree of collapse in Britain probably presented greater opportunities for newcomers and the extent of links across the North Sea doubtless encouraged a stream of movement over a longer time-span than was the case elsewhere (with the exception of the Rhineland). Especially with Saxon settlement under Magnus Maximus, the close interconnections and cultural influences between the areas surrounding the North Sea surely also explains the spread of cultural forms, such as the types of buildings used in settlements, and, to some extent, the similarity of material cultural responses to the crisis of 400. The movement of people played a part – probably a significant one – but this should not be seen as the primary, let alone the sole, explanation.

---

[78] *HE* 5.9, to the contrary.

[79] Heather (2005), p. 446, n. 20, justifies exclusion of Britain from his analysis because the Anglo-Saxons did not cause the British provinces to drop out of the system. However, it is difficult to find any invasions that *did* directly cause a province to drop out of the imperial system, even the Vandal invasion of Africa in the late 420s–430s.

[80] Above, pp. 197–9.

Another feature of migration from *barbaricum*, which we have encountered before, is the availability of other, new political identities around which opposition could crystallise. The resurgence of Frisian identity was perhaps one such but another came from the centre of *Germania Magna*. One factor in the continued stability of Danish society and politics, as mentioned, was their access to the Baltic–Black Sea amber route. The Elbe was another trade artery, leading from the Saxon regions ultimately to the Mediterranean, which might have served as a resource stabilising the situation in Saxony. The crises on the Danube[81] could have had some effect on this route but, more importantly, in the fifth century it was controlled by a new power in the region: the Thuringians.

Politics and migration in the Elbe valley: the Thuringians and Lombards

The Thuringians first appear in Vegetius' veterinary treatise around 400 but they really emerge as a significant force in sources relating to the later fifth century.[82] They are alleged to have provided a contingent for Attila's army in the 451 campaign[83] and seem to have been under Hunnic domination at that point but their kingdom became a significant feature of the political landscape after Attila's fall. They were one of the groups drawn into the political vacuum in the formerly imperial territories north of the Alps.[84] Their kings then appear in the correspondence of Theoderic the Great and were included in his network of marriage alliances.[85] Gregory of Tours is the first to record the story, later considerably elaborated by Fredegar, of how Childeric married the wife of the king of the Thuringians, who left her husband to join the virile Frankish ruler. This is a most peculiar story. Thuringia might, in most of this tale, be confused with the area around Tongres and the linkage of Clovis' mother Basina with Bisin, king of the Thuringians, based upon no more than alliteration.[86] Nevertheless a marriage alliance between Childeric and the Thuringians is possible. Gregory also claims that Clovis subdued the Thuringians, an event later dated to the tenth year of his reign by an

---

[81] Above, pp. 170–5.
[82] On the Thuringians, see Schmidt (1983); (1987); (1997).
[83] Sid. Ap. *Poems* 7, line 323.   [84] Eugippius, *Life of Severinus* 27.3, 31.4.
[85] Cassiodorus, *Variae*, 3.3, 4.1; Procopius, *Wars* 5.12.21–2.
[86] *LH* 2.12; Fredegar, *Chronicle* 3.11; Halsall (2001); Shanzer (2002b), p. 411.

anonymous interpolation, but the Thuringians clearly retained their independence.[87] The Thuringian kingdom was finally ended by Clovis' sons who conquered the region and killed its last ruler Hermenfrid (by pushing him off the walls of Zülpich) in 531–4.[88] It was another fifth-century kingdom destroyed in the dramatic 530s. In the tenth century Widukind of Korvei records an elaborate tale of the fall of the Thuringian kingdom, presumably from an epic poem like the *Niebelungenlied*, based on the events of the migration period and still circulating in his day.[89] Hermenfrid's niece, Radegund, was led off into captivity to become the wife of Chlothar I and later one of the most important saints of Merovingian Gaul. The last generation of Thuringian kings seem to have partitioned the realm between themselves but other than that it is difficult to say very much about the Thuringian kingdom from written sources.

The extent of the Thuringian realm has been a matter of debate. Some forms of material culture, such as particular types of brooch, cluster in the middle Elbe and suggest a 'core area' between the Thüringer Wald and the Elbe and between the area around Hannover and that around Leipzig (map 27.1). Outliers suggest that this territory might extend north of the Elbe towards Berlin and there is another heavy cluster in Bohemia. Isolated finds of Thuringian material occur across the whole region between the Danube, Rhine and Lower Saxony. Two views have emerged in judging the size of the Thuringian kingdom from this data. A minimal view sees the Thuringian kingdom as more or less commensurate with the 'core area' just discussed,[90] whereas another point of view envisages a 'Greater Thuringia' stretching from the Elbe to the mouth of the Rhine and including the Saxon areas.[91] The arguments of both turn on interpretations that, to some degree, see material culture as passively reflecting ethnic groups, the latter seen very much in primordialist terms. Thus Schmidt is unwilling to view Thuringian political power as having extended to areas where Thuringian material culture is not concentrated, while Böhme believes that anyone wearing a Thuringian brooch must have been Thuringian.[92]

---

[87] *LH* 2.27.

[88] *LH* 3.17–18; Procopius, *Wars* 5.13.1–2; Venantius, *Life of Radegund* 2.

[89] Widukind, *Deeds of the Saxons* 1.4–12. Springer (2004), pp. 75–89.

[90] Schmidt (1983); (1987).   [91] Böhme (1976).

[92] Böhme (1988).

There is no need to rehearse the arguments about ethnic interpretations of culture groups.[93] A stance can be adopted which reads
the material culture in a more active way. The distribution of
'Thuringian type' furnished inhumation cemeteries, discussed further
below, should probably be read in social terms, a point which by no
means discounts the symbolic content of some of the material
deposited in demonstrating Thuringian identity. It is interesting that
the distribution of Thuringian brooches outside the 'core area' and
Bohemia clusters along the Rhine and thus the edges of the Merovingian kingdom, with a few examples beyond the Rhine in the
territory of the Rhineland Frankish kingdom of Cologne. It can be
argued that signs of identity are likely to be strongest on the edges of a
political unit.[94] The archaeology might be read as revealing that on
the fringes of Merovingian power some people turned to the
Thuringians in competition with those who sided with the growing
Frankish power. This does not imply the presence of migrating
Thuringians but rather that Thuringian power was drawn out to these
areas. If this was so it allows us to re-read the written data.
Hermenfrid's marriage to Theoderic's niece Amalaberga is usually
dated to c.510, shortly after Clovis' defeat of the Alamans and probably when Clovis was conquering the Rhineland Frankish kingdoms.
This might have forced Hermenfrid to turn to an Ostrogothic alliance
as he found Clovis directly on his border on the Rhine and in the
angle between the upper Rhine and Danube.[95] Clovis' alleged (but
probably unlikely) victory over and subjection of the Thuringians
cannot be dated. It might have taken place at this time or earlier. If the
latter then it would, like his defeat of the Alamans,[96] have required
the assistance of the Rhineland Frankish kings. This demonstrates that
Merovingian overlordship over the frontier kings was growing in the
first decade of the sixth century and possibly suggests that the middle
Rhine was something of an area of competition between the
Merovingians and the Thuringians.

---

[93] Above, pp. 59–62.

[94] This is a similar interpretation to that proposed for the distribution of Visigothic
   material in Spain, above pp. 344–6.

[95] Procopius, *Wars* 5.12.21–2, says that the Thuringian–Ostrogothic alliance was
   born out of fear of the Franks.

[96] See *LH* 2.37.

Thuringian material in lower Saxony can probably be understood in a similar way. In the confusion of the fifth century attendant upon the collapse of the Empire, the migration to England and the break-up of the Saxon confederacy some people turned to the expanding Thuringian power for support.[97] Archaeology suggests that a competing strategy was to associate with the Franks. This does not prove that the Saxon regions were incorporated within the Thuringian kingdom (or that of the Franks) but, like the material on the middle Rhine, it does suggest that Thuringian power was drawn into this region, which might also have become part of a greater Thuringian hegemony. Nevertheless, later sources indeed list the *Angli* as having been part of the Thuringian kingdom. Charlemagne's code for the Thuringians was entitled the 'Law of the Angles and Varni, that is of the Thuringians' (*Lex Angliorum et Werinorum hoc est Thuringorum*). This might refer to the Angles of Schleswig or to another Anglian group that gave its name to the Engilin region on the middle and lower Unstrut.[98] Nevertheless the movement of a group of Angles up the Elbe might be a further indication of the turbulent politics that produced the Thuringian kingdom as well as shedding light upon their dynamics.

Historical sources certainly suggest that the Thuringian realm was larger than the archaeologically revealed 'core area'. The presence of Thuringians in Noricum, near Passau on the Inn has been mentioned. Gregory of Tours seems to have been under the impression that the Thuringian kingdom marched with that of the Franks on the Rhine.[99] The decisive battle in 531, when invading Franks routed Hermenfrid's army, took place west of the Unstrut, itself on the south-western edge of the 'core area'. Gregory describes the defeated Thuringians fleeing back into the Unstrut.[100]

The distribution of pottery may also be significant (map 27). Though usually associated with the Bavarians rather than the

[97] The lavish chamber burial 3575 at Issendorf might be the grave of a member of a family that based its local standing upon a connection with the Thuringians. Schmidt (1997).
[98] Schmidt (1983), p. 506.
[99] This is the implication of Procopius, *Wars* 5.12.10, and possibly Jordanes, *Getica* 55.280.
[100] *LH* 3.7.

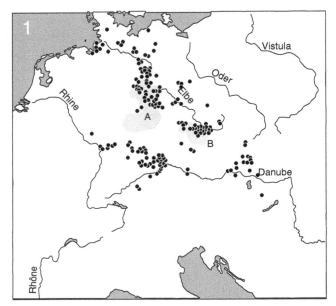

A: 'Core area' of Thuringian cemeteries   B: 'Bohemian' group of cemeteries

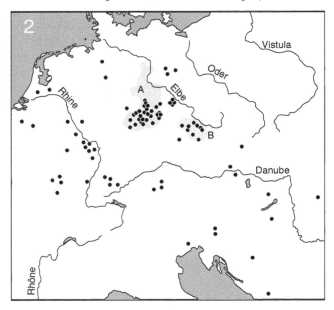

Map 27 Zones of cultural interaction on the Elbe
1: Friedenhain-Přešť'ovice pottery
2: Thuringian brooches

Thuringians,[101] fifth- to mid-sixth-century decorated ceramics of the 'Freidenhain-Přešt'ovice type' are also found distributed along the whole length of the Elbe and, like the metalwork, clustering in the Thuringian 'core area' and in Bohemia. Unlike the metalwork, however, it is slightly earlier (beginning in the late fourth century). It is also found more commonly in Lower Saxony and is distributed quite thickly on the upper Danube, in the area where the *Life of Severinus* tells us that late fifth-century Thuringian warlords were active, and between there and the Rhine, along the Main and the northern frontier of Alamannic territory. Other finds are known from the middle Danube. Rather than seeking precise ethnic ascriptions, especially when such ethnicities were fluid and, doubtless, represented only one level within a hierarchy of such identities, the distribution of material shows a network of contacts and relationships, which one group might rise to dominate. It primarily underlines the importance of the Elbe valley as a trade-route,[102] the control of which was probably important in spreading Thuringian power, just as it was suggested that control of the Baltic–Black Sea amber route played a part in the spread of Gothic hegemony.

Archaeology sheds further light upon the short-lived but important Thuringian kingdom. As elsewhere the period around 400 is represented by signs of social stress. A new group of furnished inhumations appeared in the last quarter of the century, called the Niemberger group.[103] As with the Haßleben-Leuna group that had appeared in this region a century earlier, some families responded to pressure by using a burial ritual that differentiated them more clearly from the remainder of local society. At the same time a decline in the quality of local craftsmanship is detectable.[104] Important changes took place in the middle of the fifth century. This is the date at which the metalwork forms discussed above began to appear. The new material culture exhibits significant influences from the middle Danube region – in other words the realm of Attila. The Hunnic practice of

[101] E.g. Menghin (1990), pp. 61–2, fig. 57. The interpretation is not unproblematic: H. Fehr, paper given to congress on 'Archäologie und Identität', Vienna, March 2006. The 'Bavarian' identification seems to be based essentially on a literal reading of the etymology of the name Bavarian ('men from Bohemia': see below, pp. 403–5) and, on this basis, a concentration on the material's spread from Bohemia to Bavaria, and a neglect of its distribution along the Elbe.
[102] See, e.g. Steuer (1998). [103] Schmidt (1983), pp. 515, 518.
[104] Schmidt (1983), p. 536.

skull-deformation, sometimes (albeit probably wrongly) attributed to the Huns,[105] is also attested in this region. The Thuringians' presence in the Hunnic army in 451 has been alluded to and the Hunnic connection might have been vital in producing Thuringian hegemony. The connections with Ostrogothic Italy mentioned in the written sources are also manifested by the discovery of an Ostrogothic *Spangenhelm* at Stößen.[106]

In addition to playing a significant role in the expansion of Thuringian power, it is also clear that the Elbe valley was a route used in the movement of groups of people. Thus the Heruls who appear on the Danube at this period probably migrated from southern Scandinavia along this axis. They might have represented a losing faction in politics in that region. Saxons too moved up the Elbe valley, joining up with the Lombards in their move ultimately to Italy. This group might have been another faction that lost out in the earlier fifth-century confusion in the lower Elbe–Weser region. So too might the *Angli* documented within the Thuringian kingdom on the middle Elbe.

The Lombards themselves, however, are perhaps the most important group to move up the Elbe.[107] Originally thought to have been located in what became the Saxon region, according to early Roman sources, one group was repelled from the Danube, having presumably campaigned up the Elbe, in the later second century.[108] By the later fifth century the Lombards, or Langobards, seem to have been located in the north of the Danube in lower Austria. The date of this group's move from Lower Saxony cannot be pinpointed and might possibly have been another consequence of the fragmentation of the Saxon confederacy. The connections between the Thuringians and the Lombards were close. The Thuringian king, Bisin, was married to a Lombard and his daughter wed the first definitely historical Lombard king, Wacho.[109] At this stage the Lombards seem to have been a part of the Thuringian hegemony. However, in the early

---

[105] Whereby the skull of a child was bound with boards so that it grew into an artificially elongated shape. Schmidt (1983), p. 541–2.

[106] Schmidt (1983), p. 544.

[107] For an introduction to early Lombard history and archaeology, see Christie (1995), pp. 1–68. Barbiera (2005) for interesting social analysis of the cemeteries.

[108] Dio Cassius, *Roman History* 72.3.1; Strabo, *Geography* 7.1.3.291; Tacitus, *Germania* 40.1; Velleius Paterculus, *Roman History* 2.106.

[109] Procopius, *Wars* 7.35.

sixth century they moved into *Pannonia*, where they fought with the Heruls.[110] It seems likely that this was connected with the break-up of the Thuringian hegemony under Frankish pressure. The move to *Pannonia* is usually dated to 526, thus shortly before the final Frankish conquest, and Wacho betrothed his daughter Wisigard to the son of Theuderic I, the conqueror of the Thuringians. Eventually, in spite of victories over the Gepids, in the third quarter of the fifth century the Lombards found themselves once again in the position of a losing political faction when the Avars, moved to the Danube region by the eastern Romans, emerged as the area's dominant power. The Lombard king Alboin therefore took his followers across the Alps to Italy in 568.

The creation of the Thuringian kingdom was a product of the turmoil that the crisis of the Empire produced in the middle band of barbarian territories, attested also in the migrations of the Burgundians, Vandals, Sueves and Saxons.

SETTLEMENTS AND CEMETERIES ALONG THE OLD RHINE FRONTIER: THE FRANKS AND *ALAMANNI*[111]

The Franks seem to have been affected by the end of the western Empire, but slowly. They fought to help defend the Rhine in 406 and seem to have launched some inroads into Gaul slightly later; Castinus and Aëtius are recorded fighting them in the 420s.[112] Trier is recorded as having been sacked four times by Franks drawn into the power vacuum in northern Gaul. By the later fifth century the Franks had established several kingdoms astride the old Rhine frontier and had extended control into Belgica Secunda, although the real stimulus for Frankish political dominance was their role in the Loire army. With the Merovingian dynasty's acquisition of supremacy as a result of commanding that force the history of the Franks becomes central to that of the final decades of the western Empire.

Archaeologically, the settlements along the northern frontier seem if anything to have undergone a late boom around the end of the fourth

---

[110] Procopius, *Wars* 6.14.
[111] On the *Alamanni* see Geuenich (ed.) (1998); Christlein (1991); for the Franks, see above, p. 346, n. 101.
[112] Above, pp. 233, 249.

century.[113] The high-status site at Gennep continued in use through the fifth century, although experiencing some decline in its last quarter, before being abandoned in the early sixth century.[114] Change is also manifest in the appearance of furnished burials along the Rhineland and then in the Frankish homelands.[115] The development of Frankish society within the homelands, as revealed archaeologically, then runs parallel with the developments described for their northern Gaulish territories, especially once the Merovingians had established domination of Gaul by the end of the fifth century.

The dramas of the fifth century produced numerous changes among the *Alamanni* but, as among the Franks, generally later in the fifth century. Fifth-century Alamannic political history is but dimly known. A king Gibuld or Gebavult is recorded both in Noricum and in Troyes.[116] It is difficult to know whether he could be considered an overking.[117] Gregory of Tours, writing of Clovis' defeat of the *Alamanni* some time between 496 and 506, refers to a king of the *Alamanni* but his account of Clovis' reign is highly stylised and the demands of his narrative required that each of the peoples subjected by Clovis be ruled by a single king.[118] Nevertheless, Alamannic political power does seem to have spread. As noted, Alamans are attested amongst the barbarians taking over former frontier regions in Noricum and even spreading some sort of power into Champagne in the middle third of the fifth century.[119] This expansion brought the Alamans into conflict with the Franks. Gregory tells us that Sigibert 'the Lame', a Frankish king based in Cologne, acquired his nickname from a wound suffered in battle against the *Alamanni* at Zülpich.[120] Clovis' triumph over the Alamans came when he responded to an appeal for help by Sigibert. The date of this victory is vexed.[121] There might of course have been more than one campaign. Theoderic's letter to Clovis also refers to the death of their un-named king,

---

[113] Theuws and Hiddink (1997), pp. 78–80.

[114] Heidinga (1993), p. 206; Theuws and Hiddink (1997), p. 77.

[115] Böhme (1974); Theuws and Hiddink (1997), p. 78.

[116] Gibuld/Gebavult: Eugippius, *Life of Severinus* 19.1; *Life of Lupus of Troyes* 10. The king's appearance in both areas might result from the dependence of one saint's life on the other.

[117] Hartung (1983), pp. 80–90, argues forcefully against any increase in Alamannic centralisation in the fifth century.

[118] James (1988), pp. 79–80.   [119] Above, n. 116.   [120] *LH* 2.37.

[121] Above, pp. 304–5.

possibly confirming some sort of political unity by this time.[122] Such centralisation might help explain the Alamans' rapid demise as an independent political unit. The *Alamanni* nevertheless remained a unit within the Frankish polity, ruled by a duke from the mid-sixth century.[123]

Archaeological data reveal that this was a period of ongoing change in the Alamannic regions, although in the current state of knowledge it remains difficult to paint a consistent picture that might relate to the sketchy outlines available of Alamannic political history. The high-status hilltop settlements, the *Höhensiedlungen*, continued to be occupied in the fifth century.[124] A number were abandoned in the middle of that century, however, although others, such as the Runder Burg remained in use. It could be that the gradual decline in the numbers of *Höhensiedlungen* attests to a gradual political centralisation and the reduction of the bases of rival leaders. However, given the changes in the cemetery evidence (see below), it might equally be that these sites' abandonment suggests that Alamannic society entered some sort of crisis in the mid-fifth century, thus later than areas further into *barbaricum*. The fact that a single functional interpretation does not seem to hold for all of the hillforts suggests caution in accepting a blanket explanation.

As elsewhere, and further underlining the points made earlier about the need to place the evidence for Saxon migration in broader context, there were important developments around 400. In the region's cemeteries, changes in custom took place and some sites were abandoned.[125] On the other hand, many new sites begin to be used. For example, at Lampertheim the old cremation cemetery was abandoned around 400, and soon replaced by a new inhumation cemetery. Inhumation became more common and from the middle of the century communal cemeteries began to be founded. In these cemeteries – at this stage still fairly small – the dead were inhumed with grave-goods. Isolated lavish burials, such as had characterised the preceding period, persisted but became more rare. These transformations must imply some sort of social change. Their occurrence at the same time as the abandonment of many of the *Höhensiedlungen* may also be suggestive of a breakdown of secure local power. There seems to have been more competition manifested in the region's

---

[122] Cassiodorus, *Variae* 2.41.   [123] Geuenich (1997).   [124] Hoeper (1998).
[125] Quast (1997) is a useful survey. Christlein (1991), pp. 50–62.

cemeteries. This could stem from an erosion of the power of local
leaders by an overking (as in Merovingian Francia), or from a more
general crisis, produced by the final collapse of the old relationships
between Empire and *Alamanni*. There is little in the evidence to help
us decide and the alternatives need not be mutually exclusive.

More changes took place around 500.[126] The last of the *Höhensiedlungen* were abandoned, not to be reoccupied until the later
seventh century, and new cemeteries were founded. On other sites
there is a break around 500 and the artefacts change in form at that
time. Crisis might be suggested by the fact that pollen evidence from
around the Bodensee suggests that the early sixth century was a period
when forest expanded at the expense of farmland.[127] These changes
must stand in some sort of relationship with the incorporation of the
Alamannic territories into the Frankish kingdom, though precisely
how must be debatable.[128] By the middle of the sixth century, the
cemeteries look rather like those known in Frankish territory, with
the families of entire communities participating in a competitive rite.
However, in Alamannia this ritual is far more extreme than in the
core of the Frankish kingdom. As elsewhere around the fringes of
Merovingian power, grave-goods are very elaborate. Suits of armour,
helmets and whole horses (sometimes more than one) are interred
with men, and more overt displays of jewellery are found in female
graves. Lavish burials (again, from around 500) are often in elaborately
constructed chambers. As in Francia, analysis shows that the patterns
of distribution are closely related to age and gender and the interpretation must be very similar.[129] Families competed with each other
by burying their dead with the most appropriate assemblages of
grave-goods, to the greatest possible extent. Feasting and gift-giving
doubtless accompanied such lavish displays. We can interpret this as
the continuation of a process, beginning in the mid-fifth century,
whereby local authority was more open to competition from other
local families. This might have begun as part of a centralisation of
power by the Alamannic kings, investing local authority in those who
had a connection with the king. If so, this might explain why the

[126] Koch (1997), though care should be taken with the ascription of the artefactual
data to precise historical events.

[127] Rösch (1997), p. 328.

[128] Samson (1994) casts doubt on this, though I am unconvinced.

[129] See, e.g. Brather (2004); Donié (1999); Jørgensen, Alt and Vach (1997).

military defeat of the Alamannic rulers by the Franks brought about such a rapid and dramatic collapse and their replacement by the Merovingians. As we might expect, competition for local power was greater on the fringes of the Frankish kingdom, where royal authority was rarely felt.

The Bavarians[130]

East of the Alamans another new people emerged in the former *barbaricum* at the very end of the period covered by this book: the Bavarians, whose origins are a matter of great (and sometimes bitter) historical debate.[131] They appear in the 'Vorberg' of the Alps, on both sides of the Danube in sources of the mid-sixth century.[132] Their name is generally held to derive from a word meaning 'men from Bohemia' – Baiawarioz.[133] Quite who these 'men from Bohemia' were, or indeed if the whole notion was fictitious, is impossible to know. Some archaeological evidence has been read in line with this etymology, although it dates from well before the Bavarians' appearance, and overlaps with other material culture in the Elbe valley.[134] It seems a fruitless exercise to try to unravel different ethnic groups from each other, especially in eras before they are historically attested, and more particularly in an area of clearly shared material cultural traditions.[135] This does not allow the archaeology to speak for itself.

It has been proposed that the Bavarians were a buffer state created by Theoderic of Italy. This supposition is based not upon evidence but upon two unverifiable suppositions. The first is that Cassiodorus mentioned these people in his lost Gothic history, and the second is a rule of thumb invented by Herwig Wolfram that the first mention of a people occurs a generation after their formation. The second supposition need not detain us; the first is based upon a demonstrably

---

[130] On the archaeology of the Bavarians, see Menghin (1990). For a recent survey in English, with extensive bibliography, see Hardt (2003).

[131] Bowlus (2002), pp. 249–56, for very useful English summary.

[132] The earliest reference is Jordanes, *Getica* 55.280.

[133] Hardt (2003), p. 430.

[134] See above, pp. 395–7, for a linkage with Thuringian power.

[135] A 'Kulturraum' in the words of Hauptfeld (1985), p. 121, who, rightly in my view, feels that the formation of different peoples in this region in the sixth century cannot be disentangled.

false assumption that all the information in Jordanes' *Getica* was drawn from Cassiodorus' work.[136] It seems much more likely that the appearance of the Bavarians stems from three circumstances. The first is the Frankish absorption of the *Alamanni*, destroying one powerful group in southern Germany. The second is the end of Theoderic's Ostrogothic hegemony, and then of the Italian kingdom, which put an end to another powerful political unit that kept some order in the regions north of the Alps. The third is the collapse of the Thuringian kingdom, again at Frankish hands.[137] The Thuringians might have dominated the area north of the Alps in the late fifth century, at least until the establishment of the kingdom of Italy's hegemony in the former Trans-Alpine provinces. Certainly they had been the major power further north in what became Bavaria and were allies of the Ostrogoths. These three circumstances produced a regional power vacuum. It seems that the Bavarians were an amalgam of peoples in that area. Bavarian legal tradition spoke of five main lineages.[138]

The region's fifth-century instability is manifest, as elsewhere along the frontier, by the appearance of furnished inhumation cemeteries similar to those found in the north of the Frankish kingdom and Alamannia. These appeared in the fifth century and, as elsewhere, by the start of the sixth had evolved into large communal necropoleis. The competitive grave-goods rite seems to reveal competition for local authority, probably as a result of the end of the imperial system. It is notable that these cemeteries are found overwhelmingly on what had been the Roman side of the frontier.[139]

The Bavarian ruler was always a duke, never a king, and initially, it seems, installed by the Franks. The evidence for this is flimsy, comprising a reference in the Bavarian law code, but seems to fit Gregory of Tours' account of Chlothar I bestowing the widow of his great-nephew Theudebald on Garibald the first named Bavarian duke.[140] Interestingly, Garibald had close ties with that other new power emerging in the region following the break-up of Thuringian hegemony, the Lombards, a number of his descendants later being Lombard kings in Italy. The Bavarians seem in general to have been closely linked with the Lombards, perhaps unsurprisingly given their origins. Much of their material culture is very similar. Nevertheless,

[136] Hardt (2003), p. 436.
[137] As Hauptfeld (1985): a decisive impulse for Bavarian ethnogenesis (p. 127).
[138] *Bavarian Law* 3.1.   [139] Menghin (1990), p. 80, fig. 65.   [140] *LH* 4.9.

the Bavarians also displayed a number of Roman traditions. When their law was written down, at a disputed date (probably in the late seventh century), it reveals heavy influences from late Roman legislation.

AROUND THE AFRICAN FRONTIER[141]

Some of the most interesting and illuminating transformations in non-Roman society to take place in the fifth centuries occurred around the edges of the former Roman provinces of North Africa. As was outlined in chapter 4, it is more difficult to draw a line between Roman and non-Roman society on the southern edges of the western Empire than anywhere else. In chapters 7 and 8 we saw how North Africa had gradually been cut off from the centre of Roman politics after the failure of a series of rebellions and how developments in the region's towns bear witness to new responses to this situation. This can only have been exacerbated with the Vandal conquest. The Vandals seem to have shown little or no interest in projecting their power to the extremes of the former provinces, which must have exaggerated the degree to which the outlying areas became political grey areas or power vacuums.

In the fifth and sixth centuries a number of kingdoms came into existence around the fringes of the former provinces (map 28). These are known but sketchily from inscriptions (an interesting fact in itself) and from occasional references to campaigns against the Moors in written sources, most notably Procopius' *Wars*.[142] Indeed even the precise number of such realms is a matter of debate, with some authorities postulating large kingdoms stretching for hundreds of miles from northern Morocco to the Aurès, and others much smaller political units. It would appear that these realms were based in the crucial geographical border zone between the more fertile areas of the Roman provinces and the more arid steppe and desert regions. Political authorities here could control the interaction between the

---

[141] Modéran (2003b) is monumental and definitive, although coming to hand too late to permit more than cursory use here. Courtois (1955), pp. 325–52, remains valuable, although some of its interpretations have been challenged by more recent studies. In English: Brett and Fentress (1996), pp. 70–80; Rushworth (2000); (2004). I have drawn heavily on Rushworth's interpretation.

[142] Esp. *Wars*, book 4.

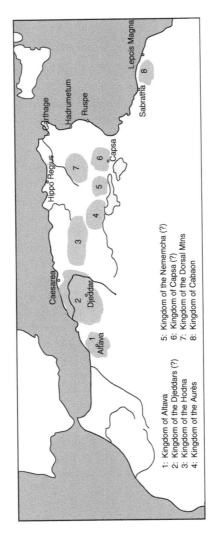

Map 28 Moorish kingdoms in North Africa

1: Kingdom of Altava
2: Kingdom of the Djeddars (?)
3: Kingdom of the Hodna
4: Kingdom of the Aurès

5: Kingdom of the Nememcha (?)
6: Kingdom of Capsa (?)
7: Kingdom of the Dorsal Mtns
8: Kingdom of Cabaon

more settled and the transhumant or even nomadic elements of the North African population.

The Moorish kingdoms made use of the Roman towns of the region as bases for their authority, although deciding which cities were and which were not under their command is a difficult issue. Some certainly were however. Volubilis in the far west was one such, where Roman traditions such as epigraphy continued. Volubilis appears to have been the town earliest abandoned by the Empire and it is interesting to note that it maintained its Roman identity so clearly and for so long.[143] Further east, another such town was Altava (Lamoricière) in *Mauretania Caesariensis*, which has yielded a famous and important inscription revealing the nature of Moorish rule.[144] This refers to one Masuna, styled 'king of the Moorish and Roman peoples' (*rex gentium Maurorum et Romanorum*). Masuna had, according to the inscription, built a fort, through several of his officers who are listed as Masguin, prefect of Safar, Iider, procurator of Castra Severiana, and Maximus, the procurator of Altava. Masuna, as his title implied, used Romans and Moors in his administration, which was clearly based around towns and employed Roman official titles. It has been suggested that the title 'king of the Moors and Romans' was a deliberate counter to the title adopted by the kings in Carthage, 'king of the Vandals and Alans'. It has been debated whether Masuna is the same as the Mas(s)onas mentioned by Procopius.[145] If the names are the same, that no more proves their bearers to be the same person than the two, much better documented, generals called Aëtius active in 452 were one and the same. If they were, then Masuna must have ruled a very large kingdom, although this remains possible. The problem remains impossible to resolve.[146]

Moving east again a number of large funerary monuments (*djedar*) at Ternaten and Djebel Lakhdar, constructed (from the date of inscriptions used in their foundations and at least one C[14] date) after the late fifth century seem to manifest the power of Moorish rulers.[147] These are elaborate dressed stone mausolea and were associated with buildings for mortuary or other ceremonies. Like many of the

---

[143] Akerraz (1985); Lenoir (1985).
[144] *CIL* 8.9835; Courtois (1955), p. 378, no. 95.   [145] *Wars* 4.13.19.
[146] Modéran (2003b), p. 376: 'un problème quasi insoluble'. Modéran leans towards the theory of separate personages.
[147] Courtois (1955), plates 11 and 12 for illustration.

barrows and other above-ground monuments constructed in Anglo-Saxon England and on the mainland of Europe just after the close of our period these were built as permanent marks on the landscape, visible from afar and apparently manifesting a control over the steppe. Whether or not the builders and occupants of these tombs were the rulers of Altava is unknown: Camps believes so; Courtois thought not.[148] The issue might have been resolved by the inscriptions on Djedars A and B at Djebel Lakhdar, that on Djedar B in Greek and Latin.[149] Alas these are now illegible. Procopius says that a king called Mastinas (or Mastigas) ruled *Mauretania Caesariensis* (which includes Altava).[150]

Another ruler with a similar name[151] is the Masties attested on an inscription from Arris in the Aurès Mountains of Numidia. Masties, according to this inscription, had been a *dux* for sixty-seven years and, he claimed, fascinatingly, *imperator* for ten.[152] There was much debate about the date at which a Moorish leader would have taken the title of emperor, whether with the Vandal sack of Rome in 455 or with the deposition of Romulus twenty-one years later. The evidence does not seem strong enough to support such precise interpretations. Leaders in the area had rebelled against Rome since the late fourth century and Firmus had styled himself *augustus*.[153] Masties' adoption of the imperial title does not necessarily imply an awareness of the constitutional or *de facto* 'end of the Roman Empire'. Yves Modéran argues persuasively that Masties' two titles, *dux* and *imperator*, parallel Masuna's title of *rex gentium Maurorum et Romanorum*, and relates to his rulership of two peoples.[154] He had been *dux* of Moors for sixty-seven years and *imperator* of Romans for ten. His acquisition of

---

[148] Camps (1985); Courtois (1955), p. 335.

[149] This point led Courtois to suppose that it should date to the period after the re-establishment of Byzantine rule in 533. This would still just about fall within the 490 +/−50 C[14] date from Djedar B: Rushworth (2004), p. 82. The 'Great Djedar' of Ternaten belongs to the late sixth century: Rushworth (2000), p. 92; (2004), p. 82.

[150] *Wars* 4.20.31. Modéran (2003b), pp. 377–80, for the identification of Mastigas and Mastinas.

[151] Names beginning with 'Mas-' are very common among the Moors, as far back as the Masinissa of Hannibal's day.

[152] Courtois (1955), p. 382, no. 132. Illustrated in Modéran (2003b), facing p. 398. The old reading that Masties was emperor for forty years appears to be based upon a misreading of the inscription: Modéran (2003b), pp. 398–401.

[153] Above, p. 137.   [154] Modéran (2003b), pp. 401–15.

rulership over Romans, Modéran associates with the Moorish rebellion and conquest at the end of Huneric's reign (484). In this argument, while *dux* was (like *rex*) an appropriate title for the leadership of a non-Roman *gens*, it was unsuitable for legitimate rule over Romans: hence Masties adopted the title of emperor. If Modéran is right, this would be a fascinating example, in reverse, of the process whereby rulers who *left* the legitimate Roman political sphere adopted the gentile title of 'king'.[155] Furthermore, Masties, says the inscription, had always been faithful to Romans and Moors, associating the two peoples in a similar way to the Altava inscription.

This would date Masties' death to 494 but a different chronological index is implied by the name of the erector of the building bearing the inscription, a certain Vartaia, identified with the Ortaïas named by Procopius as a Moorish ruler in the 530s. Modéran claims that Vartaia/Ortaïas, participating in a Byzantine campaign against the local leader, Iaudas, restored the inscription and added two lines about himself, in an effort to claim political legitimacy through association with the first independent Moorish ruler of the area.[156]

Other Moorish polities are attested further east along the line of the Aurès as far as the region around Capsa (Gafsa in modern Tunisia), not apparently within the same realm as that ruled by Masties. Another, ruled by Antalas, arose in the late Vandal period in the mountains in the heart of the Vandal kingdom in Byzacena.[157] This is the best known of the Moorish kingdoms because it features most heavily in the narratives of the wars against the Moors by Procopius and Corippus. Finally, pastoral nomads from the Sahara appear to have begun to spread their raids westwards into the Vandal kingdom and to have brought some of the Moors on the kingdom's fringes under their sway.[158]

The character of these Moorish realms is difficult to investigate in detail but some points can be made. The first dwells further on the titles adopted by the Moorish kings, as rulers of Moors and Romans.[159] These were to some extent Romanised polities. They

---

[155] Above, pp. 202–6, 266–7, 279–80, 281.
[156] Modéran (2003b), pp. 412–13; also pp. 382–3. Modéran admits that the identification is far from secure, but it makes little difference to his argument about Masties.
[157] Modéran (2003b), pp. 315–24.
[158] Above, pp. 295–6; Modéran (1991); (2003b), pp. 289–310.
[159] Rushworth (2000); (2004).

were based largely in the peripheral regions that had been abandoned by the Empire in the late third century. Clearly they used the vestigial towns of the area and officials of the Moorish kings continued to bear Roman titles. The kings themselves persisted in their desire for Roman recognition, coming in to Belisarius' camp after the defeat of the Vandals to receive imperial legitimation.[160] The Roman-ness of these states is further underlined by the continued adherence to the epigraphic tradition (in Volubilis the series of inscriptions runs down to 655) and to the dating system based upon the Mauretanian provincial era (which began in the year now designated 39 AD). The dressed stone funerary monuments of the Djedars also show Roman influence in form and decoration (and the inscriptions), although they are also to be seen as manifestations of an indigenous North African funerary tradition. There were some other 'Romanised' settlements in the rural areas of the Moorish realms, as at La Ferme Romanette.[161]

Yet the Roman element of the Moorish polities was clearly not the only one. The kings also based their power on military force, which, it has plausibly been suggested,[162] was drawn from the tribes of the mountains and, increasingly, the desert. Alan Rushworth argues convincingly that this gave the Moorish kingdoms a similar 'bi-ethnic' character to those that emerged in post-imperial western Europe, with Roman taxpayers and barbarian, in this case Moorish, soldiers.[163] The Moors controlled the crucial meeting point between two dependent ecological zones: the transhumant pastoral and even nomadic societies of the pre-desert and desert and the more settled agricultural populations of the north. In controlling this area they limited the vital access of the pastoral nomads to the goods that they needed from the north, and posed as protectors of the latter from the depredations of the nomads. Other reasons for Moorish success suggest further parallels with the post-imperial world north of the Mediterranean. Although situated beyond the Empire's frontiers, the region's élites continued to be closely integrated into the Roman government and society. They were also given military responsibilities in the areas beyond the frontier, as shown by the inscriptions from Bir ed-Dreder attesting to a series of individuals bearing the title *tribunus*.[164] The withdrawal of Rome, whose presence, as has been

---

[160] Procopius, *Wars* 3.25.2–4.　　[161] Benseddik (1980).　　[162] Rushworth (2000).
[163] Rushworth (2000); (2004).　　[164] Modéran (2003b), p. 262; Rushworth (2002).

noted, was vital to the playing out of local politics in the African provinces, will have affected them less, as it did with the rulers of the western British highlands, possibly an instructive parallel. As the Vandal state failed to integrate the Roman population fully and to make its rule effective in the further reaches of the former provinces, the Moorish rulers were able to use their political and military power to move into this political vacuum, just as, perhaps, the highland rulers did in the British lowlands. There were, thus, a number of crucial factors that made these border kingdoms, like those of the British highlands and also perhaps like those barbarian polities just beyond the Rhine frontier, most able to profit from the collapse of the Empire. These Moorish kingdoms endured and they could become large-scale units. Military success could unite large areas and the structural advantages just delineated give some coherence to greater kingdoms so formed.[165] Indeed just after the end of our period it seems that Volubilis in modern Morocco was taken over by the rulers of Altava.[166] This would argue for a kingdom stretching 500 km from one of its key centres to the other and encompassing territory that the late Roman state had not felt able to govern. The coherence of such a realm is argued for by the fact that it was to put up more prolonged resistance to the Arab conquerors of the region in the late seventh century than either the Byzantine provinces to its east or the Visigothic kingdom to its north, across the Straits of Gibraltar.[167]

CONCLUSIONS

The collapse of the western Empire was felt in varying ways in diverse parts of the former *barbaricum*. The precise effects that these political events had seem to have been dependent upon the nature and extent of the contacts between the Empire and the different areas during the fourth century. Close to the frontier, in the territories of the Franks, Alamans or Moors, the crisis of *c.*380–420 appears to have had limited effects. As was suggested in chapter 4, the fourth-century relationships between the Empire and its neighbours seem to have brought considerable power to the rulers on the frontier. These were drawn slowly into the power vacuums developing in the northern provinces.

[165] Rushworth (2004), pp. 88–95 for further discussion of mechanisms of integration in these kingdoms.
[166] Rushworth (2000), p. 96.   [167] Modéran (2003b), pp. 685–810.

Evidence of social change and competition for power is more visible within the old Roman territories than beyond the *limes*. Nevertheless, changes were taking place. Beyond the Rhine, the appearance of Hunnic power as a force that could intervene in western barbarian politics produced tensions and change became more visible at the end of the century, when the final collapse of Roman rule inevitably brought the renegotiation of the bases of power. In the areas of *barbaricum* closest to the Rhine, however, it seems to have been the expansion of Frankish power at the very end of the fifth century and in the early sixth that produced the most far-reaching changes. In an analogous situation, Moorish rulers also expanded their power into the fringes of Roman territory as power vacuums emerged there. Their power appears to have been sufficiently established not to be weakened by the end of the Empire.

It seems to have been just beyond the frontier zones that the collapse of the symbiotic relationships between the Empire and the barbarians produced the most dramatic results. The barbarians who invaded the Empire in 405/6 came from this region. The homeland of the Saxons, similarly to be viewed as that bit further from the frontier – or at least separated from the Empire by a rather broader frontier, the North Sea – also saw important changes in the early fifth century. As a result, by the second half of the century a new political unit had emerged in the centre of the northern *barbaricum*: the Thuringian kingdom, bolstered by Hunnic support and by control of the Elbe trade-routes. The southern confederation of *Picti* was projected into this intermediate band by the relocation of the British frontier and the creation of a band of territory governed by British warlords between them and the new frontier line suggested here, and this caused similar fragmentation and upheaval.

The peoples further away from the Empire seem to have been less affected by the demise of Roman imperial power. In Scandinavia the changes in trade and other connections brought renegotiations, and the altering basis of political power was made manifest in changes in art-styles, but political authority continued to grow. Finally, the least affected areas were the far north of Britain and, possibly, Ireland. These regions had had less contact with the Empire than Scandinavia and were separated from the power vacuums of lowland Britain by the chieftains of the highland zone, possibly established with imperial support in the late fourth century. Unsurprisingly, the fall of Rome appears to have made little difference at all to society and politics here, although there may have been some effects in Ireland. The discussion of the *barbaricum* during the period of the Empire's collapse and in the half century after throws into sharp relief just how interdependent Roman and barbarian politics had been. This can be further explored through consideration of the mechanics of migration.

PART III

ROMANS AND BARBARIANS IN
A POST-IMPERIAL WORLD

13

MECHANISMS OF MIGRATION
AND SETTLEMENT

·

The historiographical trend of recent decades has been to downplay the scale of the fifth-century migrations. Changes once explained in terms of mass migration, linked to primordialist concepts of ethnicity, are now accounted for by appeal to shifts in identity, cultural assimilation or integration. Migration has, however, always had its die-hard defenders[1] and recently the opponents of those who minimise the scale of late antique popular movement have invoked so-called 'migration theory' in their defence. Migration theory comprises the results of comparative study of the mechanics of migration, generally in modern historical periods. Study of well-documented population transfer has sub-divided the phenomenon into different types of migration and has isolated a number of features that characterise and indeed determine the nature of the movement of people.

Migration may, for example, be long-distance or more local. It may be circular (or tethered), where individuals move – sometimes over considerable distances – during particular periods of a usually annual cycle before returning home. This might be to take

---

[1] E.g. Welch (1992). Trafford (2000) is a useful account of the historiography of approaches to migration in British archaeology. See also Anthony (1997); Chapman and Hamerow (eds.) (1997).

flocks or herds to new pastures (whether transhumance is usefully classified as migration is, however, arguable) or to take advantage of seasonal labour opportunities. Migrations can also be called chain migrations, where some groups move but retain links to their kin in their homeland, and are then followed to the new land by other groups within this network, who themselves retain similar ties, and so on. There is career migration. And so on. Migrations have been shown to possess common features. It is, for example, usual for small groups, 'scouts', to move to the new territory first and bring or send back information about conditions there. Indeed the flow of information between new settlements and homeland is crucial and means that the movement of people is almost never one-way. Even in migrations that cannot be classified as 'circular' there are always, to some degree, people moving back to the lands of origin as others leave home and seek new lives abroad. A particularly pertinent insight is that migrations do not operate as 'floods', washing over new territories. The information flow just mentioned tends to produce migration along specified routes to particular entry points. Migration theory also takes some care to analyse the relative importance of 'push' and 'pull' factors. Are migrations driven by pressures at home forcing people out, are the attractions of the new country more important, or do both types of factor work together? Transportation costs have been claimed to play a part, although their importance has been debated.

Groups of people *did* move in late antiquity and it is helpful to think about the mechanisms by which they did so. Nevertheless, there are problems. Migration theory, as adduced in discussions of late antiquity, is essentially a series of common historical and sociological observations about population movements in the more recent past and the modern world. It is difficult to class as theory and one suspects it has been brought into play by those who believe in significant population movement to counter the theory about identities and social practice employed by those who believe that the changes of the period were produced by internal social development. More to the point, the invocation of 'migration theory' has yet to be employed to explain anything.[2] It acts in some ways

---

[2] Scull (1998). Although presenting cogent and well-informed arguments, Hamerow (1997) and (1998) contain, as far as I can see, no theory at all, in spite of their titles. The argument was originally deployed in Hamerow (1994).

as a smoke screen, neither proving migration (or its scale), nor demonstrating how the newcomers interacted with the indigenous population to produce the material cultural traces revealed by archaeology or the ethnic shifts depicted in the documents. One still has to demonstrate migration from the archaeological data before hypothesising how it might have happened. If one penetrates the discussions of the ways in which people might plausibly have moved, we find that the archaeological evidence alleged to prove migration is still analysed in the old ways. Either it provides *prima facie* evidence of the movement of people or it does not. If the material data suggest the introduction of new elements from abroad, the discussion of whether they indicate migrants or assimilated natives rapidly retreats either to an array of unsubstantiated 'must have beens' or employs social theory, instrumentalism and so on. One area where this theory has been employed to slightly greater effect concerns the examination of the demographic make-up of cemeteries in the barbarian homelands.[3] Analysis of the age-profile of the deceased in the large cemeteries of northern Germany has been argued to show that some elements of society, especially younger adult males, who generally form the 'scouts' in migrations, were leaving the area. Nevertheless the evidence is too fragmentary and uncertain, especially in regard to precise chronology, to permit any conclusions from these analyses, no matter how plausible, to be more than suggestions.

It is valuable to consider how the evidence from the 'long fifth century' relates to these observations about migration. The relationships between the Empire and the *barbaricum* provide the essential context for population movement. The Empire had long provided careers for trans-Rhenan and other barbarians. Many returned home and used their service in the Empire as the basis for local standing.[4] Others stayed on to build lives in Roman territory. This 'career migration', some circular, some not, furnished much of the background information necessary for migration: the routes along which one could move, the contacts one might need, and the conditions and opportunities of service. Trade between the Romans and their neighbours also provided a background. Individuals knew of routes into the Empire and of political, economic and social opportunities there. Those who entered the Empire and returned

---

[3] Gebühr (1998).   [4] Above, pp. 57–8, 150–61.

home, however briefly, with information might be seen as the 'scouts' in this scenario.

The relationships between the Empire and the *barbaricum* also provide the context for the 'push' and 'pull' factors. The former would include local politics in the non-Roman territories. The bulk of those who moved into the Empire outside the framework of military service or economic exchange were, this book argues, those who lost out in struggles for political dominance, and their followers. Roman 'foreign policy' furnishes the background.[5] The Romans interfered in barbarian politics, offering substantial wealth in gifts to their supporters and underscoring the attractions of serving Rome and the expectation that Rome would support her friends if they lost out, adding closely interconnected 'pull' factors to the 'push' factor of local political defeat. The connections established by individuals' previous service inside imperial territory and the attractions created by the import of Roman goods, much used as status symbols in *barbaricum*, added further 'pull' elements into the equation.

A further 'pull' during the fifth century, again indistinguishable from certain 'push' factors, is found in the political vacuums that were created around the fringes of the Empire. As the imperial government lost its ability to make its writ run effectively in places like Britain, northern Gaul and Africa, local élites frequently turned to the barbarians for support. Indeed the crisis of the Empire around 400, undermining traditional bases of political authority and legitimacy through the Romans' failure to manage their 'frontier policy',[6] created the principal context for fifth-century migration: simultaneously a mix of 'push' and 'pull' factors.

The routes of migration into the Empire probably led through the established bridgeheads over the Rhine and Danube. That migrations follow this sort of route rather than flooding over a broad front is important here. In addition to the simple necessity of knowing the way in an age before maps, peaceful immigrants into the Empire needed to know where there might be a reception from previous migrants and thus a support network within Roman society. They will also have needed some guarantees of safety and official legitimation of their settlement; it is difficult to postulate how long the knowledge that such official procedures were no longer present on the Rhine and elsewhere would have taken to filter back to

[5] See further above, pp. 147–8.   [6] Above, pp. 207–11, 217–19, 251.

barbarian homelands. Even if, as one might suspect, this did not take long, it is unlikely to have resulted in an unrestrained wave of migrants entering the Empire anywhere and everywhere. As before, they needed to know the way into the Empire, they continued to require local support networks and they had to know where land was available for settlement. All of these things were easiest closest to the frontier and in areas where their settlement could be sanctioned by political authorities who were themselves of non-Roman origin. Thus it is not surprising that the areas where there is significant evidence of population movement are those close to the former frontier in the far north of Gaul and in Britain (viewing the North Sea as a frontier).[7]

Principal routes of migration within mainland Europe followed the same major rivers as provided the principal trade-routes. This does not seem to have been a new, fifth-century development; any third-century Gothic migration also followed the Vistula–Dniester amber route and the Lombards had followed the Elbe passage. The latter route from southern Scandinavia to the imperial frontier on the Danube seems to have been repeatedly followed. Information flowed in both directions along these arteries. In the fourth century, Černjachov glass was transported towards the Baltic just as Baltic amber was carried towards the Empire and it is clear that these two-way movements continued during the fifth century.[8] If Procopius can be trusted on the matter, there were still, for example, contacts between the Heruls of the Danube frontier and those of Scandinavia in the sixth century.[9]

Most importantly, this interchange of information between old and new territories must go far towards explaining the similar developments around the North Sea during the fifth century.[10] Here the analogies deployed by 'migration theory' do provide illumination. Ironically, though, rather than allowing the explanation of the visible transformations within the archaeological data purely as the results of migration (which is usually how advocates of this 'theory' have wanted to use them), it permits the possibility of a two-way information flow (especially when one considers the close fourth-century relationships between the areas on either

---

[7] Above, pp. 198, 386–7. [8] Above, pp. 381–2.
[9] Procopius, *Wars* 6.15.1–4, 6.15.27–36. [10] Above, pp. 386–92.

side of the North Sea) to account for changes partly at least in terms of influences from the former provinces.[11]

The diversity of relationships, in terms of their frequency and nature, between the Empire and the various areas of the *barbaricum* also helps us explain the differences in the nature, scale and effects of migration on the different frontiers, such as were discussed in the previous chapter.

ADMINISTERED SETTLEMENT: THE *HOSPITALITAS* QUESTION

'Is there any other point to which you would wish to draw my attention?'
'To the curious incident of the dog in the night-time'
'The dog did nothing in the night-time'
'That was the curious incident,' remarked Sherlock Holmes.[12]

The most important debate on barbarian settlement has been concerned with the so-called *hospitalitas* question. Historians had never been entirely happy with the idea that the barbarians simply ravaged, burnt and slaughtered their way through Roman Europe, killing landowners and seizing their estates, although that remained a popular vision. In 1844 a German historian called Theodor Gaupp challenged it in a book whose much abbreviated title translates as *The Germanic Settlements and Divisions of Land in the Provinces of the Western Roman Empire*.[13] Gaupp noticed that Visigothic and Burgundian laws talked about the division of the land into thirds, with barbarians holding some of these shares and Romans the others. Some Ostrogothic Italian texts also referred to *tertia* (thirds) and to *sortes* ('lots' or 'shares') held by Goths. A law in the Theodosian code, about billeting Roman troops upon civilian householders,[14] described a similar tripartite division, the civilian host apportioning his house into thirds, one of which was given to the soldier as his lodging. Gaupp proposed that the similarity in the fractions referred

---

[11] Procopius, *Wars* 8.20.1–41, records a story of a significant movement of *Angli* back to the former *barbaricum*.

[12] A. Conan Doyle, *The Adventure of Silver Blaze*, in *The Original Illustrated 'Strand' Sherlock Holmes. The Complete Facsimile Edition* (Ware, 1989), pp. 291–306, at pp. 302–3. I thank Hilary Dane for drawing my attention to this quote in relation to the historiography of the *hospitalitas* question.

[13] Gaupp (1844).   [14] *CTh* 7.8.5 (398).

to implied that the barbarians obtained Roman land through an extension of Roman billeting law. After all, the Goths and the Burgundians had not conquered lands in Gaul, but had been settled there by the Empire after suffering heavy defeats. Gaupp's insight was decisive in changing the way in which people viewed the change from Roman Empire to barbarian kingdoms and provided the foundation for all subsequent investigations of the Visigothic, Burgundian and Ostrogothic settlements.[15]

Nonetheless, there have always been historians who have not been convinced. How could the Roman Empire simply have given away one third of its landowners' estates, especially when in a position of military and political superiority? Why did the provincials stand for it?[16] Like Sherlock Holmes, such historians found the *lack* of contemporary evidence for shock, outrage or opposition curious. The dog had *not* barked in the night. In the 1870s Fustel de Coulanges proposed that what was granted away to the Visigoths and the Burgundians was not land but the *yield* of the land, the harvest. Fustel argued that barbarian soldiers who received lands and other resources via *hospitalitas* initially held these only as *possessiones*. In other words they could work, and enjoy the usufruct of, the lands, forests and so on, but they did not own them outright (they did not have *dominium* – ownership – of them).[17] Whilst envisaging the division of land, this system did not involve – at least in its first stages – actual expropriation. This attractive proposition received a formidable critique from Julien Havet.[18] Havet, simply enough, argued that the Burgundian and Visigothic laws talked unambiguously about land, not the fruits of the land. He also pointed out that laws allowing the reclamation of land after thirty (in some cases fifty) years if wrongly occupied could hardly refer to the back-payment

[15] E.g. Bury (1958), pp. 205–6 (originally published in 1923).

[16] Dahn (1899), pp. 273–5, was not alone in explaining the peacefulness of the Italian Ostrogothic situation by pushing the blame onto Odoacer. He argued, following Procopius, that the Goths had simply taken over estates whose 'Herulian' (i.e. follower of Odoacer) landlord had been killed in battle or murdered. He thought the situation in Gaul was much less harmonious. See also Dahn (1899), pp. 407–9. Fustel de Coulanges (1904), pp. 526–8, defended the provincials against the charge of cowardice or disloyalty.

[17] Fustel de Coulanges (1904) – the second edition of the work – p. 524, drawing upon Oros. 7.32.12.

[18] Havet (1878).

of thirty harvests. Havet repeated a point made by Gaupp that there might have been several stages to the settlement, including one where the barbarians were simply billeted upon the Romans, this arrangement only later being turned into the ownership of part of the estates. This subtle argument set out very clearly the principal objections to hypotheses that deny the actual expropriation of land. In many ways, later counters to such hypotheses only restate the points made by Havet.

Following this and other work, and persistent unease that up to two thirds of the land in the Visigothic, Burgundian and Ostrogothic kingdoms was granted away to barbarian settlers, the discussion of this problem tended to revolve around land-tenure and agricultural organisation. Hans Delbrück looked at the Burgundian evidence, which is the most detailed on the division of lands.[19] His analysis was spurred by his rejection of the idea that the barbarians were num-bered in tens or hundreds of thousands. He thought that they were armies of perhaps as few as 5,000 men.[20] Burgundian law stated that the Burgundians had two thirds of the land but only one third of the *mancipia* (slaves).[21] Delbrück was neither the first nor the last to wonder how or why this could be. His solution was that those Burgundians who shared estates with the Romans were the leading aristocrats alone, and that only large aristocratic estates were parti-tioned. There would, said he, have been little point in dividing small or medium estates, as this would have ruined Burgundian *and* Roman parties to the agreement. Though basing his argument on many traditional ideas about 'Germanic' society and the footloose, freebooting, martial nature of its manhood, Delbrück proposed that the Burgundian only needed one third of the slaves. He had to settle his followers on his share and the latter would equip and provision him when he went on campaign. Delbrück also argued that only individual estates were partitioned, and not necessarily the Roman aristocrat's entire patrimony. Thus, he claimed, a small number of people could be settled in the way discussed by the law, without the expropriation of two thirds of the whole of the land of Gaul or even of two thirds of all aristocratic estates. He explained the use of a two thirds fraction in Visigothic and Burgundian Gaul compared with

[19] Delbrück (1980), pp. 317–36 (German original published in 1921).
[20] Delbrück (1980), pp. 284–99: a vitally important discussion.
[21] *LC* 54 is the key text.

only one third in Ostrogothic Italy by the fact that Theoderic, unlike the Visigothic and Burgundian kings, also paid his troops a salary. Thus they needed less land. Delbrück proposed that the administrative offices necessary for the running of this military provisioning scheme became the organs of post-Roman government and thus the seeds of 'Germanic-Romanic political formation'.[22]

Ferdinand Lot also concentrated upon the detailed provisions found in the Burgundian *Book of Constitutions*.[23] He agreed with Delbrück that the estates partitioned could only reasonably have been those of the wealthy aristocracy and that the Burgundian 'guests' were the Burgundian upper class. He also followed Fustel in arguing that in the initial stages of the settlement the Burgundians received only the *possessio* and not the *dominium* of the estate, this situation gradually changing as the Burgundian kingdom became more established. Lot's addition to the debate was to envisage the partitioned lands as 'bipartite estates' along the lines of those known from the Carolingian period, with one half (*indominicata*: the demesne) worked by slaves and the other divided up into tenancies.[24] After various sums, Lot concluded that if the Burgundian received one third of the 'demesne' (and thus one third of the slaves) and two thirds of the tenancies then the puzzling discrepancy in the law began to make sense. A Spanish scholar, Alfonso García Gallo, extended Lot's argument to the Visigothic evidence, proposing that the divisions were intended to maintain overall parity in the revenues from the land.[25]

There, essentially, the matter rested[26] until the publication in 1980 of Walter Goffart's *Barbarians and Romans 418–584: The Techniques of Accommodation*. Goffart, like Fustel and others before him, was uneasy with the idea that the Romans had granted away up to two thirds of landed estates to the barbarians, meeting no appreciable resistance from the Roman landlords. He took Sherlock Holmes' view of this absence of incident. Goffart drew attention to the fundamental fact that the Roman law of *hospitalitas* said nothing at all about payment or salary, or even food, let alone land; it was only about billeting. Goffart had been working on the evolution of late

---

[22] Delbrück (1980), p. 329.   [23] Lot (1928).
[24] See, e.g. Verhulst (2002).   [25] García Gallo (1940–1).
[26] E.g. Ensslin (1947), pp. 94–7; Jones, A. H. M. (1964), pp. 249–53; Boehm (1998), pp. 56–7 (originally 1971); Musset (1975), pp. 214–18; Wolfram (1979b), pp. 275–86, 368–71.

and post-imperial taxation[27] and this formed the basis of his approach. Goffart's book is complex and subtle – more so than many critiques make it appear – and a brief résumé scarcely does it justice. After an extremely interesting historiographical survey of attitudes to the barbarian migrations, the book discussed Roman taxation and administration. Goffart pointed out that Roman taxation worked on the basis of notional units of assessment and revenue. Some late Roman officials were paid by being given drafts on taxation.[28]

Goffart began his discussion of the fifth-century settlements with the last, that of the Ostrogoths in Italy, rather than with the Burgundians (as had Gaupp, Lot and others). He did this for the sound reason that, whereas Burgundian law had the most detailed evidence for estate division, the Ostrogothic case was the only one where *contemporary* data for the mechanisms of settlement survives, in the letters of Cassiodorus and Ennodius. The Visigothic and Burgundian data were much later than the settlements themselves and in some cases demonstrably separated from the latter by one or more modifications of the original arrangement. Goffart opened by disregarding Procopius' account of the barbarians' seizure of one third of the land of Italy.[29] Procopius states fairly clearly that Odoacer had seized Italian land from the Romans in 476 and that it was passed on to the Goths when Theoderic took over Italy in 493. Goffart pointed out that Procopius is less than reliable when dealing with events in the west beyond his own experience, and indeed much of the relevant section of his *History of the Wars* is aimed at the justification of Justinian's wars of reconquest.[30] With Procopius' testimony – probably rightly – discarded, one could turn to contemporary writings, especially Cassiodorus'.

Goffart discussed two key references in Cassiodorus' *Variae*. The first was to the *illatio tertiarum*,[31] hitherto assumed to have been a tax of a third of the revenue of all land, paid by those who had not had one third of their estates allotted to a Gothic soldier. This, alongside actual expropriation, would have made the Gothic settlement a

---

[27] E.g. Goffart (1974).   [28] Goffart (1980), pp. 40–55. Cp. Goffart (1972).

[29] Goffart (1980), pp. 62–70.

[30] On Procopius see, above all, Cameron, A. M. (1985). Halsall (2002) for discussion of the ways in which Procopius ridiculed the barbarian rulers of the formerly Roman west. Liebeschuetz (1997), p. 145 and n. 41, attempts to counter Goffart's dismissal of Procopius.

[31] Goffart (1980), pp. 73–80. The *loci classici* are *Variae* 1.14 and 2.17.

crippling burden on the Italian aristocracy. Quite apart from Ennodius' and Cassiodorus' statements that the Gothic accommodation had not impoverished the Romans – statements that in the circumstances envisaged by earlier scholars would have constituted the most crass insensitivity – it is difficult to envisage the Roman élite maintaining its prosperity, as it clearly did under the Ostrogoths, in such conditions. Goffart proposed instead that the *illatio* was simply a third of the usual tax revenues, ear-marked for the payment of Gothic troops. The 'third' therefore referred not to a fraction of an estate but to the fraction of tax revenue diverted towards the payment of the Goths. The second term discussed by Goffart was *millenarii*.[32] In most earlier readings a *millenarius* had been assumed to be a commander of 1,000 men, or *chiliarch*. Indeed it often means this but Goffart pointed out that a *millena* was a notional Roman unit of tax assessment. Roman administrative practice had allowed the diversion of the revenues of such *millenae* to new purposes. A Gothic soldier received the tax revenue from a *millena*, collected from designated taxpayers, and became a *millenarius*.[33] Such Goths additionally received periodic donatives and other rewards from the king. Conflicts recorded in Ostrogothic sources could be shown to arise where a Goth was turning his right to receive tax into actual ownership of the land.[34]

From this basis, Goffart moved on to discuss the earlier Visigothic settlement.[35] The evidence is late and fragmentary, being contained in the late fifth-century *Code of Euric* (known only from a few fragments in later palimpsests and in presumed borrowings in other codes) and late sixth-century *antiquae* (old laws) contained in the Visigothic laws. *Euric's Code* apparently distinguishes between the *sortes* (shares) of the Goths and the third (*tertia*) of the Romans, which can be glossed with the aid of an *antiqua* on land division, referring to 'the two parts of the Goth' and 'the third of a Roman'.[36] These texts make clear that the *tertia romanorum* (the third of the Romans) was a fiscal resource. Gothic seizure of such *tertiae*

---

[32] Goffart (1980), pp. 80–8. The key text is *Variae* 5.27.
[33] Mommsen (1889), p. 499, nn. 3–4, had related *millenarii* to *millenae*. Lot (1928), p. 1003, and nn. 5–6, thought *millenarii* were officers. Generally, however, it had been assumed that a *millena* was a fixed amount of land.
[34] Goffart (1980), pp. 89–100.   [35] Goffart (1980), pp. 103–26.
[36] Key texts: *CE* 277; *LV* 10.1.8. Goffart (1980), pp. 118–23.

impoverished the fisc and Euric's legislation requiring such *tertiae* to be reclaimed no less than fifty years after their seizure (Roman law generally envisaged a cut-off point of thirty years for such litigation) made it likely, according to Goffart, that the law referred to a specific royal source of revenue rather than all the land of the kingdom of Toulouse.[37] The king, said Goffart, had retained one third of the tax revenue of the realm but distributed the other two thirds to his followers. Goffart suggested that the Roman landholding élite paid their tax directly to the king and thus retained a certain social and political privilege, whereas lesser taxpayers paid their tax to designated Goths. The use, sometimes darkly ironic, of the terms *hospes* and *hospitalitas* might have stemmed from the use by the administrators of the settlement of the old quartering system to assign Gothic soldiers to Roman taxpayers.

In the last section dealing with the fifth century, Goffart moved on to the Burgundian settlement.[38] Again, the evidence was legal and late, consisting of several clauses of the early sixth-century Burgundian *Book of Constitutions*, although some laws were earlier than the period of compilation. As mentioned, the situation revealed was complex. The key title, 54, of the *Book of Constitutions*, implies at least three stages through which the division of lands and resources had gone by the time the law was issued. This clause dealt with Burgundian *faramanni* (descendants of the members of the army which had moved to Burgundy[39]) who had seized lands and *mancipia* (Goffart translated this term as bondsmen) above and beyond an earlier royal grant of two thirds of the land (*terra, agri*) and one third of the *mancipia*. Gundobad also enacted that Burgundians were not to clear woods without the consent of the Romans. Romans were to have half of the woods, dwelling-places (*curtes*) and gardens (*pomaria*). This law, with its clear discussion of lands, fields, woods, clearings, courtyards, gardens and slaves, necessitated, not for the first time, an extremely convoluted argument and explanation.

Goffart began from a premise that the Burgundians had initially been granted half of the revenue from the land. He also drew

---

[37] The counter-argument, as in, e.g., García Gallo (1940–41), was that the law was dated to fifty years after the initial settlement. There might be something in this.

[38] Goffart (1980), pp. 127–61.

[39] Previous commentators like Delbrück and Lot had understood *faramannus* to mean the head of a clan. Goffart drew his interpretation from the studies of his student Alexander Callander Murray: Callander Murray (1983), pp. 89–97.

attention to the point, noted by Lot, that the law appeared to envisage a 2:1 ratio of *mancipia* to *terra*. As such a ratio was unlikely to have really existed throughout the kingdom, Goffart argued that *terra* meant a particular kind of land. *Terra*, he claimed, were 'arable lands declared for taxation' and the accompanying *mancipia* were 'publicly registered cultivators, slave or *coloni*'.[40] Thus Goffart argued that the original settlement had involved a division of the tax revenues of the land into two. The revenue from one half, comprising lands worked by 'declared cultivators' went to the king, whilst the other half, from those lands not worked by *mancipia*, went to the Burgundian army, the *faramanni*. Later, after the Burgundian civil war of 500, the Burgundians who had backed the winning side were rewarded with an additional sixth of the realm's revenue (a third of the remaining half), thus one third of the lands worked by *mancipia*. This led to the two thirds of the land and one third of the *mancipia* mentioned in clause 54 of the *Book of Constitutions*. The grant of *mancipia* also turned some Burgundians from collectors of revenue into owners of land. Thus it was only from this point, argued Goffart, that the sale of land to, and its inheritance by, Burgundians was legally recognised. A complicated argument about maintaining parity of liability and reward between Roman and Burgundian landlords explained the shares of woods and clearings. The division of houses and gardens was accounted for by a relocation of Romans and Burgundians within the general housing 'pool' rather than involving the actual partition of houses. This is the only point of Goffart's analysis where he discussed actual settlement, the dwelling-places rather than the salary, of barbarian settlers and indeed he had no choice. The law clearly talks of houses and gardens.

After summing up what *hospitalitas* meant in the fifth-century settlements, Goffart discussed the evidence relating to Lombard settlement in Italy, which does not concern us, and set out a summary of his conclusions. Goffart's interpretation has a number of advantages, not the least of which is simplicity. No longer need one envisage either the complex surveying of estates and their division into fractions or the acquiescence of the Roman land-owning class in the loss of a significant proportion of their patrimony.

Goffart's book revitalised discussion of the settlement of the barbarians and provoked immediate criticism as well as enthusiastic

---

[40] Goffart (1980), p. 137.

support. Within a couple of years of its appearance Maria Cesa penned what is still probably the most pithy and pertinent response, providing the ground-lines for all subsequent counters to the 'Goffart thesis'.[41] Cesa's critique, like Havet's of Fustel, rested upon one key pillar: most of the texts talk unambiguously about land, not tax or yield from land. Goffart's hypothesis required one to accept that the Romans had suddenly begun to use hitherto straightforward words like *terra* (land) as shorthand for 'arable lands declared for taxation',[42] apparently reading too much into fairly transparent vocabulary.[43] Cesa also argued that Goffart had not paid attention to the 'treaty of 382'[44] and pointed out that Philostorgius had referred to the grant of 'fields' to the Goths in the settlement of 419. Cesa herself preferred the reconstructions of Fustel and Lot.[45]

A lengthy and scholarly paper by Sam Barnish also argued against Goffart's reading of the Italian Ostrogothic material, not least Cassiodorus' writings, before making a survey of the evidence for barbarian settlers actually living on the land in western Europe.[46] Unlike Delbrück, Lot or García Gallo, Barnish thought that aristocratic lands had been exempt from partition, hence the absence of opposition in the sources. Other interpretations were also proposed, suggesting that the lands used were *agri deserti* ('deserted lands')[47] or that the Goths were settled in 419 as veterans, according to usual Roman practice.[48] Thomas Burns combined some of these points to argue that the Gothic settlement in Aquitaine represented the application to an 'interior province' of frontier district regulations about the payment and billeting of troops.[49]

Ian Wood confronted Goffart's thesis as applied to the Burgundians (in many ways the most problematic part of Goffart's book),[50]

---

[41] Cesa (1982).   [42] Similar points are made by Liebeschuetz (1997).

[43] Making Goffart's criticism of an alternative reconstruction by Ferdinand Lot as calling 'for *injunctio* to carry a technical sense that it does not have' (Goffart (1980), p. 96) somewhat ironic.

[44] Cesa (1982), p. 547.

[45] Later on she preferred reconstructions based on Roman law for the settlement of veterans: Cesa (1994a), pp. 171–2.

[46] Barnish (1986).   [47] Burns (1994), pp. 263–74.

[48] Mathisen and Sivan (1998), pp. 12–14; Sivan (1987). Burns (1992) argued that Goffart's view might be correct for Spain in 409–11; by 1994 he had completely changed his mind. For a forthright, no-nonsense rejection of Goffart's view, see Nixon (1992).

[49] Burns (1994), pp. 263–74.   [50] Wood (1990b), pp. 65–9.

arguing that the evidence does not allow us to interpret the Burgundian settlement as one whereby tax revenue was redirected to the barbarian troops. Goffart had over-simplified matters in his argument for specific meanings for words like *terra*. Wood argued that the terms *iure hospitalitatis* or *sortis iure* (by right of hospitality, or by right of *sors*) were synonymous and referred to a form of land holding that was similar to *possessio*. He also drew attention to Roman involvement in a major revolt against Gundobad, suggesting that acquiescence in expropriation was not universal. The dog *had* barked in the nighttime after all. Wood also very sensibly pointed out that the evidence as we have it is all rather later than the settlement of the Burgundians and repeated Goffart's point that there were several phases or stages before the early sixth-century situation, pertaining when the Burgundian laws were codified, was arrived at. Nevertheless he disagreed with Goffart's reconstruction of that process.

Goffart also found supporters, however.[51] The most significant of these was Herwig Wolfram.[52] Despite taking umbrage at Goffart's critique of Germanist historiography he found himself in broad agreement about the Visigothic settlement. Being unsure about Goffart's reconstruction of the Italian Ostrogothic evidence, Wolfram also made a number of important criticisms of the Goffart thesis. The first concerned the hierarchical nature of Gothic society. Wolfram found it hard to believe that *bucellarii* (bodyguards) such as are discussed in *Euric's Code*, would have been given shares of tax revenue just like their masters.[53] Like Cesa, he argued that Goffart had failed to take sufficient account of the 'treaty of 382' and the evolution in the status of *foederati* since then. In later editions of Wolfram's *History of the Goths* the Goffart model is accepted as relating to the Gothic settlements not only in Gaul but in Italy too.[54]

---

[51] See the standard British textbook on the early Middle Ages: Collins (1999), p. 206.

[52] Wolfram (1983).

[53] Differences in status are also highlighted by Pampliega (1998), pp. 193–7, who rejects Goffart. Pampliega's view sees these differences as relating to Gothic familial structure. The Goths who received lands were the heads of households. This owes much to old ideas of Germanic Hausherrschaft ('household-lordship'; Sp. soberanía doméstica).

[54] Wolfram (1988), pp. 222–31, 295–300. See, especially, p. 295, on Gaupp's view of the Ostrogothic settlement and developments of the traditional interpretation: 'this view is wrong'. Wolfram (1997a), pp. 112–16.

The most important development of Goffart's thesis was put forward by the French historian, Jean Durliat. Durliat was also interested in taxation and particularly in the continuity of Roman fiscal institutions through to the Carolingian period.[55] Durliat proposed that the levying of taxation to pay the barbarians was carried out by the cities of the Empire.[56] He argued that Roman tax law permitted the cities to keep one third of the taxation that they collected and to pass two thirds on to the imperial government. This, he claimed, lay behind the two thirds to one third split between Goths (or Burgundians) and Romans. The cities retained their third but passed two thirds on to the king of the Goths, who distributed this to his followers. The king of the Goths simply replaced the emperor. This thesis has received widespread criticism. Even Goffart was not convinced.[57] Liebeschuetz has argued that the texts refer not to imperial taxation but to the revenue from municipal lands.[58] The thesis does not seem to fit the Visigothic data in any case, where two 'thirds' (in whatever form) belong to the Goths and the Roman 'third' is a fiscal resource able to be granted away by the king. This would require the cities to pass on *all* revenues to the king. Furthermore it is fairly clear[59] that, even in the south, Gallic cities were no longer functioning like this in the fifth century.

A recent article entitled 'Neglected evidence on the accommodation of barbarians in Gaul' ran to barely three pages, neatly illustrating the fact that most of the evidence on this topic has been thoroughly worked over.[60] Yet it is important to take a stance on the mechanisms used to settle the barbarians. The debate cannot simply be ignored.[61] As Goffart pointed out, barbarians settled on the land by expropriating Roman landlords would have profoundly different relationships with the remainder of the population from those paid through the delegation of taxes.

Some objections to Goffart's thesis can nevertheless be dismissed straight away. Goffart discussed how the barbarians were paid, not where or whether they settled on the land. He admitted that the barbarians could have bought land separately from any arrangement

[55] Durliat (1990).   [56] Durliat (1988); (1997a).

[57] Goffart (1992). See also Wickham (1998) for devastating critique.

[58] Liebeschuetz (1997).   [59] Above, pp. 347–8.   [60] Wolfram (1997b).

[61] As Amory (1997), p. 95, n. 45: a lapse into laziness rightly castigated by Peter Heather (2003), p. 113, n. 81.

for their subsistence (and paid tax on them) and, importantly, that rights to tax revenues could be converted (sometimes by force) into land-ownership. Even leaving aside the severe difficulties in actually detecting non-Roman settlement archaeologically, to which Barnish paid insufficient attention (such difficulties had not been very clearly recognised in 1986), evidence of occupation by barbarians has no bearing on the thrust of Goffart's argument. If traces of barbarian settlements could be found we could not be sure whether the inhabitants lived off the surrounding lands because they had been granted them by the system of *hospitalitas*, or subsisted from the revenue from estates elsewhere, or had bought land but owned other estates or revenues somewhere else. Even in the Burgundian case study, where Goffart discussed the reordering of the housing stock, archaeological evidence would not prove the case one way or another. The barbarians had to live *somewhere*. In the current state of knowledge and interpretation, this is not a debate to which archaeology can meaningfully contribute.

The fifth-century evidence of the quartering of barbarian *hospites* (guests) on Roman landlords is also largely irrelevant. In all cases the sources discuss the billeting of troops in traditional fashion. Honorius' letter requiring troops in Spain to give thanks to their hosts before leaving does not 'provide a refutation of the theory of tax-credit quartering'.[62] These troops are temporarily billeted on householders in the usual way. They are not receiving lands *or* tax revenues. Nor, indeed, had Goffart ever proposed that Roman *hospitalitas* law (about the quartering of troops) had involved tax-credits. He said that it was about providing a roof over the soldier's head and occasionally warmth, in a way entirely consistent with Honorius' letter. Paulinus of Pella suffered because his house in Bordeaux did not have a barbarian 'guest',[63] but that was *before* the 419 settlement. Furthermore, Paulinus had left the area under a political cloud, having served the usurper Priscus Attalus, and his lands might have been confiscated. Paulinus held *dominium* of an estate in Marseille, of which someone else had *possessio*. Later, a Goth paid Paulinus for this farm (not, says Paulinus, what it was worth but a price all the same).[64] Again, it is clear that this evidence must be barred from the discussion of *hospitalitas*. It is pointless to dispute the fact that barbarians

---

[62] *Contra* Burns (1994), p. 268. For the letter, see Sivan (1985), p. 275.
[63] Paulinus of Pella, *Thanksgiving*, p. 254. [64] Paulinus of Pella, *Thanksgiving*, p. 261.

owned land but this does not seem to have anything to do with the partition of estates or revenues discussed in the legal evidence.

The evidence of Sidonius, most famously the poem in which he bemoans having to live alongside Burgundian troops (apparently in Lyon),[65] likewise refers to the straightforward quartering of allied troops. Nothing in Sidonius' account suggests a permanent arrangement and there is no hint that Sidonius lost more than convenience by the arrangement; indeed he seems rather to have gained an excuse for not doing any work. His tone is condescending to be sure, but he is certainly not writing about equal partners in his estate.[66] The same is true of his allegation that Seronatus had filled the *villae* of Aquitaine with 'guests'.[67] Other probably fifth-century evidence for quartering in the usual fashion may be found in Gildas' tract.[68] He says that the Saxons came as *hospites* and received *annonae*. All this is in keeping with traditional Roman billeting law and says nothing about the partition of estates. The grant of *annonae* suggests the normal workings of the Roman quartering system, as one might expect if the situation described by Gildas belonged to the late fourth century.[69]

The proposition by a number of writers that the barbarians received *agri deserti* is important in suggesting how land could be granted to newcomers but has no relevance to the sources discussed by Goffart. The point about *agri deserti* is that such lands had no owner listed in the tax registers. The Theodosian code makes it crystal clear that no one, other than the soldiers to whom the state granted these lands, had a right to consider themselves owners of *agri deserti*.[70] Thus the situation discussed in Visigothic and Burgundian law, of the partition of land between a Roman and a barbarian, cannot have pertained. Any counter to Goffart's thesis that maintains that a third of the land was granted away, and not a third of the tax revenue, must account for the legal data: that which discusses 'thirds'. In however tortuous and possibly unconvincing a fashion, Goffart's thesis at least does this. The theory about *agri deserti* does not. Nevertheless, that does not mean that the use of *agri deserti* played no role in the settlement of the barbarians. Burns' argument

---

[65] Sid. Ap. *Poems* 12.
[66] The point was made by Fustel de Coulanges (1904), pp. 524–5.
[67] Sid. Ap. *Letters* 2.1.3.   [68] *DEB* 23.   [69] Above, pp. 197–8; Appendix.
[70] *CTh* 7.20.11.

about the Gothic settlement is, overall, unpersuasive, being founded partly on beliefs that northern Gaul was still under effective Roman control and fully garrisoned, that the north of Gaul was so militarised that there were few civilians there and that the region had been heavily settled by barbarians from beyond the Rhine. There is little support for any of these suppositions. The second is most unlikely and the third is founded upon a misreading of archaeological cemetery evidence.[71] The explanations for the division of lands put forward by Lot and his followers, notably García Gallo for the Visigothic data, are ingenious and indeed seductive but suffer from the fact that bipartite estates of the type assumed to lie behind the provisions of the *Book of Constitutions* are not attested until the later Merovingian period and indeed seem to be a creation of that era.[72] Lot was led astray by a common assumption that there was a direct line of continuity between late Roman *latifundia* and the 'grandes domaines' of the later Merovingian and Carolingian centuries.[73]

Finally, it should be emphasised that Goffart does not simply say that if we understand 'land' to be shorthand for 'lands declared for taxation purposes' then all becomes clear. His argument is also aimed at explaining the curious proportions referred to in the sources and the relationships between different shares and Burgundian or Gothic royal government. Arguments that, however rightly, point out that the legal texts talk about land still have to explain some tricky issues about land tenure and taxation. The current state of the debate seems to be that whilst important problems have been pointed out in Goffart's hypothesis, no entirely satisfactory alternative has really been brought forward. One point that must be stressed, though, is that a return to the *status quo ante Goffartum* is not possible. Whether or not one accepts his detailed replacement thesis, Goffart irreparably torpedoed the idea that the Roman system of *hospitalitas* had anything to with land or property and thus served as the basis for barbarian settlement. Any attempt to re-board that venerable vessel can only lead to a watery historiographical fate.

Alas, the principal issue concerning the mechanisms of barbarian settlement outside Italy, one raised by Ian Wood, is that there is no real evidence. Visigothic and Burgundian law is much later than the date of the settlements and there is no way by which those laws

[71] Above, pp. 153–9.   [72] Verhulst (2002).   [73] Cp. Percival (1969).

can be made to refer to the original settlements. Thus, although
Goffart's critics are quite right in pointing out that the laws talk
more convincingly about land than taxation this has no necessary
bearing on the initial arrangement. This argument can be used in
defence of Goffart's hypothesis, as he himself used it, to propose,
plausibly enough, that an original distribution of tax credits had been
converted into land ownership by the time the laws were promulgated. However, the real point is that the late date of the legislation
cuts us adrift from any certainty about the settlements' original
terms.

In what follows I shall develop a number of themes that occur in
the works of earlier writers on this subject. We should not expect a
single explanatory model for the planned settlement of barbarians to
apply in all cases. Goffart was guilty of this expectation. His method
of working back from the Ostrogothic data to the other situations
was the major flaw in his argument. Why should the 419 Visigothic
settlement have followed the same lines as that of the Ostrogoths
seventy-four years later?

We must consider the different circumstances in which the
settlements were carried out. In 419 the Goths had been brought to
terms by Constantius and despatched on campaign in Spain, before
being withdrawn by the Romans and moved to Gaul. There is
nothing in this situation that suggests an agreement between equal
parties.[74] The Roman state clearly had the upper hand. The same
was also true in 443 when the Burgundians were transferred from the
middle Rhine and settled in *Sapaudia* but in 493, by contrast,
Theoderic was in a dominant position with a conquered Italy at his
feet. In addition to the relative power of the Roman and non-
Roman parties we must also consider the location of the settlement
in the context of the wider political situation. The Visigothic army
was moved to a fertile and strategically important part of the Empire
when the latter was on the offensive against non-Roman groups
and, as it seemed, on the way to restoring its authority over the west.
The systematic expropriation of landlords makes little sense here.
Indeed, given that there seems scant reason to suppose that the

---

[74] Here, although his discussion of the texts and riposte to Durliat are entirely
sound, I disagree with Liebeschuetz (1997), p. 147. The fact that even *foedera*-
philes like Wolfram admit that there may have been no treaty as such, rather than
a simple stationing of troops, is surely significant.

arrangement was intended to be permanent,[75] the idea that the barbarians were generally settled on lands at all seems unlikely. This argument, however, runs up against Philostorgius' reference to the barbarians being given land to farm. Nevertheless, this evidence can be incorporated.[76]

In the 440s the political situation was different. There is clearer evidence to suggest a retrenchment by the Empire in the south of Gaul. We might doubt that the imperial authorities had given up hope of restoring their power in the north of Gaul and even beyond, but a policy of defending a line across the middle of Gaul using the settlement of barbarian troops seems clear. By the 440s, too, the military situation had altered, not least with the establishment of the Vandal kingdom in Africa. As well as northern Gaul, almost all of Spain now lay outside imperial government so the Empire's recruiting and tax base was limited. Not only were troops now required to defend Italy, but there were also fewer of them. In this situation the redirection of revenues, given the Empire's shrunken tax base, seems far less likely. We should also consider the location of the settlement. The Burgundians were settled, like the Alans around Auxerre at about the same time, on land not effectively governed by the Empire. This land could be given away to support non-Roman forces without weakening the Empire politically or reducing its revenues. Given that some of these territories were regarded by the central government as being in revolt against them, this use of the land as a reward for the Burgundians, bringing it under the control of Roman troops made further sense. Finally, in 493, the situation was different again, with the seizure of political control of Italy by Theoderic. With the barbarian group holding the political advantage, in this case alone of the three a permanent arrangement

[75] Again I differ from Liebeschuetz (1997), pp. 139–41. I find no reason to see the arrangement of 419 as intended to be long lasting: above, pp. 228–33. Liebeschuetz's argument that it was meant to be permanent because it lasted whereas earlier pacts had collapsed because they had not been set up to be enduring is teleological. There is also an element of circularity: the barbarians must have been given land because it was a permanent agreement; it must have been a permanent agreement because they were given land. Bleckmann (1997) is more persuasive.

[76] Goffart (1980) p. 104, n. 2, discounted Philostorgius on the reasonable grounds that his report is removed by at least two stages from his source for these events, Olympiodorus. Nevertheless we should propose an explanation that accounts for all the scanty evidence, rather than explaining away those elements that do not fit.

was presumably intended. With these differences in context there is no reason why the mechanisms used in one case should have been applied in the others.

The terms of the settlement of the Visigoths in Aquitaine must be seen in the context of Constantius' campaigns to restore the western Empire's authority throughout Spain, Gaul and perhaps beyond. In 418 the campaign to eliminate the barbarians in Spain was going well and Exuperantius' troops were restoring imperial authority in northern Gaul and perhaps even Britain. All this makes it appear that the movement of the Goths to Aquitaine was a temporary expedient, providing troops that could be transferred on 'interior lines' to either theatre of conflict without threatening key strategic communications routes and, at the same time, secure a potentially rebellious province.[77] So, how were Wallia's and Theoderic I's troops settled in Aquitaine? Goffart's thesis finds important support in the Theodosian code. Book 7, chapter 4 contains a series of laws concerning the payment of the army. In this sequence, which clusters in the 390s, troops are condemned for going to civilians and extorting money instead of the supplies (*annonae*) that are due from the latter. Not only that; they were setting their cash alternatives at very high prices.[78] Soldiers bore *delegatoria* – documents delegating tax revenue – assigning them to taxpayers from whom they collected their supplies.[79] By the early fifth century, rather than outlawing the commutation of supplies into money altogether, the law simply said that the troops should demand a fair price.[80] Whether these assignments of taxation were made on an individual (in which case the billeting systems of *hospitalitas* could indeed provide a framework) or a collective, regional basis is not clear. Nevertheless, Roman troops were assigned to taxpayers who paid them a cash sum as a draft on taxation. This looks remarkably like the system envisaged by Goffart.[81] If the Goths formed an army, we can see how the bulk of Gothic troops could have been stationed in Aquitaine and initially paid in drafts on taxation, much as Goffart proposed.

---

[77] Above, pp. 230–2.   [78] *CTh* 7.4.20.
[79] *CTh* 7.4.22. Goffart (1980), p. 89 for *delegatoria*.   [80] *CTh* 7.4.28, 30–1, 36, etc.
[81] Esp. at Goffart (1980), p. 89. In certain cases, such salaries could be passed on to heirs: *CTh* 7.4.34. It is difficult to know why Goffart did not make more of this evidence. Perhaps this stems from the fact that the barbarians were still seen as quasi-autonomous tribal/military forces rather than, as is more frequently the case today, in the context of the Roman army.

Nevertheless, one fragment of Olympiodorus' history, copied by Philostorgius and preserved in the tenth-century Byzantine anthology the *Suda*, is clear about the Goths being given Gallic lands to farm (*ton Galaton choras eis georgian*).[82] Some of the *Chronicles* hint at the same thing, though with less clarity.[83] We must return to the nature of the Goths themselves and the differences within the army. The differences I would draw attention to are based not upon social rank or the headship of households, but age. The force led by Wallia and Theoderic in 418/19 was descended from that which had found itself in the political cold under Alaric in the mid-390s. It had thus been in the field intermittently for about twenty-five years (coincidentally the length of legionary service). It would hardly be surprising if some Goths now wanted to settle down. The legislation about land for veteran soldiers and the use of *agri deserti* might validly be applied to these. This mixture of normal Roman payments to troops and the rewards for veterans seems plausible in the context of 419 and accounts for the language used in the narrative sources to describe the settlement.

What it does not account for is the situation described in the Visigothic laws. This evidence discusses lands and other resources being divided between Goths and Romans. Even using Goffart's line of argument about the conversion of drafts on taxation into ownership of land, it is difficult to derive this situation neatly from that just proposed, not least because it appears that the Romans retained civil control over *Aquitania* II in 419. It does not seem that the king of the Goths received all of the province's tax revenue to distribute to himself and his followers on a 1:2 ratio at this stage. As with the Burgundian situation, the original settlement is separated from the legal evidence not simply by the passage of time but also by a complex political history. There were a number of stages at which the Goths could have altered the terms of their settlement, especially as it became clear that this was not after all going to be a temporary expedient. Warfare between 426 and 436, perhaps more prolonged

---

[82] Olympiodorus, fr. 26.2.

[83] Hydatius 61; Prosper, *Chron.* AP 392 (=419). These references, to land *ad habitandum* ('to live in') and to *sedes* (seats) are less conclusive. I am less inclined than Wood (1998a), p. 523, to place heavy weight on their testimony. Some of the references he cites are to settlements, such as those of the Alans, Burgundians and Vandals, which were in very different circumstances from the Gothic settlement in Aquitaine.

than the sources suggest, as well as periods when the Roman government was prevented by its own civil wars from intervening in Aquitaine, provide contexts for change.[84] At any of these points the king of the Goths could have appropriated the tax-revenues of *Aquitania* II. There were also periods of warfare or hostility between 436 and the promulgation of the laws during Euric's reign (467–84), when Gothic control over land and resources could have been extended, and periods when the support of the Goths might have been bought by the Empire with additional privileges.

However, the treaty of 439 seems to have been a particularly important moment.[85] The only way of linking the original settlement with the laws, however tenuously, is to assume that the provision in *Euric's Code* allowing Roman *tertiae* occupied by Goths without royal permission to be recovered after fifty years means that the law was issued fifty years after the settlement.[86] Goffart argued that the length of this time-limit related to the special nature of the resources rather than to the date of the grant. He was surely right that Euric was protecting a royal or fiscal resource by this provision but the length of the time-span was surely chosen for specific reasons. We must consider not only the fifty-year time-limit for litigation about land seized from Romans without a royal grant, but also the usual thirty-year limit, which Euric confirmed for litigation about other land and *mancipia*.[87] It would be odd if Euric's provision allowing him to reclaim illegal seizure of Roman *tertiae* after fifty years were issued in the fiftieth year since the grant; surely the king would give himself more than a year's leeway in which to act! On the other hand Euric acceded almost thirty years after the treaty of 439 and, as noted, thirty years was the usual cut-off point for litigation about illegal seizure of land. In his code Euric seems to have been acting promptly and decisively. Whilst writing off other seizures before the treaty of 439 and progressively those since that event, he extended the usual time-limit to allow himself the right to recover any lands in the gift of the king, which had been seized without royal permission in previous reigns. This gave him the freedom to maintain control over a specific type of fiscal landed resource for the foreseeable future. The reference to the confirmation of a law of his father (Theoderic I, who signed the

---

[84] Above, pp. 245–6.   [85] Above, pp. 246–7.
[86] As, e.g. García Gallo (1940–1). Above, n. 37.   [87] *CE* 277.

treaty of 439) might strengthen this reading. The treaty of 439 was probably of more importance to the creation of the Gothic kingdom in Aquitaine than has often been appreciated.[88] This interpretation of *Euric's Code* would support that argument. It seems to have been from that date that the kings of the Goths began to have control over the distribution of lands to their followers.

The law suggests that these lands were, or could be, divided in such a way that a Goth received two thirds and the Roman one third. There is no suggestion anywhere that this split was universal throughout the kingdom or that the whole of a Roman landlord's patrimony was so partitioned, rather than just individual estates. Neither is it stated that *all* Goths have such a share in an estate, or that there were not other landholding and tenurial arrangements, with Goths owning whole estates outright. Nor is it claimed that these estates furnished a Goth's only means of support. What is under discussion in the first section of chapter 277 of *Euric's Code* is a specific type of land, one with a direct relationship to the king. In this sense Goffart seems to be correct. These divided estates could have been fiscal lands or confiscated from Roman landlords who had sided against the king, the king retaining one third (the 'Roman third'). The treaty of 439 is a plausible context, coming after a decade of weak Roman control over Aquitaine, in which fiscal resources (land and revenues) could have been formally ceded, alongside civil government, to the Gothic king. By this time, too, even the youngest of the warriors who had arrived with Theoderic I in 419 would have wanted to settle down. It is also possible that any original arrangements for the payment of the Goths through the usual means (as above) would have broken down, perhaps because of the intermittence of Roman administrative control, or that Goths had been converting such rights into the ownership of property and buying estates (like Paulinus of Pella's) elsewhere. The time was right to re-establish a formal and orderly system of rewarding the king's followers. It was important for Euric, however, to retain control over this resource. If this hypothesis is correct, the constantly evolving situation in Aquitaine, with varied means of paying and rewarding the Goths gradually changing with political circumstances and especially in times of conflict, makes the absence of protest by Roman landowners explicable. As has been pointed out before, the

[88] Above, pp. 246–7.

absence of evidence is rarely fortuitous. The dog's failure to bark was indeed a curious incident, even if not for quite the reasons that Goffart supposed.

In some ways the settlements of the Burgundians and Ostrogoths in Sapaudia and Italy are easier to explain from the evidence. The Burgundians, like the Visigoths, were settled in Sapaudia after a defeat by the Romans but, as mentioned, the political situation had changed and their settlement was located on or even beyond the frontier of the territories still governed by the Empire.[89] The evidence relating to their initial settlement is much later than the relevant period and clearly refers to a series of changes that had taken place since the original terms were established. Goffart's hypothesis should not be ruled out but it is clear that even the earliest situation described in the laws relates to the division of lands rather than revenue. This is easier to understand. The Empire had less to lose in such regions by granting away such land and less ability to organise and manage the redirection of tax revenues in areas which were in all probability not producing much fiscal income by the 440s in any case. Here the division of lands seems like the simpler solution, as long as we bear in mind the caveats above, that not all Gallo-Romans had their estates partitioned and that not the whole patrimony of a Gallo-Roman aristocrat was so divided. The reference to the Burgundians taking over lands in alliance with the local senators should imply some collaboration between the Romans and the Burgundians.[90] Indeed the senators of the region seem to have acted in concert with the Burgundians throughout. The obvious problem here, of landowners dispossessing themselves, is circumvented if one follows Wood in arguing that *ius hospitalitatis* was a form of tenure, which left eminent possession in the hands of the Roman landlord.[91] It is also, however, very possible that in this situation the lands partitioned belonged to the less powerful landowners of the region. The law stating that Burgundians should not take their share of lands, woods and so on in areas where they had been granted *hospitalitas* looks like a straightforward law about billeting.[92] Burgundians (who constituted the army) should not take shares of lands in areas where they were billeted. This would impose a double burden on the local population and the Burgundians should

---

[89] Above, p. 248, for the context.   [90] Marius of Avenches, *Chron. s.a.* 456.
[91] Wood (1990b), pp. 65–9; (1998a), p. 523.   [92] *LC* 54.1.

live off their own resources in areas where they did hold their shares. It might also be an injunction against the sorts of abuse that Goffart envisaged, whereby barbarian troops turned temporary grants of one sort into permanent possessions of another.

The involvement of Roman landowners in the Burgundian civil war of 500, however, cannot be read as an instance of 'the dog barking in the night'.[93] This was not a rebellion against oppressive Burgundian land seizures. Instead it was, again, an alliance of Roman landowners with the Burgundians, in this case supporting one political faction against another. In the aftermath, according to Gregory of Tours, Gundobad issued laws to stop the Burgundians oppressing the Gallo-Romans.[94] Even if there is any truth in this – and it may reflect no more than the fact that even by Gregory's day Burgundian law was known, erroneously, as *Lex Gundobada* – it does not support the argument that this rebellion was against barbarian seizure of lands. After all, the rebellion was against the Gundobad who, allegedly, stopped the oppression. There is no way that this evidence can be made to fit a model of Roman resentment at the rapacity of land-hungry barbarians.

Finally, we come to the Ostrogothic situation. Here, although debate continues, Goffart's interpretation finds its clearest support. The *millenarii* do seem to be holders of *millena* rather than commanders of a thousand and the Gothic 'thirds' to represent the diversion of a portion of tax revenue from land that Goffart envisaged.[95] Theoderic also paid his troops periodic donatives on top of this salary. It was the reviews of his troops at which this was paid that enabled him to subject the Goths to his ideological campaigns and distribute his patronage. This does not rule out the distribution of land as well, however. As king, Odoacer had, one imagines, held lands (not least those of the imperial patrimony), as had his chief followers. A papyrus document from the reign of Valentinian III refers to the *fiscus barbaricus* (the barbarian fisc), which presumably refers to some sort of land for the (increasingly barbarised) army.[96] These and those of any Italian supporters who had stayed with him to the end would have been confiscated by Theoderic during the purge of early 493 and redistributed to his men. After the war against

---

[93] Halsall (2003a), p. 43.   [94] *LH* 2.33.

[95] Heather accepts this interpretation: (1996), p. 242; (2003), p. 113.

[96] Cesa (1994b), p. 310.

Odoacer, Theoderic had threatened to remove citizenship and all powers of testamentary disposition (i.e. their ability to leave lands by will) from those of the Italian senatorial nobility who had not supported him.[97] This would, had he ever been able to pull it off, have given him the power to grant or regrant their land as he saw fit. It was presumably never more than a bluff but some have seen this intimidation as explaining why the Italian landowners acquiesced in a loss of a third of their lands to the Goths: at least it was better than the potential complete disinheritance of their children. This seems unlikely; it is doubtful that Theoderic could have implemented his threat and retained any sort of authority, though he could have made life very unpleasant for the senators. Nevertheless it surely inclined the Italian nobility towards acceptance of whatever confiscations took place at the expense of the ringleaders of Odoacer's faction.

The objections to Goffart's thesis that stress the internal hierarchies of the Goths have a role to play here. There were, as Heather has argued, potentially dangerous Gothic noble groups within the Goths that had, at least in the early phases of Theoderic's rule, to be kept loyal. One imagines that grants of estates would satisfy such people rather more than the simple grant of a salary or pension from the Italian tax revenue. As with the Visigoths, age too must have played some part. Many of Theoderic's Goths had been with him for twenty years by the time he became king in Italy. Such old warriors would have been looking for land to settle down upon. It is worth repeating what Goffart said, that the salary provided from Italian tax revenues gave the Goths the wherewithal to buy land for themselves – he never denied that Goths owned land. This too must have increasingly played a part as time wore on and more of the Goths grew old and wanted estates to retire to and raise their families upon. There would also, as Goffart imagined, have been opportunities for Goths to turn tax *delegatoria* into outright land-ownership, even if this was viewed as illegal by Theoderic's court. One should not lose sight of the dynamics of the situation; whatever happened in the immediate aftermath of 493 did not represent the end of the story. Similarly, when Theoderic disposed of opponents later in his reign there would, again, have been lands to redistribute. Although, especially as the reign progressed, more and more Goths will have become landowners within Italy, it does seem that the principal means by

---

[97] Ennodius, *Life of Epiphanius* 122.

which a salary was found for the Ostrogoths was by paying them from the tax registers. It is very likely that there was an initial seizure of land by Theoderic, such as is referred to in some of the sources, but the evidence does not allow us to say that a grant was made to all Theoderic's followers.[98] The implications are that as far as most Goths were concerned – especially the younger ones – it was tax, not land, that provided the bulk of their salary.

How the groups of fifth-century barbarians not discussed by Goffart were settled is difficult to say. The Vandals famously held their *sortes vandalorum*, which could refer to heritable shares of the taxation *professiones* of North African landowners or to landed estates. Modéran has argued strongly for the latter, although Schwarcz has presented persuasive counter-arguments in favour of the Vandals dwelling in towns as garrisons and being paid for by tax revenues.[99] Overall, though, it seems that, here too, the evidence points best towards a mixture of solutions: the ruling strata of the Vandals, aristocracy and church, acquired lands, often by dispossessing Roman landlords. Other, particularly older, Vandals bought lands or were granted them on retirement. Others again, especially the younger ones, probably lived in garrisons and drew a salary. As elsewhere, though, this situation contained within it the seeds of development and change so that by the sixth century it is quite likely that many if not most Vandals had settled on the land. The furore and even open mutiny that stemmed from the claims by those eastern Roman soldiers who had married Vandal women to be able to inherit the *sortes vandalorum* might make more sense if these are viewed as, by this date, permanent landed resources. This does not imply that this had always been the case.

The Franks have generally been left out of the debate on *hospitalitas*. Yet there is some evidence that the Goffart model might have applied, at least in part, to them. The patchy documentary record and the archaeology of sixth-century cemeteries suggest that the Franks formed the army in northern Gallic society and politics, just as the Goths and Burgundians did in southern Gaul, Italy and Spain. It is clear from Gregory of Tours' writings that the Franks continued the Roman practice of paying their administrators with drafts on taxation.[100] An argument can be made that *villae* in the sixth-century

---

[98] As does Heather (2003), p. 114.   [99] Modéran (2002b); Schwarcz (2004).
[100] *LH* 7.23.

Merovingian world were fiscal assets rather than unitary landholdings.[101] This might have facilitated their granting by, and reabsorption into, the fisc, something that seems to have been done regularly and with some ease in the sixth century. There is evidence that the Franks considered themselves free from at least certain forms of taxation. It seems that Frankish tax-exemption related to the poll tax (*capita*) and perhaps to the land tax when applied to certain types of estate, but that the Franks felt that this should be extended to all their landholdings. The kings, meanwhile, attempted to preserve their right to tax these lands.[102] By the time our evidence begins to survive, later in the century, it might be that individual grants of tax revenues had frequently been turned into landholdings. Around 600 it can be argued that earlier grants of the tax revenues from *villae* were transformed into actual ownership of the land.[103] On the other hand, the famous clause 59.6 of the *Pactus Legis Salicae*, postponing the inheritance by women of 'Salic land', might be understood as referring to a category of land reserved for military settlers.[104] This is a plausible argument and would suggest that Frankish warriors were granted lands rather than shares of taxation. Given the breakdown of Roman government north of the Loire this would seem to be more than likely. Nevertheless it is clear that taxation still existed in the region in the later sixth century and the precise meaning of 'Salic land' (*terra salica*) is debated. Rather than referring to the land of the Salian Franks, it might refer to the land around the *sala* or the main family homestead, a reading strengthened by the fact that the corresponding clause of seventh-century Ripuarian law refers to 'ancestral landed inheritance'.[105] In fact it has been argued that the word *salica* was only inserted into the law in later recensions,[106] at about the same time as Ripuarian law was issued.

The paucity of early sixth-century evidence from northern Gaul, however, means that it is difficult to be definitive about this situation. We might envisage a similar mixture of salaries from taxation and the grant of lands to that we have seen elsewhere.

---

[101] Halsall (1995a), pp. 188–98, 253. Durliat (1990), esp. pp. 152–6, although I do not accept all of his reasoning. See also Goffart (1982) for Merovingian taxation.
[102] *LH* 3.36, 7.15. Halsall (2003a), pp. 46–7.   [103] Halsall (1995), pp. 48–9, 263.
[104] Anderson, T. (1995).   [105] *Lex Ribv.* 57.4; Halsall (1995a), pp. 65, 67, and refs.
[106] Callander Murray (1983), pp. 201–15.

Given the Merovingian power-base in the Loire army it is likely, perhaps especially in the context of the break-up of Roman government, that the payment of the troops took place by an extension of late Roman legislation granting heritable *delegatoria* of the tax-bills of specified landowners to soldiers. In time these might have been converted into landed possessions. As soldiers grew older and wished to settle down we should envisage the use of the Roman system of land grants to veterans. If there was a continuation of the Roman situation where liability for military service was inherited, such as we might expect as military service and ethnic identity fused, then these lands would be held by later generations in return for military service. Age, the life-cycle and the dynamics that it gave to the nature of barbarian settlement have not been given enough prominence in discussions of this problem. This is a shame, as within it lie the keys to the process of how professional Roman armies were transformed into groups of landowners.[107] It certainly represents a subtler and more plausible reading of the situation than those which see large-scale social conglomerations, be they armies or (with less plausibility) peoples, sharing unified and coherent long-term aims and objectives and deciding *en masse* to become landowners.

The only area so far excluded has been Britain, where there is no very good evidence to confront this problem. Gildas portrays the rebellion of the 'Saxons', which we have placed in the 420s/430s, and their seizure of land as stemming from the Britons' inability to continue to pay their *annonae*. This would be plausible at that date, in the context of lowland British socio-economic collapse. Here we might see the forced conversion of the Roman systems whereby troops were paid from tax revenues into the occupation of landed estates. That apart, we have only the archaeological cemetery evidence that suggests that the Anglo-Saxons formed a broad military stratum within society.[108]

SETTLEMENT

The discussion of other means by which the barbarians settled within the former provinces of the Empire is very difficult. The

---

[107] The process is mapped in some detail in Halsall (2003a), pp. 40–70, but with surprisingly little attention being given to this vital factor.
[108] Below, p. 476.

problems of detecting the barbarians archaeologically, which have been repeatedly touched upon,[109] make traditional means of plotting 'barbarians' and 'Romans' from the evidence of cemeteries, especially, and settlements extremely implausible.

Another avenue employed has been that of place-name studies. The distribution of place-names with Germanic components, and which are believed to be early, can be plotted to show where barbarian incomers occupied land.[110] Similarly the spread of Germanic names for topographic features like rivers and hills can also be mapped to suggest areas where the Germanic-speaking barbarians became a dominant element of the local population (not least because the names for such features tend to be far more conservative than those of settlements).

Alas there are numerous methodological problems. The most important of these is the fact that we simply have too little linguistic and toponymic (place-name) evidence from the immediately post-imperial era. Charters and other documents that discuss and describe the landscape do not become common before the seventh century. They are in no sense numerous before the eighth and, ironically, even then most of the significant bodies of evidence relate to areas that had partly lain outside the Empire – as in the case of the monastic cartulary of Lorsch in southern Germany, which contains thousands of documents. In most cases the evidence upon which very early medieval place-name theories are founded is later still – the Domesday Book in England, for example. Chronologies of place-names founded purely upon philological theories can never be hard and fast, as is shown by the fact that some reverse the relative chronologies of others.[111] It seems that there were micro-regional preferences for particular toponymic forms, all of which seem, rather than having clearly different technical meanings, simply to be general words for 'settlement'.[112] Chronologies based around the date of earliest 'English' (or other barbarian) settlement are dependent upon the problematic ethnic readings of this data discussed above, and so cannot stand.

Another problem is that, rather than having technical meanings in Germanic languages, place-names could well be phonetic alterations

---

[109] Below, pp. 466–8 for summary.   [110] Gelling (1997).
[111] Gelling (1978); (1997). See also the discussion in Wood (ed.) (1999), pp. 90–4.
[112] See Halsall (1995a), pp. 10–12, and fig. 1.4.

of pre-existing Latin place-names. This book was mostly written in York, a city whose modern name is a contraction of Yorvik. Although Yorvik can be rationalised as a Danish word describing the site's location, it is in fact a corruption of the Anglo-Saxon word for the town: Eoferwic. Eoferwic in turn is a development from Evrawg, the Brythonic version of Eboracum, the Roman name for York (following characteristic late Latin linguistic changes, such as the softening of *b* to *v* and the loss of the word's final syllable).[113] How many other apparently non-Roman place-names with less complete records than York's represent similar phonetic translations and rationalisations? Gregory of Tours records a council at *Belsonancum* and a royal palace at *domus Mariligensis* or *Marilegio villa*.[114] The latter has become Marlenheim, explained as 'the Germanic man's name Marila, plus the Germanic 'heim', or village'[115] and the former Breslingen or Besslingen, equally a Germanic place-name. Yet, their earliest forms could both be corruptions of Latin names: Belsonacum and Marilacum. Certainly, neither has the *-ing* or *-heim* suffix, again suggesting that precise relative chronologies for such place-names are problematic.

In areas on the modern linguistic frontier, like modern Lorraine, place-names can be observed through more modern periods shifting back and forth from Germanic to Romance forms in line with political change or the language of a document's author. For example, one settlement's name alternates between Thionville and Diedenhofen. In this case, the place-name's ending changes according to French or German words for a settlement (ville, from *villa*, and Hof, meaning farm) but leaves the stem the same. Although this stem is believed to be a Germanic personal name (Theodo – the earliest [eighth-century] recorded form is *Theodonis Villa*[116]), such stems might be rationalisations of earlier non-Germanic personal or place-name elements (as in the York example).

As far as this volume is concerned, all the place-name evidence shows us is where, by whatever date the evidence becomes plentiful (and that is usually centuries after the fall of the Empire), Germanic

---

[113] Hills (2003), p. 53, uses the same example to make the same point.

[114] *LH* 9.21, 9.38, 10.18.   [115] Dauzat and Rostaing (1963), p. 436.

[116] *Theudone villa* in a charter of 770: Halsall (1995a), pp. 211–12. The 'Theud' component might just, however, be a corruption of the 'diut' component of the Roman place-name Adiutex, known just across the Moselle.

languages had come to dominate an area's place- and/or personal names. In many ways these patterns are hardly astonishing, mainly clustering in a belt along the former Rhine frontier and in lowland Britain where one might expect, from the discussion at the start of this chapter, that communities of immigrants might be formed and where newcomers might in turn be drawn.

It has been proposed that migration can be demonstrated via the study of the actual remains of early medieval people.[117] In the nineteenth century the skulls of the deceased were measured to elucidate their 'Germanic' or Roman origins.[118] This is deeply problematic, assuming that ethnic groups are physically distinct 'races', yet it has, alas, never really gone away.[119] Recently it has been proposed that the stature of weapon-bearing males in Anglo-Saxon cemeteries indicates a physically distinct incoming group.[120] This has been controversial; the argumentation is unconvincing and has been seriously challenged by subsequent studies. Other studies of dental evidence have equally suggested that there were no significant differences or changes within the skeletal remains of the post-imperial population of Britain. Results have been similar in France,[121] though the suggestion that no change in physical anthropology indicates no migration is, of course, the photographic negative of the argument that migration would be proven through skeletal differences. Another possibility is the study of stable isotope analysis of teeth. It is suggested that the geology of the regions where an individual grew up can – via the water supply – be reliably detected in the tooth enamel of the deceased. This probably has the most potential for showing the origins of the early medieval dead, although one imagines that it will need many, many more samples and close consideration before detailed conclusions are possible. Some that have been suggested so far, such as the identification of western Scotland as the origin of the occupant of an 'Anglo-Saxon' burial in Bamburgh,[122] are quite unexpected, which ought to mean that someone is doing something right!

[117] On this issue, Hills (2003), pp. 57–71, is unbetterable as a succinct, well-informed and critical survey.
[118] Above, p. 35.
[119] Simmer (1988), for example, still lists a 'cephalic index' (the ratio of a skull's breadth to its length) for each body in the cemetery.
[120] Härke (1990).   [121] Pilet (1980), p. 177.   [122] Hills (2003), p. 63.

Most famous, however, has been the intrusion of the study of DNA into the investigation of the migrations, especially in England. It has, for example, been suggested that DNA can 'prove' that there was mass migration and dramatic population change in lowland Britain in the fifth and sixth centuries.[123] The potential of DNA to show significant, precisely datable, movement within the human population of Europe since the Neolithic can, however, be seriously questioned.[124] Migration is a constant of European history; not something that occurred in specific, discrete episodes.[125] More to the point, the samples used in these (and other physical anthropological analyses) have generally been selected in accordance with a particular view of history (specifically that of migration from northern Germany to Britain). Any similarities that emerge might thus be deemed simply to reaffirm a preconception. No controls are sought from such 'unlikely' areas as Italy, France or Spain, let alone Africa. That samples from the much more mixed modern populations of the cities of England and northern Germany show greater variation than those from the highlands of north Wales or Norway might also be unsurprising. Catherine Hills has said that, just as 'historians hoped archaeologists would answer their questions, now archaeologists look to genetics ... [as a] solution to all problems.'[126] In truth, the geneticists do not often seem to be answering archaeologists' questions at all, but those of nineteenth- and early twentieth-century historians.

Most importantly, however, none of these analyses, even if possibly yielding information on geographical origins, tells us anything about what people thought they were, and ethnicity is a matter of belief. People who crossed the North Sea to Roman Britain in the third century and served in the Roman army adopted Roman culture and ethnicity. Any of their fifth-century relatives who did the same proclaimed their non-Roman identity, and may even have made different choices of which ethnicities based around their place of origin (Frisian, Angle, Saxon, Jute) they did stress. Yet their physical remains, DNA, stable isotopes in their tooth enamel, and so on, would all presumably be extremely similar. The fortuitous discovery of Stilicho's body, conveniently wrapped and labelled, in

---

[123] Weale, Weiss, Jager, Bradman and Thomas (2002). Excellent critique in Hills (2003), pp. 65–71.
[124] Evison (2000).   [125] Below, pp. 455–6.   [126] Hills (2003), p. 63.

a Ravennate grave, would tell us nothing of his own complex identity; what he thought he was, or what other people considered him to be – let alone the way in which his non-Roman antecedents were principally brought out once he had fallen from favour with the western court.

We know that people moved in the fifth and sixth centuries. The discovery of people of northern German origin in lowland Britain ought not to be a revelation to any sane scholar of this period. And, again, the absence of physical change does not imply a lack of population movement. What differentiated migration in the post-imperial world from that at other periods of history were the complex shifts in political and social identity of which it became one component, and which are studied in the next chapter. This cannot (and indeed can never) be examined through bones or teeth. The current vogue for forcing modern archaeological science to yield answers to old-fashioned and crudely formulated historical questions runs the risk of returning us to a primordialist view of ethnicity and identity, such as was popular 150 years ago.[127] These scientific techniques may yet yield interesting details about the personal histories of individuals. However, as far as the question of movement from *barbaricum* into the Roman Empire is concerned, without considerable refinement and greater sophistication, the study of the physical anthropology of the fifth- and sixth-century dead has no capacity to tell us anything that we did not already know, and every potential to set back the understanding of this period by a century or more.

In examining barbarian settlement we are forced to fall back upon the mechanisms outlined with reference to the *hospitalitas* question and those related to 'migration theory'. Imperial fiscal lands might have been used for the settlement of the newcomers, for example. Similarly, land with absentee owners (fiscal land might often have fallen *de facto* into this category) might also have provided space for the settlement of immigrants. Rulers could have expropriated opponents and bestowed their lands upon supporters from beyond the Empire. In turn these settlements could have become the focus for further immigration if the relevant information filtered back to *barbaricum*.

---

[127] Above, pp. 35–6.

Another insight into the mechanics of settlement by outsiders is provided by one clause of sixth-century Frankish law, entitled *De Migrantibus* (Concerning Migrants).[128] Essentially this clause allows any person within a *villa* (a small region) to oppose the taking over of someone's lands by an outsider, even if several people support the move.[129] The law gives an extended period (thirty days) within which the newcomer has to leave before he is called to court, at which session his opponent must provide witnesses to support the fact that he has given the newcomer due notice. If witnesses are provided and the case is upheld, then the migrant can be forcibly expelled and fined by the local court. As elsewhere in the code, the law is here giving a long period of time in order for an informal solution to the dispute to be found. The stipulation that witnesses be provided also ensures that the newcomer's expulsion has some sort of community consent. If we can assume any general applicability for the situation and mechanisms envisaged by the Frankish legislators we have an illustration of the factors, much in line with 'migration theory', that govern the ability to settle somewhere. Knowledge and connections are important, as are informal discussions within the community about the desirability or otherwise of new settlers. One assumes that people moved more easily to communities where the acceptance of newcomers could be more easily established and, in many of the contexts of the post-imperial period, these would be those with extant immigrant inhabitants. The law refers to invitations to outsiders to come and settle and it also allows anyone who has settled somewhere for over a year to remain there without let or hindrance. All this might give support to the conclusions of 'migration theory' about how the 'chains' formed by personal connections allow the flow of information and facilitate the creation of migrant communities.

In the current state of knowledge, it is very difficult to plot in any detail the location of barbarian settlement as opposed to those of the indigenous provincials. The archaeological and the toponymic evidence used to map barbarian settlement is, as we have seen, insufficient for these purposes. Though both forms might tell us about ethnic identity, either through the material culture employed to back up a claim to such identity or to give shape to ethnic groups,

---

[128] *PLS* 45.
[129] On the fiscal implications of this see Callander Murray (1983), pp. 67–79.

or in the use of personal names for the same purposes, we do not know whether the people adopting such ethnic identity were incomers from *barbaricum* or inhabitants of the former provinces. The 'long fifth century' saw numerous changes in identity and it is to those that we turn in the next chapter.

14

NEW PEOPLES, NEW IDENTITIES, NEW KINGDOMS?

Do the fourth to the sixth centuries deserve to be thought of as the period of *the* migration of peoples, or even of *the* barbarian migrations? Human beings have migrated across the planet's surface since mankind's first appearance and it cannot seriously be argued that population movement alone differentiates the period that concerns us. It is difficult, too, to argue that this era is distinguishable from others even in terms of the *scale* of such movement. It is a truism that the modern period has seen the migration of infinitely larger groups of people than migrated in the fourth and fifth centuries but the point holds even when looking only at Roman history. It is impossible to obtain an accurate figure for the numbers of people who moved between the Gothic crossing of the Danube in 376 and the Lombard invasion of Italy in 568 but even on the most maximalist interpretation they cannot have formed more than a small percentage of Europe's population. Barbarians had been entering Roman territory since the Republic. The last people before Alaric to capture Rome had been invading Gauls. An attack upon Italy by the northern German *Cimbri* and *Teutones* had required hard fighting. Caesar met the migration of the *Helvetii*, and so on. Once the Empire had established its frontiers along the Rhine and Danube, groups from *barbaricum* continued to petition for entry into Roman territory, which they were frequently granted.[1] It is difficult to estimate the size of the groups involved. They might, like those of the fourth to sixth centuries, have comprised groups smaller than whole tribes, perhaps just political and military élites and their dependants. We need not see such groups as necessarily smaller than those that moved during the period of the western Empire's collapse. Some Roman sources describe them using the same large, probably inflated, round numbers encountered in studying the late antique migrations.[2]

The people north of the Rhine–Danube *limes* did not have a monopoly on movement. In the early Roman period large numbers of people moved from the Empire's Mediterranean heartlands to its north-western provinces, and slaves and others were taken from the periphery to the core. Throughout Roman history people were moving from north to south and from east to west. The transfer of a few regiments and their dependants from one part of the Empire to another could represent a movement of people as great, or nearly so, as any barbarian migration. If this was the period of *the* migrations then it was not because of their scale.

Were the movements of the fourth to sixth centuries important, instead, because of their social, political and cultural effects? The barbarians are widely held to have been responsible for a wide range of such changes, not the least of which being the end of the western Roman Empire. However, as should have become clear, the Empire's fall cannot be laid at the door of the barbarians. The newcomers into formerly imperial territory were the focus rather than the cause of such transformations, and their migrations were themselves brought about by the period's political changes. These, and the barbarians' role in them, are most profitably explored by concentrating upon the new social and political identities that emerged in the course of the fifth and sixth centuries.

---

[1] Modéran (2004). Modéran postulates a change of scale in the third century. The upheavals of that century would certainly lead one to expect dramatic movements from *barbaricum*. Even if this is accepted, I can see nothing to suggest a further change of scale in the late fourth and fifth century.

[2] E.g. Modéran (2004), p. 349–50 and refs: 40,000 *Suevi* and *Sicambri* in 8 BC; 50,000 '*Getae*' in 5 AD; an inscription records 100,000 barbarians settled in Moesia under Nero.

NEW PEOPLES? ETHNOGENESIS

Discussion of the formation of new identities in the fifth century has focused upon the issue of ethnic change. The problem can be simply stated. In 350 most of the inhabitants (and all the politically important ones) of the territories governed by the Empire saw themselves in some way as Roman. The later Empire's cohesion had been based largely upon the absolute dominance of a particular idea of Roman identity, the adoption of which allowed participation in politics at various levels. Whoever controlled the political centre, furthermore, could validate claims to this identity. By 476, essentially as a result of competition for mastery of that centre, the western Empire had ceased to exist. It had fragmented into regional polities, in some areas quite small and based upon cities, as in Spain, but usually large-scale. In the absence of the Empire and of any claim to control the legitimacy of power or the political identities based upon it, new identities had to be forged and by 550 large numbers of people in the former provinces, especially those with a claim to political and military authority, saw themselves primarily as Gothic, Frankish, Saxon or English.[3] By the early seventh century these new ethnicities were as universal within particular regions as Romanness had been in the fourth century.

Study of the processes of ethnic change has resulted in much debate about so-called ethnogenesis.[4] Expressed, of necessity, with some simplification, the model most widely employed envisages the formation of peoples as the result of the coalescence of diverse groups of people around a small aristocratic core, as a result of the political and military success of the latter during the west's fragmentation. This group carried with it a number of foundation legends, origin myths and historical traditions, for which reason it has been dubbed the 'Traditionskern' (Tradition-core). In the model proposed by Wenskus and Wolfram, recently termed the 'Traditionskern model', the traditions of ethnic origin shared a

---

[3] I employ this term because 'Anglo-Saxon' was never used in our period and remained extremely rare (and then only in intellectual contexts) throughout the early Middle Ages. Englisc (pronounced English), was the vernacular form of 'Angle' and seems to have been used even in 'Saxon' regions.

[4] Above, pp. 14–16. The debate, and its ferocity, may be sampled in Gillett (ed.) (2002). There is an acerbic response in Wolfram (2005b), p. 11.

number of features.[5] The people was usually formed by a 'primordial act', such as the crossing of a sea or river, perhaps also the defeat or slaying of a renowned enemy. This was usually accompanied by a change in religion, from worship of the earlier Vanir gods (often in the form of brothers) to devotion to the new Aesir (with Woden as chief deity). Finally these traditions required the preservation of stories about a traditional enemy. Subscription to these traditions brought membership of the body to the newcomers. Because these groups were forged through common acceptance of stories of ethnic origins and histories, these groups are considered to have been 'peoples'. The period of the end of the Roman Empire and the barbarian migrations is thus widely considered one of the creation of peoples.

There are problems with Wolfram's model, principally that of over-systematisation. The origin myths of early medieval European peoples share a number of features, to be sure. Brothers with alliterative names (rarely specified to be twins, making the appellation *dioscuri* – technically the name of the twin brothers, Castor and Pollux – misleading) are found as leaders in the early stages: Hengest and Horsa among the Anglo-Saxons; Aio and Ibor among the Lombards, for example. Similarly migration in three ships is attested more than once: the tradition of the Anglo-Saxons' first arrival is well known but Jordanes also records that the Goths left the 'island' of Scandza in three ships. However, these stories also have profound differences. The creation of a unified corpus of *origines gentium*, which can be taken to reveal common traditional 'Germanic' motifs, is only possible by choosing certain features from some sources that resemble selected aspects of other works, alongside further stories from possibly different works again that bear some similarity with particular features from yet more sources. Episodes in one work are explained according to more detailed stories assumed to occupy the same structural position in another. For all the learning upon which it is based, this is hardly a sound method and stems ultimately from nineteenth-century Germanism. The idea that all Germanic-speaking peoples shared a unifying 'Germanic' ethos was joined to the belief that all the literary output of the early Middle Ages was in some sense 'Germanic'. On that basis, sources of diverse chronological

---

[5] A convenient English summary of traditional ethnogenesis theory can be found in Wolfram (1997a), pp. 33–4.

and geographical origin could be merged to create a 'proto-Germanic' body of tradition and custom. One cannot be other than suspicious when a modern historian, of whatever scholarly ability (and there can be no doubting Wolfram's), corrects the early medieval traditions of a people. Yet Wolfram does precisely that when he castigates Anglo-Saxon tradition for getting its Aesir and Vanir out of chronological order: surely Hengest and Horsa (Vanir 'dioscuri') should come *before* Woden (chief Aesir god), not be descended from him.[6] That, however, is what Bede and other Anglo-Saxon traditions say.[7] Rather than seeing this as revealing the constructs of Germanic philology for what they are, Wolfram instead argues that Anglo-Saxon stories had, for whatever reason, 'smoothed out' and reversed a chronology 'more faithfully' preserved in Lombard tradition! Aesir and Vanir are, of course, not recorded until the central medieval Eddas, although the *ansis* – demi-gods – referred to by Jordanes[8] have been assumed to be related to the Aesir.

The similarities between the different sources that describe the origins of early medieval peoples can be ascribed partly to the literary influence of one source on another. Paul the Deacon seems to have been influenced by Cassiodorus' or Jordanes' account of Gothic origins and he had certainly read Bede's history of the English.[9] Leaving aside the probably literary means by which tales could be transmitted (remember that the sources discussing the origins of the post-imperial peoples do not belong to one period of time but are spread across centuries), oral communication could transfer traditions once circulating about one people to another. By the Carolingian period other peoples, like the Burgundians, had acquired traditions of Scandinavian origin, unknown to earlier writers.[10] Such was the cachet acquired by the Gothic and Lombard origin myths.

Another problem is the cherry-picking of particular episodes assumed, *a priori*, to represent 'Germanic' tradition. Some stories related by Jordanes are believed to represent part of the authentic Gothic 'origin myth', such as the migration from 'Scandza', the defeat of the *Ulmerugi* who occupied the territory where the Goths made landfall, and so on.[11] Others, however, such as the Goths' defeat of the Egyptians, or the Gothic origins of the Amazons,

---

[6] Wolfram (1997a), p. 245.   [7] *HE* 1.15.   [8] *Getica* 13.78.
[9] Goffart (1988), pp. 362, 370, n. 127, 383, n. 168.   [10] Wood (2004), pp. 146–7.
[11] *Getica* 4.25–7.

are quietly left out of the discussion.[12] It has become a key tenet
of the study of antique texts that one must analyse them as unified
literary compositions, written in response to specific historical
circumstances, rather than as passive repositories of age-old
tradition.[13] Thus the authors of the works describing barbarian
origins deliberately shaped whatever material they had to hand to
make the points that they wished to make. There has been much
excellent work on the different, specific and complex agenda of
these writers. Wolfram has a tendency to disembody *origines gentium*
from these compositions and give them a life of their own, within
the Germanic philological schema mentioned above. Moreover,
these sources do not form a unified corpus of material. Quite apart
from being written by different people in distinct circumstances in
widely varying times and places, some of the works usually lumped
together in the 'canon' of 'origins of peoples' were actually written
as very different forms of literature.[14] Additional sources dipped into
to reconstruct 'Germanic' origin legends include genealogies and
works appended to legal and other material. Even perfectly
straightforward episodes in Graeco-Roman sources have been
hammered to fit the myths of 'Germanic' tradition.[15]

The idea that these *origines* and the aspects of ethnic tradition they
preserve were a specifically 'Germanic' creation is also deeply
problematic. There was a long-standing classical strand of writing
about the origins of the different peoples that formed the Mediterranean world. Cato's now fragmentary *Origines* lay at the heart of
this tradition. The stories preserved by later writers citing Cato
suggest that these classical origin myths shared a number of features
with the supposedly 'Germanic' traditions of the post-imperial
period. Aeneas, after all, was a son of Aphrodite (goddesses are also
supposed to be important in the early phases of 'Germanic' myth),
came to Italy by sea from a land far away, fought the locals and killed
the eponymous Latinus.[16] Seven (or eight) generations on, at the
origins of Rome, stood Aeneas' descendants, the alliteratively named
twins Romulus and Remus.[17] This tradition was still alive and well

---

[12] *Getica* 6.47 (war against Egyptians), 7.49–50 ff. (Amazons).
[13] Goffart (1988).   [14] Above, pp. 11–12.   [15] Gillett (2002b), pp. 1–3.
[16] Cato, *Origines* fragment 9 (Servius, *Commentary on the Aeneid* 3.16).
[17] Like the Anglo-Saxons, the Romans had clearly got their Aesir and Vanir the
wrong way round . . .

in late antiquity, as manifested in the anonymous *Famous Men of the City of Rome* and *Origin of the Roman People*, both ascribed (erroneously) to Aurelius Victor. It is all too often forgotten that Jordanes himself wrote *On the Origin and Deeds of the Roman People* (the *Romana*) to set alongside his *Getica* (*On the Origin and Deeds of the Goths*).[18] This classical tradition had a vital, but usually ignored, role in shaping the legends written about the creation of the post-imperial peoples.[19]

There are immense problems with the 'melting pot' use of selected elements of diverse works to create a systematic 'Germanic' tradition. That said, it is important not to reject everything contained within these sources as sixth-century and later literary fictions.[20] It is probably going too far to suggest that Cassiodorus and the others invented *all* of these tales from scratch. Some probably did have their origins in legends that circulated in *Germania*, though we cannot now know which, or how closely they resemble their progenitors. Many stories may well have been circulating at the time that a writer composed his account and, if they were, it seems reasonable to surmise that they might have served the sorts of functions that Wolfram and others suppose in the creation of a body of tradition, the knowledge and acceptance of which was key to incorporation within a group. What this does *not* mean, though, is that they ever formed a coherent body of tradition, or even a single, generally accepted mythic narrative. Jordanes, for example, alludes to other stories that were circulating about the Goths.[21] If he had only chosen to follow the legend of the Goths' migration via Britain, in analogous fashion to Gregory of Tours' repetition of the tale that traced the Franks to *Pannonia*,[22] one imagines that the historiography of the post-imperial period would have been that much simpler and less controversial! For one thing, no one would have tried to hammer the archaeological record into supporting such a notion. Late antique authors picked and chose elements and wove them into their own creations.

Some aspects of the ethnogenesis model nevertheless seem uncontroversial. The creation of stories, legends, and 'history' that

[18] Later on, Paul the Deacon similarly wrote a *Roman History* as well as his *History of the Lombards*.
[19] See, e.g. Amory (1997), pp. 304–5, on Capito's lost *History of the Isaurians*.
[20] Pohl (2002); (2005). [21] *Getica* 5.38. [22] *Getica* 5.38; *LH* 2.9.

told of how a people had come into being and of their struggle with old enemies – especially when justifying continued hostility to an out-group – are well-enough attested as part of the process of unification of groups.[23] Modéran has suggested that the stories of the Berbers' origins in the desert stem from an analogous migration origin myth.[24] Acceptance of the 'truth' of these tales is a means through which individuals make effective their claim to membership. Peter Heather clearly demonstrated that the 'traditions' represented in Jordanes' work were not age-old but the inventions of a new dynasty.[25] Yet subscription to the ideology manifested in such stories was a very important component of membership of the political community of the Goths and, thus, lay at the heart of the formation of this 'people'.

LAW AND ETHNICITY

As well as origin myths and histories, ethnic groups could crystallise around shared law and custom. Western European law in the post-imperial period was generally presented in ethnic terms, as the customs of a particular people. Whether such laws were imported from the Germanic-speaking *barbaricum* is another matter of heated debate.[26] Certainly, post-imperial law was very different from fourth-century Roman legislation in its workings, which operate around the compensation of one group for offences and injuries inflicted by another. It is, however, worth stressing that by the end of the period covered by this book only a few of the known 'barbarian' codes had come into existence: as a composition, Salian law in northern Gaul most plausibly dates to the very early sixth century (although it seems to contain material originating in earlier royal edicts);[27] the Burgundian code is a compilation of 516/17 but again contains royal enactments going back to the third quarter of the fifth century; the now fragmentary Visigothic code attributed to Euric probably belongs to that king's reign (467–484); and the Edict of Theoderic, probably issued by Theoderic of Italy (although it has also been linked to Theoderic II of the Visigoths), is also of

---

[23] E.g. Fewster (2002); Just (1989); Peel (1989) – the Rev. Samuel Johnson's 1921 *History of the Yoruba* bears uncanny similarities to Jordanes' work.

[24] Modéran (2003b), pp. 174–86.   [25] Above, pp. 132–3; below, p. 492.

[26] E.g. Barnwell (2000); Collins (1998); Wormald (2003).

[27] Collins (1998), pp. 11–15.

fifth-/sixth-century date.[28] 'Barbarian' law as we know it did not all come into existence at the same time. Some key texts, the Anglo-Saxon and Lombard laws for example, only began to be written down in the seventh century. This provides a long time between the demise of Roman government and the appearance of these codes, during which society changed considerably. This lengthy time-lapse is as likely as the introduction of possibly non-Roman legal practices to lie behind the differences between these laws and fourth-century Roman law. Some arguments in favour of the laws' 'Germanic' origin, based upon procedural differences (notably the supposed existence of 'feud'), can also be explained by this time lag and by a closer examination of the very last phases of Roman legislation, which sometimes sanction weapon-bearing and rights of vengeance hitherto monopolised by the Roman state.[29]

The traditional argument that these laws were imported into the Empire has worked in an analogous fashion to the creation of 'Germanic' ethnic mythology, starting from the structural similarities between various post-imperial laws and an assumption that these stem from a common 'Germanic' custom. It has then seemed possible to some to put all these laws together to reconstruct that original 'Germanic' law, and to connect this with some of the statements made by Tacitus and other Roman writers about law and justice amongst the *Germani*.[30] Gaps in the coverage of one code could then be filled in by reference to another. Ideas drawn from one body of legislation were assumed to lie behind all of the others. This has generated all kinds of misunderstandings and raises the same sorts of problems as the 'Germanist' view of origin myths. The legal codes were, equally, composed in different times and places as unitary texts, for particular reasons.[31]

---

[28] Amory (1997), p. 78, n. 187 for summary of the debate; Collins (1998), pp. 10–11.

[29] Wormald (2003) relies heavily on the existence of 'feud' as an argument in favour of the Germanic origins of post-imperial law, but ignores recent studies of feud and vengeance-killing in the west, which cast doubt on the existence of vendetta as a legal institution and upon the 'Germanic' origins of the systems that did exist: Halsall (1999b). See *CTh* 7, 8.10 (413), 7.18.14 (2 Oct. 403).

[30] The assumption is widespread. For a clear statement, see Fischer Drew (1967); (1987).

[31] The deliberate composition of the extant codes as unitary texts does not negate the fact that they usually contain within them individual clauses originating over possibly long periods of time.

The laws issued by post-imperial kings are frequently not like those issued by the emperors but we should not forget that the Visigothic and the Burgundian monarchs also issued versions of the Theodosian code. Furthermore, it is possible to trace the influence of imperial law even on supposedly straightforward 'barbarian' codes like Salic law.[32] Roman provincial governors had had the power to legislate and it has been suggested that the law promulgated by post-imperial kings was based upon those sorts of pronouncement rather than upon imperial law.[33]

The differences between post-imperial and classical Roman law have thus been explained with reference to Roman vulgar law.[34] Roman law did not only comprise the classical law of the jurists or imperial rescripts that had the power of law. There was also a stratum of vulgar law, the customs of the communities of the Empire, influenced by classical jurisprudence to be sure but significantly different from it in many ways. The similarities between the various barbarian codes can then be explained by their common derivation from the vulgar law of the different provinces. This would not be the same everywhere, hence the differences. One support for this argument is the similarity between the barbarian codes and a tract, indisputably of Roman vulgar law, from Byzantine Anatolia, known as *The Farmer's Law*. The latter can have nothing to do with 'Germanic' settlers.[35] The argument that post-imperial legislation represents the codification of provincial Roman vulgar law by barbarian leaders acting, on a precedent set by governors, in order to legitimise their rule and unify a group of followers around a particular ethnic identity, has much to recommend it.

There are nevertheless problems. One is that some codes employ Germanic technical terms. Indeed, the surviving manuscripts of Anglo-Saxon Law are all in Old English, and Bede stated in his *Ecclesiastical History* that king Æthelberht of Kent gave his people laws in English.[36] This need not mean that such laws had always been entirely vernacular. The oldest manuscript of Kentish law, the so-called *Textus Roffensis*, post-dates the reign of King Alfred,

---

[32] Callander Murray (1983), e.g. pp. 67–87.
[33] Barnwell (2000); Collins (1998).   [34] Levy (1951).
[35] Wormald (2003), pp. 29–30, argues to some extent against the use of vulgar law as an explanation of the post-imperial codes.
[36] *HE* 2.5.

who undertook an extensive programme of translation of Latin documents into Old English. It is surely possible that the text we have is an Alfredian translation. The earliest Frankish law, *Lex Salica*, contains a considerable corpus of Frankish legal terms.[37] A ninth-century translation of a seventh-century Latin code, incorporating a series of similar Old English technical terms, could have produced the late text of Kentish law, with archaic elements, that we have.[38] The hypothesis that the earliest Anglo-Saxon law resembled early Frankish or Lombard legislation, in Latin but with heavy vernacular glosses, allows us to understand Bede's statement and evade the problems raised by the supposition that Æthelberht promulgated and wrote down the law in Old English with the help of newly arrived Italian missionaries with no prior knowledge of the language (Æthelberht by contrast had access to Latin-speakers and writers, his Frankish bishop Liudhard for example, such as had enabled him to contact the Pope).

Be that as it may, the point stands that Germanic terms were employed to describe legal processes. This is probably the strongest support for the argument that post-imperial law was in some sense 'Germanic'. Nevertheless, the fact also remains that other early codes make use of analogous processes and do not give vernacular translations. It might therefore be that the post-imperial kings of barbarian origin had some Germanic terms employed for aspects of the law. In turn this might have been one way in which claims to an ethnic identity and the legal privileges that went with it were made secure. If, for example, one wished to claim Frankish status, then perhaps one had to know the correct Frankish technical terms for the legal process in which one was engaged.

We can therefore obtain a more rounded picture of how the promulgation of written law helped to unify and give a reality to new ethnic groups. In their appropriation of Roman idioms of political leadership[39] western kings naturally wished to continue the imperial tradition of issuing laws. The Bible gave a further impetus to this. The Hebrews, like the Romans, had been a people with a written law. If they were to have some sort of unity, the new peoples of the fifth and sixth centuries needed law as well as history. The texts symbolised this and the legal procedures they attest give an

---

[37] These are known as the Malberg glosses.   [38] Lendinara (1997).
[39] Below, pp. 489–91.

insight into how claims to group-membership were made effective. Nevertheless, it is worth repeating that at this stage these laws, although discussing the relationship between different ethnic groups, were territorial, like Roman legislation, applicable to all a kingdom's inhabitants. They did not, as was once believed, relate only to people of barbarian identity. It is now thought that in cases where two codes are known, one Roman and one 'barbarian' (as in the Burgundian and Visigothic kingdoms), the Roman code formed the realm's basic legislation with the 'barbarian' law providing for specific situations not covered by that law, especially the interaction of Romans and 'barbarians'.[40]

ARCHAEOLOGY AND ETHNOGENESIS

As well as subscription to a group's laws, traditions and customs, membership of the new peoples of the post-imperial world appears to have involved other, material cultural dimensions. Costume and other aspects of appearance were employed to give unity to ethnic groupings. Some sources refer to particular hairstyles being characteristic of certain peoples, for example, and there are references to distinctive dress fashions of particular groups.[41] Sidonius Apollinaris describes Frankish costume and haircut in his works.[42] This sort of thing seems to be witnessed in the archaeological record. There are, as we have seen, styles of brooch or belt-buckles with particular geographical distributions and it seems reasonable to associate these with particular ethnic groups. Making this statement must not, however, be understood to imply the old views of ethnicity (discussed in chapter 2) as meaning genetic or racial unity or that all wearers of such costumes or hairstyles were immigrants into the Empire from particular regions. The decision to adopt such styles was another aspect of incorporation.

Particular types of weaponry have also been ascribed to certain peoples. Isidore of Seville for instance, writing shortly after the close of our period, associated the name of the *francisca*, or throwing axe, with that of the Franks whose warriors used it, as described in use by

---

[40] See, e.g. Amory (1993). Collins (1998). This would be a continuation of a Roman situation. Roman law allowed for different social groups to be subject to different jurisdictions.

[41] *LH* 10.9 (Bretons/Saxons); *HL* 4.22 (Lombards).

[42] Sid. Ap. *Letters* 4.20; *Poems* 5, lines 238–53.

Sidonius and Agathias.[43] Similarly dubiously, some writers associated the *seax* or one-edged dagger, common in the post-imperial west, with the Saxons.[44] The problems of associating the throwing axe with the Franks were discussed in chapter 5. Frankish armies might have used the throwing axe more often than other forces but it is unwise to assume that everyone who used, or was buried with, a *francisca* was a Frank. Even the statistical analysis of weapons in cemeteries, ascribing ethnicities to the communities using the site according to the relative percentages of certain types of weapons, is, although perhaps a little more sophisticated, still fraught with problems.[45] Fighting styles were part of the catalogue of features that Roman ethnographers were expected to discuss when describing peoples, and these might indeed have constituted a part of the body of custom and tradition to which a group's members were expected to subscribe. The use of particular weapons, especially ones as universal as swords and spears, cannot, however, have been a significant badge of ethnicity.

It has been pointed out that although some sources list particular attributes of costume, appearance or weaponry as characteristic of a particular ethnic group, close examination of the evidence, written and especially pictorial, appears to show considerable fluidity in reality.[46] This is what one might expect. We should not assume that this renders insignificant our sources' statements. Any individual marker need not have been universal, or sufficient in itself to prove someone's membership of a group. On its own, carrying a *francisca*, or sporting a particular hairstyle, or wearing a given type of tunic or a belt-set decorated in a specific fashion, might not have automatically and clearly marked one out as a Frankish male, for example. All these signs together, however, probably made a much less ambiguous statement.[47] More importantly, what people *believe* signifies a typical custom or fashion of a group is frequently not as commonly employed in reality and is often in fact, rather than being distinctive, shared with others.[48] As discussed in chapters 2 to 4, groups sometimes employ material culture associated with other groups, in particular ways, to signify identities *within* their own

[43] Isidore, *Etymologies* 18.6.9. Sid. Ap. *Poems* 5, lines 246–8; Agathias, *Histories* 2.5.4.
[44] Springer (2004), pp. 122–30.
[45] Siegmund (1998a); (1998b); Brather (2003), esp. pp. 192–7, 517–65, for critique.
[46] Pohl (1998).   [47] Pader (1981).   [48] Above, pp. 61–2.

society. We should take seriously our sources' implications that there were recognised costumes and other 'badges' associated with the peoples of post-imperial western Europe. The new ethnic identities forged in this period required these somewhat artificial signifiers to give unity and clear signs of membership to fluid and heterogeneous groupings.

Other aspects of the archaeological record might have related to the creation of ethnic identity. Burial rites, for example, might have been among the customs to which an individual subscribed to show his or her group-membership. In Britain the cremation ritual imported from northern Germany might have functioned in this way.[49] Not everyone who cremated their relatives, or who asked to be cremated, need have been an Anglo-Saxon immigrant, even if the ritual itself was undoubtedly a new introduction. As will have become abundantly clear, furnished burial cannot be assumed to mark barbarian immigrants into the Empire. It is always much more common within the former imperial territories and seems, whether one is looking at northern Gaul, lowland Britain or the provinces north of the Alps, to be associated with the collapse of the old Roman landholding relationships. Nonetheless, one thing we cannot know from the archaeological record is what was said over the grave (where furnished burial is common we do not, at this date, have funerary liturgies). Such spoken elements might, especially with time, have included invocations of ethnic identity, as with the law. This is plausible given that some of the material, such as weaponry, probably relates to the ethnic identities constructed around the right to fight in the army.[50]

LANGUAGE, NAMES AND RELIGION

Other things served to unify the members of the newly emerging groupings, such as, in varying ways in different regions, language – linguistic change was dramatic in lowland Britain and in the Roman provinces of *Germania*,[51] Germanic legal terms were employed in other areas, and Church Gothic served as a further ethnic marker in

---

[49] Above, pp. 386–7. I am not convinced by Williams' (2002) attempts to downplay the extent to which the appearance of cremation signifies migration.

[50] Below, pp. 475–6.

[51] It is, however, worth remembering that this change took centuries to effect.

the Gothic and Vandal kingdoms.[52] By the end of the sixth century, the aristocracy across much of the former western Empire had adopted Germanic personal names. One of the best-known instances of this is the Gundulf whom we encountered at the very beginning of this book, whom Gregory of Tours claimed was his maternal great uncle.[53] He was a member of a proud senatorial house and apparently a brother of the powerful, if unpopular, metropolitan bishop Nicetius of Lyon. Yet whereas his brother had entered the church, Gundulf had taken secular service with the kings of *Austrasia*, serving as a *domesticus* (a Palatine official) before becoming a duke. Gundulf was almost certainly the name he adopted on entering royal service. The names chosen by the military aristocracy reflected the fact that new holders of political power had come ultimately from beyond the Rhine–Danube frontiers. A number of other individuals, male and female, are known to have had two names, one Germanic and one Roman (in which I include Greek and Christian/Biblical names). Gregory of Tours refers to an Avius 'who was also Vedast'.[54] A number of such names have been recorded from Ostrogothic Italy.[55] This should probably not be surprising given that in the late Empire people still bore more than one name, Flavius Abinnaeus for example. Barbarians, like Theoderic, who wished to claim a Roman pedigree, took the name Flavius, associated with the Constantinian dynasty. It should not be remarkable that people wishing to move into areas dominated by the barbarians should add a non-Roman name. People entering the church often took a Christian/Biblical name.[56]

Religion could be another unifying factor. The Goths, Sueves, Burgundians and Vandals adhered to Arianism, seen as a marker of non-Roman military identity. The Burgundians, Vandals and Sueves are sometimes recorded as Catholics in the earlier part of their histories within the Empire, and the Burgundians seem to have remained divided between Nicaean and Arian Christianity.[57] The choice of the, by the fifth century, heretical Arian doctrine must therefore have, again, been more complex than a simple matter of

---

[52] Amory (1997), pp. 102–8, and refs., for critical discussion.
[53] *LH* 6.11, 6.26.   [54] *LH* 7.3.
[55] Ademunt–Andreas; Daniel–Igila; Gundeberga–Nonnica; Minnulus–Willienant; etc. Amory (1997).
[56] E.g. *LH* 4.26.   [57] Burgundians: Oros. 7.32.11–12; Vandals: Hydatius 79.

bringing a traditional form of Christianity from *barbaricum* into the Empire. Although traditionally cited as a list of 'barbarian' introductions into the former Empire, the features employed to give shape to the ethnic groups coalescing around 'barbarian' identities were, in the overwhelming majority of cases, new creations. Clearly some elements were imported from the barbarians' homelands, though these are now (with the exception of linguistic features and some material culture, like the Anglo-Saxon cremation rite) difficult to identify for sure. Other changes once pinned on the barbarians, like the decline of towns and villas, economic decline and some types of burial cannot now, as will have become clear, be seen as having anything to do with the migration. The barbarians had become a focus for changes and renegotiations, but they were not their cause.

ETHNIC CHANGE

As with the idea that this era can be considered that of *the* migration of peoples (*Völkerwanderung*)[58] the implication of many studies, that *ethnogenesis* distinguished this period from those before and after, is misleading. New 'peoples' have come into being at all periods of history, and the focus on 'peoples' has tended to obscure other issues concerned with the renegotiation of identities in the post-imperial period. We can detect various features, as discussed above, the adoption of which served to mark out an individual as the member of a group but how easy was it for individuals to change their ethnicity? The issue of how people were able to alter their ethnic identity needs closer scrutiny.

Ethnic change in late antiquity cannot have been a simple matter. Correct Roman, masculine behaviour was the norm against which everything else was measured, possibly outside the Empire as well as within it. Recent works, principally by British archaeologists, which talk blithely about the 'rejection' of Rome (something for which there is, in any case, no evidence),[59] completely ignore this crucial issue. There were enormous brakes, cultural and socio-economic as well as political, upon the abandonment of Romanness. Correct

---

[58] Goffart (1989a).

[59] Jones, M. E. (1996); to a lesser extent (and in a different way), Dark, K. R. (1994), pp. 55–64; Higham's (1992) discussion of adaptation is more subtle, although his vision of a polarized lowland society seems questionable.

behaviour staked a claim for legitimate power at whatever level, from the local community to the highest rungs of the imperial bureaucracy. Performed *romanitas*, moreover, rendered one part of the Roman sex-gender system, at all political strata. Although no doubt modified by region, its performance distinguished the sexes, *made* one male or female, and revealed one's suitability for marriage amongst (or into) those families with any claim to local or wider authority. Throughout the west, the continued active involvement in the Empire of myriad communities bound the state together, so these dimensions of local politics (and in places like northern Gaul and Britain they could be very local indeed) are crucial to understanding the end of the western Roman Empire. In the third century the imperial state had not disintegrated because, although the mechanisms that had bound localities into the Empire in the first and second centuries had generally ceased to be very effective,[60] no alternatives emerged as legitimate bases for local authority before the state revived the attractiveness of participation in the Empire.[61] The very centrality of *romanitas* to ideas of power, status and gender was one of the Roman state's most fundamental sources of strength.

This surely lies behind the fact, discussed in chapter 11, that in several areas of the Empire the fifth century is archaeologically difficult to detect. As well as problems caused by the end of coinage and easily datable finewares, the material cultural 'vocabulary' employed to display power was heavily dependent upon Roman imperial art and styles of design. Except north of the Thames, no artistic or stylistic repertoire emerged to replace this until the Empire's final collapse in the 470s. Ethnic change was not – *it could not be* – a 'snap decision'. The process was difficult and took a generation at least to work through, as can be illustrated (via archaeological or documentary sources) throughout western Europe. This point has not been given due weight. Those who, ultimately correctly, argue that ethnicity was fluid and mutable have tended to ignore the practical difficulties of ethnic change or the time involved. Similarly, those who have opposed this thesis have based their arguments on the fact that ethnic change did not take place overnight, although such renegotiations cannot be expected to have been thorough and effective over short time-spans. Individuals' life cycles also played a role in the change of ethnic identity. The

[60] Above, pp. 71–4.   [61] Above, pp. 76–8.

broader political situation (or setting, in the terms used in chapter 2) was important, too. One ought to expect the process of change from Roman to non-Roman to work somewhat faster after the Empire's demise and this seems to have been the case. Even then it appears to have taken a generation or so.

Other potential curbs on ethnic change were the affective power of Roman identity, which was crucial but can be understood as subsumed within the issues just discussed, and the issue of acceptance into a group. The latter could have been important in individual cases but it does not generally appear to have been significant, probably because, in an era of dramatic, fluid politics and the some- times rapid movement of numerous different bodies of people around the west, few would have had the knowledge necessary to deny membership of a group.[62]

A development of this argument, proposed by Peter Heather, sees the 'Germanic' ethnic units – the 'peoples' – of this period as largely constituted by a numerous and politically important stratum of freemen. The cohesion of this group acted as a check, he argues, on ethnic change, although it did not prevent it. This is an interesting and solidly argued case and not, in itself, implausible. The evidence used is, however, problematic. Heather has supported his case partly by reference to the post-imperial western law codes. These cannot be relevant to pre-migratory 'Germanic' society. A significant body of landowners existed in the sixth century, often claiming a par- ticular ethnicity, who were not dependent upon an aristocratic lord. It is, however, mistaken to think of them as a cohesive body with a distinct political identity. Many used a connection with the king as a strategy within local politics, often in competition with other members of this 'class', in order to gain access to the ranks of the aristocracy.[63] Heather's argument comes close to a revival of the now unfashionable idea of a class of 'Königsfreie' (King's Freemen) in early medieval society.[64] Rather than being an exclusive defining characteristic, non-Roman ethnic identity appears to have some- thing that was claimed in order to join this group.

[62] Above, pp. 43–4.
[63] Above, pp. 332–6, 356–7. The archaeological cemetery evidence alluded to by Heather (2005), pp. 94–5, represents this competition for authority, rather than being, as he hints, a reflection of a broad-based free class, distinguished from slaves and freedmen.
[64] Staab (1980) for English summary.

Heather also supports his argument with interesting use of Procopius' account of the Gothic wars (535–61).[65] Again, the reality of the social group he identifies – a numerous stratum of fighting men occupying a position between the higher aristocracy and military dependants – is not in doubt.[66] They seem to be the same people as paraded at Theoderic's palace to receive donatives and witness the distribution and redistribution of royal patronage. Again, what is debatable is whether this group was in any way exclusive or had any coherent political identity. The competition within it for royal favour and the kings' use of that rivalry to undermine more established aristocracies rather suggest the opposite.

Nevertheless, given the dominance of ideas of correct Roman behaviour in the late Roman period, the replacement of 'Romanness' should have been a traumatic process that called into question all sorts of other aspects of an individual's identity. There were, however, resources within late Roman society and politics that enabled people to navigate these important changes. Ethnicity is dynamic, with constant reordering and renegotiation of the layers of identity according to the situation or setting.[67] What it meant to be Roman, and the relative importance of its different levels – tribal or municipal, regional, provincial and so on – had changed throughout the imperial period. Particularly important was the emergence of new military and Christian forms of Roman self-definition during the fourth century. The renegotiation of ethnicity would not in itself be something new to the fifth century.

The new 'peoples' constituted only one layer of the ethnic segment of the spectrum and this is most important to bear in mind. The features discussed earlier relate only to group-membership at one level. One such 'layer' could be adopted within a hierarchy of identities and then gradually stressed until it superseded the others and became that which an individual regarded as most important in self-definition.[68] Again, this requires time, possibly more than a generation. This matters for two reasons. First, it means that ethnic change for an individual is not a matter of a 'straight swap'. This in itself reduces the potential trauma of such a change of identity.

---

[65] Heather (1996), pp. 321–6; See below, pp. 499–507, for brief narrative of the wars.

[66] Halsall (2003a), pp. 40–53, for post-imperial military organisation.

[67] Above, pp. 38–43.   [68] Above, p. 43.

Second, the multi-layered nature of ethnicity enables us to counter an argument deployed by Peter Heather against the idea that ethnicity was easily changed. Heather has drawn attention to 'reappearing tribes' in late antiquity and the way in which, during the sixth-century Gothic wars, Roman troops who deserted to the Goths re-emerged to rejoin the Romans at a later point. This, says Heather, demonstrates that people were not fully integrated into the Goths (or Huns, or other groups).[69]

The issue of integration requires closer consideration. As recent controversial debates about minority populations in Britain and France illustrate, 'assimilation' and 'integration' are not politically neutral terms. Those who have castigated immigrants for 'failing' to integrate or assimilate have tended to ignore the fact that such people usually regard themselves as British or French but with other, important, forms (or levels) of identity alongside: French Muslims, British Asians and so on. These identities are important to many immigrants, especially in particular circumstances, but they do not necessarily negate any importance attached to being British or French citizens.[70] Ideas of integration and assimilation ultimately stem from the 'melting pot' view of ethnicity, an idea, common in the earlier twentieth-century United States, that immigrants would, within a generation or two, all merge into a single American population. That this never happened caused some consternation and, eventually, the idea's rejection.[71] Similarly, that individuals amongst the Goths retained a Roman identity, which, when circumstances changed, they put ahead of any Gothic persona, does not prove incomplete integration or assimilation.

As discussed in chapter 3, the Roman army had evolved its own set of identities, often consciously espousing ideas of the barbarian. It had also developed a series of ideas based around classical ethnography, which consciously, it seems, went against the civic model of Roman masculinity. One area in which this might be manifest, although the evidence is so flimsy that it cannot be more than a suggestion, concerns the control of emotions. Some army officers seem not to have conformed to the usual protocols of Roman

---

[69] 'Full integration': e.g. Heather (1996), p. 303.
[70] I wrote this on 7 July 2005, noting the statements by British Muslims condemning the terrorist attacks on central London.
[71] See also above, pp. 42–3.

behaviour. Ammianus, for example, discusses a meeting of Constantius II's *consistorium* – the emperor's inner council – at which one general, Marcellus, recently dismissed by the *caesar* Julian, was present. Marcellus accompanied his tirade against Julian with wild and dramatic gestures, apparently somewhat out of place in the staid atmosphere of consistory.[72] Ammianus, ever consciously the gentleman officer, disapproved of Valentinian I's hot temper;[73] Valentinian, like many other fourth-century emperors, was elected from the ranks of the officer corps. This behaviour may have been part and parcel of the army's adoption of identities that were the antithesis of moderate, reasoned civic masculinity.[74]

The experience of the late Roman army may also have eased the adoption of non-Roman names. As the fourth century wore on officers in high command had increasingly been barbarians who had retained their Germanic names rather than adopting Roman ones. People had, perhaps, become used to associating military authority with men bearing non-Roman names. Although this would be impossible to ascertain, some Roman aristocrats holding commands in regiments with barbarian ethnic titles might have changed their personal names to match, at least whilst with the colours. In the post-imperial west the use of several names of different ethnic origin, made easier by the Roman naming practices, was very likely one way in which the different levels of identity were manifested in varying situations.

The crucial example set by the late Roman army can also be seen in the way that ethnicity in the immediately post-imperial kingdoms was often functional. In several areas, the 'barbarians' were the army and the civil and ecclesiastical population was Roman. The evidence for this division of labour is probably clearest in Ostrogothic Italy,[75] where Theoderic's court's ideological output is specific on the matter. The Goths certainly formed the field army even if Roman Italians served in local garrisons. As discussed above, there is some evidence that Italo-Romans were taking on military roles and that this may have been a way of 'becoming' Gothic but the kingdom's short lifespan and Justinian's invasion meant that this process was never fully worked through. In northern Gaul the Franks appear, similarly, to have formed the military caste. This conclusion can be

---

[72] Amm. Marc. 16.7.2; Matthews (1989), pp. 268–9.   [73] Amm. Marc. 29.3, 30.8.
[74] Above, p. 98.   [75] Above, pp. 132–5.

reached on the basis of evidence in narrative histories like the work of Gregory of Tours and the legal evidence of Salic law.[76] The association of some adult males with weaponry in northern Gaulish furnished cemeteries might also relate to this functional basis of ethnic identity. This was probably also the case in lowland Britain, where we have no reliable written data. There too, the burial of weapons with some males has plausibly been seen as symbolising Anglo-Saxon identity.[77] Functional separation into Roman tax-payers and bureaucrats and barbarian soldiers also seems to have existed in the Vandal and Moorish areas of North Africa.[78] A similar distinction seems to have applied in Visigothic Spain,[79] though evidence from the period covered by this book is scanty and in Gaul the Goths made good use of Gallo-Roman contingents. Indeed southern Gaul seems to have been an exception to this general rule, at least after the collapse of the kingdom of Toulouse. There, Roman landlords were liable for military service, organised by *civitas*-unit.[80] This is an important point, to which we shall return.

Very clearly a continuation of the late imperial situation, this too should have been a factor easing the gradual promotion of non-Roman political and ethnic identity. The way in which it perpetu-ated the later Roman state of affairs, and was not yet a matter of birth, might be illustrated by study of the earliest Frankish law code, Salic law. In this text the ethnic terms *francus* and *romanus* are only applied to free adult males, seemingly with legal dependants.[81] When this code was issued, Frankish (or Roman) identity, seemingly linked to military service, appears to have been restricted to adult males and therefore, at least as far as Frankish identity was concerned, probably achieved through the performance of military service and the acceptance of a right to take part in the army's activities (effectively the political assembly). Younger warriors (*pueri*) do not appear to have achieved a full ethnic identity. An individual's life cycle was important in the adoption of new identities.

---

[76] Halsall (1995a), pp. 26–32. Anderson, T. (1995).

[77] Härke (1990); (1992a); (1992b). I differ from Härke in not necessarily seeing this identity as implying an individual's origins in or descent from families from the *barbaricum*.

[78] Vandals: von Rummel (2002). Moors: Rushworth (2000).

[79] Pérez Sánchez (1989).   [80] Halsall (2003a), pp. 44–5, 48.

[81] Halsall (1995a), pp. 27–9, for discussion of the text (assuming, however, a more unified period of composition than is perhaps justified). Also Halsall (2004).

The mechanisms discussed earlier in this chapter provide insights into how such an identity was achieved and maintained. Rituals such as those described in the law codes, and use of the precise legal technical language, were public means of proclaiming such an ethnic identity.[82] This would tie in with Salic law's implication that only those with a legal identity, supposing dependants that had to be spoken for at law, were assigned an ethnicity. Attendance at other assemblies, like the regular meetings of the army in Ostrogothic Italy and Frankish Gaul (where there was an annual assembly on 1 March), was another.[83] The customs manifested by archaeological cemetery data might have been a further example, as might wearing the costumes and hairstyles mentioned earlier. Most if not all of these aspects can be traced to Roman military precedent. The army had had its own courts and rituals, and, as we have seen, had long been sporting distinctive costumes.[84]

Another possible way in which new ethnicities were claimed might be in the continuation of 'barbarous' behaviour, by which is meant conduct that manifested an opposition to the traditional restraint and moderation of Roman civic masculinity. Some accounts of sixth-century Frankish kings suggest – on occasion – much more open displays of emotion, especially anger and remorse, than would have been considered appropriate within Roman notions of good government. As noted, some soldier–emperors, such as Valentinian I, were castigated for their hot tempers, but this seems more extreme with the Merovingians. Chilperic I, for example, threw himself on the ground before his bishops in one public assembly in 577 to demand their support against a bishop by whom he felt he had been wronged; Guntramn of Burgundy openly begged the citizens of Paris not to murder him; on another occasion he rather hastily had a palatine official stoned to death (shades of Valentinian here) but, unlike his Roman precursors, he then publicly expressed remorse and said that he wished he had not ordered this execution.[85] This does not suggest that the Merovingians were more emotional than the later emperors. The contrast cannot be hard and fast. Theodosius I and

---

[82] Heather (1996), p. 319, makes similar points. We disagree on whether this implies a coherent political community of freemen.
[83] Halsall (2003a), p. 43.
[84] Above, pp. 104–5. Separate jurisdiction: e.g. *CTh* 2.1.9.
[85] *LH* 5.18, 7.8, 10.10.

Valentinian I were well capable of manifesting their anger through acts of arbitrary cruelty; Theodosius was famously compelled by Ambrose of Milan to do public penance for ordering a massacre at Thessalonica;[86] and post-imperial kings could also be described (at least for particular purposes, to Roman audiences) as adopting traditionally Roman acts of moderation and restraint.[87] It might be suggested that public displays of extreme emotion had become more acceptable among the political élite, although (as before) it does not appear that these were universally approved of. Though one would not want to press the argument, it is possible that this was a display of barbarian identity.[88] Overall, like Romanness earlier on, non-Roman ethnicity was performed.

Within the Empire, some Romans had possessed a series of different levels of identity, some of which were consciously non-Roman, and had customs, costumes and behavioural codes to match. This had, nevertheless, not affected their sense of ultimately belonging to the Roman community and of changing their dress and comportment accordingly in other circumstances. This precedent provided an absolutely vital resource in enabling people in the post-imperial west to negotiate the problems involved in renegotiating, or playing down, their Roman identity. Importantly these sorts of precedent had not existed in the third century. Identity means likeness[89] and must imply some sort of pre-existing mental template. In this case, it was largely provided by the units of the late imperial army.

It seems that as time wore on, especially after the western Empire's demise, the ideologies of the ruling barbarian groups became more self-confident, moving away from justifications of power by reference to imperial legitimation.[90] This probably also enabled a change from seeing a non-Roman ethnicity as nested within other traditionally Roman forms of identity, in the way that Roman soldiers had viewed the 'non-Roman' components or levels of their personas, towards the promotion of barbarian ethnicity to a more dominant position. Again, it is important to bear in mind that ethnic change was a dynamic and contingent process.

---

[86] McLynn (1994), pp. 315–23.   [87] Sid. Ap. *Letters* 1.2.3, 1.2.6.

[88] Althoff (1998) also perceives Merovingians as more emotional than their supposedly more Christian Carolingian successors. See also my review of this book in *EME* 10 (2001), pp. 301–3.

[89] Above, p. 168.   [90] Below, pp. 493–4.

In this complex situation it is unsurprising that the Roman concepts of the barbarian themselves underwent some re-evaluation. In Ostrogothic Italy the word was very rarely used to describe the Goths in the letters of Cassiodorus but *barbarus* was used fairly unproblematically within the Edict of Theoderic to describe non-Romans interacting with the realm's Roman inhabitants.[91] A similar situation pertained in the Burgundian *Book of Constitutions*, where barbarian seems to be used as a synonym for Burgundian.[92] The Burgundians appear to have adopted a sense of pride in their barbarian identity. Salic law also contains a reference to barbarians who live according to Salic law, though it does seem to differentiate these from Franks.[93] Elsewhere in Gaul, the Roman–barbarian dichotomy appears to have been moulded by some writers, such as Gregory of Tours, to describe the difference between Christians and pagans (or at least those people or customs that were considered pagan by rigorous Christians).[94]

It is important not only to remember that ethnicities based around the peoples of the Germanic-speaking *barbaricum* formed only one level of an individual's ethnic identity, but also to bear in mind that these were not the only new kind of such identity stressed in this period. There were others that stemmed from regions within the Empire, such as the British ethnicity that came to the fore in the fifth century, especially in the highland zone, and which also became important in the Armorican peninsula of Gaul, which became Brittany.[95] By the ninth century at least, stories of British ethnogenesis were being written down, which parallel those of the 'Germanic' peoples on the mainland of Europe.[96] In the interstices between Frankish Gaul and (eventually) Gothic Spain, the Pyrenean Basques formed a core around which ethnic identities could form. Although this principally seems to have become a significant factor some time after the end of our era, it remains possible, especially given the lack of documentary data for the far south of early Merovingian Gaul and the far north of Spain, that some of the region's élites, cut off from the political centres in northern Gaul and

---

[91] E.g. *Theoderic's Edict*, 34, 43, 44.   [92] *LC* 1.11, 2.1, 10.1, 17.5, 22, 44.1, etc.
[93] *PLS* 41.1, but see also 14.2 for *barbarus salicus*.   [94] *LH* 7.29.
[95] Space has precluded discussion of the migration to Brittany and I acknowledge this serious lacuna.
[96] E.g. the *HB*.

the centre of Spain, turned to the Basques and the military support
they provided as a basis for local power.[97] Irish identities doubtless
became important in the west of Britain, particularly late in the
period covered by this book, and Moorish ethnicity became very
significant in North African local politics.[98] Far from all of the new
ethnic identities in the fifth-century west, at the level of 'peoples',
were 'Germanic'.

One form of 'Roman' identity that was brought to the fore in the
fifth century was based around the *civitas* – city-district or diocese.
This type of identity had been significant during the Empire, as
aristocrats in particular defined themselves and discussed their
families according to their *civitates* of origin.[99] It seems to have been
particularly important in Spain, although there the towns tended to
be *municipia* – foci, with particular legal privileges, for smaller units –
rather than *civitates* based on pre-Roman tribal units, as in Gaul and
Britain.[100] Again, this owed much to pre-existing Roman situations.
Because of the forms of urban organisation, cities had always been
important in Spain and, as discussed in chapter 11, Spanish politics
continued to be played out in an urban setting. Local senates are
recorded and the persistent importance of the urban *curia* in local
politics must have made one's city of origin a key determinant of
ethnic identity.

In Gaul, too, the city was important. This was especially so in
Aquitaine, where the cities survived better as higher order settlements. The *civitas* unit seems to have been fragmenting in the north,
though this change was perhaps not effective until the seventh
century.[101] Nevertheless Trier seems to have retained a particular
sense of its Roman identity, especially as far as its local senatorial
aristocracy was concerned.[102] In the south, the *civitas* was a particularly important socio-political unit. Gregory of Tours habitually
describes the people of the south as the men of particular *civitates*. In
Aquitaine armies were raised from these city-districts, giving their
inhabitants (or *populus*) a military basis to their identity.[103] Gregory
also tends to identify Gallo-Roman aristocrats by the name of
their father and their *civitas* of origin.[104] In two cities we can see a

---

[97] Collins (1990).   [98] British: Woolf, A. (2003); Moors: Rushworth (2000).
[99] Ausonius, *Order of Famous Cities* 20, lines 40–1.   [100] Kulikowski (2004).
[101] Halsall (1995a), pp. 17–18.   [102] Above, pp. 353–4.
[103] Durliat (1997b); Heather (2000b), pp. 441–3, 456.   [104] *LH* 10.2.

particular way in which this form of identity, brought to the fore in the post-imperial world, was given a focus at the very end of our period. In Vienne and Lyon, on the Rhône, inscriptions are dated by the number of years since the term of office of one of the last western consuls. However, while Vienne's inscriptions are dated by the number of years after the last consul, which seems reasonable, Lyon's are dated with regard to the penultimate consul. It seems that these urban communities chose a 'patron consul' as the focus of their own systems of measuring time, in such a way as to differentiate themselves from the neighbouring city.[105]

The use of systems of measuring time was not restricted to these two Gallic cities. It has been argued that consular dating was especially prominent in the Burgundian kingdom, though this argument has its problems.[106] The 'Spanish era' (a chronology beginning in the year we think of as 38 BC) became important and has been plausibly linked to Catholic, Hispano-Roman identity.[107] The Mauretanian era, commencing in 39 AD, continued in use in North African inscriptions and might well have had an analogous political usage, in opposition to the Vandal era, which began with their conquest of Carthage exactly 400 years later.

Another well-known area where city-based identities found a focus, not dissimilar from Lyon and Vienne's 'patron consuls', was in the promotion of their own saints' cults. This feature, common across the Empire (even, to judge from some of Gildas' comments, in Britain), and the competition that existed between cities in the celebration of their saintly protectors, is well documented.[108] All of these generally recognised features of the late antique west need to be considered as foci for local identities, within the ethnic arc of the spectrum, that came to the foreground during the upheavals of the fifth and sixth centuries, and deserve as much analysis in this regard as the 'Germanic' ethnic identities also being adopted. The regionalism that had grown since the third century provided individuals with additional resources allowing the renegotiation of

[105] Handley (2000).
[106] Handley (2000). Unfortunately Handley's argument derives in part from documents dated in Italy (thus irrelevant to Burgundian self-identification) and partly upon material forged by Jérome Vignier and included in the *MGH* edition of Avitus of Vienne's letters. My thanks to Ian Wood for these points.
[107] Handley (1999).   [108] E.g. Van Dam (1985); (1993).

Roman and other ethnic identities, which had not existed during the third-century political crises.

The fact that ethnicity is multi-layered, and the growing importance of *civitas* or municipal levels of identity, might also allow us a way of seeing how people were able to separate the political aspects of imperial Roman identity from the cultural. The church also provided means of negotiating political and ethnic change. Christians had appropriated much of the classical Roman ideas about self-control and moderation.[109] This in itself might allow people to continue with traditional ideas of correct comportment while separating this from adherence to the political entity of the Empire. Also during the 'long fifth century', however, precisely during the period at which the Empire was springing apart, another strand of Christian thought was moving towards competition in the extremes of ascetic self-denial and questioning a central concept of the Roman sex-gender system, by espousing not merely chastity but complete sexual renunciation.[110] The rise of the holy man, consciously rejecting the forms of late Roman society, was a further element in the mix.[111]

The process of ethnic change was, therefore, complex and took time to play out. Its complexity was in no small measure the result of the difficulties involved in renegotiating Roman identity. Nevertheless, the developments within Roman society during the third and fourth centuries had provided a number of resources that allowed these difficulties to be circumvented. Ethnic change in this period should not, however, be seen as a process with inevitable results. Different outcomes to some of the high-level political events of the fifth century could have changed many of the details or even reaffirmed the fourth-century supremacy of Romanness.[112]

GENDER

As has been stressed repeatedly, Roman politics were heavily gendered. What distinguished Roman from barbarian also differentiated man from woman and, as a result, the barbarian was not infrequently feminised in Roman art.[113] Any change from Roman

---

[109] See, as just one example, Caesarius of Arles, *Sermons* 214.
[110] Cooper and Leyser (2001).
[111] See, classically, Brown, P. R. L. (1971); Van Dam (1985).
[112] See further below, pp. 515–16.   [113] Ferris (1994).

to barbarian self-definition, especially one performed, as suggested above, would of necessity have a bearing upon the construction of gender, not because of a direct equation of barbarian with woman but because 'barbarisation' involved a move away from the central, gendered pole of Roman civic masculinity against which all other identities were measured. This in turn would alter the relationship between man and woman. Thus gender relations must have acted as a further brake on the processes of ethnic change in the fifth century. To participate in the politics of a community required correct behaviour within marriage, and power politics required marriage alliances between different families (at whatever level of political community). To take part in Roman politics demanded that one were gendered male or female. Failing to act 'correctly' like a Roman man could call into question one's ability to marry and thus to lead or govern. These aspects are central to how local or regional politics have a bearing upon high political developments. Unless one could adopt a new political identity without undermining one's ability to marry, and reproduce one's family, at the politically significant levels, no non-Roman polity could emerge.

There must therefore have been an intimate and reciprocal relationship between the renegotiation of ethnicities and the development of gender identities. The feminine, rather than representing a binary polarity to the masculine, was, like lesser forms of masculinity, barbarism, childhood, or the beasts, defined negatively by its inability, or judged positively according to its ability, to live up to the ideals of civic Roman masculinity. Men derived credit from the virtues (defined by men) of their women, such as chastity and modesty. These were, however, ideals that any man of the politically significant classes was, naturally, expected to possess, rather than quite distinct values. Note, too, that, on the whole, female status and power was much more closely related to sex and childbearing than male. These things could not remain fixed, however. There was always a gap between actual behaviour or performance and the ideal, meaning that gender was constantly renegotiated. Women could act, even within the parameters defined by men, to change subtly what was felt to define men in relation to women. The gradual adoption of symbols of learning by élite women in the late Empire, and the consequent stress upon other masculine characteristics, is a case in point.[114]

---

[114] Above, p. 98.

Crucially, fourth-century developments had produced a new form of masculinity, the military model discussed above, which provided the route from Roman to non-Roman ethnicity. During the period that concerns this book, as far as gender is concerned, one of the most important developments was a shift from the civic to the military model as the hegemonic form of masculinity.[115] By the later sixth century, it was weapon-bearing, and especially an association with the army (and thus an attendant ethnicity), that defined the dominant male ideal. Other forms of male identity were, increasingly, coming to be seen as inferior. In northern Gaul, for example, Salic law rated a Roman dining companion of the king as worth half the 'wergild' (the fine payable by someone who killed or injured him) of a (by implication Frankish) member of the royal bodyguard (*trustis*).[116] Roman freemen had half the 'wergild' of Frankish freemen, and within two or three generations of the end of this period, in the same region, Roman men were the legal dependants of Franks.[117] The greater relative opportunities for marriage and reproduction at high political levels constituted another reason why non-Roman identities were increasingly attractive.

It is important, however, not to see gender construction as merely reacting to changes in other forms of identity. As stated, high political change would not have been possible to come about without the ability to renegotiate gender identities. Women and men in political arenas (some local and face-to-face; others operating at broader, regional élite levels) could have made changes in self-definition politically ineffective. The social and political changes described in chapters 6–11, however, rendered the renegotiation of gender more possible in some areas. The crisis in the northern provinces, beginning around 400, produced dramatic insecurity and competition for power at a local level. This meant that, certainly by *c.*500, in the rural communities of northern Gaul and Britain, social standing was maintained by an expensive cycle of gift-giving, the purchase of support, and networks of marriage and other alliances between families. This and the importance of inheritance, which was bilateral (from father and mother's families), made marriageable women the linchpins of local politics and gave them a certain amount of status.

---

[115] See below, pp. 494–7, for how this impacted upon the definition of aristocracy.
[116] *PLS* 41.5, 41.8.   [117] *PLS* 41.1, 41.9. *Lex Ribv.*64.

Similarly the mothers of young children, vital to lasting connections between families, appear to have been significant in local communities, as can be concluded from the cemetery evidence.[118] The increased importance of marriage within such societies must have permitted people to have a say in the acceptability or otherwise of changes in political identity. This was yet another factor making ethnic transformations slow processes, taking a generation or more, particularly in the fifth century.

The subtle change in the political importance of women is perhaps manifest in aspects of their costume. Whereas imperial Roman decorative styles were not common on items of fourth-century female apparel, in the fifth and sixth centuries decorative motifs were rather more frequently transferred from masculine items such as swords and belt-sets to female jewellery. This is true of the polychrome gold and garnet metalwork that appears in Gaul and elsewhere in the 470s and of slightly earlier quoit brooch style. Style I is almost entirely found on the dress adjuncts of female costume, making its introduction at the time of the Empire's collapse even more interesting and important.[119] Style II, beginning to appear at the time that the period covered by this book was coming to an end, is, like some of the earlier styles, found on weaponry and then transferred to female items.[120] Nevertheless, close study of the grave-goods and of the nature of costume reveals strikingly that female status, quite unlike male, remained exclusively defined in terms of sex: marriage and childbearing. This created spaces within which women could act to create power for themselves, to be sure,[121] but it may be that post-imperial women were more defined by sex than their Roman predecessors.

The ways in which changes in the precise political significance of marriage entailed changes in female identity might also be explored by looking at the gendering of ethnicity. It was mentioned above that early Frankish law viewed Franks and Romans as adult males. Women and children are not, in this code, distinguished by ethnicity. This implies that ethnicity was achieved and that it was thereby performed, and also that an early Merovingian Frank or Roman was

---

[118] Halsall (1996) for northern Gallic society; the analytical method is badly misrepresented by Effros (2003), pp. 154–63. Stoodley (1999) for analogies in Anglo-Saxon England.
[119] Haseloff (1981).   [120] Høilund Nielsen (1997).   [121] Halsall (1996).

defined by opposition to women and minors – rather as the old civic Roman male had been. Similar conclusions can be reached from other, analogous material from the immediately post-imperial period. The Edict of Theoderic sees its barbarians (soldiers) as exclusively male and there are no female Goths in early Visigothic legislation.[122] Burgundian Law is the only early code to give barbarian ethnic identity to women. Generally this is in relation to marriage. Clause 24 (and, according to some manuscripts, clause 65.1) refers to the widow of a Burgundian who wishes to remarry, and clause 44.1 discusses the daughter of a Burgundian freeman who commits adultery. In all these cases the women are defined by their relationship to a Burgundian male. The only clause where this is not explicitly the case is clause 100, which allows Roman or Burgundian women to choose to marry – once again, marriage is the subject. Other indications point the same way: that ethnicity, especially non-Roman, was essentially masculine. There are, as far as I can see, no individual women in Ostrogothic Italy who are actually described as Goths.[123] Some inscriptions refer to women by ethnic descriptions and Sidonius talks of two drunken old *Getides* who kept him awake at night but this seems to be quite unusual.[124]

This was – yet again – a complex situation and certainly not a static one. Women bore non-Roman names, and three of Theoderic's relatives even had the element 'Goth' within theirs: Thiudegotho and Ostrogotha, to whom we might add his Burgundian granddaughter Suavegotho. An Ultragotho married Childebert I of the Franks.[125] Some sort of adherence to non-Roman groups was, therefore, made manifest in naming practices. This might have referred simply to relationship to Goths or other non-Romans but,

---

[122] *Theoderic's Edict*: above, n. 91. *CE* 276, 304, 312.

[123] See the prosopography of Italian Ostrogoths in Amory (1997), pp. 348–485, though with care as it contains numerous typographic errors.

[124] Dr Mark Handley has pointed out to me a *suaba* attested on an inscription in Hippo Regius (*Année Epigraphique* 1962, no. 347) and an *Alamanna* on an inscription in Florence (*CIL* 11.1731). My thanks to him for these references. Sid. Ap. *Letters* 8.3.2. Simon Loseby has suggested that these women were prostitutes (Wood (ed.) (1998), p. 283 – the comment is wrongly ascribed to me!). Such camp followers might have attracted the same ethnic affiliation as their army. From Sidonius' description it seems unlikely that they were doing much business.

[125] Thiudigotho and Ostrogotha: above, p. 288; Ultragotho: *LH* 4.20; Suavegotho: *PLRE* 2, p. 1037.

especially in the sorts of situations discussed above, the value of marriage alliances will have changed the situation – as implicit in Burgundian law. As land could bring different responsibilities and benefits according to ethnic identity, inheritance was also vital. The importance of marriage and the constantly renegotiated nature of gender identities might further be seen in the fact that a number of what are believed to have been ethnic items of costume, generally brooches such as the eagle-brooches of the Italian and (slightly later) Spanish Goths, are female dress-adjuncts. The same applies even more so to Style I. By the second half of the sixth century, King Liuvigild of the Visigoths lifted the old Roman ban on marriages between Romans and barbarians (or Goths in his law): this is the first extant Gothic legal reference to *Gotae*.[126] The original Roman law seems to have been enacted in the specific circumstances of Firmus' rebellion in North Africa in the 370s[127] and it may well have been that there was no specific need to repeal it until women began to hold non-Roman ethnic identities on a significant scale.[128] By the time that Ripuarian law was issued, probably in the 620s, northern Gaulish free women were assigned the same Ripuarian ethnicity as their menfolk. We can see something of the dynamics of how gender and ethnicity were simultaneously redefined.

It might be that male sexuality was renegotiated as Roman masculine ideals changed. It is possible that sexual continence was considered less important to good rulership than under the Empire. Frankish kings were – famously – serial monogamists, as were other post-imperial rulers. Theoderic the Ostrogoth had three wives. As before, ecclesiastics did not like this and preached long and hard against such behaviour (the church seems to have been the repository of many of the old virtues of Roman civic masculinity)[129] but it does not seem that barbarian rulers ever felt the need to subscribe to sexual continence as part of good rulership. This might have been another way in which non-Roman ethnicity was performed. Politics and gender remained as inextricably intertwined as in the Empire. The bishops' railings against sexually licentious kings manifest this and legislation against incest also seems to have been politically

---

[126] *LV* 3.1.1.   [127] Sivan (1996).   [128] See also Sivan (1998).
[129] Frankish bishops castigate the Merovingians for their sexual licence: *LH* 4.9, 4.26; *VP* 17.2.

motivated.[130] It is significant that political capital could still be made out of such tirades about marital propriety and that the concept of incest could be deployed as a political weapon.

Other changes had effects too. The working through of Christian debates on sexuality in the fifth century made the renunciation of marriage and childbearing possible (if still difficult) for members of society at all levels. This was the most drastic of all challenges to the traditional Roman sex-gender system. It also allowed women the most radical opportunities of changing their status or acquiring power without subscribing to the usual heterosexual norms of marriage and childbearing.

NEW FORMS OF POWER? I: POST-IMPERIAL RULERSHIP

Did the emerging political units of the fifth century produce new forms of rulership and authority? Kingship was a new institution in the imperial west. The kings of, and the nature of kingship in, early medieval western Europe have therefore often been supposed to be a 'Germanic' barbarian introduction. This needs reconsideration.

First of all, we must review what we know of pre-migration kingship in the barbarian territories and repeat that our information is almost entirely Roman in origin and consequently very prob-lematic.[131] Where there were kings it is very possible that the Romans created them, or that their description in the sources is moulded to fit Roman political ideas. Most of the frequently employed sources for rulership north of the Rhine, such as Tacitus and Ammianus, will not bear the weight placed upon them. Nevertheless, we have also seen that the mechanisms available to a pre-industrial ruler of a small polity – religion, defence, law – tally well enough with some of the means of governing mentioned by the Roman writers and find some support in the archaeological data. In the absence of detailed evidence it remains difficult to make these general remarks the basis for reading post-imperial kingship as an imported 'barbarian' institution.

Most historiography, even where invoking 'Germanic' precedent, has usually seen post-imperial kingship as a new development, a melding of influences on Roman soil.[132] The barbarian kings were, essentially, making it up as they went along. It is difficult to see how

---

[130] Wood (1998b).   [131] Above, pp. 121–5.
[132] E.g. James (1989b); Sawyer and Wood (eds.) (1977); Wallace-Hadrill (1971).

they could have done otherwise. As discussed in chapter 4, their ways of thinking about political power were essentially derived from those of the Romans and based around the existence of the Empire. In the breakdown and eventual absence of that Empire, they – like the provincials – were forced to develop responses and new ideas about political authority. These drew upon a range of sources, the most important, naturally enough, being Roman imperial rulership. The fourth-century Emperors had been effective, adult rulers who could present themselves as triumphant war-leaders. They had travelled widely, particularly in the strategically important regions of the Empire, and actively dispensed their patronage. They played an important part in the making of law and took the lead in doctrinal matters, even if sometimes at considerable cost to their own popularity. All these ideas fed into the nature of post-imperial kingship. Another important possible Roman inheritance was the dynastic principle. The late Empire was the era of Roman history most characterised by dynastic succession. The Constantinian dynasty reigned from 306 to 363, and the Valentinianic-Theodosian from 364 to 455. Of the post-imperial royal families, the Merovingians were by far the most successful in creating a dynasty, remaining on the Frankish throne for three centuries. Few were as successful, though all tried. Theoderic came close to establishing the Amals as securely on the Italian throne.[133] The Visigoths were ruled by the Balt family, who claimed (with what accuracy is unknown) kinship with Alaric I, between the accession of Theoderic I in 419 and the death of Amalaric in the 530s. Thereafter, however, a royal dynasty was never able to make its occupancy of the Visigothic throne permanent. Child kings soon succeeded, immediately to be deposed, or the king died childless.[134]

Although the dynastic principle was strong, post-imperial kings, like the emperors, also employed election. Sometimes, as in Rome, this took place when there was no immediate heir, but even where son succeeded father, a show of election could still be made. The kings of the Ostrogoths and of the Franks were raised on shields in front of their troops.[135] Often thought to be a survival from pre-migration 'Germanic' kingship, this is at least as likely, if not more so, to have been a custom adopted from the Roman army.[136] At either

[133] Below, p. 510. [134] Collins (1995), pp. 111–12.
[135] Cassiodorus, *Variae* 10.31; *LH* 2.40, 4.51, 7.10. [136] Above, p. 104.

end of our period, Julian and Justin II were both presented to their troops in this fashion.[137]

Indeed, post-imperial kings portrayed themselves as triumphant military commanders in the late Roman fashion, as was thoroughly demonstrated by Michael McCormick.[138] Few kings could survive without some demonstration of the ability to win wars. The later seventh-century Merovingians, outside our period, are the only significant example. This exception, however, seems to be the result of the Merovingians' extraordinary success, in the fifth and particularly the sixth centuries, in establishing the idea that only members of their family could be kings of the Franks.[139] The immediately post-imperial kings readily appropriated Roman victory ideology. Theoderic the Ostrogoth even incorporated Roman ideology about barbarians. When his troops occupied Provence he announced that it had been retaken from the barbarians – even when those barbarians were Goths ruled by a dynasty claimed by his propaganda to be inferior in status among the Goths only to his own Amal family.[140] Elsewhere, the Ostrogothic king is proclaimed *domitor gentium* (pacifier of the nations) in true imperial fashion.[141] The evidence is less clear but it appears that the Merovingians, similarly, adopted Roman ideas about the Rhine as a cultural barrier.[142]

Western kings also took over the emperors' role in doctrinal and ecclesiastical matters. Theoderic played an active part in resolving the Laurentian schism in spite of his Arian beliefs.[143] Likewise the Arian Alaric II presided over the Catholic Council of Agde (506). Just after the end of our period, the Visigothic king Liuvigild proposed his own modified form of Arianism and his contemporary Chilperic I of Neustria also dabbled in theology, as much to the disgust of their bishops as the doctrinal pronouncements of Constantius II and Valens had been to theirs.[144]

Immediately post-imperial kings adopted other trappings of Roman rule. Again, in the absence of alternative idioms of

---

[137] Amm. Marc. 20.4.17; Corippus, *In Praise of Justin* 2, lines 137 ff.

[138] McCormick (1986).   [139] Halsall (2003a), pp. 27–8.

[140] Cassiodorus, *Variae* 3.17. Cp. *Variae* 2.5.   [141] *CIL* 10.6850–2.

[142] See Gregory of Tours on the 'wild' people from beyond the Rhine: *LH* 4.49. These attitudes are all the more ironic given the Franks' own trans-Rhenan origins.

[143] Moorhead (1992), pp. 114–39. The Laurentian schism was a dispute over the papal succession.

[144] *LH* 5.44, 6.18. John of Biclaro, *Chron.* 58.

monarchical government, this should not astound us. Theudebert I of the Franks is a striking example. Writing to no less a personage than Emperor Justinian he asserted overlordship of a number of peoples in a parallel to Justinian's own adoption of titles, which claimed military success over those same peoples.[145] Theudebert, moreover, struck his own *solidi*, scandalising observers like Procopius who were well aware that to strike such coinage was an imperial prerogative. He held games in Arles, while campaigning in the south,[146] and the Frankish kings continued to present spectacles to their subjects. In the 570s Chilperic I pointedly ignored a challenge from his brother and nephew to open war, instead giving circuses in Paris and Soissons.[147] The Merovingians had inherited the imperial capital in Trier and probably the imperial palace too, which stood next to the amphitheatre. In Metz, too, which eventually superseded Trier as the Austrasian capital, it seems that the royal palace was close to an amphitheatre.[148] Like the Frankish kings, Theoderic took on the role of a provider of public buildings. Stretches of lead piping still exist inscribed with a legend proclaiming his restoration of the water supply to the citizens of Ravenna. He also legislated to preserve Roman public buildings from demolition and reuse.[149] As intimated in the case of Theudebert, post-imperial kings deployed coinage as a vehicle for propaganda. Visigothic kings used coinage to proclaim victories, in true Roman fashion, and Theoderic struck medallions to commemorate his *tricennalia* (the thirtieth anniversary of his accession to the kingship).[150]

There were new features too, however. The Merovingians stand as a good illustration here. In the sixth century it was difficult to trace the Merovingian line beyond the 450s.[151] This was a new dynasty with few or no traditions to build upon, so it had to create these on the hoof. The Merovingians' use of Roman political vocabulary has been mentioned but they added elements of their own. The most famous was their long hair. By Gregory's day the defining characteristic of a male of the royal house was long hair, and he assumed that longhaired kings (*reges criniti*) had governed the Franks

[145] *Austrasian Letters* 20.   [146] Procopius, *Wars* 7.33.5.   [147] *LH* 5.17.
[148] Halsall (1995a), p. 233.   [149] Cassiodorus, *Variae* 2.7, 3.29–31.
[150] Visigothic coins: Hillgarth (1966); Theoderic's medallions: McCormick (1986), pp. 282–3.
[151] Above, pp. 305–6.

since their entry into Roman Gaul.[152] As long hair was a distinctive mark of freedom, the hair of the Merovingians must have been very long indeed. The Merovingians also adopted a means of keeping their family distinct from others. They did not marry into their aristocrats' families, instead marrying lowborn and even slave women or foreign princesses.[153] This meant that aristocrats were never able to claim kinship with the royal family. The only exceptions appear to have been some relatives of their wives whom the Merovingians promoted into the church, such as bishops Bertram of Bordeaux and Bertram of Le Mans. Of course, once in the church such figures could not be the progenitors of rival dynasties and even these bishops' gifts to their other relatives do not appear to have raised their families to any sort of political pre-eminence. Merovingian males possibly married earlier than other Frankish men, at about fifteen, but our evidence for this usually comes from the cases of kings who acceded as minors, and where the demand to produce an heir quickly was pressing.[154]

Legitimacy was also maintained through the use of myth. In the period that concerns this volume, the Ostrogothic Amal dynasty is the best example. Peter Heather's careful analyses have shown that the image presented in the surviving version of the Amal origin myth, written by Jordanes, invented a pedigree for the family going back through the mists of time to an era that even pre-dated Troy (and thus, by implication the Romans' genealogy).[155] The Amals also mentioned pre-Christian demi-gods, called *ansis*, and the Lombards were later to claim that Woden himself had given them their name.[156] Although the evidence for this comes from after the period covered by this book, it is clear that Anglo-Saxon kings, too, claimed divine origins. All but one of the surviving genealogies originates with Woden.[157] The exception, that of the East Saxon kings, starts with the god Seaxnet, mentioned as a deity in later accounts of the conversion of the continental Saxons but otherwise little known. Conceivably, the origin legends about the Saxons' arrival in three ships under the leadership of the brothers Hengest and Horsa were beginning to circulate by the end of our period.

---

[152] *LH* 2.9, 2.41, 3.18, 8.10.   [153] *LH* 4.3, 4.25–8. Wood (1994a), pp. 121–3.

[154] E.g. Childebert II, the end to whose ten-year minority appears to have involved his marriage (cp. *LH* 7.33, 7.37).

[155] Above, pp. 334, 459–61.   [156] *Getica* 13.78; *HL* 1.8.

[157] Dumville (1976); (1977a).

The gradual move away from seeing legitimacy in Roman terms to ideologies that stressed the martial and political vigour of the barbarian dynasties might have resulted partly from unease and a lack of confidence in claiming imperial legitimacy. The Austrasian branch of the Merovingians initially had their seat at Trier, the former capital, but by the third quarter of the sixth century had removed themselves to Metz, the next city up the Moselle.[158] They were still able to create a royal complex that had all the elements of an imperial palace (audience chamber; major church; arena). Nevertheless it seems clear that in Trier, with a self-confident local aristocracy stressing its Romanness[159] and an awkward local episcopal tradition of standing up to secular power (much stressed by the powerful and long-lived metropolitan, St Nicetius[160]), the imperial buildings were difficult to appropriate. A 'second division' town like Metz presented an easier canvas upon which to inscribe the dynasty's political identity. This shift to lesser towns, away from the main cities of the late Roman world can be seen elsewhere at about the same time. The Neustrian branch of the Franks had adopted Paris as their capital. Paris had been the base of Emperor Julian and a provincial capital, but it was not a major city of Roman Gaul, being less important than Reims for example. The Merovingians' adoption of Paris might have had rather more to do with the city's association with the first two kings of the line, Childeric I and Clovis. In the mid-sixth century the Spanish Visigoths shifted their capital from Barcelona to Toledo, again a town of lesser importance in the Roman period.[161]

Something that possibly added to western rulers' insecurity in adopting imperial style was imperial ideology itself. It has been argued that the idea of the 'end of the Roman Empire' was a creation of the 520s and that before that the date 476 had had little significance.[162] This is unlikely to be the case as far as western society and local and regional politics are concerned, as we have seen. Nevertheless, it is indisputable that the 520s did see the emergence of an imperial ideology about the loss of the west to the barbarians.[163] It may be that this was itself a response to some of the more self-assertive royal

---

[158] Halsall (1995a), pp. 12–13, 231–3.   [159] Above, pp. 353–4.
[160] On whom see *VP* 17.
[161] The later Lombard choice of Pavia as a capital continued the trend: one of Theoderic's chief residences but not a major Roman city.
[162] Amory (1997), pp. 120–8; Croke (1983).   [163] Amory (1997), pp. 135–47.

ideologies emerging in the west by that date, most notably in Theoderic's Italy. Whatever the case, by early on in Justinian's reign it cannot have been easy to maintain the fiction that rule in the west was a simple matter of the old business under new management. It was difficult to claim that the western Empire simply continued under new rulers who owed their position to the emperor when the emperor himself was proclaiming those territories to have been lost and in need of reconquest.

Nonetheless, these developments show that barbarian kings were becoming ever more interested in presenting themselves in their own right rather than simply as officials of a distant emperor and in some cases this was the result of self-confidence. In Vandal Africa, although the kings took over many of the trappings of imperial rule, they also, interestingly and precociously, adopted a separate classical ideology – that of Carthage.[164] It is unfortunate that we have so little that presents Vandal rulership in its own terms but Punic symbols were adopted on Vandal coins. The kingdom dated its foundation not to the first treaty with the Romans in 434 but to its conquest of Carthage in 439. The Vandal case is interesting. Their kings were the only non-Roman dynasty to have a claim to the imperial title, through the marriage of Huneric and Eudocia, and the maintenance of the imperial cult and other aspects of Roman government have been mentioned. Yet they simultaneously presented themselves as a second Carthaginian empire. One might see in this a move to incorporate themselves in the classical Roman worldview.

Overall there is little about post-imperial kingship, beyond some claims to descent from Woden, that can convincingly be called 'Germanic' and less that can be argued to stem from the straight-forward importation of political institutions from the *barbaricum*. Post-imperial kingship was something new, but it drew most of its components from imperial ideology.

NEW FORMS OF POWER? 2: ARISTOCRACY AND NOBILITY

The period of the migrations has been held to have witnessed a change from a civil to a warrior aristocracy.[165] Barbarian war-leaders and their retinues replaced the educated noble élite of the Roman

---

[164] Clover (1986).
[165] E.g. Barnish (1988); Heather (1994); (2000b); James (1997); Wormald (1976).

world. By the close of the period that concerns this book there can be no doubt that the nature of the social élite in western Europe *had* changed, and in much the way just suggested, with increasing militarisation. This change again owed much to the pre-existing nature of Roman society. The provincial aristocracy's 'demilitarisation' has been considerably overestimated; it continued to see military service as an important aspect of its lifestyle.[166] Northern Gaul had become more and more militarised since the beginning of the fourth century and its regional élite was deploying weaponry as a symbol of its local power from the last quarter of that century, long before any barbarian take-over or significant settlement.[167] What is more, many aristocrats performed such service in regiments clad in 'barbarised' dress and with barbarian unit names. The political demise of the Empire led to the withering away of the old civic option in public service. These developments involved important renegotiations of ideas of masculinity and that the precedents set in Roman military service presented a route via which the dramatic political changes of the fifth century could be navigated.

Although the aristocrat of the fifth- and sixth-century west was increasingly likely to be armed and to have a warrior following, this was not a purely 'Germanic' feature. Certainly, the Roman aristocrats of southern Gaul, the circle and indeed the relatives of Sidonius Apollinaris, soon found themselves raising troops to fight against and later for the barbarian leaders in their region.[168] The Romans of Spain did not sit passively by as the Sueves, Vandals and Goths fought for domination of the peninsula. Some tried to resist Constantine 'III'; others fought the Goths and Sueves.[169] Even members of noble Italian dynasties incorporated military service and command into their lifestyle.[170] The *Bagaudae* of central and northern Gaul were armed Roman leaders and at least some of the Britons, particularly in the west of the diocese, fought hard against the incoming barbarians from northern Germany.[171] Others appear to have maintained some sort of Romanised force south of the Thames, and perhaps *became*

---

[166] Above, pp. 109–10. [167] Above, pp. 350–1.
[168] Sid. Ap. *Letters* 3.3; *LH* 2.37. Halsall (2003a), pp. 44–5.
[169] Oros. 7.40.5; Hydatius 81, 164; Isidore, *History of the Goths* 45; John of Biclaro, *Chron.* 32, 36, 47.
[170] Above, pp. 334–5.
[171] *Bagaudae*: above, p. 218, n. 164. Fighting Britons: *DEB* 22.

Saxons. The common ideas that the Romans needed barbarians for military protection and that the Britons were the only provincials to take up arms in their own defence are in serious need of revision.[172] So too is any view of the fifth century as a fight between 'Romans' and 'barbarians' when one considers how non-Roman political and military groups became the focus for Roman regional political factions. The militarisation of the aristocracy was not therefore a simple matter of importing barbarian ideals, though it might have been an extension of the barbarisation of the late Roman army. Essentially it was a continuation of the late Roman situation.

Nevertheless, although increasingly following the military idiom, the sixth-century aristocracy retained many features of the late Roman social élite. They continued, for example, to engage in the letter-writing that expressed *amicitia*. This is clearest, as one might expect, in areas like southern Gaul but it was also the case in the north, where the evidence survives less well. In Trier, Count Arbogast, of Frankish descent, received a flattering letter praising his *romanitas* from Sidonius, and a verse letter from the nearby bishop of Toul.[173] A century later some other letters from members of the Frankish court survive within the collection known as the *Austrasian Letters* (*Epistulae Austrasiacae*). These too fall clearly within the tradition of late Latin epistolography. They also sometimes patronised Latin poets like Venantius Fortunatus, although Fortunatus himself soon found that he could not make a living at the Frankish court and moved south to Aquitaine.[174] The hunting beloved of early medieval aristocrats also had its Roman precedents. In the south of Gaul, Spain and Italy, at least up until Justinian's wars, aristocratic life continued much as before.[175]

It is, as with kingship, difficult to identify specifically non-Roman aspects of aristocratic culture and lifestyle because of the nature of the evidence. What little we know of barbarian aristocrats before the migrations suggests that, like their kings, they were fixated with anything Roman. Certainly those who took service in the Empire were happy to adopt the trappings of Roman élite lifestyle. Other elements of their way of life that we might postulate, such as a concern with birth and descent and a love of hunting are difficult to

---

[172] For these ideas, see, e.g. Jones (1964), pp. 1058–64.
[173] Sid. Ap. *Letters* 4.17; *Austrasian Letters* 22.   [174] Brennan (1985).
[175] Barnish (1988); Mathisen (1993). Kulikowski (2004); Wormald (1976).

distinguish from identical elements in Roman aristocratic culture. Undoubtedly, barbarian aristocrats had to be warriors, but as has just been outlined, this was also an important feature of Roman élite lifestyle. The best we can say is that the importance of this aspect was enhanced in post-imperial Europe by the presence of non-Roman aristocrats.

In the bases of aristocratic power, the fall of the Empire and the barbarian migrations played little or no role at all. The Roman élite had based its social distinction upon land-ownership and office-holding. Economically, all power stemmed from the control of the surplus drawn from land, although there were differences in the ways by which it was extracted.[176] In addition to the actual ownership of large tracts of land, Roman aristocrats also drew income from their involvement in the state, which paid them in drafts on its taxation. Both of these alternatives survived the demise of the western Empire and lived on until the end of our period, the latter to atrophy around 600. There had been regional variations in the relative importance of these two elements under the Empire and these continued. It is possible that the importance of office-holding increased in the post-imperial period.

The post-imperial aristocracy made increasing use of the church in maintaining its power. Once again this was something that can be said to have continued a late Roman trend but a trend that appears to have begun comparatively late and one which was probably a response to the crisis of the Empire.[177] The senatorial aristocracy adopted Christianity only from the end of the fourth century and the move into the episcopate by such aristocrats was generally a fifth-century development.

CONCLUSION

Throughout the period between *c*.375 and *c*.535, at some levels, especially in terms of its political and institutional structures, western Europe remained recognisably part of the Roman world. Nevertheless, throughout that time, at more detailed levels vital changes were constantly taking place. Alongside the socio-economic transformations examined in chapter 11, identities were being

---

[176] For a useful survey of these means see Wickham (2005), pp. 259–302.
[177] E.g. Mathisen (1993), pp. 89–104; Van Dam (1985), pp. 141–56.

renegotiated. These changes were complex and dramatic. In places like Britain and northern Gaul a single lifetime could experience a shift from a complex urban, monetised, Romanised society, with villas, finewares and long-distance exchange to an unremittingly local and rural society with no towns and no manufacture, craft-specialisation or long-distance economic connections. At the same time, a generation could see the renegotiation of one's identities, political, ethnic and gendered. Although I have been at pains to stress that these changes could take a generation or more, and that their outcomes were never predetermined, they were still dramatic and often traumatic, and cannot and should not be summed up in glib generalisations. The changes in ethnicity were part and parcel of the renegotiation of gender identities and of the bases of political authority. All these different dimensions of identity, and the changes that took place within them, were interlinked. Bit by bit, the societies of the west moved away from the traditional Roman social ideals that had glued the Empire together. In the middle decades of the century the important changes that had taken place were exaggerated by a series of further, dramatic political events, which sounded the death-knell for the old structures of the western Roman Empire. In the last chapter of this book, we turn our attention to these final convulsions.

15

A CHANGED WORLD: THE ROOTS OF FAILURE

In late July 533 a fleet of 600 vessels left Constantinople and headed west. On board was an army of at least 17,000 men[2] under the command of Belisarius, another commander of Balkan extraction, who had distinguished himself on the Persian front and in quelling the *Nike* revolt in Constantinople. The latter – an uprising of the capital's citizens in January 532 – had come close to costing the emperor Justinian his throne and life (the rebellion drew its name from the rallying cry of '*Nike!*' or 'Victory!').[3] The dispatch of the fleet would distract attention from the emperor's unpopular domestic policies but this was not the principal reason. The expedition had been a long time in planning. Under Justinian and his predecessor and uncle, Justin I, a new, aggressive ideology had begun to emanate from Constantinople, stressing the loss of the west to the barbarians. In part, as we have seen, this was possibly a response to the increasingly self-confident ideological output of Theoderic's later years, which might have begun to be matched in the Frankish realms. Justinian's

---

[1] Moorhead (2005b), pp. 123–9, for brief narrative.
[2] According to Procopius (*Wars* 3.11.2, 11, 19): 10,000 infantry; 5,000 cavalry, and 1,000 Huns and Heruls, plus Belisarius' guards (at least 1,100 – *Wars* 3.17.1, 3.19.23).
[3] Greatrex (1997).

project for the reconquest of the west was the outcome of this ideological conflict.

Justinian's cordial relationships with the Ostrogothic queen Amalasuentha enabled Belisarius' fleet to head for Sicily but its true objective was Vandal Africa. A revolt had broken out in Sardinia, doubtless fuelled by imperial gold, and the Vandal fleet and many troops were absent from Africa quelling this uprising.[4] Another rebellion against the Vandals was provoked in Tripolitania.[5] With these distractions and the misinformation spread about the fleet's destination, on 30 August 533 Belisarius was able to land unopposed on the eastern shore of *Byzacena* at Caput Vada, in modern Tunisia.[6] The emperor justified the invasion on the grounds of Hilderic's recent deposition by Gelimer and posed as the upholder of legitimacy, not least because Hilderic was a member of the Theodosian dynasty (Valentinian III's grandson). Belisarius' force marched on Carthage and defeated the Vandal army sent against it, as much by luck as judgement, at Ad Decimum (13 September).[7] Carthage was taken without trouble. Not long afterwards the Vandal fleet returned from crushing the Sardinian uprising, however, and Belisarius' troops had to fight against the reinforced Vandal army at Tricamerum, outside Carthage, in December.[8] Again the eastern Roman army scored a victory on the basis of poor Vandal leadership rather than any tactical genius on Belisarius' part. Gelimer was besieged in the mountains, where he sheltered with the Moors, but was induced by the Gepid commander of the surrounding army to give himself up.[9] Sent back to Constantinople along with 2,000 Vandal warriors, all that was left of the people that had once terrorised the Mediterranean, Gelimer was the focus of Belisarius' triumph in the capital city in 534.

Belisarius' campaign was a dramatic success and the much-feared Vandal kingdom had collapsed. The eastern Roman reconquest of North Africa had, however, really only just begun. Belisarius and his successors in command in the region had to conduct twenty years of hard warfare against the Moors and against mutinies and rebellions within the Roman army, all of which proved much more difficult to deal with than had the ill-led Vandal forces, before the province could

---

[4] Procopius, *Wars* 3.10.25–34, 11.16.22–4.   [5] *Wars* 3.10.22–4.
[6] *Wars* 3.14.17.   [7] *Wars* 3.18–19.   [8] *Wars* 4.2–3.   [9] *Wars* 4.6–7.12–17.

truly be said to have returned to imperial government. In the process, the hitherto prosperous region was badly ravaged.[10]

The success of the Vandal campaign provided the springboard for Justinian's next and most ambitious project, the reconquest of Italy and of Rome itself. Again the pretext for invasion was provided by internal political difficulties. Theoderic had died without male children. He had married his daughter Amalasuentha to a nobleman called Eutharic, whom his propagandists claimed was a scion of the Amal royal house (supposedly a descendant of Ermenaric) found living amongst the Visigoths and declared him to be his successor.[11] In spite of imperial recognition being given to Eutharic, tensions were already arising with Constantinople, and Eutharic predeceased Theoderic, creating something of a succession crisis.[12] When the old king died, his successor was an eight-year-old, Athalaric, who acceded to the throne with his mother as regent. For eight years Amalasuentha was able, with her father's skilful mix of force and persuasion, to maintain her authority and eliminate some potential rivals.[13] However, in 534, Athalaric died, according to Procopius as a result of his excessive drunkenness and debauchery.[14] To keep her (and her family's) hold on power Amalasuentha married her cousin Theodehad, already a powerful and apparently unpopular landlord in Tuscany (Theoderic had had to rein in his land-grabbing).[15] This turned out to be an unhappy marriage, as Theodehad had no desire simply to be his cousin's consort. Amalasuentha was imprisoned and shortly afterwards murdered.[16]

Justinian was once again able to pose as the champion of legitimacy and opponent of usurpers. Belisarius' army sailed to Sicily, which was soon conquered.[17] Crossing to the mainland (May 536), the Roman

---

[10] *Wars* 4.10–28. Modéran (2003b), pp. 565–644; on damage to North Africa, see Cameron, A. M. (1989).

[11] Jordanes, *Getica* 14.80–1, 48.251, 58.298. Heather (1996), p. 233; Wolfram (1988), pp. 310–11.

[12] Above, pp. 291–2.

[13] Cassiodorus, *Variae* 11.1; Procopius, *Wars*, 5.2. Heather (1996), pp. 260–2; Wolfram (1988), pp. 334–9.

[14] *Wars* 5.3.10 – a story riddled with irony: Halsall (2002b), pp. 106–7.

[15] Procopius, *Wars* 5.3.1–2, 5.4.1–3; Cassiodorus, *Variae* 4.39.

[16] *LH* 3.31 (a very negative portrayal of Amalasuentha); Jordanes, *Getica* 59.306; Procopius, *Wars* 5.4.26–8.

[17] The Gothic wars are best followed in detail in the narratives of Procopius, *Wars* books 4–8, and Agathias, *Histories* books 1–2. There is a brief but excellent

army marched north to Naples, where the local population put up a stiff resistance. Eventually, gaining access to the city through treason, Belisarius' troops sacked the city and put much of the population to the sword, 'pour encourager les autres'.[18] Perhaps not surprisingly, the other towns of southern Italy presented little or no opposition to the Roman army and Belisarius was rapidly able to enter Rome (10 December 536).[19] By this time the Goths had tired of Theodehad's vacillation (he was attempting to make his own deal with Justinian) and murdered him. He was replaced on the throne by Wittigis, one of his military commanders, who nevertheless felt obliged to marry a princess of the Amal house in order to legitimise his position.[20] Wittigis mustered the Gothic army and besieged Belisarius in Rome. The siege of Rome by the Goths (March 537 to March 538), with its episodes of 'derring-do', is one of the highlights of Procopius' history of Justinian's wars.[21] Nonetheless, it is often forgotten that, although an eye-witness, Procopius did not write up his account until about ten years after the event and enmeshed it in the usual trappings of Graeco-Roman ethnography.[22]

Wittigis established a number of camps around Rome but was unable to blockade the city completely. As a result it was possible to get food and troops into and out of the walled area and Belisarius' aggressive sorties put the Gothic camps under as much pressure as the supposedly besieged city. Eventually, after about a year, Wittigis broke up the siege and marched away. Both sides in the war now made approaches to the dominant power in the west, that of the Franks, who had just absorbed the Burgundian kingdom. Theudebert, son of Clovis' eldest son Theuderic, had recently inherited the throne of Austrasia. He represented the new generation of increasingly confident non-Roman rulers, with no qualms about dealing with the emperor as an equal.[23] In return for his support, the Ostrogoths promised him Provence, which was, following the conquest of Burgundy, directly on the Franks' doorstep. On the

---

outline in Heather (1996), pp. 263–71. Moorhead (2005b), pp. 124–9; Wolfram (1988), pp. 342–62; (1997a), pp. 224–39; See also Kaegi (1995); Teall (1965); Thompson, E. A. (1982), pp. 77–109, for rather simplified analysis.

[18] Procopius, *Wars* 5.8.43–10.45.   [19] *Wars* 5.14.14.

[20] Procopius, *Wars* 5.11.5–9; Jordanes, *Getica* 60.310 (Wittigis' election and Theodehad's murder); Jordanes, *Getica* 60.311; *Variae* 10.32 (marriage).

[21] Procopius, *Wars* 5.16–6.10.   [22] Cameron, A. M. (1985), pp. 188–206.

[23] Above, p. 491.

other hand, Justinian promised the Franks large sums of money.[24] Theudebert had no particular interest in supporting either but every intention of sending his troops into Italy. Theudebert occupied Provence and, typically, held horse races for the populace in the circus of the great imperial city of Arles.[25] Justinian's recognition of this conquest might have been the first formal recognition of independent barbarian rule in the west.[26] His armies then entered Italy, where they slaughtered Goths and Romans alike.[27] Not for the last time, the Frankish armies in Italy were ravaged by dysentery and forced to retreat back to Gaul.[28] Nevertheless, some northern Italian cities were taken and remained under Frankish control, in shady circumstances, for decades to come.[29]

By May 540 Belisarius had penned Wittigis into Ravenna. The Gothic war could have been ended at this point. Justinian offered the Goths peace in return for a kingdom north of the river Po.[30] More than one commentator has pointed out that, strategically, this would have been very useful to the Empire, as a buffer between Roman Italy and the Franks.[31] Belisarius disagreed, however, and, taking advantage of an offer by the Goths to make him their king, seized Ravenna and captured Wittigis, who was sent east into retirement.[32] Nevertheless, the offer of the Gothic throne and Belisarius' feigned acceptance aroused Justinian's suspicion. Belisarius was recalled and the Goths endured a messy succession crisis, which threatened to fragment their kingdom.[33] A Rugian called Eraric set himself up as a candidate and claimed that the *Rugi* had never intermarried with the Goths (not a dissimilar strategy from that adopted by the Ostrogoths themselves when they broke free of Hunnic domination).[34] Nevertheless, in 541 the throne passed to a warrior usually

---

[24] Procopius, *Wars* 5.13.14, 26–9, 7.33.2–4.   [25] Procopius, *Wars* 7.33.5.

[26] *Wars* 7.33.4. I am grateful to Ian Wood for drawing my attention to this point, first noted by eighteenth-century French historians but subsequently neglected.

[27] Procopius, *Wars* 6.25.8–15.

[28] *LH* 3.32; Procopius, *Wars* 6.25.16–18, 24. On dysentery as an enemy of armies in Italy, see Halsall (2003a), p. 153.

[29] Procopius, *Wars* 8.24.6–8; James (1988), pp. 97–8.   [30] Procopius, *Wars* 6.29.1–2.

[31] E.g. Wolfram (1988), p. 348.   [32] Procopius, *Wars* 6.29.4–6, 17–40, 7.1.1–2.

[33] Procopius, *Wars* 6.30, 7.1.17, 7.1.25–49, 7.2.

[34] Procopius, *Wars* 7.2.1–2. For commentary, see Heather (1996), p. 175, with some critical comments on this reading at Halsall (1999a), pp. 139–40.

called by the name he is given in Byzantine sources: Totila.[35] Totila is
an enigmatic figure often painted, by those emploting the history of
the Italian Ostrogoths as tragedy, as the doomed hero of the Gothic
kingdom. Be that as it may, he was a skilful commander who, over the
next decade, returned most of the Italian peninsula to Gothic rule.[36]
The rapacity of Justinian's officials aided his cause. Totila's strategy
was to avoid large-scale pitched battles with the Romans but to wear
them down by constant fast-moving harrying raids and skirmishes.
As town after town fell to his forces, his armies were swelled by
Roman troops who deserted to the Goths. In desperation, Belisarius
was sent back to Italy (544–8), but even this talismanic (if probably
rather overrated) general was unable to make any headway. He was
forced to sail between the ever shrinking number of ports still in
Byzantine hands: by 549 only a handful were left.[37] Responding to
the Empire's control of the sea, Totila formed a fleet and seized Sicily,
Corsica and Sardinia, as well as ravaging the coasts of the Roman
Balkan provinces.[38]

Meanwhile, in 540, partly encouraged by the arrival of Gothic
envoys, the Persians had resumed hostilities on the eastern frontier,
distracting Roman resources away from Justinian's western endeav-
ours (it is worth repeating that campaigning continued in North
Africa). A great plague, the so-called Yellow Death, also swept
through the Mediterranean in the 540s.[39] The eastern Empire was
particularly hard hit and it has been very plausibly argued that the
losses through this calamity further eroded Roman morale. As the
war dragged on, Italy was laid waste. Rome, captured and recaptured,
was reduced to a ghost of its former self although Procopius' famous
account of the deserted city is doubtless something of an exaggeration.[40] Totila executed many of the Roman senatorial order in
exasperation at their political unreliability and others fled east to
Constantinople. The old Roman order, which had survived and even

---

[35] Procopius, *Wars*, 7.2.7–13, 18. Judging from his coins, his preferred name appears
to have been Baduila.

[36] Procopius, *Wars*, 7.3–40 *passim*. Modern commentators: Burns (1984), pp. 212–14;
Heather (1996), pp. 268–71; Moorhead (2005b), pp. 127–9; Wolfram (1988),
pp. 353–61.

[37] Procopius, *Wars* 7.30–40.   [38] *Wars* 7.39–40, 8.22.17–18, 8.24.31–3.

[39] *Wars* 8.1–17 (Persian war); 2.22 (plague). Horden (2005).

[40] Procopius, *Wars* 7.22.19. For modern views of Rome's fortunes, see the papers
collected in Smith, J. M. H. (ed.) (2000).

prospered under the rule of the Ostrogoths, was being destroyed by wars unleashed by the Roman emperor.

Eventually, in 550, Justinian was able to assemble an army large enough to put an end to Gothic resistance. Totila lost many men when the Roman navy destroyed his fleet in 551.[41] Other heavy losses in the Goths' territories in Dalmatia followed and Justinian's army, under the command of the eunuch general, Narses, entered the peninsula (not without luck) from the north in spring 552.[42] With the arrival of this overwhelming military force, the balance of power swung against the Goths. In a desperate gamble, Totila committed his troops to battle against Narses at a place called Taginae or Busta Gallorum (the Tombs of the Gauls).[43] Throwing caution to the winds the Goths hurled themselves in a wild charge at the Roman lines but were shattered by volleys of archery. Totila was mortally wounded and died during the pursuit. Later that year, his successor Teïas faced Narses in the last, cataclysmic showdown of the wars. At Mons Lactarius (Monte Lettere: Milky Mountain) in the shadow of Vesuvius, the Gothic army went down fighting.[44] For two days it fought tooth and nail against the Roman forces. Teïas himself was killed on the first day but the fighting went on for another day before the last of the Goths surrendered. After that it was a question of mopping up operations, including the defeat of further Frankish invasions (553–4) and the expulsion of some of their garrisons.[45] With the quashing of minor rebellions and the surrender of the last obdurate Ostrogothic garrisons in 561, Roman rule was re-established in Italy, although the provinces north of the Alps were never regained by the Empire and remained under Frankish hegemony. In 554 Justinian had issued his *Pragmatic Sanction*, formally recognising that the Empire once again reigned in Italy.[46]

In 555, as the Gothic wars were drawing to a close, Justinian was able to intervene in Spain. Once again, a succession dispute amongst the barbarians provided the excuse. The Visigoths had never really recovered from their defeat at Vouillé. The effectiveness of their rule in Spain at this date has probably been overestimated and seems to have taken the form of hegemony rather than outright control of the peninsula and politics there had been turbulent.[47] Theudis was

---

[41] Procopius, *Wars* 8.23.29–42.   [42] *Wars* 8.26.18–25.   [43] *Wars* 8.29–32.
[44] *Wars* 8.35.   [45] Agathias, *Histories* 1.1–2.14.   [46] Moorhead (1994), p. 111.
[47] Above, pp. 298–9.

assassinated in 548 and succeeded by his general Theudigisel or Theudisculus (Little Theudis).[48] Theudisculus was himself murdered soon afterwards,[49] the Goths, according to Gregory of Tours, having 'adopted the reprehensible habit of killing out of hand any king who displeased them and replacing him on the throne with someone whom they preferred'.[50] In this case they appear to have preferred a king called Agila. Agila was not destined to enjoy a long reign. Further illustrating the hegemonic nature of Gothic rule, he was humiliated when the citizens of Cordoba inflicted a military defeat on him, after he insulted their local saint.[51] Military defeat, not untypically, threw his regime into doubt and another Gothic nobleman called Athanagild rose in rebellion against him. In this context, Justinian sent his expedition to Spain.[52] In command was none other than Liberius, former servant of Odoacer and later mastermind of the Gothic settlement in Italy, now aged about eighty! Liberius' troops seem to have been called in by Athanagild, in something of a change from the usual Justinianic *modus operandi* of supporting the legitimate ruler (indeed, Jordanes thought the Roman force was sent to support Agila).[53] In this sequence of assassination and rebellion the claim of any Visigothic king to legitimacy was questionable.

Traditionally it was thought that the new Roman province of *Spania* extended as far inland as the Guadalquivir. However, the Roman forces appear only to have seized a coastal strip around the south-east of the Iberian peninsula.[54] Many other towns remained beyond Visigothic control and their conquest is recorded in the reign of Athanagild's successor Leuvigild. However, this does not mean that they were all under Roman authority. It is clear that Gothic authority beyond *Tarraconensis* was fragmented. These cities are likely always to have been effectively independent. Justinian's aim does not

[48] *Chronicle of Saragossa*, s.a. 544; Isidore, *History of the Goths* 43–4; *LH* 3.30.
[49] *Chronicle of Saragossa*, s.a. 545; Isidore, *History of the Goths* 44; Jordanes, *Getica* 57.303; *LH* 3.30. The *Chronicle of Saragossa*, though its absolute chronology is confused at this point, records that Theudisculus reigned for a year and seven months.
[50] *LH* 3.30.   [51] Isidore, *History of the Goths*, 45–6.
[52] Isidore, *History of the Goths* 47; Jordanes, *Getica* 57.303. Liberius had been commanding eastern Roman forces in Sicily somewhat ineptly (perhaps unsurprisingly given his age): Procopius, *Wars* 7.39.6–7, 12–13, 18; 8.24.1.
[53] Thompson, E. A. (1969), pp. 323–9, for extended hypothesis.
[54] Thompson, E. A. (1969), pp. 320–3.

seem to have been the reconquest of the Iberian peninsula although doubtless if the opportunity had presented itself he would have taken it. Instead the objective appears to have been the security of the reconquered territories in North Africa. The end of Theudis' regime, like that of Agila's, was sparked by military defeat, in this case the defeat of a Visigothic attempt to seize Ceuta on the North African coast.[55] By taking control of the Spanish littoral, Justinian put an end to the possibility of future attacks like this on his potentially prosperous territories. The Byzantine province in Spain never seems to have had a clear frontier with Gothic territory, which might result from the fact that towns to the north were effectively independent of Gothic control and acted as a buffer zone.[56]

In 565 the emperor Justinian died. At that stage his armies had reconquered Italy and North Africa and a swathe of southern Spain. He had done more to restore Roman authority in western Europe than any emperor since Theodosius but his death spared him the pain of seeing the Lombard invasion of Italy in 568.[57] The Lombards in *Pannonia* were threatened by the hegemony of the Avars in the Danube basin, ironically instigated by Justinian's transfer of that people to the region to counter other groups there. Like numerous other barbarians who lost out in the struggle for political dominance beyond the frontier, the Lombards, under their king Alboin, crossed the Alps and descended upon Italy. Before long, they had established a kingdom north of the Po and two powerful duchies based upon Spoleto in south-central Italy and around Benevento in the south. The unity of Italy was shattered.

THE ROOTS OF FAILURE (I): THE BARBARIANS

The events of the middle quarters of the sixth century, which bring this book to its close, beg two vitally important questions. Why did the 'first generation' barbarian kingdoms collapse so quickly in the middle of the sixth century, especially when we have seen that they were so Roman in nature and usually involved the active participation of the provincials? Why was the expanded empire of Justinian

---

[55] Isidore, *History of the Goths* 42.   [56] Ripoll (2001).
[57] On the Lombard background, and invasion of Italy, see: *HL* 1.23–4, 27, 2.5–9, 12, 14, 25–7; *LH* 4.41; Menander, *History*, fr. 12.1–2; Procopius, *Wars* 8.18, 25, 27. Christie (1995), pp. 73–91; Pohl (2002), pp. 195–201; Wolfram (1997a), pp. 284–8.

unable to hang on to its reconquered territories? This second question is especially interesting. One reason for the success of the early Roman Empire was its expansionist policies. Why was military expansion unable to produce similar effects for the sixth-century Empire?

We can deal with the roots of barbarian failure first. In the cases of the Vandals and the Ostrogoths, they can be sought at the top, in the failure of leadership. Gelimer proved unable to act decisively in the face of Roman invasion and twice threw away the chance to defeat Belisarius.[58] In the Vandal instance, too, one ought to consider the military balance of power. Although, according to Procopius, contemporaries and even some of the military commanders feared that any operation against the Vandals was doomed to be a failure, their pessimism was probably misplaced.[59] The Vandal navy was probably not a purpose-built fleet of war-galleys.[60] Even in 468 Gaiseric had not been confident of his chances of defeating the Roman fleet in open battle. The Vandal army had declined and had recently suffered serious defeats at the hands of the Moorish rulers who were extending their power at Vandal expense.[61] Finally it is worth repeating the size of Belisarius' army. Although Procopius gives the impression that it was considered to be a woefully small expeditionary force, an army of *c.*15,000–20,000 men (if Procopius' figures are at all accurate) was a mighty host in late antiquity, which the Vandals will have done well to have met on equal terms.[62] Procopius had his own clear reasons for presenting Belisarius' force as outnumbered yet his own account does not, in fact, suggest that the Vandal forces were very large at all.[63]

Another factor in the rapid collapse of the Vandal regime was the alienation of the Vandals from the Roman population of Africa. This might have been overplayed.[64] Procopius, for example, cannot conceal the fact that some African peasants attacked Roman stragglers to obtain the bounty placed by the Vandals on the heads of Roman troops.[65] Nonetheless, religious conflict, though sporadic, was more severe in Vandal Africa than elsewhere and we need to consider why

---

[58] Procopius, *Wars* 3.19.25–9, 4.3.11.   [59] *Wars* 3.10.3–6.

[60] Above, p. 325.   [61] Above, pp. 294–6.

[62] For the vexed question of army sizes in the early medieval west, see Halsall (2003a), pp. 119–33; for the implications of the supply demands of Byzantine armies, and the consequent restrictions upon army size, see Haldon (1999), pp. 281–92.

[63] Courtois (1955), pp. 354–6. Procopius alleges 800 dead at Tricamerum: *Wars* 4.3.24.

[64] Above, pp. 326–7.   [65] Procopius, *Wars* 3.13.1–4.

the alienation of the Vandals from the Romans might have been greater than the separation between Romans and barbarians in other areas of the post-imperial world. Partly this must be explained by the Vandal kingdom's proximity to the Roman Empire. Roman *Tripolitania* lay just across the frontier, and the sea route to Constantinople and the east was well used. This meant that access to the Roman Empire and a rival source of political authority and legitimacy was comparatively easy. Opponents of the regime habitually fled to Constantinople, where they were vocal in their calls for imperial help. The facility with which the Empire could be reached or appealed to must go a long way towards explaining the Vandals' wariness of their North African subjects. In connection with this, it is worth repeating the importance of the Moorish kings. For some time before the eastern Roman invasion the Moors had extended their power into the edges of the Vandal kingdom.[66] These kings, as we have seen, trumpeted their own credentials as legitimate heirs of Rome and their success was presumably the result of the decision of local Roman Africans to choose the 'kings of the Moors and the Romans' over the 'kings of the Vandals and the Alans'. Their military successes doubtless aided people in making this choice, strengthening the political identity based on the Moors.

In the Ostrogothic kingdom, the failure of leadership was probably even more important. Theoderic's lack of an adult male heir meant that there was no king to continue his policies. If we compare the Italian situation with that in Merovingian Gaul we see very clearly how a succession of adult rulers could produce a situation wherein the royal dynasty was unassailable in its tenure of the throne.[67] The Ostrogothic evidence argues that the Amals were well on the way towards creating a very similar situation but their succession problems stalled this and allowed opposition factions to become more significant. These crystallised especially amongst those elements of Italian society that had the most to lose from Theoderic's policies, the Gothic nobility and the Roman senatorial order, both threatened with reduction to the level of service aristocrats.[68] As with the Vandal kingdom, however, the Ostrogothic state lay close to the Empire. Communications between Italy and Constantinople were easy and frequent. As the Empire hardened its attitude towards the increasingly self-confident western rulers it became a focus for opposition to

---

[66] Above, pp. 294–6.   [67] Above, pp. 310, 356–7.   [68] Above, pp. 331–3.

Theoderic's regime and provided a rival source of ideas of political legitimacy. In competition for local power, the supporters of the Goths, who wielded power legitimised by a connection with the court at Ravenna, could be countered by claiming the higher legitimacy of a link to the emperor himself. As it became clear that Belisarius' invasion might be successful, this option became the more attractive. After 540, as the war became fragmented and fortunes swung back and forth, the choice between rival forms of power was accentuated and itself promoted the peninsula's political fragmentation.

Nevertheless it is very important to note how the state hung together after Theoderic's death.[69] The dynasty survived eight years of minority rule with a female regent and, even after Theodehad's murder, Wittigis felt obliged to marry into the house. Few early medieval dynasties could survive the accession of a child, the most obvious exception being the Merovingians, where the endurance of repeated minorities reveals the strength of their grip on legitimate rule.[70] An argument can be made that the Italian population had more experience of minority rule and of female regents than that elsewhere in Europe, having seen the power of Galla Placidia and the minorities of Honorius and Valentinian III. Nevertheless, these were almost a century in the past by the time that Athalaric succeeded his grand-father and it is perhaps doubtful that their memories could have influenced political behaviour in the 520s. The acquiescence of the Roman and Gothic populations in Athalaric's minority and the regency of Amalasuentha must be an index of how close Theoderic's policies came to success. Naples' stiff resistance also illustrates the extent to which the Ostrogothic state hung together at first, and highlights the Gothic kings' failures to deal with Belisarius' invasion.

Amongst the Visigoths, the reasons for political failure are difficult to discern. The collapse of the Balt dynasty between 507 and 532 left something of a vacuum. None of the replacement kings was able to create a lasting dynasty that could develop an ideology of legitimacy and work, as had Theoderic and the Merovingians, towards under-mining rival sources of local power. This problem was only emphasised by the fact that Visigothic power was not yet thoroughly established through the peninsula but appears to have operated

---

[69] See also above, pp. 501–2.
[70] Fouracre (2000), pp. 12–32; James (1982a), pp.127–44; Wood (1994a), pp. 55–70.

through association with locally powerful aristocratic cabals based on the Roman cities.[71] These had their own ideas of legitimacy and the Suevic kingdom in the north-west provided another alternative. The Roman enclave in the south after 550 further underlined the fact that the Visigothic rulers had no monopoly on political legitimacy. With these factors in mind it is not surprising that, even before the landing of Liberius' expeditionary force, Gothic royal power was dependent upon military success. Theudis' and Agila's reigns both failed after martial setbacks. At about this time, too, Spanish archaeology shows a period of change, suggesting other structural transformations.[72] That material culture symbolising Gothic identity was used around the fringes of the realm, in competition with other symbols might very well be a clear illustration of the competition for local authority and the different bases of power that competitors could choose in the earlier sixth century.

Some attention must be given to the two 'first generation' barbarian kingdoms whose disappearance in the middle of the sixth century was *not* a result of Justinian's campaigns: those of the Burgundians and the Thuringians. To these we might add, by way of comparison, the Alamans, who were absorbed by the Franks slightly earlier. In all of these cases failure resulted simply from military defeat. It has been argued that the Burgundians were doomed to failure, being stuck between the greater powers of the Franks and the Ostrogoths, yet this analysis cannot be sustained.[73] The Burgundian kingdom controlled prosperous territory and possessed other advantages. The power of the Franks and the Ostrogoths, barely more than a generation old by the time of the extinction of the Burgundian realm, had been built on the basis of military success. The early phase of the Gothic wars suggests that the Ostrogoths could have been as rapidly brought down by military defeat, although the ending of the legitimate dynasty also played a part. Early sixth-century Frankish power, though also possessing structural advantages, could have been stemmed by military success. The fluidity of later fifth- and sixth-century politics argues that no kingdom was yet so entrenched that its opponents were destined to lose. From one reading of the material cultural evidence, the Thuringians were a power in politics on the fringes of the Frankish hegemony. Military defeat reduced the effectiveness in local power struggles of the political identity based

---

[71] Above, pp. 340–1.　[72] Above, pp. 344–6.　[73] E.g. Musset (1975), pp. 65–6.

upon an association with them and strengthened that of the rival Frankish identity. Without more effective means of tying local societies into the core, military defeat could lead to a haemorrhage of political authority throughout a realm and, as the fate of the early barbarian kingdoms shows, it frequently did.

THE ROOTS OF FAILURE (2): THE ROMANS

The Justinianic Empire's failure to retain its western conquests can be explained by similar factors to those that account for barbarian collapse. There are however a number of more general issues. The great plague of the 540s sapped morale and caused enormous damage to the Empire's socio-economic base. The wars were expensive and Justinian's inability to pay his troops for lengthy periods of time weakened morale and promoted desertion to Totila's Goths.[74] The Empire, furthermore, seems to have overextended itself and found it very difficult to fight on several frontiers at once. Nevertheless the simple fact that the Empire was fighting on several fronts cannot provide an explanation on its own. The Roman Empire had, after all, been able to fight on several fronts before the opening of our period and even during Justinian's early years. We need to consider the nature of the enemies against which its troops were pitted. The Vandals seem to have been numerically weak and there were crucial flaws within their kingdom. The Ostrogoths, Franks and Visigoths, however, cannot be equated with the 'barbarian threat' posed by the fourth-century peoples north of the Rhine and Danube. As we saw in chapter 5, in the fourth century the military balance of power was overwhelmingly weighted towards the Empire. The barbarians could not hope to meet the Romans on equal terms. Sixth-century western kingdoms were a very different proposition from fourth-century confederacies. They were sophisticated post-imperial states, in which much of the imperial infrastructure had remained intact.[75]

We should also note that profound changes were beginning to take place in the eastern Empire itself by the middle of the sixth century. These included the end of the economic prosperity of some of the eastern Empire's provinces and the beginnings of urban decline in

---

[74] Teall (1965).
[75] On the military organization of the post-imperial western kingdoms, see Halsall (2003a), pp. 40–53.

others. The interpretation of these changes (and indeed their reality) has been a matter of considerable debate.[76] In brief, it seems that the east was starting to undergo some of the same problems that the west had experienced rather earlier. The relationships between local society and the imperial core were changing. Nevertheless these transformations would not be fully played out until well after the close of the period covered by this book, and quite how they related to the conduct of Justinian's wars is a difficult issue. The wars had a deleterious impact on the economy and economic contraction also hindered the ability to wage war. The situation seems to have spiralled.

Probably the most important factor to consider in examining the failure of the Justinianic reconquest is, once again, the nature of core–periphery relations. It was all very well to conquer new territories; the problem was how to keep them bound into a single political unit. The late Roman Republic and early Empire had absorbed enormous swathes of territory because of exceptional factors that aided their incorporation into the state.[77] No such factors existed in the sixth century, and changes in core–periphery relationships were beginning to make themselves felt even in the heartlands of the eastern Empire.

One feature that had some bearing on the ability of the Empire to hold onto and incorporate its territories was military. The early imperial army had been an important vehicle for the integration of conquered territories into the Empire. Justinian's conquering forces were able to play no such role. These armies were composed largely of mercenaries who, while effective in winning battles and in conquering territory, were less effective in a defensive garrison function.[78] Indeed many of the hired troops were sent back to their home territories outside the Empire once the war was over. This feature led to the Empire's weakness in Italy when faced with the Lombard attack.

There are other factors behind the expanding sixth-century Empire's failure to emulate the expansionist Republic and Empire of the centuries either side of the birth of Christ. One is economic. Although the Mediterranean remained unified economically, and materials from the eastern Empire were much traded with the west,

---

[76] On these issues see Cameron, A. M. (1993b), pp. 152–96, for useful overview. See also (and compare) Haldon (1990), pp. 9–49; Whittow (1996), pp. 38–68.
[77] Above, pp. 68–71.   [78] Teall (1965).

something that could, on analogy with the first-century situation, have bound the conquered territories into the state, this economic network did not penetrate far inland from the coast.[79] The economies of the west were fragmented and even, by the middle quarters of the sixth century, localised. In the later sixth century the economic unity of the Mediterranean began to break down.[80] Eastern Roman material culture did not play the same role in local politics as early Roman goods had, except perhaps around the Irish Sea.[81] These issues would have made a restored sixth-century Empire difficult to unify.

We can further explore some of these aspects by briefly examining Africa and Italy. The Romanised areas of Africa had been conquered very quickly and the local socio-political élite had been able to remain in power. This was vital, just as it had been in explaining the survival of the Roman order during the Vandal invasion. But there had been changes. Economic contraction appears to have set in before the Justinianic reconquest. Post-conquest changes weakened things further. The long period of warfare against the Moors and the mutinies within the occupying army did considerable damage. Re-imposed Roman taxation was heavy and African grain-surplus was now, as in the fourth century, transferred as a tax, rather than traded with Italy. Many African towns became small redoubts.[82] On the fringes of the reconquered province the Moors continued to provide a political alternative to Rome and a rival focus for political activity. It is notable that when the Arabs invaded the region in the later seventh century it was the Moors who provided the stiffest resistance.[83] Nevertheless, there was less of a collapse in Africa than took place in Italy. The economic decline of the post-Justinianic period might have been overplayed and some production certainly continued within the reduced militarised towns. Though reduced in extent, the eastern Roman province of North Africa retained a certain coherence and connection to the imperial core.

Italy, by contrast, was wrecked by the Gothic wars.[84] The senatorial order was destroyed and the social order in much of the

---

[79] E.g. Hitchner (1992). Above, pp. 330, 340, 349.

[80] Hodges and Bowden (eds.) (1998); Loseby (2005).

[81] Campbell (1996); Dark, K. R. (ed.) (1995).

[82] Cameron, A. M. (1989); Pringle (1981).   [83] Above, pp. 410–11.

[84] Brown, T. S. (1984), pp. 1–60.

peninsula thrown into confusion. It is not impossible that this con
have played into the hands of an expanding Empire, as truly independent local leaders were destroyed and competitors for local
authority sought legitimacy by connection with the Empire and its
patronage. This would have resembled the fourth-century situation.
Justinian, however, used his patronage to favour eastern appointees,
often resented by the locals.[85] This too need not have been decisive.
Theoderic's and the Merovingians' use of royal officers to undermine
local leaders, by making them compete for royal favour, might be
called to mind. The core of the Empire remained somewhat distant
and the emperor never visited his new territories to deploy and
redeploy patronage in a similar way to his fourth-century predecessors. The Lombard attack proved decisive in creating a series of rival
sources of authority. The peninsula fragmented into a number of
small regions and, within each, appeal could be made to a number of
different sources of authority, Lombard or Roman. There was no
unified Roman command within Italy and other figures, most notably the Pope, could provide legitimacy for people in opposition to
those wielding power on the basis of imperial service.[86] This was,
obviously, as much a problem for Lombard kings attempting to
conquer Italy as it was for Roman emperors and other leaders trying
to retain their territory. The existence of the two independent
duchies in the south provided alternative Lombard sources of power
in opposition to that stemming from the royal court in Pavia.[87] In
Spain a similar situation pertained, as we have seen, with a plurality of
different sources of legitimacy and power. Again this prevented the
secure reintegration of the new territories into the Empire.

A CHANGED WORLD, 'PARTLY DEPENDENT UPON UNHISTORIC ACTS'

This loss of a monopoly over political legitimacy was crucial. In the
fourth century the Empire had had absolute control over ideas of
legitimate political power, not only within its territories but also,
seemingly, beyond, in the territories of *barbaricum*. Bloody power
struggles could be played out for this control, precisely because it was
absolute and whoever won became the sole source of legitimacy in

---

[85] Moorhead (1994), pp. 110–11.   [86] Azzara (2002), pp. 105–9, esp. p. 107.
[87] Wickham (1981), pp. 28–47.

western Europe. After the sixth century, nobody in the west could
claim such control. No one had the sole authority to define who had
and who did not have the right to rule. This simple fact made politics
ever more fluid. The success or failure of kingdoms, inside and
outside the former Empire, could hinge on the outcomes of battles
and campaigns. The vicissitudes of political fortunes determined the
strength, in local politics, of different identities. Powerful people,
who had based their pre-eminence upon an association with a particular group and the adoption of their ethnic identity, might find
their position undermined if that group was ousted militarily and
competitors adopted the identity of the victors. In the Gothic wars
in Italy, it is clear that people reordered their ethnicities according to
the swings in the fortunes of the contending parties.[88] All kinds of
means were employed to help give shape to the local identities that
analytically occupy the 'ethnic' arc of the spectrum.[89] For all parties
it was vital to persuade people to buy into their state. When the
means of persuasion were so weak that all could be lost on another
throw of the military dice, the individuals in the local communities of
Europe had more political choice than they had had for centuries.
There was no monopoly, indeed none to be fought for, over political
legitimation. Thus ethnicity, a political identity based on that of the
wielders of armed authority, became crucial to local politics.[90]

However, ethnicity was not the only new form of identity. In the
political events of the fifth and sixth centuries, gender identities had
also been renegotiated. The adoption of non-Roman political–ethnic
identities must have led to a redefinition of the acceptable modes of
male and female behaviour.[91] This surely had an important effect
upon local community politics. The erosion of the expectation that,
in order to take part in politics and in the 'sex-gender system', a male
had to behave according to a particular code, separating him not only
from barbarians but also from women, must have led to changes in the
importance of Roman identity. These, once played out, as they seem
to have been by the early to mid-sixth century, again undermined the

---

[88] It is important to see this as a reordering of levels of identity rather than, as does
Heather (e.g. (1996), pp. 302–3), seeing it as proof of incomplete assimilation. See
above, p. 474.
[89] Above, pp. 457–70.
[90] My thinking here has been refined by an excellent paper given by Michael
Kulikowski at the eleventh International Medieval Congress, Leeds, July 2004.
[91] Above, pp. 482–8.

previous dominance of one cultural mode of behaviour, hitherto a brake on social and political change, and paved the way for much more fluid identity politics.

None of the foregoing discussion is intended to imply that Justinian could not have reconquered the west; precisely the opposite. As should have become clear, in the nature of politics in the sixth century military successes could have very dramatic results. But he could only, it seems, have succeeded in reconquering the west by reconquering the *whole* west and eliminating all of the successor states that could provide rival sources of political authority. The western Empire could only have been restored by returning to the fourth-century system of government. Only then could an effective patronage system have been employed to link local and regional élites to government at the centre and to re-establish the political dominance of Roman identity. Ultimately the lesson taught by the failures of Roman *and* barbarian regimes in the fifth century is that it was not possible to build an enduring political unit without establishing means of binding the powerful elements of local and regional society into it. These do not seem to have existed in most of sixth-century western Europe. Only in the Frankish realms was a situation evolving where legitimate local and regional power throughout the kingdom was intimately connected to the Merovingian royal court and where this could continue to be the case even through the vicissitudes of political fortunes. Kingdoms only held together according to the extent to which people identified with them in the localities. Identities, associations with the core of the kingdom, were only adopted according to the advantages they afforded.

We must, therefore, put high politics back into the analysis of local social history, but we also have to put local society and politics back into our analysis of high-level political change. Here we return to the problem with which this book opened. The aims and objectives of people in small communities, such as those discussed at the start of chapter 1, had, it can be argued, even more ability in 550 to frustrate the ambitions of kings and emperors than they had had in 375. The analysis of 'high political' events should not be dismissed as having little explanatory value or as having little relationship with broader (or deeper) issues. They played an important part in determining the nature of the options available to actors at lower levels – and it was the choices which these people made that ultimately determined the success or failure of kingdoms and empires – and thus in shaping the period's history. The history of the fifth century is 'partly dependent upon unhistoric acts; and that things are not ... as they might have been is half-owing to the number who lived faithfully a hidden life, and rest in unvisited tombs'.[92] At least their tombs have been revisited here. Understanding the way in which things turned out in late antiquity means understanding all the choices available to individual social actors, not just those which they eventually made.[93] This restores to historical actors their freedom to act, it makes the story of the fifth and sixth centuries as interesting, dramatic and unpredictable as it originally was and it means putting people back into their history.

---

[92] George Elliot, *Middlemarch* (Oxford, 1996), p. 822.   [93] Moroney (1989).

APPENDIX: GILDAS' NARRATIVE AND THE IDENTITY OF THE 'PROUD TYRANT'

In his sermon *On the Ruin of Britain* (*DEB*), traditionally supposed to have been written in the 540s but more realistically at any time between the late fifth and mid-sixth century, Gildas included a political narrative (chapters 4–26). After an introductory chapter (chapter 4), this falls into four sections: a 'Roman section' dealing with the conquest of Britain (chapters 5–6); a 'Christian 'section' detailing the evangelisation of the island (chapters 8–12); a 'northern section' relating Scottish and Pictish assaults after the Roman departure (chapters 13–21); and an 'eastern section' recounting Saxon attacks (chapters 22–6).

Gildas begins his 'northern section' by describing the departure of the legions under the *tyrannus* Magnus Maximus, leaving Britain to suffer Pictish and Scottish attacks. The Britons appealed to Rome. A legion was despatched and built a turf wall to defend the island from attack from the north. This did no good so, after a second appeal, another force was sent, constructing a second, stone wall and instructing the Britons about military defence. This was also to no avail; the barbarians seized the north of the island and ravaged Britain from sea to sea. Eventually the Britons wrote to Aëtius, the military commander in Gaul. In the famous letter, 'Groans of the Britons', Aëtius was told how the Britons were driven by the barbarians into the sea and thrown by the sea back to the barbarians. They thus had a choice between two forms of death: drowning or having their throats cut. Nevertheless Aëtius was unmoved and no help arrived. Famine broke out, some of the Britons were driven by hunger to surrender and others fled to remote mountains, heaths and caves. Yet others, however, took up arms and fought back so that, with God's help, the barbarians were driven off. Alas, says Gildas, this military success ushered in a period of sin and sexual excess.

Now, says Gildas (in the 'eastern section'), rumours abounded of impending barbarian attack. A council met, under the leadership of the 'proud tyrant' (*tyrannus superbus*), and invited the Saxons to defend the province. The latter fixed their grip on the east of the island and, when eventually the Britons withheld the increased supplies and wages demanded, rebelled. Britain was ravaged as far as the sea. Towns were destroyed and there was great slaughter. Hunger drove some of the Britons to surrender. Others, however, fled to mountains, forests and cliffs. The enemy retreated and the Britons, led by a certain Ambrosius Aurelianus (the only named figure apart from Maximus and Aëtius in these sections of Gildas' historical narrative), eventually defeated the Saxons in a war culminating at the siege of Mount Badon (the only place named in these chapters). Gildas appears to say that this occurred forty-three years and one month before he was writing, in the year of his birth. However, the result was the wreck of Britain, civil war, sin and greed. Gildas then passes on to the main point of his composition, a tirade against the kings, people and clergy of Britain.

This is usually read as a linear narrative. The 'eastern section' is held to recount the tale of the Saxon wars that followed the successful culmination of the wars in the north. This narrative begins with Maximus' rebellion (383). Another chronological fixed point is given by the mention of Aëtius, referred to as 'thrice consul'. Aëtius' third consulship took place in 446 and he died in 454,[1] so this reference should date the letter to him between 446 and 453. A third apparent fixed point is the reference to the battle of Badon taking place forty-three years and one month before Gildas' writing. This might be taken alongside the mention of grandchildren of Ambrosius Aurelianus (who, Gildas *seems* to imply, was the

---

[1] The waters may be muddied here, however, by the fact that a Fl. Aëtius held the consulate in 453. The authors of the *Consularia Constantinopolitana* and the *Fasti Vindobonenses Posteriori* (= *Consularia Italica* 570) thought this was Aëtius' fourth consulship but most scholars believe, reasonably, that it was instead the eastern Roman general who had been successful in 452 (above, p. 254).

commander at Badon, though this is far from clear) holding power in Gildas' own day. Putting these fixed points together, alongside vague references to time-lapses in Gildas' narrative, we can arrive at a date in the earlier sixth century for Gildas' writing.[2] This story became the basis for all later attempts to recreate fifth-century British political history. In 731 Bede named Gildas' *superbus tyrannus* as Vortigern (a figure also mentioned in early Welsh tradition),[3] said that the Saxon leaders were brothers called Hengest and Horsa and localised their settlement in Kent. He also added specific AD dates, using his knowledge of chronology. The late ninth-century *Anglo-Saxon Chronicle* elaborated the story further to glorify the West Saxons.[4]

Other glosses of the basic account are found in the early ninth-century *History of the Britons*, containing more stories about Vortigern[5] but seemingly dating the Saxon arrival to 428 and the appearance of Ambrosius Aurelianus to the 420s. The *Historia* consistently refers to a forty-year period of fear after Maximus' death, one thus ending in 428, at the end of which Hengest and Horsa arrived (*HB* 31). Later (*HB* 66) it says that Vortigern held *imperium* in Britain in the consulate of Theodosius and Valentinian and that the Saxons arrived in the fourth year of his reign during Felix and Taurus' consulate (again, 428). It claims that this was 401 years from the passion of Christ, also, according to its system of reckoning, in 428 AD. This is a strangely consistent chronology – strange because the rest of the account is so often demonstrably inaccurate and legendary. Dumville suggested how the *Historia*'s author could have calculated this date himself.[6] It seems likely that its author had before him either, as Dumville suggested, a version of Victorius' *cursus* with consuls added, or simply one of the many late antique consular lists (*consularia*) using Victorius' method of calculation (like Prosper of Aquitaine) and beginning in Maximus' reign. This would explain the curious comment (*HB* 26) that from Maximus' day the rulers of the Romans were called consuls.[7] The succession of consuls was known

---

[2] Dumville (1984a) demolishes the traditional use of external evidence to date Gildas to *c.*540 but then (Dumville (1984b)) reinstates the date, or one close to it, on the basis of the internal evidence of Gildas' narrative.
[3] See note 5 below.   [4] Yorke (1989).
[5] See, e.g. *HB* 31, 37–49, 66. On the *HB* in general see Dumville (1994).
[6] Dumville (1972–4), pp. 444–5.
[7] The *consularia* seems to have ended in 521 (Dumville (1972–4), pp. 443–4).

in west Britain up until the last consul in 541, as is shown by inscriptions.[8] The *Historia*'s chronology permitted John Morris to devise a whole new chronology moving Bede's and the *Anglo-Saxon Chronicle*'s dates back by a uniform twenty-one years and to hypothesise that there were two men (father and son) called Ambrosius Aurelianus![9]

Unfortunately it is not that simple. It has been suggested that Gildas himself, rather than his source, might have used the words *ter consulus* (thrice consul), meaning that the 'Groans of the Britons' could date to any time between the 420s and 454.[10] The sentence about the date of the battle of Badon has also been read as saying that it took place a month ago in the forty-fourth year of Gildas' age.[11] Gildas does not actually state that Ambrosius commanded the Britons at Badon, so there is no necessary contradiction between this reading and his statement that Ambrosius' grandchildren held power when he wrote. The first suggestion finds no support in the text and was devised simply to make Gildas concur with the date of the earliest 'Saxon' material culture in Britain, from the 430s. The second suggestion has been challenged on the grounds of Latin syntax.[12] Nevertheless, both are possible and show how ill-founded is the traditional reading of Gildas.

In an interesting argument, interpreting Gildas as meaning that Badon occurred forty-four years *after* something rather than *before* his writing, H. Wiseman argues persuasively that Gildas meant that Badon took place forty-four years and a month after the start of the war against the Saxons in the year of his birth.[13] That seems to have been how Bede[14] understood it when he placed Badon forty-four years after the coming of the English. This still, however, leaves only a relative chronology, with no fixed points.

More importantly, however, there are strong reasons to believe that Gildas' narrative of post-Roman history is not a single linear

---

[8] Handley (2001b), pp. 192–4.   [9] Morris (1973), pp. 40, 71.

[10] Casey and Jones (1990); Higham (1994), pp. 120–36; Jones, M. E. (1988).

[11] Wood (1984).

[12] McCarthy and Ó Cróinín (1987–8), pp. 237–8, who argue for a date for Badon of February 482 on the basis of an interpretation of Gildas' statement about Badon as meaning that it took place forty-four years and one month into a chronological cycle. The eighty-four-year Easter cycle available at the time would begin the cycle in 438. This is interesting but I am not sure the text supports the reading.

[13] Wiseman (2000).   [14] *HE* 1.16.

account, with the events of chapters 13–26 following each other sequentially. In the last chapter (21) of the 'northern section', after describing the civil war and sin into which the Britons had fallen, Gildas twice uses the phrase *sicut et nunc est* ('and thus it is now') and once *quod et nunc* (loosely 'nowadays'). This passage is generally cast in the past tense leading, along with a desire to create a single sequential narrative thread from these chapters, to the phrase being rendered as 'just [in the same way] as it is now' and 'nowadays too'. This is plausible but the literal reading of these phrases seems fairly unambiguous. Though discussing past events, Gildas implies that the situation continues to the present day. Moreover, the very next passage, beginning the 'eastern section' begins *interea* – meanwhile – which should imply some unspecified overlap between the two sections.[15] Gildas begins the 'Christian section' with the same word and there clearly implies an overlap as he returns from the post-Boudiccan history of Roman administration in Britain to the life of Christ in the reign of Tiberius. *Interea* could be used more poetically, not necessarily implying strict chronological overlap but still drawing the reader's attention to a change in direction.[16] Even so, Gildas' employment of the word means that the strict thread of the narrative is broken at this point.

This enables a new reading. Placing the 'eastern' and 'northern' sections alongside each other reveals (as may have become clear from the account above) that the two are very similar (figure 1: the key parallel phrases and words are emboldened). Gildas tells the story of two sets of wars in strikingly similar rhetorical fashion. A war breaks out because of the Britons' perfidy, to the Romans and to God. The barbarians ravage the island from sea to sea. Great slaughter ensues, towns are destroyed or deserted and hunger sets in. Some Britons surrender but others rally under cover of harsh terrain and fight back. With God's aid the barbarians are defeated but this victory leads to sin and civil war. There are other verbal parallels. The *cyulae* (keels) of the Saxons are mentioned in order to parallel the *curucae* (coracles) of the Picts, for example.[17] Gildas' story is heavily stylised. Lapidge has shown that the whole of *On the Ruin of Britain* follows Roman

---

[15] Miller, M. (1975) drew attention to this point but did not elaborate it.

[16] See, for example, Sid. Ap. *Poems* 7, line 230.

[17] *DEB* 19.1, 23.3. Woolf, A. (2002) argues that the whole passage containing the reference to *cyulae* is an interpolation. His argument is generally persuasive but

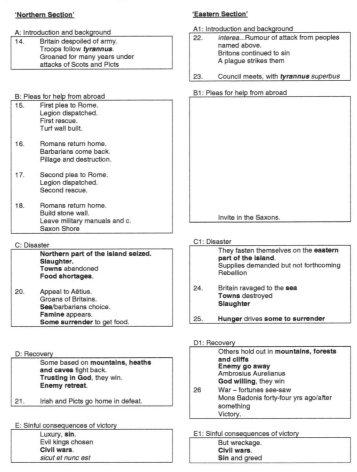

'Northern Section'

A: Introduction and background

14. Britain despoiled of army.
Troops follow **tyrannus**.
Groaned for many years under
attacks of Scots and Picts

B: Pleas for help from abroad

15. First plea to Rome.
Legion dispatched.
First rescue.
Turf wall built.

16. Romans return home.
Barbarians come back.
Pillage and destruction.

17. Second plea to Rome.
Legion dispatched.
Second rescue.

18. Romans return home.
Build stone wall.
Leave military manuals and c.
Saxon Shore

C: Disaster

Northern part of the island seized.
Slaughter.
Towns abandoned
Food shortages.

20. Appeal to Aëtius.
Groans of Britains.
Sea/barbarians choice.
Famine appears.
Some surrender to get food.

D: Recovery

Some based on **mountains, heaths**
and caves fight back.
Trusting in God, they win.
Enemy retreat.

21. Irish and Picts go home in defeat.

E: Sinful consequences of victory

Luxury, **sin.**
Evil kings chosen
Civil wars.
sicut et nunc est

'Eastern Section'

A1: Introduction and background

22. *interea*...Rumour of attack from peoples
named above.
Britons continued to sin
A plague strikes them

23. Council meets, with **tyrannus** *superbus*

B1: Pleas for help from abroad

Invite in the Saxons.

C1: Disaster

They fasten themselves on the **eastern**
part of the island.
Supplies demanded but not forthcoming
Rebellion

24. Britain ravaged to the **sea**
Towns destroyed
Slaughter

25. **Hunger** drives **some to surrender**

D1: Recovery

Others hold out in **mountains, forests**
and cliffs
Enemy go away
Ambrosius Aurelianus
God willing, they win
26   War – fortunes see-saw
Mons Badonis forty-four yrs ago/after
something
Victory.

E1: Sinful consequences of victory

But wreckage.
Civil wars.
Sin and greed

Figure 1 Gildas' narrative

rules of rhetorical composition[18] and clear rhetorical devices appear here. Take, for example, the three appeals to the Romans in the first section. Two produce a response, but the third, in classic folkloric fashion, results in no help at all. This must explain Gildas' apparently ill-informed use, and redating, of the Hadrianic and Antonine Walls

need not include the reference to keels, which, stylistically, makes sense as a counterpoise to the *curucae*.
[18] Lapidge (1984).

as exempla, something that has often puzzled historians. Gildas tells how the Britons' behaviour produced attacks by barbarians and severe catastrophe, how trust in the Lord produced victory, and how victory produced sin and corruption, which must be remedied if the Britons are not to be sorely chastised again.

There are also parallels with Gildas' 'Christian section'. A similar pattern emerges. Christianity was initially only half-hearted (similar to the feeble attempts to defend the walls against the Picts). Persecution and destruction (equating with the barbarian ravages) produced apostasy (equivalent to surrender to the Picts, Scots or Saxons) as well as the heroic actions of the Martyrs – Gildas names Alban at Verulamium and Aaron and Julius at Caerleon (religious counterparts of heroes like Ambrosius, whose greatest triumph is also localised). A *tyrannus* plays a crucial role in this section too: Diocletian. Some Christians held on in caves and other harsh terrain, paralleling the Britons who used such landscapes as the basis for resistance against the invaders, and waited until the storm of persecution had blown over, which eventually it did, just as the attacks of the barbarians also eventually ceased. After the storm had abated the rebuilding of the churches and a period of virtuous living followed, until the Arian heresy, introduced from abroad, created division. Likewise a brief period of praiseworthy rule after Badon occurred before the Britons were corrupted by sin.

Neither the 'northern' nor the 'eastern' section was presumably meant as a particularly accurate factual account, the stylised, rhetorical nature of the tale rendering attempts to assign time-spans to them futile. As the phrasing of the end of the first section and first word of the second make apparent, and as is underlined by the stylistic parallels between the two, they do not refer to episodes following on sequentially from each other. Gildas simply tells the same moralising tale twice, in regard to the two groups of barbarians attacking and settling in Britain: the Picts and Scots in the north and west, and the Saxons in the east. He tells the tale, furthermore, in a way that makes recent politics parallel Britain's Christian history. The eastern and northern sections clearly overlapped in time to some unspecified extent. Whether each phase in one section corresponded exactly in time with its counterpart in the other is certainly unknowable, probably unlikely and perhaps unimportant. The point is that it is impossible to establish a linear narrative from Gildas' historical section.

What *is* important from this reading is that we can see a striking parallel in the early parts of the 'Christian', 'northern' and 'eastern' sections. All refer to a *tyrannus*, Diocletian, Maximus, and the *tyrannus superbus* respectively. Considering the parallels between the sections it seems more reasonable to see the *superbus tyrannus*, later *infaustus tyrannus* (unlucky tyrant), of chapter 23 not as a pun on the name of a figure otherwise unattested by Gildas, and indeed not mentioned by *anyone* before the eighth century, but as a clear reference back to the *tyrannus* who *was* named, and whose unlucky fate was described, in chapter 13: Magnus Maximus. One manuscript of Gildas' work names the *superbus tyrannus* as Vortigern.[19] This appears to be an interpolation, using a later form of the name than that found in Bede's eighth-century work. It is as likely that Vortigern, whose name means 'Great Tyrant', is a legendary outgrowth of Gildas' vague reference to the *tyrannus superbus* as that Gildas' reference is a pun on Vortigern's name. Indeed historians may have only identified the *first* description – *tyrannus superbus* – as a pun and not the second – *infaustus tyrannus* – because of the *a priori* assumption, drawn from Bede, that Gildas is talking about Vortigern. Yet *infaustus tyrannus* is equally capable of being a pun (on the name Faustus for example – the *Historia Brittonum* coincidentally claims that Maximus had a son called Faustus). Alternatively, the pride of the 'proud tyrant' might refer to Magnus Maximus' name, which after all means 'Great the Greatest'. The name Vortigern itself translates *magnus tyrannus*. Vortigern's appearance in the apparently fifth-century *consularia* used by the *Historia Brittonum* might argue against this thesis but there were at least 300 years during which someone could have added comments about Vortigern into the text. Gildas generally named the tyrants in his work;[20] he did not name the *tyrannus* of chapter 23 because he had already done so: Magnus Maximus.

---

[19] Dumville (1977b).

[20] His famous diatribe against five named *tyranni* follows the historical section (*DEB* 27–36).

BIBLIOGRAPHY

———————— • ————————

To list all of the works relating to all of the topics covered by this volume, even only those written in English during the past thirty years, would require at least one book the size of this one. I have barely dipped my toe in this bibliographic ocean, and the list of works below does not include all of those that I *have* used. To save space, references were often streamlined to recent works, preferably in English, with good bibliographies, and those supporting the precise points made in the text. A number of authors from whom I have learnt much have been harshly treated by this pruning and I offer them my apologies. Absence from this bibliography is most certainly not a comment on the quality of a book or essay.

To save space and because of the wide audience at which this book is aimed, although all Latin and most Greek sources have been consulted in their original language, where I am aware of translations of all or most of a primary source, only that translation is listed, though preference is usually given to parallel texts. I have also translated the titles of many primary sources, which doubtless makes some look odd to specialists but I hope will give the novice a clearer idea of what they are about. Abbreviations of sources' titles are, however, given in their conventional forms, relating to their Latin or Greek titles. This explains the apparent lack of relationship between an abbreviation and the source's full title!

ABBREVIATIONS

A. Journals, series, collections and secondary works

An. Tard.	*Antiquité Tardive*
ASE	*Anglo-Saxon England*
BAR(B)	British Archaeological Reports (British Series)

BAR (I)	British Archaeological Reports (International Series)
BBCS	*Bulletin of the Board of Celtic Studies*
BSAA	*Boletin del Seminario de Estudios de Arte y Arqueologia*
CAH 13	*The Cambridge Ancient History*, vol. 13: *The Late Empire*, A.D. *337–425*, ed. Cameron, A. M. and Garnsey, P. (Cambridge, 1998)
CAH 14	*Cambridge Ancient History*, vol. 14: *Empire and Successors*, A.D. *425–600*, ed. Cameron, A. M. Ward-Perkins, B. and Whitby, M. (Cambridge, 2000)
CBA	Council for British Archaeology
CSSH	*Comparative Studies in Society and History*
EHD	*English Historical Documents*, vol. 1: *c.500–1042*, ed. Whitelock, D., 2nd edn (London, 1979)
EHR	*English Historical Review*
EME	*Early Medieval Europe*
ERS	*Ethnic and Racial Studies*
FmSt	*Frühmittelalterliche Studien*
FotC	Fathers of the Church
GRBS	*Greek, Roman and Byzantine Studies*
Hist.	*Historia*
HZ	*Historische Zeitschrift*
JEA	*Journal of European Archaeology*
JEH	*Journal of Ecclesiastical History*
JRA	*Journal of Roman Archaeology*
JRGZM	*Jahrbuch des römisch-germanisches Zentralmuseums Mainz*
JRS	*Journal of Roman Studies*
MGH	*Monumenta Germaniae Historica*
MIÖG	*Mitteilungen des Instituts für Österreichisches Geschichtsforschung*
NCMH 1	*The New Cambridge Medieval History*, vol. 1: *c.500–c.700*, ed. Fouracre, P. (Cambridge, 2005).
NMS	*Nottingham Medieval Studies*
NPNF	Nicene and Post-Nicene Fathers
P&P	*Past & Present*
PBA	*Proceedings of the British Academy*
PLRE	*Prosopography of the Later Roman Empire*, vol. 1, ed. Jones, A. H. M.; vols. 2–3, ed. Martindale, J. R. (Cambridge, 1971–92)
Rb	*Romanobarbarica*
RBPH	*Revue Belge de Philologie et Histoire*
RH	*Revue Historique*
RN	*Revue du Nord*
SAR	*Scottish Archaeological Review*
SCH	*Studies in Church History*
Spec.	*Speculum*
SzSf	*Studien zur Sachsenforschung*

TAPA	Transactions of the American Philological Association
TRHS	Transactions of the Royal Historical Society

B. PRIMARY SOURCES AND AUTHORS

Amm. Marc.	Ammianus Marcellinus, *Res Gestae*: *Ammianus Marcellinus*. trans. Rolfe, J.C., 3 vols. (London 1935–9)
CE	*Euric's Code*: MGH *Leges Sectio 1, Leges Nationum Germanicarum*, vol. 1: *Leges Visigothorum*, ed. Zeumer, K. (Hannover and Leipzig, 1902), pp. 1–32
Chron.	Chronicle
Chron. Gall. 452	*Gallic Chronicle of 452: From Roman to Merovingian Gaul*, trans. Callander Murray, A. (Peterborough, Ontario, 2000), pp. 76–85
Chron. Gall. 511	*Gallic Chronicle of 511: From Roman to Merovingian Gaul*, trans. Callander Murray, A. (Peterborough, Ontario, 2000), pp. 98–100
CIL	*Corpus Inscriptionum Latinarum*, 17 vols. with additional fascicules (Berlin, 1853–)
CJ	*Justinianic Code*: An English translation is available at http://www.constitution.org/sps/sps.htm
CTh	*Theodosian Code: The Theodosian Code and Novels and the Sirmondian Constitutions*, trans. Pharr, C. (Princeton, NJ, 1952).
DEB	Gildas, *On the Ruin and Conquest of Britain (De Excidio Britanniae): Gildas. The Ruin of Britain and other Documents*, ed. and trans. Winterbottom, M. (Chichester, 1978)
HB	*Historia Brittonum*: Nennius. *British History and the Welsh Annals*, ed. and trans. Morris, J. (Chichester, 1980)
HE	Bede, *Ecclesiastical History of the English People: Bede's Ecclesiastical History of the English People*, ed. and trans. Colgrave, B. and Mynors, R. A. B. (Oxford, 1969)
HL	Paul the Deacon, *History of the Lombards: Paul the Deacon. History of the Lombards*, trans. Dudley Foulke, W. (Philadelphia, 1974; originally 1907)
LC	*Book of Constitutions: The Burgundian Code*, trans. Drew, K. F. (Philadelphia, 1972)
Lex Ribv.	*Ripuarian Law: The Laws of the Salian and Ripuarian Franks*, trans. Rivers, T. J. (New York, 1986), pp. 167–214
LH	Gregory of Tours, *Histories: Gregory of Tours. The History of the Franks*, trans. Thorpe, L. (Harmondsworth, 1974)

530   *Bibliography*

LHF	*The Book of the History of the Franks: The Liber Historiae Francorum*, trans. Bachrach, B. S. (Laurence, KS, 1973)
LV	*Visigothic Law, MGH Leges Sectio 1, Leges Nationum Germanicarum*, vol. 1: *Leges Visigothorum*, ed. Zeumer, K. (Hannover and Leipzig, 1902), pp. 33–456. S. P. Scott's early twentieth-century translation is available online at http://libro.uca.edu/vcode/visigoths.htm. Note, however, that the numbering of clauses sometimes differs from that in the *MGH* edition. I have used the more accurate *MGH* numbering.
Not. Dig.	*Notitia Dignitatum: Notitia Dignitatum accedunt Notitia Urbis Constantinopolitanae et Latercula Provinciarum*, ed. Seeck, O. (Frankfurt am Main, 1876; repr. Frankfurt, 1962)
Nov. Maj.	*Novels of Majorian: The Theodosian Code and Novels and the Sirmondian Constitutions*, trans. Pharr, C. (Princeton, NJ, 1952), pp. 551–61
Oros.	Orosius, *Seven Books of History Against the Pagans*: *Paulus Orosius. The Seven Books of History against the Pagans*, trans. Deferrari, R. J. (FotC 50; Washington, DC, 1964)
PLS	*Compact of Salic Law: The Laws of the Salian Franks*, trans. Drew, K. F. (Philadelphia, 1991); *The Laws of the Salian and Ripuarian Franks*, trans. Rivers, T. J. (New York, 1987), pp. 39–144
RIB	*Roman Inscriptions of Britain*, ed. Collingwood, R. G., Wright, R. P. et al., 2 vols. and numerous fascicules, rev. edns (Stroud, 1983; 1990–5)
RICG 1	*Receuil des Inscriptions Chrétiennes de la Gaule antérieures à la Renaissance Carolingienne.* vol. 1: *Première Belgique*, ed. Gauthier, N. (Paris, 1975)
SHA	*The Scriptores Historiae Augustae*, ed. and trans. Magie, D. 3 vols. (London, 1932)
Sid. Ap.	Sidonius Apollinaris
Soc.	Socrates Scholasticus, *Ecclesiastical History*: *NPNF*, 2nd ser., vol. 2, trans. Zenos, A. C. (Reprint: Grand Rapids, MI, 1989), pp. 1–178
Soz.	Sozomen, *Ecclesiastical History*: *NPNF*, 2nd ser., vol. 2, trans. Hartranft, C. D., *NPNF*, 2nd ser., 2 (Reprint: Grand Rapids, MI, 1989), pp. 179ff.
VP	Gregory of Tours, *Life of the Fathers* (*Vita Patrum*), trans. James, E., 2nd edn. (Liverpool, 1991)

Zos.   Zosimus, *New History: Zosime: Histoire Nouvelle*, ed. and (French) trans., Paschoud, F. (Paris, 1971–89); *Zosimus. New History*, trans. Ridley, R. T. (Canberra, 1982)

PRIMARY SOURCES (ADDITIONAL TO THOSE LISTED
UNDER ABBREVIATIONS)

Agathias, *Histories: Agathias. The Histories*, trans. Frendo, J. D. (Berlin, 1975)

Airs, Waters, Places: Hippocrates, vol. 1, ed. and trans. Jones, W. H. S. (London, 1923)

Ambrose, *Letters: Ambrose of Milan: Political Letters and Speeches*, trans. Liebschuetz, J. H. W. G. (Liverpool, 2005); *St Ambrose: Letters*, trans. Beyenka, M. M. (FotC 26; Washington, DC, 1954)

Ambrose, *The Soul: St Ambrose: Seven Exegetical Works*, trans. McHugh, M. P. (FotC 26; Washington, DC, 1973).

Angers Formulary: MGH Legum Sectio V: Formulae Merovingici et Karolini Aevi, ed. Zeumer, K. (Hannover, 1886), pp. 1–25

Anonymous Valesianus: *Ammianus Marcellinus*, vol. 3, ed. and trans. Rolfe, J. C. (London, 1939), pp. 506–69

Aristotle, *Politics: Aristotle: Politics*, ed. and trans. Rackham, H. (London, 1932)

Armes Prydein: Armes Prydein: The Prophecy of Britain, from the Book of Taleisin, ed. Williams, I. (Dublin, 1982)

Augustine, *Confessions: Augustine. Confessions*, trans. Sheed, F. J. (Indianapolis 1993; revised with new intro. by P. R. L. Brown)

Augustine, *The Free Choice of the Will: St Augustine: The Teacher, The Free Choice of the Will, Grace and Free Will*, trans. Russell, R. P. (FotC 59; Washington, DC, 1968)

Ausonius, *Epigrams: Ausonius*, trans. White, H. G. E., 2 vols. (London, 1919–21), vol. 2, pp. 154–217

Ausonius, *Moselle: Ausonius*, trans. White, H. G. E., 2 vols. (London, 1919–21), vol. 1, pp. 224–67

Ausonius, *Order of Famous Cities: Ausonius*, trans. White, H. G. E., 2 vols. (London, 1919–21), vol. 1, pp. 268–85

Austrasian Letters: MGH Epistolae, vol. 3: *Merovingici et Karolini Aevi*, vol. 1, ed. Gundlach, W. (Berlin, 1892), pp. 110–53. A translated selection is available online at http:/tabula.rutgers.edu/latintexts/letters/.

Avitus, *Letters: Avitus of Vienne: Letters and Selected Prose*, trans. Shanzer, D. and Wood, I. N. (Liverpool, 2002)

Bavarian Law: (1926). The Laws of the Alamans and Bavarians, trans. Rivers, T. J. (Philadelphia, 1977)

Beowulf: Anglo-Saxon Poetry, trans. Bradley, S. A. J. (London 1982), pp. 411–94

Bede, *Life of Cuthbert: Two Lives of Saint Cuthbert*, trans. Colgrave, B. (Cambridge 1940), pp. 141–307

Bertramn of Le Mans, *Testament: Archives Historiques du Mans II. Actus Pontificum Cenomannis in Urbe Degentium*, ed. Busson, G. and Ledru, A., (Le Mans, 1901)

Bobolen, *Life of Germanus of Grandval: MGH Scriptores Rerum Merovingicarum*, vol. 5: *Passiones vitaeque sanctorum aevi Merovingici*, vol. 3, ed. Krusch, B. (Hannover, 1905), pp. 25–40

Boethius, *Consolation of Philosophy: Boethius. The Consolation of Philosophy*, trans. Watts, V. E. (Harmondsworth, 1969)

Book of the Popes: The Book of Pontiffs, trans. Davis, R. (Liverpool, 1989)

Braulio of Saragossa, *Life of Aemilianus: Lives of the Visigothic Fathers*, trans. Fear, A. T. (Liverpool, 1997), pp. 15–43

Caesar, *Gallic War: Caesar: The Gallic War*, ed. and trans. Edwards, H. J. (London, 1917)

Caesarius of Arles, *Letters: Caesarius of Arles: Life, Testament, Letters*, trans. Klingshirn, W. E. (Liverpool, 1994), pp. 77–139

Caesarius of Arles, *Sermons: Caesarius of Arles. Sermons*, 3 vols., trans. Mueller, M. M. (FotC 31, 47 and 66; Washington, DC, 1956–73)

Candidus: *The Fragmentary Classicizing Historians of the Later Roman Empire*, ed. and trans. Blockley, R. C. (Liverpool, 1981), vol. 2, pp. 463–73

Cassiodorus, *Chron.: MGH Auctores Antiquissimi*, vol. 11: *Chronica Minora saec. IV. V. VI. VII*, vol. 2, ed. Mommsen, T. (Berlin, 1894), pp. 109–61

Cassiodorus, *Variae: MGH Auctores Antiquissimi*, vol. 12: *Cassiodori Senatoris Variae*, ed. Mommsen, T. (Berlin, 1894); (selection) *Cassiodorus: Variae*, trans. Barnish, S. J. B. (Liverpool, 1992); (summaries with some translations) *The Letters of Cassiodorus: Being a Condensed Translation of the Variae Epistolae of Magnus Aurelius Cassiodorus Senator*, trans. Hodgkin, T. (London, 1886)

Cato, *Origines: Caton: Les Origines (fragments)*, ed. and (French) trans. Chassignet, M. (Paris, 1986)

Chronicle of Saragossa: MGH Auctores Antiquissimi, vol. 11: *Chronica Minora saec. IV. V. VI. VII*, vol. 2, ed. Mommsen, T. (Berlin, 1894), pp. 221–3

Cicero, *On Duties: Cicero: On Duties*, ed. and trans. Griffin, M. T. and Atkins, E. M. (Cambridge, 1991)

Cicero, *Republic (De Re Publica): Cicero. De Re Publica and The Laws*, ed. and trans. Walker Keyes, C. (London, 1943)

Claudian, *Against Eutropius: Claudian*, ed. and trans. Platnauer, M. (London, 1922), vol. 1, pp. 138–229

Claudian, *Against Rufinus: Claudian*, ed. and trans. Platnauer, M. (London, 1922), vol. 1, pp. 24–97

Claudian, *Consulship of Stilicho: Claudian*, ed. and trans. Platnauer, M. (London, 1922), vol. 1, pp. 364–93; vol. 2, pp. 2–73

Claudian, *Fourth Consulate of Honorius: Claudian*, ed. and trans. Platnauer, M. (London, 1922), vol. 1, pp. 286–335

Claudian, *Gildonic War: Claudian*, ed. and trans. Platnauer, M. (London, 1922), vol. 1, pp. 98–137

Claudian, *Gothic War: Claudian*, ed. and trans. Platnauer, M. (London, 1922), vol. 2, pp. 124–73

Claudian, *Sixth Consulship of Honorius: Claudian*, ed. and trans. Platnauer, M. (London, 1922), vol. 2, pp. 70–123

Claudius Mammertinus, *Speech of Thanks to Julian: The Emperor Julian: Panegyric and Polemic*, ed. and trans. Lieu, S. N. C., 2nd edn (Liverpool, 1989), pp. 3–38

Clovis, *Letter to the Bishops of Aquitaine: From Roman to Merovingian Gaul*, trans. Callander Murray, A. (Peterborough, Ontario, 2000), pp. 267–8

Columella, *Agriculture: Columella: On Agriculture*, trans. Ash, H. B. (London, 1941)

Constantius, *Life of Germanus: Soldiers of Christ: Saints and Saints' Lives from Late Antiquity and the Early Middle Ages*, ed. Noble, T. F. X. and Head, T. (Pennsylvania, 1995), pp. 75–106

Consularia Constantinopolitana: The Chronicle of Hydatius and the Consularia Constantinopolitana. Two Contemporary Accounts of the Final Years of the Roman Empire, ed. and trans. Burgess, R. W. (Oxford 1993), pp. 173–245

Consularia Italica (a collection of annalistic texts grouped by Theodor Mommsen under this title, highly misleading in almost every way but convenient for citation): *MGH Auctores Antiquissimi*, vol. 9: *Chronica Minora saec. IV. V. VI. VII*, vol. 1, ed. Mommsen, T. (Berlin, 1892), pp. 249–339

Corippus, *In Praise of Justin: Flavius Cresconius Corippus: In Laudem Iustini Augusti Minoris Libri IV*, ed. and trans. Cameron, A. M. (London, 1976).

Dio Cassius, *Roman History: Dio's Roman History*, trans. Cary, E., 9 vols. (London, 1914–27)

Dracontius, *Apology: MGH Auctores Antiquissimi*, vol. 14: *Merobaudes. Dracontius. Eugenius Toletanus*, ed. Volmer, F. (Berlin, 1905), pp. 114–31

Ennodius, *Life of Epiphanius: MGH Auctores Antiquissimi*, vol. 7: *Ennodi Opera*, ed. Vogel, F. (Berlin, 1885), pp. 84–109

Ennodius, *Panegyric to Theoderic: MGH Auctores Antiquissimi*, vol. 7: *Ennodi Opera*, ed. Vogel, F. (Berlin, 1885), pp. 203–14

Eugippius, *Life of Severinus: Eugippius. The Life of St Severin*, trans. Bieler, L. (Washington, 1965)

Eunapius: *The Fragmentary Classicizing Historians of the Later Roman Empire*, ed. and trans. Blockley, R. C. (Liverpool, 1981), vol. 2, pp. 1–150

Fredegar, *Chronicle: The Fourth Book of the Chronicle of Fredegar, with its Continuations*, trans. Wallace-Hadrill, J. M. (London, 1960). Selections from books 1–3 in *From Roman to Merovingian, Gaul*, trans. Callander Murray, A. (Peterborough, Ontario, 2000), pp. 591–4, 597–621

Gerald of Wales, *Journey through Wales: Gerald of Wales: The Journey through Wales/The Description of Wales*, trans. Thorpe, L. (Harmondsworth, 1978), pp. 63–209

Hilary, *Letter to Leontius:* (= *Gundlach's 'Genuine Arlesian Letters' no. 19)* *MGH Epistolae,* vol. 3: *Merovingici et Karolini Aevi,* vol. 1, ed. Gundlach, W. (Berlin, 1892), pp. 28–9.

Honorius, *Letter to Agricola: From Roman to Merovingian Gaul,* trans. Callander Murray, A. (Peterborough, Ontario, 2000), p. 169–71

Honorius, *Letter to Arcadius: Corpus Scriptorum Ecclesiasticorum Latinorum,* vol. 35: *Epistulae Imperatorum Pontificorum Aliorum inde ab A. CCCLXVII usque ad A. DLIII datae,* part 1, ed. Guenther, O. (Vienna, 1895), letter 38, pp. 85–8.

Hydatius, *Chron.: The Chronicle of Hydatius and the Consularia Constantinopolitana. Two Contemporary Accounts of the Final Years of the Roman Empire,* ed. and trans. Burgess, R. W. (Oxford, 1993), pp. 1–172

Isidore, *Etymologies: Isidori Hispalensis Episcopis Etymologiarum sive Originum libri XX,* ed. Lindsay, W. M., 2 vols. (Oxford, 1911)

Isidore, *History of the Goths: Conquerors and Chroniclers of Early Medieval Spain,* trans. Baxter Wolf, K. (Liverpool, 1990), pp. 81–110

Jerome, *Against Jovinianus: NPNF,* 2nd ser., vol. 6: *St Jerome: Letters and Select Works,* trans. Fremantle, W. H. (Grand Rapids, MI, 1989), pp. 346–416

Jerome, *Chronicle:* An online edition and English translation may be found at http://www.tertullian.org/fathers/jerome_chronicle_00_eintro.htm

Jerome, *Letters: NPNF,* 2nd ser., vol. 6: *St Jerome: Letters and Select Works,* trans. Fremantle, W. H. (Grand Rapids, MI, 1989), pp. 1–295

John of Antioch: *The Age of Attila,* trans. Gordon, C. D. (New York, 1992)

John of Biclaro, *Chron.: Conquerors and Chroniclers of Early Medieval Spain,* trans. Baxter Wolf, K. (Liverpool, 1990), pp. 61–80

John Malalas, *Chron.: The Chronicle of John Malalas,* Australian Association for Byzantine Studies, Byzantina Australiensia 4, trans. Jeffreys, E., Jeffreys, M. and Scott, R. (Melbourne, 1986)

Jordanes, *Getica: The Gothic History of Jordanes,* trans. Mierow, C. C. (New York, 1915, repr. 1966)

Jordanes, *Romana: MGH Auctores Antiquissimi,* vol. 5.1: *Iordanis Romana et Getica,* ed. Mommsen, T. (Berlin, 1882), pp. 1–52

Lactantius, *On the Deaths of the Persecutors: Lactantius: De Mortibus Persecutorum,* ed. and trans. Creed, J. L. (Oxford, 1984)

Latin Panegyrics: In Praise of Later Roman Emperors. The Panegyrici Latini. Introduction, Translation and Historical Commentary, trans. Nixon, C. E. V. and Saylor Rodgers, B. (Berkeley, CA, 1994)

Life of Caesarius: Caesarius of Arles: Life, Testament, Letters, trans. Klingshirn, W. E. (Liverpool, 1994), pp. 1–65

Life of Fulgentius of Ruspe: Fulgentius. Selected Works, ed. Eno, R. B. (Washington, 1997), pp. 4–56

Life of Genovefa: Sainted Women of the Dark Ages, trans. McNamara, J.-A., Halborg, J. E. and Whatley, E. G. (Durham, NC, 1992), pp. 17–37

Life of Lupus of Troyes: MGH Scriptores Rerum Merovingicarum, vol. 7: *Passiones Vitaeque Sanctorum Aevi Merovingici*, vol. 5, ed. Krusch, B. and Levison, W. (Hannover, 1905), pp. 284–302

Lives of the Fathers of the Jura: Vie des pères du Jura, ed. and (French) trans. Martine, F. (Paris, 1968)

Lives of the Fathers of Mérida: Lives of the Visigothic Fathers, trans. Fear, A. T. (Liverpool, 1997), pp. 45–105

Lucretius, *Nature of Things: Lucretius: De Rerum Natura*, trans. Rouse, W. H. D. (London, 1924)

Malchus: *The Fragmentary Classicizing Historians of the Later Roman Empire*, ed. and trans. Blockley, R. C. (Liverpool, 1981), vol. 2, pp. 401–62

Marcellinus, *Chron.: The Chronicle of Marcellinus*, ed. and trans. Croke, B. (Sydney, 1995)

Marius of Avenches, *Chron.: From Roman to Merovingian Gaul*, trans. Callander Murray, A. (Peterborough, Ontario, 2000), pp. 101–8.

Menander, *History: The History of Menander the Guardsman*, ed. and trans. Blockley, R. C. (Liverpool, 1985)

Narrative of the Emperors of the Valentinianic and Theodosian Houses: MGH Auctores Antiquissimi, vol. 9: *Chronica Minora saec. IV. V. VI. VII*, vol. 1, ed. Mommsen, T. (Berlin, 1892), pp. 629–30

Olympiodorus: *The Fragmentary Classicizing Historians of the Later Roman Empire*, ed. and trans. Blockley, R. C. (Liverpool 1981), vol. 2, pp. 151–220

On Matters Military (De Rebus Bellicis): A Roman Reformer and Inventor, ed. and trans. Thompson, E. A. (Oxford, 1952)

Orientius, *Commonitorium: Commonitorium et Carmina Orientio Tributa*, ed. Rapisarda, C. A. (Catania, 1958)

Passion of St Saba the Goth: The Goths in the Fourth Century, ed. and trans. Matthews, J. F. and Heather, P. (Liverpool, 1991), pp. 109–17

Patrick, *Confession: St Patrick. His Writings and Muirchu's Life*, ed. and trans. Hood, A. B. E. (Chichester, 1978), pp. 23–34, 41–55

Patrick, *Letter to Coroticus: St Patrick. His Writings and Muirchu's Life*, ed. and trans. Hood, A. B. E. (Chichester, 1978), pp. 35–8, 55–9

Paul the Deacon, *Book of the Bishops of Metz: MGH Scriptores 2*, ed. Waitz, G. (Hannover, 1878), pp. 260–70

Paul the Deacon, *Roman History: MGH Scriptores Rerum Germanicarum in usum Scolarum*, vol. 49: *Pauli Historia Romana*, ed. Droysen, H. (Berlin, 1879)

Paulinus of Milan, *Life of St Ambrose: The Western Fathers*, trans. Hoare, F. R. (London, 1954), pp. 147–88

Paulinus of Nola, *Poems: The Poems of Saint Paulinus of Nola*, trans. Walsh, P. G., Ancient Christian Writers 40 (New York, 1975)

Paulinus of Pella, *Thanksgiving: The Last Poets of Imperial Rome*, trans. Ibsell, H. (Harmondsworth, 1971), pp. 242–62

Plato, *Republic: Plato: The Republic*, ed. and trans. Shorey, P., 2 vols. (London, 1930–5)

Pliny the Elder, *Natural History: Pliny: Natural History*, ed. and trans. Rackham, H., Jones, W. J. S. and Eichholz, D. E., 10 vols. (London, 1938–62)

Possiduis, *Life of Augustine: The Western Fathers*, trans. Hoare, F. R. (London, 1954), pp. 189–244

Priscus: *The Fragmentary Classicizing Historians of the Later Roman Empire*, ed. and trans. Blockley, R. C. (Liverpool, 1981), vol. 2, pp. 221–400

Procopius, *Wars: Procopius*, ed. and trans. Dewing, H. B., vols. 1–5 (London, 1914–28)

Propertius, *Elegies: Propertius: Elegies*, ed. and trans. Goold, G. P. (London, 1990)

Prosper of Aquitaine, *Chron.: From Roman to Merovingian Gaul*, trans. Callander Murray, A. (Peterborough, Ontario, 2000), pp. 62–76

Prudentius, *Against Symmachus: Prudentius*, ed. and trans. Thomson, H. J., 2 vols. (London, 1949–53), vol. 1, pp. 344–401; vol. 2, pp. 2–97

Querolus: *Selections: From Roman to Merovingian Gaul*, trans. Callander Murray, A. (Peterborough, Ontario, 2000), pp. 171–3; *People, Personal Expression and Social Relations in Late Antiquity*, ed. and trans. Mathisen, R. W. (Ann Arbor, 2003), vol. 1, pp. 17–19, 43–4, 62–4, 114–18, 219–21

Ravenna Annals: Bischoff, B. and Koehler, W., 'Eine illustrierte Ausgabe der spätantiken Ravennater Annalen', in *Medieval Studies in Memory of A. Kingsley Porter* (Cambridge, 1939), vol. 1, pp. 125–38

Remigius, *Letter to Clovis: From Roman to Merovingian Gaul*, trans. Callander Murray, A. (Peterborough, Ontario, 2000), p. 260

Remigius, *Testament: People, Personal Expression and Social Relations in Late Antiquity*, ed. and trans. Mathisen, R. W. (Ann Arbor, 2003), vol. 1, pp. 242–8

Ruricius, *Letters: Ruricius of Limoges and Friends. A Collection of Letters from Visigothic Gaul*, trans. Mathisen, R. W. (Liverpool, 1998)

Rutilius Namatius, *On his Return. The Last Poets of Imperial Rome*, trans. Ibsell H. (Harmondsworth, 1971), pp. 221–41

Salvian, *On the Governance of God: The Writings of Salvian the Presbyter*, trans. O'Sullivan, J. F. (New York, 1947)

Sidonius Apollinaris, *Letters: Sidonius: Poems and Letters*, ed. and trans. Anderson W. B., vol. 1 (London, 1936), pp. 329–483; *Sidonius: Poems and Letters*, ed. and trans. Anderson W. B., with Warmington, E. H., vol. 2 (London, 1965)

Sidonius Apollinaris, *Poems: Sidonius: Poems and Letters*, ed. and trans. Anderson W. B., vol. 1 (London, 1936), pp. 1–327

Strabo, *Geography: The Geography of Strabo*, trans. Jones, H. L., 8 vols. (London, 1917–32)

Sulpicius Severus, *Dialogues: The Western Fathers*, trans. Hoare, F. R. (London, 1954), pp. 68–144

Synesius, *Kingship: Synésios de Cyrène: Discours sur la royauté*, ed. and (French) trans. Lacombrade, C. (Paris, 1951)

Tacitus, *Agricola: Tacitus on Britain and Germany*, trans. Mattingly, H. (Harmondsworth, 1971), pp. 51–98

Tacitus, *Germania: Tacitus: Germania*, trans. Rives, J. (Oxford, 1999).

Tacitus, *Histories: Tacitus: Histories and Annals*, trans. Moore, C. H. and Jackson, J., 4 vols. (London, 1925–37)

Tertullian, *Pallium: Tertullianus, De Pallio*, ed. and (Dutch) trans. Gerlo, A. (Wetteren, 1940). English translation online at: http://www.tertullian. org/articles/hunink_de_pallio.htm

Themistius, *Orations: Politics, Philosophy and Empire in the Fourth Century: Select Orations of Themistius*, trans. Heather, P. and Moncur, D. (Liverpool, 2001)

Theodoret, *Ecclesiastical History: NPNF*, 2nd ser., vol. 3: *The Ecclesiastical History, Dialogues and Letters of Theodoret*, trans. Jackson, B. (reprint: Grand Rapids, MI, 1989)

Theoderic's Edict: MGH Legum, vol. 5, ed. Bluhme, F. (Hanover, 1875–89), pp. 145–79.

Vegetius, *Epitome: Vegetius. Epitome of Military Science*, trans. Milner, N. P. (Liverpool, 1993)

Velleius Paterculus, *Roman History: Velleius Paterculus: Compendium of Roman History*, ed. and trans. Shipley, F. W. (London, 1924)

Venantius, *Life of Radegund: Sainted Women of the Dark Ages*, trans. McNamara, J.-A., with Halborg, J. E. and Whatley, E. G. (Durham, NC, 1992), pp. 70–86

Venantius, *Miracles of Hilary*: R. Van Dam, *Saints and their Miracles in Late Antique Gaul* (Princeton, 1993), pp. 155–61

Victor of Tunnuna, *Chron.: MGH Auctores Antiquissimi*, vol. 11: *Chronica Minora saec. IV. V. VI. VII*, vol. 2, ed. Mommsen, T. (Berlin, 1894), pp. 184–206

Victor of Vita, *History of the Vandal Persecution: Victor of Vita: History of the Vandal Persecution*, trans. Moorhead, J. (Liverpool, 1992)

Vitruvius, *Architecture: Vitruvius: On Architecture*, ed. and trans. Granger, F., 2 vols. (London, 1931–4)

Widukind, *Deeds of the Saxons: MGH Scriptores Rerum Germanicarum in usum Scholarum. Widikundi Manachi Corbeiensis Gestarum Regum Saxonicarum Libri Tres*, ed. Waitz, G. and Kehr, K. A., 5th edn (Hanover, 1935)

Wissembourg Cartulary: *Traditiones Wizenburgenses: Die Urkunden des Klosters Weissenburg, 661–864*, ed. Glöckner, K. and Doll, A. (Darmstadt, 1979)

SECONDARY WORKS

Akerraz, A. (1985). 'Note sur l'enceinte tardive de Volubilis', in Lancel (ed.) (1985), pp. 429–36.

Alcock, L. (1971). *Arthur's Britain* (Harmondsworth).

(1972). *'By South Cadbury is that Camelot...' Excavations at Cadbury Castle 1966–70* (London).

(1987). *Economy, Society and Warfare among the Britons and Saxons* (Cardiff).

(1992). 'Message from the dark side of the moon: western and northern Britain in the age of Sutton Hoo', in Carver (ed.) (1992), pp. 205–15.

(2003). *Kings and Warriors, Craftsmen and Priests in Northern Britain, AD 550–850* (Edinburgh).

Alföldi, A. (1952a). *A Conflict of Ideas in the Late Roman Empire. The Clash between the Senate and Valentinian I* (Oxford).

(1952b). 'The moral barrier on Rhine and Danube', in *The Congress of Roman Frontier Studies 1949*, ed. Birley, E. (Durham, 1952), pp. 1–16.

Alföldi, M. R.- (1997). '*Germania magna* – *nicht* libera. Notizen zum römischen Wortgebrauch.' *Germania* 75: 45–52.

Allison, P. (2003). 'An empire of cities', in *The Cambridge Illustrated History of the Roman World*, ed. Woolf, G. (Cambridge), pp. 202–31.

Althoff, G. (1998). '*Ira regis*: prolegomena to a history of royal anger', in *Anger's Past: The Social Uses of an Emotion in the Middle Ages*, ed. Rosenwein, B. H. (Ithaca, NY), pp. 59–74.

Amory, P. (1993). 'The meaning and purpose of ethnic terminology in the Burgundian laws', *EME* 2: 1–28.

(1997). *People and Identity in Ostrogothic Italy, 489–554* (Cambridge).

Anderson, B. (1983). *Imagined Communities* (Cambridge).

Anderson, T. (1995). 'Roman military colonists in Gaul, Salian ethnogenesis and the forgotten meaning of Pactus Legis Salicae 59.5', *EME* 4.2: 129–44.

Anthony, D. (1997). 'Prehistoric migrations as social process', in Chapman and Hamerow (eds.) (1997), pp. 21–32.

Applebaum, S. (ed.) (1971). *Limeskongress 7* (Tel Aviv).

Arce, J. (1994). 'Constantinopla, Tarraco y Centcelles', *Buttleti Arqueológic*, 5th ser., 16: 147–66.

(2003). 'The enigmatic fifth century in Hispania: some historical problems', in Goetz, Jarnut and Pohl (eds.) (2003), pp. 135–57.

Arjava, A. (1996). *Women and the Law in Late Antiquity* (Oxford).

(1998). 'Paternal power in late antiquity'. *JRS* 88: 147–65.

Armit, I. (1998). *Scotland's Hidden History* (Stroud).

(2003). *Towers in the North. The Brochs of Scotland* (Stroud).

Armit, I. (ed.) (1990). *Beyond the Brochs: Changing Perspectives on the Later Iron Age in Atlantic Scotland* (Edinburgh).

Armit, I. and Ralston, I. B. M. (2003). 'The Iron Age', in Edwards and Ralston (eds.) (2003), pp. 168–93.

Arnheim, M. T. W. (1972). *The Senatorial Aristocracy in the Later Roman Empire* (Oxford).

Arnold, C. J. (1984). *From Roman Britain to Saxon England* (London).

(1988). 'Territories and leadership: frameworks for the study of emergent polities in early Anglo-Saxon southern England', in Driscoll and Nieke (eds.) (1988), pp. 111–27.

Ausbüttel, F. M. (1991). 'Die Verträge zwischen den Vandalen und Römern.' *Rh* 11: 1–20.

(2003). *Theoderich der Große: der Germane auf dem Kaiserthron* (Darmstadt).

Ausenda, G. (ed.) (1995). *After Empire: Towards an Ethnology of Europe's Barbarians* (Woodbridge).

Autorenkollektiv (1983). *Die Germanen. Geschichte und Kultur der germanischen Stämme in Mitteleuropa. Ein Handbuch in zwei Bänden*, vol. 2 (Berlin).

Axboe, M. (1995). 'Danish kings and dendrochronology: archaeological insights into the early history of the Danish state', in Ausenda (ed.) (1995), pp. 217–51.

(1999). 'Towards the kingdom of Denmark', in Dickinson and Griffiths (eds.) (1999), pp. 109–18.

Azkarate Garai-Olaun, A. (1992). 'The western Pyrenees during the late antiquity: reflections for a reconsideration of the issue', in *Il Territorio tra tardoantico e altomedioevo: Metodi di indagine e risulati*, ed. Brogiolo, G. -P. and Castelleti, L. (Florence), pp. 179–91.

Azzara, C. (2002). 'The papacy', in *Italy in the Early Middle Ages*, ed. La Rocca, C. (Oxford).

Baker, J. R. (1974). *Race* (London).

Ballin Smith, B. and Bainks, I. (eds.) (2002). *In the Shadow of the Brochs: The Iron Age in Scotland* (Stroud).

Balsdon, J. P. V. D. (1979). *Romans and Aliens* (London).

Banton, M. (1998). *Racial Theories*, 2nd edn (Cambridge).

Barbiera, I. (2005). *Changing Lands in Changing Memories: Migration and Identity during the Lombard Invasions* (Florence).

Barker, G. (1995). *A Mediterranean Valley: Landscape Archaeology and Annales History in the Biferno Valley* (London).

Barnes, T. D. (1982). *The New Empire of Diocletian and Constantine* (Cambridge, MA).

(1998). *Ammianus Marcellinus and the Representation of Historical Reality* (Ithaca).

Barnish, S. J. B. (1986). 'Taxation, land and barbarian settlement in the western Empire', *Papers of the British School at Rome* 54: 170–95.

(1988). 'Transformation and survival in the western senatorial aristocracy, c.400–700', *Papers of the British School at Rome* 56: 120–55.

(1992). 'Old Kaspars: Attila's invasion of Gaul in the literary sources', in Drinkwater and Elton (eds.) (1992), pp. 38–47.

Barnwell, P. S. (1992). *Emperor, Prefects and Kings: The Roman West, 395–565* (London).

    (2000). 'Emperors, jurists and kings: law and custom in late Roman and early medieval west', *P&P* 168: 6–29.

Barry, T. (ed.) (2000). *A History of Settlement in Ireland* (London).

Barth, F. (1969a). 'Introduction', in Barth (ed.) (1969), pp. 9–38.

    (1969b). 'Pathan identity and its maintenance', in Barth (ed.) (1969), pp. 117–34.

Barth, F. (ed.) (1969). *Ethnic Groups and Boundaries: The Social Organization of Culture Difference* (Bergen/London).

Bartholemew, P. (1982). 'Fifth-century facts', *Britannia* 13: 261–70.

    (1984). 'Fourth-century Saxons', *Britannia* 15: 169–85.

Bassett, S. (1989). 'In search of the origins of Anglo-Saxon Kingdoms', in Bassett (ed.) (1989), pp. 3–27.

Bassett, S. (ed.) (1989). *The Origins of Anglo-Saxon Kingdoms* (London).

Behr, C. (2000). 'The origins of kingship in early medieval Kent', *EME* 9.1: 25–52.

Bemmann, J. (1999). 'Körpergräber der jungeren römischen Kaiserzeit und Völkerwanderungszeit aus Schleswig Holstein. Zum Aufkommen einer neuen Bestattungssitte im überregionalen Vergleich', *SzSf* 13: 5–45.

Bender, H. (2001). 'Archaeological perspectives on rural settlement in late antiquity in the Rhine and Danube area', in Burns and Eadie (eds.) (2001), pp. 185–98.

Benseddik, N. (1980). 'La ferme Romanette, Ain Benia, Ain bent Soltaine: fortins ou fermes fortifiées?', in Hanson and Keppie (eds.) (1980), pp. 977–98.

Benseddik, N. and Potter, T. W. (1993). *Fouilles du forum de Cherchel*, 2 vols. (Algiers).

Bentley, G. C. (1987). 'Ethnicity and practice', *CSSH* 29: 24–55.

Bergengruen, A. (1958). *Adel und Grundherrschaft im Merowingerreich* (Wiesbaden).

Bertrandy, F. and Coltelloni-Trannoy, M. (2005). *L'Afrique romaine de l'Atlantique à la Tripolitaine, 69–439. Enjeux historiographiques, méthodologie, bibliographie commentée* (Paris).

Bierbrauer, V. (1994a). 'Archeologia e storia dei Goti dal I al IV secolo', in Bierbrauer, Arslan and von Hessen (eds.) (1994), pp. 22–47.

    (1994b). 'Archeologia degli Ostrogoti in Italia', in Bierbrauer, von Hessen and Arslan (eds.) (1994), pp. 170–213.

Bierbrauer, V., von Hessen, O. and Arslan, E. A. (eds.) (1994). *I Goti* (Milan).

Bintliff, J. and Hamerow, H. (eds.) (1995). *Europe between Late Antiquity and the Middle Ages: Recent Archaeological and Historical Research in Western and Southern Europe*, BAR (I) 617 (Oxford).

Blackhurst, A. (2004). 'The house of Nubel: rebels or players?', in Merrills (ed.) (2004), pp. 59–75.

Blagg, T. F. C. and Millett, M. (eds.) (1990). *The Early Roman Empire in the West* (Oxford).

Blazquez, J. M. (1974). 'Der Limes im Spanien des vierten Jahrhunderts', in *Actes du IXe Congrès International d'Etudes sur les Frontières Romaines. Mamaïa, 6–23 Sept. 1972*, ed. Pippidi, D. M. (Cologne), pp. 485–502.

(1980). 'Der Limes hispaniens im 4. und 5. Jahrhunderts Forschungstand; Niederlassung der Laeti oder Gentiles am Flusslauf der Duero', in Hanson and Keppie (eds.) (1980), pp. 345–96.

Bleckmann, B. (1997). 'Honorius und das Ende der römischen Herrschaft in Westeuropa', *HZ* 265: 561–95.

Blockley, R. C. (1980). 'The date of the 'Barbarian Conspiracy', *Britannia* 11: 233–5.

(ed. and trans.) (1983). *The Fragmentary Classicizing Historians of the Later Roman Empire* (Liverpool).

(1998). 'The dynasty of Theodosius', *CAH* 13, pp. 111–37.

Boehm, L. (1998). *Geschichte Burgunds: Politik, Staatsbildungen, Kultur*, 2nd edn (Wiesbaden).

Böhme, H.-W. (1974). *Germanische Grabfünde des 4 bis 5 Jahrhunderts zwischen untere Elbe und Loire. Studien zur Chronologie und Bevölkerungsgeschichte* (Munich).

(1976). 'Das Land zwischen Elb- und Wesermündung vom 4. bis 6. Jahrhundert. Die Sachsen und ihre Beziehungen zum römischen Westen', *Führer zu vor- und frühgeschichtliche Denkmäler* 29: 205–26.

(1986). 'Das Ende der Römerherrschaft in Britannien und die angelsächsische Besiedlung Englands im 5. Jahrhundert', *JRGZM* 33: 469–574.

(1988). 'Les Thuringiens dans le nord du royaume franc'. *Revue Archéologique de Picardie* 3/4: 57–69.

Böhner, K. (1963). 'Zur historischen Interpretation der sogenannten Laetengräber', *JRGZM* 10: 139–67.

(1994). 'Die frühmittelalterlichen Spangenhelme und die nordischen Helme der Vendelzeit', *JRGZM* 41: 471–549.

Bona, I. (1991). *Das Hunnenreich* (Stuttgart).

Bourdieu, P. (1977). *Outline of a Theory of Practice* (Cambridge).

Bowden, W., Lavan, L. and Machado, C. (eds.) (2004). *Recent Research on the Late Antique Countryside* (Leiden).

Bowersock, G. (1988). 'The dissolution of the Roman Empire', in *The Collapse of Ancient States and Civilizations*, ed. Yoffee, N. and Cowgill, G. L. (Tucson), pp. 166–75.

Bowersock, G., Brown, P. R. L. and Grabar, O. (eds.) (1999). *Late Antiquity: A Guide to the Postclassical World* (Cambridge MA, and London).

Bowes, K. (2001). 'Villa-churches, rural piety and the Priscillianist controversy', in Burns and Eadie (eds.) (2001), pp. 323–48.

Bowlus, C. R. (2002). 'Ethnogenesis: the tyranny of a concept', in Gillett (ed.) (2002), pp. 241–56.

Brather, S. (2004). *Ethnische Interpretationen in der frühgeschichtlichen Archäologie: Geschichte, Grundlagen und Alternativen* (Berlin).

Breeze, D. J. (1987). 'Britain', in Wacher (ed.) (1987), pp. 198–222.

Brennan, B. (1985). 'The career of Venantius Fortunatus', *Traditio* 41: 49–78.

Brett, M. and Fentress, E. (1996). *The Berbers* (Oxford).

Bright, D. F. (1987). *The Miniature Epic in Vandal Africa* (Norman, OK).

Brink-Kloke, H. and Meurers-Balke, J. (2003). 'Siedlungen und Gräber am Oespeler Bach (Dortmund) – eine Kulturlandschaft im Wandel der Zeiten', *Germania* 81: 47–146.

Brogiolo, G.-P. (ed.) (1996a). *Early Medieval Towns in the Western Mediterranean. Documenti di Archeologia 10* (Mantua).

  (ed.) (1996b). *La fine delle ville Romana. Trasformazioni nelle campagne tra tarda antichità e alto medioevo. Documenti di Archeologia 11* (Mantua).

Brogiolo, G.-P. and Cantino Wataghin, G. (eds.) (1998). *Sepolture tra IV e VIII secolo. Documenti di Archeologia 13* (Mantua).

Brogiolo, G. P., Christie, N. and Gauthier, N. (eds.) (2002). *Towns and their Territories between Late Antiquity and the Early Middle Ages* (Leiden).

Brogiolo, G. P., and Ward Perkins, B. (eds.) (1999). *The Idea and the Ideal of the Town between Late Antiquity and the Early Middle Ages* (Leiden).

Brown, P. R. L. (1961). 'Religious dissent in the later Roman Empire: the case of North Africa', *History* 46: 83–101.

  (1971). 'The rise and function of the holy man in late antiquity', *JRS* 61: 80–101.

  (1978). *The Making of Late Antiquity* (Cambridge, MA).

  (1988). *The Body and Society: Men, Women and Sexual Renunciation in Early Christianity* (London).

  (1992). *Power and Persuasion in Late Antiquity: Towards a Christian Empire* (Madison).

  (1995). *Authority and the Sacred: Aspects of the Christianization of the Roman World* (Cambridge).

  (1998a). 'Asceticism, pagan and Christian', *CAH* 13, pp. 601–31.

  (1998b). 'Christianization and religious conflict', *CAH* 13, pp. 632–64.

  (2002). *The Rise of Western Christendom: Triumph and Diversity, AD 200–1000* (Oxford).

Brown, T. S. (1984). *Gentlemen and Officers: Imperial Administration and Aristocratic Power in Byzantine Italy, AD 554–800* (British School at Rome).

Brulet, R. (1993). 'Les dispositifs militaires du Bas-Empire en Gaule septentrionale', in Vallet and Kazanski (eds.) (1993), pp. 135–49.

  (1997). 'La tombe de Childéric et la topographie funéraire de Tournai à la fin du Vᵉ siècle', in Rouche (ed.) (1997), pp. 59–78.

Burgess, R. W. (1992). 'From Gallia Romana to Gallia Gothica: the view from Spain', in Drinkwater and Elton (eds.) (1992), pp. 19–27.

(ed. and trans.) (1993). *The Chronicle of Hydatius and the Consularia Constantinopolitana: Two Contemporary Accounts of the Final Years of the Roman Empire* (Oxford).

Burns, T. S. (1973). 'The battle of Adrianople: a reconsideration', *Hist.* 22: 336–45.

(1984). *A History of the Ostrogoths* (Bloomington, IN).

(1992). 'The settlement of 418', in Drinkwater and Elton (eds.) (1992), pp. 53–63.

(1994). *Barbarians within the Gates of Rome. A Study of Roman Military Policy and the Barbarians, ca.375–425* (Bloomington, IN).

Burns, T. S. and Eadie, J. W. (eds.) (2001). *Urban Centers and Rural Contexts in Late Antiquity* (East Lancing, MI).

Burrus, V. (1995). *The Making of a Heretic. Gender, Authority and the Priscillianist Controversy* (Berkeley, CA).

Bury, J. B. (1919). 'Justa Gratia Honoria.' *JRS* 9: 1–13.

(1958). *History of the Later Roman Empire from the Death of Theodosius I to the Death of Justinian* (reprint; New York).

Callander Murray, A. (1983). *Germanic Kinship Structure: Studies in Law and Society in Antiquity and the Early Middle Ages* (Toronto).

(1986). 'The position of the Grafio in the constitutional history of Merovingian Gaul', *Spec.* 61: 787–805.

(1988). 'From Roman to Frankish Gaul: 'centenarii' and 'centenae' in the administration of the Merovingian kingdom', *Traditio* 44: 59–100.

(1994). 'Immunity, nobility and the Edict of Paris', *Spec.* 69: 18–39.

(2002). 'Reinhard Wenskus on "Ethnogenesis", ethnicity and the origin of the Franks', in Gillett (ed.) (2002), pp. 39–68.

Cameron, A. D. (1970). *Claudian: Poetry and Propaganda at the Court of Honorius* (Oxford).

Cameron, A. D. and Long, J. (1993). *Barbarians and Politics at the Court of Arcadius* (Berkeley).

Cameron, A. M. (1985). *Procopius and the Sixth Century* (London).

(1989). 'Gelimer's laughter: the case of Byzantine Africa', in Clover and Humphreys (eds.) (1989), pp. 171–90.

(1991). *Christianity and the Rhetoric of Empire. The Development of a Christian Discourse* (Berkeley, CA).

(1993a). *The Later Roman Empire, 284–430* (London).

(1993b). *The Mediterranean World in Late Antiquity, 395–600* (London).

Cameron, A. M. (ed.) (1995). *The Byzantine and Early Islamic Near East 3: States, Resources and Armies* (Princeton, NJ).

Cameron, A. M. and King, G. R. D. (eds.), (1994). *The Byzantine and Early Islamic Near East 2. Land Use and Settlement Patterns* (Princeton, NJ).

Campbell, E. (1996). 'Trade in the Dark Age west: a peripheral activity?', in *Scotland in Dark Age Britain*, ed. B. Crawford (St Andrews), pp. 79–91.

Camps, G. (1985). 'De masuna à Koceila: les destines de la Maurétanie aux VIe et VIIe siècles', in Lancel (ed.) (1985), pp. 307–24.

Capelle, T. (1998). *Die Sachsen des frühen Mittelalters* (Stuttgart).

Carile, A. (ed.) (1995). *Teodorico e i Goti tra Oriente e Occidente* (Ravenna).

Carlyle, T. (1830). 'On history', reprinted in F. Stern (ed.), *Varieties of History* (New York, 1973), pp. 91–101.

Carozzi, C. (1992). 'Le Clovis de Grégoire de Tours', *Le Moyen-Age* 98: 169–85.

Carreté, J.-M., Keay, S. and Millett, M. (1995). *A Roman Provincial Capital and its Hinterland: The Survey of the Territory of Tarragona, Spain, 1985–1990* (Ann Arbor).

Carroll, M. (2001). *Romans, Celts and Germans. The German Provinces of Rome* (Stroud).

Carver, M. O. H. (1989). 'Kingship and material culture in early Anglo-Saxon East Anglia', in Bassett (ed.) (1989), pp. 141–58.

Carver, M. O. H. (ed.) (1992). *The Age of Sutton Hoo: The Seventh Century in North-western Europe* (Woodbridge).

Casey, P. J. and Jones, M. E. (1990). 'The date of the letter of the Britons to Aëtius', *BBCS* 37: 281–90.

Castellanos, S. (1996). 'Aristocracias y dependientes en el alto Ebro (siglos V-VIII)', *Studia Historica, Historia Medieval* 14: 29–46.

(2000). 'Propiedad de la tierra y relaciones de dependencia en la Galia del siglo VI. El *Testamentum Remigii*', *An. Tard.* 8: 223–7.

Castellanos, S. and Martín Viso, I. (2005). 'The local articulation of central power in the north of the Iberian Peninsula (500–1000)', *EME* 13: 1–42.

Cesa, M. (1982). 'Hospitalitas o altre "techniques of accommodation"? A proposito di un libro recente', *Archivio Storico Italiano* 140: 539–52.

(1984). 'Überlegungen zur Föderatenfrage', *MIÖG* 92: 307–16.

(1992–3). 'Il matrimonio di Placidia ed Ataulfo sullo sfondo dei rapporti fra Ravenna e i Visigoti', *Rb* 12: 23–53.

(1994a). *Impero Tardoantico e Barbari. La crisi militare da Adrianopli al 418* (Como).

(1994b). 'Il regno di Odoacre: la prima dominazione germanica in Italia', in *Germani in Italia*, ed. Scardigli, B. and Scardigli, P. (Rome), pp. 307–20.

Chapman, J. and Hamerow, H. (eds.) (1997). *Migrations and Invasions in Archaeological Explanation*, BAR (I) 664 (Oxford).

Charles-Edwards, T. (2003). 'Nations and kingdoms: a view from above', in Charles-Edwards (ed.) (2003), pp. 25–58.

Charles-Edwards, T. (ed.) (2003). *After Rome* (Oxford).

Chastagnol, A. (1973). 'Le repli sur Arles des services administratifs gaulois en l'an 407 de notre ère', *RH* 97: 23–40.

(1978). *L'album municipal de Timgad* (Bonn).

Chavarría Arnau, A. (2004). 'Interpreting the transformation of late Roman villa: the case of Hispania', in Christie (ed.) (2004), pp. 67–102.

(2005). 'Dopo la fine delle ville: le campagne Ispaniche in epoco Visigota (VI–VII secolo)', in *Dopo la fine delle ville: Le campagne dal VI al IX secolo*, ed. Brogiolo, G.-P., Chavarría Arnau, A. and Valenti, M. (Mantua), pp. 263–85.

Chavarría Arnau, A. and Lewit, T. (2004). 'Archaeological research on the late antique countryside: a bibliographic essay', in Bowden, Lavan and Machado (eds.) (2004), pp. 3–51.

Childe, V. G. (1929). *The Danube in Prehistory* (Oxford).

Christie, N. (1995). *The Lombards* (Oxford).

(1996). 'Barren fields? Landscapes and settlements in late Roman and post-Roman Italy', in Shipley and Salmon (eds.) (1996), pp. 254–83.

(2006). *From Constantine to Charlemagne: An Archaeology of Italy, AD 300–800* (Aldershot).

Christie, N. (ed.) (2004). *Landscapes of Change: Rural Evolutions in Late Antiquity and the Early Middle Ages* (Aldershot).

Christie, N. and Loseby, S. T. (eds.) (1996). *Towns in Transition: Urban Evolution in Late Antiquity and the Early Middle Ages* (Aldershot).

Christlein, R. (1991). *Die Alamannen. Archäologie eines lebendigen Volkes*, 3rd edn (Stuttgart).

Clark, D. F. (2000). *A Methodological Examination of Aspects of Chronological and Social Analysis of Early Anglo-Saxon Cemeteries with Particular Reference to Cemetery I, Mucking, Essex* (unpub. PhD Dissertation, University of London).

Clark, G. N. (1993). *Women in Late Antiquity: Pagan and Christian Lifestyles* (Oxford).

Clarke, G. N. (1979). *Winchester Studies 3: Pre-Roman and Roman Winchester Part II, The Roman Cemetery at Lankhills* (Oxford).

Clarke, H. and Ambrosiani, B. (1995). *Towns in the Viking Age*, rev. edn (Leicester).

Close-Brooks, J. (1983). 'Dr Bersu's excavations at Traprain Law, 1947', in *From the Stone Age to the 'Forty-Five*, ed. O'Connor, A. and Clarke, D. V. (Edinburgh), pp. 206–23.

(1987). 'Comment on Traprain Law', *SAR* 4.2: 92–4.

Clover, F. M. (1978). 'Carthage in the age of Augustine', in *Excavations in Carthage 1976*, ed. Humphrey, J. H. (Ann Arbor), pp. 1–14 (repr. as Clover (1993), no. V).

(1982). 'Carthage and the Vandals', in *Excavations in Carthage 1978*, ed. Humphrey, J. H. (Ann Arbor), pp. 1–22 (repr. as Clover (1993), no. VI).

(1986). 'Felix Karthago', Dumbarton Oaks Papers 40: 1–16 (repr. as Clover (1993), no. IX).

(1989). 'The symbiosis of Romans and Vandals in Africa', in *Das Reich und die Barbaren*, ed. Chrysos, E. and Schwarcz, A. (Vienna and Cologne), pp. 57–73 (repr. as Clover (1993), no. X).

(1993). *The Late Roman West and the Vandals* (London).

Clover, F. M. and Humphreys, R. S. (eds.) (1989). *Tradition and Innovation in Late Antiquity* (Madison, WI).

Collins, R. J. H. (1980). 'Merida and Toledo, 550–585', in James (ed.) (1980), pp. 189–219.

(1990). 'The ethnogenesis of the Basques', in Wolfram and Pohl (eds.) (1990), pp. 35–44.

(1995). *Early Medieval Spain. Unity in Diversity, 400–1000*, 2nd edn (London).

(1998). 'Law and ethnic identity in the western kingdoms in the fifth and sixth centuries', in *Medieval Europeans: Studies in Ethnic Identity and National Perspectives in Medieval Europe*, ed. Smyth, A. P. (London), pp. 1–23.

(1999) *Early Medieval Europe, 300–1000*, 2nd edn (London).

(2004). *Visigothic Spain, 409–711* (London).

Collis, J. (1984). *The European Iron Age* (London).

Conant, J. (2004). 'Literacy and private documentation in Vandal North Africa: the case of the Albertini Tablets', in Merrills (ed.) (2004), pp. 199–224.

Cooney, G. (2000). 'Reading a landscape manuscript: a review of progress in prehistoric settlement studies in Ireland', in Barry (ed.) (2000), pp. 1–49.

Cooney, G. and Grogan, E. (1994). *Irish Prehistory: A Social Perspective* (Dublin).

Cooper, K. (1992). 'Insinuations of womanly influence: an aspect of the Christianization of the Roman aristocracy', *JRS* 82: 150–64.

(1996). *The Virgin and the Bride: Idealized Womanhood in Late Antiquity* (Cambridge, MA).

(1999). 'The widow as impresario: gender, legendary afterlives and documentary evidence in Eugippius' *Vita Severini*', in Pohl and Diesenberger (eds.) (1999), pp. 53–63.

Cooper, K. and Leyser, C. (2001). 'The gender of grace', in Stafford and Mulder-Bakker (eds.) (2001), pp. 6–21.

Corcoran, S. (1996). *The Empire of the Tetrarchs* (Oxford).

Cotterill, J. (1993). 'Saxon raiding and the role of late Roman coastal forts of Britain', *Britannia* 24: 227–40.

Courcelle, P. (1964). *Histoire littéraire des grandes invasions germaniques* (Paris).

Courtois, C. (1955). *Les Vandales et l'Afrique* (Paris).

Crawford, B. (ed.) (1994). *Scotland in Dark Age Europe* (St Andrews).

Croke, B. (1983). '476: The manufacture of a turning point', *Chiron* 13: 81–119 (repr. as B. Croke, *Christian Chronicles and Byzantine History, 5th–6th Century* (London, 1992), no. V).

Croke, B. (ed. and trans.) (1995). *The Chronicle of Marcellinus* (Sydney).

Cunliffe, B. and Keay, S. (eds.) (1995). *Social Complexity and the Development of Towns in Iberia* (= PBA 86).

Cüppers, H., (ed.) (1984). *Trier. Kaiserresidenz und Bischofssitz* (Mainz).

Curran, J. (1998). 'From Jovian to Theodosius', *CAH* 13, pp. 78–110.

Curta, F. (2005). 'Frontier ethnogenesis in late antiquity: the Danube, the Tervingi, and the Slavs', in *Borders, Barriers, and Ethnogenesis: Frontiers in Late Antiquity and the Middle Ages*, ed. Curta, F. (Turnhout), pp. 173–204.

(1999). *Pagan City and Christian Capital. Rome in the Fourth Century* (Oxford).

Dahn, F. (1899). *Die Goten: Ostgermanen – Die Völker der Gotischen Gruppe*, 4 vols. (Berlin; repr. Breslau, n.d., in 1 vol.).

Daly, W. M. (1994). 'Clovis: how barbaric, how pagan?', *Spec.* 69: 619–64.

Daniell, C. (1994). 'The geographical perspective of Gildas', *Britannia* 25: 213–17.

Daniels, C. (1987). 'Africa', in Wacher (ed.) (1987), pp. 223–65.

Dark, K. R. (1992). 'A sub-Roman re-defence of Hadrian's Wall?', *Britannia* 23: 111–20.

(1994). *From Civitas to Kingdom: British Political Continuity, 300–800* (Leicester).

(1995). *Theoretical Archaeology* (London).

(2002). *Britain and the End of the Roman Empire* (Stroud).

Dark, K. R. (ed.) (1996). *External Contacts and the Economy of Late Roman and Post-Roman Britain* (Woodbridge).

Dark, S. P. (1996). 'Palaeoecological evidence for landscape continuity and change in Britain ca A.D. 400–800', in Dark, K. R. (eds.) (1996), pp. 23–51.

Dauzat, A. and Rostaing, C. (1963). *Dictionnaire étymologique des noms de lieux en France* (Paris).

Davies, W. (2005). 'The Celtic kingdoms', in *NCMH* 1, pp. 232–62.

Delbrück, H. (1980). *History of the Art of War, Volume II: The Barbarian Invasions*, trans. of German 3rd edn (Lincoln, Nebraska).

Dench, E. (1995). *From Barbarians to New Men. Greek, Roman and Modern Perceptions of Peoples from the Central Apennines* (Oxford).

De Palol, P. (1977). 'Romanos en la Meseta: el Bajo Imperio y la aristocracia indígena', in *Segovia. Symposium de Arqueologia Romana* (Barcelona), pp. 297–308.

De Paor, L. and De Paor, M. (1958). *Early Christian Ireland* (London).

De Ste Croix, G. (1981). *The Class Struggle in the Ancient Greek World from the Archaic Age to the Arab Conquest* (London).

Dickinson, T. M. (2005). 'Symbols of protection: the significance of animal-ornamented shields in early Anglo-Saxon England', *Medieval Archaeology* 49: 109–63.

Dickinson, T. M. and Griffiths, D. (ed.) (1999). *The Making of Kingdoms*, Anglo-Saxon Studies in History and Archaeology 10 (Oxford).

Dierkens, A. and Périn, P. (2000). 'Les *sedes regiae* mérovingiennes entre Seine et Loire', in Ripoll and Gurt (eds.) (2000), pp. 267–304.

(2003). 'The fifth-century advance of the Franks in Belgica II: history and archaeology', in *Essays on the Early Franks*, ed. Taayke, E., Looijenga, J. H., Harsema, O. H. and Reinders, H. R. (Groningen), pp. 165–93.

Diesner, H.-J. (1966). *Das Vandalenreich: Aufstieg und Untergang* (Leipzig).

Dietz, S., Sebaï, L. L. and Ben Hassen, H. (eds.) (1995). *Africa Proconsularis: Regional Studies in the Segermes Valley of North Tunisia* (Copenhagen/ Aarhus).

Dixon, P. (1982). 'How Saxon is the Saxon house?', in *Structural Reconstruction: Approaches to the Interpretation of the Excavated Remains of Buildings*, ed. Drury, P., BAR(B) 110 (Oxford), pp. 275–86.

Dolley, M. (1976). 'Roman coin hoards from Ireland and the date of Saint Patrick', in *Proceedings of the Royal Irish Academy*, pp. 181–90.

Donié, S. (1999). *Soziale Gliederung und Bevölkerungsentwicklung einer frühmittelalterlichen Siedlungsgemeinschaft: Untersuchungen zum Gräberfeld bei Schretzheim* (Bonn).

Dopsch, A. (1937). *The Economic and Social Foundations of European Civilization* (New York and London).

Dörfler, W. (2003). 'Rural economy of the continental Saxons from the migration period to the tenth century', in Green and Siegmund (eds.) (2003), pp. 133–48.

Dornier, A. (1971). 'Was there a coastal *Limes* in western Britain in the fourth century?', in Applebaum (ed.) (1971), pp. 15–20.

Dreyfus, H. L. and Rabinow, P. (1982). *Michel Foucault. Beyond Structuralism and Hermeneutics* (London).

Drijvers, J. W. and Hunt, D. (eds.) (1999). *The Late Roman World and its Historian. Interpreting Ammianus Marcellinus* (London).

Drinkwater, J. F. (1983). *Roman Gaul* (London).

(1989). 'Patronage in Roman Gaul and the problem of the Bagaudae', in *Patronage in Ancient Society*, ed. Wallace-Hadrill, A. (London), pp. 189–203.

(1992). 'The Bacaudae of fifth-century Gaul', in Drinkwater and Elton (eds.) (1992), pp. 208–17.

(1996). '"The Germanic threat on the Rhine frontier": a Romano-Gallic artefact?', in Mathisen and Sivan (eds.) (1996), pp. 20–30.

(1997). 'Julian and the Franks and Valentinian I and the Alamanni: Ammianus on Roman-German relations', *Francia* 24: 1–16.

(1998). 'The usurpers Constantine III (407–411) and Jovinus (411–413)', *Britannia* 29: 269–98.

Drinkwater, J. F. and Elton, H. (eds.) (1992). *Fifth-century Gaul: A Crisis of Identity?* (Cambridge).

Driscoll, S. (1988a). 'Power and authority in early historic Scotland: Pictish symbol stones and other documents', in *State and Society: The Emergence and Development of Social Hierarchy and Political Centralization*, ed. Gledhill, J., Bender, B. and Larsen, M. T. (London), pp. 215–36.

(1988b). 'The relationship between history and archaeology: artifacts, documents and power', in Driscoll and Nieke (eds.) (1988), pp. 162–87.

Dumville, D. N. (1972–4) 'Some aspects of the chronology of the *Historia Brittonum*', *BBCS* 25: 439–45.

(1976). 'The Anglian collection of royal genealogies and regnal lists', *ASE* 5: 23–50.

(1977a). 'Kingship, genealogies and regnal lists', in Sawyer and Wood (eds.) (1977), pp. 72–104.

(1977b). 'Sub-Roman Britain – History and legend', *History* 62: 173–92.

(1984a). 'Gildas and Maelgwn: problems of dating', in Lapidge and Dumville (eds.) (1984), pp. 51–60.

(1984b). 'The chronology of *De Excidio Britanniae* book I', in Lapidge and Dumville (eds.) (1984), pp. 61–84.

(1989a). 'The tribal hidage: an introduction to its texts and their history', in Bassett (ed.) (1989), pp. 225–30.

(1989b). 'Essex, Middle Anglia and the expansion of Mercia in the south-east midlands', in Bassett (ed.) (1989), pp. 123–40.

(1994) *Historia Brittonum*: An insular history from the Carolingian Age', in Scharer & Scheibelreiter (ed.) (1994), pp. 406–34.

Duncan Jones, R. (1974). *The Economy of the Roman Empire: Quantitative Studies* (Cambridge).

(1990). *Structure and Scale in the Roman Economy* (Cambridge).

Durliat, J. (1988). 'Le salaire du paix sociale dans les royaumes barbares', in *Annerkennung und Integration. Zu den Wirtschaftlichen Grundlagen der Völkerwanderungszeit (400–600)*, ed. Wolfram, H. and Schwarcz, A. (Vienna), pp. 21–72.

(1990). *Les finances publiques de Dioclétien aux Carolingiens (284–889)* (Sigmaringen).

(1997a). 'Cité, impôt et intégration des barbares', in Pohl (ed.) (1997), pp. 153–79.

(1997b). '*Episcopus, civis et populus dans les Historiarum Libri de Grégoire*', in Gauthier and Galinié (eds.) (1997), pp. 185–93.

Dyson, S. L. (2003). *The Late Roman Countryside* (London).

Edwards, N. (1990). *The Archaeology of Early Medieval Ireland* (London).

Edwards, K. J. and Ralston, I. B. M. (eds.) (2003). *Scotland after the Ice Age: Environment, Archaeology and History, 8000 BC–AD 1000* (Edinburgh).

Effros, B. (2003). *Merovingian Mortuary Archaeology and the Making of the Early Middle Ages* (Berkeley).

Eger, C. (2001). 'Vandalische Grabfunde aus Karthago', *Germania* 79: 347–90.

Ehling, K. (1996). 'Zur Geschichte Constantins III', *Francia* 23: 1–12.

Ellis, L. (1996). 'Dacians, Sarmatians and Goths on the Roman–Carpathian frontier: second–fourth centuries', in Mathisen and Sivan (eds.) (1996), pp. 105–25.

Elton, H. (1992). 'Defence in fifth-century Gaul', in Drinkwater and Elton (eds.) (1992), pp. 167–76.

    (1996a). *Warfare in Roman Europe, 350–425* (Oxford).

    (1996b). *Frontiers of the Roman Empire* (London).

    (1996c). 'Defining Romans, barbarians and the Roman frontier', in Mathisen and Sivan (eds.) (1996), pp. 126–35.

Ensslin, W. (1947). *Theoderich der Grosse* (Munich).

Eriksen, T. H. (1993). *Ethnicity and Nationalism: Anthropological Perspectives* (London).

Esmonde-Cleary, S. (1989). *The Ending of Roman Britain* (London).

Étienne, R. and Mayet, F. (1993–4). 'La place de la Lusitanie dans le commerce Méditerranéen', *Conimbriga* 32–3: 201–18.

Euzennat, M. (1986). 'La frontière d'Afrique', in *Studien zur Militärgrenzen Roms*, pp. 573–83.

Evans Grubbs, J. (1995). *Law and Family in Late Antiquity: The Emperor Constantine's Marriage Legislation* (Oxford).

Evison, M. P. (2000). 'All in the genes? Evaluating the biological evidence of contact and migration', in Hadley and Richards (eds.) (2000), pp. 277–94.

Ewig, E. (2001). *Die Merowinger und das Frankenreich*, 3rd edn, rev. J. Jarnut (Stuttgart).

Fanning, S. (1992). 'Emperors and empires in fifth-century Gaul', in Drinkwater and Elton (eds.) (1992), pp. 288–97.

    (2002). 'Clovis Augustus and Merovingian *imitatio imperii*', in Mitchell and Wood (eds.) (2002), pp. 321–35.

Faulkner, N. (2000). *The Decline of Roman Britain* (Stroud).

Favrod, J. (1997). *Histoire politique du royaume Burgonde, 443–534* (Lausanne).

Feachem, R. W. (1955–6). 'The fortifications of Traprain Law', *Proceedings of the Society of Antiquities for Scotland* 89: 284–9.

Fehr, H. (2002). '*Volkstum* as paradigm: Germanic people and Gallo-Romans in early medieval archaeology since the 1930s', in Gillett (ed.) (2002), pp. 177–200.

Fentress, E. (ed.) (2000). *Romanization and the City: Creation, Transformations, and Failures* (Portsmouth, RI).

Ferreiro, A. (ed.) (1999). *The Visigoths: Studies in Culture and Society* (Leiden).

Ferrill, A. (1986). *The Fall of the Roman Empire: The Military Explanation* (London).

Ferris, I. (1994). 'Insignificant others: images of barbarians on military art from Roman Britain', in *TRAC 94. Proceedings of the Fourth Annual Theoretical Roman Archaeology Conference, Durham 1994*, ed. Cottam, S. Dunworth, D., Scott, S. and Taylor, J. (Oxford), pp. 24–31.

Fewster, D. (2002). 'Visions of national greatness: medieval images, ethnicity and nationalism in Finland, 1905–1945 ', in Gillett (ed.) (2002), pp. 123–46.

Fischer Drew, K. (1967). 'The barbarian kings as law-givers and judges', in *Life and Thought in the Early Middle Ages*, ed. Hoyt, R. S. (Minneapolis), pp. 7–29, repr. in Fischer Drew (1988).

   (1987). 'Another look at the origins of the middle ages: a reassessment of the role of the Germanic kingdoms', *Spec.* 62: 803–12.

   (1988). *Law and Society in Early Medieval Europe* (London).

Fitz, J. (ed.) (1977). *Limes. Akten des 11. Internationalen Limeskongresses* (Budapest).

Foster, S. (1992). 'The state of Pictland in the age of Sutton Hoo', in Carver (ed.) (1992), pp. 217–34.

   (1996). *Picts, Gaels and Scots* (Edinburgh).

Fouet, G. (1983). *La Villa gallo-romaine de Montmaurin (Haute-Garonne)* (Paris).

Fouracre, P. (1990). 'Merovingian history and Merovingian hagiography', *P&P* 127: 3–38.

   (2000). *The Age of Charles Martel* (Manchester).

Fowden, G. (1993). *Empire to Commonwealth: Consequences of Monotheism in Late Antiquity* (Princeton, NJ).

   (1999). 'Religious communities', in Bowersock, Brown and Grabar (eds.) (1999), pp. 82–106.

Francovich, R. and Hodges, R. (2004). *Villa to Village. The Transformation of the Roman Countryside in Italy, c.400–1000* (London).

Freeman, P. (2001). *Ireland and the Classical World* (Austin, TX).

Frend, W. H. C. (1952). *The Donatist Church* (Oxford).

Frye, N. (1968). *Anatomy of Criticism: Four Essays* (New York).

Fuchs, R., et al. (eds.) (1997). *Die Alamannen*, 2nd edn (Stuttgart).

Fuentes Domínguez, A. (1989). *La necrópolis tardorromana de Albalate de las Nogueras (Cuenca) y el problema de las denominadas 'necrópolis del Duero'* (Cuenca).

Fulford, M. (1993). 'Silchester: the early development of a civitas capital', in Greep (ed.) (1993), pp. 17–33.

Fuller, J. F. C. (1954). *Decisive Battles of the Western World and their Influence upon History* (London).

Fustel de Coulanges, N. D. (1904–8). *Histoire des institutions politiques de la France*, 6 vols., 2nd edn, ed. C. Jullian (Paris).

(1904). *L'invasion germanique et la fin de l'Empire* (Paris) = Fustel de Coulanges (1904–8), vol. 2.

Galinié, H. (1988). 'Reflections on early medieval Tours', in Hodges and Hobley (eds.) (1988), pp. 57–62.

(1999). 'Tours from an archaeological standpoint', in Karkhov et al. (eds.) (1999), pp. 87–105.

García Gallo, A. (1940–1). 'Notas sobre el reparto de terras entre Visigodas y Romanos', *Hispania* 1: 40–63.

García Moreno, L. A. (1990). 'Zamora del dominio imperial romano al visigodo. Cuestiones de Historia militar y geopolítica', *I. Congresso de Historia de Zamora*, pp. 455–66.

(1991). 'El hábitat rural disperso en la peninsula Ibérica durante la antigüedad tardía (siglos V–VII)', *Antigüidad Cristiana* 8: 265–73.

(1999). 'El hábitat rural agrupado en la peninsula Ibérica durante la antigüedad tardía (siglos V–VII)', in *Homenaje a Jose Maria Blázquez*, ed. Alvar, J. (Madrid), pp. 99–117.

Garnsey, P. (1998). *Cities, Peasants and Food in Classical Antiquity* (Cambridge).

Garnsey, P. and Humfress, C. (2001). *The Evolution of the Late Antique World* (Cambridge).

Garnsey, P. and Saller, R. (1987). *The Roman Empire: Economy, Society and Culture* (London).

Garnsey, P. and Whittaker, C. R. (1998). 'Rural life in the late Roman Empire', in *CAH* 13, pp. 277–311.

Gastaldo, G. (1998). 'I corredi funerari nelle tombe "tardo romane" in Italia settentrionale', in Brogiolo and Cantino Wataghin (eds.) (1998), pp. 15–59.

Gaupp, T. (1844). *Die germanischen Ansiedlungen und Landtheilungen in den Provinzen des römischen Westreiches in ihrer völkrechtlicher Eigenthümlichkeit und mit Rücksicht auf verwandte Erscheinungen der alten Welt und des späteren Mittelalters* (Breslau).

Gauthier, N. and Galinié, H. (eds.) (1997). *Grégoire de Tours et l'espace gaulois* (Tours).

Gautier, E. F. (1932). *Genséric, roi des Vandales* (Paris).

Geary, P. J. (1983). 'Ethnic identity as a situational construct in the early Middle Ages', *Mitteilungen der Anthropologischen Gesellschaft in Wien* 113: 15–26.

(1988). *Before France and Germany: The Creation and Transformation of the Merovingian World* (Oxford).

(1999). 'Barbarians and ethnicity', in Bowersock, Brown and Grabar (eds.) (1999), pp. 107–29.

(2002). *The Myth of Nations: The Medieval Origins of Europe* (Princeton, NJ).

Gebuhr, M. (1998). 'Angulus Desertus?', *SzSf* 11: 43–85.

Gelichi, S. (1996). 'Note sulle Città Bizantine dell'Esercato e della Pentapoli tra IV e IX secolo', in Brogiolo (ed.) (1996a), pp. 67–76.

Gelling, M. (1978). *Signposts to the Past: Place-names and the History of England* (London).

(1997). *Signposts to the Past: Place Names and the History of England* (3rd edn; Chichester).

Gellner, E. (1973). 'Scale and nation', *Philosophy of the Social Sciences* 3: 1–17.

George, J. W. (2004). 'Vandal poets and their context', in Merrills (ed.) (2004), pp. 133–43.

Gerberding, R. (1987). *The Rise of the Carolingians and the Liber Historiae Francorum* (Oxford).

Geuenich, D. (1997). 'Wiedersacher der Franken: expansion und Konfrontation', in Fuchs et al. (eds.) (1997), pp. 144–8.

Geuenich, D. (ed.) (1998). *Die Franken und die Alemannen bis zur "Schlacht bei Zülpich"* (Berlin).

Giardina, A. (ed.) (1986). *Società romana e impero tardoantico*, 4 vols. (Rome).

(1993). *The Romans* (Chicago).

Gidlow, C. (2004). *The Reign of Arthur. From History to Legend* (Stroud).

Giese, W. (2004). *Die Goten* (Stuttgart).

Gillam, J. (1979). 'Romano-Saxon pottery: an alternative explanation', in *The End of Roman Britain*, ed. Casey, P. J., BAR (B) 71 (Oxford), pp. 103–118.

Gillett, A. (1999). 'The accession of Euric'. *Francia* 26.1: 1–40.

(2002a). 'Was ethnicity politicized in the earliest medieval kingdoms?', in Gillett (ed.) (2002), pp. 85–121.

(2002b). 'Introduction: ethnicity, history and methodology', in Gillett (ed.) (2002), pp. 1–18.

(2003). *Envoys and Political Communication in the Late Antique West* (Cambridge).

Gillett, A. (ed.) (2002). *On Barbarian Identity: Critical Approaches to Ethnicity in the Early Middle Ages* (Turnhout).

Goetz, H.-W. (1980). 'Orosius und die Barbaren. Zu den umstrittenen Vorstellungen eines spätantiken Geschichtstheologen', *Hist.* 29: 356–76.

Goetz, H.-W., Jarnut, J. and Pohl, W. (eds.) (2003). *Regna and Gentes: The Relationship between Late Antique and Early Medieval Peoples and Kingdoms in the Transformation of the Roman World* (Leiden).

Goffart, W. (1957). 'Byzantine policy in the west under Tiberius II and Maurice: the pretenders Hermengild and Gundovald (579–585)', *Traditio* 13: 73–118.

(1972). 'From Roman taxation to medieval seigneurie: three notes', *Spec.* 47: 165–87, 373–94.

(1974). *Caput and Colonate: Towards a History of Late Roman Taxation* (Toronto).

(1980). *Barbarians and Romans* AD *418–585: The Techniques of Accommodation* (Princeton, NJ).

(1982). 'Old and new in Merovingian taxation', *P&P* 96: 3–21.

(1988). *The Narrators of Barbarian History, AD 550–800: Jordanes, Gregory of Tours, Bede, Paul the Deacon* (Princeton, NJ).

(1989a). 'The theme of the barbarian invasions in Later Antique and modern historiography', in *Das Reich und die Barbaren*, ed. Chrysos, E. and Schwarcz, A. (Vienna), pp. 87–107, reprinted in Goffart (1989c), pp. 111–32.

(1989b). 'An Empire unmade: Rome, AD 300–600', in Goffart (1989c), pp. 33–44.

(1989c). *Rome's Fall and After* (London).

(1992). Review of Durliat (1990), *EHR* 107: 675–6.

(1995). 'Two notes on Germanic antiquity today', *Traditio* 50: 9–30.

(2002a). 'Does the distant past impact upon the invasion age Germans?', in Gillett (ed.) (2002), pp. 21–37.

(2002b). 'Conspicuously absent: martial heroism in the Histories of Gregory of Tours and its likes', in Mitchell and Wood (eds.) (2002), pp. 365–93.

Grahame, M. (1998). 'Redefining Romanization: material culture and the question of social continuity in Roman Britain', in *TRAC 97. Proceedings of the Seventh Annual Theoretical Roman Archaeology Conference*, ed. Forcey, C., Hawthorne, J. and Witcher, R. (Oxford), pp. 1–10.

Grahn-Hoek, H. (1976). *Der fränkische Oberschicht im 6 Jahrhundert. Studien zu ihrer rechtlichen und politischen Stellung* (Sigmaringen).

Grant, M. (1967). *Gladiators* (Harmondsworth).

(1990). *The Fall of the Roman Empire. A Reappraisal*, rev. edn (London).

Greatrex, G. (1997). 'The Nika riot: a reappraisal', *JHS* 117: 60–86.

Green, D. H. (1998). *Language and History in the Early Germanic World* (Cambridge).

Green, D. H. and Siegmund, F. (eds.). (2003). *The Continental Saxons from the Migration Period to the Tenth Century: An Ethnographic Perspective* (Woodbridge).

Grew, F. and Hobley, B. (eds.) (1985). *Roman Urban Topography in Britain and the Western Empire*. CBA (London).

Griffiths, D. W. (1994). 'Trade and production centres in the post-Roman north: the Irish Sea perspective', in Nielsen, Randsborg and Thrane (eds.) (1994), pp. 184–8.

Groenewoudt, B. J. and van Nie, M. (1995). 'Assessing the scale and organisation of Germanic iron production in Heeten, the Netherlands', *JEA* 3.2: 187–215.

Grünewald, T. (2004). *Bandits in the Roman Empire: Myth and Reality* (London).

Guibernau, M. and Rex, J. (1996). *The Ethnicity Reader: Nationalism, Multiculturism and Migration* (Cambridge).

Gutiérrez Lloret, S. (1996). 'Le città della Spagna tra romanità e islamismo', in Brogiolo (ed.) (1996a), pp. 55–66.

Haarnagel, W. (1979). *Die Grabung Feddersen Wierde: Methode, Hausbau, Siedlungs- und Wirtschaftsformen, sowie Sozialstruktur* (Wiesbaden).

Hadley, D. M. and Richards, J. D. (eds.) (2000). *Cultures in Contact: Scandinavian Settlement in England in the Ninth and Tenth Centuries* (Turnhout).

Haldon, J. F. (1990). *Byzantium in the Seventh Century: The Transformation of a Culture* (Cambridge).

(1999). *Warfare, State, and Society in the Byzantine World, 565–1204* (London).

Hall, E. (1989). *Inventing the Barbarian* (Oxford).

Halsall, G. R. W. (1992). 'The origins of the *Reihengräberzivilisation*: forty years on', in Drinkwater and Elton (eds.) (1992), pp. 196–207.

(1995a). *Settlement and Social Organization: The Merovingian Region of Metz* (Cambridge).

(1995b). *Early Medieval Cemeteries: An Introduction to Burial Archaeology in the Post-Roman West* (Skelmorlie).

(1995c). 'The Merovingian period in north-east Gaul: transition or change?', in Bintliff and Hamerow (eds.) (1995), pp. 38–57.

(1996). 'Female status and power in Merovingian central Austrasia: the burial evidence', *EME* 5.1: 1–24.

(1997). 'Archaeology and historiography', in *The Routledge Companion to Historiography*, ed. Bentley, M. (London), pp. 807–29.

(1998). 'Burial, ritual and Merovingian society', in Hill and Swan (eds.) (1998), pp. 325–38.

(1999a). Review article. 'Movers and Shakers: the barbarians and the fall of Rome', *EME* 8.1: 131–45.

(1999b). 'Reflections on early medieval violence: the example of the "blood feud"', *Memoria y Civilización* 2: 7–29.

(2000). 'Archaeology and the late Roman frontier in northern Gaul: the so-called Föderatengräber reconsidered', in *Grenze und Differenz im früheren Mittelalter*, ed. Pohl, W. and Reimitz, H. (Vienna), pp. 167–80.

(2001). 'Childeric's grave, Clovis' succession and the origins of the Merovingian kingdom', in Mathisen and Shanzer (eds.) (2001), pp. 116–33.

(2002a). 'Nero and Herod? The death of Chilperic and Gregory's writing of the Histories', in Mitchell and Wood (eds.) (2002), pp. 337–50.

(2002b). 'Funny foreigners: laughing with the barbarians in late antiquity', in Halsall (ed.) (2002), pp. 89–113.

(2003a). *Warfare and Society in the Barbarian West, 450–900* (London).

(2003b). 'Burial writes: graves, "texts" and time in early Merovingian northern Gaul', in *Erinnerungskultur im Bestattungsritual. Archäologisch-Historisches Forum*, ed. Jarnut, J. and Wemhoff, M. (Munich), pp. 61–74.

(2004). 'Gender and the end of empire', *Journal of Medieval and Early Modern Studies* 34.1: 17–39.

(2005a). 'The sources and their interpretation', in *NCMH* i, pp. 56–90.

(2005b). 'The barbarian invasions', in *NCMH* i, pp. 35–55.

Halsall, G. R. W. (ed.) (2002). *Humour, History and Politics in Late Antiquity and the Early Middle Ages* (Cambridge).

Hamerow, H. (1994). 'Migration theory and the migration period', in *Building on the Past: Papers Celebrating 150 Years of the Royal Archaeological Institute* (London), pp. 164–77.

(1997). 'Migration theory and the Anglo-Saxon "identity crisis"', in Chapman and Hamerow (eds.) (1997), pp. 33–44.

(1998). 'Wanderungstheorien und die angelsächsische "Identitätskrise"', *SzSf* 11: 121–34.

(2002). *Early Medieval Settlements: The Archaeology of Rural Communities in North-West Europe 400–900* (Oxford).

(2005). 'The earliest Anglo-Saxon kingdoms', in *NCMH* i, pp. 263–88.

Handley, M. (1998). 'The early medieval inscriptions of Western Britain: function and sociology', in Hill and Swan (eds.) (1998), pp. 339–61.

(1999). 'Tiempo y identidad: La datación por la Era en las inscripciones de la España tardorromana y visigoda', *Iberia. Revista de la Antigüedad* 2: 191–201.

(2000). 'Inscribing time and identity in the kingdom of Burgundy', in Mitchell and Greatrex (eds.) (2000), pp. 83–102.

(2001a). 'Beyond hagiography: epigraphic commemoration and the cult of the saints in late antique Trier', in Mathisen and Shanzer (eds.) (2001), pp. 187–200.

(2001b). 'The origins of Christian commemoration in late antique Britain', *EME* 10: 177–99.

(2003). *Death, Society and Culture: Inscriptions and Epitaphs in Gaul and Spain, AD 300–750*, BAR(I) 1135 (Oxford).

Hansen, H. J. (1989). 'Dankirke: affluence in late Iron Age Denmark' in Randsborg (ed.) (1989), pp. 123–8.

Hanson, W. S. and Keppie, L. J. F. (eds.) (1980). *Roman Frontier Studies 1979, Papers Presented to the 12th International Congress of Roman Frontier Studies*, BAR(I) 71 (Oxford).

Harbison, P. (1988). *Pre-Christian Ireland* (London).

Hardt, M. (2003). 'The Bavarians', in Goetz, Jarnut and Pohl (eds.) (2003), pp. 429–61.

Härke, H. (1989). 'Early Saxon weapon burials: frequencies, distributions and weapon combinations', in *Weapons and Warfare in Anglo-Saxon England*, ed. Chadwick-Hawkes, S. (Oxford), pp. 49–61.

(1990). '"Weapon graves"? The background of the Anglo-Saxon weapon burial rite', *P&P* 126: 22–43.

(1992a). *Angelsächsische Waffengräber des 5. bis 7. Jahrhunderts* (Cologne).

(1992b). 'Changing symbols in a changing society: the Anglo-Saxon weapon rite', in Carver (ed.) (1992), pp. 149–65.

Harries, J. D. (1994). *Sidonius Apollinaris and the Fall of Rome* (Oxford).

(1999). *Law and Empire in Late Antiquity* (Cambridge).

Hartmann, M. (2003). *Aufbruch ins Mittelalter: Die Zeit der Merowinger* (Darmstadt).

Hartung, W. (1983). *Süddeutschland in der frühen Merowingerzeit: Studien zu Gesellschaft, Herrschaft, Stammesbildung bei Alamannen und Bajuwaren* (Wiesbaden).

Haseloff, G. (1973). 'Zum Ursprung der germanischen Tierornamentik – die spätrömische Wurzel', *FmSt* 6: 406–42.

(1981). *Germanische Tierornamentik der Völkerwanderungszeit*, 3 vols. (Berlin).

Häßler, H.-J. (1991). *Ur- und Frühgeschichte in Niedersachsen* (Stuttgart).

Hauptfeld, G. (1985). 'Die Gentes im Vorfeld von Ostgoten und Franken im sechsten Jahrhundert', in *Die Bayern und ihre Nachbarn*, ed. Wolfram, H. and Schwarcz, A. (Vienna), vol. 1, pp. 121–34.

Havet, J. (1878). 'Du partage des terres entre les romains et les barbares chez les Burgondes et les Visigoths', *Revue Historique* 3: 87–99.

Hawkes, J. (1997). 'Symbolic lives: the visual evidence', in Hines (ed.) (1997), pp. 311–38.

Hayes, J. W. (1972). *Late Roman Pottery* (London).

Haynes, I. P. (1993). 'The romanisation of religion in the auxilia of the Roman imperial army from Augustus to Septimius Severus', *Britannia* 24: 141–57.

(1999). 'Military service and cultural identity in the auxilia', in A. K. Goldsworthy and I. P. Haynes (eds.), *The Roman Army as a Community in War and Peace* (Portsmouth, RI), pp. 165–74.

Hays, G. (2004). '*Romuleis libicisque litteris*: Fulgentius and the "Vandal renaissance"', in Merrills (ed.) (2004), pp. 101–32.

Heather, P. J. (1988a). 'The anti-Scythian tirade of Synesius' *De Regno*', *Phoenix* 42: 152–72.

(1988b). 'Cassiodorus and the rise of the Amals: genealogy and the Goths under Hun domination', *JRS* 78: 103–28.

(1991). *Goths and Romans, 332–489* (Oxford).

(1994). 'State formation in the first millennium A.D.', in Crawford (ed.) (1994), pp. 47–70.

(1995a). 'The Huns and the end of the Roman Empire in western Europe', *EHR* 110: 4–41.

(1995b). 'Theoderic, king of the Goths', *EME* 4.2: 145–73.

(1996). *The Goths* (Oxford).

(1997). '*Foedera* and *foederati* of the fourth century', in Pohl (ed.) (1997), pp. 57–74.

(1998a). 'Senators and senates', in *CAH* 13, pp. 184–210.

(1998b). 'Disappearing and reappearing tribes', in Pohl and Reimitz (eds.) 1998, pp. 95–111.

(1998c). 'Goths and Huns, c.320–425', in *CAH* 13, pp. 487–515.

(1999). 'The barbarian in late antiquity: image, reality and transformation', in Miles (ed.) (1999), pp. 234–58.

(2000a). 'The Western Empire, 425–76', in *CAH* 14, pp. 1–32.

(2000b). 'State, lordship and community in the west (c. AD 400–600)', in *CAH* 14, pp. 437–68.

(2001). 'The late Roman art of client management: imperial defence in the fourth-century west', in Pohl, Wood and Reimitz (eds.) (2001), pp. 15–72.

(2003). *Gens* and *regnum* among the Ostrogoths', in Goetz, Jarnut and Pohl (eds.) (2003), pp. 85–133.

(2005). *The Fall of Rome: A New History* (London).

Heather, P. (ed.) (1999). *The Visigoths: From the Migration Period to the Seventh Century* (Woodbridge).

Heather, P. and Matthews, J. (trans.) (1991). *The Goths in the Fourth Century* (Liverpool).

Heather, P. and Moncur, D. (trans.) (2001). *Politics, Philosophy and Empire in the Fourth Century: Select Orations of Themistius* (Liverpool).

Hedeager, L. (1987). 'Empire, frontier and the barbarian hinterland: Rome and northern Europe from AD 1–400', in *Centre and Periphery in the Ancient World*, ed. Rowlands, M., Larsen, M. and Kristiansen, K. (Cambridge), pp. 125–40.

(1992). *Iron Age Societies: From Tribe to State in Northern Europe, 500 BC to 700 AD* (London).

(2000). 'Migration period Europe: the formation of a political mentality', in Theuws and Nelson (eds.) (2000), pp. 15–57.

(2005). 'Scandinavia', in *NCMH* 1, pp. 496–523.

Heidinga, H. A. (1994). 'Frankish settlement at Gennep: a migration period settlement in the Dutch Meuse area', in Nielsen, Randsborg and Thrane (eds.) (1994), pp. 202–8.

Hemphill, P. (2000). *Archaeological Investigations in Southern Etruria*, vol. 1: *The Civitella Cesi Survey* (Stockholm).

Hendy, M. (1995). 'Coinage and exchange', in Carile (ed.) (1995), pp. 151–8.

Herrin, J. (1987). *The Formation of Christendom* (Oxford).

Higham, N. J. (1992). *Rome, Britain and the Anglo-Saxons* (London).

(1994). *The English Conquest: Gildas and Britain in the Fifth Century* (Manchester).

(2002). *King Arthur: Myth-Making and History* (London).

Hill, J. and Swan, M. (eds.), (1998). *The Community, the Family and the Saint: Patterns of Power in Early Medieval Europe* (Turnhout).

Hill, P. (1987). 'Traprain law: the Votadini and the Romans', *SAR* 4.2: 85–91.

Hillgarth, J. N. (1966). 'Coins and chronicles: propaganda in sixth-century Spain and the Byzantine background', *Hist.* 15: 483–508.

Hills, C. (2003). *The Origins of the English* (London).

Hills, C. and Hurst, H. (1989). 'A Goth at Gloucester?', *Antiquaries Journal* 69: 154–8.

Hines, J. (1995). 'Cultural change and social organization in early Anglo-Saxon England', in Ausenda (ed.) (1995), pp. 75–88.

(1998). 'Culture groups and ethnic groups in northern Germany in and around the Migration Period', *SzSf* 13: 219–32.

(2003). 'Society, community and identity', in Charles-Edwards (ed.) (2003), pp. 61–100.

Hines, J. (ed.) (1997). *The Anglo-Saxons from the Migration Period to the Eighth Century: An Ethnographic Perspective* (Woodbridge).

Hitchner, B. (1992). 'Meridional Gaul, trade and the Mediterranean economy in late antiquity', in Drinkwater and Elton (eds.) (1992), pp. 122–31.

Hodges, R. (1989). *The Anglo-Saxon Achievement* (London).

Hodges, R. and Bowden, W. (eds.) (1998). *The Sixth Century: Production, Distribution and Demand* (Leiden).

Hoeper, M. (1998). 'Die Höhensiedlungen der Alamannen und ihre Deutungsmöglichkeiten zwischen Fürstensitz, Heerlager, Rückzugsraum und Kultplatz' in Geuenich (ed.) (1998), pp. 325–48.

Hoeper, M. and Steuer, H. (1999). 'Eine völkerwanderungszeitliche Höhenstation am Oberrhein – der Geißkopf bei Berghaupten, Ortenaukreis – Höhensiedlung, Militärlager oder Kultplatz?' *Germania* 77: 185–246.

Hoffmann, D. (1969–70) *Das Spätrömische Bewegungsheer und die Notitia Dignitatum*, 2 vols. (Düsseldorf).

Høilund Nielsen, K. (1997). 'Animal art and the weapon-burial rite – a political badge?', in *Burial and Society: The Chronological and Social Analysis of Archaeological Burial Data*, ed. Kjeld Jensen, C. and Høilund Nielsen, K. (Aarhus), pp. 129–48.

Holum, K. G. (1982). *Theodosian Empresses: Women and Imperial Dominion in Late Antiquity* (Berkeley).

Hopkins, K. (1978). 'Economic growth and towns in classical antiquity', in *Towns and Societies*, ed. Abrams, P. and Wrigley, E. A. (Cambridge), pp. 35–77.

Horden, P. (2005). 'Mediterranean plague in the age of Justinian', in *The Cambridge Companion to the Age of Justinian*, ed. Maas, M. (Cambridge), pp. 134–60.

Humphries, M. (1996). 'Chronicle and chronology: Prosper of Aquitaine, his methods and the development of early medieval chronography', *EME* 5: 155–75.

　　(2000a). 'Italy, AD 425–605', in *CAH* 14, pp. 525–51.

　　(2000b). 'Introduction: the city between late antiquity and the Middle Ages', in Lançon (2000), pp. xvi–xxii.

Hunt, E. D. (1998). 'The church as a public institution', in *CAH* 13, pp. 238–76.

Huskinson, J. (1999). 'Women and learning: gender and identity in scenes of intellectual life on late Roman sarcophagi', in Miles (ed.) (1999), pp. 190–213.

Hutchinson, J. and Smith, A. D. (1996). *Ethnicity* (Oxford).

Hvass, S., (1983). 'Vorbasse: the development of a settlement through the first millennium AD', *Journal of Danish Archaeology* 2: 127–36.

　　(1989). 'Rural settlements in Denmark in the first millennium AD', in Randsborg (ed.) (1989), pp. 91–9.

Irsigler, F. (1969). *Untersuchungen zur Geschichte des frühfränkischen Adels* (Bonn).

Jackson, K. H. (1964). *The Oldest Irish Tradition: A Window on the Iron Age* (Cambridge).

James, E. F. (1982a). *The Origins of France: From Clovis to the Capetians, 500–1000* (London).

　　(1982b). 'Ireland and Western Gaul in the Merovingian period', in D. Whitelock, R. McKitterick and D. Dumville (eds.), *Ireland in Medieval Europe: Studies in Memory of Kathleen Hughes* (Cambridge), pp. 362–86.

　　(1988). *The Franks* (Oxford).

　　(1989a). 'Burial and status in the early medieval West.' *TRHS*, 5th ser., 39: 23–40.

　　(1989b). 'The origins of barbarian kingdoms: the continental evidence', in Bassett (ed.) (1989), pp. 40–52.

　　(1997). 'The militarisation of Roman society, 400–700', in Nørgård Jørgensen and Claussen (eds.) (1997), pp. 19–24.

　　(2001). *Britain in the First Millennium* (London).

James, S., Marshall, A. and Millett, M. (1985). 'An early medieval building tradition', *Archaeological Journal* 141: 182–215.

Jarnut, J. (1994). 'Gregor von Tours, Frankengeschichte II.12: *Franci Egidium sibi regem adiscunt*: Faktum oder Sage?', in *Ethnogenese und Überlieferung Angewandte Methoden der Frühmittelalterforschung*, ed. Brunner, K. and Mertens, B. (Vienna), pp. 129–34

(2004). 'Germanisch. Plädoyer für die Abschaffung eines obsoleten Zentralbegriffes der Frühmittelalterforschung', in Pohl (ed.) (2004), pp. 107–13.

Jarrett, M. G. (1967). 'The Roman frontier in Wales', in *Studien zu den Miltärgrenzen Roms* (1967), pp. 21–31.

Johnson, S. (1979) *The Roman forts of the Saxon Shore*, 2nd edn (London).

(1980). *Later Roman Britain* (London).

Jones, A. H. M. (1948). *Constantine and the Conversion of Europe* (London).

(1953). 'Inflation under the Roman Empire', *Economic History Review* 5: 293–318 (reprinted in Jones (1974), pp. 187–227).

(1954). 'The cities of the Roman Empire: Political, administrative and judicial functions', *Receuil de la Société Jean Bodin* 6: 135–73 (repr. in Jones (1974), pp. 1–34).

(1955). 'The economic life of the towns of the Roman Empire', *Receuil de la Société Jean Bodin* 7: 161–92 (repr. in Jones (1974), pp. 35–60).

(1962). 'The constitutional position of Odoacer and Theoderic', *JRS* 52: 126–30 (repr. in Jones (1974), pp. 365–74).

(1964). *The Later Roman Empire, 284–602* (Oxford).

(1974). *The Roman Economy: Studies in Ancient Economic and Administrative History*, ed. Brunt, P. A. (Oxford).

Jones, M. E. (1988). 'The appeal to Aëtius in Gildas', *NMS* 32: 141–55.

(1996). *The End of Roman Britain* (Ithaca).

Jones, R. F. J. (1987). 'A false start? The Roman urbanization of western Europe', *World Archaeology* 19.3: 47–57.

(1991). 'The urbanization of Roman Britain', in Jones, R.F.J. (ed.) (1991), pp. 53–65.

Jones, R. F. J. (ed.) (1991). *Britain in the Roman Period: Recent Trends* (Sheffield).

Jones, W. R. (1971). 'The image of the barbarian in medieval Europe', *CSSH* 13: 376–407.

Jørgensen, L., Alt, K. W. and Vach, W. (1997). 'Families at Kirchheim am Ries: analysis of Merovingian aristocratic and warrior families', in Nørgård Jørgensen and Claussen (eds.) (1997), pp. 102–12.

Jørgensen, L., Storgaard, B. and Gebauer Thomsen, L. (eds.) (2003). *The Spoils of Victory: The North in the Shadow of the Roman Empire* (Copenhagen).

Just, R. (1989). 'Triumph of the ethnos', in Tonkin, McDonald and Chapman (eds.) (1989), pp. 71–88.

Kaegi, W. E. (1995). 'The capability of the Byzantine army for operations in Italy', in Carile (ed.) (1995), pp. 79–99.

Kaiser, R. (2004). *Die Burgunder* (Stuttgart).

Kapelle, W. E. (1979). *The Norman Conquest of the North: The Region and its transformation, A.D. 1000–1135* (London).

Kazanski, M. (1991). *Les Goths (Ier–VIIe après J.-C.)* (Paris).

Kazanski, M., Mastykova, A. and Périn, P. (2002). 'Byzance et les royaumes barbares d'occident au début de l'époque mérovingienne', in *Probleme der frühen Merowingerzeit im Mitteldonauraum* (Brno), pp. 159–93.

Keay, S. (1988). *Roman Spain* (London).
     (1996). 'Tarraco in late antiquity', in Christie and Loseloy (eds.) (1996), pp. 18–44.
     (2003). 'Recent archaeological work in Roman Iberia (1990–2002)', *JRS* 93: 146–211.

Keay, S. and Terrenato, N. (eds.) (2001). *Italy and the West: Comparative Issues in Romanization* (Oxford).

Kelly, C. (1998). 'Emperors, government and bureaucracy', in *CAH* 13, pp. 138–83.
     (2004). *Ruling the Later Roman Empire* (Cambridge, MA).

King, C. E. (1992). 'Roman, local and barbarian coinages in fifth-century Gaul', in Drinkwater and Elton (eds.) (1992), pp. 184–95.

Kirby, D. P. (2000). *The Earliest English Kings*, 2nd edn (London).

Kirk, J. P. and Leeds, E. T. (1954). 'Three early Saxon graves from Dorchester, Oxon', *Oxoniensia* 17–18: 63–76.

Kleemann, J. (1999). 'Zum Aufkommen der Körperbestattung in Niedersachsen', *SzSf* 13: 253–62.

Klingshirn, W. J. (1994). *Caesarius of Arles: The Making of a Christian Community in Late Antique Gaul* (Cambridge).

Knight, J. (1999). *The End of Antiquity: Archaeology, Society and Religion AD 235–700* (Stroud).

Knowles, D. (1963). *Great Historical Enterprises: Problems in Monastic History* (London).

Koch, U. (1997). 'Besiegt, beraubt, vertrieben: die Folgen der Niederlagen von 496/7 und 506', in Fuchs, Kempa, Redies, Theune-Großkopf & Wais (ed.) (1997), pp. 191–201.

Krantheimer, R. (1980). *Rome: Profile of a City, 312–1308* (Princeton).

Kristoffersen, S. (1999). 'Migration period chronology in Norway', in *The Pace of Change: Studies in Early Medieval Chronology*, ed. Hines, J., Høilund Nielsen, K. and Siegmund, F. (Oxford), pp. 93–114.

Kuhnen, H. P. (1997). 'Zwischen Reichs- und Stadtgeschichte – Trier in Spätantike und Frühmittelalter', in Wieczorek, Périn, von Welck and Menghin (eds.), (1997), pp. 138–44.

Kulikowski, M. (2000a) 'The *Notitia Dignitatum* as a historical source', *Hist.* 49: 358–77.

   (2000b). 'Barbarians in Gaul, usurpers in Britain', *Britannia* 31: 325–45.

   (2000c). 'The career of the *comes hispaniarum* Asterius', *Phoenix* 54: 123–40.

   (2001). 'The interdependence of town and country in late antique Spain', in Burns and Eadie (eds.) (2001), pp. 147–61.

   (2002a). 'Nation versus army: a necessary contrast?', in Gillett (ed.) (2002), pp. 69–84.

   (2002b). 'Marcellinus "of Dalmatia" and the dissolution of the fifth-century Empire', *Byzantion* 72: 177–91.

   (2002c). 'Fronto, the bishops, and the crowd: episcopal justice and communal violence in fifth-century Tarraconensis', *EME* 11.4: 295–320.

   (2004). *Late Roman Spain and its Cities* (Baltimore).

   (2006). *Rome's Gothic Wars from the Third Century to Alaric* (Cambridge).

Ladner, G. B. (1976). 'On Roman attitudes toward barbarians in late antiquity', *Viator* 7: 1–26.

Lamm, J. P. and Nordstrom, H. (eds.) (1983). *Statens Historiska Museum, Studies 2: Vendel Period* (Stockholm).

Lancel, S. (ed.) (1985). *Histoire et archéologie de l'Afrique du Nord: IIe colloque international (Grenoble, 5–9 Avril 1983)* (= *Bulletin archéologique du Comité des travaux historiques et scientifiques*, n.s. 19 (Paris).

Lançon, B. (2000). *Rome in Late Antiquity* (Edinburgh).

Lane, A. (1994). 'Trade, gifts and cultural exchange in Dark Age western Scotland', in Crawford (ed.) (1994), pp. 103–15.

Lapidge, M. (1984). 'Gildas' education and the Latin culture of sub-Roman Britain', in Lapidge and Dumville (eds.) (1984), pp. 37–50.

Lapidge, M. and Dumville, D. N. (eds.) (1984). *Gildas: New Approaches* (Woodbridge).

Larrick, R. (1986). 'Age grading and ethnicity in the style of Loikop (Samburu) spears', *World Archaeology* 18: 269–83.

Lavan, L. (2001). 'The late-antique city: a bibliographic essay', in *Research in Late-Antique Urbanism*, ed. Lavan, L. (Portsmouth, RI), pp. 9–26.

Lebecq, S. (1990). *Les origines franques, Ve–IXe siècle* (Paris).

Lee, A. D. (1998). 'The army', in *CAH* 13, pp. 211–37.

Leeds, E. T. (1913). *The Archaeology of the Anglo-Saxon Settlements* (Oxford).

Lendinara, P. (1997). 'The Kentish laws', in Hines (ed.) (1997), pp. 211–30.

Lenoir, E. (1985). 'Volubilis du bas-empire à l'époque Islamique', in Lancel (ed.) (1985), pp. 425–8.

Lenski, N. (1995). 'The Gothic civil war and the date of the Gothic conversion', *GRBS* 36: 51–87.

(2002). *The Failure of Empire: Valens and the Roman State in the Fourth Century* A.D. (Berkeley).

Lepelley, C. (1979). *Les cités de l'Afrique romaine au bas-empire*, vol. 1 (Paris).

(1992). 'The survival and fall of the classical city in late Roman Africa', in Rich (ed.) (1992), pp. 50–76.

Lepelley, C. (ed.) (1991). *L'Armée et les affaires militaires: IVe colloque international d'histoire et d'archéologie de l'Afrique du Nord* (Paris).

Leveau, P. (1984). *Caesarea de Maurétanie: une ville romaine et ses campagnes* (Rome).

Levy, E. (1951). *West Roman Vulgar Law: The Law of Property* (Philadelphia).

Lewis, C. T. and Short, C. (1879). *A Latin Dictionary* (Oxford).

Liebeschuetz, J. H. W. G. (1991). *Barbarians and Bishops: Army, Church and State in the Age of Arcadius and Chrysostom* (Oxford).

(1992). 'Alaric's Goths: nation or army?', in Drinkwater and Elton (eds.) (1992), pp. 75–83.

(1997). 'Cities, taxes and the accommodation of barbarians: the theories of Durliat and Goffart', in Pohl (ed.) (1997), pp. 135–51.

(2001). *The Decline and Fall of the Roman City* (Oxford).

(2003). '*Gens* into *Regnum*: the Vandals', in Goetz, Jarnut and Pohl (eds.) (2003), pp. 55–83.

Little, L. K. and Rosenwein, B. H. (eds.) (1998). *Debating the Middle Ages* (Oxford).

Livens, R. G. (1974). 'Litus Hibernicum', in Pippidi (ed.) (1974), pp. 333–9.

(1986). 'Roman defences in north Wales, Holyhead Mountain and Caergybi', in *Studien zur Militärgrenzen Roms* (1986), pp. 58–9.

Lomas, K. (1998). 'Roman imperialism and the city in Italy', in *Cultural Identity in the Roman Empire*, ed. Laurence, R. and Berry, J. (London), pp. 64–78.

López-Pardo, F. (1991). 'Los problemas militares et la inclusión de Mauretania Tingitana en la *Diocesis Hispaniarum*', in Lepelley (ed.) (1991), pp. 445–53.

López Sánchez, F. (2002). 'Le monnayage d'Olybrius ou l'affirmation de l'Occident face à l'Orient', *Cahiers Numismatiques* 39, no. 153 (September): 31–43.

L'Orange, H. P. (1965). *Art and Civic Life in the Later Roman Empire* (Princeton, NJ).

Lorren, C. and Périn, P. (1997). 'Images de la Gaule rurale au Vie siècle', in Gauthier and Galinié (eds.) (1997), pp. 93–109.

Loseby, S. T. (1992). 'Marseille: a late antique success story?', *JRS* 82: 165–85.

(1996). 'Arles in late antiquity: *Gallula Roma Arelas* and *Urbs Genesii*', in Christie and Loseby (eds.) (1996), pp. 45–70.

(1998a). 'Marseille and the Pirenne Thesis I: Gregory of Tours, the Merovingian kings and 'un grand port', in Hodges and Bowden (eds.) (1998), pp. 203–29.

(1998b). 'Gregory's cities: urban functions in sixth-century Gaul', in Wood (ed.) (1998), pp. 239–70.

(2000a). 'Urban failures in late-antique Gaul', in *Towns in Decline* AD *100–1600*, ed. Slater, T. (Aldershot), pp. 72–95.

(2000b). 'Power and towns in late Roman Britain and early Anglo-Saxon England', in Ripoll and Gurt (eds.) (2000), pp. 319–70.

(2005). 'The Mediterranean economy', in *NCMH* 1, pp. 605–38.

Lot, F. (1928). 'Du régime de l'hospitalité', *RBPH* 7: 975–1011.

(1933). 'Le serment de fidélité à l'époque franque', *RBPH* 12: 569–82.

Louis, E. (2004). 'A de-Romanised landscape in Northern Gaul: The Scarpe valley from the fourth to the ninth century AD', in Bowden, Lavan and Machado (eds.) (2004), pp. 479–504.

Lowe, C. (1999). *Angels, Fools and Tyrants: Britons and Anglo-Saxons in Southern Scotland* (Edinburgh).

Lucy, S.J. (1997). 'Housewives, warriors and slaves? Sex and gender in Anglo-Saxon burials', in Moore, J. and Scott, E. (eds.) *Invisible People and Processes: Writing Gender and Childhood into European Archaeology* (London).

(2002). 'Burial practice in early medieval eastern Britain: constructing local identities, deconstructing ethnicity', in Lucy and Reynolds (eds.) (2002), pp. 72–87.

Lucy, S. and Reynolds, A. (eds.) (2002). *Burial in Early Medieval England and Wales* (London).

Lütkenhaus, W. (1998). *Constantius III. Studien zu seiner Tätigkeit und Stellung im Westreich 411–421* (Bonn).

Luttwak, E. (1976). *Grand Strategy of the Roman Empire: From the First Century A.D. to the Third* (Baltimore).

MacGeorge, P. (2003). *Late Roman Warlords* (Oxford).

Mackensen, M. and Schneider, G. (2002). 'Production centres of African Red Slip (third–seventh centuries) in northern and central Tunisia: archaeological provenance and reference groups based upon chemical analysis', *JRA* 15: 121–58.

MacMullen, R. (1984). *Christianizing the Roman Empire* (AD *100–400*) (New Haven).

(1988). *Corruption and the Decline of Rome* (New Haven).

Mac Niocaill, G. (1972). *Ireland before the Vikings* (Dublin).

Maenchen-Helfen, O. von (1973). *The World of the Huns: Studies in their History and Culture* (Berkeley).

Magnou-Nortier, E. (1989). 'La gestion publique en Neustrie: les moyens et les hommes (viie – ixe siècles)', in *La Neustrie: Les pays au nord de la Loire de 650 à 850*, ed. Atsma, H. (Sigmaringen), pp. 271–318.

Magnus, B. (1997). 'The firebed of the serpent: myth and religion in the migration period mirrored through some golden objects', in Webster and Brown (eds.) (1997), pp. 194–207.

Manares, T. (1980). *La cerámica tardoromana-visigoda, anaranjada y gris con decoración estampada en la España Nor-occidental (Studia Archaeologica 65)* (Valladolid).

Mann, J. C. (1979). 'Power, force and the frontiers of the empire', *JRS* 69: 175–83.

Marcone, A. (1998). 'Late Roman social relations', in *CAH* 13, pp. 338–70.

Markus, R. A. (1964). 'Donatism: the last phase', *SCH* 1: 118–26.

(1972). 'Christianity and dissent in Roman north Africa: changing perspectives in recent work', in *SCH* 9: 21–36.

(1986). 'Pelagianism: Britain and the continent', *JEH* 37: 191–204.

(1990). *The End of Ancient Christianity* (Cambridge).

Martin, M. (1997). 'Zwischen den Fronten', in Fuchs, Kempa, Redies, Theune-Großkopf and Wais (eds.) (1997), pp. 119–24.

(1998). 'Alamannen im römischen Heer – eine verpaßte Integration und ihre Folgen', in Geuenich (ed.) (1998), pp. 407–22.

Martín Viso, I. (2002). *Fragmentos del Leviatán: La Articulación política del espacio zamorano en la alta edad media* (Zamora).

Massa, S. (1996). 'La necropoli del Lugone (Salò): analisi della struttura sociale', in Brogiolo (ed.) (1996b), pp. 71–9.

Mathisen, R. W. (1979a). 'Resistance and reconciliation: Majorian and the Gallic aristocracy after the fall of Avitus', *Francia* 7: 597–627.

(1979b). 'Sidonius on the reign of Avitus: a study in political prudence', *TAPA* 109: 165–71.

(1992). 'Fifth-century visitors to Italy: business or pleasure?', in Drinkwater and Elton (eds.) (1992), pp. 228–38.

(1993). *Roman Aristocrats in Barbarian Gaul: Strategies for Survival in an Age of Transition* (Austin, TX).

(1999). 'Sigisvult the patrician, Maximinus the Arian and political stratagems in the Western Roman Empire, c.425–40', *EME* 8: 173–96.

Mathisen, R. W. (ed.) (2001). *Law, Society and Authority in Late Antiquity* (Oxford).

Mathisen, R. W., and Shanzer, D. (eds.) (2001). *Society and Culture in Late Roman Gaul: Revisiting the Sources* (Aldershot).

Mathisen, R. W. and Sivan H. S. (1999). 'The kingdom of Toulouse and the frontiers of Visigothic Aquitania (418–507)', in Ferreiro (ed.) (1999), pp. 1–62.

Mathisen, R. W. and Sivan, H. S. (eds.) (1996). *Shifting Frontiers in Late Antiquity* (Aldershot).

Matthews, J. F. (1975). *Western Aristocracies and Imperial Court, A.D. 364–425* (Oxford).

(1989). *The Roman Empire of Ammianus Marcellinus* (London).

(2000a). *Laying Down the Law: A Study of the Theodosian Code* (New Haven).

(2000b). 'Roman law and barbarian identity in the late Roman west', in Mitchell and Greatrex (eds.) (2000), pp. 31–44.

Mattingly, D.J. (1995). *Tripolitania* (London).

(2004). 'Being Roman: expressing identity in a provincial setting', *JRA* 17: 5–25.

Mattingly, D.J. and Hitchner, R.B. (1995). 'Roman Africa: An archaeological review', *JRS* 85: 165–213.

Mattingly, D.J. and Salmon, J. (eds.) (2001). *Economies beyond Agriculture in the Classical World* (London).

Maxfield, V.A. (1987). 'Mainland Europe', in Wacher (ed.) (1987), pp. 139–87.

Maxfield, V.A. (ed.) (1989). *The Saxon Shore: A Handbook* (Exeter).

Mazzarino, S. (1973). *L'Impero Romano*, vol. 3 (Rome and Bari).

McCarthy, D. and Ó Cróinín, D. (1987–88). 'The "lost" Irish 84 year Easter table rediscovered', *Peritia* 6–7: 227–42.

McCormick, M. (1986). *Eternal Victory: Triumphal Rulership in Late Antiquity, Byzantium and the Early Medieval West* (Cambridge).

McLynn, N. (1994). *Ambrose of Milan* (Berkeley).

Meier, D. (2003). 'The North Sea coastal area: settlement history from Roman to early medieval times', in Green and Siegmund (eds.) (2003), pp. 37–67.

Menghin, W. (1990). *Frühgeschichte Bayerns* (Stuttgart).

Merrills, A.H. (2004a). 'Introduction: Vandals, Romans and Berbers: understanding late antique North Africa', in Merrills (ed.) (2004), pp. 3–28.

(2004b). 'The perils of panegyric: the lost poem of Dracontius and its consequences', in Merrills (ed.) (2004), pp. 145–62.

Merrills, A.H. (ed.) (2004). *Vandals, Romans and Berbers: New Perspectives on Late Antique North Africa.* (Aldershot).

Mertens, J. (1963). 'Oudenburg, camp du Litus Saxonicum en Belgique?', in Novak (ed.) (1963), pp. 123–31.

(1971). La nécropole du castellum de Oudenburg', in Applebaum (ed.) (1971), pp. 59–70.

(1977). 'Quelques considérations sur le Limes Belgicus', in Fitz (ed.) (1977), pp. 63–72.

(1980). 'Recherches récentes sur le limes en Gaule Belgique', in Hanson and Keppie (eds.) (1980), pp. 423–70.

(1986). Recherches récentes sur le Bas-Empire en Belgique', in *Studien zur Militärgrenzen Roms* (1986), pp. 192–99.

Miles, R. (ed.) (1999). *Constructing Identities in Late Antiquity* (London).

Millar, F. (1981). *The Roman Empire and its Neighbours* (New York).

Miller, D. (1985). *Artefacts as Categories: A Study of Ceramic Variability in Central India* (Cambridge).

Miller, D. H. (1996). 'Frontier societies and the transition between late antiquity and the middle ages', in Mathisen and Sivan (eds.) (1996), pp. 158–71.

Miller, M. (1975) 'Bede's use of Gildas', *EHR* 305: 241–61.

Millett, M. (1990). *The Romanization of Britain: An essay in Archaeological Interpretation* (Cambridge).

Milne, G. (1993). 'The rise and fall of Roman London', in *Roman Towns: The Wheeler Inheritance. A Review of 50 Years of Research*, ed. Greep, S. J. (York), pp. 11–15.

   (1995). *Roman London* (London).

Minor, C. (1996). 'Bacaudae – a reconsideration', *Traditio* 51: 297–307.

Mitchell, K. and Wood, I. N. (eds.) (2002). *The World of Gregory of Tours* (Leiden).

Mitchell, S. and Greatrex, G. (eds.) (2000). *Ethnicity and Culture in Late Antiquity* (London).

Modéran, Y. (1991). 'Les premiers raids des tribus Sahariennes en Afrique et la Johannide de Corippus', in Lepelley (ed.) (1991), pp. 479–90.

   (2002a). 'Les Vandales et la chute de Carthage', in Briand, C. and Crogiez, S. (eds.), *L'Afrique du Nord antique et médiévale: mémoire, identité et imaginaire, Actes des journées d'études organisées par le GRHS, Université de Rouen, 28 Janvier et 10 Mars, 1999* (Rouen), pp. 97–132.

   (2002b). 'L'établissement des Vandals en Afrique', *An. Tard.* 10: 87–122.

   (2003a). *L'Empire romain tardif, 235–293, ap. J.-C.* (Paris).

   (2003b). *Les Maures et l'Afrique romaine* (Rome).

   (2004). 'L'établissement de barbares sur le territoire romain à l'époque impériale', in *La mobilité des personnes en Méditerranée de l'antiquité à l'époque moderne*, ed. Moatti, C. (Rome), pp. 337–97.

Moerman, M. (1968). 'Being Lue: use and abuses of ethnic identification', in *Essays on the Problem of Tribe Proceedings of the 1967 Annual Spring Meeting of the American Ethnological Society*, ed. Helm, J. (Seattle), pp. 153–69.

Mommaerts, T. S. and Kelley D. H. (1992). 'The Anicii of Gaul and Rome', in Drinkwater and Elton (eds.) (1992), pp. 111–21.

Mommsen, T. (1889). 'Ostgotische Studien', *Neues Archiv* 14: 223–49, 451–544.

Moorhead, J. (1978). 'Boethius and Romans in Ostrogothic service', *Hist.* 27: 604–12.

   (1983). 'The last years of Theoderic', *Hist.* 32: 106–20.

   (1992). *Theoderic in Italy* (Oxford).

   (1994). *Justinian* (London).

   (1999). *Ambrose: Church and Society in the Late Roman World* (London).

   (2005a). 'Ostrogothic Italy and the Lombard invasions', in *NCMH* 1, pp. 140–61.

   (2005b). 'The Byzantines in the West in the sixth century', in *NCMH* 1, pp. 118–39.

Moroney, M. G. (1989). 'Teleology and the significance of change', in Clover and Humphreys (ed.) (1989), pp. 21–6.

Morris, J. (1973). *The Age of Arthur* (London).

Musset, L. (1975). *The Germanic Invasions* (London).

Myres, J. N. L. (1960). 'Pelagianism and the end of Roman rule in Britain', *JRS* 50: 21–36.

(1977). *A Corpus of Anglo-Saxon Pottery of the Pagan Period*, 2 vols. (Cambridge).

(1986). *The English Settlements* (Oxford).

Myhre, B. (1992). 'The royal cemetery at Borre in Vestfold: a Norwegian centre into a European periphery', in Carver (ed.) (1992), pp. 301–13.

(1997). 'Boathouses and naval organisation', in Nørgård Jørgensen and Claussen (eds.) (1997), pp. 169–83.

(2003). 'The Iron Age', in *The Cambridge History of Scandinavia*, vol. 1: *From Prehistory to 1520*, ed. Helle, K. (Cambridge), pp. 60–93.

Mytum, H. (1992). *The Origins of Early Christian Ireland* (London).

Näsman, U. (1998). 'The Justinianic era of south Scandinavia: an archaeological view', in Hodges and Bowden (ed.) (1998), pp. 255–78.

(1999). 'The ethnogenesis of the Danes and the making of a Danish kingdom', in Dickinson and Griffiths (ed.) (1999), pp. 1–10.

Nathan, G. S. (1992), 'The last emperor: The fate of Romulus Augustulus', *Classica et Mediaevalia* 43: 261–71.

(2000). *The Family in Late Antiquity: The Rise of Christianity and the Endurance of Tradition* (London).

Neumaier, H. (1997). 'Freies Germanien'/, Germania libera' – Zur Genese eines historischen Begriffs.' *Germania* 75: 53–67.

Nielsen, P. O., Randsborg, K. and Thrane, H. (eds.) (1994). *The Archaeology of Gudme and Lundeborg* (Copenhagen).

Nietzsche, F. (1994). *On the Genealogy of Morality*, ed. Ansell-Pearson, K. (Cambridge; original edn, 1887).

Nixon, C. E. V. (1992). 'Relations between Visigoths and Romans in fifth-century Gaul', in Drinkwater and Elton (eds.) (1992), pp. 64–74.

Noble, T. F. X. (1999). 'The transformation of the Roman world: reflections on five years of work', in *East and West: Modes of Communication, Proceedings of the First Plenary Conference at Mérida*, ed. Chrysos, E. and Wood, I. N. (Leiden), pp. 259–77.

Noonan, T. S. (1997). 'Scandinavians in European Russia', in *The Oxford Illustrated History of the Vikings*, ed. Sawyer, P. H. (Oxford), pp. 134–55.

Nørgård Jørgensen, A. and Claussen, B. L. (ed.) (1997). *Military Aspects of Scandinavian Society in a European Perspective AD 1–1300* (Copenhagen).

Novak, G. (ed.) (1963). *Archeolski Radovi I Rasprave (Acta et Dissertationes Archaeologiae) III. Quintus Congressus Internationalis Limitis Romani Studiosorum (17–23 Sept. 1961)* (Zagreb).

Noyé, G. (1996). 'Les villes des provinces d'Apulie-Calabre et de *Bruttium*-Lucanie du IVe au VIe siècle', in Brogiolo (ed.) (1996a), pp. 97–120.

Nuber, H. U. (1993). 'Der Verlust der obergermanisch-raetischen Limesgebiete und die Grenzsicherung bis zum Ende des 3. Jahrhunderts', in Vallet and Kazanski (eds.) (1993), pp. 101–8.

(1998). 'Zur Entstehung des Stammes der *Alamanni* aus römischer Sicht', in Geuenich (ed.) (1998), pp. 367–83.

Ó Cróinín, D. (1995). *Early Medieval Ireland 400–1200* (London).

Okamura, J. Y. (1981). 'Situational ethnicity', *ERS* 4.4: 452–65.

Okamura, L. (1996). 'Roman withdrawals from three transfluvial frontiers', in Mathisen and Sivan (eds.) (1996), pp. 11–19.

Oost, S. I. (1968). *Galla Placidia Augusta: A Biographical Essay* (Chicago).

Orlandis, J. (1987). *Historia de España: Época Visigoda (409–711)* (Madrid).

Padel, O. J. (1994). 'The nature of Arthur', *Cambrian Medieval Celtic Studies* 27 (summer): 1–31.

Pader, E. J. (1981). *Symbolism, Social Relations and the Interpretation of Mortuary Remains*, BAR(I) 130 (Oxford).

Palol, P. de (1977). 'Romanos en la meseta: el bajo imperio y la aristocracia indígena', in *Segovia, Symposium de Arqueologia Romana* (Barcelona), pp. 297–308.

Palol, P. de and Ripoll, G. (1999). *Die Goten: Geschichte und Kunst in Westeuropa* (Augsburg).

Pampliega, J. (1998). *Los Germanos en España* (Pamplona).

Paschoud, F. (ed. and trans.) (1986). *Zosime: Histoire Nouvelle, Livre V* (Paris).

(1989). *Zosime: Histoire Nouvelle, Livre VI* (Paris).

Peacock, D. P. S., Bejaoui, F. and Ben Lazreg, N. (1990). 'Roman pottery production in central Tunisia', *JRA* 3: 59–84.

Pearce, S. (ed.) (1982). *The Early Church in Western Britain and Ireland: Studies Presented to C. A. Ralegh Radford*, BAR(B) 102 (Oxford).

Pearson, A. (2002). *The Roman Shore Forts: Coastal Defences of Southern Britain* (Stroud).

Peel, J. D. Y. (1989). 'The cultural work of Yoruba ethnogenesis', in Tonkin, McDonald and Chapman (eds.) (1989), pp. 198–215.

Percival, J. (1969). 'Seigneurial aspects of late Roman estate management', *EHR* 82: 449–73.

(1976). *The Roman Villa: An Historical Introduction* (London).

Perez, Rodriguez, F. and García, Rozas, M. del Rosario (1989). 'Nuevos datos acerca de la produccion de Terra Sigillata Hispanica Tardiva', *BSAA* 55: 169–91.

Pérez, Sánchez, D. (1989). *El Ejército en la Sociedad Visigoda* (Salamanca).

Périn, P. (1997). 'Paris, merowingische Metropol', in Wieczorek, Périn, von Welck and Menghin (eds.) (1997), pp. 121–8.

(1998). 'La progression des Francs en Gaule du nord au Ve siècle: histoire et archéologie', in Geuenich (ed.) (1988), pp. 59–81.

(2002a). 'Paris', in *Reallexikon der germanischen Altertumskunde*, ed. Müller, R. (Berlin), vol. 22, pp. 488–96.

(2002b). 'Settlements and cemeteries in Merovingian Gaul', in Mitchell and Wood (eds.) (2002), pp. 67–99.

(2004). 'The origin of the village in early medieval Gaul', in Christie (ed.) (2004), pp. 255–78.

Périn, P. and Feffer, L. C. (1987). *Les Francs*, 2 vols. (Paris).

Perrin, O. (1968). *Les Burgondes: leur histoire des origines à la fin du premier royaume (534)* (Neuchâtel).

Perring, D. (1991). *Roman London* (London).

Pietri, C. (1980). 'L'espace chrétien dans la cité: le *vicus christianorum* et l'espace chrétien de la cité arverne (Clermont)', *Revue de l'histoire de l'église de France* 66: 177–210.

Piganiol, A. (1947). *L'Empire Chrétien (325–395)* (Paris).

Pilet, C. (1980). *La nécropole de Frénouville*, BAR (I) 83 (Oxford).

Pippidi, D. M. (ed.) (1974). *Actes du IXe congrès international d'études sur les frontières romaines, Mamaïa, 6–23 Sept. 1972* (Cologne).

Pirenne, H. (1939). *Mohammed and Charlemagne* (London).

Pitts, L. F. (1989). 'Relations between Rome and the German "kings" on the middle Danube in the first to fourth centuries AD', *JRS* 79: 45–58.

Pohl, W. (1988). *Die Awaren* (Munich).

(1998a). 'Telling the difference: signs of ethnic identity', in Pohl and Reimitz (eds.) (1998), pp. 17–69.

(1998b). 'Conceptions of ethnicity in early medieval studies', in Little and Rosenwein (ed.) (1998), pp. 15–24.

(2000). *Die Germanen (Enzyklopädie deutscher Geschichte)* (Munich).

(2001). 'History in fragments: Montecassino's politics of memory', *EME* 10: 343–74.

(2002). *Die Völkerwanderung: Eroberung und Integration* (Stuttgart).

(2004). 'The Vandals: fragments of a narrative', in Merrills (ed.) (2004), pp. 31–47.

(2005). 'Aux origines d'une Europe ethnique: transformations d'identités entre antiquité et moyen âge', *Annales: Histoire, Sciences Sociales* 60: 183–208.

Pohl, W. (ed.) (1997). *Kingdoms of the Empire: The Integration of Barbarians in Late Antiquity* (Leiden).

(ed.) (2004). *Die Suche nach den Ursprüngen: Von der Bedeutung des frühen Mittelalters* (Vienna).

Pohl, W. and Diesenberger, M. (ed.) (1999). *Eugippius und Severin: Der Autor, der Text und der Heilige* (Vienna).

Pohl, W. and Reimitz, H. (ed.) (1998). *Strategies of Distinction: The Construction of Ethnic Communities, 300–800* (Leiden).

Pohl, W., Wood, I. N. and Reimitz, H. (eds.) (2001). *The Transformation of Frontiers: From Late Antiquity to the Carolingians* (Leiden).

Popa, A. (1997). 'Die Siedlung Sobari, Kr. Soroca (Republik Moldau)', *Germania* 75: 119–31.

Potter, T. W. (1979). *The Changing Landscape of South Etruria* (London).

   (1987). *Roman Italy* (London).

   (1995). *Towns in Late Antiquity: Iol Caesarea and its Context* (Sheffield).

Proceedings of the Royal Irish Academy (1976). *Colloquium on Hiberno-Roman Relations and Material Remains (September 1974)*.

Prévot, F., Blaudeau, P., Voisin, J.-L. and Najar, L. (2006). *L'Afrique Romaine, 69–439* (Neuilly).

Pringle, D. (1981). '*The defence of Byzantine Africa from Justinian to the Arab conquest: an account of the military history and archaeology of the African provinces in the sixth and seventh centuries*', BAR(I) 99 (Oxford).

Proudfoot, B. (1977). 'Economy and settlement in rural Ireland', in *Studies in Celtic Survival*, ed. Laing, L. BAR(B) 37 (Oxford), pp. 83–106.

Quast, D. (1997). 'Vom Einzelgrab zum Friedhof: Beginn der Reihengräbersitte im 5. Jahrhundert', in Fuchs et al. (1997), pp. 171–90.

Rahtz, P. A. (1976). 'Irish settlements in Somerset', in *Proceedings of the Royal Irish Academy* (1976), pp. 223–30.

Ralston, I. B. M. and Armit, I. (2003). 'The early historic period: an archaeological perspective', in Edwards and Ralston (eds.) (2003), pp. 217–39.

Rance, P. (2001). 'Attacotti, Déisi and Magnus Maximus: the case for Irish federates in late Roman Britain', *Britannia* 32: 243–70.

Randsborg, K. (ed.) (1989). *The Birth of Europe: Archaeology and Social Development in the First Millennium A.D.* (Rome).

Rathbone, D. W. (1983). 'The slave mode of production in Italy', *JRS* 73: 160–8.

Raven, S. (1993). *Rome in Africa*, 3rd edn (London).

Reece, R. (1981). 'The third century, crisis or change?', in *The Roman West in the Third Century*, ed. King, A. and Hennig, M., BAR(I) 109 (Oxford), pp. 27–38.

   (1999). *The Later Roman Empire: An Archaeology, AD 150–600* (Stroud).

Reichmann, C. (1997). 'Frühe Franken in Germanien', in Wieczorek, Périn, von Welck and Menghin (eds.) (1997), pp. 55–65.

Reuter, M. (1996). 'Germanische Siedler des 3. und 4. Jahrhunderts in römischen Ruinen: Ausgrabungen des bade- sowie des Wirtschaftsgebäudes de Villa Rustica von Wurmlingen, Kreis Tuttlingen', *Archäologische Ausgrabungen in Baden Württemberg, 1995* (Stuttgart), pp. 204–8.

Reydellet, M. (1995). 'Théodoric et la *civilitas*', in Carile (ed.) (1995), pp. 285–96.

Reynolds, P. (1993). *Settlement and Pottery in the Vinalopó Valley (Alicante, Spain)*, BAR(I) 588 (Oxford).

(1995). *Trade in the Western Mediterranean, AD 400–700: The Ceramic Evidence*, BAR(I) 604 (Oxford).

Reynolds, V. (1980a). 'Sociobiology and the idea of primordial discrimination', *ERS* 3.3: 303–15.

(1980b). 'Sociobiology and discrimination: a rejoinder', *ERS* 3.4: 482–3.

Rich, J. (ed.) (1992). *The City in Late Antiquity* (London).

Rich, J. and Wallace-Hadrill, A. (eds.) (1991). *City and Country in the Ancient World* (London).

Richards, J. D. (1995). 'The archaeology of early Anglo-Saxon England', in Ausenda (ed.) (1995), pp. 51–74.

Richardson, J. S. (1996). *The Romans in Spain* (Oxford).

Riggs, D. (2001). 'The continuity of paganism between the cities and countryside of late Roman Africa', in Burns and Eadie (eds.) (2001), pp. 285–300.

Ripoll, G. (1994). 'Archeologia visigota in *Hispania*', in Bierbrauer, von Hessen and Arslan (eds.) (1994), pp. 301–27.

(1998a). *Toréutica de la Bética (siglos VI y VII D.C.)* (Barcelona).

(1998b). 'The arrival of the Visigoths in Hispania: population problems and the process of acculturation', in Pohl and Reimitz (eds.) (1998), pp. 153–87.

(1999a). 'Symbolic life and signs of identity in Visigothic times', in Heather (ed.) (1999), pp. 403–31.

(1999b). 'The transformation and process of acculturation in late antique Hispania: select aspects from urban and rural archaeological documentation', in Ferreiro (ed.) (1999), pp. 263–302.

(2001). 'On the supposed frontier between the *Regnum Visigothorum* and Byzantine *Hispania*', in Pohl, Wood and Reimitz (eds.) (2001), pp. 95–115.

Ripoll, G. and Gurt, J. M. (eds.) (2000). *Sedes Regiae (ann.400–800)* (Barcelona).

Rives, J. (trans.) (1999). *Tacitus: Germania* (Oxford).

Rivet, A. L. F. (1969). *The Roman Villa in Britain* (London).

Roberts, M. (1984). 'The Mosella of Ausonius: an interpretation', *TAPA* 114: 343–53.

(1992). 'Barbarians in Gaul: the response of the poets', in Drinkwater and Elton (eds.) (1992), pp. 97–106.

Roberts, W. I. (1982). *Romano-Saxon Pottery*, BAR(B) 106 (Oxford).

Robinson, O. F. (1992). *Ancient Rome: City Planning and Administration* (London).

Rodriguez-Aragon, F. Perez, (1992). 'Los cingula militiae tardorromanos de la peninsula Iberica', *BSAA* 58: 239–61.

Rodríguez Martín, F. G. (1995). 'La villa romana de Torre Águila (Barbaño Montijo, Badajoz)', *JRA* 8: 313–16.

Rösch, M. (1997). 'Ackerbau und Ernährung: Pflanzenreste aus alamannischen Sielungen', in Fuchs et al. (1997), pp. 323–30.

Roskams, S. P. (1991). 'London – new understanding of the Roman city', in Jones, R. F. J. (ed.) (1991), pp. 67–8.

    (1996a). 'The urban transition in the Maghreb', in Brogiolo (ed.) (1996a), pp. 43–54.

    (1996b). 'Urban transition in North Africa: Roman and medieval towns of the Maghreb', in Christie and Loseby (eds.) (1996), pp. 159–83.

    (forthcoming). 'Carthage, AD 400–500 – an archaeological perspective', Proceedings of conference on Vandals at Institute for Research in Social Stress, San Marino (Woodbridge).

Rouche, M. (1979). *L'Aquitaine des Wisigoths aux Arabes, 418–781: naissance d'une région* (Paris).

Rouche, M. (ed.) (1997). *Clovis: histoire et mémoire*, tome 1: *Clovis, son temps, l'événement* (Paris).

Rubin, G. (1975). 'The traffic in women: notes on the "political economy" of sex', in *Toward an Anthropology of Women*, ed. Reiter, R. R. (New York), pp. 157–210.

Rubin, Z. (1986) 'The Mediterranean and the dilemma of the Roman Empire in late antiquity', *Mediterranean Historical Review* 1: 13–62.

Rundkvist, M. (2003). *Barshalder 2: Studies of Late Iron Age Gotland* (Stockholm).

Rushworth, A. (2000). 'From periphery to core in late antique Mauretania', in *TRAC 99. Proceedings of the Ninth Annual Theoretical Roman Archaeology Conference*, ed. Fincham, G., Harrison, G., Holland, R. R. and Revell, L. (Oxford), pp. 90–103.

    (2002). '*Defensores provinciae*: the militarization of frontier zone elites in third-century Mauretania', in *Limes XVIII: Proceedings of the XVIIIth International Congress of Roman Frontier Studies Held in Amman, Jordan (Sept., 2000)*, BAR(I) 1084 (Oxford), pp. 349–60.

    (2004). 'From Arzuges to Rustamids: state formation and regional identity in the pre-Saharan zone', in Merrills (ed.) (2004), pp. 77–98.

Saggioro, F. (2004). 'Late antique settlement on the plains of Verona', in Bowden, Lavan and Machado (eds.) (2004), pp. 505–34.

Salin, E. (1950–9). *La civilisation mérovingienne d'après les textes, les sépultures et la laboratoire*, 4 vols. (Paris).

Salzman, M. R. (2002). *The Making of a Christian Aristocracy: Social and Religious Change in the Western Roman Empire* (Cambridge, MA).

Samson, R. (1987). 'Social structures in Reihengräber: mirror or mirage?', *SAR* 4.2: 116–26.

(1994). 'The end of Alamannic princely forts and the supposed Merovingian hegemony', *JEA* 2.2: 341–60.

Sawyer, P. H. and Wood, I. N. (eds.), (1977). *Early Medieval Kingship* (Leeds).

Scharer, A. and Scheibelreiter, G. (eds.) (1994). *Historiographie im frühen Mittelalter* (Vienna).

Scharf, R. (1993). 'Iovinus – Kaiser im Gallien', *Francia* 20: 1–13.

(1999) 'Ripari und Olibriones? Teilnehmer an der Schlacht auf dem katalaunischen Feldern', *MIÖG* 107: 1–11.

Scheibelreiter, G. (1994). 'Vom Mythos zur Geschichte. Überlieferung zu den Formen der Bewahrung von Vergangenheit im Frühmittelalter', in Scharer and Scheibelreiter (eds.) (1994), pp. 26–40.

Schmidt, B. (1983). 'Die Thüringer', in *Autorenkollektiv* (1983), pp. 502–48.

(1987). 'Das Königreich der Thüringer und seine Provinzen', in Menghin (ed.) (1987), pp. 471–80.

(1997). 'Das Königreich der Thüringer und seine Eingliederung in das Frankenreich', in Wieczorek, Périn, von Welck and Menghin (eds.) (1997), pp. 285–97.

Schön, M. (1999). *Feddersen Wierde, Fallward, Flögeln: Archäologie im Museum Burg Bederkesa, Landkreis Cuxhaven* (Bremerhaven).

Schwarcz, A. (2001). 'The Visigothic settlement in Aquitania: chronology and archaeology', in Mathisen and Shanzer (eds.) (2001), pp. 15–25.

(2004). 'The settlement of the Vandals in North Africa', in Merrills (ed.) (2004), pp. 49–57.

Scott, E. (1990). 'Romano-British villas and the social construction of space', in *The Social Archaeology of Houses*, ed. Samson, R. (Edinburgh), pp. 149–72.

Scull, C. (1995). 'Approaches to material culture and social dynamics of the migration period of eastern England', in Bintliff and Hamerow (eds.) (1995), pp. 71–83.

(1998). 'Migration theory and early England: contexts and dynamics of cultural change', *SzSf* 11: 177–85.

Sfameni, C. (2004). 'Residential villas in late antique Italy: continuity and change', in Bowden, Lavan and Machado (eds.) (2004), pp. 335–75.

Shanzer, D. (1998a). 'Two clocks and a wedding: Theoderic's diplomatic relations with the Burgundians', *Rb* 14: 225–58.

(1998b). 'Dating the baptism of Clovis: the bishop of Vienne vs. the bishop of Tours', *EME* 7.1: 29–57.

(2002a). 'Laughter and humour in the early medieval Latin west', in Halsall (ed.) (2002), pp. 25–47.

(2002b). 'History, romance, love and sex in Gregory of Tours' *Decem Libri Historiarum*', in Mitchell and Wood (eds.) (2002), pp. 395–418.

Shanzer, D. and Wood, I. N. (trans.) (2002). *Avitus of Vienne: Letters and Selected Prose* (Liverpool).

Shaw, B. D. (1980). 'Archaeology and knowledge: the history of the African provinces of the Roman Empire', *Florilegium: Carleton University Papers on Late Antiquity and the Middle Ages* 2: 28–60, (repr. in Shaw (1995a)).

(1982). 'Fear and loathing: the nomad menace and Roman Africa', in *Roman Africa/L'Afrique Romaine, The 1980 Governor-General Vanier Lectures, Revue de l'Université d'Ottowa* 52, ed. Wells, C. M. (Ottawa), pp. 25–46 (repr. in Shaw (1995b)).

(1984a). 'Bandits in the Roman Empire', *P&P* 105: 4–52.

(1984b). 'Latin funerary inscriptions and family life in the later Roman Empire', *Hist.* 33: 457–97.

(1986). 'Autonomy and tribute: mountain and plain in Mauretania Tingitana', *Desert et montagne au maghreb: hommage à Jean Dresch, Revue de l'Occident Musulman et de la Méditerranée* 41–2, ed. Baduel, P. pp. 66–89 (repr. in Shaw (1995b)).

(1987). 'The family in late antiquity: the experience of Augustine', *P&P* 115: 3–51.

(1993). 'The bandit', in Giardina (ed.) (1993), pp. 300–41.

(1995a). *Environment and Society in Roman North Africa* (Aldershot).

(1995b). *Rulers, Nomads and Christians in Roman North Africa* (Aldershot).

Shipley, G. and Salmon, J. (eds.) (1996). *Human Landscapes in Classical Antiquity* (London).

Siegmund, F. (1998a). 'Alemannen und Franken: Archäologisch überlegungen zu ethnischen Strukturen in der zweiten Hälfte des 5. Jahrhunderts', in Geuenich (ed.) (1998), pp. 558–80.

(1998b). 'Social structure and relations', in Wood (ed.) (1998), pp. 177–99.

(2003). 'Social relations among the old Saxons', in Green and Siegmund (eds.) (2003), pp. 77–95.

Simmer, A. (1988). *Le cimetière mèrovingien d'Audun-le-Tiche* (Paris).

Sivan, H. (1985). 'An un-edited letter of the Emperor Honorius to the Spanish soldiers', *Zeitschrift für Papyrologie und Epigraphik* 61: 273–87.

(1987). '*On foederati, hospitalitas* and the settlement of the Goths in AD 418', *American Journal of Philology* 108: 759–72.

(1992). 'Town and country in late antique Gaul: the example of Bordeaux', in Drinkwater and Elton (eds.) (1992), pp. 132–43.

(1996). 'Why not marry a barbarian? Marital frontiers in late antiquity (the example of CTh 3.14.1)', in Mathisen and Sivan (eds.) (1996), pp. 136–45.

(1998). 'The appropriation of Roman law in barbarian hands: "Roman-barbarian" marriage in Visigothic Gaul and Spain', in Pohl and Reimitz (eds.) (1998), pp. 189–203.

Smith, A. D. (1979). 'Towards a theory of ethnic separatism', *ERS* 2.2: 21–37.

(1986). *The Ethnic Origins of Nations* (Oxford).

Smith, J. M. H. (2001). 'Did women have a transformation of the Roman world?', in Stafford and Mulder-Bakker (eds.) (2001), pp. 22–41.

Smith, J. M. H. (ed.) (2000). *Early Medieval Rome and the Christian West: Essays in Honour of Donald A. Bullough* (Leiden).

Smith, J. T. (1997). *Roman Villas: A Study in Social Relations* (London).

Smith, R. R. R. (1997). 'The public image of Licinius I: portrait sculpture and imperial ideology in the early fourth century', *JRS* 93: 170–202.

Snyder, C. A. (1998). *An Age of Tyrants: Britain and the Britons A. D. 400–600* (Stroud).

Solberg, B. (1999). 'Development of a hierarchical society in western Norway – demography, property rights and social structure', *SzSf* 13: 367–79.

Southern, P. and Dixon, K. R. (1996). *The Late Roman Army* (London).

Sparey Green C. (1982). 'The cemetery of a Romano-British Christian community at Poundbury, Dorchester, Dorset', in Pearce (ed.) (1982), pp. 61–76.

(1993) *Excavations at Poundbury, Dorchester, Dorset, 1966–1982: 2. The Cemeteries* (Dorchester).

Speidel, M. (1975). 'The rise of ethnic units in the Roman imperial army', *Aufstieg und Niedergang des Römischen Welt* 2.3: 202–31.

(1985). 'The master of the dragon standards and the golden torc: an inscription from Prusias and Prudentius' *peristephanon*', *TAPA* 115: 283–7.

Spencer, M. (1994). 'Dating the baptism of Clovis', *EME* 3.1: 97–116.

Springer, M. (2004). *Die Sachsen* (Stuttgart).

Staab, F. (1980). 'A reconsideration of the ancestry of modern political liberty: the problem of the "King's Freemen" (Königsfreie)', *Viator* 11: 51–69.

Stafford, P. and Mulder-Bakker, A. B. (eds.) (2001). *Gendering the Middle Ages* (Oxford).

Stancliffe, C. (2005). 'Religion and society in Ireland', in *NCMH* 1, pp. 397–425.

Stein, E. (1959). *Histoire du bas empire*, 2 vols. (Paris).

Steuer, H. (1998). 'Theorien zur Herkunft und Entstehung der Alemannen. Archäologische Forschungsantätze', in Geuenich (ed.) (1998), pp. 270–334.

Stickler, T. (2002). *Aëtius: Gestaltungsspielräume eines Heermeisters im ausgehenden Weströmischen Reich* (Munich).

Stoodley, N. (1999). *The Spindle and the Spear: A Critical Enquiry into the Construction and Meaning of Gender in the Early Anglo-Saxon Burial Rite*, BAR (B) 288 (Oxford).

Storms, G. (1970). 'The significance of Hygelac's raid', *NMS* 14: 3–26.

Stout, M. (1997). *The Irish Ringfort*, Irish Settlement Studies 5 (Dublin).

(2000). 'Early Christian Ireland: settlement and environment', in Barry (ed.) (2000), pp. 81–109.

Studien zu den Militärgrenzen Roms (1967). *Studien zu den Miltärgrenzen Roms. Vorträge des 6. Internationalen Limeskongresses in Süddeutschland, Beihefte der Bonner Jahrbücher* 19 (Cologne).

Studien zur Militärgrenzen Roms (1986). *Studien zur Militärgrenzen Roms III.13, Internationaler Limeskongress Aalen 1983. Vorträge Forschungen und Berichte zur Vor- und Frühgeschichte in Baden-Württemberg* 20 (Stuttgart).

Suzuki, S. (2000). *The Quoit Brooch Style and Anglo-Saxon Settlement* (Woodbridge).

Swift, E. (2000). *The End of the Roman Empire: An Archaeological Investigation* (Stroud).

Tainter, J. A. (1988). *The Collapse of Complex Societies* (Cambridge).

Teall, J. L. (1965). 'Barbarians in Justinian's armies', *Spec.* 40: 294–322.

Teitler, H. C. (1992). 'Un-Roman activities in late antique Gaul: the cases of Arvandus and Seronatus', in Drinkwater and Elton (eds.) (1992), pp. 309–17.

Theuws, F. and Alkemade M. (2000). 'A kind of mirror for men: sword depositions in late antique northern Gaul', in Theuws and Nelson (eds.) (2000), pp. 401–76.

Theuws, F. and Hiddink H. (1997). 'Der Kontakt zu Rom', in Wieczorek, Périn, von Welck and Menghin (eds.), (1997), pp. 66–80.

Theuws, F. and Nelson, J. L. (eds.) (2000). *Rituals of Power: From Late Antiquity to the Early Middle Ages* (Leiden).

Thomas, C. (1973). 'Irish colonists in south-west Britain', *World Archaeology* 5: 5–13.

(1982). 'East and west: Tintagel, Mediterranean imports and the early insular church', in Pearce (ed.) (1982), pp. 17–34.

(1994). *And Shall these Mute Stones Speak? Post-Roman Inscriptions in Western Britain* (Cardiff).

Thomas, S. (1966). 'Die provinzialrömischen Scheibenfibeln der römischen Kaiserzeit im freien Germanien', *Berliner Jahrbuch für Vor- und Frühgeschichte* 6: 119–78.

(1967). 'Die germanischen Scheibenfibeln der römischen Kaiserzeit im freien Germanien', *Berliner Jahrbuch für Vor- und Frühgeschichte* 7: 1–187.

Thompson, E. A. (1948). *A History of Attila and the Huns* (Oxford).

(1952). 'Peasant revolts in late Roman Gaul and Spain', *P&P* 2: 11–23.

(1956). 'The settlement of the barbarians in southern Gaul', *JRS* 46: 65–75 (= Thompson, E. A. (1982), ch. 2).

(1961). 'The Visigoths in the time of Ulfila', *NMS* 5: 3–32.

(1965). *The Early Germans* (Oxford).

(1966). *The Visigoths in the Time of Ulfila* (Oxford).

(1969) *The Goths in Spain* (Oxford).

(1977). 'Britain, AD 406–410', *Britannia* 8: 303–18.

(1982). *Romans and Barbarians: The Decline of the Western Empire* (Madison, WI).

(1996). *The Huns* (= Thompson, E. A. (1948), rev. Heather, P.) (Oxford).

Thompson, L. A. (1989). *Romans and Blacks* (London).

Tipper, J. (2004) *The Grubenhaus in Anglo-Saxon England: An Analysis and Interpretation of the Evidence from Anglo-Saxon England's most Distinctive Building Type* (Yedingham).

Todd, M. (1972). *Everyday Life of the Barbarians: Goths, Franks and Vandals* (London).

(1975). *The Northern Barbarians, 100 BC – AD 300*, 1st edn (London).

(1987). *The Northern Barbarians, 100 BC – AD 300*, rev. edn (Oxford).

Tomlin, R. S. O. (1972). '*Seniores–iuniores* in the late Roman field army', *American Journal of Philology* 93: 253–78.

(1974). 'The date of the "barbarian conspiracy"', *Britannia* 5: 303–9.

(1987). 'The army of the late empire', in Wacher (ed.) (1987), pp. 107–23.

Tonkin, E., McDonald, M. and Chapman, M. (eds.) (1989). *History and Ethnicity* (London).

Trafford, S. (2000). 'Ethnicity, migration theory and the historiography of the Scandinavian settlement of England', in Hadley and Richards (eds.) (2000), pp. 17–33.

Tremoleda, J. et al. (1995). 'Recent work on villas around Ampurias, Gerona, Mura and Barcelona (NE Spain)', *JRA* 8: 271–307.

Trigger, B. G. (1989). *A History of Archaeological Thought* (Cambridge, 1989).

Trout, D. E. (1999). *Paulinus of Nola: Life, Letters, and Poems* (Berkeley, CA).

Underwood, R. (1999). *Anglo-Saxon Weapons and Warfare* (Stroud).

Valenti, M. (1996). 'La Toscana tra VI e IX secolo: città e campagne tra fine dell'età tardoantica ed altomedioevo', in Brogiolo (ed.) (1996b), pp. 81–110.

Vallet, F. and Kazanski, M. (eds.) (1993). *L'armée romaine et les barbares du IIIe au VIIe siècle* (Paris).

Van Dam, R. (1985). *Leadership and Community in Late Antique Gaul* (Berkeley, CA).

(1986). '"Sheep in wolves' clothing": the letters of Consentius to Augustine', *JEH* 37: 515–35.

(1993). *Saints and their Miracles in Late Antique Gaul* (Princeton, NJ).

van den, Berghe P. L. (1978). 'Race and ethnicity: a sociobiological perspective', *ERS* 1.4: 401–11.

(1980). 'Sociobiology and discrimination: a comment on Vernon Reynolds', *ERS* 3.4: 475–81.

Van Es, W. (1967). *Wijster: A Native Village beyond the Imperial Frontier 150–425 AD* (= *Palaeohistoria* 11).

van, Ossel, P. (1992). *Etablissements ruraux de l'antiquité tardive dans le nord de la Gaule*, 51e supplément à Gallia (Paris).

(1995). 'Insécurité et militarisation en Gaule du Nord au bas-empire: l'exemple des campagnes', *Revue du Nord* 77: 27–36.

van, Ossel P. and Ouzoulias, P. (2000). 'Rural settlement economy in northern Gaul in the late Empire: an overview and assessment', *JRA* 13: 133–60.

Velay, P. (1992). *From Lutetia to Paris: The Island and the Two Banks* (Paris).

Verhulst, A. (2002). *The Carolingian Economy* (Cambridge).

Verlinde, A. D. and Erdrich, M. (1998). 'Eine germanische Siedlung der späten Kaiserzeit mit umwehrter Anlage und umfangreicher Eisenindustrie in Heeten, Province Overijssel, Niederlande', *Germania* 76: 693–719.

Verlinden, C. (1954). 'Frankish colonization: a new approach', *TRHS*, 5th ser., 4: 1–17.

Vogt, J. (1967). *The Decline of Rome: The Metamorphosis of Ancient Civilisation* (London).

Volpe, G. (ed.) (1998). *San Giusto: la villa, le ecclesiae* (Bari).

von Rummel, P. (2002). 'Habitus vandalorum? Zur Frage nach einer gruppen-spezifischen Kleidung der Vandalen in Nordafrika', *An. Tard.* 10: 131–41.

(2003). 'Zum Stand der afrikanischen Vandalenforschung nach den Kolloquien in Tunis und Paris', *An. Tard.* 11: 13–19.

(2005). *Habitus Barbarus: Kleidung und Repräsentation spätantiker Eliten im 4. und 5. Jahrhundert n. Chr.* (Doctoral dissertation, Albert-Ludwigs-Universität Freiburg im Breisgau).

(forthcoming). 'North African towns and the Vandal kingdom', Proceedings of conference on Vandals at Institute for Research in Social Stress, San Marino (Woodbridge).

Wacher, J. S. (1974). *The Towns of Roman Britain* (London).

Wacher, J. S. (ed.) (1987). *The Roman World* (London).

Wainwright, F. T. (ed.) (1955). *The Problem of the Picts* (London).

Walbank, F. W. (1969). *The Awful Revolution: The Decline of the Roman Empire in the West* (Liverpool).

Walker Bynum C. (1982). 'Did the twelfth century discover the individual?', in Walker Bynum, C., *Jesus as Mother: Studies in the Spirituality of the High Middle Ages* (Berkeley, CA), pp. 82–109.

Wallace-Hadrill, J. M. (1962). *The Long-Haired Kings* (London).

(1971). *Early Germanic Kingship in England and on the Continent* (Oxford).

Ward-Perkins, B. (1984). *From Classical Antiquity to the Middle Ages: Urban Public Building in Northern and Central Italy AD 300–850* (Oxford).

Ward-Perkins B. (1998). 'The cities', *CAH* 13, pp. 371–410.

Warmington, B. H. (1954). *The North African Provinces from Diocletian to the Vandal Conquest* (Cambridge).

Warner, R. B. (1988). 'The archaeology of early historic Irish kingship', in Driscoll and Nieke (eds.) (1988), pp. 47–68.

Watson, B. (1998). ' "Dark earth" and urban decline in late Roman London', in Watson (ed.) (1998), pp. 100–6.

Watson, B. (ed.) (1998). *Roman London: Recent Archaeological Work* (Portsmouth, RI).

Weale, M. E. et al. (2002). 'Y chromosome evidence for Anglo-Saxon mass-migration', *Molecular Biology and Evolution* 197(7): 1008–21.

Webster, J. and Cooper, N. (eds.) (1996). *Roman Imperialization: Post-Colonial Perspectives* (Leicester).

Webster, L. and Brown, M. (eds.), (1997). *The Transformation of the Roman World*, AD 400–900 (London).

Welch, M. (1992). *Anglo-Saxon England* (London).

(1993). 'The archaeological evidence for federated settlements in Britain in the fifth century', in Vallet and Kazanski (eds.) (1993), pp. 269–78.

Wells, P. S. (1980). *Culture Contact and Culture Change: Early Iron Age Central Europe and the Mediterranean World* (Cambridge).

(2001). *Beyond Celts, Germans and Scythians: Archaeology and Identity in Iron Age Europe* (London).

Wenskus, R. (1961). *Stammesbildung und Verfassung. Das Werden der frühmittelalterlichen Gentes* (Cologne).

Werner, J. (1950). 'Zur Entstehung der Reihengräberzivilisation', *Archaeologica Geographica* 1: 23–32.

Wharton, A. J. (1995). *Refiguring the Post-Classical City: Dura Europos, Jerash, Jerusalem and Ravenna* (Cambridge).

White, D. A. (1961). *Litus Saxonicum: The British Saxon Shore in Scholarship and History* (Madison, WI).

White, H. (1978). *The Tropics of Discourse: Essays in Cultural Criticism* (Baltimore).

White, L. (ed.) (1966). *The Transformation of the Roman World. Gibbon's Problem After Two Centuries* (Berkeley, CA).

White, R. and Barker, P. A. (1998). *Wroxeter: Life and Death of a Roman City* (Stroud).

Whittaker, C. R. (1976). 'Agri deserti', in *Studies in Roman Property*, ed. Finley, M. I. (Cambridge), pp. 137–65, 193–200, repr. in Whittaker (1993), no. 3.

(1993). *Land, City and Trade in the Roman Empire* (London).

(1994). *Frontiers of the Roman Empire* (Baltimore, MD).

Whittow, M. (1996). *The Making of Orthodox Byzantium, 600–1025* (London).

Whyman, M. C. (2001) *Late Roman Britain in Transition, AD 300–500: A Ceramic Perspective from East Yorkshire* (Unpublished D.Phil. thesis, University of York).

Wickham, C. J. (1981). *Early Medieval Italy: Central Power and Local Society, 400–1000* (London).

(1998). 'The fall of Rome will not take place', in Little and Rosenwein (eds.) (1998), pp. 45–57.

(2005). *Framing the Early Middle Ages: Europe and the Mediterranean 400–800* (Oxford).

Wieczorek, A., Périn P., von Welck K. and Menghin, W. (eds.) (1997). *Die Franken: Wegbereiter Europas*, 2nd edn (Mainz).

Wightman, E. M. (1970). *Roman Trier and the Treveri* (London).

(1985). *Gallia Belgica* (London).

Williams, D. F. (1989). 'The impact of the Roman amphora trade on pre-Roman Britain', in *Centre and Periphery: Comparative Studies in Archaeology*, ed. Champion, T. C. (London), pp. 142–50.

Williams, H. (2002). 'Remains of pagan Saxondom? – The study of Anglo-Saxon cremation rites', in Lucy and Reynolds (eds.) (2002), pp. 47–71.

Williams, S. (1985). *Diocletian and the Roman Recovery* (London).

Williams, S. and Friell, G. (1994). *Theodosius: The Empire at Bay* (London).

Wilmott, T. (1997). *Birdoswald: Excavations of a Roman Fort on Hadrian's Wall and its Successor Settlements, 1987–92* (London).

Wilson, R. J. A. (1983). *Piazza Armerina* (New York).

Wirth, G. (1997). 'Rome and its Germanic partners in the fourth century', in Pohl (ed.) (1997), pp. 13–55.

Wiseman, H. (2000). 'The derivation of the date of the Badon entry in the Annales Cambriae from Bede and Gildas', *Parergon* n.s. 17.2: 1–10.

Witschel, C. (2004). 'Re–evaluating the Roman west in the third century', *JRA* 17: 251–81.

Wolfram, H. (1975) 'Gotische Studien I. Das Richtertum Athanarichs', *MIÖG* 83: 1–32.

(1979a). 'Gotisches Königtum und römisches Kaisertum von Theodosius dem Großen bis Justinian I', *FmSt* 14: 1–28.

(1979b). *Geschichte der Goten* (Munich).

(1983). 'Zur ansiedlungen reichsangehöriger Föderaten. Erklärungsversuche und Forschungsziele', *MIÖG* 91: 5–35.

(1988). *History of the Goths*, trans. of revision of 2nd German edn (Berkeley).

(1997a). *The Roman Empire and its Germanic Peoples* (Berkeley, CA).

(1997b). 'Neglected evidence on the accommodation of barbarians in Gaul', in Pohl (ed.) (1997), pp. 181–3.

(2005a). 'Frühes Königtum', in *Das frühmittelalterliche Königtum: Ideelle und religiose Grundlagen*, ed. Erkens, F.-R. (Berlin), pp. 42–64.

(2005b). *Gotische Studien: Volk und Herrschaft im frühen Mittelalter* (Munich).

Wolfram, H. and Pohl, W. (eds.) (1990). *Typen der Ethnogenese unter besondere Berücksichtigung der Bayern* (Vienna).

Wood, I. N. (1977). 'Kings, kingdoms and consent', in Sawyer and Wood (eds.) (1977), pp. 6–29.

(1983). *The Merovingian North Sea* (Alingsås).

(1984). 'The end of Roman Britain: continental evidence and parallels', in Lapidge and Dumville (eds.) (1984), pp. 1–26.

(1985). 'Gregory of Tours and Clovis', *RBPH* 63: 249–72.

(1987). 'The fall of the western Empire and the end of Roman Britain', *Britannia* 18: 251–62.

(1988). 'Clermont and Burgundy 511–34', *NMS* 32: 119–25.

(1990a). 'Administration, law and culture in Merovingian Gaul', *in The Uses of Literacy in Early Medieval Europe*, ed. McKitterick, R. (Cambridge), pp. 63–81.

(1990b). 'Ethnicity and the ethnogenesis of the Burgundians', in Wolfram and Pohl (eds.), (1990), pp. 53–69.

(1992). 'Continuity or calamity: the constraints of literary models', in Drinkwater and Elton (eds.) (1992), pp. 9–18.

(1993). 'The "secret histories" of Gregory of Tours', *RBPH* 71: 253–70.

(1994a). *The Merovingian Kingdoms, 450–751* (London).

(1994b). *Gregory of Tours* (Bangor).

(1998a). 'The barbarian invasions and first settlements', in *CAH* 13, pp. 516–37.

(1998b). 'Incest, law and the Bible in sixth-century Gaul', *EME* 7: 291–303.

(1999). 'The monastic frontiers of the *Vita Severini*', in Pohl and Diesenberger (eds.) (1999), pp. 41–51.

(2003). 'Gentes, kings and kingdoms – the emergence of states: the kingdom of the Gibichungs', in Goetz, Jarnut and Pohl (eds.) (2003), pp. 243–69.

(2004). 'Misremembering the Burgundians', in Pohl (ed.) (2004), pp. 139–48.

Wood, I. N. (ed.) (1998). *Franks and Alamanni in the Merovingian Period: An Ethnographic Perspective* (Woodbridge).

Woods, D. (1996). 'The Saracen defenders of Constantinople in 378', *GRBS* 37: 259–79.

(2002). 'Ammianus and the blood-sucking Saracen', in *Pleiades Setting: Essays for Pat Cronin on his Sixty-Fifth Birthday*, ed. Sidwell, K. (Cork), pp. 127–45.

Woolf, A. (2002). 'An interpolation in the text of Gildas' *De Excidio Britanniae*', *Peritia* 16: 161–7.

(2003). 'The Britons: from Romans to Barbarians', in Goetz, Jarnut and Pohl (eds.) (2003), pp. 345–80.

Woolf, G. (1998). *Becoming Roman: The Origins of Provincial Civilization in Gaul* (Cambridge).

Wormald, C. P. (1976). 'The decline of the western empire and the survival of its aristocracy', *JRS* 66: 217–26.

(2003). 'The *leges barbarorum*: law and ethnicity in the post-Roman West', in Goetz, Jarnut and Pohl (eds.) (2003), pp. 21–53.

Yorke, B. A. E. (1989). 'The Jutes of Hampshire and Wight and the origins of Wessex', in Bassett (ed.) (1989), pp. 84–96.

(1990). *Kings and Kingdoms of Early Anglo-Saxon England* (London).

(2003). 'Anglo-Saxon *gentes* and *regna*', in Goetz, Jarnut and Pohl (eds.) (2003), pp. 381–407.

Young, B. K. (1975). *Merovingian Funeral Rites and the Evolution of Christianity: A Study in the Historical Interpretation of Archaeological Material* (unpublished Univ. of Pennsylvania Ph.D. thesis).

Zeumer, K. (1898). 'Ueber zwei neuentdeckte westgothische Gesetze', *Neues Archiv* 22: 78.–112.

INDEX

•

Praetorian Prefecture of the Gauls

Diocese of the Britains

1 Britannia I
2 Britannia II
3 Flavia Caesariensis
4 Maxima Caesariensis
5 Valentia

Diocese of the Gauls

6 Germania I
7 Germania II
8 Belgica I
9 Belgica II
10 Lugdunensis I
11 Lugdunensis II
12 Lugdunensis III
13 Lugdunensis Senonia
14 Maxima Sequanorum
15 Alpes Poeniae

Diocese of the Seven Provinces

16 Aquitania I
17 Aquitania II
18 Narbonensis I
19 Narbonensis II
20 Novempopulana
21 Vienensis
22 Alpes Maritimae

Diocese of the Spains

23 Tarraconensis
24 Carthaginiensis
25 Gallaecia
26 Lusitania
27 Baetica
28 Baleares
29 Mauretania Tingitana

The Praetorian Prefecture of Italy

The Diocese of Italia Annonaria

30 Raetia I
31 Raetia II
32 Aemilia
33 Venetia & Histria
34 Alpes Cottiae
35 Liguria
36 Flaminia & Picenum Annonaria

The Diocese of Italia Suburbicaria

37 Tuscia & Umbria
38 Picenum Suburbicarium
39 Valeria
40 Roma
41 Samnium
42 Campania
43 Apulia & Calabria
44 Lucania & Bruttium
45 Sicilia
46 Corsica
47 Sardinia

The Diocese of Illyria

48 Noricum Ripense
49 Noricum Mediterraneum
50 Pannonia I
51 Pannonia II
52 Savia
53 Valeria
54 Dalmatia

The Diocese of Africa

55 Mauretania Caesariensis
56 Mauretania Sitifensis
57 Numidia
58 Africa Proconsularis
59 Byzacena
60 Tripolitania

Cambridge Medieval Textbooks

Already published

Germany in the High Middle Ages c. 1050–1200
HORST FUHRMANN

The Hundred Years War
England and France at War c. 1300–c. 1450
CHRISTOPHER ALLMAND

Standards of Living in the Later Middle Ages:
Social Change in England, c. 1200–1520
CHRISTOPHER DYER

Magic in the Middle Ages
RICHARD KIECKHEFER

The Papacy 1073–1198: Continuity and Innovation
I.S. ROBINSON

Medieval Wales
DAVID WALKER

England in the Reign of Edward III
SCOTT L. WAUGH

The Norman Kingdom of Sicily
DONALD MATTHEW

Political Thought in Europe 1250–1450
ANTONY BLACK

The Church in Western Europe from the Tenth
to the Early Twelfth Century
GERD TELLENBACH
Translated by Timothy Reuter

The Medieval Spains
BERNARD F. REILLY

England in the Thirteenth Century
ALAN HARDING

Monastic and Religious Orders in Britain 1000–1300
JANET BURTON

Religion and Devotion in Europe *c.* 1215–*c.* 1515
R. N. SWANSON

Medieval Russia, 980–1584
JANET MARTIN

The Wars of the Roses: Politics and the Constitution in England, *c.* 1437–1509
CHRISTINE CARPENTER

The Waldensian Dissent: Persecution and Survival, *c.* 1170–*c.* 1570
GABRIEL AUDISIO
Translated by Claire Davison

The Crusades, *c.* 1071–*c.* 1291
JEAN RICHARD
Translated by Jean Birrell

A History of Business in Medieval Europe, 1200–1550
EDWINS S. HUNT, JAMES MURRAY

Medieval Economic Thought
DIANA WOOD

Medieval Scotland
A. D. M. BARRELL

Roger II of Sicily
A Ruler between East and West
HUBERT HOUBEN

The Carolingian Economy
ADRIAAN VERHULST
Translated by Graham A. Loud, Diane Milburn

Women in Early Medieval Europe, 400–1100
LISA M. BITEL

Southeastern Europe in the Middle Ages, 500–1250
FLORIN CURTA

The Jews of Medieval Western Christendom, 1000–1500
ROBERT CHAZAN

The Byzantine Economy
ANGELIKI E. LAIOU & CÉCILE MORRISSON

Medieval Russia, 980–1584 Second Edition
JANET MARTIN

Barbarian Migrations and the Roman West, 376–568
GUY HALSALL

Lightning Source UK Ltd.
Milton Keynes UK
UKHW01f2148010818
326654UK00001B/7/P